DOCTOR WHO

THE LEGEND

Published by BBC Books, BBC Worldwide Limited, 80 Wood Lane, London W12 0TT

First published 2003. Copyright © Justin Richards 2003
Reprinted 2003
The moral right of the author has been asserted.

Printed in Great Britain by Butler & Tanner Ltd, Frome and London

ISBN 0563 48602 3

Commissioning Editor: Ben Dunn
Project Editors: Sarah Emsley and Vicki Vrint
Copy Editors: Vicki Vrint and Sarah Emsley
Consultant: Andrew Pixley
Design Manager: Sarah Ponder
Design: Siân Rance, Emil Dacanay and Nadine Levy for Wherefore Art?
Cover Design: Emil Dacanay for Wherefore Art?
Production Controller: Kenneth McKay

With additional thanks to:
Everyone at the BBC's Written Archives Centre, and especially Trish Hayes
The staff of the BBC Photographic Library
Paul Cornell, James Goss and all at BBCi
John Ainsworth
Peter Anghelides
Mark Ayres
Rhianwen Bailey
J Jeremy Bentham
Tessa Clark
Davy Darlington
Robert Dick
Gary Gillatt
Clayton Hickman
David J Howe
Nick Pegg
Gary Russell
Mike Tucker
Paul Vanezis
Jan Vincent-Rudzki

*There is not space or time, even in a book this size, to mention every one of the thousands of people who has ever worked on **Doctor Who**. But we remember and thank them for the journey.*

BBC Books would like to thank the following for providing photographs and for permission to reproduce copyright material. While every effort has been made to trace and acknowledge all copyright holders, we would like to apologise should there have been any errors or omissions.

All images © BBC except:
page 13 (top) and page 62 (right) Barry Newbery
page 118 (top), page 118 (merchandise strip), page 388 (Legend continues strip) Panini UK Ltd.
page 73 (top), page 79 (bottom), p110 (background), page 112 (bottom), page 113 (main) Tony Cornell
page 138 (background), page 137 - courtesy of Steve Cambden

Spelling and Capitalisation

In compiling this book we have taken the decision to work as far as possible from the actual narrative of **Doctor Who** – this is after all a celebration of that story. Of course, not every weird and wonderful alien (and not so alien) creature, device or place has been spelled out for us on screen, so the main source for both spelling and capitalisation has been the original television scripts.

But these scripts are not consistent – between stories, or even within a single story. And occasionally what is seen or said in the transmitted programme is obviously different again. Our decision has been to go by on-screen pronunciation and spelling first – so Sutekh in *Pyramids of Mars* is an Osiran, as pronounced by the Doctor, Sutekh and Horus, rather than an Osirian as the script suggests. The scripts then form our secondary source (which makes for some interesting inconsistencies – in *The Twin Dilemma*, for example, the people of the planet Jaconda are Jocondans).

But even so we had to make pragmatic decisions. Is the Grand Marshall in *The Seeds of Death* a spelling mistake or an intended Martian variation of Grand Marshal? Is Brigadier Lethbridge-Stewart's name hyphenated? In *The Three Doctors* it has no hyphen on the notice board outside UNIT HQ, but in *The Android Invasion* it is hyphenated on the door of his office, and in *Battlefield* his guncase is initialled A L-S. We have decided that, in this instance, the Brig would know if his own name is hyphenated. So Lethbridge-Stewart it is.

Another character with a problematic name is the second Doctor's companion Jamie. As it is never seen written within a story, we decided that the correct spelling of Jamie's surname is 'Macrimmon' – as specified in the camera scripts for *The Highlanders* and *The Moonbase*. But it then becomes McCrimmon in some later scripts, while it is given as 'McCrimmond' throughout the camera scripts for *The Web of Fear*. *Radio Times* for The Five Doctors in 1983 gave the name as 'McCrimmon' but the same listing also misspells Zoe Heriot's surname as 'Herriot'. Our preferred spelling is the originally intended Macrimmon.

Capitalisation is perhaps more difficult. Camera scripts give all directions in capitals, so the main source for preferred capitalisation is within the dialogue, and often inconsistent. Even if it is consistent within a script, it may be inconsistent between stories or with similar names/titles. We have taken the scripts as a starting point, but then rationalised certain things (such as components of the TARDIS, for example) for consistency.

If the reader disagrees with any of the decisions we have taken, they can always take comfort from the fact that it is all undoubtedly much clearer in the original Gallifreyan.

BBC
BOOKS

DOCTOR WHO

THE LEGEND

40 YEARS OF TIME TRAVEL

JUSTIN RICHARDS

About this Book

This book is a celebration of 40 years of **Doctor Who.**

Although it is a big book, it would take many volumes of this size to document every aspect of **Doctor Who**, so we have decided to concentrate on the narrative – the adventure itself.

Almost every **Doctor Who** story ever broadcast has now been released on video (or as a soundtrack if the original is missing), and all but four have been published in the form of novels. So rather than spend time recounting those stories in detail, we have decided to concentrate on the wider tapestry – the information we learn about the Doctor, his companions and enemies, and the worlds he visits as the stories unfold. The detail that is so often neglected, but which gives such depth and colour to the enormous **Who**niverse of space and time.

Of course, no celebration of **Doctor Who** would be complete without some behind the scenes discussion. Again, the history of the series' production – a history which mirrors and illustrates the development of the British television industry as a whole – could fill many books. Here we touch on the most important aspects, using them to put the narrative discussion in context.

We do not have space to go into the social and demographic background and influence of **Doctor Who** in detail, but in many ways that is an exercise for the reader. As you leaf through the pages and glance at the stunning photographs, as you remind yourself of the stories and characters, as you travel again to so many make-believe worlds and imagined times, allow yourself to slip back in time and remember watching those stories – whether on video, on their original transmission or even from behind the sofa.

This book is about nostalgia. It is a testament to the fact that the memory does not lie. It proves that **Doctor Who** really *was* that good. And some time soon, in some space nearby, it will be again...

Contents

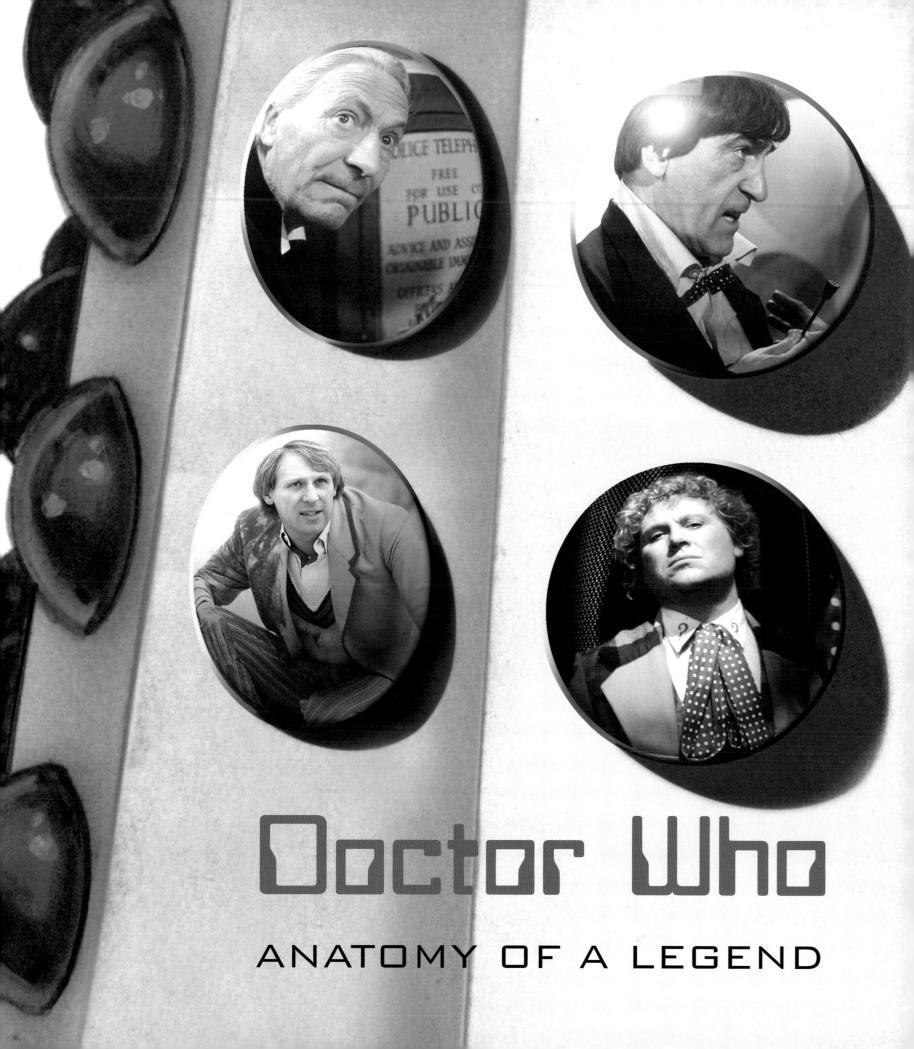

Doctor Who

ANATOMY OF A LEGEND

At about tea time on Saturday 23 November 1963, a legend was born.

From the opening shot of a pillar of smoke apparently rising through a void, accompanied by television's first electronically realised theme music, it was clear that **Doctor Who** was something different. Nobody knew quite how different, or how successful and enduring it would turn out to be...

Forty years on, we can look back on that success and celebrate it. Over that 40 years **Doctor Who** has probably touched the lives of everyone living in Britain, and a good proportion of the rest of the world. Is there anyone who looks at a police box and thinks of anything other than **Doctor Who**? Is there anyone who does not recognise that distinctive theme music? Anyone who doesn't 'get' the *Knock-knock, who's there?, Doctor...* joke? Or associate long scarves and floppy hats with time travel?

Is there anyone who does not know what a Dalek is? An image so potent it still appears on everything from biscuit advertisements to postage stamps...

For all the millions of people who have hidden from the Daleks – and the Cybermen, Ice Warriors, Yeti and even giant maggots – there are also thousands, if not tens of thousands, who have worked directly or indirectly on **Doctor Who**. Not just the television series, but the books, the audio adventures, the feature films, the vast range of merchandise from wallpaper to colouring-in books, from model kits to underpants...

It is hard to define exactly what has made the series so successful. But at its heart, **Doctor Who** is a transcendent idea. There are resonances of so many things in the basic format, which in part accounts for the appeal. It is at once morality play and melodrama. It is recognisably Gothic horror as well as Jules Verne adventure and modern techno-thriller.

The basic idea – the notion of the loner, a moral, almost prophetic figure – resonates with so many other things. In many ways, **Doctor Who** is like the archetypal Western, though that format itself is almost mythic in derivation. The *Outsider* walks into town from the desert wilderness. He has no name, no explicit background, but the town is in crisis and he is exactly the right person to resolve matters before disappearing again. He can help society, he can set it back on its right tracks – for his own reasons, and perhaps at some cost – but there is no way he can ever fit into it. During the course of events, it is apparent that the Outsider will resolve matters in his own way; that the treatment, while essential and ultimately successful, may be more dangerous, risky and painful than the original canker that must be rooted out. The story takes place on a knife-edge, within a society teetering on the brink of sophistication, caught on the very cusp of civilisation – in the metaphorical no-man's-land between the desert and the city.

It has been said that **Doctor Who** is a British institution. More than that, it is a part of British life. It has changed our cultural vocabulary in ways that nobody could even begin to suspect 40 years ago. We now live in a society where a place that seems deceptively large is TARDIS-like; where pure evil is equated with the Daleks; where time travel is more likely to be associated with 'the Doctor' than with H.G. Wells; where hiding behind the sofa is shorthand for that thrill one gets from the ambivalence of wanting and yet not wanting to see what happens next...

The Doctor may have saved our world on countless occasions, but he has also changed it.

WHO IS THE DOCTOR?

In the beginning, the Doctor was a mystery, an enigma. The title of the series – **Doctor Who**? – was a valid and very real question. We now know that he is a Time Lord from the planet Gallifrey who can change his form when he 'dies'. But this tells us very little about him.

Over the years we learn that he absconded from his people, stealing the TARDIS, because he was bored. For all their great powers, the Time Lords did nothing but observe, whereas the Doctor wanted to get out there and experience the wonders of the Universe. Since then, he has come to realise that there is evil that must be fought.

The Doctor is *Renaissance man* made real. He is a man of knowledge and wisdom. The limits of his abilities and talents, if indeed there are any, are unknown and unknowable. To outside observers he is an enigma. He is at once incredibly simple: demonstrating a well-defined moral stance and 'mission'; and incredibly complex: his motivation, and originally his background, are a total mystery. Even his lack of a name is an enigma. Essentially a loner and lonely, he walks forever in eternity. And he walks alone, lost in his own wanderlust and rocked between boundless enthusiasm and numbing ennui. Companions may come and go, but he is never that close to any of them. The only real feeling the Doctor demonstrates is his utter abhorrence of evil.

THE TARDIS

Outwardly a police telephone box of the type common in London in the early 1960s, the TARDIS is an unbelievably advanced vehicle that travels through time and space and is bigger inside than out.

The original intention was that the TARDIS should be a vehicle for transporting its occupants between stories (it is often referred to as 'the ship' in early stories), and a home for these 'wanderers in the fifth dimension'. Since it could not be steered with any accuracy, its role within the story was limited to that of a safe haven – somewhere the travellers must go to reach safety.

At first we know only that it is an incredibly advanced (almost magic) time and space vehicle. It looks like a London police telephone box because one of its incredibly advanced mechanisms – an ability to blend in with its surroundings – has failed. It contains everything necessary to support and sustain its crew and passengers – from bedrooms to food machines to clothing. We do not know whether the Doctor built it, or why, or when.

Over time we learn it is a Type 40 TT Capsule built by the Time Lords of Gallifrey. There is a suggestion that the TARDIS is female, is alive and has some symbiotic relationship with the Doctor...

MONSTERS OF THE UNIVERSE

To an extent, the Doctor is defined by his enemies. You can tell the class of a hero by the quality of his opponents.

For all the villains and super-villains the Doctor has faced, for all the maniac scientists and misguided leaders, the warmongers and the megalomaniacs, for all the alien creatures and monsters, two races stand out.

The Daleks are the quintessential monsters – not just in **Doctor Who** but in their own right. They were there almost from the beginning, and are as potent a symbol of evil now as ever. Part of their appeal is that they were humans before they became totally and irredeemably evil.

The Cybermen come a close second. Over the years they have evolved and changed in appearance far more than the Daleks. But the Cyberman is still an iconic design and – like the Daleks – a powerful image of what we might ourselves one day become...

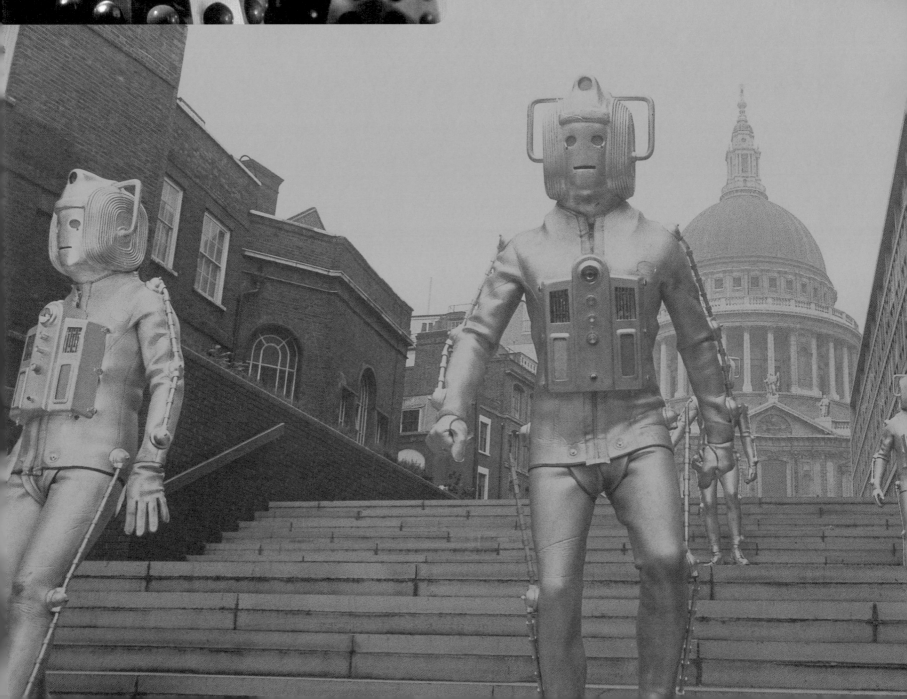

IN THE BEGINNING...

1963 was an interesting year in Britain. It was a time of contrasts. Prime Minister Macmillan maintained that we had never had it so good, yet the recent Cuban missile crisis reminded everyone of the fragility of the nuclear peace with the USSR. The young, dynamic President Kennedy signalled a move away from the old order and his optimism and charm gave people hope for the future. But those aspirations were shattered by an assassin's bullets in Dallas on 22 November 1963.

The day after Kennedy was gunned down, **Doctor Who** began.

Watching stories made and screened 40 years ago from a modern perspective is as misleading as it is unfair. Those early **Doctor Who**s were never intended to be repeated for a modern, more sophisticated audience. They were produced for tiny 405-line black-and-white screens in the days before domestic video recorders were even dreamed of, and shown in an era when the family ritually gathered round the television of a Saturday night with a severely limited choice of channels.

Perhaps the most obvious difference between the viewer of today and that of the original broadcasts is that – often – today's viewer knows what will happen. But the original audience had rather less information than maybe we realise.

It is perhaps obvious, but it is worth restating, that the viewers of *The Daleks* had no idea what a Dalek was, still less what it might look like. They had no idea whatsoever that they were about to meet a creature that would inspire the imaginations of a generation of children and toy manufacturers.

In fact, they had no idea either how many episodes the Dalek story would run for. *Radio Times* billed each episode

with its own title – and even when this gave way to overall story titles and episode numbers, none of the black and white **Doctor Who** stories were billed as in later years with an indication of the overall number of episodes. When the Doctor and his companions returned to the TARDIS towards the end of the fourth episode of *The Daleks*, there was no reason for the viewer not to believe he was finally escaping from Skaro and abandoning the Thals to their fate. Equally, many a nervous viewer must have thought the travellers safe as they escaped back to the TARDIS at the end of Episode 5 of *Marco Polo* – only to catch their breath as Tegana grabbed Susan from behind...

It is perhaps difficult to believe that the original viewers of first-transmission **Doctor Who** were as close to the Second World War as we are now to the Falklands conflict. This was a society that could implicitly see the echoes of Nazism in the Daleks. The alien symbols on Nelson's column were to them pseudo-swastikas, just as *The Dalek Invasion of Earth* portrayed a Nazi invasion of Britain that the older viewers had feared in reality.

Even closer to home, the depiction of Skaro as a world devastated by atomic warfare came just a year after the world had held its breath during the Cuban missile crisis and waited for the nuclear end. One of the most poignant and powerful portrayals of the awful possibilities was Nigel Kneale's teleplay *The Road* – broadcast less than three months before the Doctor and his companions set foot on the devastated planet of Skaro...

Today it is all too easy to watch the Daleks and to see them merely as successful science-fiction monsters. But even before *Genesis of the Daleks* in 1975, their real impact was that they showed us what our own fate might one day be – or even, by paralleling relatively recent events in Germany, what the human race had *already* become.

THE BIRTH OF DOCTOR WHO

Soon after he joined the BBC as Head of Drama at the end of 1962, Sydney Newman decided he wanted a science-fiction series to go out on Saturday evenings between the sports magazine **Grandstand** and the pop-quiz **Juke Box Jury.**

The BBC had produced successful science fiction for television before – most notably the three classic **Quatermass** serials written by Nigel Kneale. What Newman proposed was an ongoing series to be called **Doctor Who**. The brief that he passed on to the head of the Script Department (later to become Head of Serials), Donald Wilson, was that the central figure should be an old man who travelled in a time machine. While Newman always saw **Doctor Who** as science fiction, he advocated a mixture of future and historical stories and made it clear that he wanted no 'bug-eyed monsters'.

Wilson in turn passed the development of the project on to one of his staff: Cecil Webber. It was C.E. Webber who fleshed out the idea, defined the central character and the young girl and two teachers who would be drawn into his worlds, and decided that the time machine should be a variation on the sort of 'magic door' through which adventures were to be had in novels such as *Alice Through the Looking Glass* and *The Lion, the Witch and the Wardrobe*.

Webber's work went through several iterations of comment and amendment, but essentially he defined what **Doctor Who** would become. Sadly, he was never commissioned to write a broadcast episode of the series. Material from his proposed opening story was added into the script that became *An Unearthly Child*, by Anthony Coburn – the first episode of **Doctor Who**.

Coburn elaborated on Webber's foundations, but the concepts remained essentially unchanged. Biddy, the young girl, became the enigmatic Doctor's granddaughter Susan, and the teachers' names changed from Lola McGovern and Cliff to Barbara Wright and Ian Chesterton. The time machine, which had been mooted as 'some common object in the street such as a night-watchman's shelter' and would be found to be 'a marvellous contrivance of quivering electronics' became a police telephone box, which Coburn named TARDIS.

Right up to the production of this first episode details and amendments were added and made by the appointed story editor David Whitaker and the new young producer Verity Lambert – who took over from Rex Tucker who moved on to other projects.

Lambert cast the principal roles, deciding on William Hartnell for the crucial part of the Doctor. Ian was to be played by William Russell, who viewers would remember from **Ivanhoe**, and Barbara by Jacqueline Hill. The role of 15-year-old Susan was given to Carole Ann Ford, who was actually 23 at the time.

The Doctor: 'I tell you, before your ancestors had turned the first wheel the people of my world had reduced movement through the farthest reaches of space to a game for children.'

While Verity Lambert sorted out her cast, David Whitaker was working hard to get scripts written. It was decided that the stories would alternate between those set in the future and those in the past.

The first episode of **Doctor Who** was recorded at the BBC's Lime Grove studios on Friday 27 September 1963. As with all studio-based television of the time it was recorded as if it were live, since editing videotape was extremely difficult and involved taking a pair of scissors or a razor blade to the recorded tape, and guessing where to make the cut and splice. Filmed material – from location or the BBC's Ealing film studios – would be copied on to videotape in real time. The first episode of **Doctor Who**, unusually, contains a single edit – the cut between Ian and Barbara entering the police box and their finding themselves in the TARDIS.

Before filming had started, it had been decided that because of the narrative and technical complexities of the planned series, the first episode would be recorded as a 'pilot'. If it went well, and the characters and narrative worked as everyone hoped they would, this pilot would be transmitted as the first episode. But if there were things that could be improved, there was the leeway to make the necessary changes in the script and the technical planning, and then record the episode again in revised form.

This is indeed what happened. The decision was taken by Sydney Newman, the 'father' of **Doctor Who**. After watching the first episode he felt that there were several changes that could and should be made. Most important of these was a mellowing of the character of the Doctor who is rather more abrasive and confrontational in the pilot.

With a slightly revised script that made the Doctor less acerbic, *An Unearthly Child* was recorded again on Friday 18 October.

On the strength of the pilot, Donald Wilson decided to accept 13 episodes of **Doctor Who** initially, with the option of commissioning more later. While the future of the series remained in the balance for a long time, it ran every year until 1989.

The direction of the series changed forever on 21 December 1963 – when the first episode of *The Daleks* was broadcast. It closed with a shot of a Dalek's sucker arm menacing Barbara... The following week, the full Dalek was revealed, and while the BBC was still not decided about the show's future – and Sydney Newman was angry that the bug-eyed monsters he had outlawed were already appearing – the public took the series to its heart.

Three years later, not even the departure of the lead actor could stop the Doctor's travels through space and time...

The Doctor: 'We are not of this race, we are not of this Earth. We are wanderers in the fourth dimension of space and time cut off from our own planet and our own people by aeons and universes far beyond the reach of your most advanced sciences.'

EXTRACTS FROM THE ORIGINAL FORMAT DOCUMENTS

THE DOCTOR

DR. WHO — A name given to him by his three earthly friends because neither he nor they know who he is. Dr. Who is about 650 years old.* Frail looking, but wiry and tough like an old turkey — is amply demonstrated whenever he is forced to run from danger. His watery blue eyes are continually looking around in bewilderment and occasionally a look of utter malevolence clouds his face as he suspects his earthly friends of being part of some conspiracy. He seems not to remember where he comes from but he has flashes of garbled memory which indicate that he was involved in a galactic war and still fears pursuit by some unidentified enemy. Because he is somewhat pathetic his three friends continually try to help him find his way 'home', but they are never sure of his motives.
[* This is amended to 'over 60' in later versions]

THE TARDIS

Doctor Who has a 'ship' which can travel through space, through time, and through matter. It is a product of the year 5733 and cannot travel forward from that date (otherwise the Doctor and Sue could discover their own destinies), the authorities of the 50th-century deeming forward sight unlawful. This still enables Ian and Barbara (and the audience) to see into environments and existences far beyond the present day. The ship, when first seen, has the outward appearance of a police box, but the inside reveals an extensive electronic contrivance and comfortable living quarters with occasional bric-a-brac acquired by the Doctor on his travels. Primarily, the machine has a yearometer, which allows the traveller to select his stopping place. In the first story, however, the controls are damaged and the ship becomes uncertain in performance, which explains why Ian and Barbara, once set upon their journey, are never able to return to their own time and place in their natural forms.

SUSAN

The Doctor's grand-daughter, aged fifteen. She is a sharp, intelligent girl, quick and perky. She makes mistakes, however, because of inexperience. Addicted to 20th-century contemporary slang and likes pop records — in fact she admires the life teenagers enjoy in 1963. At the beginning of the story, she has persuaded her grandfather to stay in 1963 so that she can go to school and create at least one complete section of experience. Since she has been visiting all sorts of existences and places with her grandfather, Susan has a wide general knowledge and on some subjects can be brilliantly factual. On other matters, she is lamentably ignorant. She has something of a crush on Ian Chesterton.

IAN

[Ian Chesterton is] 27, red-brick university type, a teacher of applied science at Susan's school. A good physical specimen, a gymnast, dextrous with his hands and fortunate to possess the patience to deal with Doctor Who and his irrational moods. He occasionally clashes with the Doctor on decisions but for all the Doctor's superior scientific knowledge, is able to make intelligent enquiry and bring sound common sense to bear at moments of stress.

BARBARA

[Barbara Wright is] 23, attractive. A history teacher at the same school [as Ian]. Timid but capable of sudden courage. Although there is no question of a developing love story between her and Ian, her admiration for him results in undercurrents of antagonism between her and Susan.

One

THE FIRST DOCTOR AND THE TARDIS

THE DOCTOR

From the very beginning, the Doctor is an enigma. In appearance he is an elderly man with a shock of white hair. 'I'm not a doctor of medicine,' he says, but we never discover quite what he is a doctor of.

Unlike the avuncular, joking know-all of later years, the First Doctor is abrasive and brash. He tells Ian, 'Your arrogance is nearly as great as your ignorance.' It is perhaps because he dismisses Ian and Barbara as annoying and irrelevant that they get the better of him and manage to force their way inside the TARDIS. If he had been more accommodating when they first met, they might never have joined him on his travels.

During their time together, the Doctor's attitude to his companions mellows. Particularly after their ordeals on the planet Skaro (*The Daleks*) and the subsequent problems inside the TARDIS itself (*The Edge of Destruction*) he treats them more as companions and less as unwelcome stowaways.

But the one thing he never trusts them with is information about himself. Ian works out very quickly that his surname is not Foreman like his granddaughter Susan's. 'That's not his name,' he tells Barbara. 'Who is he? Doctor *who?* Perhaps if we knew his name we might have a clue to all this.'

In fact the biggest – almost the only – clue they get is when they first meet him. When Ian complains that he is treating himself and Barbara like children, the Doctor rounds on him: 'Children of my civilisation would be insulted... I tolerate this century but I don't enjoy it. Have you ever thought what it's like to be wanderers in the fourth dimension, have you? To be exiles? Susan and I are cut off from our own planet without friends or protection. But one day we shall get back. Yes, one day... One day...'

Two things that are immediately apparent are the Doctor's attachment to the TARDIS, and his love of his granddaughter, Susan. Rather than risk her leaving him, the Doctor transports himself together with Susan and the intruders Ian and Barbara away from London and 1963 (*An Unearthly Child*). It is this same love that drives him to lock Susan out of the TARDIS in *The Dalek Invasion of Earth* when he realises that she has reached the place that will be her ideal home – that she has found someone to love her and look after her in the way her grandfather has done up until now...

THE MAN BEHIND THE DOCTOR – WILLIAM HARTNELL

Born in 1908, William Hartnell was an actor from the age of 16. His first film parts came in the 1930s (he was credited as Billy Hartnell). For the most part he played small comedy roles, but in 1943 that changed when he was cast by Carol Reed as a tough army sergeant in the acclaimed World War Two propaganda film, *The Way Ahead*.

The result was more work, but Hartnell was typecast as a tough man – villains, detectives, prison officers. He was also the eponymous sergeant in the very first 'Carry On' film – *Carry On Sergeant*. Later he became well known for his role in the television series **The Army Game**.

It was in his role as a rugby talent scout in Lindsay Anderson's 1963 film *This Sporting Life* that he caught the attention of **Doctor Who**'s first producer, Verity Lambert.

After he left **Doctor Who** Hartnell did little other work. His health was deteriorating and by the time he returned to the role for *The Three Doctors*, he was not well enough to appear in the studio with the other actors, and his part was shot on film and used as inserts on scanner screens. William Hartnell died in April 1975.

'A citizen of the Universe. And a gentleman to boot.'

(THE DOCTOR –
THE DALEKS' MASTER PLAN)

THE TARDIS

The TARDIS has the outward appearance of a police telephone box of the type used by London's Metropolitan Police from 1929 until it became obsolete in 1969. But it is actually a machine that can travel through time and space. It dematerialises from a location, and reappears at its destination – which could be absolutely anywhere, at any point in history or the future.

The outside 'shell' of the TARDIS houses a much larger interior. While the Doctor gives various explanations for how this can be, he usually puts it down to the TARDIS being 'dimensionally transcendental'. Certainly he understands much of its function and construction. But we get the impression that to a large extent he is learning about it as we do. The Doctor admits that he cannot really control the TARDIS and does not even fully understand it. But all the time he is struggling to further his expertise.

On the face of it, the TARDIS seems absurd. As Ian says: 'Let me get this straight. A thing that looks like a police box, standing in a junkyard – it can move anywhere in time and space?' It even appears to have a Yale lock, though in *The Daleks* we learn there is more to this than meets the eye.

The TARDIS is supposed to camouflage its appearance when it lands so that it blends in with its surroundings. So it takes on the form of a police telephone box when it lands in London in 1963. Yet when it moves back to prehistoric Earth, its appearance does not change to match the new surroundings in *An Unearthly Child*. 'How very disturbing,' the Doctor comments. Susan tells Ian and Barbara that in the past the TARDIS has been an Ionic column and a sedan chair.

As they travel with the Doctor and Susan, Barbara and Ian discover more of the capabilities and secrets of the TARDIS. It has many rooms, a food machine, a mechanism for self-diagnosing faults…

> Ian: 'Time doesn't go round and round in circles. You can't get on and off whenever you like in the past and the future.'
> Doctor: 'Really, where does time go then?'
>
> *(AN UNEARTHLY CHILD)*

BEHIND THE SCENES: THE TARDIS

The way in which the TARDIS was intended to materialise at its destination and to dematerialise when it left was something that was relatively difficult to achieve on television in the 1960s. Apart from the recording of the opening title sequence, the first studio work done on **Doctor Who** was an experimental recording session on Friday 13 September 1963 at the BBC's Lime Grove studios. The sole purpose of this session was to confirm that the desired effect could be achieved. The day got off to a shaky start when the police box TARDIS prop turned out to be too big to fit into the lift, but the day was a success.

In the earlier years of **Doctor Who**, various techniques were used to achieve the TARDIS's materialisation and dematerialisation. These included editing the sequence on film, cross-fading between the set and a photograph of the same set with or without the TARDIS in place, and simply not showing it at all. In later years, the standard (but not the only) technique for making the TARDIS fade in and out of existence was called 'roll back and mix'. This involved recording the location where the TARDIS would arrive or from which it would depart with a camera that was 'locked off' – fixed in position. The TARDIS prop was then removed (or added), and the camera continued recording. When the material shot by the camera was wound (rolled) back and the two pictures mixed together – the location both with and without the police box prop – the TARDIS could be made to fade in or out of existence.

While the designer for the first transmitted **Doctor Who** story was Barry Newbery, the pilot episode – and the TARDIS interior – had been designed by Peter Brachaki. Brachaki's idea was that the TARDIS should be designed to be operated by a single pilot. This led to the main hexagonal console with its central column. The original intention was that this column would rise on take-off, turn during flight, then fall again on landing.

Another of Brachaki's ideas was that all the controls on the console should be custom-made and moulded to the shape of the pilot's hands. He also considered glowing transparent walls, but both of these ideas were too costly.

While some of the elements of the huge set were simplified for later stories, the TARDIS interior remains one of the most recognisable sets for television. The main elements – the roundelled walls and central console – have been retained through various redesigns of varying magnitude (see, for example, *The Time Monster*, *The Masque of Mandragora* and *The Five Doctors*) including the one for *Doctor Who – The Movie* where the increased budget was used to enhance and extend the initial design rather than replace it.

The distinctive sound of the TARDIS's arrival and departure was created by Brian Hodgson of the BBC Radiophonic Workshop – the department that provided sound effects for **Doctor Who**. The main sound of the TARDIS engines was actually the sound of Hodgson scraping his front-door key up and down the strings of an upright piano.

'I made up the name from the initials -
Time And Relative Dimension In Space.
I thought you'd both understand when you
saw the different dimensions inside from
those outside.' (SUSAN FOREMAN – *AN UNEARTHLY CHILD*)

THE TELEVISION STORIES

STORY AND EPISODE TITLES

When **Doctor Who** first started, the stories were not titled. Rather, each individual episode had a title (see Appendix). Although most stories were given titles in publicity material, in *Radio Times*, and other internal BBC sources, it was not until *The Savages* in 1966 that the individual episode titles were dropped in favour of an overall title and episode number. As a result, there are several stories for which there is some dispute about the title. But there *are* overall story titles on some internal BBC production documents. So over the years some stories have been referred to both by these internal titles, by other titles thought to relate to them, or by the title of their first episode.

In this book, we have used the title most often and most sensibly attributed to the story. This practice also matches the BBC Video releases of the stories.

'I was born in another time. Another world.'

(SUSAN – *AN UNEARTHLY CHILD*)

SUSAN FOREMAN

Whether Susan was really the Doctor's granddaughter is a matter of much debate. But there is no doubt that there is a close bond between them. There is never any suggestion during the time we see them travel together that this is not the case.

Susan's name is probably not Foreman, any more than the Doctor's is. This is merely the name on the gates of the junkyard where the TARDIS is hidden.

Susan looks and behaves like a typical 15-year-old girl. It is at her insistence that she attends Coal Hill School, and it is here that her strange breadth of knowledge is noticed by her teachers. Ian Chesterton says, 'She lets her knowledge out a bit at a time so as not to embarrass me... She knows more science than I'll ever know. She's a genius.' Yet, as the history teacher Barbara Wright points out, her knowledge is patchy: 'I don't know how you explain the fact that a teenage girl does not know how many shillings there are in a pound... She said she thought we were on the decimal system.'

But Susan is not human. While she likes pop music, she can read a thick textbook in an evening and, as we will later discover, under certain circumstances she can communicate telepathically (*The Sensorites*).

Susan is an adventurer. 'I like walking through the dark,' she tells her teachers. 'It's mysterious.' In *The Daleks*, she braves the dangers of the petrified jungle and the mutated Thals to retrieve the drugs her grandfather and friends desperately need. In *The Aztecs*, she is headstrong enough to refuse to marry the Perfect Victim who can demand anything of anyone on pain of death.

When we first meet Susan, she is enjoying life as a 'normal' schoolgirl on twentieth-century Earth. 'I love your school,' she tells Ian. 'I love England in the twentieth century. The last five months have been the happiest of my life...' Her strong feelings are emphasised by the fact that she would rather leave her grandfather than the twentieth century.

But Susan is growing up fast. She may have a bit of a crush on Ian, and see Barbara as a mature confidante, but she falls completely in love with David Campbell (*The Dalek Invasion of Earth*). Realising that his granddaughter will never willingly leave him, believing him to be dependent on her, the Doctor locks her out of the TARDIS.

IAN CHESTERTON

As a science teacher, Ian Chesterton believes only when he can see the proof. This makes him initially a sceptic when he finds himself inside the TARDIS, asked to believe that it can travel in time and space. As he tells the Doctor, it is a scientific dream he does not expect to find fulfilled in a junkyard. The Doctor's response is typically unforgiving: 'Your arrogance is nearly as great as your ignorance.'

TARDIS DATA BANK:

DESCRIPTION:
FEMALE, DOCTOR'S
GRANDDAUGHTER,
APPARENT EARTH
AGE: 15 YEARS
TRAVELLED: PRE-*AN
UNEARTHLY CHILD –
THE DALEK
INVASION OF
EARTH; THE FIVE
DOCTORS*

TARDIS DATA BANK:

DESCRIPTION: MALE,
HUMAN, SCIENCE
TEACHER AT COAL
HILL SCHOOL
TRAVELLED: *AN
UNEARTHLY CHILD –
THE CHASE*

20

TARDIS DATA BANK:

DESCRIPTION: FEMALE, HUMAN,
HISTORY TEACHER AT COAL HILL SCHOOL
TRAVELLED: *AN UNEARTHLY CHILD – THE CHASE*

In fact, Ian is neither arrogant nor ignorant. 'But I want to understand,' he tells the Doctor, and once he has proof, once he has seen and convinced himself, he turns out to be the most practical of the travellers. It is Ian who struggles to free them from the ropes that bind them in the Cave of Skulls, and it is Ian who eventually manages to make fire. In *The Daleks* he loses no opportunity to quiz the Doctor about the TARDIS systems and how they work.

Ian is not short of common sense. He can see the strength of Barbara's desire to return to the TARDIS rather than explore the Dalek City on Skaro (*The Daleks*) and stands up to the Doctor to make sure they leave safely. He is also headstrong and stubborn. When one of the travellers must go back for drugs, Ian insists it must be him – despite the fact that his legs have been paralysed by the Daleks, and that only Susan and the Doctor can unlock the TARDIS doors. This same headstrong stubbornness is what drives him to risk his life and warn the Thals that the Daleks are about to ambush them, and later to persuade the pacifist Thals they must fight to survive.

Never short on bravery and courage, Ian wins the Doctor's respect to the point where the old man treats him almost as an equal, almost as a friend. Before long he is revelling in his new-found life – and is even knighted by King Richard the Lionheart (*The Crusade*). But he never loses sight of the fact that he wants more than anything else to get home.

'I'm sorry, Doctor, but
you rattle off explanations
that would have baffled
Einstein and you expect
Barbara and I to know what
you're talking about.'

(IAN CHESTERTON – *THE CHASE*)

BARBARA WRIGHT

Barbara accepts the apparent impossibilities of travel through time and space more readily than Ian. But like Ian, her first inclination is to try to rationalise what she sees and hears: 'Susan, can't you see that all this is an illusion? It's a game that you and your grandfather are playing, if you like. But you can't expect us to believe it.' She is practical, realistic, and once she realises the truth she is prepared to accept it entirely.

Barbara is more instinctive than Ian. As they wait outside the Totters Lane junkyard, she tells him: 'Funny, isn't it. I feel frightened. As if we're about to interfere in something that is best left alone.'

This combination of intuition and practicality make Barbara the ideal mediator in the TARDIS. From the start it is she who manages to smooth the way between the Doctor and Ian. But when she is convinced of something, she is more than capable of standing up for it. She is fiercely defensive when accused of sabotaging the TARDIS in *The Edge of Destruction*, but it is when they encounter *The Aztecs* that Barbara is most assertive.

With her interest in history, she can see the inherent good in Aztec civilisation as well as the evil. She knows what will happen when the Conquistadors arrive, and she is determined to change things for the better.

Again, once Barbara comes to accept she cannot alter history she has the strength of character to live with it. It is this strength of character that enables her to survive the hardships of working for the Zarbi on Vortis (*The Web Planet*) and being captured and threatened with torture by El Akir (*The Crusade*).

Like Ian, she has a single-minded determination to get home, no matter how interesting her time with the Doctor may be. It is this that makes her decide to risk her life in the Dalek time ship and leave the TARDIS when the opportunity arises.

TARDIS DATA BANK:

DATE: AUTUMN 1963;
UNKNOWN, PRIOR
TO ICE AGE
LOCATION: COAL HILL
AREA, LONDON,
EARTH

WHEN SCHOOLTEACHERS
BARBARA WRIGHT AND IAN
CHESTERTON FOLLOW THEIR
PUPIL SUSAN FOREMAN BACK
TO THE JUNKYARD WHERE
SHE LIVES WITH HER
GRANDFATHER, THEY
DISCOVER A TIME MACHINE
SHAPED LIKE A POLICE BOX.
THEY ARE TAKEN BACK TO
PREHISTORIC EARTH WHERE
THEY MUST HELP A PRIMITIVE
TRIBE REDISCOVER THE
SECRET OF FIRE IF THEY ARE
TO SURVIVE…

AN UNEARTHLY CHILD

In which two schoolteachers find a very strange police box in a junkyard, and the adventure in space and time begins...

BY ANTHONY COBURN

4 EPISODES, FIRST BROADCAST 23 NOVEMBER–14 DECEMBER 1963

JOURNEY INFORMATION

ZA

Za's father was leader of the tribe, and the Firemaker. But when he died the secret of fire died with him. Now with 'Orb', the sun, getting colder again, the tribe desperately needs fire. Finding out how to make it has become an obsession for Za. Only when he can make fire like his father will the tribe regard him as the true leader. Only then will Horg allow him to take his daughter Hur as his partner.

Za understands more than anyone that fire is essential to the tribe's survival, and the importance of the strangers. He also appreciates the help they give him when he is wounded. Za risks his own life to save the tribe and he really seems to believe that if his rival Kal were leader, the tribe would be doomed. His stubborn position is not without personal risk: 'My father made fire,' Za tells his mother. 'Yes,' she agrees, 'and they killed him for it.'

The Doctor:
'If you could touch the alien sand and hear the cries of strange birds and watch them wheel in another sky, would that satisfy you?'

KAL

Kal is the last survivor of another tribe that died in the last cold spell. Because of this he too appreciates the importance of fire. When he witnesses the Doctor making fire (lighting his pipe with a match), the significance is not lost on him. At the first opportunity he makes an attempt to wrest control of the tribe from Za.

But Kal lacks Za's intelligence. The Doctor easily tricks him into showing off the bloodstained knife which he used to kill an old woman, and he is driven away by the angry tribe.

Whether he returns out of a desire for revenge, or his ambition to lead the tribe, Kal kills the guard at the Cave of Skulls without any remorse, believing that if he can defeat Za then the tribe will be his.

BEHIND THE SCENES

THEME MUSIC AND OPENING TITLES

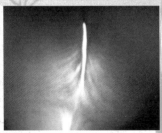

The theme music for **Doctor Who** was written by Ron Grainer, and producer Verity Lambert was keen for it to be realised by the BBC's Radiophonic Workshop. Grainer was a respected and accomplished composer who provided the themes for many popular television programmes, including **Maigret**, **Steptoe and Son**, and later **The Prisoner**, **Man in a Suitcase** and **Tales of the Unexpected.**

The job of interpreting Grainer's score and bringing the music to life was given to Delia Derbyshire at the Radiophonic Workshop. With help from Dick Mills (who later provided sound effects for **Doctor Who** from the Third Doctor's era onwards), she produced the music wholly electronically. In simple terms, the approach was to use signal generators to create the tones needed and record them. The finished music was then put together note by note.

A version of Ron Grainer's theme music was used on every episode of **Doctor Who** throughout its history (though the end titles of *Earthshock*, Episode 4, were run silently). With slight alterations, Delia Derbyshire's realisation of that music was used until 1980, then an updated version – again realised at the Radiophonic Workshop, this time by Peter Howell – replaced it for *The Leisure Hive*. Several other arrangements were used in later years.

To accompany the music, the opening titles were created by Bernard Lodge. In fact, they were the first filmed work to be done on **Doctor Who**. On 20 August 1963, with the help and technical supervision of Norman Taylor, Lodge filmed the footage from which he would cut together the opening titles.

The technique used was called 'visual howlaround'. This involved pointing a television camera at a screen showing that same camera's own output. The resulting feedback created swirling images and fog patterns, which Lodge was interested in using. He also discovered that when he fed in the lettering for the programme's title, this created its own feedback patterns. Lodge subsequently used the technique, with the addition of an image of the Doctor's face, to create the title sequences for the Second and Third Doctors.

Like many other aspects of the series, the titles and theme music for **Doctor Who** have always been innovative, distinctive and immediately recognisable.

THE DALEHS

In which the Daleks make their first appearance, and nothing will ever be the same again...
BY TERRY NATION
7 EPISODES, FIRST BROADCAST 21 DECEMBER 1963–
1 FEBRUARY 1964

TARDIS DATA BANK:

DATE: UNKNOWN (BUT 'GENERATIONS' PRIOR TO 2540)
LOCATION: PLANET SKARO

THE TRAVELLERS ARE CAPTURED BY THE MUTATED DALEKS, SURVIVORS OF A NUCLEAR WAR, WHO EXIST INSIDE TRAVEL MACHINES IN THEIR CITY IN THE MIDST OF A PETRIFIED JUNGLE. THE DOCTOR AND HIS COMPANIONS MUST CONVINCE THE PACIFIST HUMANOID THALS THAT THEY HAVE TO FIGHT THE DALEKS IF THEY ARE TO SURVIVE...

Dalek: 'The only interest we have in the Thals is their total extermination... Tomorrow we will be the masters of the planet Skaro.'

JOURNEY INFORMATION

SKARO

Skaro is the 12th planet in its solar system. The Thals, who have mapped as far as their legerscopes will allow, have records of other solar systems as well (on hexagonal plates).

According to the Daleks, over five hundred years previously, there were two races on the planet – the Daleks, and the Thals. 'After the neutronic war, our Dalek forefathers retired into the city protected by our machines... Most of [the Thals] perished in the war, but we know that there are survivors. They must be disgustingly mutated, but the fact that they have survived tells us they must have a drug that preserves the life force.' The Thal Alydon says Skaro '... was once a great world full of ideas and art and invention. In one day it was destroyed.'

THE PETRIFIED JUNGLE

White and ashen, misty ... the travellers' first thought is that there has been a forest fire of indescribable heat. A breeze blows through the jungle, yet the branches and trees do not move. As Ian discovers, the wood of the trees is like 'very brittle stone. It crumbles when you touch it.'

THE LAKE OF MUTATIONS

The Lake of Mutations lies behind the Dalek City. There is a chemical in the water that makes it glow in the moonlight.

Ganatus, one of the Thals, recounts how 'Five of us went there in search of food, and only my brother and I came back... We found what was left of one of them. The lake is alive with mutations, bred and cross-bred until the original has long been replaced by...' He leaves the result to the imagination, though we do see a giant caterpillar and a round, glowing-eyed creature that rises from the lake.

THE DALEKS

The Daleks have a xenophobic dislike of the Thals and any other life forms. They follow Susan's journey back to the TARDIS on rangerscopes, though they cannot track within the jungle. A lazerscope transmits pictures of the Thals.

The only glimpse we are afforded of the Dalek creatures that live inside the protective machines is a hideous clawed hand that emerges from under Susan's cloak.

The Dalek leaders are a 'Council', located on the fourth level of the City, although the Daleks' 'Control Room' is on level ten. The background noise is not unlike a heartbeat and is heard in all subsequent Dalek stories with the exception of *Resurrection of the Daleks*.

THE THALS

Before the war, the Thals were a race of warriors and the Daleks were teachers and philosophers. Now the Thals have evolved into a race of pacifists – absolutely opposed to conflict.

Examining the Thals' historical records, the Doctor deduces: 'There was a neutron war here. Most died and the survivors mutated. In the case of the Thals the mutation came round in full circle then refined itself into what you see... It took hundreds of years of course. In the second example [the Daleks] the mutation has not completed its full circle.' The Thals' records call the Daleks' ancestors Dals.

NEW INFORMATION

THE DOCTOR

The Doctor tells the Thals: 'I'm much too old to be a pioneer, although I was once, amongst my own people.'

With Ian and Barbara he is as self-assured and proud as ever: 'The mind will always triumph. With me to lead them, the Thals are bound to succeed.'

THE TARDIS

Susan says all TARDIS journeys are recorded and explains, 'There's a meter fixed to a great big bank of computers. If you feed it with the right sort of information it can take over the controls of the ship and deliver you to any place you want to go...'

Just as when it landed on prehistoric Earth in *An Unearthly Child*, the outside world is visible through the doors of the TARDIS.

The fault locator shows the reference number of a faulty or damaged TARDIS component. For example, the fluid link (a mercury-filled 'fuse' with a screw end) is listed as 'K7'.

Susan explains that, as a defence the whole lock comes away from the door of the TARDIS: 'There are 21 different holes inside the lock. There's one right place and twenty wrong ones. If you make a mistake, the whole inside of the lock will melt.'

Ian: 'What victory are you going to show these people when most of them have been killed? A fluid link? Is this what you're going to hold up to them and say "Thank you very much, this is what you've fought and died for"?'

BEHIND THE SCENES

GENESIS OF THE DALEKS

When **Doctor Who**'s script editor, David Whitaker, asked Terry Nation to write for the series neither of them could have guessed where it would lead. Nation almost didn't write for **Doctor Who**, but finding himself unexpectedly out of work he agreed to take on the job. Later he would admit that his intention was simply to 'take the money and fly like a thief'.

The initial storyline went through various revisions – most notably to remove the third race of aliens that originally arrived at the end of the story to confess they had started the neutronic war and had returned to settle the dispute between the Daleks and the Thals.

For his villains, the Daleks, Nation wanted creatures that were different from anything that had been seen before. He was inspired by the Georgian State Dancers – the women in their long skirts seemed to glide across the stage, and this was something he took as a starting point. His other objective was that the Daleks should have no recognisably human features. What he definitely did not want were creatures that were obviously actors dressed in suits.

The descriptions in Terry Nation's scripts, however, gave little idea of the tremendous visual impact the Daleks would achieve. The first appearance of a Dalek is at the end of Episode 1, where just a sucker arm is seen pointing at Barbara:

'Seen only by the audience, a panel slides open and there emerges from it a pair of mechanical arms. Barbara hears the sound behind her and turns in time to see the thing advancing on her. Only its arms are seen by the audience as they pin Barbara's arm to her side and she starts to scream.'

'Standing in a half circle in front of them are four hideous machine-like creatures. They are legless, moving on a round base. They have no human features. A lens on a flexible shaft acts as an eye. Arms with mechanical grips for hands (we have seen these arms before, moving up behind Barbara). The creatures hold strange weapons in their hands. One of them glides forward. It speaks with an echoing metallic voice.'

It was the job of BBC designer Raymond Cusick to bring these descriptions to life. Cusick based his design around the shape of a man sitting on a chair. To this basic shape he added the sucker arm and gun (originally at different levels) and an eye at the top of the creature.

The job of building the four Dalek machines was subcontracted to a company called Shawcraft Models. The voices were provided by actors Peter Hawkins, who provided voices for many children's programmes including **The Flowerpot Men** and **Captain Pugwash**, and David Graham who provided many voices for various Gerry Anderson series (including Brains and Parker in **Thunderbirds**). Their voices were treated using a 'ring modulator' device to achieve the distinctive metallic, grating quality.

Despite slight modifications for later stories – most notably the addition of 'slats' over the middle-section bands round the Daleks – the basic design remained unchanged. It is testament to Terry Nation's imagination and Raymond Cusick's design vision that it is as recognisable and potent today as it ever was.

THE EDGE OF DESTRUCTION

In which the Doctor and his companions spend a whole story inside the TARDIS...

BY DAVID WHITAKER

2 EPISODES, FIRST BROADCAST 8–15 FEBRUARY 1964

TARDIS DATA BANK:

DATE: NO SPACE, NO TIME
LOCATION: INSIDE THE TARDIS

ODD THINGS HAPPEN IN THE TARDIS – THE SCANNER SHOWS STRANGE IMAGES, THE DOORS OPEN IN FLIGHT AND CLOCK FACES SEEM TO MELT. HAS SOME LIFE FORM GOT INTO THE SHIP, OR IS THE TARDIS ITSELF TRYING TO WARN THE TRAVELLERS OF TERRIBLE DANGER...

Barbara: 'How dare you? Do you realise, you stupid old man, that you'd have died in the Cave of Skulls if Ian hadn't made fire for you? ... Accuse us? You ought to go down on your hands and knees and thank us. But gratitude's the last thing you'll ever have, or any sort of common sense either.'

NEW INFORMATION

THE DOCTOR

When the Doctor cuts his head, Susan binds it with a special bandage. The bandage is striped with bands of coloured ointment which disappear as the ointment goes into the wound. When the bandage is completely white, the wound is healed.

THE TARDIS

Susan's S-shaped bed folds down out of the wall when a control is pressed. Barbara and Susan share a room, while Ian has a room of his own. We do not see where the Doctor sleeps.

The Doctor refers to the 'main units' of the TARDIS. He also mentions the 'memory banks' that record the TARDIS journeys. Susan calls a ringing buzzer alarm that sounds from the console 'the danger signal'.

The central column is called simply 'the column' and the heart of the machine is under it. When the column moves, it proves the extent of the power thrust. If it were to come out of the console completely, the power would be free to escape. The Doctor says that if you felt the power, 'You wouldn't live to speak of it. You'd be blown to atoms in a split second.'

The 'fast return switch' takes the TARDIS back in time at an accelerated rate, and operates for as long as it is held down. The longer it is held down, the further back the TARDIS travels. It is labelled 'FAST RETURN' in felt pen.

The Doctor mentions the TARDIS's 'very extensive wardrobe', which includes an Ulster cape that belonged to Gilbert and Sullivan.

At one point, he remarks, 'My machine can't think.' This contrasts with his later contention that the TARDIS is, in a sense, alive.

The Doctor: 'It means that the ship is on the point of disintegration. You're not to blame. All four of us are to blame...'

The Doctor: 'What does he think it is — a potting shed, or something?'

TARDIS DATA BANK:

DATE:
APRIL–SEPTEMBER
1289
LOCATION: ASIA, EARTH

THE DOCTOR AND HIS
FRIENDS MEET MARCO POLO,
WHO DECIDES TO TAKE THE
TARDIS AS A GIFT TO PRESENT
TO KUBLAI KHAN. AS THEY
CROSS THE GOBI DESERT,
NOT ONLY MUST THE DOCTOR
RECOVER THE TARDIS KEY,
BUT HE MUST ALSO DEAL
WITH THE WARLIKE TEGANA
WHO IS OUT TO ASSASSINATE
THE KHAN…

MARCO POLO

In which the time travellers make an epic journey across China and meet Kublai Khan...
BY JOHN LUCAROTTI
7 EPISODES, FIRST BROADCAST 22 FEBRUARY–4 APRIL 1964

Marco Polo: 'A caravan that flies. Do you imagine what that will mean to Khan? It will make him the most powerful ruler the world has ever known. Stronger than Hannibal. Mightier than Alexander the Great.'

JOURNEY INFORMATION

MARCO POLO

Marco Polo is determined above all to gain permission from the Khan to return home to Venice. He explains that he left his home for Cathay in 1271. He impressed the Khan with his intelligence and was appointed to his service in 1277. 'Since then, I have travelled to every corner of his domain and beyond it. Two years ago, my father, my uncle and I asked the Khan for permission to go home. He refused. I think we had all served him too well... I have not seen my home for 18 years. I want to go back... I intend to [ask the Khan again.] But this time, I shall offer him a gift so magnificent that he will not be able to refuse me.' He means to give Kublai Khan the TARDIS.

PING-CHO

Ping-Cho is 16. She comes from Samarkand where her father is a government official. She misses her home and is going to Kublai Khan's summer palace at Shang-Tu for an arranged marriage, though she has never seen her future husband. 'I know only two things about him. He's a very important man. And he's 75 years old.'

The young girl strikes up a friendly relationship with Susan, even stealing the TARDIS key for her. Equally loyal, Susan is captured by Tegana when she risks going to say goodbye to her friend.

TEGANA

A ruthless killer and a cunning strategist, the war lord Tegana is single-minded in his plan to assassinate Kublai Khan. He sees life as a game of chess: '... a fascinating game of the strategy of war. Two equally balanced armies deployed upon a field of battle, and each commander determined to be the one who cries "Shah mat"... It means the king is dead.'

NEW INFORMATION

THE DOCTOR

The Doctor confesses he can't see anything without his glasses. He describes himself to Polo as 'a man of superior intellect'. Yet he sulks when Polo won't let him have access to the TARDIS. As Barbara says, the Doctor 'has a wonderful machine, capable of all sorts of miracles, and it is taken away from him by a man he calls a primitive.' He refuses to eat, and won't even confide in Susan.

Despite his later stance on carrying weapons, the Doctor uses a sword to take on one of the Mongol warriors during an attack on the camp.

When Kublai Khan and the Doctor discuss the pains of getting old, the Doctor says, 'I am not a doctor of medicine, sir, otherwise I should be able to cure these pains.'

THE TARDIS

The TARDIS is suffering from a burnt-out component that needs replacing (possibly after the events of *The Edge of Destruction*). There is no power, and therefore no light, no heat and apparently no water.

There is only one TARDIS key, which the Doctor gives to Marco Polo. He says that Marco Polo won't be able to use it, and later tells him, 'Put the key in that lock, Polo, and you will destroy the ship... You need more than a key to enter my ship. You need knowledge. Knowledge you will never possess.'

In *An Unearthly Child* both the Doctor and Susan had keys, but the Doctor used Susan's to fuse Dalek equipment in *The Daleks*. By *The Dalek Invasion of Earth*, the Doctor has made her another TARDIS key – which she discards when she leaves him.

COMPANIONS

SUSAN: Susan mentions 'the metal seas of Venus'. She tells Ping-Cho that her home is 'as far away as a night star'.

BEHIND THE SCENES

MISSING STORIES

In the 1960s and 1970s the BBC rarely repeated television programmes, and domestic video recorders had yet to arrive on the scene. In fact, there were only two **Doctor Who** repeats during the 1960s.

The BBC's Film and Television Archive stored the master videotapes of **Doctor Who** stories, but space was limited and videotape – which could be reused – was expensive. During the 1970s the BBC decided to 'junk' many older television programmes – there was little prospect of ever repeating them, and overseas sales were limited as more countries moved over to colour television. During this period there was a systematic destruction of the television archive and many programmes now deemed valuable, including **Doctor Who**, were destroyed.

Today, the value of early television is appreciated and with video and DVD offering opportunities for resale the BBC is keen to recover missing material.

Huge amounts of **Doctor Who** have in fact been recovered. BBC Enterprises (now BBC Worldwide), the commercial arm of the BBC, retained black-and-white film prints of episodes from the first three Doctors for overseas sales. Material was returned from abroad, and has been located by private collectors. But, sadly, much is still missing, including some colour episodes that have only survived in black and white.

Listed below are the episodes currently missing in their entirety, though various clips do exist from many of them.

THE MISSING EPISODES:

STORY	BBC STORY CODE	EPISODES MISSING
Marco Polo	D	1, 2, 3, 4, 5, 6, 7
The Reign of Terror	H	4, 5.
The Crusade	P	2, 4.
Galaxy 4	T	1, 2, 3, 4
Mission to the Unknown	T/A	1
The Myth Makers	U	1, 2, 3, 4
The Daleks' Master Plan	V	1, 2, 3, 4, 6, 7, 8, 9, 11, 12
The Massacre	W	1, 2, 3, 4
The Celestial Toymaker	Y	1, 2, 3
The Savages	AA	1, 2, 3, 4
The Smugglers	CC	1, 2, 3, 4
The Tenth Planet	DD	4
The Power of the Daleks	EE	1, 2, 3, 4, 5, 6
The Highlanders	FF	1, 2, 3, 4
The Underwater Menace	GG	1, 2, 4
The Moonbase	HH	1, 3
The Macra Terror	JJ	1, 2, 3, 4
The Faceless Ones	KK	2, 4, 5, 6
The Evil of the Daleks	LL	1, 3, 4, 5, 6, 7
The Abominable Snowmen	NN	1, 3, 4, 5, 6
The Ice Warriors	OO	2, 3
The Enemy of the World	PP	1, 2, 4, 5, 6
The Web of Fear	QQ	2, 3, 4, 5, 6
Fury from the Deep	RR	1, 2, 3, 4, 5, 6
The Wheel in Space	SS	1, 2, 4, 5
The Invasion	VV	1, 4
The Space Pirates	YY	1, 3, 4, 5, 6

THE KEYS OF MARINUS

In which the Doctor and his friends have several separate adventures and William Hartnell takes a holiday for two episodes...
BY TERRY NATION
6 EPISODES, FIRST BROADCAST 11 APRIL–16 MAY 1964

Arbitan: 'If you help me find the keys of Marinus I will let you have free access to your machine when you have delivered all the keys to me. If not, you will stay on the island without food or water. The choice is yours.'

JOURNEY INFORMATION

ARBITAN AND MARINUS

The island where the Conscience Machine is housed inside a pyramid-like building has beaches of glass and is surrounded by a sea of acid.

Arbitan, the Keeper of the Conscience, tells the travellers that technology on Marinus reached its peak over 2,000 years ago:

'All our knowledge culminated in the manufacture of this. At the time it was called the Conscience of Marinus. Marinus – that is the name of our planet. At first this machine was simply a judge and jury that was never wrong and unfair, and then we added to it, improved on it, made it more and more sophisticated until finally it became possible to radiate its power and influence the minds of men throughout the planet. They no longer had to decide what was wrong or right – the machine decided for them... Marinus was unique in the Universe – robbery, fear, hate, violence were unknown among us... For seven centuries we prospered. And then a man named Yartek found a means of overcoming the power of the machine. He and his followers, the Voords, were able to rob, exploit, kill, cheat. Our people could not resist because violence is alien to them... We always hoped to find a way of modifying [the machine] and making it again irresistible. So instead of destroying it we removed the five key microcircuits... One of them I kept... The other four were taken and put in places of safety all over Marinus. Only I know where they are. And now the time has come when they must be recovered...'

TRAVEL-DIALS

Arbitan explains that travel-dials are devices that '... enable you to move from place to place... The principle is much the same as that of your ship... They are all programmed to the same destination. You have only to twist the dial.'

The Doctor: 'Ah, now this might be helpful. Yes, if I can have instruments like these, I might be able to overcome the fault in the time mechanism aboard the ship.'

YARTEK AND THE VOORDS

The Voords wear protective suits for a submarine journey to the island. One of these suits is all that is left when the submarine leaks and one of the Voords is dissolved by the acid sea.

All of the Voords except Yartek have an antenna with a circular, forked or triangular top attached to their forehead. This is never explained but may be related to how they were able to block or resist the power of the Conscience Machine.

THE BRAINS OF MORPHOTON

The disembodied brains of Morphoton exist in glass tanks and rule a city on Marinus where one of the keys is hidden. They tell Barbara, 'We are the masters of this place. Our brains outgrew our bodies. It is our intelligence that has created this whole city. But we need the help of the human body to feed us and to carry out our orders... The human body is the most flexible instrument. No single mechanical device could reproduce its mobility and dexterity.'

NEW INFORMATION

THE TARDIS

While we see the TARDIS arrive at, and leave from, Marinus, there is no sound. Arbitan describes seeing the TARDIS 'materialise' – the first time this description is used. The Doctor mentions a 'fault in the time mechanism' of the TARDIS.

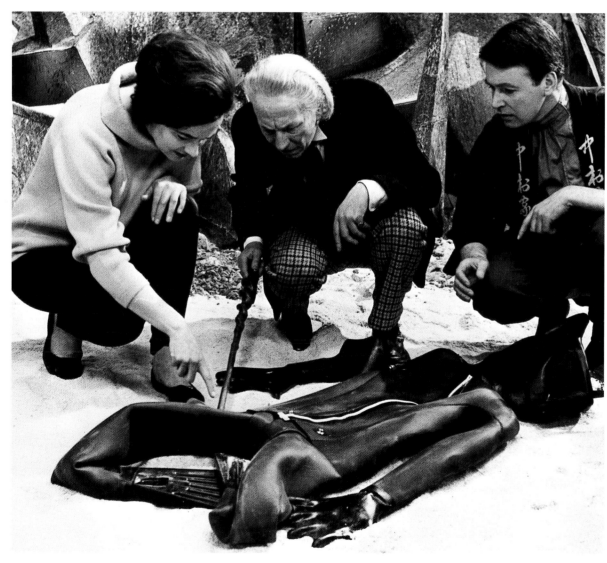

THE AZTECS

In which Barbara is hailed as a goddess and learns that history cannot be changed...
BY JOHN LUCAROTTI
4 EPISODES, FIRST BROADCAST 23 MAY–13 JUNE 1964

The Doctor: 'But you can't rewrite history — not one line... What you are trying to do is utterly impossible. I know. Believe me, I know.'

TARDIS DATA BANK:

DATE: AFTER 1430
LOCATION: MEXICO, EARTH

BARBARA IS MISTAKEN FOR THE REINCARNATION OF AZTEC HIGH PRIEST YETAXA AND TREATED AS THE GOD. BUT WHEN SHE TRIES TO FORBID THE PRACTICE OF HUMAN SACRIFICE, SHE MAKES AN ENEMY OF THE HIGH PRIEST TLOTOXL. MEANWHILE, SUSAN IS TO BE MARRIED TO THE PERFECT VICTIM, IAN TRIES TO FIND A WAY BACK INTO THE TOMB WHERE THE TARDIS IS, AND THE DOCTOR ACCIDENTALLY PROPOSES MARRIAGE TO THE LADY CAMECA...

JOURNEY INFORMATION

AUTLOC AND TLOTOXL

Autloc and Tlotoxl represent the two sides of Aztec culture. As Barbara points out, the Aztecs are a paradox. On the one hand they are civilised and advanced, creators of great beauty and art. But on the other, they indulge in human sacrifice and inflict painful punishment in the names of their gods.

Autloc, as High Priest of Knowledge, personifies the better side of Aztec culture. As a man he is considerate, open-minded, aristocratic in bearing. His departure for the wilderness at the end of the story may represent a personal salvation, but it also serves to demonstrate that Barbara – and Autloc – have lost the ideological argument.

At the end of the story, Tlotoxl, High Priest of Sacrifice – 'the local butcher' – is very much in charge. Throughout the story he questions Barbara's divinity and seeks to destroy her. To our eyes, Tlotoxl is an ugly, scheming bigot. But it is his interpretation of what is important to his culture that ultimately prevails. 'How shall a man know his gods?' he asks Barbara. How indeed?

CAMECA

Cameca resides in the Garden of Peace, where the Doctor is taken. Autloc tells the Doctor, 'Of all those here, her advice is most sought after... You will find her a companion of wit and interest.' Sure enough, the Doctor strikes up a friendship with the Aztec lady, and accidentally proposes marriage to her by making cocoa for them to share...

NEW INFORMATION

THE DOCTOR

For the first, and probably the only, time we see the Doctor in love. Or at the very least, demonstrating a depth of regard and respect for the Aztec lady Cameca that is rarely equalled again. He might be ignorant of the implications when he makes cocoa for her, but there is a hint of pride as well as amused embarrassment when he tells Ian that he is

engaged. The true depth of his feelings is revealed when he decides to keep a brooch that Cameca has given him.

As is often the case, the Doctor is quick to point out that he is not a doctor of medicine. He proudly describes himself to Cameca as '… a scientist and engineer. I'm a builder of things.'

COMPANIONS

IAN: In *Marco Polo*, Ian was quick to point out that he is no fighter or swordsman. But he is able to stun an Aztec Warrior, Ixta, with a nerve pinch to the neck, and later defeats him in single combat.

BARBARA: Barbara's idealism is nowhere more obvious than here. Although she eventually accepts the Doctor's contention that she cannot change a single line of history, she is determined to try. Her goal is to save what is good and honourable in Aztec society and drive out the horrors and ignorance of human sacrifice, hoping the Aztecs will be better equipped to deal with Cortez and the Spaniards when they arrive to conquer.

When referring to Barbara's relationship with Autloc the Doctor says, 'You failed to save a civilisation, but at least you helped one man.'

Barbara: 'I warn you Tlotoxl, you say one word against me to the people and I'll have them destroy you.'

34

THE SENSORITES

In which Susan demonstrates her telepathic powers, and **Crackerjack** presenter Peter Glaze appears under make-up as an alien villain...

BY PETER R. NEWMAN

6 EPISODES, FIRST BROADCAST 20 JUNE–1 AUGUST 1964

TARDIS DATA BANK:

DATE: 28TH CENTURY
LOCATION: THE SENSE-SPHERE

THE TARDIS LANDS INSIDE A SPACESHIP WHERE THE CREW SEEM TO BE DEAD. BUT THEY REVIVE AND WARN THE DOCTOR AND HIS FRIENDS THEY ARE PRISONERS OF THE SENSORITES. THE DOCTOR MUST BARGAIN FOR ALL THEIR LIVES BY HELPING THE SENSORITES TO FIND THE TRUE SOURCE OF A STRANGE ILLNESS THAT IS KILLING THEM...

The Administrator: 'Weakling, betrayer of our people, coward! I should imprison you in some room wherein no light can shine and fill that room with noise.'

JOURNEY INFORMATION

THE SENSORITES

Ten years earlier, five humans had visited the Sense-sphere. They wanted molybdenum (a valuable metal that can withstand great temperature) and argued amongst themselves. Two left the Sense-sphere in their ship, and the Sensorites assumed the others had hidden on board and fought for control as the ship exploded one mile above the planet's surface. Since then the Sensorites have been dying in increasing numbers. The Doctor discovers this is due to deadly nightshade that is being put into their water supply by the humans they thought were dead...

The Sensorites are telepathic and can control human minds, inducing deep, death-like sleep. They communicate over distances with each other using telepathic amplifiers – small discs that they touch to their foreheads. The Sensorite weapons can temporarily paralyse up to a range of 30 yards. It is implied they can be set to kill.

They are not used to darkness (their eyes are fully dilated), do not like noise and talk in soft whispers. Their heart is in the centre of their chests, and they can apparently survive in space without a protective suit.

The Sensorites have a caste system, with uniforms indicating rank and status. Their leader, the First Elder, has two sashes across his chest and the Second Elder has a single sash. The City Administrator's uniform has a dark band round the neck. The warriors have three

The Doctor:

'I'd like to talk to him, face to face... Tell him we're not pirates or plunderers. There's only one treasure we desire from him — freedom!!'

bands on their arm, and are led by a captain. Scientists have a spiral design on their chest.

Referring to how the human John has reacted to the Sensorites' manipulation of his mind, a scientist says, 'We discovered long ago that in our brain there were many different compartments or divisions. When fear or alarm is at work, that section becomes "open" – a veil is lifted... That is what happened to the man John. But the veil will not lower itself, thus he is constantly afraid.'

NEW INFORMATION

THE DOCTOR

The Doctor says that he once threw a parson's nose at Henry VIII so as to be sent to the Tower of London – where the TARDIS was being held. He also says Beau Brummel (famous dandy and protegé of the Prince Regent) told him he looked better in a cape.

He also reveals that, like his granddaughter, he is telepathic to some degree and sometimes knows what Ian is thinking.

The Doctor tells the Sensorites he's never had an argument with Susan before (from past evidence, he is exaggerating). He does not refuse an offered weapon (though in fact it is Ian who carries it), saying: 'I have never liked weapons at any time, however they are handy little things.'

THE TARDIS

The Sensorites remove the entire TARDIS lock, so the doors cannot be opened. The Doctor says forcing the doors will 'disturb the field of dimensions inside'.

COMPANIONS

SUSAN: Susan describes her home to the Sensorite First Elder: 'It's ages since we've seen our planet. It's quite like Earth ... but at night the sky is a burnt orange, and the leaves on the trees are bright silver.'

Susan mentions visiting the planet Esto, where the plants communicate telepathically. She can read Sensorite thoughts only when they allow it, though she can 'transmit' to them.

When Susan leaves the Sense-sphere she loses her ability for thought transference – the Sense-sphere apparently aids the ability as it has many ultra-high frequencies. The Doctor says she has an obvious talent for telepathy and can develop it when they return to their home world. Susan wants to know when they will return – she isn't unhappy, but she says she wants to 'belong' somewhere rather than being a wanderer.

THE REIGN OF TERROR

In which the Doctor and his friends try to escape the guillotine and Ian and Barbara keep watch on Napoleon...
BY DENNIS SPOONER
6 EPISODES, FIRST BROADCAST 8 AUGUST–12 SEPTEMBER 1964

JOURNEY INFORMATION

JAMES STIRLING

An English spy, James Stirling, has lived in France in the guise of Citizen Lemaitre for several years. Since England and France are at war, Stirling is in constant danger of execution. Even though the rebel Jules Renan and his friends oppose the government, they are wary of helping the English. Stirling himself prefers to work alone – unsurprising in a country where anyone may turn out to be a traitor to their friends and comrades.

An expert at his job, Stirling even tricks the Doctor into revealing that he is Barbara's friend, and guesses that Susan is his granddaughter. He is also a man of his word, helping secure Susan's release after Ian and Barbara have spied on Barrass and Napoleon for him.

JULES RENAN

Jules Renan is a rebel opposed to Robespierre and the revolution. He explains his position and philosophy to Barbara when justifying his killing of the traitor Leon Colbert: 'Do you ever wonder why I'm doing these things, hiding in shadows, fighting in corners? ... There can be no loyalty

TARDIS DATA BANK:

DATE: 24–27 JULY 1794
LOCATION: EARTH – IN AND AROUND PARIS, FRANCE

THE TARDIS LANDS IN FRANCE DURING THE TERROR. THE DOCTOR PLAYS THE ROLE OF A LOCAL OFFICIAL TO TRY TO RESCUE HIS COMPANIONS FROM PRISON. IAN PROMISES WEBSTER, A FELLOW PRISONER, THAT HE WILL FIND STIRLING, AN ENGLISH SPY. ABOVE ALL, THEY MUST AVOID BEING GUILLOTINED...

Webster: 'One day soon, France will stop this madness and turn her full attention across the Channel. We must be ready for that day. There's a man in France — an Englishman — working to that end... Find him if you can... Promise to find James Stirling...'

or honour where anarchy prevails... There are only two sides today, Barbara. Those who rule by fear and treachery, and those who fight for reason and justice. Anyone who betrays these principles is worse than the devil in hell.'

NEW INFORMATION

THE DOCTOR

The Doctor decides to put Ian and Barbara off the TARDIS and refuses to change his mind. He reacts with annoyance to the suggestion that he is not in total control: 'I'm rather tired of your insinuations that I am not master of this craft. Oh, I admit, it did develop a fault – a minor fault on one occasion, perhaps twice. But, nothing I couldn't control.' Eventually he agrees to the face-saving compromise of seeing them safely home.

The Doctor displays a rare streak of violence, hitting a roadworks overseer over the back of the head with a spade in order to escape. Later he hits the Conciergerie jailer over the head with a bottle.

The Doctor reiterates that history cannot be changed: 'The events will happen, just as they are written. I'm afraid so, and we can't stem the tide. But at least we can stop being carried away with the flood.'

COMPANIONS

SUSAN: Barbara tells Jules that Susan does not sleep for long, and tells a physician that the girl has an 'enormous appetite'.

BARBARA: Barbara strikes up a very friendly relationship with Leon Colbert. She is distraught when she learns of his death.

Despite the fact that Jules killed him to rescue Ian, and in self-defence, Barbara defends Colbert's treachery: 'The revolution isn't all bad, and neither are the people who support it. It changed things for the whole world, and good, honest people gave their lives for that change... You check your history books, Ian, before you decide what people deserve.'

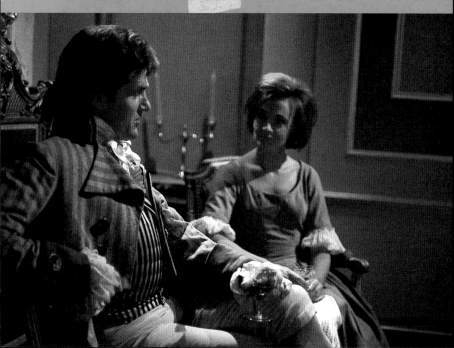

PLANET OF GIANTS

In which the travellers are reduced to an inch in height and also lose an episode...
BY LOUIS MARKS
3 EPISODES, FIRST BROADCAST 31 OCTOBER–14 NOVEMBER 1964

TARDIS DATA BANK:

DATE: PRESUMABLY 'PRESENT DAY'
LOCATION: RURAL ENGLAND

REDUCED TO JUST AN INCH HIGH, THE DOCTOR AND HIS FRIENDS FACE 'GIANT' CATS AND HOMICIDAL HUMANS AS THEY STRUGGLE TO STOP THE PRODUCTION OF A DEADLY PESTICIDE THAT WILL DESTROY ALL INSECT LIFE – AND THE ECOSYSTEM...

Smithers: 'DN6. It kills everything. Even worms, Forrester. And the cat... It'll poison people.'

JOURNEY INFORMATION

DN6

DN6 is a revolutionary new insecticide created by Smithers, and Forrester is determined to manufacture it. But DN6 is not discriminating – it destroys all insect life, not just pests, and unlike other insecticides it does not break down and lose its effect over time.

Government inspector Farrow explains the dangerous problem of DN6 to Forrester: 'The very exhaustive tests I have made show that DN6 is totally destructive... There are many insects which make a vital contribution to agriculture, and these insects must not die...'

NEW INFORMATION

THE DOCTOR

For the first time, the Doctor takes the opportunity to apologise to Barbara for his brusque manner: 'My dear Barbara, was I rude to you just now? If so, I'm so sorry – I always forget the niceties under pressure. Please forgive me.'

Susan describes the explosion of a spray can as 'just like that air raid.' The Doctor remembers and says, 'What infernal machines those Zeppelins were.'

THE TARDIS

Susan says the moment of materialisation is the most dangerous part of a journey.

When the TARDIS doors open in flight, a white void is all that can be seen outside. The Doctor says the doors

opened 'because the space pressure was far too great'. This 'pressure' he later says, was what reduced their size. The Doctor is not absolutely sure he can restore them to normal size, telling Ian: 'Yes of course I can... I hope...'

The scanner is damaged – the screen apparently shattering, and the Doctor wonders if this is because outside there is 'something too big to explain'.

The TARDIS's materialisation and dematerialisation are silent, although the materialisation in future London at the end of the story is heard inside the TARDIS.

> Susan: 'These things haven't been made bigger. We've been made smaller... The doors of the TARDIS opened, that means the space pressure forced us to reduce.'

BEHIND THE SCENES

THE MISSING EPISODE: THE URGE TO LIVE

While *Planet of Giants* was transmitted in three episodes, it was originally scripted and produced as a four-part story. On 19 October 1964, less than two weeks before transmission of the first episode, it was decided to edit the story down to three parts by combining material from the last two episodes into a single episode. The decision was taken by the BBC's Head of Serials, Donald Wilson, and Head of Drama, Sydney Newman – both of whom had been instrumental in setting up **Doctor Who**.

Although made as the penultimate story in **Doctor Who**'s first recording 'block', *Planet of Giants* was to be broadcast as the first story of the second season. Wilson and Newman both thought that it lacked the 'punch' of a season opener and would have preferred to have kicked off with *The Dalek Invasion of Earth*. However, this was not possible as the character of Susan leaves at the end of the Dalek story, so the stories could not simply be swapped round. This left three choices: to proceed as originally planned; to drop *Planet of Giants* completely; or to cut the number of episodes to strengthen the storyline by editing the already-recorded material.

In his memo to Newman summarising their decision to go with the third choice, Wilson says: '... I am not satisfied that it will get us off to the great start that we must have if it runs to its full length. Much of it is fascinating and exciting but by its nature and the resources needed we could not do everything we wanted to do to make it wholly satisfactory...'

The editing of Episodes 3 and 4 was supervised by Douglas Camfield, who had directed Episode 4. Camfield would go on to become one of the most prolific and respected of **Doctor Who** directors.

THE DALEK INVASION OF EARTH

In which the Daleks return and conquer the Earth, and Susan departs...
BY TERRY NATION
6 EPISODES, FIRST BROADCAST 21 NOVEMBER–26 DECEMBER 1964

TARDIS DATA BANK:

DATE: c2167

LOCATION: EARTH – MAINLY LONDON AND BEDFORDSHIRE

TWO HUNDRED YEARS IN THE FUTURE, THE DALEKS ARE THE MASTERS OF A DEVASTATED EARTH, TURNING THE POPULATION INTO SLAVES OR DEHUMANISED 'ROBOMEN'. THE DOCTOR AND HIS FRIENDS JOIN WITH A RESISTANCE GROUP TO ATTACK THE DALEKS. AT THE DALEK MINE WORKINGS IN BEDFORDSHIRE, THE DOCTOR DISCOVERS THE DALEKS' TERRIFYING PLAN AND BATTLES TO SAVE THE WORLD...

JOURNEY INFORMATION

THE DALEKS

The Daleks can now travel outside the confines of their City, and invade other planets. They have enlarged 'fenders', and pick up power and transmissions through a receiver dish on the back of their casings. Their bases are revealed to be completely flat when one is lifted up by rebelling miners.

The Daleks are led by the Black Dalek – also called the 'Supreme Controller'. There is also mention of a separate 'Supreme Command'. The invading Daleks are the 'Dalek Earth Force'. A 'Saucer Commander' is seen briefly – a predominantly black Dalek, but with alternating black and silver flanges. This Dalek is later replaced as Saucer Commander by the 'proper' Black Dalek.

The firebombs the Daleks use to destroy London are trunk-like boxes with three circular dials on the front. David Campbell, one of the rebels, and Susan defuse one of the bombs by dissolving the casing with acid (from one of the rebels' bombs) then removing the timer.

THE DALEK INVASION: Ten years before the story, Earth was bombarded with meteorites, which scientists called a 'cosmic storm'. The people began to die of a new plague. Apparently, 'whole continents of people were wiped out – Asia, Africa, South America. They used to say Earth had a smell of death about it...'

David says, 'The plague had split the world into tiny little communities, too far apart to combine and fight, and too small individually to stand any chance against invasion... About six months after the meteorite fall, that's when the saucers landed. Cities were razed to the ground, others were simply occupied. Anyone who resisted was destroyed.'

The Daleks plan to drill through the Earth's crust and blow out the planet's core with a penetration explosive capsule. They will then install a guidance system so as to pilot the Earth like a giant spaceship.

ROBOMEN

Because there are relatively few Daleks on Earth, they operate on some prisoners and turn them into living robots – Robomen. David explains that the 'transfer' operation controls the human brain '...at least for a time... I've seen the Robos when they break down. They go insane. They smash their heads against walls, they throw themselves off buildings or into the river...'

THE SLYTHER

The revolting Slyther is a sort of 'pet' of the Black Dalek, used to enforce the curfew at the mine. It roams the mine area at night in search of human food. The Slyther's horrific, screaming cries strike terror into the mine workers.

Dalek: 'We are the masters of Earth.'

NEW INFORMATION

THE DOCTOR

The Doctor has no qualms about knocking out a Roboman with his stick. But he stops the rebel Tyler shooting it: 'I never take life, only when my own is reasonably threatened...'

Throughout the story, the Doctor's love of his granddaughter is evident, and he is not oblivious to her developing relationship with David. He leaves Susan behind, locking her out of the TARDIS, because he fiercely believes this is the best thing for her. Perhaps, also, it is an admission that he knows that he can never take her home...

THE TARDIS

The TARDIS outer door closes when the Doctor closes the inner doors. The Doctor can double-lock the doors so that, even with a key, Susan cannot enter. He can talk to her outside 'through' the scanner.

COMPANIONS

SUSAN: Susan confides in David that she has no real home. 'I never felt that there was any time or place that I belonged to. I've never had any real identity.'

Susan says of the Doctor: 'He's a pretty fantastic sort of man.' Although she loves David, she cannot bring herself to leave the Doctor, until he locks her out of the TARDIS.

BEHIND THE SCENES

LOCATION FILMING

With external location shooting now commonplace in television drama, it is surprising to learn that the first location footage shot for **Doctor Who** was a set of five short insert shots of the Doctor walking down the road for Episode 2 of *The Reign of Terror*. The 35mm film was shot in a single day – 15 June 1964 – and did not even feature the *real* Doctor. Actor Brian Proudfoot took the place of William Hartnell in these sequences, filmed on two locations in Buckinghamshire.

Film had been used before to augment the video material shot in the recording studio. It was common practice right from the first episode to film material that was too complicated or dangerous at the BBC's film studios in Ealing. This included, for example, the fight between Kal and Za (*An Unearthly Child*) which needed complex editing that just could not be achieved on videotape in those days.

Material filmed in the Ealing studios, and later location film, would be shot ahead of the main studio recordings, then edited into video material. This practice continued, generally, throughout the run of **Doctor Who**. In the earlier years, it could mean that some or all of the regular actors and actresses had to be released from rehearsals or even studio time in order to fulfil their location filming commitments.

The Doctor: 'One day, I shall come back — yes, I shall come back. Until then there must be no regrets, no tears, no anxieties. Just go forward in all your beliefs, and prove to me that I am not mistaken in mine. Goodbye, Susan. Goodbye, my dear.'

As there was a gap between the film and video sessions, designs occasionally changed. A good example of this is the change in the make-up and masks used for the Menoptra in *The Web Planet*. Having seen the filmed footage, the production team decided the masks would need to be redesigned for the more discerning video cameras and planned close-up video shots. The difference is apparent in the finished programme, and very obvious when publicity photographs of different scenes are seen together (as on page 47).

The Dalek Invasion of Earth was only the second story to require external location filming. The film work for Episodes 1, 3, 4 and 6 is impressive and accomplished. It is also extensive. The logistics of filming Daleks against the backdrop of a deserted London – including the impressive shots of Daleks on Westminster Bridge, the Embankment and in Trafalgar Square – were especially tricky, and planned shots on the Mall including Buckingham Palace were abandoned. The filming of these sequences for Episode 3 was done in the early hours of Sunday 23 August 1964.

There is a discernible difference in 'texture' between film and videotape, which makes the change between location and studio apparent in many television series. Although video can now be treated to look like film (and vice versa), the differences were there for **Doctor Who** viewers to see right up until the use of Outside Broadcast (OB) video for location work. OB was adopted as standard for the series from *The Trial of a Time Lord* onwards though it had been used as early as *Robot* in 1974.

Vicki: 'Of course I know about the Beatles I've been to their memorial theatre in Liverpool... They're marvellous, but I didn't know they played classical music.'

VICKI

After Vicki's mother died her father wanted to get away from Earth, and took a job on the planet Astra in 2493. This is where Vicki and her father were going when the spaceship they were on crash landed on the planet Dido. She appears to be in her teens.

In *The Web Planet* we learn that Vicki studied medicine, but has never heard of aspirin (which the Doctor has in his first-aid kit). She tells Barbara that she took a certificate in medicine, physics, chemistry and other subjects when she was ten years old. She studied for almost an hour a week on a machine. When she hears what Barbara taught, she wonders if she was a teacher in a nursery school.

Until she meets the Doctor, Ian and Barbara, Vicki takes fellow passenger Bennett's account of how the natives of Dido killed her father and the rest of the crew and passengers for granted: 'They killed all the crew. When we landed, we made contact here. Everyone on board was invited to a grand sort of meeting. I couldn't go – I was ill, a fever or something. I stayed here that night. I remember waking up – a thunderstorm, I thought. But it was an explosion. Bennett – Bennett dragged himself back. I was ill for days. I didn't know about it till later. I came around and found Bennett. He can't walk. We just wait...'

Once she leaves Dido, Vicki is keen to start on the adventures she has been promised. She is bored at the villa where the travellers stay in *The Romans*, desperate for adventure and disappointed it doesn't all happen at once.

Vicki's relationship with the Doctor is very similar to that between the Doctor and Susan. 'Oh yes, I like the Doctor,' she tells Ian and Barbara. 'It's funny, but as soon as he walked in I felt you could trust him. But why does he wear those funny clothes and that long white hair?'

Throughout her travels with the Doctor, Vicki retains her sense of wonder and awe. When she first sees Nero, she is literally bouncing with excitement. Even the spectacle of Rome burning enthuses the young girl – 'My first real sight of history,' she tells the Doctor. It is not to be her last...

THE RESCUE

In which the Doctor, Ian and Susan rescue Vicki from the planet Dido...
BY DAVID WHITAKER
2 EPISODES, FIRST BROADCAST 2–9 JANUARY 1965

The Doctor: 'You destroyed a whole planet to save your skin — you're insane.'

JOURNEY INFORMATION

DIDO

The Doctor says that the last time he visited Dido the total population of the planet was barely a hundred people. 'Peace, friendship, happiness – this means everything to the people here.' Because there are so few of them, life is so much more precious. Ian and Barbara see the ruined buildings, destroyed in the explosion.

The natives of Dido who appear at the end of the story do not speak. They are dressed in white, and seem to know that Bennett, who engineered the explosion to cover up for a previous crime, is the villain responsible for the destruction of their race.

CONSTRUCTION TOOL

The claw-like device Koquillion uses as a weapon is described by the Doctor as emitting '... a ray used in construction work... when I was here last time... they'd just perfected this thing.'

THE SAND BEAST

The Sand Beast Vicki has 'adopted' and calls 'Sandy' is a large shuffling creature with green eyes on stalks. Although it looks fierce, it is vegetarian. Vicki has trained 'Sandy' to come to the space ship for food. She is distraught when Barbara – assuming it is attacking – kills her pet with a flare pistol.

The ceremonial robes and masks (worn by Bennett masquerading as 'Koquillion') are based on the creature, as are engravings and the hand-hold rings in the walls.

NEW INFORMATION

THE DOCTOR

The Doctor obviously misses Susan and sleeps through the TARDIS landing, which Ian says he has never done before. Then he absent-mindedly tells Susan to open the doors.

The Doctor has been to Dido before. He recognises the smell of the planet, and tests a rock sample to be sure. His thoughts on discovering this is indeed Dido are interesting: 'Well, I must say it will be rather nice to meet these friendly people again after all these years... I wonder if I was to tell Ian it was deliberate whether he'd believe me or not. Oh no, of course, I was asleep. Pity...'

Ian describes the Doctor's cursory examination of him after a rockfall as 'the most thorough-going medical I've ever had'. To this, the Doctor replies with amusement: 'Yes, it's a pity I didn't get that degree, isn't it?'

When circumstances make it necessary, the Doctor attacks Bennett – first with the Dido construction tool, then with a sword and finally, in desperation, a cushion.

THE TARDIS

When Barbara says they have landed, the Doctor corrects her: 'Materialised, I think, is a better word.' (His first use of the word.)

Ian uses the Doctor's key to open the doors (when the Doctor is unconscious). So, he is able to unlock the doors without melting the lock (as Susan described in *The Daleks*). Possibly the Doctor has disabled this mechanism as it is not mentioned again.

COMPANIONS

BARBARA; While Barbara takes immediately to Vicki, and is distraught when she accidentally kills the girl's pet, she is less than amused at Vicki's suggestion that if she is from 1963 she must be 'about five hundred and fifty years old'.

Koquillion: 'Remember, I am the only one who can save you from my people. You should be grateful — I am your only protection.'

Doctor: 'Oh, so you want a fight, do you?!'

THE ROMANS

In which the Doctor indulges in some comic relief with the help of Derek Francis as Emperor Nero...
BY DENNIS SPOONER
4 EPISODES, FIRST BROADCAST 16 JANUARY–6 FEBRUARY 1965

TARDIS DATA BANK:

DATE: JUNE–JULY 64AD
LOCATION: ROME, EARTH

THE DOCTOR IS MISTAKEN FOR A FAMOUS LYRE PLAYER CALLED PETTULIAN, AND PROVOKES EMPEROR NERO'S JEALOUSY. IAN AND BARBARA ARE CAPTURED BY SLAVE TRADERS. BARBARA BECOMES A SLAVE AT NERO'S COURT, ATTRACTING THE EMPEROR'S UNWANTED ATTENTIONS AND UPSETTING HIS WIFE. IAN BECOMES A GALLEY SLAVE, BEFORE BEING SENT TO FIGHT IN THE ARENA. CAN THEY ALL ESCAPE BEFORE THE FIRE OF ROME…

JOURNEY INFORMATION

EMPEROR NERO

Nero is grotesque and spoilt. He is used to getting everything he wants, be it Barbara or a fight between gladiators and does not care who suffers in the process. He takes pleasure in humiliating his personal slave Tigilinus – giving him a drink he suspects has been poisoned.

Equally casually, after Ian and his friend Delos escape he kills the guard at the amphitheatre because 'he didn't fight hard enough' to stop them. When 'Maximus Pettulian' (actually the Doctor) gets too much applause, Nero decides to have him killed in the arena.

Vain and arrogant, Nero wonders whether to call his new city: 'Neropolis, Nero Caesum, or just plain Nero?' He is exhilarated by the idea of burning down Rome itself simply to get his own way and prove a point to the Senate.

TAVIUS

Tavius is the slave buyer for the court of Nero and is involved in helping the real Pettulian to assassinate Nero.

Despite his intrigues and plotting, Tavius is a man of principle, revealed at the last to be a Christian as he wishes

Barbara well – clutching the crucifix that hangs hidden around his neck. Tavius buys Barbara at the slave auction because she shows kindness to a fellow prisoner. 'Most people would have looked after themselves. You're kind and considerate.'

Perhaps Tavius sees in Barbara someone who reflects the Christian values he himself aspires to, and which are so rare at the court of Nero.

NEW INFORMATION

THE DOCTOR

The Doctor gleefully attacks a mute assassin, Ascaris. He tells Vicki, 'You know, I am so constantly outwitting the opposition, I tend to forget the delights and satisfaction of the gentle art of fisticuffs…'

After his silent lyre recital – so 'soft and delicate' that only those with keen musical perception will be able to hear it – the Doctor claims he gave Hans Andersen the idea for the *Emperor's New Clothes*.

He takes great joy in punning with Nero about the secret plan to feed him to the lions, and chuckles mischievously as he watches Rome burn. But, having lectured Vicki on the dangers of interfering with history, he vigorously insists, 'It's got nothing to do with me.'

THE TARDIS

The Doctor says the TARDIS can take off from any angle, and it has evidently survived falling from the cliff.

COMPANIONS

IAN: During his five days as galley slave, Ian confesses to Delos that he is 'not a great swimmer'. He is, however, adept in the sword fight with Delos (so he has improved since *Marco Polo*).

BARBARA: Once again, Barbara displays her knowledge of history: 'Bad? Have you any idea how the Romans treated their slaves? Or how many escaped?'

Nero gives Barbara a gold bracelet – which she still wears in *The Web Planet*.

THE WEB PLANET

In which the travellers meet giant ants, butterflies and woodlice, and one of the butterflies is actor Martin Jarvis…

BY BILL STRUTTON

6 EPISODES, FIRST BROADCAST 13 FEBRUARY–20 MARCH 1965

The Doctor: 'Apart from rubbing our back legs together like some sort of grasshopper, I doubt that we could get on speaking terms with them.'

TARDIS DATA BANK:

DATE: UNKNOWN
LOCATION: VORTIS, IN THE ISOP GALAXY

CAPTURED BY THE ANT-BEETLE-LIKE ZARBI, WHICH ARE CONTROLLED BY THE ALIEN ANIMUS, THE DOCTOR AND HIS FRIENDS TRY TO HELP THE BUTTERFLY-LIKE MENOPTRA TO RECLAIM THEIR PLANET. BARBARA IS SENT TO WORK IN THE CRATER OF NEEDLES, WHILE IAN MEETS THE UNDERGROUND OPTERA. THE DOCTOR AND VICKI, MEANWHILE, BECOME PRISONERS OF THE ANIMUS…

Hetra: 'We will consult the chasm of light and if you come from above, you will die.'

JOURNEY INFORMATION

VORTIS

The barren planet Vortis is in the Isop Galaxy. It has several moons (one named Taron), attracted by the same force that attracts the TARDIS – the Animus.

THE MENOPTRA

Like giant butterflies, the Menoptra are the intelligent natives of Vortis. They move in a stylised manner and gesticulate with their fingerless hands while speaking in accented, shrill tones. They were driven from their home world by the Animus and fled to a nearby moon before massing their force to retake it on the nearby planet Pictos.

THE ANIMUS

The Doctor believes the Carsenome web-city has taken 100 to 200 years to grow to its present size. The Animus, at the centre of the web (over the magnetic pole), controls the Zarbi and larvae guns. It communicates with the Doctor through a transparent dome lowered from the ceiling. A gun 'arm' appears from the wall and fires on the TARDIS and smothers the Doctor and Vicki in cobwebs.

The Animus is a mass of tentacles, a cross between a spider and an octopus. It can control anyone who comes into contact with gold. An elderly Menoptra, Prapillus, says that the Animus is 'an alien from the darkness of space.' It was only discovered 'when it was already thinking itself into the crannies of Vortis and the minds of the Zarbi.'

THE ZARBI

The Zarbi are a giant cross between ants and beetles, controlled by the power of the Animus. The Menoptra Vrestin tells Ian: 'The Zarbi are not an intelligent species, but they were essential to the life pattern here. We lived at peace with them until they were made militant by the dark power…'

LARVAE GUNS

The larvae guns are grub-like creatures, with armoured shells and many thin legs, like woodlice. They have a long proboscis that can fire a bolt of energy, powerful enough to kill Menoptra and blast through the walls of the Carsenome. Only the Zarbi can control them.

The Menoptra plan to destroy the Animus with the Isoptope developed by their wise men. This is a living cell destructor, intended to reverse the Carsenome's growth process.

Prapillus explains that, 'Before the Animus came, the flower forest covered the planet in a cocoon of peace.' The ancient song-spinners sang of the beauty of the long-lost Temples of Light.

OPTERA

Dwarfed, legged caterpillar-like creatures, the Optera live underground. They call the Animus 'Pwodarauk', and their language is an amalgam of both surface and underground ideas and images.

The Optera do not remember that they were once Menoptra, who they now regard as their gods. Vrestin explains, 'Your wings withered on your bodies while you crawled blindly underground like slugs. You were born to the greatest freedom of all creatures: to peace, beauty and light...'

NEW INFORMATION

THE DOCTOR

Although the Doctor has not been to Vortis before, he knows of the planet.

He is as absent-minded as ever, sending Vicki into the TARDIS for a red box, and then claiming he asked for a white one. The box she brings contains a dead spider which the Doctor describes as one of his specimens.

THE TARDIS

For the first time we fully see the 'other side' of the TARDIS Control Room, which contains a small equipment annexe with filing, a cluttered desk, the Astral Map, a chair, various equipment and a first aid kit.

The TARDIS central console spins round under the influence of the Animus. The TARDIS light flashes as the ship is dragged away to the Carsenome. The Doctor remarks that with no power 'the ship is useless'. He uses his ring to provide power to open the doors – shining a light from equipment at the jewel set in it.

A Zarbi is repelled and stunned when it tries to enter the TARDIS. The Doctor says the interior of the ship is inviolable. The TARDIS power is in opposition to the Animus, so the Doctor is able to subvert one of the Animus's wishbone control necklets.

COMPANIONS

IAN: Ian uses his Coal Hill School tie as a belt. He says, 'I've seen a colony of ants eat their way right through a house. That size, they could eat their way through a mountain.'

VICKI: Vicki says the aspirin tablets that Barbara gives her are old-fashioned. She wonders (sarcastically) if Barbara's school was a nursery when Barbara says that the main subjects were 'the three Rs'. Vicki herself had, she says, certificates in medicine, physics, chemistry and other subjects by the age of ten.

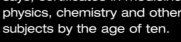

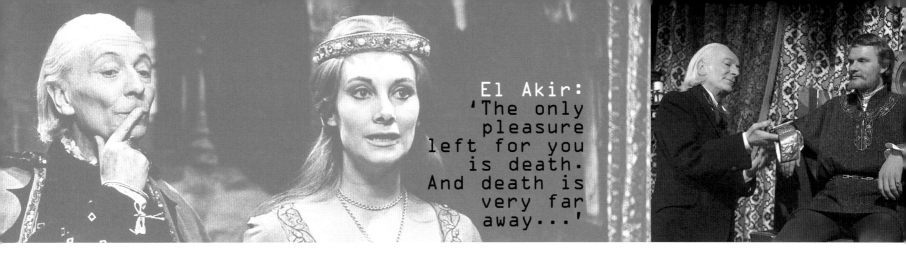

El Akir: 'The only pleasure left for you is death. And death is very far away...'

THE CRUSADE

In which Julian Glover appears as King Richard the Lionheart, and Jean Marsh as his sister Joanna...
BY DAVID WHITAKER
4 EPISODES, FIRST BROADCAST 27 MARCH–17 APRIL 1965

TARDIS DATA BANK:

DATE: AUTUMN 1191
LOCATION: PALESTINE – MAINLY JAFFA, RAMLAH AND LYDDA

BARBARA IS KIDNAPPED BY THE EVIL SARACEN WARLORD EL AKIR. IAN GOES TO HER RESCUE, WHILE THE DOCTOR AND VICKI GET INVOLVED IN POLITICS AT THE COURT OF KING RICHARD THE LIONHEART WHEN RICHARD DECIDES TO TRY TO MARRY HIS SISTER TO SALADIN'S BROTHER AND SUE FOR PEACE...

King Richard: 'In the name of God, St. Michael and St. George, we dub you Sir Ian, Knight of Jaffa. Arise Sir Ian and be valiant.'

JOURNEY INFORMATION

KING RICHARD

King Richard is weary of war. He respects, but does not understand, the Saracen leader Saladin. He is a proud man, who refuses to deal with the men who killed his friends, and assumes his sister Joanna will go along with his plans. Without consulting her, he writes to Saladin, offering his sister in marriage to Saladin's brother Saphadin as part of a peace treaty. But ultimately he knows that his plans will come to nothing and he will be forced to continue the war.

SALADIN

Saladin is a man of honour, sending Richard gifts when he is ill. He trusts Richard's sincerity, but being more pragmatic and realistic than his opponent, he doubts his ability to persuade others.

'Strategy is worth a hundred lances,' Saladin tells Saphadin. 'If you can marry with this sister of the English king then do so and I will help you to it... Have England,

France and all the rest come here to cheer a man and woman and a love match? No, this is a last appeal for peace from a weary man.'

HAROUN AND EL AKIR

Haroun gives insight into the character of El Akir as much as his own plight when he relates his story to Barbara:

'Last year my house was a fine and happy place – a gentle wife, a son who honoured and obeyed me and two daughters who adorned whatever place they visited. Then El Akir came to Lydda and imposed his will. He desired my eldest daughter, Maimuna, but I refused him... when Safiya and I were away he came and burned my house. My wife and son were put to the sword.'

Haroun knows enough of El Akir to ask Barbara to kill his surviving daughter, Safiya, rather than let El Akir take her. He lives now for only two things – his daughter and the death of El Akir. It is a moment of triumph and grim satisfaction for him that in killing El Akir he also finds and frees Maimuna.

NEW INFORMATION

THE DOCTOR

The Doctor knocks out one Saracen attacker, and has a sword fight with another. He is not averse to stealing clothes from a local trader – after he discovers they are already stolen.

Joanna tells the Doctor, 'There's something new in you, yet something older than the sky itself. I sense that I can trust you.' But she feels betrayed when the Doctor keeps her brother's confidence although the Earl of Leicester reveals Richard's plans to her.

The Doctor immediately brands the Earl a fool – his words turning the Earl into a powerful enemy: 'I admire bravery and loyalty, sir. You have both of these. But, unfortunately you haven't any brain at all. I hate fools.'

COMPANIONS

IAN: Ian shows his ability with a sword, and is knighted by King Richard.

His fear of ants when he is staked out in the desert and daubed with honey to attract them is presumably heightened by the fact that he once saw ants eat through a house (as mentioned in *The Web Planet*) and also by his recent meeting with the Zarbi.

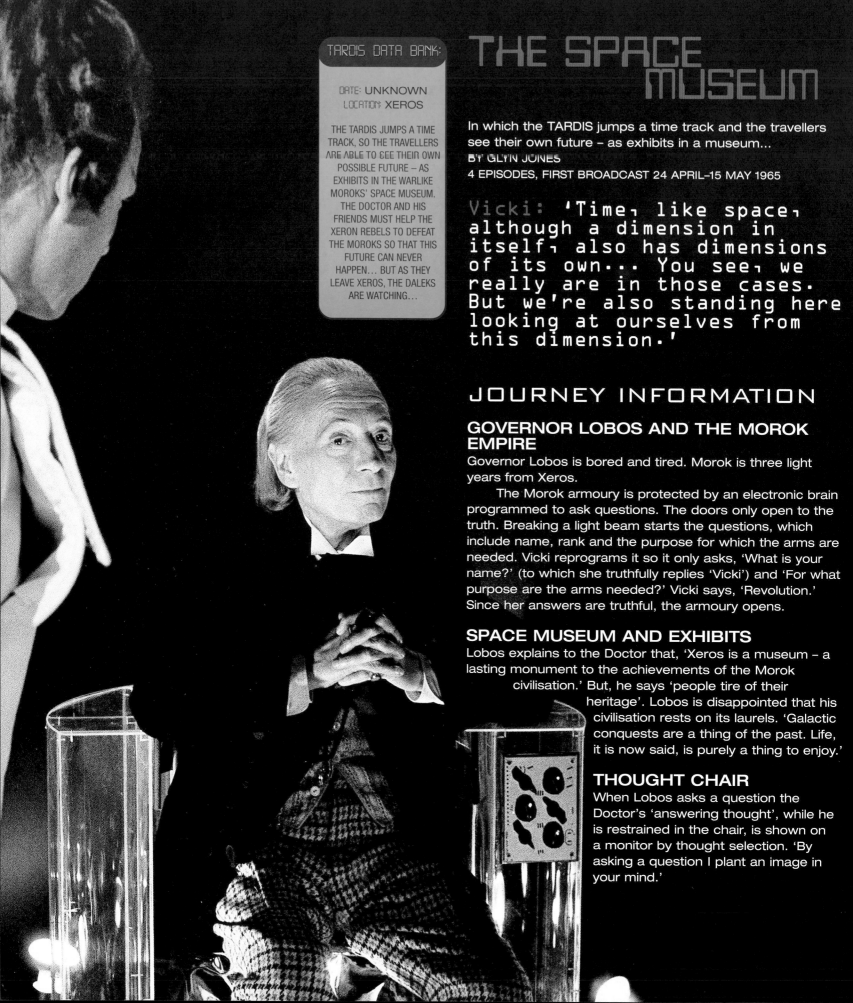

THE SPACE MUSEUM

In which the TARDIS jumps a time track and the travellers see their own future – as exhibits in a museum...
BY GLYN JONES
4 EPISODES, FIRST BROADCAST 24 APRIL–15 MAY 1965

TARDIS DATA BANK:

DATE: UNKNOWN
LOCATION: XEROS

THE TARDIS JUMPS A TIME TRACK, SO THE TRAVELLERS ARE ABLE TO SEE THEIR OWN POSSIBLE FUTURE – AS EXHIBITS IN THE WARLIKE MOROKS' SPACE MUSEUM. THE DOCTOR AND HIS FRIENDS MUST HELP THE XERON REBELS TO DEFEAT THE MOROKS SO THAT THIS FUTURE CAN NEVER HAPPEN... BUT AS THEY LEAVE XEROS, THE DALEKS ARE WATCHING...

Vicki: 'Time, like space, although a dimension in itself, also has dimensions of its own... You see, we really are in those cases. But we're also standing here looking at ourselves from this dimension.'

JOURNEY INFORMATION

GOVERNOR LOBOS AND THE MOROK EMPIRE

Governor Lobos is bored and tired. Morok is three light years from Xeros.

The Morok armoury is protected by an electronic brain programmed to ask questions. The doors only open to the truth. Breaking a light beam starts the questions, which include name, rank and the purpose for which the arms are needed. Vicki reprograms it so it only asks, 'What is your name?' (to which she truthfully replies 'Vicki') and 'For what purpose are the arms needed?' Vicki says, 'Revolution.' Since her answers are truthful, the armoury opens.

SPACE MUSEUM AND EXHIBITS

Lobos explains to the Doctor that, 'Xeros is a museum – a lasting monument to the achievements of the Morok civilisation.' But, he says 'people tire of their heritage'. Lobos is disappointed that his civilisation rests on its laurels. 'Galactic conquests are a thing of the past. Life, it is now said, is purely a thing to enjoy.'

THOUGHT CHAIR

When Lobos asks a question the Doctor's 'answering thought', while he is restrained in the chair, is shown on a monitor by thought selection. 'By asking a question I plant an image in your mind.'

But the Doctor's thought-answers are not what Lobos expects or wants. The question 'How did you get here?' for example, produces a picture of a penny-farthing.

XERONS

The Xeron rebels wear black, have pronounced eyebrows and are little more than children. Dako, one of the rebels, says that the Moroks invaded without warning. 'Xeros was a place of peace and knowledge...' Tor elaborates: 'They destroyed everything, even our people. Only the children were spared – to work... When we grow older we are taken to other planets.'

NEW INFORMATION

THE DOCTOR

Ian asks, 'Doctor, why do you always show the greatest interest in the least important things?' The Doctor replies, 'The least important things sometimes, my dear boy, lead to the greatest discoveries. Like steam for instance coming out of a kettle. I was with him at the time...'

Once he understands the principles of the interrogation device that Lobos uses, the Doctor can control his thoughts to thwart the interrogation techniques.

The Moroks freeze the Doctor to turn him into an exhibit

and as he recovers he suffers from rheumatism, telling Ian, 'It always happens to me when I'm cold.' He says, 'I was merely frozen stiff... My brain was working with the speed of a mechanical computer. I was asking myself questions and the answers were arriving with remarkable alacrity.'

THE TARDIS

The Doctor says he is 'quite unable to measure the time dimension that the TARDIS jumped'. The reason the TARDIS has materialised in what is essentially an alternative reality is that a small component got stuck. Until it clicked into place the travellers had not actually arrived.

COMPANIONS

IAN: Governor Lobos says to Ian, 'You'll achieve nothing if you kill me.' To this, Ian replies (perhaps bluffing), 'Possibly, but it might be enjoyable.'

VICKI: It is Vicki who ultimately saves the travellers from their fate by inciting the young Xeron rebels to action: 'Sitting here planning and dreaming of a revolution isn't going to win your planet back.'

She demonstrates her analytical and technological ability by reprogramming the Morok armoury's computer to allow the rebels access to it.

DATE: UNKNOWN;
1966; 1872; 1996;
UNSPECIFIED
FUTURE; 1965
LOCATION: THE PLANET
ARIDIUS; NEW
YORK; *MARY
CELESTE*, NORTH
ATLANTIC; GHANA;
THE PLANET
MECHANUS;
LONDON

THE DALEKS PURSUE THE
TARDIS THROUGH TIME AND
SPACE TO EXTERMINATE
THEIR 'GREATEST ENEMIES'.
THE TRAVELLERS EVADE
THEM ON THE DESERT
PLANET ARIDIUS, AS WELL AS
IN THE EMPIRE STATE
BUILDING, A HAUNTED HOUSE
AND ON BOARD THE *MARY
CELESTE*... EVENTUALLY THE
TRAVELLERS ESCAPE AS THE
DALEKS BATTLE THE
MECHONOIDS ON THE PLANET
MECHANUS, AND IAN AND
BARBARA DECIDE IT IS TIME
TO GO HOME – COURTESY OF
THE DALEKS' (WORKING) TIME
MACHINE...

THE CHASE

In which the Daleks pursue the TARDIS through time and space to exterminate the Doctor and his companions...
BY TERRY NATION
6 EPISODES, FIRST BROADCAST 22 MAY–26 JUNE 1965

Dalek: 'The assassination group will embark at once in our time machine. They will pursue the humans through all eternity. They must be destroyed.'

JOURNEY INFORMATION

THE DALEKS

Most of the Daleks in this story have 'slats' over the bands round their mid-sections, including the black Dalek Supreme that dispatches the Dalek force in Episode 1.

One Dalek is fitted with a 'perceptor' that can track and locate the TARDIS travellers. This is a device like a compass that replaces the sucker. The Daleks can detect the TARDIS buried on Aridius with their seismic detectors – which they also use to detect the lift that travels to the Mechonoid City. They use an 'Electrode Unit' (a rotating dish-like device that replaces the sucker arm) to remotely activate the lift.

The Dalek guns are referred to as 'neutralisers', and are ineffective against the TARDIS. The Daleks add to their destructive vocabulary of 'exterminate' with various synonyms including: 'Obliterate', 'Eradicate' and 'Annihilate.'

DUPLICATE DOCTOR

The Daleks construct a robot duplicate of the Doctor from 'photo images and relevant data'. The duplicate is then produced in the Cell Renovator Chamber. The computer feeds its memory cells with data. Micro-units contain personality and vocal mannerisms.

TIME-SPACE VISUALISER

The time-space visualiser (on which the travellers watch Shakespeare, the Beatles, Abraham Lincoln and the Daleks) was a gift from the Xeron Space Museum. It is a large circular device that converts neutrons of light energy into electrical impulses to show past images on a monitor screen.

ARIDIUS

Aridius's two suns have dried up the seas, and the Daleks describe the area where the TARDIS lands as the Sagaro Desert. It was once a vast ocean, where the Aridians lived in a city beneath the sea and there are strange sculptures in the sand. The Aridians themselves are humanoid amphibians with gills for ears, spines on their backs, and scaly bodies.

The flesh-eating mire beasts are the only other creatures to have survived the drying up of the seas. They lived in the slime at the bottom of the ocean and moved underground, attacking and invading the Aridian city. The only way the Aridians can control their numbers is by blowing up sections of their city that the beasts have overrun.

HAUNTED HOUSE

While the Daleks know that the haunted house is on Earth, the Doctor's theory is rather more fanciful – he believes it is a creation of the collective imagination of the human mind.

After both time machines have left the house we see the truth – a kiosk labelled 'Festival of Ghana 1996'. Beneath this a poster advertises: 'Frankenstein's House of Horrors Price $10'. There is a sticker across it: 'Cancelled by Peking'.

MECHANUS AND THE MECHONOIDS

Mechanus is a swampy, jungle planet where huge mushroom-like plants (which Ian calls 'fungoids') can move, though they shy away from light. The Mechonoid city stands on stilts 1,500 feet above the ground. The Mechonoids are geodesic spheres, about 6 feet across.

Stranded pilot Steven Taylor says, 'About fifty years ago, Earth decided to colonise this planet. It landed a rocket full of robots programmed to clear landing sites, get everything ready for the first immigrants... The Earth got involved in interplanetary wars. I suppose this place was forgotten.' The immigrants would have been carrying a code to identifiy them to the Mechonoids. Steven cannot crack the code, so the Mechonoids treat him as a specimen for study.

The Mechonoids are armed with flame-throwers that emerge from their sides. The Daleks get a report on the Mechons (as they call the Mechonoids) from Skaro.

NEW INFORMATION

THE DOCTOR

The Doctor's stubbornness comes to the fore when Ian and Barbara want to risk using the Dalek time machine to return to their own time. 'I will not aid and abet suicide,' he tells them emphatically. But once he knows they will be all right he admits he will miss them. The Doctor says he 'tried for two years' to get Ian and Barbara home.

THE TARDIS

The Doctor gives Ian a 'TARDIS Magnet' – a green light indicates the direction the TARDIS is in.

The time-path detector shows the Daleks are in pursuit. The Doctor says it has 'been in the ship ever since I constructed it.' He does not remember it registering before.

We get the first mention of the 'time rotor' – a control on the console that slows down when the TARDIS is landing. It takes 12 minutes for the TARDIS computers to 'reorientate and gather power' so that they can leave again.

COMPANIONS

IAN: When telling the Doctor he wants to go home, Ian says, 'I want to sit in a pub and drink a pint of beer again. I want to walk in a park and watch a cricket match. Above all, I want to belong somewhere, do something, instead of this aimless drifting around in space.'

BARBARA: Barbara is the first to realise that she and Ian could get home. She tells the Doctor, 'I know we thrust ourselves upon you, but we've been through a great deal together since then. And all we've been through will remain with us always. It will probably be the most exciting part of my life. But Doctor, we're different people, and now we have a chance to go home. We want to take that chance...'

VICKI: Vicki recognises 'ancient New York... There were pictures of it in our history books, it was destroyed in the Dalek invasion.'

Vicki is terrified of heights, so the Doctor has to blindfold her before she is lowered 1,500 feet from the Mechonoid city.

TARDIS DATA BANK:

DESCRIPTION:
MALE, HUMAN,
ASTRONAUT
TRAVELLED:
*THE CHASE –
THE SAVAGES*

STEVEN TAYLOR

'There's more to this time travelling than meets the eye.'

(STEVEN TAYLOR – *THE TIME MEDDLER*)

Steven Taylor is a spaceship pilot who crashed on the planet Mechanus. He tells the Doctor and his friends that he crashed in the jungle and then wandered around for days trying to avoid the hostile plant life. He was then captured by the Mechonoids and has been their prisoner, so far as he can tell, for two years.

It is never suggested he was part of a crew, and so presumably was flying solo. He asks the Doctor and his friends 'who won the wars?' which suggests he may have been a military pilot, though this is never actually stated or refuted. When Steven says he is 'Steven Taylor, Flight Red Fifty', he could be giving the military unit to which he is attached or the name of his mission or flight.

Steven has a panda mascot called Hi Fi which he evidently cares about – when the Mechonoid city burns, he goes back to find it. It is only by chance and luck that he finds the TARDIS (*The Chase*) and stumbles inside before the Doctor and Vicki leave.

Generally good-humoured, Steven has a sarcastic side to him. When (in *The Time Meddler*) the TARDIS lands on the Northumbrian beach, Steven asks why the Doctor chose such an unusual design for his ship. The Doctor explains, 'The TARDIS is required to land and blend in with the surroundings... For instance, if we were to land in the middle of the Indian Mutiny, well I'm sure the ship could possibly take on the appearance of a howdah...' Steven's response to this is to comment that if it landed on the beach against a cliff, it would presumably take on the appearance of a large rock. When the Doctor agrees, Steven says to Vicki, 'And you wonder why I don't believe you? You know that large rock over there looks exactly like a police telephone box to me.'

But ultimately it is Steven's independence and his leadership skills that motivate him to leave the TARDIS in *The Savages*. He rises to the challenge of rebuilding a civilisation, perhaps at last realising the potential of his training as well as of his experiences with the Doctor.

THE TIME MEDDLER

In which the Doctor meets Peter Butterworth playing a member of his own race – disguised as a monk and meddling with history...
BY DENNIS SPOONER
4 EPISODES, FIRST BROADCAST 3–24 JULY 1965

The Monk: 'A few hints and tips from me and they'd be able to have jet airliners by 1320. Shakespeare would be able to put Hamlet on television.'

JOURNEY INFORMATION

THE MONK

The Doctor describes the Monk as 'a time meddler'. The Monk has with him all the comforts of a later age – a cooked breakfast is prepared using a toaster and hob, he has a wristwatch, takes snuff and uses binoculars to look out for the Vikings whom he plans to destroy with an atomic cannon so that Harold's army will be fresh for Hastings.

He is mischievous rather than evil, and in fact he means well – treating the wounded villager Eldred despite the inconvenience.

Vicki and Steven discover that the Monk has a 'private collection' in his TARDIS – including 'something from every period and every place', such as furniture, pictures, statues... In his diary, Vicki finds: 'Met Leonardo da Vinci and discussed with him the principles of powered flight... Put £200 in a London bank in 1968, nipped forward 200 years and collected a fortune in compound interest...'

The Monk's behaviour is actually not far off what we come to expect of the Doctor himself in later lives. The argument the Doctor gives the Monk about not meddling is the charge that will be levied against the Doctor in *The War Games.* But whereas the Doctor's defence of his actions and interventions will be that there is evil in the Universe that must be fought, the Monk's motives are less high-minded. 'It's more fun my way,' he tells the Doctor. 'I can make things happen ahead of their time... For instance, do you really believe the Ancient Britons could have built Stonehenge without the aid of my anti-gravitational lift?'

CHANGING HISTORY

The complications of changing history are touched on when Vicki postulates, 'If the monk changes it, I suppose our memories will change as well.' This gives Steven pause for thought: 'That means that the exact minute, the exact second that he does it, every history book, the whole future of every year and time on earth will change just like that and nobody will know that it has... There's more to this time travelling than meets the eye.'

TARDIS DATA BANK:

DATE:
SEPTEMBER, 1066
LOCATION:
NORTHUMBRIA

ARRIVING IN 1066, THE DOCTOR FINDS THE LOCAL MONASTERY HAS ITS OWN GRAMOPHONE AND TOASTER – AND ONLY ONE MONK. VICKI AND STEVEN FIND A WRISTWATCH. THE MONK IS ANOTHER TIME TRAVELLER, WITH HIS OWN TARDIS, WHO IS PLANNING TO ARRANGE FOR KING HAROLD TO DEFEAT WILLIAM AND THE NORMANS AT THE BATTLE OF HASTINGS...

The Doctor: 'What do you think it is? A space helmet for a cow?'

NEW INFORMATION

THE DOCTOR

The Doctor enjoys a drink of mead. He tricks the Monk into believing he has a gun when it's just a stick: 'I have a Winchester '73 right in the middle of your spinal cord.'

Steven asks if the Doctor and the Monk 'come from the same place'. The Doctor's reply is, 'Yes, I regret that we do. But I would say that I am 50 years earlier.'

THE TARDIS

The TARDIS is submerged under water with no ill effects.

A 'dimensional controller' regulates the internal dimensions of the TARDIS and removing it makes the inside fit in the outside of the TARDIS.

THE MONK'S TARDIS

The camouflage device of the Monk's TARDIS works. His TARDIS is disguised as a Saxon sarcophagus. Inside, it is identical to the Doctor's, although the control unit is taller.

The Monk's TARDIS is a 'Mark IV' – more advanced than the Doctor's own ship. 'It's a splendid machine. Though I do note there's been quite a few changes.' The Monk says it is fitted with automatic drift control, allowing it to suspend itself in space.

The Doctor removes the Monk's dimensional circuit from the end of a cable underneath the console. So as not to be trapped inside, he ties a string to it and pulls it through the doors. The circuit that comes free is a transparent box with circuitry inside.

PROGRESS CHART

1. Arrival in Northumbria
2. Position atomic cannon
3. Sight Vikings
4. Light Beacon Fires
5. Destroy Viking Fleet
6. Norman Landing
7. Battle of Hastings
8. Meet King Harold

GALAXY 4

In which the beautiful female Drahvins try to enlist the Doctor's help against the ugly alien Rills and their Chumbley robots – but who are the real villains...
BY WILLIAM EMMS
4 EPISODES, FIRST BROADCAST 11 SEPTEMBER–2 OCTOBER 1965

TARDIS DATA BANK:

DATE: UNKNOWN
LOCATION: AN UNNAMED PLANET

TWO SHIPS HAVE CRASHED AFTER A SPACE BATTLE, BUT THE PLANET THEY HAVE LANDED ON IS ABOUT TO BE DESTROYED. THE BEAUTIFUL FEMALE DRAHVINS SEEM FRIENDLY, BUT IN FACT IT IS THE UGLY RILLS THAT ARE MORE TOLERANT AND FORGIVING – OFFERING THE DRAHVINS THE SHELTER OF THEIR OWN SHIP WHICH CAN BE REPAIRED. THE DOCTOR, VICKI AND STEVEN GET INVOLVED IN A BATTLE THAT ONLY ONE RACE CAN SURVIVE...

Rill: 'Not all the dominant species in the Universe look like humans. Our appearance might be a shock to you as it shocked the Drahvins.'

JOURNEY INFORMATION

THE DRAHVINS

The belligerent Drahvins come from the planet Drahva in Galaxy 4. There are too many people on Drahva. In charge, Maaga has been sent with her crew of soldiers to find other planets to colonise.

Most Drahvins are female; they keep as many men as they need and kill the rest. Soldier Drahvins are cultivated in test tubes. They have limited intelligence and exist only to kill. When not needed, they switch off, sitting silent and still, heads bowed. Maaga believes the soldiers are less than useful in space exploration: 'If you were to conquer space, they said, you will need soldiers. So here I am, confronted with danger, and the only one able to think.'

Put off by the appearance of the Rills, the Drahvins refuse to work together with these former enemies to escape the imminent destruction of the planet. Instead they still seek to destroy the Rills. This intolerance, in effect, condemns them to death.

THE RILLS

The Rills are (subjectively) ugly and look like a cross between a tusked walrus and a scaly reptile. They have no vocal cords but communicate through thought. They breathe ammonia, and live within a protective environment behind a glass partition on board their ship.

They claim not to kill, and it is the Drahvins who are the aggressors – attacking the Rill ship in space when it turns to leave after a four-day stand-off and driving off the Chumblies sent to negotiate. The Rill ship is not too damaged to leave, but they need the Doctor's help to generate the necessary power before the planet explodes.

THE CHUMBLIES

The robotic servants of the Rills are nicknamed 'Chumblies' by Vicki because of the sound they make. They consist of multiple 'domes' and can communicate with the Rills (a light on top flashes). The domes can open up or close down like a telescope, and each Chumbley has various kinds of equipment (including weaponry) and rod-like arms that extend.

NEW INFORMATION

THE DOCTOR

The Doctor claims that he never kills anything. He tells the Rills that, unlike the Drahvins, he does not care what they look like: 'Importance lies in the character and what use is made of intelligence. We respect you as we respect all life.'

THE TARDIS

Sounds from outside can be heard in the TARDIS, and external explosions rock the inside. The TARDIS is surrounded by a force barrier, which the Doctor implies he built.

The Doctor connects the TARDIS to the Rill ship to power it up so the Rills can escape. He uses the TARDIS Astral Map (seen in *The Web Planet*) to predict the time left before the planet is destroyed.

COMPANIONS

VICKI: Vicki is skilled at cutting hair. It is she who names the Chumblies, and who first communicates with the Rills.

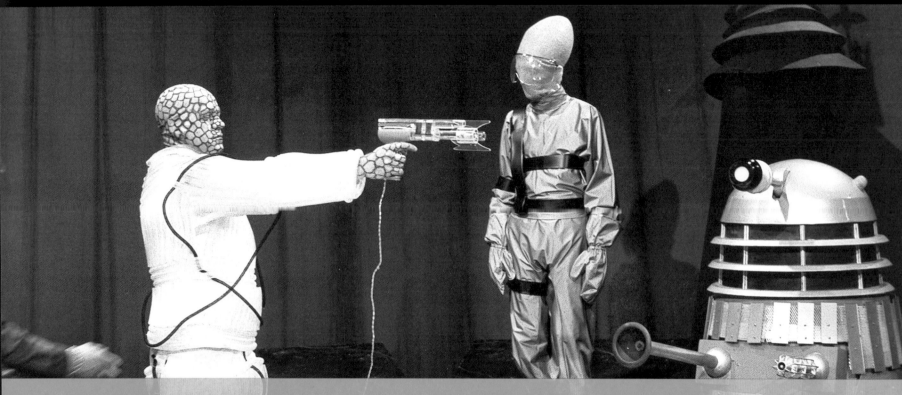

MISSION TO THE UNKNOWN

Marc Cory: 'The Daleks are planning the complete destruction of our galaxy. Together with the powers of the outer galaxies, a war force is being assembled... If our galaxy is to be saved, whoever receives this message must relay this information to Earth immediately.'

In which the Doctor and his companions do not appear, but the Daleks do...
BY TERRY NATION
1 EPISODE, FIRST BROADCAST 9 OCTOBER 1965

TARDIS DATA BANK:

DATE: AD 4000, OR SHORTLY BEFORE
LOCATION: KEMBEL

SPACE AGENT MARC CORY IS INVESTIGATING THE SIGHTING OF A DALEK SHIP AND DISCOVERS THEY HAVE A BASE ON KEMBEL. BUT HIS CREW ARE INFECTED BY VARGA PLANTS, IMPORTED FROM SKARO, AND START TO MUTATE INTO VARGAS. THE DALEKS ARE NEGOTIATING WITH REPRESENTATIVES OF THE OUTER GALAXIES TO DESTROY THE SOLAR SYSTEM. CORY RECORDS A MESSAGE OF WARNING, BUT BEFORE HE CAN SEND IT HE IS FOUND AND EXTERMINATED...

JOURNEY INFORMATION

CORY AND THE SSS

Marc Cory is a member of the SSS, which may stand for Space Security Service (which crew member Lowery reads from Cory's ID) or Special Security Service (as Cory identifies himself in his recording). Cory is licensed to kill, and has the authority to enlist the aid of any persons, civil or military.

The ship Cory has commandeered (acting on a hunch) has 'UN Deep Space Force Group 1' and a Union Jack on each tail fin.

THE DALEKS

The Daleks are led by the black Dalek Supreme. They have not been active in Earth's galaxy for a long time. In the 500 years before this story, they have gained control of over 70 planets in the Ninth Galactic System and 40 in the constellation of Miros (both millions of light years away from Earth's galaxy).

The Daleks' circular conference table has a star map on its surface, with planets as raised hemispheres. The delegates at the conference are from: Gearon, Trantis, Malpha, Sentreal, Beaus, Warrien and Celation.

VARGA PLANTS

The Varga plants are large, semi-mobile cactus-like plants indigenous to Skaro. The Daleks have brought some to Kembel to act as a defence. The thorns are poisonous – the sting of a Varga leads victims to mutate and become Vargas themselves. There is no known cure.

KATARINA

'Can we have reached the place of perfection so soon?'

(KATARINA – *THE DALEKS' MASTER PLAN*)

Katarina is barely more than a slave – handmaiden to Cassandra, Princess of Troy. She believes she is doomed to die – the auguries have foretold it.

Initially sent by Cassandra to spy on Vicki, Katarina helps the wounded Steven back to the TARDIS – and leaves with Steven and the Doctor. She never really understands what has happened to her or where she is. She believes that the Doctor is a god who is taking her on the journey through Beyond and despite his protestations to the contrary, she sees the TARDIS as his temple. She believes she is on a divine journey to her 'place of perfection' – and perhaps she is.

Katarina dies in Episode 4 of *The Daleks' Master Plan*. Always loyal to her new 'master' the Doctor, she uses what little knowledge she has acquired to open the airlock door on Chen's spaceship rather than allow herself to be held hostage by the homicidal Kirksen who is demanding the Doctor return the ship to Kembel and the Daleks. 'She wanted to save our lives,' the Doctor tells Steven. 'And perhaps the lives of all other beings of the solar system. I hope she found Perfection.'

TARDIS DATA BANK:

DESCRIPTION: FEMALE, HUMAN, HANDMAIDEN OF CASSANDRA

TRAVELLED: *THE MYTH MAKERS – THE DALEKS' MASTER PLAN*

THE MYTH MAKERS

In which the Doctor is mistaken for Zeus and suggests using a wooden horse to end the siege of Troy...

BY DONALD COTTON

4 EPISODES, FIRST BROADCAST 16 OCTOBER–6 NOVEMBER 1965

TARDIS DATA BANK:

DATE: c1184 BC
LOCATION: TROY AND THE SURROUNDING AREA

THE TARDIS LANDS OUTSIDE TROY DURING THE SIEGE. THE DOCTOR IS CAPTURED BY THE GREEKS AND GIVEN TWO DAYS TO DEVISE A PLAN FOR TAKING THE CITY. STEVEN AND VICKI ARE CAPTURED BY THE TROJANS, AND GIVEN TWO DAYS TO DEVISE A MEANS OF BANISHING THE GREEKS...

The Doctor: 'Have you ever thought of a horse, hmm? ... It should be a huge horse, about forty feet high...'

JOURNEY INFORMATION

THE GREEKS
Kings Agamemnon and Menelaus, Odysseus and the Greeks are camped outside Troy, which has been besieged for ten years. They worship the god Zeus.

THE TROJANS
King Priam, his daughter Cassandra and youngest son Troilus are embroiled in the war caused by Priam's son Paris stealing Menelaus's wife Helen.

While he is distracted by the TARDIS Priam's other son Hector is killed by Achilles of Greece.

THE TROJAN WAR

Historians disagree as to whether or not the Trojan War actually took place, but tales of it are told in Homer's *Odyssey* and *Iliad*, and Virgil's *Aeneid*. Paris, son of King Priam of Troy, fell in love with Helen, wife of King Menelaus of Sparta, and stole her away to Troy. Menelaus's brother, King Agamemnon, led the rest of the Greek world in a war against the Trojans that lasted for ten years. In the ninth year, Achilles killed Hector of Troy in revenge for Hector's killing of Patroclus, Achilles's closest friend. In the tenth year, the Greek fleet sailed away from Troy, but concealed itself nearby. Believing the Greeks had truly left, the Trojans thought it was safe to bring a wooden horse they had left behind into the city – despite being warned against doing this by the prophetess Cassandra, who was cursed never to be believed. The Greeks hidden in the horse, led by Odysseus, opened the city's gates to let the rest of their force in, and Troy was destroyed.

NEW INFORMATION

THE DOCTOR

The Greeks initially believe the Doctor is the god Zeus (appearing in the guise of an old beggar). But he convinces them he is merely a time and space traveller.

Having dismissed the wooden horse story as fanciful storytelling by Homer, the Doctor is forced to 'invent' it himself so the Greeks can capture the city of Troy. This is after he abandons the idea of catapulting troops over the city walls in gliders (he uses a paper plane to demonstrate this) when Odysseus suggests he try it himself first.

THE TARDIS

The Trojans prepare to burn the TARDIS, but stop when Vicki emerges.

Odysseus claims the TARDIS for himself when the Greeks capture Troy.

COMPANIONS

VICKI: Vicki knows of the Greek heroes and the Trojan horse. She eats meat (in this case, peacock). She's not much younger than 17.

Vicki meets and falls in love with a young Trojan called Troilus. She adopts the name Cressida, and she and Troilus leave Troy with his cousin Aeneas...

STEVEN: Steven adopts the name of Diomede. He is wounded in the shoulder by a sword thrust, and suffers blood poisoning.

KATARINA: Katarina believes in prophecy – she is certain that her death has been foretold by augury. She is sent by Cassandra to get evidence that Cressida (Vicki) is actually a Greek spy. Vicki sends her to help the Doctor get the wounded Steven back to the TARDIS.

Vicki: 'The main thing is I belong here now with you. If you'll have me.'

THE DALEKS' MASTER PLAN

In which the Daleks form an alliance of aliens to conquer the galaxy in an epic adventure across space and time...

BY TERRY NATION AND DENNIS SPOONER FROM AN IDEA BY TERRY NATION

12 EPISODES, FIRST BROADCAST 13 NOVEMBER 1965–29 JANUARY 1966

The Doctor: 'I'm afraid, my friends, that the Daleks have won.'

TARDIS DATA BANK:

DATE: 4000 AD; 1965–6; 1920S; c2600 BC.
LOCATION: KEMBEL; DESPERUS; EARTH; MIRA; TIGUS.

FOLLOWING ON FROM *MISSION TO THE UNKNOWN*, THE DALEKS' PLAN IS NEARING COMPLETION WHEN THE TREACHEROUS GUARDIAN OF THE SOLAR SYSTEM – MAVIC CHEN – DELIVERS THE TARANIUM CORE OF THEIR TIME DESTRUCTOR TO KEMBEL. BUT THE DOCTOR MANAGES TO STEAL THE TARANIUM AND ESCAPE IN CHEN'S SHIP. THE DALEKS AND CHEN PURSUE THE DOCTOR AND HIS FRIENDS THROUGH SPACE AND TIME – FROM THE PRISON PLANET DESPERUS TO ANCIENT EGYPT (WHERE HE AGAIN MEETS THE MEDDLING MONK) THE DOCTOR TRIES TO KEEP THE TARANIUM FROM THE DALEKS. FINALLY, BACK ON KEMBEL, THE DOCTOR OPERATES THE TIME DESTRUCTOR...

JOURNEY INFORMATION

SARA KINGDOM

Agent Kingdom of the SSS was a loyal agent of Mavic Chen. Bret Vyon is her brother (perhaps they had different fathers, or Kingdom may be her married name).

She is tricked by Chen into killing her brother, and as a result is unwilling at first to accept the Doctor's assertion that Chen is the traitor. Once convinced, she helps the Doctor and Steven to destroy the Daleks, even at the cost of her own life. She ages to death on Kembel when the Time Destructor is activated.

After her death, the Doctor claims that the one thing she lived for was to see the total destruction of the Daleks, and he knows that without her help it would not have been achieved.

BRET VYON

Bret was bred on Mars Colony 16. He joined the Space Security Service in AD 3990. He gained First Rank in AD 3995 and Second Rank in AD 3998. Sara Kingdom is his sister.

THE MONK

The Monk has bypassed the 'dimensional controller' of his TARDIS (see *The Time Meddler*), and has been pursuing the Doctor to take his revenge. The Doctor refers to him as 'an amateur'.

The Monk claims to know of the Daleks through reputation only.

THE DALEKS

The Daleks are again led by the Dalek Supreme. Some Daleks have 'pyroflame' arms. Their plan is to conquer the solar system; later this changes to 'conquer the Universe'. They plan to do this with the Time Destructor – for which they need a full emm of Taranium. They treat Mavic Chen as their ally as the Taranium can only be found on Uranus and it has taken 50 years to mine.

The Time Destructor rolls back the evolutionary process for Daleks caught in its field. 'Millions of years of progress, reversed back,' the Doctor says. Their casings collapse, and they are left as starfish-like creatures flopping on the ground.

MAVIC CHEN

Mavic Chen is the part-Oriental Guardian of the solar system. He joins with the Daleks in their plan to capture Earth and all the other planets in the Solar System.

He presents the Daleks with the Taranium core of their time destructor. Never one to miss an opportunity to give a speech, once the Taranium core is recovered from the Doctor, Chen addresses the Dalek Alliance delegates (and kills any who disagree with him) – while the Daleks ready the Time Destructor and calmly imprison them.

Not content merely to rule the solar system, Chen plans to betray the Daleks and take overall control at the first opportunity – he has a fleet of Earth security vessels ready to seize control of Kembel. But the Daleks are just as perfidious: the Dalek Supreme has him

Mavic Chen: 'This Council is now under my power. I will give the orders and you will obey them.'

taken out of the Control Room (so as not to damage the equipment) and executed.

THE DALEK ALLIANCE

The members of the Dalek Alliance (apart from Mavic Chen) are the rulers of the outer galaxies: Zephon, Master of the Fifth Galaxy; the Masters of Celation and Beaus; Trantis, the representative of the largest of the outer galaxies; Malpha and Gearon. Zephon is a new arrival since *Mission to the Unknown*, and previous delegates Sentreal and Warrien have disappeared since *Mission to the Unknown*.

DESPERUS

Desperus is a prison planet. The prisoners live in caves, and the ground is swampy. Giant bats – screamers – are the native fauna.

MIRA AND THE VISIANS

Mira is a jungle planet, nearer to Earth than Kembel. Its only inhabitants are the Visians, which are eight-foot-tall, invisible and vicious. They become briefly visible when exterminated.

NEW INFORMATION

THE DOCTOR

The Doctor is the inventor of a 'magnetic chair' which he uses to keep Bret Vyon immobile when he doesn't trust him – boasting that it could hold a herd of elephants.

The Daleks imply that while the Doctor has adopted a humanoid form, that is not his actual appearance.

THE TARDIS

It is possible to communicate to the outside from within the TARDIS. The shield that protects the ship is similar to a field of gravity power that Steven creates.

The scanner eye is located on the TARDIS roof (although by *Full Circle* an image translator is used instead).

The Doctor changes the Monk's TARDIS into various forms – finally a police box – to confuse the Daleks.

COMPANIONS

STEVEN: Steven comes from a time at least several centuries before AD 4000.

KATARINA: Katarina manages to work out how the airlock on Chen's spaceship *Spar* operates when taken hostage inside by the killer Kirksen. She opens the outer door and blasts both herself and Kirksen into space to prevent the Doctor being forced back to Kembel to face the Daleks.

THE MASSACRE

In which the Doctor and Steven try to avoid being caught up in historical events while André Morell and Leonard Sachs hold positions of office...

BY JOHN LUCAROTTI AND DONALD TOSH

4 EPISODES, FIRST BROADCAST 5–26 FEBRUARY 1966

TARDIS DATA BANK:

DATE: 20–24 AUGUST 1572; 1960S
LOCATION: PARIS; LONDON

ARRIVING IN PARIS DURING THE FRENCH WARS OF RELIGION, SHORTLY BEFORE THE MASSACRE OF THE HUGUENOTS, STEVEN BELIEVES THE DOCTOR IS IMPERSONATING THE ABBOT OF AMBOISE. HE IS HORRIFIED WHEN HE SEES THE ABBOT'S DEAD BODY DUMPED IN THE GUTTER. BUT THE ABBOT IS THE DOCTOR'S DOUBLE, AND THE REAL DOCTOR IS ALIVE AND WELL. BOTH STEVEN AND THE DOCTOR ARE CAUGHT UP IN EVENTS, AND KNOW THAT THEIR NEW FRIENDS WILL SHORTLY FACE DEATH...

JOURNEY INFORMATION

THE CATHOLICS

Charles IX and his mother, Catherine de Medici, are both Catholics. Marshall Tavannes and the Abbot of Amboise are part of the plan to assassinate the Protestant Admiral de Coligny, allegedly on Catherine's orders.

THE HUGUENOTS

Most of the Huguenots have been in the service of Admiral de Coligny. Coligny, their chief military leader, has been invited on to the King's Council in an effort to bring peace between Protestants and Catholics.

THE FRENCH WARS OF RELIGION

The French Wars of Religion between the Catholics and the Protestant Huguenots last from 1562 to 1598. The massacre of Protestants at Vassy in 1562 led to the First War, which lasted until the Treaty of Amboise of 1563. The Second War (1567–8) and the Third War (1568–70) were

also ended by treaties, but none of them were particularly acceptable to Protestants or Catholics. Catherine de Medici attempted to create peace between the two sides, and arranged a marriage between the Catholic Princess Marguerite and the Huguenot Henry of Navarre.

However, the Catholics do not want peace – they blame the Protestants for everything that is wrong with society. When the Huguenot de Coligny is attacked, the Protestants threaten to riot and Catherine allegedly persuades her son, Charles IX, to massacre them all. This is the St Bartholomew's Day Massacre of 1572. The killing spreads across the country, and a huge number of Protestants are murdered. The wars continue until 1598, when the Protestants are finally given freedom of worship by the Edict of Nantes.

NEW INFORMATION

THE DOCTOR

The Doctor is the double of the Abbot of Amboise. He dare not change the course of history, so must allow the massacre to take place.

COMPANIONS

STEVEN: Steven claims to be a Protestant.

Saddened by the way the Doctor seems to have abandoned his Huguenot friends, especially Anne Chaplet, Steven leaves the TARDIS when it lands on Earth in 1966, but returns to warn the Doctor that two policemen are coming.

DODO: Dodo enters the TARDIS in 1966 believing it to be a real police box. She wants to report that a small boy has been hurt in an accident.

TARDIS DATA BANK:

DESCRIPTION: FEMALE, HUMAN

TRAVELLED: *THE MASSACRE – THE WAR MACHINES*

DODO CHAPLET

'Wait a minute, if this isn't a police box, what is it? And who are you?' (DODO – *THE MASSACRE*)

Dodo's full name is Dorothea Chaplet. She is an orphan, and not long out of school (assuming she has actually left). She may be a Cockney (her accent varies), and her grandfather was French – which leads the Doctor to speculate that she may be descended from Anne Chaplet whom Steven was friends with in *The Massacre* (though this is unlikely as Anne Chaplet's children would have taken their father's surname).

Dodo lives with her great-aunt, and believes she won't be missed. She takes the notion of travelling through time and space in the TARDIS in her stride and seems equally excited to be on the Ark (although she believes at first it might be Whipsnade Zoo) or back in the Wild West in *The Gunfighters*. Steven sums her up when he says in *The Savages*, 'If it isn't allowed, Dodo would be the first in the queue.'

She does get frustrated with Cyril and the Toymaker's games in *The Celestial Toymaker*, and is mortified to learn that her own cold is responsible for a plague that affects the inhabitants of the Ark.

The Doctor seems close to Dodo, especially after Steven leaves in *The Savages*. As soon as he first sees her, he remarks to Steven that she reminds him of his granddaughter, Susan. But in *The War Machines*, she is taken over by the computer WOTAN and conditioned to betray the Doctor. While the Doctor is able to resist WOTAN and break Dodo's conditioning, he sends her to the country to recuperate. She does not return, but sends a message – and her TARDIS key – back with Polly and Ben to say she has decided to stay in London. The Doctor is deeply disappointed that she does not tell him in person...

THE ARK

In which the Doctor encounters the one-eyed Monoids and the Earth plunges into the sun...

BY PAUL ERICKSON AND LESLEY SCOTT

4 EPISODES, FIRST BROADCAST 5–26 MARCH 1966

Steven: 'The nature of Man, even in this day and age, hasn't altered at all. You still fear the unknown like everyone else before you.'

JOURNEY INFORMATION

THE ARK

The Ark is a spaceship travelling from Earth to Refusis II, a journey that will take over 700 years. It carries the whole of the Earth's population miniaturised in suspended animation.

Its crew are the human Guardians of the Human Race, and their servants, the Monoids. The Ark contains a jungle, in which animals including Indian elephants, monitor lizards, chameleons and locusts live.

The name 'the Ark' is given to the ship by Dodo, as a reference to Noah's Ark. The humans watch Earth's destruction on the ship's screen.

When the travellers first arrive on the Ark, a giant statue of a human being is under construction. When they return 700 years later, they find it has been completed – but the head that has been added is of a Monoid. The head contains a fission bomb, which the Monoids plan to use to destroy the Ark after they have evacuated to Refusis II.

MONOIDS

The Monoids came to Earth 'many years ago', when their own planet was dying. They offered their services in return for a place on the Ark. They are tall, green and reptilian in appearance, with one eye and no mouth. They are mute, and apparently ingest food through holes in their necks.

When the TARDIS returns to the Ark, the Monoids have taken control. They now talk, using artificial voice boxes built into collars round their necks. They refer to themselves by numbers rather than names (the numbers are printed on their collars). The human Guardians apparently encouraged the Monoid research that developed the voice boxes and their burning weapons – the heat prods.

REFUSIS II AND THE REFUSIANS

Refusis II is a jungle planet. The Refusians once had shape and form, but a galaxy accident – a giant solar flare – caused them to become invisible and formless. They can sense other Refusians, but cannot see each other.

They have the power to move objects – from flowers to the huge statue containing the fission bomb, which a Refusian manoeuvres into the Ark's airlock so that it can be ejected into space.

They could sense the Ark approaching and built castles for its inhabitants.

TARDIS DATA BANK:

DATE: THE 57TH SEGMENT OF TIME (THE EVENTS OF EPISODES 3 AND 4 TAKE PLACE 700 YEARS AFTER THE EVENTS OF EPISODES 1 AND 2)

LOCATION: THE ARK, TRAVELLING TO REFUSIS II; REFUSIS II

TEN MILLION YEARS IN THE FUTURE, THE SURVIVORS OF EARTH ARE TRAVELLING TO A NEW WORLD – REFUSIS II. BUT THE HUMAN GUARDIANS AND THEIR MONOID SERVANTS HAVE NO RESISTANCE TO DODO'S COLD – AND THE TRAVELLERS ARE PUT ON TRIAL FOR STARTING AN EPIDEMIC. THE DOCTOR FINDS A CURE, AND THEY LEAVE. BUT THE TARDIS ARRIVES BACK IN THE SAME SPOT ON THE ARK 700 YEARS LATER – WHEN THE PREVIOUSLY PASSIVE MONOIDS HAVE TAKEN CONTROL...

Monoid 1: 'They were a simple people... They were totally unprepared for the conflict when it came.'

NEW INFORMATION

THE DOCTOR

The Doctor is able to cure the cold virus by injecting a vaccine developed from animal membranes (a cure apparently first used back in the twentieth century, but then lost in the time of primal wars).

The Doctor realises that the Monoids are 'far more knowledgeable than most people realise,' from the help they give him in developing the vaccine.

THE TARDIS

Steven claims that 'the TARDIS made the decision' to return to the Ark 700 years later.

COMPANIONS

STEVEN: Steven has no immunity to the cold virus.

DODO: Dodo went to Whipsnade Zoo as a child. She knows a lot about nature.

She has a cold which she inadvertently passes on to the humans and Monoids aboard the Ark. They have no resistance to the virus.

THE CELESTIAL TOYMAKER

In which Michael Gough plays the enigmatic Toymaker and the Doctor becomes invisible...

BY BRIAN HAYLES

4 EPISODES, FIRST BROADCAST 2–23 APRIL 1966

TARDIS DATA BANK:

DATE: UNKNOWN

LOCATION: THE CELESTIAL TOYMAKER'S DOMAIN

THE DOCTOR BECOMES INVISIBLE IN THE DOMAIN OF THE TOYMAKER – WHOSE GAMES THE TRAVELLERS MUST PLAY AND WIN IF NOT TO BECOME HIS PLAYTHINGS FOR ETERNITY. STEVEN AND DODO COMPETE IN VARIOUS GAMES AGAINST THE CLOWNS JOEY AND CLARA, THE KING, QUEEN AND KNAVE OF HEARTS, MRS WIGGS AND SERGEANT RUGG, AND THE OBNOXIOUS SCHOOLBOY CYRIL. THE DOCTOR, MEANWHILE, MUST WIN THE TRILOGIC GAME AGAINST THE TOYMAKER HIMSELF... BUT IN THIS DOMAIN, TO WIN IS TO LOSE...

Dodo: 'He can bring them to life, but they have wills and minds of their own. I'll never be able to look at a doll or a playing card again with an easy mind. They really do have a secret life of their own.'

JOURNEY INFORMATION

THE TOYMAKER

The Toymaker is immortal, and has lived for thousands of years, playing games. If he loses a game the price he pays is the loss of his world, but he is powerful enough to rebuild it. If the contestant loses, he is added to the domain as a toy (and if he wins, destroyed with it). The Doctor describes The Toymaker as '...a power for evil. He manipulates people and makes them into his playthings.'

All the Toymaker's subjects are actually toys – the clowns Joey and Clara, for example, are first seen as dolls being taken from their house by the Toymaker. When Dodo looks back at their slumped figures after they have lost the game, she sees that they are again just dolls... The Toymaker threatens to break Sergeant Rugg and Mrs Wiggs like a stack of plates.

The games that Dodo and Steven have to play are: Blind Man's Buff, against Joey and Clara; a lethal version of musical chairs, against the King, Queen and Knave of Hearts; finding a key in Mrs Wiggs's kitchen, supervised by Sergeant Rugg (the key unlocks a door to a hall where Steven and Dodo risk partnering the dancing dolls for all eternity). Finally, they must play hopscotch across an electrified floor, against the unpleasant practical-joking schoolboy Cyril.

RIDDLES

The riddles that Dodo and Steven are posed are:

Four legs, no feet, of arms no lack,
It carries no burden on its back.
Six deadly sisters, seven for choice,
Call the servants without voice.

This refers to seven chairs – one is safe but six are fatal. Dodo and Steven 'test' some of them with dolls.

Hunt the key, to fit the door
That leads out on the dancing floor.
Then escape the rhythmic beat
Or you'll for ever tap your feet

This refers to finding the key in the kitchen, then evading the dancing dolls.

Lady Luck
Will show the way,
Win the game
Or here you'll stay.

This challenges Dodo and Steven to win the game of hopscotch or become playthings of the Toymaker.

THE TRILOGIC GAME

The trilogic game consists of a pyramid of numbered layers, and three points: A, B and C. The player has to move the pyramid from point A to point C, moving one layer at a time, and never placing a larger piece on top of a smaller piece. The new pyramid has to be completed at C in exactly 1,023 moves.

NEW INFORMATION

THE DOCTOR

The Doctor knows of the Toymaker, telling him, 'You and your games are quite notorious. You draw people here like a spider does to flies... and should they lose the games they play, you condemn them to become your toys forever.'

The Toymaker reveals that the Doctor has been to his domain before, but did not stay long enough to play any games. This time the Toymaker makes the Doctor invisible (and for a while dumb) and denies him the TARDIS.

The Doctor is able to complete the trilogic game, and imitates the Toymaker's voice in order to complete the final move from within the safety of the TARDIS.

THE TARDIS

The TARDIS survives the destruction of the Toymaker's domain, though it does not protect the occupants from his initial attack.

> The Doctor:
> 'The Toymaker is immortal. He's lasted thousands of years and very occasionally, of course, he loses a game and then he has to pay the price...'

BEHIND THE SCENES

SCRIPT CHANGES

The Celestial Toymaker was originally written by Brian Hayles, but he was unable to perform the required rewrites. Therefore the scripts were extensively reworked by script editor Donald Tosh, who cut scenes which would be too complex or expensive to film, and added elements such as the trilogic game.

Producer John Wiles had planned to replace William Hartnell, whose contract was up for renewal, and decided that the Doctor would disappear for most of the story, and return at the end with a different appearance.

The story also featured characters called George and Margaret. George and Margaret were the eponymous 'stars' of a play by the then BBC Head of Serials Gerald Savory – a play in which the characters were often mentioned but never actually appeared. Savory gave permission for them finally to appear in this serial, but at a late date withdrew his permission – after the parts had been cast.

The scripts were reworked once more by the new script editor Gerry Davis, who changed George and Margaret to characters such as Joey and Clara, as well as making many other alterations. With Wiles and Tosh having moved on, Hartnell's contract was renewed, and the Doctor now reappeared as himself at the end of the story. Ex-producer John Wiles made an official complaint to Gerald Savory about the extensive changes made to his story after he left the programme.

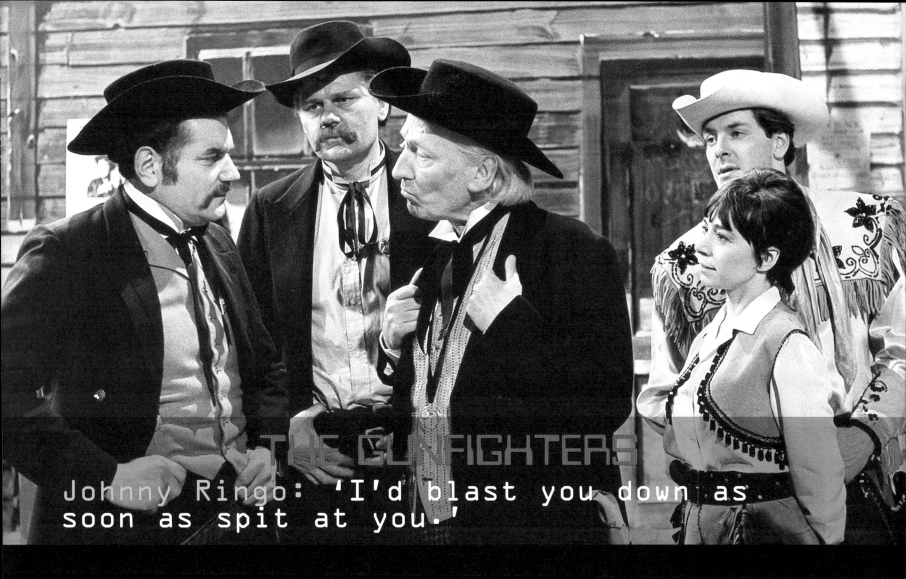

Johnny Ringo: 'I'd blast you down as soon as spit at you.'

In which the Wild West seems much smaller than on the big screen, and history is rewritten...
BY DONALD COTTON
4 EPISODES, FIRST BROADCAST 30 APRIL–21 MAY 1966

TARDIS DATA BANK:

DATE: 24–26 OCTOBER 1881
LOCATION: TOMBSTONE

THE DOCTOR GETS HIS TOOTH PULLED BY DOC HOLLIDAY IN TOMBSTONE WHILE DODO AND STEVEN LITERALLY SING FOR THEIR LIVES. THE TRAVELLERS ARE CAUGHT UP IN THE EVENTS LEADING UP TO THE FAMOUS GUNFIGHT AT THE OK CORRAL, WITH THE 'DOC' MISTAKEN FOR HOLLIDAY. CAN THEY EVADE THE GUNFIRE AND THE ASSASSIN JOHNNY RINGO? WILL THEY ESCAPE WITH THEIR COWBOY OUTFITS – AND THEIR ARTISTIC INTEGRITY – INTACT...

JOURNEY INFORMATION

DOC HOLLIDAY
Holliday killed gunfighter Reuben Clanton. He's a gambler, a drinker – and a dentist. He now runs a practice in Tombstone, which has a giant tooth hanging outside as an advertisement (or possibly a deterrent) to potential customers. His father was a colonel in the army in Alabama.

JOHNNY RINGO
Ringo is a top gun, and a wanted man – with a $1,000 reward offered by Dodge City. He's been on the trail of Holliday and Kate for nearly two years. He and Kate used to be lovers – now she's engaged to Doc Holliday.

Completely unscrupulous, he murders the Last Chance Saloon barman Charlie, just so that Charlie won't tell Earp that he is in town.

WYATT EARP
Earp is Marshal of Tombstone, and a close friend of Holliday. He (along with Sheriff Masterson) is one of the few men of integrity in Tombstone.

THE CLANTONS
Phineas, Ike and Billy Clanton are gunfighters, intent on taking revenge on Doc Holliday. With 'Pa' Clanton, they're running a huge rustling operation.

NEW INFORMATION

THE DOCTOR
The Doctor claims he doesn't touch alcohol, and disapproves of violence. That said, Steven takes a

The Doctor: 'You can't walk into the middle of a western town and say you've come from outer space. Good gracious me, you would be arrested on a vagrancy charge.'

six-shooter from the TARDIS that the Doctor claims is part of his 'favourite collection'.

The Doctor adopts the pseudonym Doctor Caligari.

When he becomes the first customer to have his tooth pulled by Doc Holliday the Doctor inquires about anaesthetic. Holliday offers: 'I can give you a rap on the cranium with this six-shooter' or failing that a slug of rattlesnake oil (whisky).

COMPANIONS

STEVEN: Although Steven fancies himself as 'Dead-eye Steve, the fastest, meanest gun in the West', the Doctor introduces him as 'Mr Steven Regret, tenor'. He can indeed sing and plays the piano.

DODO: Dodo can play the piano. She's always wanted to meet Wyatt Earp.

The Doctor introduces her as 'Miss Dodo Dupont, wizard of the ivory keys'.

By the end of the story, the Doctor tells her that she is 'fast becoming a prey to every cliché-ridden convention in the American West.'

BEHIND THE SCENES

RATING SUCCESS AND FAILURE

For a long time it was generally believed that *The Gunfighters* achieved the lowest audience viewing figures of any **Doctor Who** story. While it is among the lowest for the First Doctor's era, that was not the case.

Initially BBC and ITV measured their viewing figures independently, using companies such as JICTAR. From 1981, joint viewing figures were measured by BARB, the Broadcasters' Audience Research Board. They prepare estimates of total viewing figures based on a representative sample of television-watching households. In 1963, 13.6 million homes had a television (but of course each home could have more than one occupant, so 13.6 million would not be the maximum viewing figure). The majority of these homes could receive both BBC and ITV. By 1989, this figure had increased to 21.1 million homes.

The highest and lowest average ratings for stories for each Doctor are shown right:

First Doctor:
Highest:	*The Web Planet* –	12.6 million
Lowest:	*The Smugglers* –	4.5 million

Second Doctor:
Highest:	*The Moonbase* –	8.3 million
Lowest:	*The War Games* –	4.9 million

Third Doctor:
Highest:	*The Three Doctors* –	10.3 million
Lowest:	*Inferno* –	5.6 million

Fourth Doctor:
Highest:	*City of Death* –	14.5 million

(but this was while ITV was on strike). The highest outside the ITV strike is:

	The Robots of Death –	12.7 million
Lowest:	*Meglos* –	4.7 million

Fifth Doctor:
Highest:	*Black Orchid* –	10 million
Lowest:	*The King's Demons* –	6.5 million

Sixth Doctor:
Highest:	*Attack of the Cybermen* –	8.1 million
Lowest:	*The Trial of a Time Lord*	
	Episodes 1–4 –	4.4 million

Seventh Doctor:
Highest:	*Silver Nemesis* –	5.5 million
Lowest:	*Battlefield* –	3.7 million

Eighth Doctor:
	Doctor Who – The Movie –	9.1 million

THE SAVAGES

In which the Doctor does some moralising and Steven makes a decision...

BY IAN STUART BLACK

4 EPISODES, FIRST BROADCAST 28 MAY–18 JUNE 1966

TARDIS DATA BANK:

DATE: UNKNOWN, FUTURE
LOCATION: AN UNNAMED PLANET

THE TARDIS ARRIVES ON AN APPARENTLY IDYLLIC WORLD. BUT THE DOCTOR AND HIS FRIENDS DISCOVER THAT THE 'CIVILISED' ELDERS ARE LIVING OFF THE LIFE FORCE OF A GROUP OF 'SAVAGES' WHO LIVE OUTSIDE THEIR CITY. THE DOCTOR PROTESTS, BUT IS TAKEN TO THE LABORATORY TO HAVE HIS OWN LIFE FORCE DRAINED AND DONATED TO THE LEADER, JANO...

Jano: 'We absorb only a very special form of animal vitality.'

JOURNEY INFORMATION

JANO

Jano is the leader of the Council of Elders. He has been following the Doctor's travels for some time.

He tries to convince the Doctor of the value of the Elders' way of life – of the advantages of draining life force from others to 'feed' themselves – and explains that the process can make the brave man braver, the wise man wiser, the strong man stronger, and the beautiful girl even more beautiful. He explains, 'We have learned how to transfer the energy of life directly to ourselves. We can tap it at its source. It is as though we were able to recharge ourselves with life's vital force.'

But after he absorbs some of the Doctor's life force, Jano begins to see the error of his people's ways. For a while he is confused – he thinks himself to be the Doctor and refers to Dodo and Steven as his young friends... The Doctor explains that as well as acquiring his intellect, Jano has acquired some of his conscience. Seeing how morally wrong the Elders' way of life is, Jano destroys the laboratory.

CHAL

Chal is the leader of the 'Savages'. He counsels against revenge and killing.

The Savages were once great artists, he says – as is apparent from the intricate carvings in the caves where they take refuge. Chal says they are on an island. It is Chal who first turns to his new friend Steven, and asks him to lead the two races after the scientist Senta's laboratory is destroyed.

The Doctor: 'Jano is now saddled with the states of right and wrong, which makes him an explosive element in a civilisation such as this.'

NEW INFORMATION

THE DOCTOR

The Elders know of the Doctor and respect him. They have been following his journey through time and space for many light years and predicted his arrival. They know him 'as a record in our charts of space and time', calling him 'The Traveller from Beyond Time'. The Elders' leader Jano says that the Doctor is recognised as the 'greatest specialist in time–space exploration'. But they did not expect anyone to be travelling with the Doctor.

The Doctor says that if he accepts the gifts they offer him, that would mean he endorses their way of life – so he would like to know about it. When he hears from Jano how the Elders transfer the life energy from others to themselves, he is horrified. 'The sacrifice of even one soul would be too great,' he tells Jano.

He has his own life force drained (to 'feed' Jano), and becomes unconscious. Later he says, 'I must have fallen into some kind of a coma. It was as though ... all my powers had been sapped.'

THE TARDIS

The Doctor tells Steven to go to the TARDIS Emergency Cabinet and bring back a container with capsules marked D 403, which he thinks will help one of the drained Savages to recover.

COMPANIONS

STEVEN: The Doctor lends Steven the TARDIS key, which suggests that Steven does not have one.

Steven agrees to Chal's invitation (previously turned down by the Doctor) that he stay behind and help the two races live together peacefully.

DODO: Typically, wandering off on her own, it is Dodo who discovers Senta's laboratory where the life-force transference takes place. The life force is stored in vats as a thick, black liquid.

POLLY

'I haven't got it wrong, have I?
You do have orange sellers, don't you?
I mean Nell Gwyn and all that?'

(POLLY – *THE HIGHLANDERS*)

Polly is in her twenties and from contemporary London. When we first meet her, she is working as secretary to Professor Brett (and bemoaning the fact that the computer WOTAN's typing is faster and more accurate than her own).

Her surname is never given, but Ben calls her 'Duchess' because of her upper-class accent and sophistication. He also calls her 'Poll' – which becomes Paul in *The Smugglers* when she pretends to be a boy.

When she is not pretending to be a boy, Polly has no qualms about using her feminine appeal to advantage – for example to enlist the help of Algernon ffinch in *The Highlanders*. But she is more than just a pretty face. In *The Moonbase*, it is Polly who realises that the plastic components of the Cybermen can be attacked with solvents just as nail varnish remover dissolves the plastic of nail varnish – though it is Ben who comes up with a practical means of delivering 'Polly Cocktail' using fire extinguishers.

Polly has a deep affection for Ben, although she masks it behind banter and teasing. She chats him up at the Inferno nightclub, and in a sense she is still chatting him up when they leave together in *The Faceless Ones*. Polly is rarely completely serious, except when she believes her friends are in trouble. And she is most serious when Ben is threatened.

TARDIS DATA BANK:

DESCRIPTION: FEMALE, HUMAN, SECRETARY TO PROFESSOR BRETT
TRAVELLED: *THE WAR MACHINES – THE FACELESS ONES*

BEN JACKSON

'When I was a kid, we used to live opposite a brewery. You could take a walk and get tipsy all in one go.'

(BEN JACKSON – *THE POWER OF THE DALEKS*)

Ben is in his twenties and a Cockney. He's a sailor in the British navy – his ship is HMS *Teazer*. During his time with the Doctor he never loses sight of the fact that what he wants, more than anything, is to get back to his ship.

Ben is a practical man and a realist. It takes him a while to believe that the TARDIS really does travel through time and space. When the Doctor changes, it is Ben who is most sceptical – for a long time he is sure that this is not the Doctor at all but an impostor. Ironically, it is only when a Dalek recognises the Doctor that Ben realises the strange little man really is who he says.

Never one to shirk action and danger, Ben is also clever and practical. In *The Tenth Planet*, he is sensible enough to realise that it would be a mistake to take on a Cyberman with a screwdriver. But he does dazzle a Cyberman with a film projector before killing it with its own weapon when it leaves him no choice. Later in the same story, it is Ben who works out that the Cybermen are avoiding radiation and helps devise a plan to destroy them with the Snowcap Base's reactor fuel rods.

While they only meet in the Inferno nightclub shortly before departing, accidentally, with the Doctor in the TARDIS, Ben and Polly have become good friends and trust each other. Their relationship is punctuated by good-natured teasing and banter, but they complement each other well. It is no surprise that they leave, together, at the first opportunity – arriving back in London in *The Faceless Ones* on the same day as they left.

TARDIS DATA BANK:

DESCRIPTION: MALE, HUMAN, SAILOR
TRAVELLED: *THE WAR MACHINES – THE FACELESS ONES*

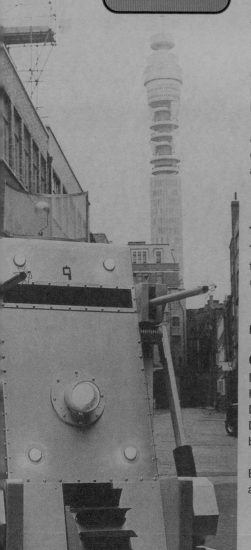

TARDIS DATA BANK:

DATE: 12–20 JULY 1966
LOCATION: LONDON

ARRIVING BACK IN
CONTEMPORARY LONDON,
THE DOCTOR IS STRANGELY
UNSETTLED BY THE SIGHT OF
THE NEW POST OFFICE
TOWER. THE TOWER HOUSES
THE OFFICES OF PROFESSOR
BRETT AND HIS
SUPERCOMPUTER WOTAN,
WHICH IS TO BE LINKED TO
OTHER COMPUTERS ACROSS
THE GLOBE. BUT, ABLE TO
THINK FOR ITSELF, WOTAN
HAS DECIDED THAT
PROGRESS WOULD BE MORE
EFFECTIVE WITHOUT
MANKIND – SO IT
CONSTRUCTS MOBILE
COMPUTERIZED WAR
MACHINES TO DESTROY
HUMANITY. CAN THE DOCTOR
ESCAPE FROM AND DESTROY
A SUPERCOMPUTER THAT
CAN HYPNOTIZE PEOPLE
DOWN A TELEPHONE LINE…

THE WAR MACHINES

In which the newly completed Post Office Tower houses a deadly threat to the security of London…

BY IAN STUART BLACK, BASED ON AN IDEA BY KIT PEDLER
4 EPISODES, FIRST BROADCAST 25 JUNE–16 JULY 1966

JOURNEY INFORMATION

PROFESSOR BRETT

WOTAN is Brett's life's work. He is a computer genius and his offices are in the Post Office Tower. Brett is happy to explain and demonstrate WOTAN to the Doctor and Dodo when they come to his offices.

He is the first to be taken over by WOTAN, and his mind is freed when WOTAN is destroyed by a reprogrammed War Machine.

WOTAN AND THE WAR MACHINES

WOTAN – Will Operating Thought ANalogue – is a computer at least ten years ahead of its time, according to its creator Professor Brett. It is the most advanced computer in the world, and even knows what TARDIS stands for. It is housed in the Post Office Tower in London.

On 'C-Day' WOTAN will be linked to, and take control of, other computers in organisations all round the world – including Parliament, the White House, the European Free Trade Association, Woomera, Telstar, the European Launcher Development Organisation, Cape Kennedy and the Royal Navy.

Able to hypnotise people – even down the telephone – WOTAN takes over Brett. It then orders the War Machines to be built, to take over the world's capital cities. Since it can think more efficiently than humans, it does not need them and believes the world needs to evolve beyond mankind if it is to progress.

The War Machines are developed, assembled and tested in secret in a warehouse. They are large, tank-like mobile-computers controlled by WOTAN (orders are received through a dish on their tops) and armed with guns and large swinging arms with heavy hammer-heads attached. The War Machines can jam guns and each one is numbered.

NEW INFORMATION

THE DOCTOR

The Doctor gets a strange prickling sensation when the Daleks are near. He attributes this to the Post Office Tower, but it may be because of the Daleks' link to Waterfield's antiques shop (see *The Evil of the Daleks*).

According to WOTAN, the Doctor is a human called Doctor Who.

The Doctor can break WOTAN's hypnotic conditioning and is also able to stop a War Machine (number 9), and reprogram it to destroy WOTAN.

COMPANIONS

DODO: Dodo is taken over by WOTAN, but the Doctor manages to break her conditioning. He sends her to the country to recuperate, and she decides to remain on earth, sending the Doctor a message with Polly and Ben.
Dodo has her own TARDIS key (unlike Steven in *The Savages*), which she asks Polly to give back to the Doctor.

BEN: Ben's ship has gone to the West Indies and he has a shore posting for six months. He and Polly return Dodo's TARDIS key to the Doctor and enter the TARDIS as it dematerialises.

Pike: 'Sawbones, ye Neptune's curse. Ye laid a trap, and for that you'll die by the pike... I'm coming for ye. See if your magic will help you now.'

THE SMUGGLERS

In which Polly and Ben do some swashbuckling in Cornwall...
BY BRIAN HAYLES
4 EPISODES, FIRST BROADCAST 10 SEPTEMBER–1 OCTOBER 1966

> **TARDIS DATA BANK:**
>
> DATE: LATE 17TH CENTURY
> LOCATION: CORNWALL
>
> THE DOCTOR, POLLY AND BEN ARE CAUGHT UP IN A STRUGGLE BETWEEN SQUIRE EDWARDS AND THE VICIOUS CAPTAIN PIKE AS THEY TRY TO FIND PIRATE AVERY'S HIDDEN TREASURE. THE DOCTOR HAS A CLUE TO ITS LOCATION, BUT CAN HE AND HIS COMPANIONS STAY ALIVE LONG ENOUGH TO FIND IT...

JOURNEY INFORMATION

SQUIRE EDWARDS
The local publican, Kewper, says, 'the Squire's the law in these parts'. The Squire is the magistrate of the borough, and revels in his authority. But while he is a rogue and a smuggler he is not callous and has a respect for life. He refuses to kill Ben and Polly for the treasure, and saves the Doctor's life.

He sums himself up when he says, 'I've been a rogue. I frankly admit it. But, the generosity of this stranger has shamed me. But, I never spilled blood in my villainy. I beg you – as a fellow rogue, if you must – spare my poor villagers.'

CAPTAIN PIKE AND AVERY'S CREW
Pike is a blackguard with a pike-shaped 'hook' in place of his right hand. He is after Avery's treasure and is willing to sacrifice anyone to get it. He kills his crewman Jamaica simply for allowing the Doctor and Kewper to escape.

His crewmate Cherub is of a similar disposition and character to his captain – willing to leave and betray Pike if it means he can get the treasure for himself.

Longfoot: 'Remember these words: This is Deadman's secret key – Smallbeer, Ringwood, Gurney.'

Avery himself died a pauper – 'rotten with rum and madness in his tongue'. Legend has it that '... he bargained for his life: his soul in return for the souls of those who come after, seeking and finding the cursed treasure.'

'Holy' Joe Longfoot was mate on Avery's ship, *the Black Albatross,* and has hidden Avery's treasure. The names mentioned in the clue he leaves when he is killed are all members of Avery's crew. Jack Ringwood, the master gunner, had a wooden leg. Zeb Gurney was ship's chandler and sewed the shrouds for dead sailors. Daniel Smallbeer was renowned as a tough fighter, and Tim Deadman was Avery's galley boy.

The Doctor realises that Longfoot has changed the names on various stones in the crypt so that the intersection of lines drawn between the stones indicates the flagstone under which the treasure is hidden.

Whether the treasure is cursed is a matter of conjecture. But Polly points out: 'They're all dead ... the ones who wanted the treasure.' The Doctor's reply is circumspect: 'Yes, superstition is a strange thing, my dear, but sometimes it tells the truth.'

NEW INFORMATION

THE DOCTOR

The Doctor relocates Longfoot's dislocated finger, and when Pike asks if he is a sawbones, he replies, 'I would prefer you to use the correct term, sir. I am a doctor.'

In contrast to his early exhortations not to interfere in history and events, the Doctor refuses to leave the village when he has the chance, telling Ben and Polly that they cannot go as he feels under a 'moral obligation' to help. 'It's this village,' he explains, 'I feel that I might be responsible for its destruction. And therefore I must at least try and avoid this danger...'

THE TARDIS

The Doctor admits he does not know where they are headed and says this is 'the cause of half my troubles through my journeys. I never know ... I have no control over where I land. Neither can I choose the period in which I land.'

When the TARDIS lands at the South Pole, its interior gets noticeably colder – either because the outside environment affects the interior of the ship (though it can materialise in space with no such effects) or possibly as an indication to the crew of the conditions outside.

COMPANIONS

BEN: Ben is anxious to be back at his ship. He also mentions getting back to his 'barracks', which suggests he serves in the Royal Navy (as he tells Cutler in *The Tenth Planet*) rather than as a merchant seaman.

Polly describes him as having a 'bell-bottom sense of humour'. He has no qualms about engaging in hand-to-hand combat with Pike's men.

POLLY: Ben describes Polly as 'our little dolly-rocker Duchess'. Later he calls her 'Paul' – to cover up for calling her 'Poll' when she is pretending to be a boy.

THE TENTH PLANET

In which the Cybermen arrive in the worlds of **Doctor Who**, and William Hartnell leaves...

BY KIT PEDLER AND GERRY DAVIS

4 EPISODES, FIRST BROADCAST 8–29 OCTOBER 1966

TARDIS DATA BANK:

DATE: DECEMBER 1986
LOCATION: EARTH – MAINLY THE 'SNOWCAP'
SOUTH POLAR BASE

EARTH'S LOST TWIN PLANET, MONDAS, RETURNS TO THE SOLAR SYSTEM AND ENERGY DRAINS AWAY FROM EARTH. ARRIVING AT A SOUTH POLE SPACE CENTRE THE DOCTOR, POLLY AND BEN ARE CAUGHT UP IN AN INVASION BY THE INHABITANTS OF MONDAS – CYBERMEN. AS THE CYBERMEN PLAN TO DESTROY THE EARTH TO SAVE THEIR OWN PLANET, THE DOCTOR WEAKENS…

The Doctor: 'Millions of years ago there was a twin planet to Earth...'

JOURNEY INFORMATION

GENERAL CUTLER

'Impossible is not in my vocabulary,' General Cutler, the commander of Snowcap Base, says. He is determined and brash, used to getting his own way. Cutler's preference is for a small team, which he works so hard its members only do a couple of months' duty each.

The only thing that matters to Cutler more than his command is the safety of his son. Ultimately, and wrongly, Cutler blames the Doctor for his son's death and has no hesitation in threatening to kill him.

Z BOMB

The Z Bomb is a 'doomsday weapon' that could split the planet in half. There are two or three at strategic positions around the globe. Mounted in the warhead of a Demeter rocket, the Z Bomb could destroy Mondas, though the Cybermen plan to use it to destroy Earth.

MONDAS

Mondas was an ancient name for Earth, and the land masses of the planets are very similar. The Cybermen explain, 'Aeons ago the planets were twins then we drifted away from you on a journey to the edge of space. Now we have returned...'

THE CYBERMEN

The leading Cyberman says, 'We are called Cybermen... We were exactly like you once but our cybernetic scientists realised that our race was getting weak... Our lifespan was getting shorter. So our scientists and doctors devised spare parts for our bodies until we could be almost completely replaced... Our brains are just like yours, except that certain weaknesses have been removed... You call them emotions, do you not?' The heart is another of the weaknesses that has been removed (the chest unit seems to replace the heart and lungs).

'We are equipped to survive,' another Cyberman explains. 'We are only interested in survival. Anything else is of no importance.'

The Cybermen carry weapons hooked below their belts and the 'victims' fall down dead with smoke pouring from them. They can also render a human unconscious by pressing their hands to his head. But the Cybermen are susceptible to radiation – weakened to the point of collapse by its effects. They draw the power that keeps them alive from their home planet. When Mondas absorbs too much energy and explodes, the human material of the Cybermen 'dissolves', leaving just a shrivelled husk.

NEW INFORMATION

THE DOCTOR

When the Doctor falls unconscious, Ben describes his pulse and breathing as 'normal'. Polly says he just seems to be worn out. The Doctor's own feeling is that some outside influence may have affected him. 'This old body of mine is wearing a bit thin,' he adds.

REGENERATION

(The term 'regeneration' is not used until *Planet of the Spiders*.)

The TARDIS seems to play a part in the Doctor's regeneration – its central column rises and falls before dematerialisation, and other controls operate themselves.

The Doctor then regenerates as the TARDIS dematerialises – a bright light covering his face as his features (and clothes) blur and change.

COMPANIONS

BEN: Throughout this story, Ben takes the initiative – getting a machine gun to Cutler, destroying the Cyberman that is guarding him in the Projection Room, sabotaging the rocket, working out how to oppose the Cybermen with radiation and persuading scientist Barclay and the others to go along with his plan.

BEHIND THE SCENES

THE CREATION OF THE CYBERMEN

The Cybermen were the creation of Dr Kit Pedler, who became, for a while, unofficial scientific adviser to **Doctor Who**. Pedler was a medical researcher when he was recommended to script editor Gerry Davis as someone who might be useful as an adviser.

According to Davis, Pedler was presented with hypothetical, fictional problems and asked to extrapolate what would happen. One of the questions Davis posed was: 'What if some alien intelligence gets inside the top of the Post Office Tower [which was visible from Davis's office window] and decides to take over London?' Pedler's considered reply formed the basis for *The War Machines*.

Another of Davis's scenarios concerned a new planet that was a mirror image of Earth drifting into our solar system. Pedler's answer again formed the basis of a **Doctor Who** story, but this time one he wrote himself (albeit in collaboration with Gerry Davis when Pedler was taken ill): *The Tenth Planet*.

Pedler told Davis that as a doctor his greatest phobia was 'dehumanising medicine.' He foresaw a time when spare-part surgery had reached the stage where it was commonplace, possibly even cosmetic. There would come a point where it was impossible to tell how much of the original human being remained. Such creatures, he reasoned, would be motivated by pure logic coupled with the overriding desire to survive. They would sacrifice their entire bodies and their minds in the quest for immortality...

The Cybermen were first described in the script at the end of Episode 1 of *The Tenth Planet*:

    We now see them as tall, thin, clad
    in a silver link one-piece suit...

Disguised in army parkas, one of the Cybermen then reaches for the body of a dead soldier:

    ... the sleeve on the arm of one of
    them slips back. Instead of flesh there
    is a transparent 'arm-shaped' forearm
    containing shining rods and lights.
    There is a normal hand at the end of
    it. A close-up of one of their heads
    reveals a metal plate running between
    centre hair line front and occiput...

The job of designing the Cybermen from these, and later, descriptions fell to costume supervisor Sandra Reid, working on her first (of many) **Doctor Who** stories. While the look of the Cybermen would change and evolve almost with every story in which they appeared, the initial design included the main elements that make the Cybermen recognisable: the blank mask-like face, 'jug handles' connected to a light in the head, cables and rods to enhance the limbs, and the large chest unit.

The voices of these early Cybermen, however, were markedly different from their successors. In the script, the Cyberman voice was described as 'flat but not Dalekish, hard in tone'.

Voice artist Roy Skelton came up with a stilted, eerily mechanical-sounding voice with the pitch, intonation and inflection all different from normal human speech. However, while it was distinctive, this voice did not continue through to other stories and by the time the Cybermen returned in *The Moonbase*, they had indeed become more electronic sounding and 'Dalekish'.

The scripts for *The Tenth Planet* (and also in places for *The Moonbase*) gave the individual Cybermen names. These were never used in the story, but for *The Tenth Planet* they were retained in the cast listings.

Kit Pedler continued to write Cybermen scripts – *The Moonbase* and (with Gerry Davis) *The Tomb of the Cybermen*. He went on to contribute story ideas for *The Wheel in Space* and *The Invasion*. Later the two would collaborate to create the landmark BBC ecological thriller series **Doomwatch**, and also to write three related novels.

Apart from **Doomwatch** and the creation of the Cybermen, Dr Kit Pedler is best remembered for his book and series **Mind Over Matter**. He died in 1981 at the age of 53.

SCENIC DESIGN

The job of a television designer in the 1960s was arduous enough (with responsibility for the design and construction of all sets as well as for providing props) but for the early seasons of **Doctor Who** this work was compounded. The BBC had a small Visual Effects Department, but they made it clear that they were not staffed up to serve an effects-intensive show like **Doctor Who**. Rather than allocate more money and resources to Visual Effects, it was decided that the designer for each story would also handle special props and effects.

Much of this work was farmed out to contract companies, such as Shawcraft Models (Uxbridge) Ltd which built the original Dalek props as well as the TARDIS interior set and the model of the Dalek City on Skaro. But the bulk of the work still fell to the Design Department. Though this would change and Visual Effects would take over the special-effects work for the series during the Second Doctor's era, in the earliest days the designer's role was even more key.

During the First Doctor's tenure, two designers in particular contributed to the look of the series. The first of these was Barry Newbery, who designed many of the lavish historical stories such as *Marco Polo* and *The Crusade,* as well as some science-fiction-based tales like *The Ark.* Newbery continued to work on the series, though less frequently, right up until *The Masque of Mandragora* in 1976.

Also pivotal to the development of **Doctor Who**'s design look was Raymond P. Cusick – who designed the Daleks. Cusick also designed many of the other innovative science-fiction-based stories including *The Sensorites* and *The Rescue,* as well as some historical tales such as *The Romans*. Both these talented and prolific designers worked on the epic 12-part story *The Daleks' Master Plan*.

Even without the additional burden of handling effects, the designer on **Doctor Who** had a difficult and crucially important role. As with any other BBC production, the designer was not just responsible for the design and creation of the studio sets. He or she also handled the 'look' of the show on location – providing furnishings and dressing the location. A tunnel entrance might become the hi-tech back door to the villain's lair in *The Pirate Planet*; a quarry becomes the snowy wastes of Antarctica in *The Seeds of Doom;* London streets are taken back to Victorian times (which involved tipping a pile of straw over a car) in *The Talons of Weng-Chiang...*

Doctor Who was like no other BBC production. Even the series' science-fiction 'cousin' **Blake's 7** took place in a single time and hence had an established unity of design. The TARDIS might arrive anywhere at any time for a given story – or, as with *The Chase* or *The Hand of Fear*, even travel to several different times and places within a single story.

COSTUME DESIGN

Many of the problems that the scenic designer faced on **Doctor Who** were also challenges for the costume designer. Only in contemporary stories could costumes be used from stock, hired in, or even bought off the shelf. The saving of effort and cost in this case was one of the reasons behind stranding the Third Doctor on Earth for the majority of his tenure. At a time when inflation was high and costs rising faster than television budgets, it was a sensible production decision as well as one that took the series in an interesting narrative direction.

As with scenic design, the early years of **Doctor Who** were handled by just a few costume designers – notably Daphne Dare during the First Doctor's era and later Sandra Reid and Martin Baugh – while in later years, a costume designer was assigned to each story depending on availability and the director or producer's requests.

The extent of the costume designer's remit is perhaps more apparent than that of the scenic designers. Obviously there needs to be a synergy between the set design and the costumes of the people or creatures who inhabit that environment. But there can also be an overlap with other departments including Visual Effects and Make-up.

The monsters and alien creatures that appeared on **Doctor Who** were created by the various BBC design departments. Construction was often subcontracted, but the design process was almost always in-house.

Whether a creature was designed by the scenic designer, the costume designer or realised through make-up varied according to the perceived requirements of the script as well as the skills and preferences of the people involved. While, as a general guideline, Design was responsible for 'props' (like the Daleks and the Zarbi) and Costume for costumes that were 'worn' by an actor (like the Menoptra and the Voord), there was considerable overlap. Some of the most memorable of the Second Doctor's alien enemies were created by costume designer Martin Baugh – including the Ice Warriors, the Yeti and the box-like robotic Quarks in *The Dominators*.

From the Second Doctor's era onwards the BBC's Visual Effects Department was also involved and often

The most challenging stories were those set in an alien environment or the future. With only a standard drama budget, the designer was called upon to realise a world where little or nothing could be bought off the shelf or furnished from stock materials and props – be it the alien jungle of Zeta Minor, the Dalek City on Skaro, the inside circuitry of a miniscope, or the honeycomb-like tombs of the Cybermen on Telos. Even the historical stories, while allowing for research, could often make use of standard props and scenery flats. As a result, many of the alien and future cultures the Doctor encountered were reminiscent of periods from Earth's past – simply to save on time, effort and money.

Even contemporary stories can create problems. For *The Web of Fear,* the writers and the director assumed that an actual London Underground station and tunnels could be used. But London Transport in effect refused to grant permission for filming to take place on its premises by demanding a large fee and stipulating that filming could only take place between 2 a.m. and 5 a.m. As a result, all the sequences that took place in the London Underground were achieved at the BBC's Lime Grove and Ealing studios, using detailed sets that could be rearranged to form different stations and sections of tunnel. It is a testament to the skill of the BBC's Design Department that London Transport believed the production team had gone ahead and filmed in the real Underground without permission.

provided design and/or realisation of part of a creature or components of the costume. The Make-up Department was responsible for the area of the Ice Warriors' mouths and eyes visible through the helmet, for example. Visual Effects provided claws for the Yeti's hands and feet...

As with the series as a whole, the creatures of **Doctor Who** were a collaborative effort that showcased the expertise of the diverse BBC design departments and the talents of the people who worked in them.

MAKE-UP DESIGN

In the early years of the series, a make-up designer was assigned to the show rather than to individual stories. Sonia Markham and later Sylvia James were responsible for many of the First and Second Doctors' stories, though others worked on the programme too.

Most of the make-up artist's job is invisible – making the actors' features look right for the camera. But – as with every area of design – **Doctor Who** often had very special requirements. Not only were there Stone Age savages to be

made up (one of whom refused to take off her artificial eyelashes – she did not appear in the finished *An Unearthly Child*), but there were also cloned Drahvin women, survivors of a Dalek invasion of Earth... As the programme continued there were demands for an even greater variety of alien life forms, from green Swampies in *The Power of Kroll* to a race of time-sensitive leonine creatures in *Warriors' Gate*, Often Make-up worked in collaboration with half-masks provided by Visual Effects to create Ogrons, Draconians, Davros and even (in *The Daemons*) the devil himself.

Only on **Doctor Who** would a make-up artist be asked to provide victims of alien plagues, burned mutants, people who have fallen into acid baths, the scarred and scorched face of Sharaz-Jek in *The Caves of Androzani* or the bent and distorted face of Greel – seen only for a few seconds in *The Talons of Weng-Chiang* despite Heather Stewart spending hours making up actor Michael Spice for the shot...

The 'look' of a **Doctor Who** story is very much a collaborative effort. Occasionally, of course, there are problems when the disparate elements of design come together. Sometimes the problem can be overcome in the studio. You never see any Zygons actually going through any of the doors on their

spaceship, for example, any more than you will see K-9 entering or leaving the TARDIS without both doors being open – because they don't fit. But sometimes it is impossible to disguise the fact that the designs do not gel – why are Drathro's guards so grimy and dirty when the tunnels they live in are so bright and clean (*The Trial of a Time Lord*)?

But in the vast majority of cases the work of the various departments blends together seamlessly. The opening sequence of *The Robots of Death,* to pick just one example from many, demonstrates how startlingly effective this combination of talents can be. It shows a model Sandminer (from visual effects designer Richard Conway) crossing a model desert. The camera moves in to show a view into the control deck (designed by Kenneth Sharp) where we meet the Voc and Dum Robots together with the human crew, their costumes (designed by Elizabeth Waller) perfectly in keeping with their surroundings and the crew's make-up (designed by Ann Briggs) reflecting the stylistic design of the robots.

Two

THE SECOND DOCTOR

THE DOCTOR

'He's a very different Doctor,' Polly tells Ben at the start of *The Power of the Daleks*, and indeed he is. The scratchy, arrogant old man that had been the Doctor is replaced with a younger and seemingly far softer character. The First Doctor's cold, analytical abilities give way to apparent bluster and a tendency to panic under pressure.

But with the Second Doctor, more than any other, first impressions are misleading. This is a Doctor who can defeat the Daleks on Vulcan without apparently having any idea of what he has done or how he did it. Yet often when he wins the day it is apparent that the solution is one he has been planning for a while. This is a Doctor who can be saddened by the trivial, mindless destruction of Kent's crockery in *The Enemy of the World* yet electrifies the entrance and controls of the Cybermen's tombs on Telos to give a fatal shock to anyone who tries to enter.

The Doctor's apparent bluster and ineptitude mask a deeper, darker nature. When his companion Jamie tells him that their association is over in *The Evil of the Daleks,* that the Doctor simply uses people for his own ends, the audience agrees more readily with Jamie than with the Doctor. We have seen the Doctor's cold manipulation of Jamie for the Human Factor experiment, and even if his ultimate triumph over the Emperor Dalek does something to mitigate his actions, the knowledge remains that a cold, calculating alien lurks inside the bumbling exterior. In many ways the Second Doctor is very much a reincarnation of the First. Perhaps, through age, the First Doctor has simply become bored with this pretence and dropped it.

But there are moments when the Second Doctor's humanity also shines through. There is ultimately no doubt that his *raison d'être* is to fight the evil in the universe – as he tells his friends in *The Moonbase* and his own people in *The War Games*. And there is a personal as well as a universal cost. It is in moments when the whole façade of the bumbler and the cold warrior drops that we glimpse the true Doctor, the man that he would like to be if circumstances allowed – moments like his description of his family to Victoria in *The Tomb of the Cybermen*; his simple comment to Jamie that he was fond of the departing Victoria too (*Fury from the Deep*); his sad farewell to his companions Jamie and Zoe in *The War Games* before he turns his righteous anger and indignation on his own people – the ones who have chosen the easy option, have ignored the evils that must be fought, have lived the life that perhaps he wishes he himself could have had...

'I am not a student of human nature. I am a professor of a far wider academy of which human nature is merely a part.'

(THE DOCTOR –
THE EVIL OF THE DALEKS)

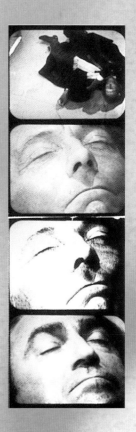

THE MAN BEHIND THE DOCTOR – PATRICK TROUGHTON

Born in 1920, Patrick Troughton was a highly respected character actor when he was offered the title role of **Doctor Who.** It is reported that William Hartnell believed that Troughton was the only actor capable of taking over, though this was not a factor in his casting.

To the television audience of late 1966, Troughton was remembered for playing Robin Hood and Paul of Tarsus, and Quilp in the BBC's 1962 production of *The Old Curiosity Shop.*

Troughton later claimed that he initially refused the role, believing (with typical modesty) that the series would last only about six weeks if he took over. He tended to avoid press interviews and media attention, though towards the end of his life his renewed association with **Doctor Who** led

him to attend several **Doctor Who** conventions, including the BBC's massive gathering in Longleat in 1983.

After leaving **Doctor Who**, Troughton had no difficulty securing other roles – including Father Brennan in *The Omen* and the Duke of Norfolk in the BBC's prestigious *The Six Wives of Henry VIII.* Perhaps his best remembered children's television work of later years was as the mysterious magician Cole Hawlings in the BBC's 1984 production of *The Box of Delights.*

Having reprised his role of the Doctor on three occasions, most recently in *The Two Doctors* alongside Colin Baker in 1985, Patrick Troughton died in 1987 while at a **Doctor Who** convention in the USA.

THE POWER OF THE DALEKS

In which Patrick Troughton takes over as the Doctor, and the Daleks claim to be friendly...

BY DAVID WHITAKER

6 EPISODES, FIRST BROADCAST 5 NOVEMBER–10 DECEMBER 1966

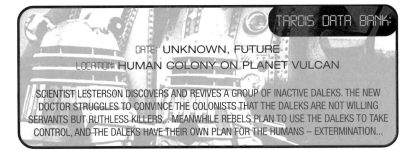

TARDIS DATA BANK:

DATE: UNKNOWN, FUTURE
LOCATION: HUMAN COLONY ON PLANET VULCAN

SCIENTIST LESTERSON DISCOVERS AND REVIVES A GROUP OF INACTIVE DALEKS. THE NEW DOCTOR STRUGGLES TO CONVINCE THE COLONISTS THAT THE DALEKS ARE NOT WILLING SERVANTS BUT RUTHLESS KILLERS... MEANWHILE REBELS PLAN TO USE THE DALEKS TO TAKE CONTROL, AND THE DALEKS HAVE THEIR OWN PLAN FOR THE HUMANS – EXTERMINATION...

The Doctor: 'I'd like to see a butterfly fit into a chrysalis case after it spread its wings.'

JOURNEY INFORMATION

VULCAN

What we see of Vulcan beyond the colony's buildings is a mercury swamp – composed of mercury pools and geysers. The atmosphere is breathable, but the fumes render Polly and Ben unconscious. It is also hot in the swamp (the TARDIS read-outs give the temperature as '86') and the colonists wear goggles and protective clothing.

The colony supports itself at least partly by mining. The miners live mainly on the 'Perimeter'. Lesterson, a scientist, has a device that computes meteorite storms approaching the colony's weather satellites, so as to cut down on satellite losses and damage.

THE DALEKS

The Doctor says the capsule containing the Daleks has been buried for at least 200 years when he goes inside it. The Daleks evidently recognise him.

Outnumbered and unarmed, the Daleks, for once forced to operate from a position of weakness, are at their most cunning. They scheme throughout to get the power supply that will place them in a dominant position from which they can destroy the colony. To this end, they pander to Lesterson, telling him what he wants to hear and offering him all the help they can. As one of them says: 'We understand the human mind.' When they are done with Lesterson they have no qualms about killing him, commenting with typical bluntness, 'Your usefulness is over.'

The Daleks can store power, but they require a static electrical circuit for permanent energy. The Doctor explains that Daleks are 'powered by static electricity. It's like blood to them - a constant life-stream... They've conquered static, just as they've conquered antimagnetics.' He wonders at one point 'how much longer they'll be able to move around on these floors? They're not metal.'

When their weapons are returned, their firepower is as awesome as ever. One Dalek gun fires through two-inch thick tungsten steel in a demonstration to the rebel leaders.

The Daleks reproduce on a conveyor-belt production line that assembles empty casings, into which Dalek creatures are placed. The Dalek itself is seen as a frothing, many-tentacled thing. A claw-like creature glimpsed in the capsule may be a Dalek, but this is not made clear.

Daleks: 'Exterminate all humans. Exterminate, annihilate, destroy. Daleks conquer and destroy. Daleks conquer and destroy!'

NEW INFORMATION

THE DOCTOR

'Life depends on change and renewal,' the Doctor says, by way of explaining his new body. But at first even his companions are not convinced that this is the Doctor.

The Doctor speaks about himself as if he were another person: 'The Doctor was a great collector wasn't he... The Doctor kept a diary, didn't he?'

It is difficult to know how much of the Doctor's apparent bluster is act, and how much really is the absent-mindedness of genius. Having defeated the Daleks, he doesn't seem to know how or even if he has succeeded. 'What happened? What did I do? What did I do?' he asks.

THE TARDIS

The Doctor implies that the TARDIS is essential to his regeneration. 'I've been renewed,' he tells Ben. 'It's part of the TARDIS – without it, I couldn't survive.'

COMPANIONS

BEN: When he was small, Ben lived opposite a brewery. He once had a headmaster who 'got nicked for not paying his bus fare'.

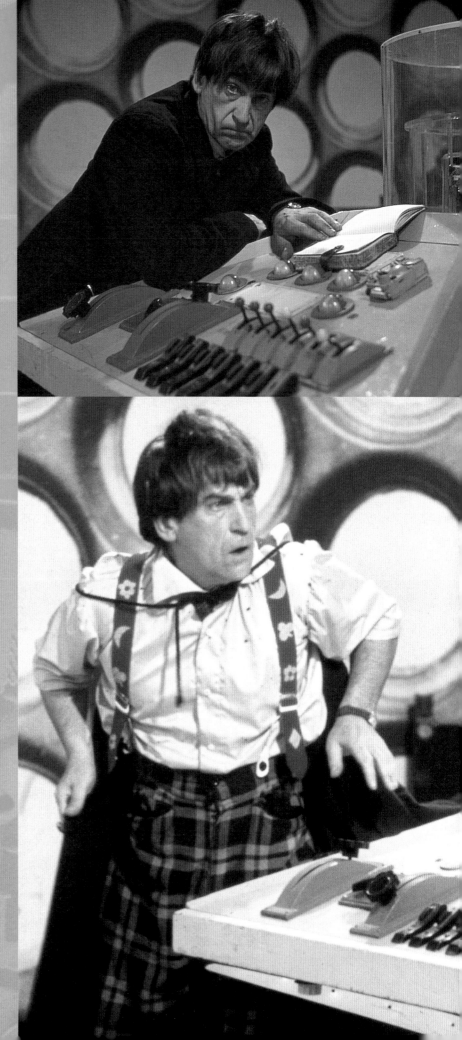

BEHIND THE SCENES

CREATING A NEW DOCTOR

Two suggestions lie at the core of the Second Doctor's character. The first was made by the BBC's Head of Drama, Sydney Newman, who felt that the Doctor should be a 'cosmic hobo'. The second was Patrick Troughton's own idea that his Doctor would be a 'listener' who took in information, assimilated it and synthesized his own brilliant solution. Troughton's idea was born, at least in part, from his hope that this approach would result in him having to learn fewer lines.

Patrick Troughton and script editor Gerry Davis worked out a more detailed character for the Doctor. Davis later commented, 'I thought it would be very interesting to have a character who never quite says what he means – who, really, uses the intelligence of the people he is with. He knows the answer all the time... He is watching, he's really directing...'

One thing that Troughton was reportedly keen to include was a catchphrase for his Doctor. While many people recall the Second Doctor's cries of 'When I say run, run. Run!' (a variation of which he uses in *The Power of the Daleks*), Troughton's favoured phrase was: 'I should like a hat like that.'

Variations of this occur in several early stories. 'I would like a hat like that,' he declares in *The Power of the Daleks*. In *The Highlanders*, he says it both of Ben's tam-o'-shanter, and a Highland bonnet he finds near an abandoned cannon. At the feast in *The Underwater Menace* Polly remarks, 'I've never seen him go for food like this before. It's usually hats.' Even when reading early scripts for *The Two Doctors*, Troughton suggested an additional sequence where his Doctor runs through a crowded market, to be glimpsed several times by the camera – each time in a different hat...

JAMIE MACRIMMON

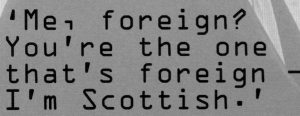

'Me, foreign?
You're the one
that's foreign —
I'm Scottish.'

(JAMIE – *THE EVIL OF THE DALEKS*)

James Robert Macrimmon is the son of Donald Macrimmon, and a piper like his father and his father's father.

Because of his background he is simple and straightforward, but he is also intelligent and blessed with a good deal of common sense. When the Dominators examine his brain, they discover that he shows signs of recent rapid learning. In many ways, Jamie's travels with the Doctor are a voyage of discovery. Almost everything is new to him, and while he struggles to understand he also enjoys the experience.

It is in Jamie's nature to accept things, and this helps him to assimilate the worlds around him. He relates new experiences to his own world where he can – aeroplanes become flying beasts, a Cyberman is the legendary phantom piper that appears to members of his clan on their deathbeds. But what he cannot find an analogy for he simply accepts with wonder but no worry.

It is this straightforward view of life that often puts him ahead of his more sophisticated companions. In *The Dominators*, as the Doctor and Zoe admire their handiwork and take pride in the fact that the planet Dulkis has been

saved and there will only be a minor volcanic eruption confined to an island, it is Jamie who points out that this is all very well – but they happen to be on the island. It is Jamie who contrives to capture a Yeti in *The Abominable Snowmen*.

Certainly Jamie is brave, never one to shirk a fight or run away. Despite knowing how dangerous and foolish the expedition is, because they tease him he accompanies Zoe and Isobel (her friend in *The Invasion*) into the London sewers to hunt for Cybermen.

Ultimately, despite occasional reservations, Jamie sees the Doctor as a friend as well as a mentor. While he relishes the chance to travel and learn and have adventures, he also believes that the Doctor really does need his help. He tells Ben at the end of *The Faceless Ones* that he will look after the Doctor and with the help of Victoria and then Zoe, this is what he does.

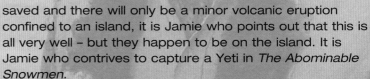

TARDIS DATA BANK:

DESCRIPTION: MALE, HUMAN, JACOBITE REBEL FROM 1746
TRAVELLED: *THE HIGHLANDERS – THE WAR GAMES*
(ALSO *THE TWO DOCTORS*)

THE HIGHLANDERS

In which Jamie joins the Doctor on his travels...
BY ELWYN JONES AND GERRY DAVIS
4 EPISODES, FIRST BROADCAST 17 DECEMBER 1966–7 JANUARY 1967

Trask: 'In case you're thinking of escaping, there's Jim Hughes for 'e. He didn't find it a happy ship, and I finds him another berth where he'll be happy. Once aboard the Annabelle, that's the only way you'll get off her. Straight downwards.'

TARDIS DATA BANK:

DATE: APRIL 1746
LOCATION: NEAR CULLODEN, AND INVERNESS, SCOTLAND

IN THE AFTERMATH OF THE BATTLE OF CULLODEN, THE DOCTOR AND BEN ARE CAPTURED AND CAUGHT UP IN A PLOT BY EX-SOLICITOR GREY TO SHIP PRISONERS AS SLAVES TO THE WEST INDIES. POLLY OUTWITS AND BEGUILES REDCOAT OFFICER ALGERNON FFINCH, AND THE YOUNG PIPER JAMIE MACRIMMON FINDS HIMSELF STARTING AN ADVENTURE IN SPACE AND TIME...

JOURNEY INFORMATION

THE JACOBITES

Colin McClaren is an important Jacobite. His daughter, Kirsty, tells Polly, 'I'm not used to fetching and carrying, you know. We used to have our own servants.'

McClaren is important enough for Bonnie Prince Charlie to have given him his ring to keep safe. 'The Prince gave it to my father off his own hand in heat of battle,' Kirsty explains. 'My father saved the Prince's life.' McClaren also has the Prince's standard concealed round his waist.

COMMISSIONER GREY

Grey, His Majesty's Commissioner for Disposal of Rebel Prisoners, tells the Jacobite prisoners held on Captain Trask's ship that they have the choice of betraying their honour and their countrymen, or being hanged for refusing to turn King's Evidence. He then offers a third alternative: 'Plantation workers are required to work in His Majesty's colonies in the West Indies. I have here seven-year contracts. Sign your name to these, and you will receive free transportation to your new homes.'

But the offer is not as attractive as it sounds. As one prisoner says, 'Not one of your men that sign will live out your seven years. Better a quick and honourable death at the end of a rope, than a long slow one...'

The Doctor:
'They're bound to have heaps of weapons as souvenirs. You don't know the English soldier. He'd sell his grandmother for tuppence ha-penny.'

LIEUTENANT ALGERNON THOMAS ALFRED FFINCH

ffinch is an archetypal English officer of the time. He is an arrogant bumbler – allowing Polly and Kirsty to get the better of him. He is loyal to king and country, and values his reputation.

But ffinch emerges as someone with genuine, though suppressed, feelings whose admiration and affection for Polly grows despite her teasing and rudeness. He may not empathise with his men, but he is loyal to his superior officer, and he is honourable and astute enough to bring Grey to justice.

NEW INFORMATION

THE DOCTOR

The Doctor disguises himself at various stages as a German doctor (Doctor von Wer), a washerwoman and a redcoat soldier complete with false moustache.

In his German doctor persona, he takes delight in tricking Grey – threatening him with a pistol: 'I'm not very expert with these things and it just might go off in your face.' When Grey's credulous assistant, Perkins, says he doesn't suffer from headaches, the Doctor bangs Perkins' head on a table and asks him again. He diagnoses 'print blindness – you read too much' and assures Perkins that the sound of Grey hammering to be let out of a cupboard is all in his mind.

But the Doctor's more serious nature comes to the fore when necessary. He holds Perkins at gunpoint at an inn, later explaining: 'It's not loaded. They're dangerous things.'

The Doctor is willing and able to supply the arms necessary for the prisoners on board the *Annabelle* to revolt, though he does not admit how or where he gets a barrowload of weapons. Kirsty suggests he 'must have robbed the Duke's arsenal'. The Doctor's reply is typically enigmatic: 'Yes, something like that.'

COMPANIONS

BEN: Ben is as headstrong and impetuous as ever. He asks if he can sign Grey's contract, then rips it up. He uses an old Houdini trick to escape when bound: 'You flex your muscles when they tie you up. Then, when you're ready, you relax them. Well that way you're half the size you were before.'

POLLY: It is Polly who takes the initiative with Kirsty, suggesting that the girls lure ffinch into a pit and then take his money, identity disc, and even a lock of his hair. 'Crying's no good,' she tells Kirsty. 'We're going to create a diversion.'

Polly's affection for Ben is evident – much to his embarrassment. 'Oh, don't overdo it Poll,' he tells her as she hugs him.

Polly also strikes up a relationship with ffinch, teasing him whenever they meet and calling him 'Algy'. She is astute enough to realise that ffinch has developed an admiration for her, and although he describes his arrest of Grey as 'a chance to put paid to a villain', Polly comments, 'It wasn't just that, was it?' Formal and correct as ever, he admits: 'Not quite, ma'am.'

JAMIE: Colin McClaren describes Jamie as 'son of Donald Macrimmon, a piper, like his father and his father's father.'

Jamie cannot swim – though he seems to cope in *The Underwater Menace*.

TARDIS DATA BANK:

DATE: AFTER 1968
LOCATION: ATLANTIS, EARTH

IN THE UNDERWATER KINGDOM OF ATLANTIS, 'FISH PEOPLE' WITH PLASTIC GILLS HARVEST FOOD FROM THE SEA. PROFESSOR ZAROFF CLAIMS HE CAN RAISE ATLANTIS ONCE MORE ABOVE THE WAVES, BUT THE DOCTOR REALISES THAT HE IS ACTUALLY PLANNING TO DESTROY THE WORLD BY DRILLING THROUGH THE THINNEST PART OF THE EARTH'S CRUST...

THE UNDERWATER MENACE

In which the travellers find Atlantis, and Polly nearly becomes a Fish Person...
BY GEOFFREY ORME
4 EPISODES, FIRST BROADCAST 14 JANUARY–4 FEBRUARY 1967

The Doctor: 'Ben and I will try and get into the generating station. We'll turn up the power on the reactor, break down the sea walls and flood the laboratory. There's only one thing that's worrying me... Can we all swim?'

JOURNEY INFORMATION

ATLANTIS

The community, architecture, religion and livelihood of Atlantis are all based on the sea. There are stylised pictograms on the rocky walls, and ceremonial Fish masks are worn, or held in front of faces, at religious occasions. 'The living goddess Amdo sees and hears all,' says the priest, Lolem, of 'Mighty Amdo, goddess of land and sea.'

Zaroff recounts how, 'When Atlantis was submerged, at the time of the flood, some life continued in air pockets in the mountain's caves, thanks to the natural air shaft provided by the extinct volcano.'

When the crisis is past and the Doctor is believed to have died, Thous, the ruler of Atlantis, says they will raise a stone to him in the temple. But Damon, an Atlantean, is a voice for change and progress: 'No. No more temples. It was temples and priests and superstition that made us follow Zaroff in the first place. When the water's found its own level, the temple will be buried forever. We shall never return to it. But we will have enough left to build a new Atlantis, without gods, and without Fish People.'

Zaroff: 'The process has started. My nuclear reactor is activated, and when the desired figure is reached, fission will take place, and none of all this will matter for any of us.'

THE FISH PEOPLE

The Fish People are human beings who have been operated on by Damon to insert plastic gills so they can breathe underwater and harvest food beneath the sea.

They are not native Atlanteans, as Damon explains, 'We pick up survivors from shipwrecks who would otherwise be corpses and convert them to Fish People.'

NEW INFORMATION

THE DOCTOR

The message that the Doctor sends to Zaroff is: 'Vital secret will die with me. Dr W.' At first, the Doctor seems in awe of him. When Zaroff shows off his laboratory and asks the Doctor if he is impressed, the Doctor replies, 'No, not a bit, not a bit,' admitting, 'I expected nothing less from the great Professor Zaroff.'

The Doctor describes himself to Thous as 'a man of science' and, once convinced that Zaroff must be stopped, demonstrates Zaroff's plan to Ramo by heating up a sealed earthenware pot with water in it till it explodes.

Ben persuades a guard that the Doctor is a wanted man by telling him, 'Well, blimey, look at him. He ain't normal, is he?' The Doctor is impressed: 'I'm not quite sure about that not being normal bit, but very well done.'

THE TARDIS

Jamie's enthusiasm for the TARDIS is tempered by his realisation that the Doctor is not in control. 'Can you not exactly make it go where you mean it to?' he asks, and the Doctor tells him, 'If I wanted to. It's just that I've never wanted to.' In response to Ben and Polly's scepticism, the Doctor insists, 'Right, just for that, I'll show you. Now, where shall we go? I know, let's go to Mars.' The next story is set on the Moon.

PROFESSOR ZAROFF

Zaroff led the field in producing cheap food from the sea. The Doctor calls him the 'greatest scientific genius since Leonardo' and comments that he disappeared twenty years ago. The East blamed the West, and the West blamed the East.

Zaroff has found a point in a fissure where the Earth's crust is less than fifteen miles thick, and says they have been working on drilling for 'many years'. But the Doctor realises that 'the water will be converted into superheated steam, the pressure will grow, and crack the crust of the Earth. Destroy all life, maybe even blow the planet apart.'

Zaroff is completely mad: 'I shall have redeemed my promise to lift Atlantis from the sea. Lift it to the sky. It will be magnificent... The achievement, my dear Doctor. The destruction of the world. The scientists' dream of supreme power.'

Thous, ruler of Atlantis, is blind to Zaroff's insanity, believing him to be 'the prophet who would raise us above the sea.' But the Atlantean Ramo describes Zaroff as 'a destroyer. He appeals to all that is base in our people. He should never have come to Atlantis.'

The Doctor's diagnosis is more direct: 'The Professor is as mad as a hatter... Completely. No answer. It's sad.'

THE MOONBASE

In which the Cybermen return, redesigned, and attack Earth's weather...
BY KIT PEDLER
4 EPISODES, FIRST BROADCAST 11 FEBRUARY–4 MARCH 1967

The Doctor: 'There are some corners of the Universe which have bred the most terrible things. Things which act against everything that we believe in. They must be fought.'

TARDIS DATA BANK:

DATE: 2070
LOCATION: THE MOON

THE CREW OF A MOONBASE THAT OPERATES THE GRAVITRON TO CONTROL EARTH'S WEATHER ARE BEING STRUCK DOWN BY A STRANGE PLAGUE. THE DOCTOR DISCOVERS THAT THE CYBERMEN ARE RESPONSIBLE, TAKING CONTROL OF THE INFECTED HUMANS AND PLANNING TO DESTROY EARTH'S POPULATION WITH SEVERE WEATHER SYSTEMS. BUT HE ALSO REALISES THAT THE CYBERMEN NEED THE HUMANS TO WORK THE EQUIPMENT AS THEY ARE ALSO SUSCEPTIBLE TO THE EFFECTS OF GRAVITY...

JOURNEY INFORMATION

THE MOONBASE

The main function of the Moonbase – officially called Weather Control Moon, or occasionally Moonport – is to operate the Gravitron which controls and regulates the weather on Earth. The Moonbase is run by International Space Control under Controller Rinberg in Geneva.

Chief Hobson introduces key members of his international staff: 'Roger Benoit ... is my assistant. He takes over as Chief Scientist if anything happens to me. He's a physicist like us and Joe Benson. Nils, our mad Dane, is an astronomer and mathematician, as is Charlie here. Ralph, Jules and Franz are geologists. When they are not acting as cooks, lookouts, general handymen.'

Hobson is reluctant to accept the reality of the Cybermen, but once convinced he is a fierce and determined opponent. Having seen the respect and admiration with which his team treat him, there is no doubt that they will stand by him 'to the last man'. Typically, when the threat is past, Hobson's first thought is to get the Gravitron working again.

THE GRAVITRON

The Gravitron is a long cylindrical device that 'controls the tides, the tides control the weather'. According to Hobson, every schoolchild knows about the Gravitron.

According to Benoit, the machine produces very intense sonic fields. Without protective close-fitting helmets, the operators inside the Gravitron Room would be driven insane in a short time, possibly 12 hours.

THE CYBERMEN

'There were Cybermen,' Hobson says, 'every child knows that. But they were all destroyed ages ago.'

The Cybermen are a different design to those in *The Tenth Planet*. The human hands are now three-fingered metal claws, the chest unit is more streamlined and the body is a silver suit with tubular exoskeleton and cabling. The face is a blank, metal skull-like helmet. The 'light' is now integrated into the headpiece. When they speak, a metal flap over the mouth tilts open.

A small aerial extends from the chest unit when a Cyberman communicates by radio. The Cybermen can fire a

Rinberg:

'We've just had a report from Miami, Florida. Thirty minutes ago they were enjoying clear skies and a heatwave. Now hurricane Lucy is right overhead.'

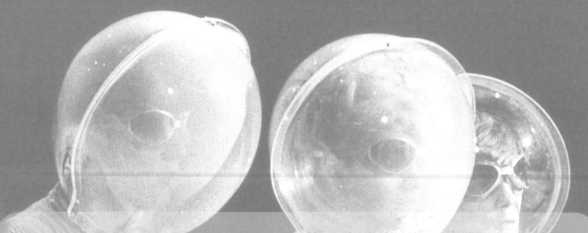

'spark' from their fingers that renders their victim unconscious. Unlike the large weapons carried by the Cybermen in *The Tenth Planet*, their new small arms are rod-like devices that slot into the bottom of their chest units.

The 'altered' humans that the Cybermen control wear probes attached to their foreheads and held together in a 'mesh'. They are controlled from a box with aerials using a sonic beam.

The Cybermen use a cylindrical capsule to transfer humans between their ship and the Moonbase without the need for spacesuits.

NEUROTROPE X

The Cybermen are 'altering' the humans with Neurotrope X, which the Doctor dexcribes as 'a large, infective agent that only attacks the nerves. That's why the patients have got these lines on their faces and their hands. It follows the course of the nerves under the skin.'

Since the food the Cybermen have contaminated is sugar, the disease affects different people at different times, as not everyone takes sugar.

NEW INFORMATION

THE DOCTOR

When Polly asks if he is a medical doctor, the Doctor says: 'Yes, I think I was once, Polly. I think I took a degree in Glasgow – 1888, I think... Lister.' In *The Rescue* he implies that he failed a medical degree, though that may have been a different occasion.

A Cyberman tells the Doctor, 'You are known to us.'

THE TARDIS

The TARDIS makes a bumpy landing because of the Gravitron. The spacesuits are kept in the chest in the Control Room.

As they leave, the Doctor demonstrates the time scanner. He explains, 'Instead of the normal picture showing where we are it gives you a glimpse of the future.' It shows a Macra claw.

COMPANIONS

POLLY: Polly discovers how to attack the Cybermen with 'Cocktail Polly', a solvent mixture that includes acetone, benzene, ether and epoxypropane.

JAMIE: There is a legend in Jamie's clan of a phantom piper that appears to a Macrimmon just before he dies, and Jamie assumes that the Cyberman in the sickbay is this piper.

THE MACRA TERROR

In which a human colony is threatened by giant crabs...
BY IAN STUART BLACK
4 EPISODES, FIRST BROADCAST 11 MARCH–1 APRIL 1967

TARDIS DATA BANK:

DATE: UNKNOWN, FUTURE
LOCATION: AN EARTH COLONY ON AN UNNAMED PLANET

THE DOCTOR AND HIS FRIENDS DISCOVER THAT A COLONY IS ACTUALLY UNDER THE MESMERIC CONTROL OF THE MACRA – GIANT CRAB-LIKE CREATURES WHO ARE USING THE HUMANS AS SLAVES TO MINE THE GAS THEY NEED TO SURVIVE. BEN IS TURNED AGAINST HIS FRIENDS, AND THE DOCTOR BATTLES TO CONVINCE THE PILOT THAT HE AND THE OTHER COLONISTS ARE BEING CONTROLLED...

JOURNEY INFORMATION

THE MACRA

The Macra are giant, crab-like creatures dependent on the gas from a mine for survival. The Doctor says, 'The Macra that have come to the surface of this planet have not found sufficient gas in the atmosphere, so they've had to get somebody to pump it up from down below.'

He tells Polly, 'They're like germs in the human body. They've got into the body of this colony. They're living as parasites.'

THE GAS

The purpose of the colony, so far as the Macra are concerned, is to mine and refine the gas the Macra need.

Officia, the colonist in charge of the mine, explains, 'The rock foundation is a type of salt. In its depths it generates gases, over the years, and these gases are extremely valuable.' But as the rebellious Medok says, 'You don't survive long in this atmosphere. It's the gas – it gets everywhere.' The gas makes the workers cough, and they wear masks and goggles for protection. Apparently, no-one has ever escaped from the mine.

THE COLONY

The colony seems idyllic when the travellers first arrive. The Pilot, who is in day-to-day charge, tells them that the colonists regulate the day by music, and offers them the chance to take advantage of the 'refreshing department'. The colony's figurehead is the 'Controller' – a face on ubiquitous screens. The colonists are confined to rest cubicles at night by order of Control and anyone who wanders around the colony at night may be killed.

The colonists have been brainwashed by the Macra who use scented air and a thin strand of wire in the wall above the subject's head, which the Doctor likens to a 'nerve tapping the subconscious of the human brain'. The

final element of the processing is a voice telling the sleeper to relax and obey orders...

Once released from the Macra's mind control, the colonists realise their predicament and express their gratitude. The Pilot officially thanks 'the strangers, for they have saved our colony. A dance festival will be held every year in their memory, and the winners will be awarded the Strangers' Trophy.'

NEW INFORMATION

THE DOCTOR

The Doctor is less than impressed with the colony's 'clothes reviver' machine. Rather than remain smart and unrumpled, he climbs into the 'rough and tumble machine, for toning up the muscles' and emerges as his usual crumpled self.

'You have destroyed three nerve circuits, Doctor,' the Pilot tells him when he sabotages the processing equipment. 'You have burned them out. What have you to say?' The Doctor is unrepentant and shows the Pilot a piece of wire: 'Rather neat, don't you think? And so simple. I did it with this.' The Pilot is astonished: 'You admit it?' 'I'm proud of it,' the Doctor assures him.

COMPANIONS

BEN: Ben is the only one of the travellers who succumbs to the hypnotic processing. But he struggles to resist it. He fails to report Jamie for taking an official's keys, and the Doctor later remarks, 'Ben, you're recovering. I always thought you were a tough customer.'

POLLY: Polly takes the opportunity of a 'makeover' at the colony to have her hair styled short for a change.

Medok: 'There are things – horrible things. Creatures, infesting this camp at night.'

JAMIE: Jamie does the Highland Fling when he is mistaken for a dancer by a team of Cheerleaders while escaping. 'Why do you call it the Highland Fling?' one of the Cheerleaders asks. 'Because we finish the dance by flinging ourselves out the door,' he replies, demonstrating.

BEHIND THE SCENES

TITLE SEQUENCE

The first episode of *The Macra Terror* featured a new opening title sequence. Producer Innes Lloyd was keen to update the titles and asked Bernard Lodge, who devised the original opening title sequence, for something along the same lines but different.

The original titles (page 23) were created using a technique called visual howlaround which basically involved a video camera recording the feedback from its own output – the visual equivalent of the 'shriek' when a microphone and speaker are brought too close together. These feedback images could be shaped by feeding a 'real' image into the camera as a starting point for the distortion.

Lodge recalled that an interesting effect was achieved when a human face was used in the sequence – the face tearing away and distorting. For the new titles, he suggested using a photograph of Patrick Troughton's – the Doctor's – face. A film wipe using scrunched-up polystyrene was used to add a gritty texture to the sequence.

Accompanied by a reworked version of the well-known signature theme that incorporated more 'sound effects' into the music, the new title sequence set the trend for future **Doctor Who** opening titles – all of which (with the exception of *Dr Who – The Movie*), whatever technique was used to create them, included the image of the current Doctor's face.

THE FACELESS ONES

In which Wanda Ventham and Pauline Collins help the Doctor against aliens who are kidnapping holidaymakers from Gatwick Airport...

BY DAVID ELLIS AND MALCOLM HULKE

6 EPISODES, FIRST BROADCAST 8 APRIL–13 MAY 1967

JOURNEY INFORMATION

THE CHAMELEONS

In their native form, the Chameleons are humanoids with dark, scarred, globby faces and bodies. In this form they would suffocate in Earth's atmosphere.

The Chameleon Meadows tells the Doctor, 'We had a catastrophe on our planet. A gigantic explosion... We have lost our identities. My people are dying out... Our scientists devised a process so that we could take on the physical

The Doctor:
'Well, in view of the facts that I've already presented, the ray gun, this pen and, um, one or two other things. I think we're dealing with people who are not from this planet.'

characteristics of another being.' Armbands maintain the link between the 'donor' and the Chameleon, removing the band or changing the controls on it can break the connection. The controls can modify the Chameleon's speech (the Chameleon versions of Crossland and Jamie lack the accents of the originals). The Chameleon Crossland has perfect eyesight, whereas the original wears glasses.

The Chameleons plan to abduct 50,000 young people 'this time'. While the real versions of the Chameleon team at Gatwick are kept unconscious in cars in the airport car park (with the exception of Nurse Pinto in the Medical Centre), the majority are held miniaturised on the Chameleon space station. The Chameleon Tours planes are themselves miniaturisation chambers.

The Chameleon Spencer uses a pen-like device to 'freeze' both Polly and Ben when he captures them. The Doctor later uses the same device on him and demonstrates how it works by firing at a cup of tea – the tea turns to ice.

As a race, the Chameleons are arrogant, believing they are superior to the humans they are using. 'They're only human beings,' the Director tells the Doctor. 'We are the most intelligent race in the universe.' In the end, the Doctor persuades them to stop their plan and return the humans not by moral argument, but by threats.

NEW INFORMATION

THE DOCTOR

The Doctor evades arrest by the police by brandishing what appears to be a grenade and threatening: 'One step nearer and I'll blow you all to smithereens.' As he escapes, he tosses the 'grenade' to the Gatwick Commandant – who finds it is a rubber ball.

When Polly and Ben have the chance to leave, Ben says they won't 'if you really need us.' Polly tells the Doctor, 'The thing is, it is our world.' The Doctor quietly replies, 'Yes, I know. You're lucky, I never got back to mine.'

'I'm sad to see them go,' Jamie says. 'Yes Jamie,' the Doctor admits. 'So am I.'

COMPANIONS

POLLY: The fake Chameleon Polly claims she is Michele Leuppi from Zurich and has never been to England before. The real Polly is less able to mask her desire to stay at home than Ben is.

JAMIE: Jamie initially thinks the aeroplanes are 'beasties' and is fascinated by Gatwick Airport.

When Samantha Briggs, whose brother has disappeared on a Chameleon Tours flight, tells Jamie it costs £28 to get to Rome, he thinks this is a fortune: 'I've never seen that much money in my life.' He kisses and hugs Samantha before she leaves for her flight – but this is, at least partly, so he can steal her ticket. Once on the plane, Jamie gets airsick.

The Chameleon duplicate of Jamie does not have a Scottish accent, and says of the Doctor, drawing on memories inherited from Jamie, 'He is not of this Earth or of this century. He has travelled through time and space. His knowledge is even greater than ours.'

TARDIS DATA BANK:

DATE: 20TH JULY 1966
LOCATION: GATWICK AIRPORT

PASSENGERS ON CHAMELEON TOURS FLIGHTS FROM GATWICK AIRPORT ARE DISAPPEARING. THE DOCTOR DISCOVERS THAT THE COMPANY IS RUN BY ALIENS WHO HAVE LOST THEIR IDENTITIES IN A PLANETARY CATASTROPHE. THEY ARE KIDNAPPING HUMANS AND STORING THEM ABOARD A SPACE STATION, ALIENS TAKING THEIR PLACES ON EARTH...

The Doctor: 'So long as you keep your side of the bargain, you may return to your own planet unharmed. Perhaps your scientists will be able to find some way out of their dilemma. I may be able to give them one or two ideas of my own.'

VICTORIA WATERFIELD

Victoria is a reluctant adventurer, travelling with the Doctor through necessity rather than choice.

At the end of *The Evil of the Daleks*, Victoria is stranded on the Dalek planet Skaro, and an orphan. Her mother, whom Victoria closely resembles, has been dead for a while. Her father, the scientist Edward Waterfield, dies saving the Doctor's life in the Dalek City. His final request to the Doctor is that he look after Victoria.

Being aware of her father's experiments, and having seen the Daleks' technology and city, Victoria is prepared to encounter civilizations more scientifically advanced than her own. But it is in her nature always to look to the more human side of circumstances.

She has led a sheltered and unsophisticated life up until her abduction, but she is able to hold her own in the verbal sparring with Captain Hopper in *The Tomb of the Cybermen*, and puts up with Jamie's teasing. Her reaction to the Doctor's explanation of his travels through time and space is not to wonder at the technology of the TARDIS, but to worry about how old he must be. And having established he is hundreds of years old, Victoria lets him sleep rather than wake him for his watch in the City of Telos.

Unsophisticated she may be, but Victoria is not gullible. She is clever and intelligent and gets the better of Kaftan twice after the woman has tricked her into drinking drugged coffee in *The Tomb of the Cybermen*. First she screams as if a dead Cybermat is about to attack again, distracting Kaftan; later she tells Kaftan and Klieg that there is another weapon in the Testing Room where they have locked the Doctor's group. Because of her apparent innocence and naivety, they are inclined to believe her.

There is no doubt that Victoria misses her home and her father. She loves the Doctor and Jamie, and enjoys her time in their company, but she remains forever an unwilling adventurer. She tells as much to the Doctor in *The Tomb of the Cybermen*, and her enthusiastic memories of the recipe for Kaiser pudding in *The Enemy of the World* remind us of how much she misses home.

Never afraid to scream at danger, it is fitting that Victoria's screams provide the solution to the seaweed creature in *Fury from the Deep*. It is also no surprise, with hindsight, that Victoria takes the first real opportunity to settle down in an established, caring family unit and decides to stay with the Harrises rather than remain with the Doctor and Jamie and seek out new worlds and dangers.

'I don't really like being scared out of my wits every second.'

(VICTORIA – *FURY FROM THE DEEP*)

TARDIS DATA BANK:

DATE: 20 JULY 1966; JUNE 1866; UNKNOWN
LOCATION: LONDON; MAXTIBLE'S HOUSE NEAR CANTERBURY; SKARO

THE DOCTOR AND JAMIE ARE TAKEN BACK TO 1866 WHERE THE DALEKS FORCE THE DOCTOR
TO RUN A TEST ON JAMIE TO DISTILL THE HUMAN FACTOR, AS UNDERSTANDING THAT WILL
ALLOW THE DALEKS TO DEFEAT HUMANITY. IN FACT, THE DALEKS INTEND THE DOCTOR TO
INFECT EARTH WITH THE DALEK FACTOR. ON THE DALEK PLANET SKARO, THE DOCTOR
MANAGES TO INFECT A NUMBER OF DALEKS WITH THE HUMAN FACTOR AND ENGINEERS A
REBELLION OF 'HUMANIZED' DALEKS AGAINST THEIR EMPEROR...

The Doctor:
'Somewhere in the Dalek race there are three Daleks with the Human Factor. Gradually, they will come to question. They will persuade other Daleks to question. You will have a rebellion on your planet.'

THE EVIL OF THE DALEKS

In which Marius Goring does a deal with the Daleks, and the Doctor triggers a Dalek civil war...
BY DAVID WHITAKER
7 EPISODES, FIRST BROADCAST 20 MAY–1 JULY 1967

JOURNEY INFORMATION

THE DALEKS

The Emperor is a massive Dalek built into the Dalek City. It is not completely destroyed in the civil war; a light is still flashing. The Emperor's guards are black-domed Dalek Leaders. The Doctor says the Dalek City is huge, mainly below ground.

When the top is blown off a Dalek, glutinous gunge erupts from inside.

TIME TRAVEL: The Daleks are able to appear from the time cabinet invented by Maxtible and Waterfield and establish a link to Waterfield's antiques shop. When the Daleks abandon the twentieth century, their equipment fades away.

THE DALEK PLAN: Maxtible tells the Doctor that, 'the Daleks tell me they have always been defeated by human beings ... possibly because of some factor, possessed by human beings... Perhaps they want to find out what it is and transplant it into their race.'

When Jamie is tricked into rescuing Victoria each and every one of his reactions is recorded by the Dalek equipment and it is up to the Doctor to select the major feelings that make up the Human Factor. Having defined the Human Factor, it is then imprinted on three positronic brains. Each of these is implanted in a dormant test Dalek.

But rather than using the Human Factor to understand how humans have consistently defeated them – their stated goal – the Daleks use it to discover the Dalek Factor. This they will then use to infect all of Earth's history in a stream that will be sprayed into the atmosphere.

THE TEST DALEKS – ALPHA, BETA, OMEGA: Once revived, the three Test Daleks are just like children. 'But they will grow up very fast.' The Doctor names them Alpha, Beta and Omega and marks their names on their casings. In their child-like state, the Test Daleks play 'trains' and spin the Doctor round as he rides on their fenders.

EDWARD WATERFIELD

Since the death of his wife, Waterfield's daughter Victoria is his closest relative and greatest love. The fact that she is the image of his late wife as a young girl only adds to his heartache when she is taken from him. Not realising he has been betrayed by Maxtible, he blames himself when she is taken hostage: 'Creatures burst out of the cabinet, invaded the house, took away my daughter... We had opened the way for them with our experiments.' Maxtible maintains their innocence: 'No English judge or jury would find it in their hearts to convict us of one solitary thing.'

Maxtible is right to think his friend is naïve. But it is Waterfield's compassion and conscience that mark him out. Without hesitation he throws himself in front of a group of Daleks firing on the Doctor. Instinctively he knows that the Doctor's is 'a good life to save', just as he knows that in the Doctor he has found the best possible person to care for and protect his daughter.

THEODORE MAXTIBLE

Maxtible's obedience to his Dalek masters is complete. 'I have done everything you have asked me to,' he tells them. 'You wanted an agency here on Earth to plan and prepare things for you. I have been that agency.'

The driving force behind Maxtible's dealings with the Daleks is the promise of the secret of alchemy: 'To possess such a secret would mean power and influence beyond all imagination.' He will go to any lengths to achieve his ambitions. He hypnotises Victoria and takes her to the Daleks so that Waterfield is compelled to help him. He even allows the Daleks to control the thoughts and actions of his future son-in-law. It is only when the Daleks destroy his house to cover their tracks that he becomes angry with them.

MAXTIBLE'S TIME EXPERIMENTS: Maxtible's time cabinet contains 144 separate mirrors. Each is subjected to electric charges. 'Like repels like in electricity, Doctor, and so next, Waterfield and I attempted to repel the image in the mirror... Negative and positive electricity had failed, so we tried static.'

ARTHUR TERRALL

Ruth Maxtible's fiancé, Arthur Terrall, hears the Dalek commands in his head and is controlled by a small black box on his neck. Mollie says that Terrall is usually a kind man, and attributes his being 'a bit odd' to his experiences in the Crimean War. But the Doctor uses a sword to test his theory – and finds it behaves as if magnetised. 'If I didn't know better, Mr. Terrall, I'd say that you were full of some sort of electricity.'

NEW INFORMATION

THE DOCTOR

The Doctor has reservations about sending Jamie to perform the test, but also relishes the experiment. Right from the start he sees a way to destroy the Daleks, and seems willing to sacrifice even Jamie.

The Doctor is not human, but the Daleks know he understands the Human Factor. A Dalek tells the Doctor 'You have travelled too much through time. You are more than human.'

The Doctor tells Victoria the Daleks cannot easily persuade him to take the Dalek Factor to Earth: 'You see, there isn't a persuasion strong enough. Not even the offer of all the lives in this room... Five lives against a whole planet? Well, it's not a choice is it?'

THE TARDIS

The Daleks threaten to destroy the TARDIS if the Doctor refuses to help them. They assume that the Doctor can control the TARDIS and use it to spread the Dalek Factor throughout the entire history of Earth. The Doctor tells Victoria, 'Even if they set us free, we still couldn't go back to Earth.'

COMPANIONS

JAMIE: When the Doctor says that the experiment is nearly over, Jamie finally loses his temper: 'Anyone would think this was a little game... People have died. The Daleks are all over the place, fit to murder the lot of us, and all you can say is you've had a good night's work... Look, I'm telling you this. You and me – we're finished. You're just too callous for me. Anything goes by the board, anything at all... You don't give that much for a living soul except yourself.'

VICTORIA: We first see Victoria as she is being reprimanded by the Daleks for feeding the 'flying pests' at the window of her room. She is both frightened and defiant.

THE TOMB OF THE CYBERMEN

In which their tombs are opened and the Cybermen emerge once again...
BY KIT PEDLER AND GERRY DAVIS
4 EPISODES, FIRST BROADCAST 2–23 SEPTEMBER 1967

Klieg: 'I shall leave you to the Cybermen. I am sure they will have some use for you. Or part of you.'

TARDIS DATA BANK:

DATE: UNKNOWN, FUTURE
LOCATION: TELOS

THE DOCTOR, JAMIE AND VICTORIA MEET AN EXPEDITION THAT AIMS TO UNEARTH THE LAST REMAINS OF THE CYBERMEN. BUT IT IS FINANCED BY KAFTAN AND KLIEG WHO INTEND TO REVIVE THE DORMANT CYBERMEN FROM THEIR FROZEN TOMBS. CAN THE DOCTOR AND HIS FRIENDS SURVIVE THE CYBERMEN, THEIR RODENT-LIKE CYBERMATS AND HUMAN VILLAINS? THE DOCTOR MUST FIND A WAY TO FREEZE THE CYBERMEN ONCE MORE...

JOURNEY INFORMATION

TELOS

While there is mention of the 'City of Telos,' no name is given specifically to the planet.

The massive double doors to the Cyber City seem to be the only entrance. Embossed Cyber 'insignia' are everywhere and the doors are operated by symbolic logic. For example, an 'OR-gate' operates the concealed doors. Klieg tries to solve the logic problem to operate the controls, but it is the Doctor who is able to decipher the Cybermen's puzzle.

THE CYBERMEN

The Cyber Controller is a taller Cyberman with no chest unit and less piping. The Controller's head has an enlarged cranium, lit from within, with visible veins. It lacks the usual 'handles' of the other Cybermen.

Professor Parry, the expedition leader, says that 'Telos was their home' and they had 'been dead for the last 500 years'. Archaeologist Viner explains: 'We know they died out many centuries ago, what we don't know is why they died out.' The two men also refer to the Cybermen's 'early dynasties' (though this may be an archaeological term).

Cybermen need to be revitalised periodically. When the Cyber Controller's energy levels are low, his speech slows and slurs, and he has to be helped into a recharging cabinet.

The Cybermen set their trap and retreated into tombs as 'Our machinery had stopped and our supply of replacements been depleted.' The Controller knows of the Doctor from the Cyber History Computer, and attributes the Cybermen's problems at least in part to the Doctor's previous intervention: 'You had destroyed our first planet and we were becoming extinct.'

CYBERMATS

The Doctor describes Cybermats as 'a form of metallic life'. They are small creatures with faceted eyes, antennae and a segmented tail. They move on rows of filaments, and they have what seem to be rows of teeth.

THE EXPEDITION

Parry explains that his expedition is 'searching the Universe for the last remains of the Cybermen'. He implies that Telos is just one of the sites they are investigating.

KAFTAN AND ERIC KLIEG

While Kaftan has the money to back the expedition, it is Klieg who seems more overtly ambitious. Their aim is to find and revive the Cybermen, then ally the power of the Cybermen with the intelligence of the Brotherhood of Logicians on Earth.

'Everything yields to logic,' Klieg tells the Doctor. 'Our basic assumption.'

Kaftan's aims are simple. 'We are going to build a better world,' she says. But it is to Kaftan herself, rather than her aims and ambitions, that her servant Toberman is loyal.

NEW INFORMATION

THE DOCTOR

When Victoria, saddened by the memory of her father, says she expects the Doctor cannot remember his own family, he tells her, 'Oh yes, I can when I *want* to. And that's the point really – I have to really want to – to bring them back in front of my eyes. The rest of the time they sleep in my mind and I forget...'

He wears a cloak on the surface of Telos and in the caverns below ground, suggesting he feels the cold to some extent. When the Doctor meets the expedition for the first time, Viner says the Doctor has 'archaeologist written all over him.' The Doctor's amused reply is, 'Really, does it show?'

The Doctor is so determined the Cybermen should never again be revived, that he electrifies the doors, hatch and control panel to deliver a fatal shock.

THE TARDIS

The Doctor tells Victoria the TARDIS has been, 'my home ... for a considerable number of years', and says that her father and Maxtible were, '... working on the same problem, but I have perfected a rather special model which enables me to travel through the universe of time.'

COMPANIONS

JAMIE: Jamie seems as surprised as Victoria to learn the Doctor's age: 'in Earth terms... about 450 years old.' He is annoyed that he cannot open the doors: 'Aye, well, I've not had much exercise lately.'

VICTORIA: Victoria is able to shoot a Cybermat from several yards away with Kaftan's pistol.

Controller: 'To die is unnecessary. You will be frozen and placed in our tombs until we are ready to use you.'

THE ABOMINABLE SNOWMEN

In which an alien Intelligence uses robot Yeti to attack a Tibetan monastery...
BY MERVYN HAISMAN AND HENRY LINCOLN
6 EPISODES, FIRST BROADCAST 30 SEPTEMBER–4 NOVEMBER 1967

Padmasambhava: 'We must make certain the Doctor learns nothing of what is happening. He is a man of great knowledge and intelligence. But he may not have sympathy for the powers that guide us. He may even seek to hinder the great plan.'

JOURNEY INFORMATION

THE GREAT INTELLIGENCE AND THE YETI

The Great Intelligence is 'formless in space'. The monk Padmasambhava 'astral travelled' and made mental contact with it. It used his mind and body and kept him alive for many years, telling him that it wished to conduct an experiment. To help it, Padmasambhava, 'laboured for nearly two hundred years. With the help of the Intelligence he built the Yeti creatures and the other wonderful machines.'

In fact the Intelligence plans to take on physical form, at the expense of the world itself. The pyramid that Songsten, the Abbot of the monastery, takes to a cave allows the Intelligence to focus on Earth so that its wanderings in space will come to an end.

Small Yeti models are used to direct the movements of the actual robotic creatures on a relief map of the monastery and surrounding area. The Yeti are themselves governed by a Controller – a machine that relays the orders – which is concealed in the small sanctum behind Padmasambhava's throne.

The robot Yeti are incredibly strong. They are controlled by silver control spheres that fit into a covered cavity in the chest and 'bleep' when active outside the Yeti.

The Doctor likens the sphere to a brain and implies that the control spheres are empty, containing a portion of the will of the Intelligence. Without its control sphere, a Yeti becomes dormant, but the sphere (or another closer one) is recalled to the Yeti to reactivate it.

Professor Travers, the leader of an expedition to find an abominable snowman, insists that the real Yeti are 'shy creatures... afraid of men'. But recently, the monks reveal, they have changed. One senior monk, Khrisong, says that they were rarely seen: 'Timid. Then, suddenly, they become savage...'

PADMASAMBHAVA AND THE MONKS

More than anything, Padmasambhava now longs to be free to die. Once he realises the Intelligence's true plans he is mortified: 'This was not your plan. But if you continue to expand... I have brought the world to its end...' Yet despite his realisation and horror, Padmasambhava must do what he is compelled to do. The Intelligence will not let him die.

More than anyone, Padmasambhava's old friend the Doctor understands his anguish and

his predicament. As he dies, Padmasambhava tells him gratefully, 'At last peace, Doctor.'

TRAVERS

Travers is a man driven by his determination to find the Yeti. He has been searching for 20 years, and staked his reputation and money on the expedition. As we later discover in *The Web of Fear*, he does not catch up with the real abominable snowman. But he does take back to England relics and mementoes of the robot Yeti built by the Great Intelligence...

NEW INFORMATION

THE DOCTOR

The Doctor visited Detsen 300 years earlier (in 1630, he says) and took away a sacred bell, the holy ghanta, for safe keeping. He also met Padmasambhava. Padmasambhava says that, 'The Doctor is wise. His eyes are not closed in ignorance... But his mind is on a complex plane. It is hard to fathom. There is a chance he will oppose what we have to do.'

The Doctor breaks Padmasambhava's hypnotic conditioning of Victoria with hypnotism of his own. Jamie admits he did not know the Doctor could do that sort of thing. 'No, neither did the person who hypnotised Victoria,' the Doctor tells him.

COMPANIONS

JAMIE: Jamie is delighted to find bagpipes in the TARDIS trunk, and says he could mend them.

When the companions first arrive in Tibet, Jamie refuses to wear warm clothing, saying, 'I tell you I'm a Highlander, the cold doesn't affect me.'

VICTORIA: Victoria is not willing to wait in the TARDIS getting bored. She is curious, and her curiosity gets the better of her when she asks a young monk, Thonmi, about the inner sanctum. Victoria is also stubborn, refusing to go to safety with the monks.

The Doctor: 'Ah, they were clever machines. Almost a pity to have had them destroyed.'

THE ICE WARRIORS

In which Bernard Bresslaw plays the first Ice Warrior, and Peter Barkworth tries to stop him taking over the world...
BY BRIAN HAYLES

6 EPISODES, FIRST BROADCAST 11 NOVEMBER–16 DECEMBER 1967

JOURNEY INFORMATION

BRITANNICUS BASE

Under the command of Leader Clent, Britannicus Base is a converted Georgian mansion preserved inside a protective plastic bubble, spared from redevelopment because it was classified as being of historic interest.

Clent's number two, Miss Garrett, refers to the base computer as 'the Great Computer' and Clent refers to 'World Computer Control', suggesting the two are linked.

LEADER CLENT AND ERIC PENLEY

Clent trusts the computer implicitly. He also admits that, 'This is the most important job I've ever had... I was chosen because I never fail. In my handling of the team, I made one vital mistake.' He means Penley, who he believes to be irresponsible because of his temperament and lack of trust in the computer. Clent describes Penley as the 'best man in Europe for ionisation studies. And he turned out hopelessly temperamental.'

For Penley, it is supremely important that Man should be in control of his own destiny. He describes his world as 'up here', meaning in his head, 'private, and no admittance'. Eventually, it is Penley who offers reconciliation with Clent. Clent is not above returning the favour: 'Penley, you are the most insufferably irritating and infuriating person I've ever been privileged to work with... Can't write a report though, can you?'

THE IONISER

Ionisation is a method of intensifying the sun's heat on to the Earth in particular areas. The Doctor likens it to a magnifying glass. Miss Garrett says that Ionisation can produce temperatures intense enough to melt rock. Varga, the leading Ice Warrior, sees the Ioniser as a weapon – which is ironic as the Ioniser is ultimately used to destroy him.

THE ICE WARRIORS

Walters, the scientist who first finds Varga, describes him as a 'proper "Ice Warrior"'. Once revived, Varga tells Victoria he is from the 'red planet'. He explains that his spaceship crashed at the foot of the ice mountain. 'As we came out to investigate, a great avalanche of snow buried us.'

First and foremost the Martians are warriors. Varga is determined to triumph: 'We only fight to win.' He laughs at the strategic naivety of his opponents, a rasping, coughing sound.

TARDIS DATA BANK:

DATE: POSSIBLY AD c3000
LOCATION: BRITANNICUS BASE, EUROPE (IN BRITAIN, POSSIBLY SCOTLAND) AND SURROUNDING AREA

VARGA, A MARTIAN SPACE CAPTAIN, HAS BEEN FROZEN IN THE ICE FOR THOUSANDS OF YEARS. WHEN HE IS REVIVED AND AWAKENS HIS CREW, HE SEES THE HUMANS BATTLING AGAINST A NEW ICE AGE AS HIS ENEMIES, AND THE IONISER HOLDING BACK THE GLACIERS AS A WEAPON. THE DOCTOR MUST CONVINCE THE ICE WARRIORS OTHERWISE, OR DEFEAT THEM...

Clent: 'Then suddenly, one year, there was no spring. Even then it wasn't understood. Not until the ice caps began to advance.'

Knowing that the atmosphere of Mars is (or was) mainly nitrogen with almost no hydrogen or oxygen, the Doctor deduces that the Martians will choke on ammonium sulphide.

WEAPONRY: Each warrior has a weapon built into their right forearm, which is fired by clenching the clamp-like fist. This is a sonic gun. 'It will burst your brain with noise.'

The main armament on the ship is a sonic cannon. The Doctor says this 'works on the basis that sound waves produce reverberations in the objects in their path'.

NEW INFORMATION

THE DOCTOR

'What do you mean – I'm only human?' the Doctor demands. 'Well as a matter of fact...' but he does not complete the thought.

The Doctor is able to tell there is something wrong with the Ioniser from the pitch of its sound. After checking, he concludes that 'in 2 minutes 38 seconds, you're going to have an almighty explosion.' Clent is of course sceptical, but the computer confirms the Doctor's analysis to within a second.

The Doctor solves the 'hypothetical' problem of the encroaching ice age in 45 seconds. Scientist Arden later remarks that this same conclusion 'took us at the Academy of Scientists years.'

The Doctor's dislike of computers comes through strongly in this story (and explains his affinity with Penley). The Base Computer itself says of the Doctor: 'High IQ but undisciplined for our needs... could be obstructive in certain situations.' The Doctor's own methods of working are in evidence – paper notes everywhere, some scrunched up, covering floor and tables.

THE TARDIS

The TARDIS materialises on its side at the start of the story, the Doctor saying it was a 'blind landing'. At the end of the story, the TARDIS is seen to be upright again.

Varga: 'They would not help me. They would keep me as a curiosity, and they would leave my warriors for dead, or destroy them... But with my men, I can talk from strength. Then we shall decide... Whether to go back to our own world, or to conquer this.'

THE ENEMY OF THE WORLD

In which Patrick Troughton plays both the hero and the villain...
BY DAVID WHITAKER
6 EPISODES, FIRST BROADCAST 23 DECEMBER 1967–27 JANUARY 1968

JOURNEY INFORMATION

SALAMANDER

Salamander mentions a 'World Authority' and Bruce is 'Head of World Security', but Leader Salamander's actual status is not clear.

Salamander is popular because he has apparently saved the world from starvation by inventing a sun-store. This collects rays from the sun and stores them in concentrated form. Salamander is then able to direct conserved energy to areas starved of sun.

Salamander himself is arrogant and assured. He is urbane – his wine is specially made in Alaska – and sophisticated. But he is also a cold-blooded, power-hungry killer. He must control the world, even if it means keeping a group of people captive in a secret bunker and lying to them that there has been a nuclear war; even if it means engineering massive 'natural' disasters in which thousands die; even if it means blackmailing the people who work for him, such as Fariah and Fedorin – and killing them when they cease to have any use.

He is also a master of initiative and improvisation. Defeated by the Doctor's deception, Salamander learns from the mistake and turns that same trick back on itself – imitating the Doctor in order to make his escape.

GILES KENT

Kent's story is that he was once a high official in the World Zone Authority: 'Deputy Security Leader for North Africa and Europe, but Salamander discredited and ruined me because he realised I was beginning to get suspicious.'

Although Kent's colleagues, including Astrid, don't know it, he was Salamander's right-hand man and instrumental in setting up the underground base from which Salamander engineers 'natural' disasters. Now Kent, having fallen out with Salamander, wants to seize control and take over the operation.

NEW INFORMATION

THE DOCTOR

The Doctor is able to imitate Salamander from seeing a televised speech. He works out from Salamander's accent that, 'He must have come from Mexico, Quintana Roo or Yucatan or somewhere.' In fact, Salamander was born in Merida, the state capital of Yucatan. The Doctor says it would take him three weeks, perhaps four, to master the accent.

The Doctor goes to the extreme of 'interrogating' Jamie and Victoria in the guise of Salamander so that Bruce will be convinced they are telling the truth about Salamander. To convince them afterwards that he really is the Doctor, he mimes playing the recorder – and makes the exact noise. He tells his companions he has to mime it as they themselves forced him to leave his actual recorder in the TARDIS.

The Doctor tells Kent that he suspected him all along: 'Any man who resorts to murder as eagerly and as rapidly as you must be suspect. You didn't just want to expose Salamander, you wanted to kill him and take his place.'

THE TARDIS

At the end of the story, Jamie says that the Doctor has told him 'never to touch the controls'.

Salamander is sucked into the black void outside when the TARDIS dematerialises with the doors open. This is the first time an intruder has operated the TARDIS.

COMPANIONS

JAMIE: As ever, Jamie is fiercely protective of Victoria, telling Salamander's henchman Benik that if he lays a finger on her, he'll kill him. 'You must have been a nasty little boy,' he tells Benik. But Benik is unimpressed by Jamie's bravado: 'Oh I was. But I had a very enjoyable childhood.'

VICTORIA: When sent to work in the kitchens, Victoria enthusiastically recalls the recipe for Kaiser pudding. 'We used to have a lovely pudding at home, with lots of almonds, eggs, lemon peel, candy peel, oranges, cream and, oh it was lovely... It's quite simple, really. You sort of whoosh it up all together.' The chef, Griff, is unimpressed: 'Oh that's great, just great. Yes, I've got a job for you, all right. Peel those spuds.'

Astrid: 'You resemble very closely a man who is determined to be dictator of the world. A man who will stop at nothing.'

TARDIS DATA BANK:

DATE: c2017
LOCATIONS: EARTH –
TEN MILES WEST OF
CAPE ARID IN
AUSTRALIA;
KANOWA
RESEARCH STATION
(200 MILES AWAY);
PRESIDENTIAL
PALACE IN
HUNGARY

WORLD LEADER
SALAMANDER HAS
DEVELOPED A SUN-STORE
THAT WILL ALLEVIATE FAMINE.
HE IS PLOTTING TO BECOME A
WORLD DICTATOR BY
ENGINEERING 'NATURAL'
DISASTERS – AND HE IS THE
DOUBLE OF THE DOCTOR.
JOINING FORCES WITH GILES
KENT TO DISCOVER THE
TRUTH, JAMIE AND VICTORIA
GO UNDERCOVER, WHILE THE
DOCTOR IMITATES
SALAMANDER AND
INFILTRATES HIS BASE...

Salamander: 'My predictions are accurate. The entire Eperjes-Tokaj ranges are in eruption. Fedorin, come and look. It's very pretty. The history of Hungary is about to be rewritten.'

THE WEB OF FEAR

In which the Yeti return – spreading deadly cobwebs through the London Undergound...
BY MERVYN HAISMAN AND HENRY LINCOLN
6 EPISODES, FIRST BROADCAST 3 FEBRUARY–9 MARCH 1968

JOURNEY INFORMATION

THE GREAT INTELLIGENCE AND THE YETI

The Yeti of *The Web of Fear* are slightly altered from *The Abominable Snowmen* – less bulky, with glowing eyes. When the control sphere returns to a Yeti exhibited in a museum, the Yeti changes as it comes to life. The Doctor calls it 'a sort of Mark 2'. The Yeti now 'bleep' all the time when active. When the Doctor dismantles a control sphere he discovers it has a mechanism inside.

The web is a mist above ground and web below. It is also referred to as a fungus, and seems to grow by a form of cell replication. Captain Knight tells the Doctor that the army has tried 'chemicals, flame-throwers, explosives, all to no avail.'

The mist was evident by the fifth of an unspecified month, and the affected area was cordoned off. By the following day, the affected area had expanded to include South Kensington tube station. The mist continued to spread, and was first reported in the London Underground on the seventh. The tube system was immediately abandoned. The Yeti themselves were first sighted on the ninth.

Travers initially has four Yeti models from Tibet. The Intelligence uses them to summon the Yeti to destroy or to kill.

Travers, possessed by the Intelligence, tells the Doctor that he has fallen into 'the trap that I have so carefully prepared for you'. What it wants is the Doctor himself – or rather, his mind: 'I have invented a machine that will drain all past knowledge and experience...' The machine is a glass pyramid with a triangular seat in the middle.

But the Doctor has crossed the wires on the headset: 'The Intelligence wouldn't have drained me, I would have drained the Intelligence. As it is, all it got was a crossed circuit.'

As Travers' daughter Anne says, all they have done is, '...cut off its contact with Earth ... it's still out there in space somewhere, flying around...'

TRAVERS

Travers is 40 years older than when the Doctor and his friends last met him. He now has a white beard and glasses, and – to his annoyance – his hands shake. He also has his daughter, Anne, who has become a scientist. Anne is devoted to her father, allowing for his eccentricity and absent-mindedness.

'When I came back from Tibet,' Travers tells the Doctor, 'I brought quite a bit of stuff with me – you know, broken Yeti, bits of control sphere, things like that... One of the control spheres was intact. So naturally, I wanted to find out how it worked... I fiddled with the thing on and off for years, and then one day...' The Doctor can guess – the sphere disappeared once Travers got it working, as the Intelligence resumed control.

COLONEL LETHBRIDGE-STEWART

In the first story in which he appears, Lethbridge-Stewart – later to play a major role in the life of the Third Doctor – is a colonel sent in to take charge of the Fortress after the death of Colonel Pemberton who has been killed during the operation against the Intelligence.

Although they are initially wary of each other, the Doctor and Lethbridge-Stewart come to trust and respect each other. Already there is evidence of the characteristics that will endear the Brigadier (as he becomes) to the Doctor.

Not afraid to lead his men by example, or to take risks, he comments, 'I think it's pointless, but at least we'll be doing something active.' This dislike of inaction is a sentiment that will be echoed in his later adventures.

NEW INFORMATION

THE DOCTOR

Although the Doctor has a plan to deal with the Intelligence once he knows its intentions, he is prepared for the worst, telling Jamie and Victoria, 'If what the Intelligence says is true, my mind will be like that of a child. You'll have to look after me until I grow up.'

THE TARDIS

The Doctor explains that at the end of the *The Enemy of the World*, 'Salamander started the TARDIS without first closing the doors. He was sucked out... He's not in a very enviable position, you know, at the moment, floating around in time and space.'

Jamie knows which is the door switch and he and Victoria help check the readings for gravity, power, control and flight.

TARDIS DATA BANK:

DATE: 1975 OR LATER
LOCATION: LONDON

THE DOCTOR, JAMIE AND VICTORIA ARRIVE IN THE LONDON UNDERGROUND TO FIND THAT LONDON IS COVERED IN A STRANGE MIST AND HAS BEEN EVACUATED. THE YETI ARE BACK, ONCE AGAIN CONTROLLED BY THE GREAT INTELLIGENCE, AND THE DOCTOR JOINS FORCES WITH AN ELDERLY PROFESSOR TRAVERS AND HIS DAUGHTER, ANNE, IN A MILITARY OPERATION LED BY COLONEL LETHBRIDGE-STEWART. BUT WHO IS THE AGENT OF THE INTELLIGENCE WORKING AGAINST THEM? AND WHAT DOES THE INTELLIGENCE PLAN FOR THE DOCTOR...

Travers / Intelligence: 'Through time and space, I have observed you, Doctor. Your mind surpasses that of all other creatures... Your mind will be invaluable to me. Therefore I have invented a machine that will drain all past knowledge and experience from your mind.'

Lethbridge-Stewart: 'That's why we're dependent on you three coming up with the answers. If you fail, London's finished — England itself, perhaps. Now the army will, of course, give you all the support you need.'

Baxter: 'This sound — at first I thought it was something to do with the pumps but it isn't. Most peculiar sound. A sort of regular thumping, pulsating. Like a heartbeat.'

FURY FROM THE DEEP

In which deadly seaweed takes people over – including Victor Maddern...
BY VICTOR PEMBERTON
6 EPISODES, FIRST BROADCAST 16 MARCH–20 APRIL 1968

JOURNEY INFORMATION

THE WEED CREATURE

From Victoria's description and his own observations, the Doctor finds a picture of the Weed Creature in an old book of legends and superstitions. 'This particular drawing is supplied by ancient mariners in the North Sea in the middle of the eighteenth century,' he explains. 'There's obviously some connection between the Weed and the Creatures themselves.'

The Doctor believes the Weed to be a living organism capable of exercising telepathic control. The Creature is part of a colony that derives its intelligence parasitically from the human brains of its hosts.

Robson, chief of sea-gas operations in the North Sea and infected by the Creature, tells the Doctor that its aim is, 'the conquest of the human planet... The mind does not exist. It is tired. It is dead. It is obsolete. Only our new masters can offer us life... The body does not exist. Soon we shall all be one.'

OAK AND QUILL

The Weed was first drawn up by one of the drilling rigs. Oak and Quill were probably the engineers assigned to clear the blockage. Coming into direct contact with the Weed they were among the first – if not actually the first – to be controlled.

The two engineers are instrumental to the Weed's plan to control the gas complex. They infect Maggie Harris, one of the refinery workers, by breathing out toxic gas from their mouths. Weed grows down their arms and is visible on their hands and at their cuffs.

JOHN ROBSON

Robson is chief of the Euro Sea Gas HQ and UK operations. The complex supplies the gas for the whole of southern England and Wales. Six rigs pump gas to a central control rig which then pumps it ashore to be refined. Underneath the impeller shaft is a vast gasometer buried in the earth.

Robson prides himself that the flow has never been shut off since he took charge. He resents his deputy

TARDIS DATA BANK:

DATE: NEAR FUTURE
LOCATION: NORTH SEA COAST AND GAS RIG, ENGLAND

AN INTELLIGENT SEAWEED CREATURE IS 'TAKING OVER' PERSONNEL ON NORTH SEA GAS RIGS. THE DOCTOR, JAMIE AND VICTORIA MUST CONVINCE PEOPLE OF THE DANGER, AND DISCOVER WHO HAS BEEN INFECTED. VICTORIA MAY BE THE KEY TO DEFEATING THE CREATURE, BUT SHE IS TIRING OF LIVING A LIFE OF ENDLESS DANGER...

Harris's university rather than practical background. Robson himself spent four years on a rig without a break and has a reputation built on 30 years of experience.

Once he has recovered from the infection, we see the Robson who is respected and revered by Chief Baxter and his other staff.

NEW INFORMATION

THE DOCTOR

The Doctor has a stethoscope in his pocket which he uses to listen to the heartbeat in the pipeline on the beach. He also uses his sonic screwdriver for the first time, explaining, 'It's a sonic screwdriver. Never fails... All done by sound waves.' On the last morning he apparently goes for a swim in the sea.

The Doctor flies a helicopter (somewhat erratically) back from the control rig. 'I've been dying to get my hands on one of those things,' he says. 'It's a very primitive machine, you know. It should be easy to control.' But he doesn't know how to land.

The Doctor sets up a system to use the amplified sound of Victoria's screams to destroy the Weed Creature. This includes a 'little toy of my own' which 'together with the amplifiers ... should produce a sonic layer sound wave' which travels along the pipeline to destroy the Weed's nerve centre.

The Doctor realises before she tells him that Victoria does not want to leave with them: 'You don't want to come with us, do you, Victoria? ... Well, I suspected as much.'

THE TARDIS

When it materialises, the TARDIS lands on the sea, and floats. The Doctor examines the seaweed sample in a small laboratory on board the TARDIS.

COMPANIONS

JAMIE: Down in the impeller shaft, Jamie's instinct tells him that something is wrong: 'Let's get out of here. I feel as if something evil is lurking down here.'

His fondness for Victoria is as evident as ever. 'If anything happened to you, I'd never forgive myself,' he says, thinking she is unconscious. 'Oh Jamie. I didn't know you cared,' she teases him.

VICTORIA: Victoria manages to pick locks with a hairpin.

Throughout the story, Victoria is feeling she has had enough of adventuring with the Doctor and Jamie. 'Why is it that we always land up in trouble?' she asks the Doctor. He tells her it is the spice of life, but she is not so sure: 'I don't really like been scared out of my wits every second.'

Victoria knows she can never go home: 'I wouldn't be at ease back in Victorian times,' she says. 'I have no parents or family left there anyway.' So the Doctor asks Maggie Harris on her behalf: 'I wonder if you'd mind if Victoria stayed with you for a little while. You see, she's got no parents or home and it is a bit difficult...'

ZOE HERIOT

TARDIS DATA BANK:

DESCRIPTION: FEMALE, HUMAN, FROM THE 21ST CENTURY
TRAVELLED: *THE WHEEL IN SPACE – THE WAR GAMES*

'Suppose that we do get ourselves out of this mess — what have I got left? A blind reliance on facts and logic.'

(ZOE – *THE WHEEL IN SPACE*)

Zoe Heriot is a young astrophysicist and astrometricist, first class, aboard Station Three, known as the Wheel. She meets the Doctor and Jamie in *The Wheel in Space* and tells them she is 'an astrophysicist, pure-mathematics major'. Dr Gemma Corwyn adds that this is 'with honours'.

On the Wheel, Gemma Corwyn describes Zoe as the 'librarian', and it is later revealed that she has a photographic memory.

Zoe's training has left her emotionally undeveloped. From an early age she has been taught the value of logic, which leads her into conflict with other members of the Wheel's crew. Leo Ryan, another crew member of the Wheel, upbraids her for her apparent lack of personal interest in the fate of the Wheel when the meteorites are due to strike: 'It's all a problem in solid geometry to you isn't it?' he chides. 'Just like a robot. Facts, calculations... Proper little brain-child – all brain and no heart.'

'I don't want to be thought of as a freak,' Zoe complains. 'Leo said that I was like a robot, a machine. I think he's right. My head has been pumped full of facts and figures which I reel out automatically when needed, but I want to feel things as well.'

When the Doctor tells her that 'logic ... merely enables one to be wrong with authority,' it actually makes an impression on her. In the Doctor, Zoe has a perfect case study for the success of the illogical and the power of intuitive action and lateral thinking. 'There's too much I don't know,' she tells Jamie. 'I was trained to believe that logic and calculation would provide me with all the answers. Well I'm just beginning to realise there are questions which I can't answer... What good am I? I've been created for some false kind of existence where only known kinds of emergencies are catered for.'

It is because of this growing realisation that there is more to knowledge than facts, more to life than logic, that Zoe hides on board the TARDIS. She has learned as much as she can in the closeted environment of the Wheel where her abilities and role are compartmentalised and defined. Now she is ready to discover the Universe, and her own place in it.

THE WHEEL IN SPACE

In which the Cybermen return – again – hatching from eggs to attack a space station...
BY DAVID WHITAKER, FROM A STORY BY KIT PEDLER
6 EPISODES, FIRST BROADCAST 27 APRIL–1 JUNE 1968

TARDIS DATA BANK:

DATE: 21ST CENTURY
LOCATION: STATION THREE (ALSO KNOWN AS 'THE WHEEL');
THE SILVER CARRIER

THE DOCTOR AND JAMIE ARRIVE ON A SPACE STATION AND FIND THAT ITS STOCKS OF BERNALIUM HAVE BEEN DESTROYED BY CYBERMATS. TWO CYBERMEN SECRETLY ARRIVE, CONCEALED IN NEW STOCKS PLANTED ON A NEARBY DRIFTING SPACESHIP, THE SILVER CARRIER. THE CYBERMEN ARE PLANNING TO ATTACK THE EARTH FROM THE WHEEL IN SPACE, UNLESS THE DOCTOR, JAMIE AND THEIR NEW FRIEND, ZOE, CAN STOP THEM...

The Doctor: 'Now listen everyone, the Cybermen are here, in this Wheel. They took over this poor fellow to stop you sending to Earth or signalling for help.'

JOURNEY INFORMATION

THE WHEEL
The Wheel is officially Station Three, call sign LX 88J. It is mainly 'a radio-visual relay for Earth, a halfway house for deep-space ships, a space research station, stellar early warning station for all types of space phenomena...'

The Wheel is staffed by a multinational and multi-ethnic crew. Dr Gemma Corwyn says that 'all spacemen are protected against brain control by drugs'.

JARVIS BENNETT
Bennett is Controller of the Wheel and takes his orders from Earth Central. He has an almost pathological desire that everything run to order, and unexplained and illogical events fuel his increasing paranoia. Gemma Corwyn says that he 'is simply a man that can't accept phenomena outside the laws of physics... He can't face the truth.'

THE SILVER CARRIER
Hijacked by the Cybermen, the Silver Carrier is a Phoenix Mark IV. It is a service and supply ship for Station Five, reported overdue nine weeks previously and now 87 million miles off course. At last contact, the Silver Carrier had 7 million miles to touchdown and enough fuel for 20 million.

THE CYBERMEN
The Cybermen's bodies and their external tubing and hydraulics are more streamlined than in earlier encounters, and their eyes have 'teardrop' holes at the outside lower corners with a similar hole below their mouths. Their chest units are now mounted upside down, although a Cyberman caught in the Wheel's doors has his the other way up.

The Cybermen are given orders by a Cyber Planner. This is a large bulbous metal object with thin filament attachments within a cradle.

To absorb and neutralise the Cyber control, the Doctor tells Gemma Corwyn, 'A metal plate and a transistor will do. Tape them to the back of the neck.'

The Cybermen are able to project mental images from crewman Vallance's brain to the Cyber Planner, which advises that, 'The Doctor is known and recorded.'

CYBERMATS
The Cybermats are similar to those seen in The Tomb of the Cybermen, except their eyes are 'solid' rather than facetted, they have spines down their backs and they lack antennae. They are controlled initially by telemeter guidance. The eyes flash when they attack and the Doctor says they have a range of 'at least ten feet'.

They are carried to the Wheel in egg-like protective projectiles of small mass and high density which sink through the hull causing slight drops in air pressure.

The Cybermats tune in to human brainwaves. The Doctor destroys them by having an audio frequency transmitted that causes them to whirl, crash, smoke and then disintegrate.

Cyber Planner: 'Positive. The Doctor is known and recorded. An enemy. He must be lured outside the force field and destroyed.'

NEW INFORMATION

THE DOCTOR
When treating the Doctor for concussion, Dr Corwyn describes his skull X-ray as 'extraordinary'.

Jamie gives the Doctor the alias that is most often associated with him – 'John Smith' – which he takes from the manufacturer or supplier's name printed on the front panel of the electronic stethoscope Doctor Corwyn is using: 'John Smith & Associates'.

THE TARDIS
The fault locator has a read-out under a flap on the console. The Doctor needs mercury to refill the fluid link, and pours it into the console through a funnel.

Trying to warn the Doctor to go somewhere more pleasant, the TARDIS scanner shows: a lake with cranes taking flight; a large moonlit waterfall; a tropical beach with palm trees…

THE TIME VECTOR GENERATOR: The time vector generator is about 18 inches long, 'gold, with a gold tip at one end and a white one at the other'. It is housed in a compartment close to the main door. Once removed, it alters the size of the TARDIS. The inside becomes an ordinary police box again. The tips can be removed and the energy inside projected. This destroys a Servo Robot, and Jamie uses it to signal to the Wheel. The Doctor fixes the time vector generator to the Wheel's laser-gun circuit to boost the power to destroy the Cyberman spaceship.

COMPANIONS

JAMIE: Jamie gives his full name as James Robert Macrimmon. He does not know what meteorites are, and does not understand Zoe's tape recorder.

BEHIND THE SCENES

REPEAT SUCCESS

The Wheel in Space was the final story of the fifth season of **Doctor Who**, after which there was a break before the next season started with *The Dominators*. For the first time this break was filled with a repeat of a previous story – *The Evil of the Daleks*.

The very first episode of **Doctor Who** was repeated the week after its original broadcast, immediately ahead of the second episode. But this was the first time that a complete story had been repeated, and is the only time that such a repeat has been incorporated into the narrative of the series.

Reproduced here are the script pages for the final scene of *The Wheel in Space* where the Doctor shows Zoe the events of *The Evil of the Daleks*. (Note that there are slight differences as recorded – for example the Doctor sees Zoe hiding inside a trunk rather than crawling into the TARDIS.)

THE DOCTOR IS TOPPING UP THE MERCURY LEVEL FROM THE BOTTLE HE FOUND EARLIER.
HE MOVES TO THE CONTROL COLUMN AND PRESSES A BUTTON AND STARES INTO A SQUARE OSCILLATOR WHICH RECORDS ANY FAULT WHICH MIGHT BE IN EVIDENCE.
JAMIE WALKS IN THROUGH THE DOORS.
JAMIE: All set?
DOCTOR WHO: Oh, yes. I've even got a little mercury left over.
JAMIE: Then we can go?
DOCTOR WHO: Yes, Jamie we …
HE STOPS AS HE TURNS TO JAMIE. WE SEE FROM HIS P.O.V. AS ZOE CRAWLS IN ON HER HANDS AND KNEES. SHE IS UNAWARE SHE IS OBSERVED. THE DOCTOR SMILES.
DOCTOR WHO: Just one little matter to settle first, Jamie.
HE WALKS ACROSS TO THE CHAIR BEHIND WHICH ZOE HAS HIDDEN HERSELF.
SLOWLY HER HEAD APPEARS OVER THE CHAIR.
JAMIE: Hey, I told you…
ZOE: I want to go with you!
JAMIE: It's impossible.
DOCTOR WHO: No, Jamie, it isn't impossible. What we have to decide is… is it wise. You may change your mind.
ZOE: I won't.
DOCTOR OPENS A PANEL, BRINGS OUT A HEADPIECE ATTACHED TO A HEADBAND. HE GOES TO THE ARMCHAIR AND SITS DOWN, ADJUSTING THE HEADPIECE TO HIS HEAD.

DOCTOR WHO: I wonder, look at the screen up there… above the control panel.
JAMIE: What are you going to do?
DOCTOR WHO: I'm going to show Zoe exactly the kind of thing she could be in for.
ZOE: Thought patterns?
DOCTOR WHO: Yes, but I'll make them up into a complete story. Have you ever heard of the Daleks?
ZOE: No.
DOCTOR WHO: Then watch.
HE PRESSES THE HEAD PIECE AND CLOSES HIS EYES. A CLIP FROM THE EVIL OF THE DALEKS APPEARS ON THE SCREEN.

For the repeat showing, the beginning of the first episode of *The Evil of the Daleks* was slightly amended to include a voice-over from Patrick Troughton as the Doctor and Wendy Padbury as Zoe, to remind viewers of the reason for the repeat:

DOCTOR WHO: Now, as I remember, Zoe, it all started when Jamie and I discovered somebody making off with the TARDIS.
ZOE: But what about those Daleks you showed me?
DOCTOR WHO: We're coming to that, Zoe. Just let me show you the story from the beginning.

THE DOMINATORS

In which the robot Quarks help their Dominator masters to attack a barren island...
BY NORMAN ASHBY
5 EPISODES, FIRST BROADCAST 10 AUGUST–7 SEPTEMBER 1968

TARDIS DATA BANK:

DATE: UNKNOWN
LOCATION: PLANET
DULKIS:'THE ISLAND
OF DEATH' AND
CAPITAL CITY

TWO DOMINATORS – RAGO
AND TOBA – AND THEIR
ROBOT QUARKS ARRIVE ON A
FORMER NUCLEAR-TEST
ISLAND ON THE PEACEFUL
PLANET OF DULKIS. THE
DULCIANS ARE COMMITTED
TO PEACE, BUT THE
DOMINATORS ARE PLANNING
TO ENSLAVE THEM AND
DESTROY THE PLANET TO
PROVIDE FUEL FOR THEIR
FLEET. CAN THE DOCTOR AND
HIS FRIENDS CONVINCE THE
DULCIANS OF THE DANGER
AND DEFEAT THE
DOMINATORS BEFORE THE
PLANET IS DESTROYED...

JOURNEY INFORMATION

DULKIS

Dulkis is ruled by a council, of which Senex is Director. For centuries the Dulcians have lived in peace. War is outlawed on Dulkis and there are no prisoners. Rago discovers the Dulcians have two hearts.

The Seventh Council under Director Manus had initiated research 172 years earlier that led to the development of atomic energy. The 'Island of Death' was used to test an atomic explosive device, after which all further research was prohibited and the island preserved as both a museum and a warning. A war museum was set up on the island to exhibit weapons and teach the horrific results of warfare. There is an atomic shelter under the war museum.

THE DOMINATORS

The Dominators are 'the Masters of the Ten Galaxies'. Rago tells Senex: 'Dominators do not seek assistance. What we need, we take... We control an entire galaxy, our war mission is spreading to colonise others. Our Quarks must be released for this task. Therefore we must replace their workforce on our home planet.'

The leader of the invasion fleet is the 'Fleet Leader', and there are over 30 ships in the fleet en route for Epsilon IV.

The Dominators' ship is a circular saucer-shaped craft. There are star charts on the wall, and also two maps of the island. Illuminated Quark symbols are arranged in two columns of eight (suggesting there are 16 Quarks). When a Quark is destroyed, the corresponding symbol flashes.

The Dominators' ship stores radioactive particles and converts the energy to power. Rockets are to be fired through holes drilled in the crust of Dulkis into magma, creating a volcano. When a seed device explodes in this eruption, the whole planet will become a molten mass of radioactive material that will act as a fuel store for the fleet. The Doctor intercepts the seed device, confining the resulting eruption to the island.

THE QUARKS

The Dominators' robots, the Quarks, are powered by ultrasound. They can use their arm-like force units to shoot to kill or paralyse or give an electric shock, as well as for communications and power (for example for the drills). They use molecular force to bind the Doctor and Jamie to a wall/table. A Quark is able to record all technical data pertaining to the survey unit base just by turning round through 360 degrees.

The Quarks communicate in high-pitched speech, and various high-pitched sounds. For example, a 'double-bleep' indicates confirmation of an order. When a Quark is tripped and covered with a blanket by Jamie, it emits a warning alarm signal.

NEW INFORMATION

THE DOCTOR

Exhausted from projecting his thought patterns, the Doctor says he wants a holiday. He has been to Dulkis before: 'Some time ago mind you... It was so peaceful I didn't want to leave.'

To persuade the Dominators that he and Jamie are not dangerous, the Doctor deliberately fails the intelligence tests set by Rago and Toba. But Rago is not convinced. 'Are you such a fool?' he wonders. 'You have intelligent eyes.'

The Doctor: 'An unintelligent enemy is far less dangerous than an intelligent one, Jamie... Just act stupid – do you think you can manage that?'

The Doctor has a telescope as well as a Geiger counter in his pocket. The Doctor mixes medical chemicals to make explosives. 'It's surprising what you can do with a few simple chemicals and a little ingenuity.' The sonic screwdriver converts to a simple blow-torch which the Doctor uses to cut through a wall.

COMPANIONS

JAMIE: Rago's initial assessment of Jamie is that he is vulnerable as he has only one heart. He has a simple brain which shows signs of recent rapid learning. It is Jamie's idea to dig through to the borehole and intercept the seed device – an idea which the Doctor says is so simple that only Jamie could have thought of it.

ZOE: Zoe says that the war museum reminds her of 'the old atom test islands on Earth'. She is initially dismissive of the Quarks, saying, 'They're only robots.'

BEHIND THE SCENES

COMIC ROBOTS

Although the Quarks appeared only once in televised **Doctor Who** (apart from a cameo at the end of *The War Games*), they were popular enough to feature more often than any other enemy except the Cybermen in the *TV Comic* strip stories featuring the Second Doctor.

Despite disagreements between BBC Enterprises and the authors who created the Quarks (Mervyn Haisman and Henry Lincoln, credited as Norman Ashby for this story) as to who owned what proportion of the copyright and the design of the robots, they returned to battle the Doctor several times in the comics, where they became their own masters, the Dominators not being mentioned.

The robots' design remained true to their television counterparts, apart from the omission of the front and back 'spikes' from the Quarks' heads. In this slightly revised form,

the Quarks came to see the Doctor and Jamie as their greatest enemy and set out to destroy them.

Apart from being forced to fight a duel against a Quark, the Doctor and Jamie also came up against the aggressive robots in a Scottish castle. Perhaps most bizarre is the story in which Quarks send giant wasps to destroy their greatest foes (and end up fighting against the wasps themselves)...

Cully: 'For centuries we have lived in peace. We have proved that universal gentleness will cause aggression to die.'

THE MIND ROBBER

In which the Doctor and his companions arrive in the Land of Fiction and are chased by toy soldiers...
BY PETER LING
5 EPISODES, FIRST BROADCAST 14 SEPTEMBER–12 OCTOBER 1968

JOURNEY INFORMATION

THE LAND OF FICTION

The Doctor tells Jamie and Zoe that he thinks the Land of Fiction may be a place where 'nothing is impossible'.

In the the Master's Citadel, Jamie finds machines retelling fiction (*Treasure Island* on a screen, *Little Women* being read aloud...). The 'current' story of himself, Zoe and the Doctor emerges from a ticker-tape machine – which the Doctor is later able to use to rewrite the fiction and change events...

To accept the 'rules' of the Land is to become fictional and submit to the Master.

THE 'MASTER'

The Master is an elderly writer who was taken from his desk when he dozed off on a hot summer's day in 1926. He

created 'The Adventures of Captain Jack Harkaway' for *The Ensign*, a boys' magazine, and wrote 5,000 words every week for 25 years – which is why he was selected for the post in the Land of Fiction. He claims he has everything he wants including a vast and comprehensive library that contains all the known works of fiction written by Earthmen since the dawn of time.

His imagination and creativity give life to the inhabitants of the Land. This presumably includes the life-size toy soldiers with huge keys in their backs that walk with a lurching gait, and 'see' through a light in their hats. There are also White Robots that exist in both the void and the Land of Fiction.

The Master is controlled by a computer. He describes his controller(s) as 'Another power, higher than any of you can begin to imagine.' He also calls it 'the Intelligence I serve', and says that 'they' need Man as a creative powerhouse. Later the Master refers to the Master Brain, which the Doctor realises is a computer that feeds off his thoughts.

NEW INFORMATION

THE DOCTOR

The Doctor has a mirror in his pocket, which he uses to look safely at Medusa. He has never heard of the fictional hero the Karkus, though he has been in the year 2000, 'but I hardly had time to follow the strip cartoons.'

He is seen to type rapidly (a useful skill he still retains in *Robot*).

THE TARDIS

The Doctor is forced to use the emergency unit, which he says shifts the TARDIS out of the space–time dimension – out of reality. It is a black box with a button on it, which plugs into the console. The TARDIS arrives 'nowhere' and none of the controls register. The unit has a built-in timing mechanism to restore the companions to normal space–time.

The Doctor:
'If we move outside the TARDIS, we step into a dimension about which we know nothing. We should be at the mercy of the forces outside time and space as we know it.'

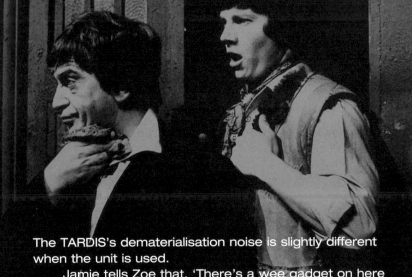

The TARDIS's dematerialisation noise is slightly different when the unit is used.

Jamie tells Zoe that, 'There's a wee gadget on here somewhere that warns you to go elsewhere if there's any danger.'

We see the Doctor working on repairs in the small TARDIS power room.

A meter indicates the power usage against storage. If it falls below 1,000 that means the TARDIS is using more power than it is storing.

The TARDIS appears to break up, depositing its occupants in the Land of Fiction, but comes together again at the end of the story.

COMPANIONS

JAMIE: After being lured out of the TARDIS, he hears bagpipes and sees Scotland on the scanner. Jamie can read the proverbs and sayings of the Forest of Words, and also (with some difficulty) the ticker-tape account of the Doctor and Zoe's encounter with Medusa.

ZOE: After being lured out of the TARDIS, she sees her 'home city' on the scanner. Zoe recognises the Karkus from the hourly telepress of the year 2000. She is able to defeat him in a fight and he therefore becomes submissive to her... It is Zoe who finally overloads the Computer.

BEHIND THE SCENES

THE DOCTOR'S DREAM?

It is possible that the bulk of this story takes place only in the Doctor's mind.

At the start of the next story (*The Invasion*) the Doctor is sitting in exactly the same position in the same chair as at the end of Episode 1 of *The Mind Robber* when Jamie and Zoe are safely back in the TARDIS but before it explodes. So the last four episodes may all be his dream, or an internal mental battle with the forces of 'nowhere'.

Or possibly the dream begins even sooner than this, as Jamie's line at the start of the next story – 'Doctor, it's all right, it worked.' – fits better with the use of the emergency unit than with escaping the Land of Fiction...

If the bulk of the story is indeed a dream or internal mental battle of the Doctor's, that would also explain how Zoe can observe, 'There must be somebody here, these candles are alight,' in *The Mind Robber*, when in *The Space Pirates*, she does not know what candles are and has to ask 'how do they work?'

The Doctor's inherent dislike of computers would also motivate the 'villain' behind the Land of Fiction. The computer in charge may be a manifestation rather than actuality – either a rationalisation of another force or being, or given form by the Doctor's distrust and dislike of computers...

There is some evidence that this was the intention from the script for *The Invasion*, (which was written by Derrick Sherwin, who also wrote – uncredited – the first episode of *The Mind Robber*) which opens with the observation:

```
THE CAMERA IS DEFOCUSED AND AS ITS PICTURE
SHARPENS WE SEE THE DOCTOR SEATED IN HIS CHAIR
WHERE WE LEFT HIM BEFORE THE TARDIS BROKE UP
IN THE PREVIOUS STORY.
```

THE INVASION

In which UNIT first appears, and the Cybermen return – yet again – to emerge from the sewers and invade London...
BY DERRICK SHERWIN, FROM A STORY BY KIT PEDLER
8 EPISODES, FIRST BROADCAST 2 NOVEMBER–21 DECEMBER 1968

TARDIS DATA BANK:

DATE: NEAR FUTURE c1979
LOCATION: ENGLAND, LONDON

THE DOCTOR, JAMIE AND ZOE HELP THE NEWLY FORMED UNIT ORGANISATION, LED BY THEIR FRIEND LETHBRIDGE-STEWART, IN AN INVESTIGATION INTO INTERNATIONAL ELECTROMATICS. THEY DISCOVER THE COMPANY'S DIRECTOR, TOBIAS VAUGHN, IS IN LEAGUE WITH THE CYBERMEN – WHO ARE PREPARING TO LAUNCH AN INVASION. MANKIND IS PARALYSED BY SIGNALS FROM IE COMPONENTS, AS THE CYBERMEN EMERGE FROM THE SEWERS AND TAKE OVER LONDON...

JOURNEY INFORMATION

UNIT AND BRIGADIER LETHBRIDGE-STEWART

Colonel Lethbridge-Stewart has been promoted to Brigadier and put in charge of the recently formed United Nations Intelligence Taskforce, which he describes as 'an independent intelligence group'. He says UNIT's remit is to investigate people rather than arrest them.

UNIT's headquarters is a military operations room in the back of a transport plane. For most of the story, the plane (piloted by Wing Commander Robins) is located somewhere outside London. A map shows where UNIT forces are.

Major General Rutlidge at the Ministry of Defence is the Brigadier's immediate superior, although he can bypass Rutlidge and go to UNIT Central Command in Geneva.

INTERNATIONAL ELECTROMATICS

International Electromatics is the world's biggest electronics manufacturer, having made a breakthrough in micro-monolithic circuit designs. The TARDIS lands in the IE compound. All the local people have been bought out, most of them joining the company. UNIT has been unable to trace those who did not. IE also has high-rise London offices near Chapron Street.

TOBIAS VAUGHN

At his first meeting with IE's Managing Director Tobias Vaughn, the Doctor realises his blink-rate is very slow.

Security Chief Packer's incompetence drives Vaughn to violent anger on several occasions, but generally he is calm and controlled. When Professor Watkins – a scientist imprisoned by Vaughn and forced to work for him – says he would kill Vaughn given the chance, Vaughn hands him a gun. He cajoles Watkins into firing it – to no effect, as Vaughn's body is cybernetic.

Vaughn tells the Doctor that he has worked with the Cybermen for five years. He eventually agrees to help the Doctor: 'because I hate them... The world is weak, vulnerable, a mess of uncoordinated and impossible ideals. It needs a strong man, a single mind. A leader.'

He has Watkins working on a Cerebratron Mentor – a machine that produces excessively powerful emotional pulses as an aid to learning – a weapon he can mass produce to use against the Cybermen after the invasion so as to avoid being converted into a full Cyberman. Even if this fails, he believes he will have an escape route – the Doctor's TARDIS.

THE CYBERMEN

Vaughn's contact with the Cybermen is via the Cyber Director behind a wall in his office at the IE building in London. When Vaughn turns against the Cyber Director, it repels him with a blaze of light. Vaughn destroys the Cyber

Director with the Cerebratron Mentor, suggesting that the Director is itself a form of Cyberman.

The Cybermen claim they have not been on Earth before, but the Doctor and Jamie have been recognised 'on Planet Fourteen' and must be destroyed.

The Cybermen arrive at the IE Compound in spaceships and are then shipped to London in crates by rail. They are kept deactivated in protective cocoons.

The Cybermen use circuits built into IE equipment to paralyse most humans on Earth. Vaughn and his team are protected by implanted audio-rejection capsules. The Cybermen plan to land and select humans for conversion to Cybermen – unsuitable humans will be destroyed.

Vaughn demands that he be put in control of Earth and supplies the minerals the Cybermen require. The Cyber Director insists that to control Earth, Vaughn must: 'undergo complete conversion and become one of us'. But Vaughn is adamant: 'My body may be cybernetic but my mind stays human. That is final.'

NEW INFORMATION

THE DOCTOR
The Brigadier tells UNIT Captain Turner not to underestimate the Doctor: 'They may look like amateurs but that man has an incredible knack of being one jump ahead of everyone.' For the first time we see the Doctor driving, when he takes a Land Rover to get to IE. He uses the Cerebratron Mentor to destroy a Cyberman that kills Packer.

THE TARDIS
The TARDIS landing mechanism jams and it is stuck in space. The visual stabiliser is also on the blink – removing it (for repair) makes the TARDIS invisible. The Doctor says the TARDIS 'merely needs an overhaul ... just like any piece of machinery.'

IE's Head of Research, Gregory, says the TARDIS circuits '... don't make sense. The material isn't any known metal alloy, in fact the structure's more like that of a plastic. What's more, the connections seem to be to be completely illogical.'

COMPANIONS
JAMIE: Jamie seems not to know what a missile is. When he is wounded in the leg during Packer's attack, Zoe says, 'It's just a slight flesh wound. But he's furious, because the army doctor won't let him walk on it.'

ZOE: Determined not to be 'beaten by this stupid tin box', Zoe enjoys destroying the IE reception computer by giving it an insoluble problem in Algol. She computes the attack pattern for missiles to set up a chain reaction and destroy the formation of incoming Cyberships. She tells the officer in charge, Major Branwell, 'It's all quite logical really, hardly any calculation needed at all. Except the simple stuff like speed, angle of descent and relative positions of the spaceships.'

Vaughn: 'Do you wish to be totally converted? Do you prefer to be one of them? Completely inhuman? That's what would happen if they take over. We will cease to be human.'

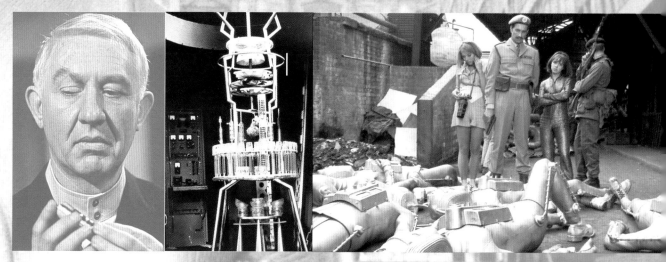

122

THE KROTONS

In which the Doctor combats the Krotons – creatures that look like they are partly made of egg boxes...
BY ROBERT HOLMES
4 EPISODES, FIRST BROADCAST 28 DECEMBER 1968–
18 JANUARY 1969

TARDIS DATA BANK:

DATE: UNKNOWN
LOCATION: UNNAMED PLANET INHABITED BY THE GONDS

THE DORMANT, CRYSTALLINE KROTONS USE THE MENTAL ENERGY OF THE PEACEFUL GONDS TO SUSTAIN THEMSELVES. BUT THE COMBINED MENTAL ENERGIES OF THE DOCTOR AND ZOE REVIVE THE KROTONS. THE DOCTOR AND HIS FRIENDS MUST CONVINCE THE GONDS THAT THE KROTONS ARE NOT BENEFACTORS, AND ESCAPE BEING DISPERSED...

JOURNEY INFORMATION

THE GONDS

The planet where the Gonds live has twin suns and normal gravity. The air is a mixture of ozone and sulphur, according to the Doctor, and has an unpleasant, sulphurous smell.

The architecture of the Gonds settlement is, the Doctor says, more typical of a low-gravity planet. The Dynotrope is a huge geodesic sphere overshadowing their dwellings. No-one goes into the wasteland because it is poisoned and they will die.

It is the law of the Krotons that everyone uses the 'teaching machines' when young. The Gonds are therefore dependent on the Krotons for their patchy knowledge. They know little about electricity (what electrical devices they have work off stored solar power). They have relatively advanced medicines, but know little general chemistry – they are taught nothing that could threaten the Krotons.

The teaching machines provoke an emotional response in the user. The Doctor says the Krotons 'use these machines to plant impressions in the mind. That's how they've enslaved these people.'

The Gonds are led by a council – Eelek takes over from Selris as leader when he gains enough popular support, although Selris says the position is hereditary and his son Thara will succeed him.

THE KROTONS

The Dynotrope is the Krotons' spaceship, part of a battlefleet, it operates through mental power – a focusing device will transfer the Dynotrope back into the Krotons' own cosmos. Four 'high brains' are needed in relay to operate it, but two Krotons were exhausted by enemy fire.

The Dynotrope was set in perpetual stability to preserve power and the systems were instructed to educate the primitive Gonds to the level needed to reanimate the surviving Krotons. The Gonds were tested at intervals, and their mental energy absorbed into the active Dynotrope circuits before the 'waste matter' (the Gonds themselves) was rejected and dispersed.

The Krotons, like the Dynotrope, are crystalline. The Krotons are based on tellurium – even the Dynotrope is made of this material. A Kroton tells Jamie that they cannot die, but function permanently until they 'exhaust'. The 'exhaust procedure is merely a reversion to basic molecules, but the matter can be reanimated'.

The Krotons are blind outside the Dynotrope, unable to see in the light. When one of the Krotons goes after the Doctor and Zoe, the other guides it using scanners in the Dynotrope.

The Krotons' heads spin when the Dynotrope becomes unbalanced. As it gets closer to exhaustion, it starts to leak a dark liquid. The Doctor says if the Dynotrope exhausts there will be a colossal explosion that will destroy most of the planet.

NEW INFORMATION

THE DOCTOR

After saving the Gond girl Vana from the Krotons, the Doctor tells Zoe he is 'not a doctor of medicine'. He hypnotises Vana as part of her 'treatment', using a pocket watch on a chain. He is irritated by Zoe's intelligence. He scores higher

than her on the Kroton tests – after a shaky start – but he answers more questions.

The Doctor demonstrates an expertise in chemistry, getting Gond scientist Beta to create a variation of sulphuric acid with which to destroy the tellurium-based Dynotrope.

THE TARDIS

The TARDIS light continues to flash after it has landed and the Doctor and his companions have left it.

The TARDIS hostile action displacement system – HADS – is activated by the Kroton's attempt to disperse it. The HADS detects whether the TARDIS is in danger, and automatically moves it to a safe location nearby (if the Doctor has remembered to set it).

COMPANIONS

ZOE: Zoe scores more than double the score of the best Gond student on the Teaching Machines. When Selris wonders whether the Doctor can answer the questions, she tells him that of course he can: 'The Doctor's almost as clever as I am.'

Zoe knows all about tellurium – one of the exceptional elements in the periodic table.

Selris: 'Silver men caused a poisonous rain to fall, killing hundreds of our people and turning the earth black... It was said that ever afterwards anyone who set foot there would die in terrible pain.'

THE SEEDS OF DEATH

In which the Ice Warriors take over a Moonbase and spread a deadly foam-like fungus across the Earth...
BY BRIAN HAYLES
6 EPISODES, FIRST BROADCAST 25 JANUARY–1 MARCH 1969

TARDIS DATA BANK:

DATE: UNKNOWN – c21ST CENTURY
LOCATION: T-MAT CONTROL, LONDON; ELDRED'S MUSEUM; WEATHER CONTROL STATION AND T-MAT STATION ON THE MOON

THE TARDIS LANDS IN AN ERA WHEN EVERYTHING – PEOPLE AND GOODS – IS TRANSPORTED BY T-MAT. ICE WARRIORS TAKE OVER T-MAT CONTROL ON THE MOON, AND TRANSPORT MARTIAN SEED PODS TO EARTH. AS THE OXYGEN-REMOVING FUNGUS IN THE PODS GROWS AND SPREADS ACROSS THE PLANET, THE DOCTOR, JAMIE AND ZOE ARE TRAPPED ON THE MOON. CAN THEY REPAIR T-MAT, STOP THE SPREADING FUNGUS AND DEFEAT THE ICE WARRIORS BEFORE THEIR INVASION FLEET ARRIVES...

The Doctor: 'You know, a complete blanket of this would reduce the oxygen content of the Earth's atmosphere quite drastically... It would make the atmosphere of the Earth uninhabitable to the human race, but exactly like the atmosphere of Mars. '

JOURNEY INFORMATION

PROFESSOR DANIEL ELDRED

It was Eldred who designed the ion-jet rocket that was to take man beyond the moon. He has been in rocketry all his life – his father engineered the first lunar passenger module and he travelled on the last trip back to Earth 'before it all finished'.

He is bitter that T-Mat put an end to space travel. He lost government backing and his project was abandoned, though he was offered a job working on T-Mat.

COMMANDER JULIAN RADNOR

Radnor is the commander of T-Mat Control in London. He used to be a friend of Professor Eldred, until he walked out on him and joined the T-Mat administration for the government.

Radnor reports to Sir James Gregson – United Nations plenipotentiary, and Minister with special responsibility for T-Mat.

T-MAT

The full name for T-Mat is 'Travelmat Relay'.

According to the publicity material, 'Travelmat is the ultimate form of travel. Control centre of the present system is the Moon, serving receptions at all major cities on Earth. Travelmat provides an instantaneous means of public travel, transports raw materials and vital food supplies to all parts of the world. Travelmat supersedes all conventional forms of transport. Using the principle of dematerialisation at the point of departure, and rematerialisation at the point of arrival in special cubicles, departure and arrival are almost instantaneous. Although the system is still in its early stages, it is completely automated and foolproof against power failure.'

The cities listed on Moonbase control board are: New York, Moscow, Toronto, Calcutta, Bombay, Stockholm, Washington, Athens, Izmir, Rome, Ottawa, Tokyo, London, Canberra. Seed pods are sent to some of these cities and also to Oslo, Paris, Zurich, Hamburg and Berlin.

THE ICE WARRIORS

The Ice Warriors are commanded by Slaar (whose name is only mentioned by the Grand Marshal, and by Zoe). Slaar has a more streamlined helmet, and does not wear the shell of body armour that the warriors wear.

Slaar's superior is the Grand Marshal. He is similar to Slaar, but with a more ornate helmet – and he speaks 'normally' as he is in his own atmosphere.

One of the Moon personnel, Phipps, builds a weapon that can destroy the Ice Warriors using a solar amplifier. Focusing dishes attached to a solar power line seem to melt the warriors so that just a pool of fluid is left on the floor.

The Doctor says, 'Mars is a dying planet, I imagine they're trying to find a new home...'

MARTIAN SEED PODS

The seed pods are white spheres that grow and burst, releasing a mist of spores. Sixteen reception centres receive pods (and one is dispatched to Zurich later on), resulting in four deaths from oxygen starvation.

The foam appears to be the by-product of a large fungus that bursts, spreading its spores over a large area. The rate of growth is such that acres are covered in minutes, destroying crops...

The Doctor finds the fungus has a molecule, composed of five atoms, which absorbs oxygen. A complete blanket of the fungus would reduce the Earth's oxygen content to about one twentieth of normal – uninhabitable for humans but exactly like Mars. In desperation, the Doctor tries dousing a pod with hydrochloric acid, sulphuric acid, nitric acid ... and water – which shrinks the pod and kills it.

Grand Marshal: 'You have failed us, Slaar — we shall all die. We are being drawn into the orbit of the sun.'

NEW INFORMATION

THE DOCTOR

The Doctor is careful not to lie to Eldred about how they entered his museum: 'The usual way, we just materialised,' he explains, which Eldred takes to mean by T-Mat.

The Doctor is the only person to be directly 'hit' by an exploding seed pod and survive, though he is rendered unconscious for a while (in *Pyramids of Mars* he mentions a respiratory bypass mechanism).

He destroys an Ice Warrior at Weather Control with a solar energy weapon. He destroys another when he first arrives back on the Moon, and redirects the last surviving Warrior's gun so it kills Slaar, before he electrocutes the Warrior. By disconnecting the satellite signal he destroys the entire Martian fleet. He justifies this by saying, 'You were trying to destroy an entire world.'

BEHIND THE SCENES

SCRIPT EDITING

The script editor (for a time called the story editor) is responsible for ensuring that scripts are commissioned, delivered, and available for production. Together with the producer, the script editor has more narrative control over the series' development than anyone else. The typical process of developing a script for **Doctor Who** is outlined below. Of course, there were exceptions to this at every stage.

INITIAL IDEAS: The process of coming up with ideas for a story is a vague one. Some story ideas have been sent in by writers 'on spec', like the Robert Holmes outline that eventually became *The Krotons*. Some come when a writer is invited to submit ideas for a script – as with Terry Nation's *The Daleks*. Others are worked up from discussions between the writer and script editor.

STORYLINE: The next stage is for the writer to work up a short, rough storyline. This is usually several pages long and tells the story the writer wishes to script in general terms. Sometimes a script is commissioned directly from the initial ideas or a discussion between script editor and writer.

For *The Time Warrior*, writer Robert Holmes, who had been persuaded, despite some initial reluctance, by script editor Terrance Dicks to work up a story set in medieval times, submitted his storyline in the form of a Sontaran citation for Commander Linx.

STORY BREAKDOWN: A story breakdown, if required, is a scene-by-scene telling of the story in outline form. Logistically it is a very useful document, as it is detailed enough to allow the director to begin the planning process in earnest, as the writer moves on to the draft script.

REWRITES AND EDITING: How much a script will be rewritten depends on the quality of the drafts, the time available and the extent to which the requirements of the production team may have changed.

If the rewrites are extensive and time is short, it may be that the script editor takes over at this point. So, for example, Gerry Davis's draft scripts for *Revenge of the Cybermen* were extensively rewritten by script editor Robert Holmes to include the Vogans and allow for location filming.

Sometimes the rewrites are extreme enough to merit the script editor receiving a credit as author. But this is often down to the inclination of the script editor. *Pyramids of Mars*, rewritten entirely by Robert Holmes, for example, was credited to Stephen Harris, whereas Holmes took a credit in his own name for his rewritten version of *The Ark in Space*.

Similarly, David Fisher's *Gamble with Time* was entirely rewritten by script editor Douglas Adams and producer Graham Williams (under the pseudonym David Agnew), and retitled *City of Death*. Because it was derived from Fisher's story, the original author still retained copyright and received most of the fee and subsequent royalties.

Unhappy with rewrites performed on their scripts by Derrick Sherwin, Mervyn Haisman and Henry Lincoln opted to use the pseudonym Norman Ashby for *The Dominators*. Terrance Dicks, unhappy with Robert Holmes's rewrites on *The Brain of Morbius* (while Dicks was unavailable to rewrite it himself), insisted that Holmes devise some 'bland pseudonym' on the script – which is therefore credited to Robin Bland.

Terrance Dicks himself was frequently required to rewrite extensively while he was script editor. Sometimes – as with *The Ambassadors of Death*, which was largely written in final draft by Malcolm Hulke (Episode 1 by Trevor Ray) – he employed another writer to 'rescue' a script. But often he did the job himself, uncredited. Dicks is in fact responsible for writing the bulk of *The Seeds of Death* (and would later write most of another Ice Warrior story *The Monster of Peladon*).

But Terrance Dicks, Robert Holmes and Derrick Sherwin were by no means the only script editors who found themselves scripting extensive material under other names...

IN THE STUDIO: By the time the programme reaches the studio, the scripts should be completely final. However, this is not always the case. On occasion, circumstances are such that changes need to be made at the filming stage – almost always by the script editor and/or the director. In *The Claws of Axos*, for example, a line was added in filming to explain the 'freak weather' the production crew had encountered on location.

Script editor Eric Saward was called upon to write new material for Episode 2 of *Timelash* when it under-ran. This was recorded with the subsequent story. For *The Green Death* and *The Mind Robber* new material was required to cover for the unavoidable absence of cast members (see *Miss Cast* on page 183), but generally, by the time a story reaches the studio, everyone hopes the scripts are complete and final.

TARDIS DATA BANK:

DATE: UNKNOWN, FUTURE
LOCATION: VARIOUS LOCATIONS IN THE FOURTH (NEW SARUM) SECTOR OF THE GALAXY

AFTER BEING STRANDED ON A SECTION OF A SPACE BEACON BLOWN UP BY SPACE PIRATES, THE DOCTOR, JAMIE AND ZOE MEET UP WITH VETERAN PROSPECTOR MILO CLANCEY. TOGETHER THEY MANAGE TO EVADE THE INTERSTELLA SPACE CORPS, AND TRACK THE PIRATES TO THE PLANET TA. HERE CLANCEY MEETS A LONG-DEAD FRIEND AS THE AUTHORITIES CLOSE IN ON THE PIRATES...

THE SPACE PIRATES

In which the Doctor, Jamie and Zoe join in a space opera...
BY ROBERT HOLMES
6 EPISODES, FIRST BROADCAST 8 MARCH–12 APRIL 1969

JOURNEY INFORMATION

BEACONS

There are 18 beacons, millions of miles apart, scattered across the Fourth Sector to help spaceships navigate. They are made almost entirely of 1,600 tonnes of pure argonite. They are each built out of eight sections assembled in space and held together by solar-powered magnets. The beacons are powered by a solar energy store, but also have emergency power – which is used to send a Mayday if main power fails.

THE PIRATES

The pirates use scissor charges to blow the beacons apart along the lines of their electro-magnetic fields. They then attach rockets to send them on to the planet Ta so that they can break the sections up for the argonite at their leisure.

The pirates have a Beta Dart called *Beta Buccaneer*. This is one of the finest and fastest ships in the galaxy, which costs in excess of a hundred million credits.

Clancey:
'There's about a hundred thousand things I don't understand, but I don't stand around asking fool questions about them, I do something useful.'

General Hermack: 'These old mining prospectors, like Clancey, were the first men to go out into deep space. For a time they had the place to themselves — roaming the space-ways, looking for planets, jumping each other's claims. They were a wild breed... and they learned to live without the law.'

MAURICE CAVEN

Caven is the pirate leader, and a 'master pilot.' Ruthless even with his own people, he threatens to blow up Dervish and the Beta Dart if they don't complete their work refuelling the rockets to take the beacon sections to planet Lobos.

DERVISH

Dervish is an engineer. He devised the UHF-detonated charges the pirates use. It is therefore ironic that Caven threatens him with one. He has been blackmailed by Caven into helping – 'I made a mistake once,' he admits. 'Just once. Caven found out about it.'

MADELEINE ISSIGRI

The Issigri Mining Corporation has been run by Madeleine since the supposed death of her father, Dom Issigri. She belives that mining inspector Clancey, while Dom's partner, was responsible for his death.

While she is in league with Caven and his pirates to make money, Madeleine will not be party to murder. 'When all this started,' she reminds Caven, 'it was going to be a salvage operation – space flotsam you said. But then piracy and now murder?'

Madeleine is haunted by the memory of her father. She has kept his study locked since his death – which makes it the ideal place for Caven to keep the old man hidden.

Issigri Mining is based on the planet Ta in the Pliny System – the first planet mined by Clancey and Dom Issigri.

MILO CLANCEY

Clancey is an old-fashioned mining prospector who 'prefers an astral pointer and a piece of string to the new star charts.'

Once a legend in 'Reja Magnum', Clancey now has mines on Lobos that are nearly exhausted. He runs the Milo Clancey Space Mining Company.

Clancey's ship, the LIZ 79, is practically falling apart. It is a C-class freighter – old and very slow. Clancey says he lost the registration 'about thirty years ago'.

NEW INFORMATION

THE DOCTOR

The Doctor says he needs less oxygen than Jamie and Zoe. He explains that Zoe calls him 'Doctor' out of 'sheer politeness'.

He keeps drawing pins in his pocket – which makes for an uncomfortable landing – explaining, 'I like drawing pins – normally.' He also has a tuning fork ('I usually carry them') with which he opens an audio lock, and a bag of marbles. But he refuses to use the green one in a trap for the pirates as it is one of his favourites.

COMPANIONS

JAMIE: Having been airsick in *The Faceless Ones*, Jamie feels spacesick on the LIZ 79 en route to Ta.

ZOE: It is Zoe who deduces that the pirates' base must be on Ta, working it out from the trajectory of the beacon segments. As ever, she is scrupulously polite. She tells Clancey, 'It's very rude to point, you know. Especially with a gun.'

Zoe does not know what argonite is, to Milo Clancey's surprise. In Dom Issigri's study she does not know what candles are and asks, 'How do they work?'

THE WAR GAMES

In which the Doctor is recaptured by his own people, the Time Lords, and put on trial...
BY TERRANCE DICKS AND MALCOLM HULKE
10 EPISODES, FIRST BROADCAST 19 APRIL–21 JUNE 1969

JOURNEY INFORMATION

THE TIME ZONES
There are 11 triangular time zones and the central Alien Headquarters. The Aliens' map shows the 1917 War zone, American Civil War zone, 30 Years War zone, Boer War zone, English Civil War zone, Russo-Japanese War zone, Crimean War zone, Peninsular War zone, Roman zone, Greek zone, Mexican Civil War zone.

There is 'fog' between the zones which the Doctor says is a force field. Humans cannot recall details such as how long they have been at the front, and Lady Jennifer (a volunteer ambulance driver) cannot remember where her hospital is.

THE WAR GAMES
The War Chief explains that the war games are simply the means to an end. 'The Aliens intend to conquer the entire galaxy – a thousand inhabited worlds...' Humans are, he says, '...the most suitable recruits for our armies. Man is the most vicious species of all... Consider their history, for half a million years they have been systematically killing each other. Now we can turn this savagery to some purpose – we can bring peace to the galaxy.'

So the humans continue to fight so that the 'best' – the ones who survive – can be selected for the Alien army.

PROCESSING
The Alien Scientist gives a lecture on the processing technique used on the kidnapped humans to convince them they are still fighting their own wars on Earth: 'The problem is to retain the specimen's personality as a fighting man while at the same time putting him under our control ... however, in the case of certain humans of particularly strong character and individuality ... the processing tended to fade, and the specimens developed the ability to pass through the time zone barriers. Some formed themselves into resistance groups which have considerably hampered the progress of our plan.'

THE WAR CHIEF
The War Chief is a Time Lord who recognises, and is recognised by, the Doctor. 'You may have changed your appearance,' he tells the Doctor, 'but I know who you are.'

He came to the Aliens of his own accord: 'I was promised efficiency and cooperation. Without the knowledge I have, this complete venture would be impossible.' He has shown the Aliens how to operate the time–space machines he provided, but not how to construct them. He now plans to betray and abandon his allies.

He kills the Security Chief, describing it as 'a personal debt I had to settle', but the Security Chief has already reported his treachery to the War Lord, who has the War Chief executed.

THE WAR LORD
After the War Games have ended, the alien leader, the War Lord, is put on trial by the Time Lords. But he refuses to recognise the court, and pleads that the humans would have killed each other anyway. He also tries to implicate the Doctor. He is found guilty of all charges and 'will be dematerialised – it will be as though you had never existed'.

The Doctor: 'The only people who can put an end to this ghastly business and send everyone back to their own times — The Time Lords... They're my own people.'

THE TIME LORDS

The Doctor says that the Time Lords are 'the only people who can put an end to this ghastly business and send everyone back to their own times.'

He summons them, knowing they will capture him, by sending 'a very special sort of box' containing all the information about what's been going on. It is mentally assembled from six metal plates the Doctor has in his pocket.

The Doctor says that, 'The Time Lords holding trial is a very rare event... Normally they don't interfere with the affairs of other planets, but they had to when I called for help.' The Time Lords say that the Doctor's defence at his own trial for intefering in the affairs of others has raised 'difficult issues'. Ultimately, his contention that they must fight the evils of the Universe rather than merely observe them seems to signal a change in Time Lord philosophy and culture...

NEW INFORMATION

THE DOCTOR

The Doctor reveals for the first time that he is a Time Lord, and says he ran away because he was bored... 'The Time Lords are an immensely civilised race – we can control our own environment, we can live forever barring accidents, and we have the secret of space-time travel... We hardly ever use our great powers, we're content simply to observe and gather knowledge...' But the Doctor was not content with this: 'With a whole galaxy to explore – millions of planets, eons of time, countless civilisations to meet.' In his defence at his trial the Doctor pleads: 'All these evils I have fought, while you have done nothing but observe. True, I am guilty of interference – just as you are guilty of failing to use your great powers to help those in need.'

The Time Lords' verdict is: 'We have accepted your plea that there is evil in the Universe that must be fought and that

you still have a part to play in that battle... We have noted your particular interest in the planet Earth, the frequency of your visits must have given you special knowledge of that world and its problems... For that reason you will be sent back to that planet... In exile... You will be sent to Earth in the twentieth century, and will remain there for as long as we deem proper. And for that period, the secret of the TARDIS will be taken from you... Your appearance has changed before, it will change again – that is part of the sentence.'

TARDIS TRAVEL MACHINES

The Doctor says that the controls for the Aliens' time machines are of a 'slightly different design' to those of the TARDIS. The machines take the shape of a dark green box with doors that slide out. Inside they are very large, with several rooms. The controls are geometric shapes and rods attached to a board. They are moved round and reconfigured to operate the machines.

The Doctor calls them 'TARDIS Travel Machines' (although they are referred to on one occasion as SIDRATs) and compliments the War Chief on their dimensional flexibility and remote control. 'In my day these things were impossible to achieve without shortening the life of the time control units... You haven't solved it, have you? Your machines have a limited lifespan...'

COMPANIONS

JAMIE: When he leaves, Jamie tells the Doctor, 'I won't forget you, you know.' But in fact the Time Lords remove both Zoe and Jamie's memories of their travels with the Doctor. He arrives back in Scotland and chases off a redcoat who fires at him.

ZOE: 'Will we ever meet again?' Zoe asks the Doctor when she says goodbye. The Doctor reminds her, 'You and I know, time is relative isn't it?'

Zoe is sent back to the Wheel (rather than the *Silver Carrier*), where she says to her friend, Tanya Lernov, 'I thought I'd forgotten something important, but it's nothing.'

BEHIND THE SCENES

ALL CHANGE

With the end of the Second Doctor's era, **Doctor Who** underwent some fundamental changes. One was the move from black-and-white to full-colour production. But narrative, as well as technical, changes were called for.

Producer Peter Bryant and script editor Derrick Sherwin had already decided to move on. Patrick Troughton had also decided to leave after three years in the role of the Doctor, and despite initial thoughts that one or both might stay on for a while with a new Doctor, Wendy Padbury (Zoe) and Frazer Hines (Jamie) also decided the time was right to leave.

A problem that had faced the production team for a while was one of increasing costs in real terms. The move

to colour was likely to exacerbate the financial problems. This, added to the increased technical complexity, helped motivate the move to a six-monthly rather than all-year season of episodes, even though the number of episodes produced had already been reduced.

Another way of saving money was to find a reason to set most, if not all, of the stories on contemporary Earth. This would make location filming easier and reduce the cost of costume and design since much more could be used or built from 'stock'.

But Derrick Sherwin realised that a series set entirely on present-day Earth with the Doctor and a couple of companions as the only regular characters would not be credible. What was needed was an organisation that the Doctor could be affiliated with – that had been set up to investigate exactly the sort of alien menaces **Doctor Who**'s viewers were used to seeing.

As a 'pilot' for this new format Sherwin wrote *The Invasion*, which introduced the United Nations Intelligence Taskforce – UNIT. For *The Invasion*, UNIT was commanded by Brigadier Lethbridge-Stewart, who had featured in *The Web of Fear* and proved popular.

Sherwin, together with Peter Bryant, developed this as the basis for the new series format to include UNIT, Lethbridge-Stewart and a new companion called Liz. It stated that a new actor was being introduced to play the Doctor, though the character would remain essentially the same.

Lethbridge-Stewart was originally the creation of writers Mervyn Haisman and Henry Lincoln. He had undergone a name change in the final drafts of *The Web of Fear*, but Sherwin was keen that the original writers get the credit and royalties they deserved. Writing to John Henderson, the BBC's Assistant Head of Copyright, he observed:

```
The character of Brigadier Lethbridge-Stewart was first introduced in
serial "QQ" (The Web of Fear) — written by Mervyn Haisman and Henry
Lincoln. We did change the character's name in the original, but despite
that he was 'created' by the authors. We used him again in serial "VV"
(The Invasion) by yours truly, and paid copyright to the authors for
this privilege! In "VV" I also introduced a force called U.N.I.T. at the
head of which was Brigadier Lethbridge-Stewart. As you will see from the
revised format we intend to continue with U.N.I.T. and consequently
Lethbridge-Stewart.

We do wish to retain this character but of course, should the authors
prove difficult over granting copyright, we could change our minds.
```

One of the reasons cited for reusing Lethbridge-Stewart was that the team 'very much like the actor who played him' – Nicholas Courtney.

With UNIT in place and under the Brigadier's command, all that was now needed was a reason for the Doctor to remain on Earth and associate himself with the organisation. When other scripts fell through, Terrance Dicks, who had taken over from Derrick Sherwin as script editor, was called upon at short notice to provide the final ten episodes of the Second Doctor's era. Not only was a ten-part story needed in a hurry, but it had to explain how the Doctor would come to be stranded on Earth.

Under these difficult circumstances, Dicks called in his friend, writer Malcolm Hulke, to help. Together they wrote *The War Games* – which established that the Doctor was a Time Lord, and which ended with his own people exiling him to Earth. The secret of the TARDIS was taken from him, along with part of his memory. In addition, the Doctor's appearance was to change – although, even while *The War Games* was being recorded, the new Doctor had yet to be cast...

Time Lord: 'There is no escape, Doctor. Return the TARDIS immediately to our home planet... You have broken our laws. You must face your trial.'

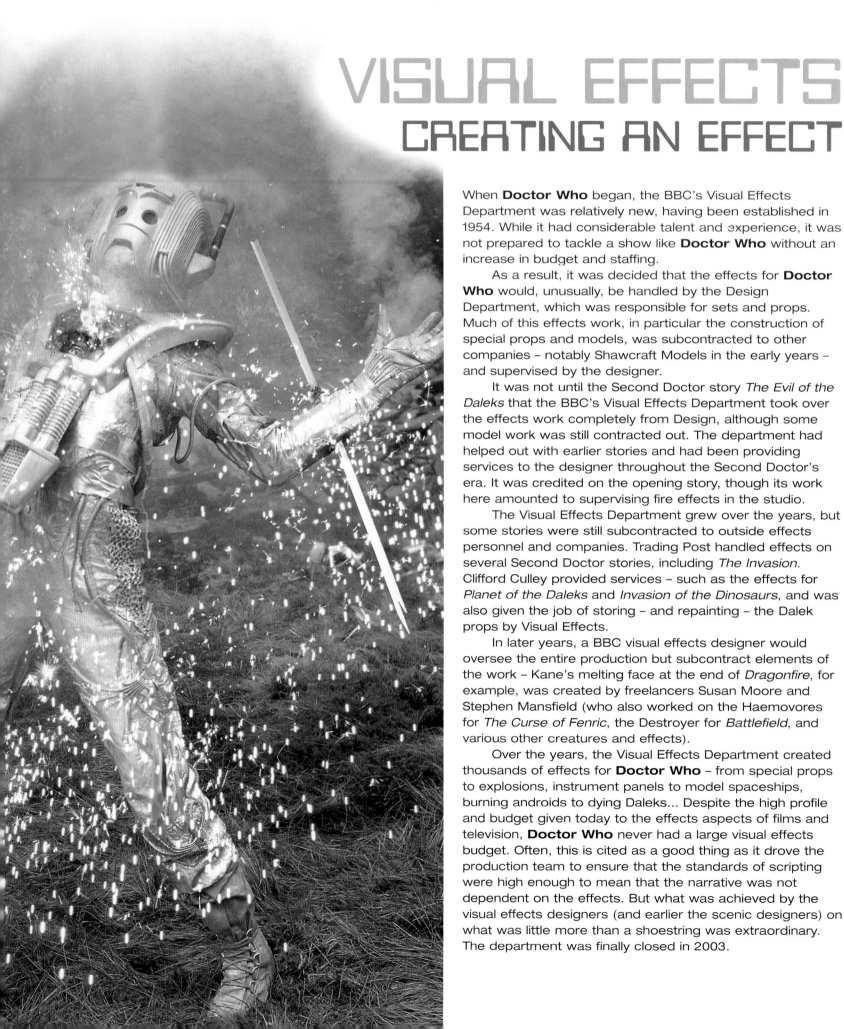

VISUAL EFFECTS
CREATING AN EFFECT

When **Doctor Who** began, the BBC's Visual Effects Department was relatively new, having been established in 1954. While it had considerable talent and experience, it was not prepared to tackle a show like **Doctor Who** without an increase in budget and staffing.

As a result, it was decided that the effects for **Doctor Who** would, unusually, be handled by the Design Department, which was responsible for sets and props. Much of this effects work, in particular the construction of special props and models, was subcontracted to other companies – notably Shawcraft Models in the early years – and supervised by the designer.

It was not until the Second Doctor story *The Evil of the Daleks* that the BBC's Visual Effects Department took over the effects work completely from Design, although some model work was still contracted out. The department had helped out with earlier stories and had been providing services to the designer throughout the Second Doctor's era. It was credited on the opening story, though its work here amounted to supervising fire effects in the studio.

The Visual Effects Department grew over the years, but some stories were still subcontracted to outside effects personnel and companies. Trading Post handled effects on several Second Doctor stories, including *The Invasion*. Clifford Culley provided services – such as the effects for *Planet of the Daleks* and *Invasion of the Dinosaurs*, and was also given the job of storing – and repainting – the Dalek props by Visual Effects.

In later years, a BBC visual effects designer would oversee the entire production but subcontract elements of the work – Kane's melting face at the end of *Dragonfire*, for example, was created by freelancers Susan Moore and Stephen Mansfield (who also worked on the Haemovores for *The Curse of Fenric*, the Destroyer for *Battlefield*, and various other creatures and effects).

Over the years, the Visual Effects Department created thousands of effects for **Doctor Who** – from special props to explosions, instrument panels to model spaceships, burning androids to dying Daleks... Despite the high profile and budget given today to the effects aspects of films and television, **Doctor Who** never had a large visual effects budget. Often, this is cited as a good thing as it drove the production team to ensure that the standards of scripting were high enough to mean that the narrative was not dependent on the effects. But what was achieved by the visual effects designers (and earlier the scenic designers) on what was little more than a shoestring was extraordinary. The department was finally closed in 2003.

SPECIAL PROPS

What counts as an effect, and what is part of 'normal' design is debatable. This was decided between the director, designer and visual-effects designer for each story during the planning stages. There was no hard and fast rule, but anything that could not be sourced from stock or built using the normal scenic techniques and processes was often allocated to Visual Effects.

Some of the special props are obvious examples – the Doctor's sonic screwdriver, Ace's futuristic ghetto blaster in *Silver Nemesis*; futuristic guns and communicators; a Sontaran gravity bar for *The Sontaran Experiment*... Control panels and equipment were sometimes constructed by Design, sometimes given to Visual Effects, and sometimes they could be hired in. For *The Green Death*, *The Ark in Space*, and a variety of other stories, scenery was hired from the Century 21 company – and is often recognisably from their live-action series **UFO**.

But often, Visual Effects was also responsible for less obvious props – be it a 'working' prop like the Ultima coding machine in *The Curse of Fenric* or the Marconiscope in *Pyramids of Mars*, or something rather more static and innocuous like the coin that is caught in a time rift at the start of *Warriors' Gate*...

MODELS

Models are very much the work of Visual Effects. These can vary from a complete landscape – the stone circle in *The Stones of Blood* (so that the real road at the location was 'removed') or the Tower and surrounding area in *State of Decay* – to the smallest part of a set or prop, like a piece of floor that has to melt or explode, or a bolt that needs to be removed by the Doctor's sonic screwdriver in *The Ark in Space*.

When something existed both as a model and as a full-sized prop or set, the two obviously needed to match. Usually, the model was made to match the designer's requirements, but occasionally things worked the other way round. For *City of Death*, visual-effects designer Ian Scoones produced a painting of the landscape of prehistoric Earth before the set designs were done. The director and designer agreed that this would form the basis of the set – and that Scoones could build a model landscape based on the impressive painting. The resulting sequence, with its exploding Jagaroth spaceship, is one of the most impressive model shots in **Doctor Who**. When Bernard Wilkie, who set up the BBC's Visual Effects Department with Jack Kine, chose a photograph for the cover of a new edition of his book *The Technique of Special effects in Television*, he picked a shot of Scoones working on this

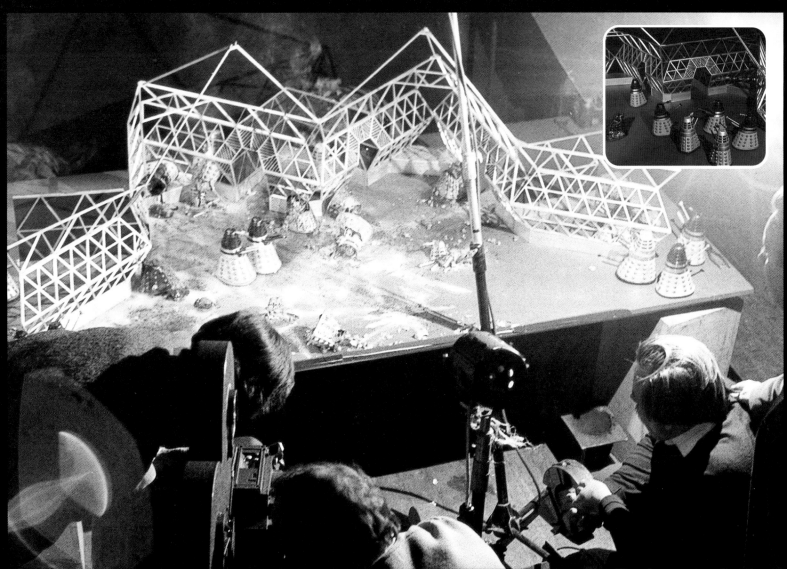

landscape model – and sent Scoones a copy of the book with a note saying how easy it had been to pick this out as an example of the very best of Visual Effects' work.

As well as producing models that are seen on their own in effects shots, there was often a requirement for a model that could be seen in situ, as if it were the real thing. The doors to the City of Telos in *The Tomb of the Cybermen* are a 'foreground miniature' – a model positioned closer to the camera than the background it appears to belong to. This method was often used on **Doctor Who**, a variation of glass painting – where the camera shoots through a piece of glass on which a painting enhances or replaces part of the background. This technique was used, for example, to add turrets to Leeds Castle so it became Castle Gracht in *The Androids of Tara*. In later years, electronic techniques were used to generate and merge images like these (and are discussed in the separate section on Electronic Effects).

SPACESHIPS

Be it the wobbly Dalek saucer flying over a devastated future London, or the impressive motion-controlled 'fly-round' the space station at the start of *The Trial of a Time Lord*, spaceships have featured heavily in **Doctor Who**.

Although **Doctor Who** has never been as dependent on spaceship models and effects as, say, **Star Trek** or **Blake's 7**, it has certainly had its fair share. The series has featured relatively few 'space opera' stories – *The Space Pirates*, *Frontier in Space* and arguably *The Invisible Enemy* – but there have been spaceships in many stories.

Most spaceship shots have been achieved with models flown (sometimes upside down, so the strings are *beneath* the model and therefore less visible) against a starscape. But electronic techniques have also been used to position models on their background – as in *Nightmare of Eden*, for example.

In *Remembrance of the Daleks*, a model of the Dalek shuttle craft was used for the sequences of it leaving and returning to the mother ship. But to land it on Earth, a full-size prop spaceship was built by Visual Effects and flown into the school playground by a crane.

Perhaps the most bizarre spaceship of all is the TARDIS. There have been many different TARDIS models, and we have seen the Doctor's time-and-space ship spinning impressively through space, materialising in model landscapes, even landing on the sea. It has pulled a neutron star off course (*The Creature from the Pit*), been attacked in space by cobwebs (*The Web of Fear*) and even suffered the indignity of being ripped apart in *The Mind Robber*.

CREATURES

The most famous of the creatures that the Visual Effects Department has 'handled' on **Doctor Who** are, of course, the Daleks and K-9.

K-9 was a radio-controlled prop, often operated by Nigel Brackley. K-9 was not as simple a prop as it might appear, however – unable to travel over rough ground he was often pulled along by a fishing line, or even on a trolley. His gears and motors needed almost constant attention, and he often broke down. When K-9 was first used in the television studio in *The Invisible Enemy*, the radio-control signals conflicted with the frequencies used by the cameras, and he was apt to go crazy and career off and crash...

The Daleks, despite their robotic appearance, and in keeping with their supposed purpose as life-support and travel machines, were actually operated by actors who sat inside them. But, from the Second Doctor's era onwards, it was the Visual Effects Department that was responsible for maintaining, amending, repainting and building the Dalek props.

'Special' Daleks created by Visual Effects have included those rigged to explode – complete with dead (or dying) Dalek creatures inside (*Resurrection of the Daleks* and *The Five Doctors*), lightweight props that could be 'walked' through a quarry (*Destiny of the Daleks*) and an impressive Special Weapons Dalek (*Remembrance of the Daleks*).

Visual Effects has produced almost as many alien creatures as the Doctor has defeated monsters. As well as being totally responsible for life forms as diverse as the Drashigs, giant maggots and giant spiders, the Destroyer, Horda and the impressive animatronic Fifi in *The Happiness Patrol*, the department has also produced parts of other creatures. The heads of Silurians and Sea Devils, mask components of Draconians and Ogrons, Yeti feet and claws, Davros's chair and mask... All these – and much more – were provided by Visual Effects.

EXPLOSIONS

The one thing that the Visual Effects Department did as impressively as it built things, was blow them up.

The number of explosions featured in **Doctor Who** – from a tiny component on the TARDIS console to entire planets and space fleets – is huge. The variety is almost as large – from the Sea Devils' underwater base to spaceships; from control consoles to Daleks; from a Gothic arched gateway between universes to a village church...

One of the most impressive explosions was the destruction of a group of Daleks exterminated under Waterloo station by a Special Weapons Dalek in *Remembrance of the Daleks*. In fact, this was such an impressive explosion that it set off all the car alarms in the area and the emergency services arrived on the scene within minutes of having been called, they thought, to the site of a bomb explosion. It was with some surprise they discovered the culprits were the Daleks...

THE MEASURE OF SUCCESS

The best visual effects are those that the audience does not even notice. If the viewer accepts as reality what is actually a planned, designed and executed effect, then the Visual Effects Department has done its job to perfection.

How many viewers realise that when Melkur burns the plans for the Source Manipulator in *The Keeper of Traken* they are actually clasped not by Neman, but in an artificial hand that won't get scorched? Who guessed that the ground moving under the Doctor and Romana's feet in *Destiny of the Daleks* is really a raised wooden platform with two effects assistants standing in for Tom Baker and Lalla Ward? Who can tell that the TARDIS never went on location in *Planet of Fire* – it isn't really there at all...

And there are countless other examples of visual effects that go unremarked, or are taken at face value. It may be a rather negative form of praise, but for the Visual Effects Department this is often the greatest accolade. Consider the well-deserved self-congratulation, as well as the amused smiles, when a viewer wrote an angry letter to the **Doctor Who** office to complain that a pretty village church that he had enjoyed visiting should have been blown up simply to make a television programme. Little did he realise that the explosion at the end of *The Dæmons* was not in the Wiltshire village of Aldbourne at all, but on a BBC Visual Effects model stage.

SPECIAL EFFECTS SHOWCASE:

CREATING 'THE FINAL END'

The first story on which the BBC's Visual Effects Department was wholly responsible for effects was in the Second Doctor's era: *The Evil of the Daleks*. It is hard to think of a story from the black-and-white era of **Doctor Who** that would have been more of a challenge. It is hard to think of *any* **Doctor Who** story that has such an effects-intensive or impressive conclusion. It is a great shame that no known copy of the final episode (or any episode apart from Episode 2) exists.

The final climactic battle between the humanised Daleks and the Daleks still loyal to the Emperor was achieved using a combination of filmed live-action and model work, video material, music and sound effects. The result is remembered as one of the most spectacular sequences in the history of **Doctor Who**.

The bulk of the film work for the battle sequence was directed by Tim Combe, the production assistant, as director Derek Martinus was busy with other aspects of the production. Combe went on to become a director himself, overseeing the Third Doctor's *The Silurians* and *The Mind of Evil*.

We can get an idea of the planning and thought that went into the finished results from surviving production documentation as well as surviving photographs, film footage and audio recording. The information below is taken from material held in the BBC's archived production files. It has been collated from various sources and edited for clarity.

DO NOT FIGHT IN HERE

Tim Combe's intentions come across in a memo to Brian Hodgson of the BBC's Radiophonic Workshop (dated 11 May 1967) in which he summarises the sequences for which he needs sound effects. The following text is taken from that memo.

In the full text, Combe is at pains to point out that while this is his suggestion Hodgson is the expert on sound effects. 'I leave it to you... you're the expert.'

What happens is this — Dalek fires at Dalek, picture to negative, the head is knocked off the Dalek and falls to the ground. After a beat the head slowly dissolves into jelly — a throbbing jelly. The headless Dalek then blunders about bumping into things before finally coming to a halt with its gun and feeler depressed! Lots of the inside of the Dalek has spewed out too.

It would be rather nice if when the headless Dalek is charging about the place we could get some sort of pig screams — really horrific and painful. As more Daleks are blown up so more screams come into force.

We have other scenes too with the Emperor Dalek slowly disintegrating as the Daleks fire upon it. Its cables burst and all the time its "heart" continues to beat (a light inside), until finally the Control Room is a complete mess of broken Daleks with smoke etc. Throughout this sequence lights go haywire of course — up and down on the dimmers. A few lighting effects. Eventually the Emperor Dalek gets weaker and weaker and dies!

DESTRUCTION OF THE DALEK CITY

The memo below was sent by visual-effects designer Michaeljohn Harris to director Derek Martinus describing how he proposed to depict the destruction of the Dalek City.

Two film sequences were to be shot of the model city, and Harris said they could, 'within reason, be stopped and started again between shots, but it must be appreciated that it is a one-off effect and therefore two high-speed cameras should be used throughout.'

PROPOSED SEQUENCE OF DESTRUCTION OF DALEK CITY
FIRST SECTION
(this could in fact be a series of takes)
1. City seen under harsh black-and-white lighting. A Dalek middle foreground patrols slowly towards camera. 2nd Dalek appears mid-distance. Approaches and fires (small flash flame). 1st Dalek scoots for cover. An explosion at point it has just been standing.
2. A small explosion takes place on base of facetted dome building left middle ground, where 1st Dalek has just taken refuge.
3. One or two small explosions and fires, etc in distance. Middle distance overhead cables burn out.
4. Angular building foreground explodes with flying debris leaving angular base smoking and burning.
THIS ENDS FIRST SEQUENCE OF DESTRUCTION.

SECOND SEQUENCE OPENS
5. Smoke and small fires continue. TV screen-type building right middle ground explodes and collapses.
6. Facetted dome building melts and collapses in flames and glare of white heat from basement of building. (Source of glare unseen)
7. A patch of fire and smoke develop in centre of city. Ground cracks and falls in, edges of pit fold downwards. Buildings twist and collapse into pool of glaring, smoking, bubbling lava.
Track in and finish.

THE FINAL RESULT

Although Episode 7 of *The Evil of the Daleks* no longer exists in the BBC Archives, it is possible to get an impression of the finished result from a short behind-the-scenes film shot by Effects Assistant Tony Cornell at the BBC's Ealing Film Studios and called *The Last Dalek*. This material, together with a commentary by visual-effects designers Michaeljohn Harris and Peter Day, is included on the BBC DVD release of *The Seeds of Death*.

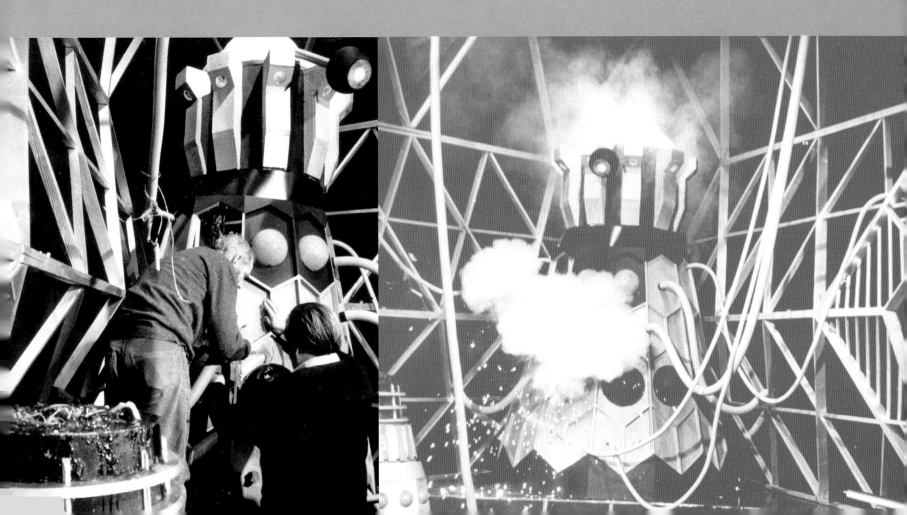

Three

THE THIRD DOCTOR

After the childlike enthusiasm and apparent muddling-through of his predecessor, the Third Doctor represented a return to a more authoritarian figure. Rather than the bumbling but occasionally brilliant 'sibling' that the Second Doctor had been to his companions, this new Doctor was once again paternal – an intellectual man of action respected by his colleagues in UNIT and looked up to by his companions.

By allying himself, however unwillingly at first, with an official organisation, the Doctor became more overtly a figure of authority than ever before. True, the First Doctor had helped in a semi-official capacity in *The War Machines* and the Second Doctor had freely lent his somewhat unorthodox skills to the army in *The Web of Fear* and to UNIT in *The Invasion*. But now the Doctor had the United Nations organisation as his base, his employer, even his home. For all his two hearts, his historical anecdotes and his Venusian Aikido, the Doctor had come down to Earth in more ways than one.

In fact, for the first half of his tenure, the Third Doctor might as well be a brilliant, athletic and eccentric human scientist. It is in the detail rather than the big picture that the Doctor is so alien and so interesting. For here is a 'man' who can drop the names of Nelson, Henry VIII and Napoleon without embarrassment or fear of contradiction. He can confidently and assuredly regale his companions with tales of meeting a giant rabbit, a pink elephant, and a purple horse with yellow spots, or of picking flowers with an old hermit on the mountain behind his home.

But between these quiet moments of alien memory and trans-temporal history, the Doctor is ready to explode into action or anger. Particularly in his earlier times, when his enforced exile is so unpalatable, the Doctor is ready to brand any lesser intellect a fool and any figure of authority a buffoon. He seems to take pleasure in putting down the Professor Stahlmans and the Chinns of this world, and others. He proudly eschews UNIT passes with an arrogance that belies his reliance on that organisation's continued good will.

He may not carry the pass, but he is more than ready to use the name and reputation – and power – of the organisation. 'As an associate of UNIT,' he tells Meredith with some satisfaction in *The Silurians*, 'I think you will find that I have the authority to do precisely as I please.' By the time he makes the acquaintance of Sarah Jane Smith in *The Time Warrior*, the Doctor's almost revered position within UNIT is something he feels he can boast about, mentioning oh-so-casually how they have asked *him* to look into the matter of some missing scientists. A far cry from his resentful accusations and insults when the Brigadier destroys the Silurians, or his parting words to the Brigadier when he believes he can escape Earth at the end of *Inferno*.

If the Doctor's relationship with UNIT is ambivalent, it is nowhere near as complex as his relationship with the Master. On the one hand, the evil Time Lord is the Doctor's nemesis and antithesis. The Master is clearly opposed to everything that the Doctor holds dear, from freedom of choice through to the very survival of humanity itself. Yet the Doctor feels able to confess he is looking forward to their next encounter. He may be miffed that the Master's degree in cosmic science is better than his own, but the Doctor displays a healthy respect for

'History books? My dear Captain Hart, Horatio Nelson was a personal friend of mine.'

(THE DOCTOR – *THE SEA DEVILS*)

him behind his back. To his face, the Doctor is always careful to deride his overambitious, overcomplicated machinations. Yet when they team up in *The Claws of Axos*, it is all too easy to suspect with Bill Filer that the Doctor really is preparing to sell out Earth itself for the sake of his errant former friend.

Each very evidently is trying to hide more than just a sneaking admiration for the other. And while the Master all too often tries to kill the Doctor, he also saves him from the Daleks (*Frontier in Space*), just as the Doctor argues publicly against the suggestion that the Master should be executed for his heinous crimes (*The Sea Devils*).

But beneath the sometimes arrogant exterior, the Doctor still retains the same depth of compassion and contempt for oppression and injustice. He takes time to teach Codal the value of courage in *Planet of the Daleks*, and risks his life to accuse the Controller of being a quisling in *Day of the Daleks*. He is a man who feels things deeply – be it sadness at the loss of a friend at the close of *The Green Death* as he drains his champagne and slips quietly away from Jo's engagement party, or the remorse at having had to trick Omega in *The Three Doctors*.

At his hearts, the Doctor has a love of life in all its forms – a love epitomised by his story of the 'daisiest daisy' in *The Time Monster* – and a thirst for knowledge. It is ironic that in *Planet of the Spiders* these two defining characteristics come into direct conflict and become, in effect, the death of him...

THE MAN BEHIND THE DOCTOR – JON PERTWEE

Born in 1919 in London, John Pertwee later changed his first name to Jon, having seen it misspelled this way on a poster.

Following in his actor-father's footsteps, Pertwee went from school to RADA and worked in the theatre before becoming involved in radio and then joining the Royal Navy during the Second World War.

After the war, Pertwee's career in radio flourished and in 1959 he joined the original cast of *The Navy Lark* – a programme with which he would remain associated all his life. It gave him ample opportunity to demonstrate his remarkable vocal talents.

From this, Pertwee moved into films. A consummate character actor, he appeared in several *Carry On* films – including *Carry On Screaming!* in 1966, in which he played the short-lived scientist Dr Fettle (with Kenneth Williams playing Dr Watt).

When Patrick Troughton left the role of **Doctor Who**, Pertwee persuaded his agent to put his name forward for the part. They were both surprised to find that he had already been shortlisted.

In many ways, Pertwee played the Doctor 'against type'. Having been a comedic character actor, he played the role 'straight' and took it seriously. This was a distinct contrast with the radio and cabaret work he continued to do.

With Pertwee in the lead role, the series flourished and became more popular than ever. The so-called 'UNIT years' are remembered by many as its golden age, with the 'family' rapport of the Doctor, Brigadier, Yates, Benton and Jo Grant battling the suavely evil Master as played by Roger Delgado.

After leaving the role in 1974, Jon Pertwee hosted the aptly named ITV **Whodunnit?** programme. Any fears that he might be typecast as the Doctor for all time were dispelled when he later, memorably, brought Worzel Gummidge to life.

Jon Pertwee returned to play the Doctor on several occasions, on stage, radio and television. His most notable return was in *The Five Doctors* in 1983. He continued to enjoy his numerous appearances at **Doctor Who** conventions around the world until his death in 1996.

UNIT

In *The Mind of Evil,* the Doctor says that the United Nations Intelligence Taskforce has been set up, '... to deal with new and unusual menaces to mankind'.

UNIT in the United Kingdom is under the command of Brigadier Lethbridge-Stewart. It is a military organisation, the personnel seconded from the armed forces of the host nation. UNIT Headquarters is in Geneva, though in times of war or international crisis the local UNIT forces are at the disposal of the host nation.

The remit of UNIT as explained in *The Invasion* is rather vague, the Brigadier describing it merely as 'an independent intelligence group' that investigates situations rather than actually arresting people.

Perhaps because of the attempted Cybermen invasion, that remit seems to have broadened by *Spearhead from Space*. 'We're not exactly spies here at UNIT,' Lethbridge-Stewart tells the newly recruited Dr Elizabeth Shaw. 'We deal with the odd, the unexplained. Anything on Earth, or even beyond...'

He explains that Earth is now more likely than ever to be attacked by aliens. 'In the last decade we've been sending probes deeper and deeper into space. We have drawn attention to ourselves, Miss Shaw... Since UNIT was formed there have been two attempts to invade this planet... We were lucky enough to be able to stop them. There was a policy decision not to inform the public...'

UNIT's brief is in fact quite wide. In *The Silurians*, UNIT is called in to investigate events which are merely 'outside the normal security pattern'.

We learn in *Robot* that, technically, the Brigadier should have a captain and a major reporting to him, but the UNIT budget won't run to it. (In fact a Major Cosworth appears in *The Mind of Evil*.) Apart from the Brigadier himself, the regular members of UNIT (who appear in more than one story) include:

SERGEANT BENTON – a corporal in *The Invasion*, promoted to regimental sergeant major for *Robot*. A keen ballroom dancer, he retires from UNIT to run a second-hand car dealership.

CAPTAIN MIKE YATES – who misguidedly betrays the organisation to Operation Golden Age in *Invasion of the Dinosaurs*, and is allowed to resign quietly. He discovers the link between K'anpo's meditation centre and the giant spiders of Metebelis Three in *Planet of the Spiders*.

CORPORAL BELL – the Brigadier's long-suffering personal assistant, she runs the administrative side of UNIT HQ.

DR ELIZABETH SHAW – the Doctor's assistant. Recruited from Cambridge University, she returns there following the events of *Inferno*.

JOSEPHINE GRANT – the Doctor's assistant. She gets a job with UNIT at the instigation of her uncle at the UN, and leaves to marry Professor Clifford Jones in *The Green Death*.

SURGEON LIEUTENANT HARRY SULLIVAN – seconded from the Royal Navy. He travels for a while with the Doctor and Sarah Jane Smith, before deciding in *Terror of the Zygons* that the train is a safer method of transport than the TARDIS.

BRIGADIER LETHBRIDGE-STEWART

'I'm not quite so much of a sceptic as I was since that little escapade,' Alistair Gordon Lethbridge-Stewart, newly promoted to Brigadier, tells the Second Doctor in *The Invasion*.

A straightforward career soldier, Lethbridge-Stewart may initially find it hard to accept the robot Yeti and the Great Intelligence in *The Web of Fear*. But once in charge of the newly formed UNIT, he takes such matters in his stride. 'Chap with wings there, five rounds rapid,' he famously orders when confronted with a murderous gargoyle in *The Dæmons*.

Perhaps the hardest things he has to accept are to do with the face-changing, time-travelling Doctor rather than the alien menaces he fights against. By *Terror of the Zygons*, he has become accustomed to such strange goings-on – assuring the Duke of Forgill who has just (apparently) learned that aliens are using a robotic Loch Ness monster to attack North Sea oil rigs: 'Before I joined UNIT I was highly sceptical of such things.'

Above all, however, the Brigadier is as calm in a crisis as he is when all is running smoothly. In *The Dæmons*, having been updated on recent events while he is still in bed, the Brigadier concludes, 'I see, Yates. So the Doctor was frozen stiff at the barrow, was then revived by a freak heatwave, Benton was beaten up by invisible forces, and the local white witch claims she's seen the devil.' Hearing this matter-of-fact summation of his own experiences of six impossible things before breakfast, Captain Yates confesses: 'Yes sir. I know it sounds a bit wild.'

But this cool acceptance of the impossible is not an acquired skill – Lethbridge-Stewart is similarly sanguine in *The Invasion*. As the Doctor makes his way through the sewers to confront Vaughn, and Captain Turner heads for Russia, there are Cybermen on the streets of London and the population of the world is paralysed by the Cyber hypnotic signal. 'Well, don't look so worried,' the Brigadier tells Zoe. 'Fancy a cup of tea?'

'But Doctor, it's exactly your cup of tea. This fellow's bright green apparently, and dead.'

(BRIGADIER LETHBRIDGE-STEWART – *THE GREEN DEATH*)

> **TARDIS DATA BANK:**
> DESCRIPTION: MALE, HUMAN
> APPEARED: *THE WEB OF FEAR, THE INVASION, SPEARHEAD FROM SPACE – ROBOT* (MOST STORIES), *TERROR OF THE ZYGONS, MAWDRYN UNDEAD, THE FIVE DOCTORS, BATTLEFIELD*

'I deal with facts, not science-fiction ideas.'

(DOCTOR ELIZABETH SHAW – *SPEARHEAD FROM SPACE*)

LIZ SHAW

> **TARDIS DATA BANK:**
> DESCRIPTION: FEMALE, HUMAN
> APPEARED: *SPEARHEAD FROM SPACE – INFERNO.*

Dr Elizabeth Shaw has an important research programme going ahead at Cambridge when she is invited to join UNIT. The Brigadier has decided he needs a scientific adviser and Liz Shaw is an expert in meteorites, with degrees in 'medicine, physics, and a dozen other subjects'.

Liz is initially sceptical of the Brigadier's stories about 'little blue men with three heads...' telling him, 'I deal with facts, not science-fiction ideas.' But after meeting the Doctor – and experiencing the events of the attempted Nestene invasion – she is more willing to accept the unexpected.

Although she does not spend much time as the Doctor's colleague, Liz demonstrates her scientific and medical abilities on many occasions and he soon comes to regard her almost as an equal. They also share a distrust and dislike of military organisation and discipline.

Perhaps this is one of the reasons why, following the events at the Inferno project, Liz decides to return to Cambridge and continue with her research...

SPEARHEAD FROM SPACE

In which shop window-dummies come to life, and Jon Pertwee is the Doctor – exiled to Earth, and in colour...

BY ROBERT HOLMES

4 EPISODES, FIRST BROADCAST 3–24 JANUARY 1970

The Doctor: 'What do you think of my new face, by the way? I wasn't too sure about it myself to begin with, but it sort of grows on you. Very flexible, you know. Could be useful on the planet Delphon, where they communicate with their eyebrows.'

JOURNEY INFORMATION

THE NESTENES

The Nestenes are a collective intelligence, brought to Earth in meteorites. They are actually energy units, each containing part of the Nestene consciousness. If they are not found and recovered, they 'increase their pulsation signals'.

The Nestene leader, Channing, tells the suborned Hibbert, 'We are the Nestenes. We have been colonising other planets for a thousand million years. Now we have come to colonise Earth.'

Channing does not know what the creature being grown in the tank will look like. 'I made nothing. I merely provided an environment tank in which the energy units can create the perfect life form.' He explains to the Doctor that this means: 'A life form perfectly adapted for survival and conquest on this planet.' When the Doctor asks if this is what the Nestenes look like on their own planet, Channing replies, 'No, we have no individual identity... We are indestructible...' The Doctor likens the creature to a 'collective brain and nervous system,' and observes that by killing it he will kill them all. The creature – like the Autons and a facsimile of the Brigadier's superior, General Scobie, before it – is destroyed by an EEG/UHF machine. Liz describes this as 'basically the same as an ECT machine – electroconvulsion therapy. Only much more powerful.' The replicas 'revert' to blank-Auton state. Channing also 'reverts' and the Autons collapse.

TARDIS DATA BANK:

DATE: NEAR FUTURE
LOCATION: ASHBRIDGE AREA, OXLEY WOODS IN ESSEX; LONDON.

THE NEW DOCTOR ARRIVES IN OXLEY WOODS IN THE MIDDLE OF A FREAK METEORITE SHOWER. USING FACELESS KILLER AUTONS DISGUISED AS SHOP-WINDOW DUMMIES, THE NESTENES ARE PLANNING TO INVADE THE WORLD – REPLACING MILITARY, POLITICAL AND CIVIL LEADERS WITH FACSIMILES DISPLAYED AT MADAME TUSSAUDS. THE CONVALESCENT DOCTOR WORKS WITH BRIGADIER LETHBRIDGE-STEWART AND DR ELIZABETH SHAW OF UNIT TO THWART THE NESTENE PLANS, EVEN AS THE INVASION BEGINS...

Brigadier: 'All over the country — window dummies coming alive. Attacking police stations, barracks, communications centres...'

AUTONS

'Crude weapons with a single offensive function', the Autons are blank-faced, plastic humanoids. Each has a gun concealed inside its hand – the fingers dropping away to allow the gun to emerge and fire. Bullets and even shotguns have no effect on Autons.

NEW INFORMATION

THE DOCTOR

In the hospital, it is discovered that the Doctor has two hearts (seen on his X-ray). His blood is seen to be red when he is shot, but Lomax in the pathology lab claims that the blood sample '... wasn't human blood... it is not a human blood type, the platelet stickiness shows that.' Dr Henderson says, 'His whole cardiovascular system is quite unlike anything I've ever seen...' The Doctor's pulse eventually 'settles down' to ten a minute. He goes into a self-induced coma after his skull suffers a bullet graze.

The Doctor has the TARDIS key hidden in his shoe, and is seen to have a tattoo (of a snake) on his right forearm. He claims he has lost his memory, and when Liz asks what he's a doctor of, he tells her, 'Practically everything, my dear.' The Doctor has a watch that 'homes in on the TARDIS'.

After trying to leave in the TARDIS, the Doctor says, 'I couldn't bear the thought of being tied to one planet and one time.' He agrees to help the Brigadier on certain 'terms' including: 'Facilities to repair the TARDIS, laboratory, equipment, help from Miss Shaw here...' He says that he doesn't want money – 'got no use for the stuff', but he does need clothes, and has taken to the vintage car he 'borrowed' from the hospital: 'I took to that car. It had character...'

THE TARDIS

The Yale-type TARDIS key does not work for the Brigadier – 'But it will for me,' the Doctor says, telling Liz that 'the lock has a metabolism detector'. He also tells her he has an entire laboratory inside which is possible because the TARDIS is 'dimensionally transcendental'.

When the Doctor tries to operate it, smoke escapes from the TARDIS even before the door opens. 'The TARDIS no longer works,' the Doctor explains sadly. 'They've trapped me here... They've changed the dematerialisation code.'

UNIT

UNIT is a top-secret security organisation. Liz is searched when she arrives at UNIT HQ, and has obviously never heard of UNIT. The press, though, *has* heard of it – and associates it with 'a man from space' as well as the meteorites.

COMPANIONS

BRIGADIER LETHBRIDGE-STEWART: Liz is initially sceptical of the Brigadier's abilities and even his sanity: 'You really believe in a man who's helped to save the world twice, with the power to transform his physical appearance... An alien who travels through time and space in a police box.'

But his matter-of-fact approach to bizarre events leads to her respecting and trusting him.

BEHIND THE SCENES

FILMING THE IMPOSSIBLE

Spearhead from Space is the only **Doctor Who** story, with the exception of *Doctor Who – The Movie*, to be made entirely on film. But it was almost not made at all.

Although the exterior filming was already 'in the can' and studio sessions were booked for the interior sequences of the Third Doctor's first story, BBC Television Centre in London was in the midst of industrial action taken by the Association of Broadcast Staff. The strike meant that some series due to be made were cancelled, while others were rescheduled.

Doctor Who was among the series affected. Outgoing producer Derrick Sherwin decided, however, that it would be possible to complete the story entirely on 16mm film – in effect making the entire programme on location.

Director Derek Martinus found the BBC's Wood Norton training centre near Evesham in Worcestershire to be an ideal location, with interiors that could match the work already filmed elsewhere. He also appreciated the opportunity to improvise, so that an antique shower, for example, was incorporated into a sequence of the Doctor escaping from his hospital confinement.

Filming also benefited the new star, Jon Pertwee. He was understandably nervous and was not used to television studio work, whereas he was a veteran of the feature film business. So the chance to make *Spearhead from Space* in the same way as a large-scale film suited his methods of working, and allowed him time to settle into the role before his first work on video in the television studios for the following story, *The Silurians*.

The end result was a tightly edited and richly textured story with a realistic feel that would have been diluted by the usual mixture of film and video work.

THE SILURIANS

In which prehistoric reptilian creatures emerge from caves in Derbyshire to reclaim the Earth from the upstart apes...

BY MALCOLM HULKE

7 EPISODES, FIRST BROADCAST 31 JANUARY–14 MARCH 1970

TARDIS DATA BANK:

DATE: NEAR FUTURE
LOCATION: EARTH –
WENLEY MOOR,
AND LONDON

INVESTIGATING MYSTERIOUS POWER FAILURES AND A DEATH AT AN UNDERGROUND RESEARCH CENTRE, THE DOCTOR DISCOVERS A COLONY OF SILURIANS – PREHISTORIC, INTELLIGENT REPTILES WHO WENT INTO HIBERNATION BEFORE MAN EVOLVED. BUT NOW THEY HAVE WOKEN UP, AND THEY ARE PREPARED TO WIPE OUT MANKIND WITH A KILLER PLAGUE TO GET THEIR PLANET BACK...

JOURNEY INFORMATION

WENLEY MOOR RESEARCH ESTABLISHMENT

The Wenley Moor Research Establishment is an atomic research centre built into the caves. Major Baker is in charge of security. Dr Lawrence explains, 'This establishment consists basically of a device for research into the nature of the atom – a cyclotron, otherwise known as a proton accelerator. It bombards atoms with subatomic particles... We are on the verge of discovering a way to provide cheap, safe atomic energy for virtually every one of us.'

Senior scientist Dr Quinn claims, 'We're developing a new kind of nuclear reactor. One which converts nuclear energy directly to electrical power.'

There is an unusually high level of personnel problems at the centre – absenteeism, nervous breakdowns, accidents... Liz says that minor neuroses are '200 per cent above the normal, even for a place like this'. There are also unexplained power losses. These problems have been going on for three months.

THE SILURIANS

The Silurians believe the Earth to be their planet. 'We were here before Man. We ruled this world millions of years ago,' the Silurian Leader claims. But '... a small planet was approaching the world. We calculated that it would draw off our atmosphere, destroying all life. We built this place and suspended our lives until the atmosphere should return.'

But the Silurians continued in hibernation while Man evolved and became dominant. Now they have been disturbed by the work of the Research Establishment, and are drawing off their power until they are ready to make their own.

The Silurians' third eye can stun, open cage doors, and also revives Major Baker when he is set free. The Silurians are able to melt a tunnel through the rock to capture the Doctor from the lab. They are also able to produce cave walls to trap UNIT troops. The third eye is used to remove the cave walls again.

DISEASE

The Silurian Scientist says, 'When the apes used to raid our crops we used to use this. Millions were wiped out. Now we could conduct an experiment on this ape...' The effects of the disease are not unlike bubonic plague – pustules develop, the skin becomes discoloured and the victim falls unconscious then dies.

While the Silurians realise that the 'apes' may be more resistant to the disease now, they still believe that it will effectively wipe Man out, 'They are only apes. They will not develop a cure.'

NEW INFORMATION

THE DOCTOR

The Doctor is able to analyse the Silurian plague bacteria and discover a cure, though he finds it difficult and frustrating, and remarks at one point, 'You know I'm beginning to lose confidence for the first time in my life. And that covers several thousand years.'

Once the threat has receded, the Doctor shows his enthusiasm for exploring the Silurian base, 'There's a wealth of scientific information down here, Brigadier. And I can't wait to get started on it.' When the Brigadier destroys the Silurians, the Doctor is appalled and devastated.

BESSIE

The Doctor has his new car, Bessie, for the start of this story. The car is a bright yellow Edwardian roadster which the Doctor describes to Liz as 'a car of great character'. Bessie starts when the Doctor pats the bonnet.

COMPANIONS

BRIGADIER LETHBRIDGE-STEWART: Whether it is the Brigadier's decision to destroy the Silurians in the end or whether he is obeying orders from above, as Liz suggests, is never made clear. But he is obviously keen to be rid of the Doctor before he explodes the charges, and believes that what he is doing is for the best.

LIZ SHAW: Liz demonstrates her medical expertise – taking a blood sample from an infected ambulance driver and administering antibiotics to combat the plague.

The Doctor:
'That's murder.
They were intelligent, alien beings. A whole race of them.
And he's just wiped them out.'

BEHIND THE SCENES

OPENING AND CLOSING TITLES

A new title sequence was devised for the Third Doctor. It was created by Bernard Lodge, who had created the two previous versions, and used the same technique of a camera recording its own feedback.

Again, Lodge incorporated a photograph of the actor playing the Doctor – in this case Jon Pertwee. He experimented with a three-quarter-length shot, but again used a portrait photograph.

Although the titles were to be in colour, Lodge found that using feedback from a colour camera gave disappointing results. So, again, black-and-white images were used, which were then coloured afterwards using an optical printer.

For the first time, Lodge also produced a closing title sequence (without the use of the Doctor's face) to be run under the end credits. (For Episodes 2, 5 and 6 of *The Green Death* these end titles were run backwards and upside down to save rewinding the film.)

To accompany the new titles, a slightly revised version of the theme music was created by the BBC's Radiophonic Workshop.

Silurian Leader: 'This is our planet. We were here before Man. We ruled this world millions of years ago...'

THE AMBASSADORS OF DEATH

In which astronauts on a mission to Mars return and kill...
BY DAVID WHITAKER
7 EPISODES, FIRST BROADCAST 21 MARCH–2 MAY 1970

TARDIS DATA BANK:

DATE: NEAR FUTURE
LOCATION: ENGLAND INCLUDING SPACE CONTROL CENTRE; SPACE; ALIEN SPACESHIP

ASTRONAUTS RESCUED FROM A MISSION TO MARS ARE KIDNAPPED WHEN THEY ARRIVE BACK ON EARTH. THEY SEEM TO HAVE BEEN IRRADIATED, AND CAN NOW KILL PEOPLE MERELY BY TOUCHING THEM. BUT THE DOCTOR DISCOVERS THE ASTRONAUTS HAVE BEEN REPLACED WITH ALIEN AMBASSADORS WHO ARE BEING FORCED TO BEHAVE IN A HOSTILE MANNER. WITH THE DOCTOR TRAVELLING TO THE ALIEN MOTHER SHIP, AND LIZ KIDNAPPED, THE BRIGADIER IS LEFT WONDERING WHO TO TRUST...

JOURNEY INFORMATION

SPACE CONTROL

Space Control is the UK equivalent of NASA's Mission Control. From here the Mars Probe missions are launched and monitored. Space Control is under the command of Ralph Cornish.

The entrance to Space Control is through a tunnel into a hill. It is close to (or in) London – seven miles from the warehouse where Carrington sends his signal to the aliens.

GENERAL CARRINGTON

General Carrington is the head of the newly formed 'Space Security Department'. He was an astronaut on Mars Probe 6, and blames the aliens for the death of his colleague, Jim Daniels (in fact, the aliens did not realise that their touch was fatal to humans).

He believes that arranging for the destruction of the aliens is his 'moral duty', and will go to any lengths to save the Earth.

REEGAN

Reegan is a ruthless killer whose only loyalty is to himself and whose only interest is money and power. He has no qualms about killing the scientists who accompany the astronauts when he kidnaps them. He arranges for his thugs to ride in the back of the van with the Ambassadors – so that the thugs die of radiation poisoning.

As a disguise Reegan's van changes its side markings from 'Hayhoe Launderers Ltd' to 'Silcock Bakeries'. The number plates change from KBF979H to YLD259H.

Reegan is planning to raid a bank when the Brigadier arrives to arrest him. Realising he needs all the favours he can get, it is Reegan who suggests they use the aliens to get into Space Control. 'You won't forget it was my idea,' he tells the Brigadier.

THE AMBASSADORS

The Alien vessel is a half-mile diameter discoid. The ship emits radio impulses like those emitted by pulsars that jam NASA's satellite cameras. Inside the alien ship, the Doctor finds an environment prepared for him – a glowing orange cave.

The space-suited Ambassadors are emitting over two million rads. Bullets have no effect on them, and are flattened. The Doctor thinks they are 'deflected by some kind of force field'. The Ambassadors kill with an electric charge from the hand. However, their energy blasts may not always kill – a Space Control guard is later back on duty after being electrocuted. Also, a policemen attacked at an isotope store recovers and dives out of the way of Reegan's van.

When one of the Ambassadors removes its helmet, it reveals a globular, pustuled face beneath. The Ambassadors are not susceptible to g-force, so they can be sent back to the alien ship in a rocket fuelled with pure M3 variant.

THE DOCTOR

The Doctor has heard the Ambassadors' 'message' sound before – but he can't remember where or when.

When preparing to pilot the mission to recover the human astronauts, the Doctor tells Cornish, 'I've spent more time in space than any astronaut on your staff. Not, I'll admit, in the rather primitive contraptions that you use, but I'll manage... I can also withstand considerably more g-force than most people.' When Cornish gets the Doctor's medical report, he comments, 'This is incredible...'

THE TARDIS

The TARDIS console is removed from the TARDIS and positioned in the Doctor's UNIT lab.

The Doctor is trying to reactivate the time vector generator (which he used in *The Wheel in Space*) and he sends Liz into the future – she disappears, and so does he. Eventually they both reappear together.

LEFEE

BESSIE

Carrington and his associate Grey get stuck to Bessie when the Doctor presses a switch marked 'anti-theft device'. He tells them not to worry as '... it'll switch itself off. Eventually.'

UNIT

When triangulating Carrington's signal to the aliens, UNIT is able to get every national radio station to triangulate.

Benton is still working for UNIT. He previously appeared as a corporal in *The Invasion* and has now been promoted to sergeant.

COMPANIONS

LIZ SHAW: Liz speaks French on the phone to the triangulation team in Nancy. Misguided scientist Lennox met Liz when she was doing research at Cambridge.

BEHIND THE SCENES

COLOUR SEPARATION OVERLAY

Colour Separation Overlay (CSO), also known as Chromakey or Blue-screen, is a way of combining two images. The technique works by having areas of a specified colour in one image replaced by elements from a second image. Blue is typically used as the so-called 'keying' colour, though yellow was also used on **Doctor Who** – not least because the TARDIS is blue, and would disappear if blue was the keying colour.

CSO is a remarkably versatile tool. A single key-coloured rectangular area can become a large screen display showing the whole of another video image. Or a character standing alone in front of a key-colour backdrop can be added to another set – even a model. In the opposite case, a model can be added to a live-action scene and appear full-size.

The disadvantages of CSO were that it could take a long time to set up, and often there was a coloured 'haze' around the CSO area. Reflective surfaces also gave problems as they could reflect the key colour and therefore 'disappear' into the other image.

The very first use of CSO on **Doctor Who** was in *The Silurians* where it was used to provide a 'false' cave wall in the background of the scene where Major Baker is captured by the Silurians (Episode 4). It was also used in that story to put pictures on the Silurians' monitor, and to provide shots of a giant dinosaur kept by the Silurians keep.

The dinosaur was actually a suit worn by visual effects assistant Bertram A. Collacott (and was referred to in the camera scripts as 'Bertram the Friendly Monster'). For the scenes where the dinosaur appeared with the Doctor and Liz, it was recorded acting against a blue backdrop. The blue colour was then replaced by the video images of Jon Pertwee and Caroline John 'reacting' to the creature.

Only after the programme had been completed did it occur to the production staff that a model could have been used, as the actual size of the dinosaur prop was of no importance. (This was the approach later taken with similar monsters like the Drashigs and a Plesiosaur, in *Carnival of Monsters*, and the dinosaurs in *Invasion of the Dinosaurs*.)

In *The Ambassadors of Death*, CSO was used even more ambitiously. Amongst other things, the technique was employed to provide images on the screens at Space Control as well as the effects for the alien captain, and the Doctor's arrival inside the alien space ship. The technique was used extensively throughout the colour years of **Doctor Who** – more effectively in some cases than others.

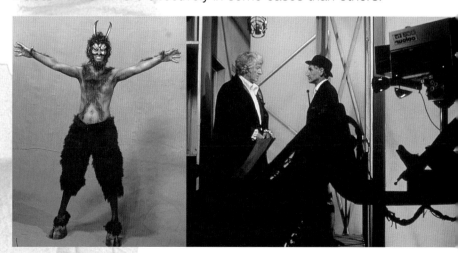

INFERNO

In which drilling into the Earth's crust releases forces that transform people into primordial monsters...

BY DON HOUGHTON

7 EPISODES, FIRST BROADCAST 9 MAY–20 JUNE 1970

JOURNEY INFORMATION

PROJECT 'INFERNO'

We do not learn the official name of the project, but as Sir Keith Gold, its executive director, says, 'Some of the technicians have nicknamed this place "the Inferno".'

The drill head itself is the only one of its kind in the world. When consultant Greg Sutton arrives it is 20 miles deep. 'You're liable to wake up Old Nick going that deep,' he comments. The project intends to tap pockets of gas beneath the Earth's crust and harness their energy.

THE PRIMORDS

Maintenance worker Harry Slocum is infected when he touches the green seepage from Number Two Output Pipe. He staggers out of the drill-head area in a daze, and almost immediately becomes homicidal. He make an inhuman grunting, screeching sound. As Slocum mutates, hair grows on his hands and his face. He is shot twice at point-blank range through the heart with a rifle, and still manages to kill a soldier. Slocum's attacks infect a technician and UNIT soldier Private Wyatt.

The Doctor describes what has happened as, 'Some sort of retrogression of the body cells...'

Fire extinguishers can be used to fight off the Primords as they are unable to cope with the cold. Heat actually seems to accelerate their mutation: 'The hotter it is, the stronger they grow.'

ALTERNATIVE EARTH

In the alternate world, the drilling project is at a more advanced stage. The scientists on the alternate project all wear numbered, white uniforms – including Stahlmann (note the double 'n' spelling in the alternate world) and his assistant Petra Williams, who is Dr Williams, assistant director of the project. The project is in fact a scientific labour camp..

The guards are members of the Republican Security Forces (replacing UNIT). Benton's rank is Platoon Under Leader.

The Brigade Leader has authority to execute the Doctor under the Defence of the Republic Act, 1943. He says the royal family were 'executed – all of them'. While this suggests the republic has been in existence since at least 1943, Sir Keith still has a knighthood. He has been killed in a motor accident en route to the ministry in London.

The Doctor says that taking anyone back to the 'real' world would '... create a dimensional paradox. It would shatter the space–time continuum of all the universes.'

THE BRIGADE LEADER

Unlike the Brigadier, the Brigade Leader has no moustache and wears an eyepatch over his scarred left eye. By the end of the world, the Brigade Leader has become dangerously unstable, trying to force the Doctor to take him to the 'real' world. He even shoots drilling expert Sutton when provoked, although there are no bullets in the gun.

SECTION LEADER ELIZABETH SHAW

In the alternate world, Elizabeth Shaw is not a scientist, but a Section Leader in the Republican Security Forces. But she did read physics at university, prompting the Doctor to realise that there are vestiges of the Liz he knows.

The Doctor: 'But I don't exist in your world.'
Brigade Leader: 'Then you won't feel the
bullets when we shoot you.'

NEW INFORMATION

THE DOCTOR

The Doctor says he has heard the noise Slocum makes before: 'Krakatoa, in the Sundra Straits. During the volcanic eruption of 1883.'

The Doctor uses what he calls 'Venusian karate' to immobilise Stahlman when he tries to destroy the computer's microcircuit to stop it warning against his drilling. 'It's very effective,' he tells the Brigadier. 'Hold it long enough and the subject becomes permanently paralysed.'

In the alternate world, hearing that the royal family has been executed, the Doctor observes, 'Pity, a charming family. I knew her great-grandfather in Paris.'

On his return to the 'real' world, the Doctor goes into a coma. Liz says his hearts are beating steadily. When he wakes he says his pulse is more or less 'normal' – at 170. He then checks his own hearts – finding that the right one seems a fraction faster: 'Still, that's only to be expected, isn't it?'

Preparing to escape from Earth with the TARDIS console, the Doctor says of the Brigadier, 'I've had about all I can stand of this pompous self-opinionated idiot here.' Later, the Doctor is forced into as much of an apology as he can manage: 'We don't want to bear a grudge for a few hasty words, do we? No, not after all the years that we've worked together...'

THE TARDIS

The TARDIS console has been removed from the TARDIS and is in a workshop.

The Doctor describes his 'trial trip' with the console: 'I seemed to be in some sort of limbo. There was a barrier I couldn't break through...' In the alternate world, the Doctor says that he has arrived by accident. 'The TARDIS console slipped me sideways in time.'

THE MASTER

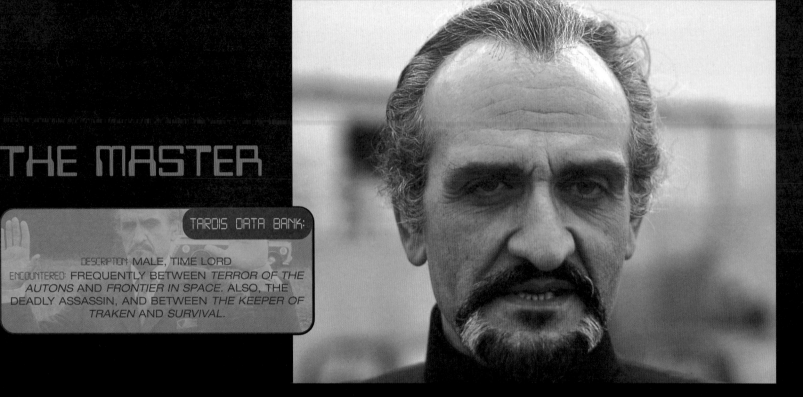

TARDIS DATA BANK:

DESCRIPTION: MALE, TIME LORD
ENCOUNTERED: FREQUENTLY BETWEEN *TERROR OF THE AUTONS* AND *FRONTIER IN SPACE*. ALSO, *THE DEADLY ASSASSIN*, AND BETWEEN *THE KEEPER OF TRAKEN* AND *SURVIVAL*.

The Master is urbane, sophisticated and charming. His face – especially his eyes – hint at his terrible power. He can hypnotise the weak-minded with a few words, and destroy worlds on a whim.

Like the Doctor, the Master is a renegade Time Lord – in *The Sea Devils*, the Doctor tells Jo, 'He used to be a friend of mine once. A very good friend. In fact you might almost say that we were at school together.' (In *Terror of the Autons*, we learn that the Master's degree in cosmic science was of a higher class than the Doctor's.) Certainly the Time Lords are aware of their association and antipathy, and warn the Doctor of the Master's arrival on Earth.

never falters and is tempered only by a black sense of humour and a passion for destruction. The Master would revive the Sea Devils and provoke a war with humanity merely, he says, for the pleasure of seeing the human race exterminated. In *The Claws of Axos*, he will strike a bargain with Axos that trades his life and his TARDIS for the Earth itself, and in *The Dæmons* he effectively sells his soul to the devil in a bid for ultimate power.

Yet through it all, we get the impression that the Master and the Doctor are twin facets of the same persona. It seems almost as if neither can bring himself to kill the other – the Doctor saves the Master from execution after *The*

'I am usually referred to as the Master... Universally.'

(THE MASTER – *TERROR OF THE AUTONS*)

For his part, the Doctor pretends to be unimpressed, branding the Master 'an unimaginative plodder', but his respect for him is undeniable. They might be at opposite ends of the moral spectrum, but each has an empathy with the other.

Why or when the Master left his people is never stated, and in *The Deadly Assassin* we discover that he has destroyed all traces of his existence. He has also plundered the Time Lord files for information – information that leads him to the Doomsday Weapon in *Colony in Space* as well as allowing him to contact the Sea Devils.

While he is charming yet ruthless, suave but evil, one thing about the Master is indisputable: he is hungry for power. Whether it be power over the individuals he hypnotises, or dominion over the Universe itself, this ambition

Dæmons, and from being killed by Kronos in *The Time Monster*... The Master always seems to leave an escape route for the Doctor, and prevents the Daleks from executing him in *Frontier in Space*.

After using up all his regenerations, the Master returns in *The Deadly Assassin* as a bitter, emaciated husk of a man, motivated only by hate. But after he acquires a new body in *The Keeper of Traken*, a degree of his charm and wit returns, albeit tempered by a more overtly sadistic streak. Even after he is executed by the Daleks in *Doctor Who – The Movie*, he returns from the grave to haunt the Doctor – still charming and darkly humorous, still evil and manipulative, but now after the Doctor's remaining regenerations to replace his own misspent life. Perhaps this is a further admission of the affinity between them...

TARDIS DATA BANK:

DESCRIPTION: FEMALE, HUMAN
TRAVELLED: *TERROR OF THE AUTONS – THE GREEN DEATH*

JOSEPHINE GRANT

On the face of it, Jo Grant is ill-equipped to be a UNIT agent. When she is foisted on the Brigadier against his will at the insistence of her uncle – a high-ranking official in the UN – he hits on the idea of assigning her to be the Doctor's assistant after Liz's return to Cambridge. But his assertion that what the Doctor needs is someone to hold his test tubes and tell him how wonderful he is, and that Miss Grant will fulfil that role 'admirably' is perhaps a cover for his hope that the Doctor's attitude will convince Jo that UNIT is not for her.

If that is the case, then he has miscalculated. Jo may start by being 'clumsy' and 'ham-fisted', as the Doctor says – ruining an experiment of his by mistaking it for a fire – but her failures and mistakes only fuel her determination to succeed. 'I've really got off to a terrific start, haven't I?' she tells Captain Yates. 'I find the man everybody's looking for, I forget where he is, and I end up by trying to blow you all sky-high.' But rather than wallow for long in self-recrimination, Jo disobeys orders and follows the Doctor to Rossini's circus – where she is able to rescue him.

Jo tells the Doctor that she is a fully qualified agent, but since she also tells him she took an A-level in General Science, only to point out later 'I didn't say I passed', this may be an exaggeration. But Jo's abilities in escapology and her enthusiasm are never in doubt. Very quickly, the Doctor and the Brigadier come to realise what an asset she really is.

In an organisation as professional and disciplined as UNIT, Jo – like the Doctor – will always stand out as an individual who is not afraid to speak her mind and follow her own instincts. In *The Green Death*, she tells the Brigadier she is going to Llanfairfach even if it means resigning from UNIT (ironically, as he has come to order her there anyway): 'I am a member of UNIT – orders, court martials and all that. But unless you arrest me, I mean unless you actually seize me and fling me into a dungeon...'

Once in Llanfairfach, she meets Professor Cliff Jones, whom she has come to admire and respect from reports of his work and ideals. Before long they are firm friends, and she admits to the Doctor that he 'reminds me of a sort of younger you'. When she agrees to marry Cliff, Captain Yates is disappointed and saddened, yet he is able to put a brave face on things and join in the celebratory party. But the Doctor is devastated. He downs his champagne in a single swallow, then leaves, alone, to drive off into the sunset.

In which the Master makes his first appearance, and so does Jo Grant...
BY ROBERT HOLMES
4 EPISODES, FIRST BROADCAST 2–23 JANUARY 1971

TARDIS DATA BANK:

DATE: NEAR FUTURE
LOCATION: UNIT HQ; FARREL PLASTICS; ROSSINI'S CIRCUS (AT TARMINSTER); 'MINISTRY OF TECHNOLOGY BEACON HILL RESEARCH ESTABLISHMENT'

A TIME LORD WARNS THE DOCTOR THAT AN OLD ADVERSARY OF HIS HAS ARRIVED ON EARTH – THE MASTER. THE MASTER IS IN LEAGUE WITH THE NESTENES WHO ARE PLANNING ANOTHER INVASION ATTEMPT (SEE *SPEARHEAD FROM SPACE*). THIS TIME, AS WELL AS CREATING THE AUTONS, THEY PLAN TO KILL HALF A MILLION PEOPLE WITH PLASTIC DAFFODILS THAT SPRAY A SUFFOCATING PLASTIC FILM OVER THEIR VICTIMS' FACES. IN THE CONFUSION, THE NESTENES WILL ARRIVE AND TAKE OVER – UNLESS THE DOCTOR, JOINED BY HIS NEW ASSISTANT JO GRANT, CAN STOP THEM…

JOURNEY INFORMATION

THE NESTENES AND AUTONS

The Doctor describes the Nestenes as '... a ruthlessly aggressive intelligent alien life form.'

Later he says, 'The Nestenes change the molecular structure of plastic... they energise it in some way and turn it into quasi-organic matter, almost like flesh and blood.' Also, 'Any plastic artefact, anything at all, can, in the Nestene sense of the word, be alive.'

The Nestenes 'animate' a murderous plastic armchair, a grotesque troll-like doll (activated by heat), a telephone flex, plastic daffodils and, of course, the Autons.

An Auton knocked over a cliff by Yates in his car simply gets up and climbs back up again. The leading Auton speaks in an electronic voice.

The invading Nestenes are a white amorphous mass manifested between two radio telescope dishes.

DAFFODILS

The killer daffodils have their instructions imprinted on every cell as a program-pattern, which reveals a nose and mouth when converted to 'visual symbols'. Activated by radio transmission, the daffodils spray plastic film over the noses and mouths of their victims. This film is then dissolved by the carbon dioxide from the lungs as the victims die.

The Master plans to set off the daffodils with a radio impulse '... which the Nestenes will send. I shall open a channel for them... When 450,000 people fall dead the country will be disrupted.' In the chaos, the Nestenes will land.

The Master describes the 'Nestene Autojet' as 'my own small contribution to their invasion plan.' The Doctor tells him it is 'vicious, complicated and inefficient'.

The Doctor: 'You know, Jo, I sometimes think that military intelligence is a contradiction in terms.'

NEW INFORMATION

THE DOCTOR

The Doctor says he should have destroyed the remaining Nestene energy sphere (found after *Spearhead from Space*), but it would have felt too much like murder.

A Time Lord tells the Doctor that the Tribunal felt he should be warned about the Master: 'You are incorrigibly meddlesome, Doctor, but we've always felt that your hearts are in the right places.' The Time Lord has come 29,000 light years.

THE TARDIS

The dematerialisation circuit is first mentioned (and seen).

The Master's TARDIS arrives at Rossini's circus as a horsebox. The Doctor uses a device with an earpiece to listen for 'certain vibrations' and then (possibly) unlock it. Scientist Philips has a Yale-type key, and the Doctor takes it from his dead hand (and makes use of it in *Colony in Space*).

The dematerialisation circuits from the two TARDISes look the same, but are incompatible. The Doctor says 'My TARDIS uses a Mark 1 dematerialisation circuit, and I tried to replace it with a Mark 2.'

UNIT

There is a river or coast (possibly a harbour) outside the UNIT Lab window.

THE MASTER

The Doctor describes the Master as, 'That Jack-a-napes, all he ever does is cause trouble,' and '... an unimaginative plodder.' The Time Lord says, 'The Master has learned a great deal since you last met him.'

The Master kills scientist Goodge and leaves his miniaturised body in his own lunch box.

The Doctor says, 'The Master can completely control the human mind... Some minds are stubborn

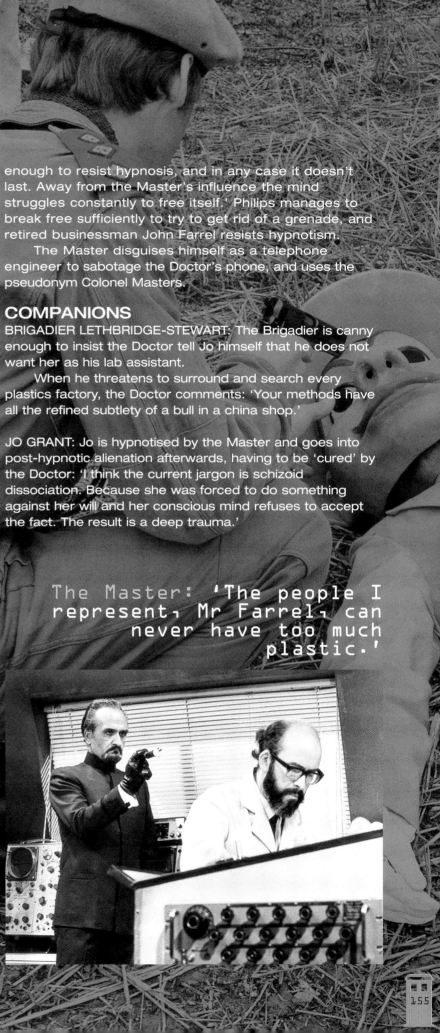

enough to resist hypnosis, and in any case it doesn't last. Away from the Master's influence the mind struggles constantly to free itself.' Philips manages to break free sufficiently to try to get rid of a grenade, and retired businessman John Farrel resists hypnotism.

The Master disguises himself as a telephone engineer to sabotage the Doctor's phone, and uses the pseudonym Colonel Masters.

COMPANIONS

BRIGADIER LETHBRIDGE-STEWART: The Brigadier is canny enough to insist the Doctor tell Jo himself that he does not want her as his lab assistant.

When he threatens to surround and search every plastics factory, the Doctor comments: 'Your methods have all the refined subtlety of a bull in a china shop.'

JO GRANT: Jo is hypnotised by the Master and goes into post-hypnotic alienation afterwards, having to be 'cured' by the Doctor: 'I think the current jargon is schizoid dissociation. Because she was forced to do something against her will and her conscious mind refuses to accept the fact. The result is a deep trauma.'

The Master: 'The people I represent, Mr Farrel, can never have too much plastic.'

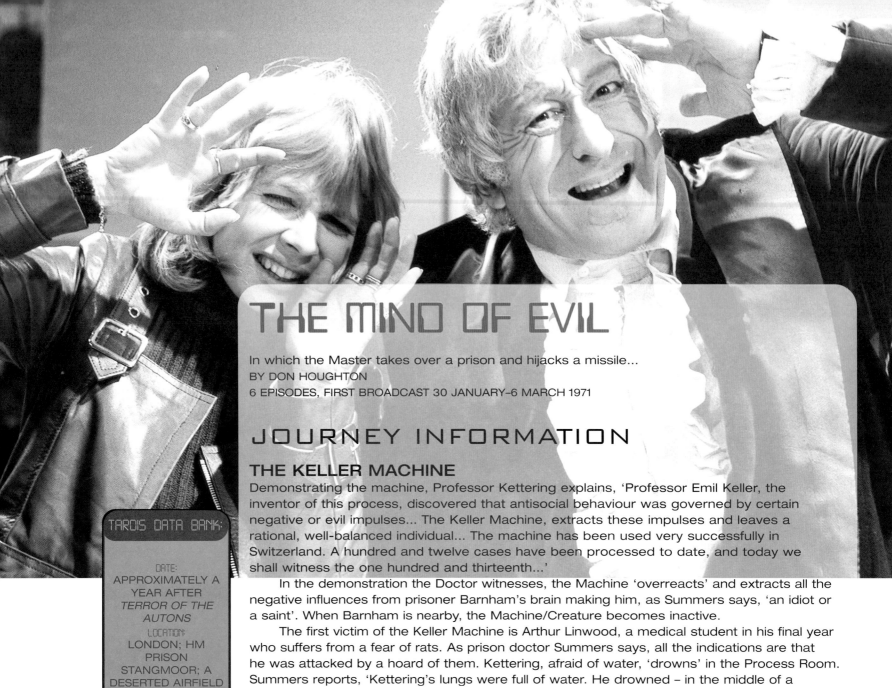

THE MIND OF EVIL

In which the Master takes over a prison and hijacks a missile...
BY DON HOUGHTON
6 EPISODES, FIRST BROADCAST 30 JANUARY–6 MARCH 1971

JOURNEY INFORMATION

THE KELLER MACHINE

Demonstrating the machine, Professor Kettering explains, 'Professor Emil Keller, the inventor of this process, discovered that antisocial behaviour was governed by certain negative or evil impulses... The Keller Machine, extracts these impulses and leaves a rational, well-balanced individual... The machine has been used very successfully in Switzerland. A hundred and twelve cases have been processed to date, and today we shall witness the one hundred and thirteenth...'

In the demonstration the Doctor witnesses, the Machine 'overreacts' and extracts all the negative influences from prisoner Barnham's brain making him, as Summers says, 'an idiot or a saint'. When Barnham is nearby, the Machine/Creature becomes inactive.

The first victim of the Keller Machine is Arthur Linwood, a medical student in his final year who suffers from a fear of rats. As prison doctor Summers says, all the indications are that he was attacked by a hoard of them. Kettering, afraid of water, 'drowns' in the Process Room. Summers reports, 'Kettering's lungs were full of water. He drowned – in the middle of a perfectly dry room.'

Inside the machine is a creature that feeds on the evil of the mind. It is a slimy brain-like creature, with an eye set in it, and the Doctor describes it as incredibly resilient: 'It would take an atomic explosion or an enormous charge of electricity to destroy that.'

As it grows in power, the machine can move by 'rippling' and dematerialising/materialising. The Doctor puts together a device that sends an electric current through a coil of cable that alternates on much the same frequency as the beta rhythms of the human brain. Once the coil is over the Keller Machine it confuses it enough to take away its power of movement. But later the machine burns through the coil and escapes. It is eventually destroyed when the Thunderbolt nerve-gas missile explodes.

NEW INFORMATION

THE DOCTOR

The Doctor tells Chinese peace conference delegate Fu Peng that Mao Tse-Tung himself gave him leave to use his personal name, Tse-Tung. Doctor speaks Hokkien fluently to Fu Peng, and Cantonese to Chinese security officer Captain Chin Lee.

TARDIS DATA BANK:

DATE:
APPROXIMATELY A
YEAR AFTER
TERROR OF THE
AUTONS
LOCATION:
LONDON; HM
PRISON
STANGMOOR; A
DESERTED AIRFIELD
AT STANHAM

THE DOCTOR AND JO
WITNESS A DEMONSTRATION
OF THE KELLER MACHINE,
WHICH ABSORBS THE EVIL
FROM HARDENED CRIMINALS.
BUT THE DOCTOR REALISES
THE MACHINE CONTAINS AN
ALIEN MIND-PARASITE
BROUGHT TO EARTH BY THE
MASTER. MEANWHILE UNIT
HANDLES SECURITY AT A
PEACE CONFERENCE AND THE
MASTER HELPS THE
PRISONERS AT STANGMOOR
TAKE CONTROL OF THE
PRISON AND HIJACK A
THUNDERBOLT NERVE-GAS
MISSILE TO FIRE AT THE
CONFERENCE...

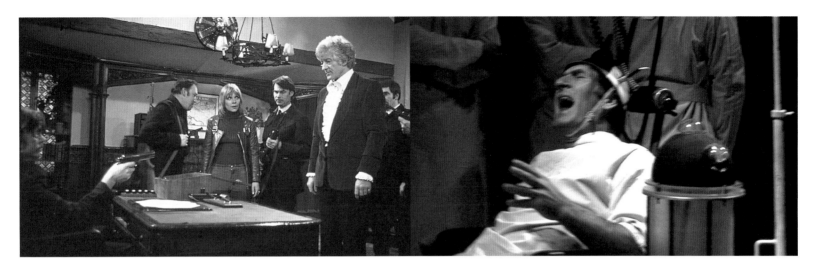

The Doctor: 'I knew there was something evil about that machine.'

When he is attacked by the Keller Machine, the Doctor hears Daleks and sees Koquillion, a Dalek, a Zarbi, Slaar, a War Machine, a Cyberman... He knows he cannot hold out against the machine.

Dr Summers says the Doctor's physical make-up is extraordinary: 'He's just not human.' The Doctor refuses the pills Summers has left, saying, 'Wrong metabolism, Jo. They'd probably kill me...'

When Jo offers him a gun, he hands it back: 'You were trained to use those things. They only make me nervous.' When she beats him at draughts he says the game is too simple, and that he is more used to three-dimensional chess.

The Doctor tells Jo about his time in the Tower of London: 'I shared a cell with a very strange chap called Raleigh... Sir Walter Raleigh. He'd got into some trouble with Queen Elizabeth – Elizabeth I that is – and he kept going on about this new vegetable of his he'd discovered called the potato...' (In *The Sensorites* the Doctor says he was sent to the Tower by Henry VIII.)

UNIT
The Brigadier has a new office in a big terraced town house. It is number 24, and near Cornwall Gardens.

THE MASTER
The Master's plan, basically, is to start a world war by destroying the peace conference with the Thunderbolt missile '... and later, when this planet is in ruins, I shall take over.'

He is again disguised as a telephone engineer, this time to tap into UNIT phone lines. He smokes a cigar, and has a large chauffeur-driven car. He reads the *Financial Times*.

In the persona of Emil Keller, he visits Stangmoor and sees Mailer – next prisoner in line to be processed. When threatened, he grabs Mailer's hand and forces him to the floor, then offers to help him take over the prison.

The Doctor is wearing a hypnotic amplifier which transmits and amplifies its power and the Master leaves the Doctor to be attacked by the Keller Machine. After the Doctor is attacked, the Master restarts one of his hearts with heart massage.

When he is himself attacked by the machine, the Master sees a huge, vampire-like Doctor laughing at him...

COMPANIONS
BRIGADIER LETHBRIDGE-STEWART: The Brigadier agrees to sort out the Keller Machine in order to get the Doctor to investigate the Chinese peace conference delegate's death. He will back up the Doctor's call for a complete ban on the Keller Process, get on to the Home Secretary '... and if that doesn't do any good, I personally will go down to Stangmoor and blow the blasted machine up myself.'

To get his team into Stangmoor, the Brigadier disguises himself as a delivery man complete with flat cap and accent: 'Morning, mate. Provisions... Nosh. Food... I've got a week's supply of food in there. And booze for the governor. Am I s'posed to go back and tell 'em you don't want it? They'll think you're barmy.'

The Brigadier: 'Throbbing in the head? Fainting? You're too delicate for intelligence work, Benton. You'd better go and lie down.'

THE BEAUTIFUL, GOLD-
SKINNED AXONS OFFER
MANKIND AXONITE, A
REMARKABLE 'THINKING
MOLECULE'. BUT THE
DOCTOR DISCOVERS THAT
THE AXONS, THEIR ORGANIC
SPACESHIP AXOS, AND THE
AXONITE ARE ALL PART OF
THE SAME VAMPIRIC
CREATURE THAT IS PLANNING
TO DRAIN ALL ENERGY FROM
THE EARTH. TO PREVENT THE
DISTRIBUTION OF AXONITE
AND DEFEAT AXOS, THE
DOCTOR IS FORCED INTO AN
UNEASY ALLIANCE WITH THE
MASTER – BUT JO SOON
WONDERS IF EITHER OF THEM
CAN BE TRUSTED…

The Master: 'I
suppose you can
take the normal
precautions
against nuclear
blast. Like
sticky tape on
the windows,
and that sort
of thing.'

THE CLAWS OF AXOS

In which the Axons transform from golden humanoids into nasty tentacled creatures…
BY BOB BAKER AND DAVE MARTIN
4 EPISODES, FIRST BROADCAST 13 MARCH–3 APRIL 1971

JOURNEY INFORMATION

NUTON NATIONAL POWER COMPLEX

The Nuton complex, on the south coast of England, provides power for the whole of Britain. Sir George Hardiman is in charge, and Winser is Head of Research.

Winser hopes to use a cyclotron to accelerate particles beyond the speed of light so they are travelling through the fourth dimension … and then investigate the nature of time itself.

AXOS

The Axon 'man' explains, 'Our worlds are uncountable light years away, on the far rim of the galaxy. Our planetary system has been crippled by extreme solar flare activity. Axos is all that remains of our culture. As you can see, our science, unlike yours, has taken an organic path. This "ship" was not built for our journey, it was grown… Grown from a single cell.'

Axonite is the source of Axos's growth technology: 'Axonite can absorb, convert, transmit and program all forms of energy … [even radiation] … Axonite is, shall we say, the chameleon of the elements. It is a thinking molecule. It uses the energy it absorbs not only to copy but to re-create and restructure any given substance.'

In fact, it is by distributing Axonite across the world that Axos will absorb the Earth's energy to feed itself. For the maximum nutrient value, Axonite must be distributed worldwide within 72 hours.

Axos tells the Doctor that, 'All things must die… Axos merely hastens the process… Slowly we will consume every particle of energy, every last cell of living matter. Earth will be sucked dry.'

While the Axons at first appear as golden humanoids, their true appearance is tentacled, blobby aliens. An Axon is able to transmit power from the Nuton reactor just by walking into it.

Axos is telepathic. Demanding the secrets of time travel from the Doctor, Axos tells him he has 'only to think the equation, the mind of Axos will do the rest.'

Axos discovers it needs '10 to the 9 mega K-tonnes' of power to create a time field big enough for Axos.

The Axons are immune to bullets. An Axon monster extrudes a tentacle that blows up a UNIT soldier – disintegrating him entirely. It then kills (but does not disintegrate) two UNIT soldiers with a touch.

The Doctor gives Axos the time travel it requires – locking it into a time loop.

NEW INFORMATION

THE DOCTOR

When the Doctor enters Axos he is identified as an 'extraterrestrial' and suffers an 'attack'.

The Doctor tells the Master, 'I don't want to spend the rest of my life as a heap of dust on a second-rate planet to a third-rate star… We either escape together or we die together.' He explains he needs the Master because: 'The Time Lords have put a block on my knowledge of dematerialisation theory…'

When leaving, the Doctor shoots American agent Bill Filer's gun from his hand with the Master's laser pistol. He offers Axos time travel if it will help him to attack the 'High Council of the Time Lords' (the first mention of this body).

He is less than happy to discover that, 'The Time Lords have programmed the TARDIS always to return to Earth.'

THE TARDIS

The Master gets into the Doctor's TARDIS with a device he uses on the lock. Trying to get the ship to work, he describes it as '... an overweight, underpowered museum piece. No proper stabiliser... Might as well try to fly a second-hand gas stove.' The Master says the TARDIS can theoretically store all the power of the Nuton complex.

A roundelled TARDIS corridor is clearly visible leading from the Control Room to the main doors. One of the roundels in the Control Room is a scanner.

Linking the TARDIS and Axos drive systems means that Axos will become a TARDIS and the TARDIS will become a part of Axos.

To escape the time loop the Doctor 'simply boosted the circuits and broke free'.

The Master's TARDIS is seen as a plain box.

UNIT

American agent Bill Filer has been sent over from Washington to help search for the Master.

UNIT in the UK is under investigation by a Ministry of Defence committee headed by an officious civil servant called Chinn, but the Brigadier says UNIT is not within the MoD. He says he is personally responsible for the Doctor – for whom there is no file.

THE MASTER

The Master has made a bargain with Axos: 'If we spared you and your TARDIS, you would lead us to this planet in return for the death of the Doctor' – and the destruction of all life on Earth.

When trying to repair the TARDIS, the Doctor tells the Master: 'You're the mechanic.'

He refuses to join with the Doctor and Axos to attack the High Council of Time Lords.

The Doctor: 'The claws of Axos are already deeply embedded in the Earth's carcass. Soon it will activate its nutrition cycle and the feast will begin.'

COLONY IN SPACE

In which the Doctor is able to leave Earth at last, on a mission for the Time Lords – and meets the Master...
BY MALCOLM HULKE
6 EPISODES, FIRST BROADCAST 10 APRIL–15 MAY 1971

TARDIS DATA BANK:

DATE: 2–5 MARCH 2472
LOCATION: UXARIEUS

THE TARDIS IS SENT BY THE TIME LORDS TO A PLANET WHERE COLONISTS ARE BEING INTIMIDATED BY A MINING COMPANY THAT WANTS THEM TO MOVE ON SO THEY CAN GET THE MINERAL RIGHTS. AN ADJUDICATOR ARRIVES FROM EARTH – THE MASTER, WHO IS ACTUALLY AFTER THE DOOMSDAY WEAPON CREATED BY AN ANCIENT RACE THAT HAS NOW DEGENERATED INTO PRIMITIVES. THE DOCTOR AND JO ARE CAUGHT IN THE CONFLICT BETWEEN MINERS AND COLONISTS, WHILE THE MASTER PLANS TO CONTROL THE UNIVERSE...

JOURNEY INFORMATION

UXARIEUS

The Doctor says the planet's atmosphere is quite healthy: 'Similar to Earth before the invention of the motor car.' Jo finds a flower with different-coloured petals. Otherwise there seems to be no vegetation and the colony's crops have repeatedly failed. Colonist Mary Ashe tells Jo, 'There's no animal life. Just a few birds and insects.' The mining company's computer predicts there is enough duralinium to build a million living units on Earth.

THE COLONY

The colony consists of a main geodesic dome, with a rocket nearby. There are 21 smaller domes across the area, which are identified by number.

Colonist Jane Leeson's calendar says Tuesday 3 March 2472 and Mary Ashe says they left Earth in 2471.

INTERPLANETARY MINING CORPORATION

IMC is a large mining combine based on Earth. Its spaceship is labelled IMC 157, although Captain Dent identifies himself as 'Survey Ship Four Three.'

Dent has ordered his subordinate Morgan to fake attacks on the colonists by giant lizards (using a robot fitted with 'claws' and a projector), to scare the colonists off the planet. But they are not easily intimidated, and after several battles, IMC is forced to leave.

THE DOOMSDAY WEAPON

The Master explains that the Primitive City was 'once the centre of a great civilisation... By genetic engineering they developed a super-race. That priest we saw must be a remnant of it... This super-race developed a Doomsday Weapon. But it was never used... Maybe it was due to a degeneration of the life strain...' The Doctor realises that the super-race became '... priests of a lunatic religion worshipping machines instead of gods.'

The Doomsday Weapon, according to the Master, '... stretches for miles all around us'. It destroys suns by making them explode. The Crab Nebula was the result of the super-race testing the weapon.

The Guardian of the Doomsday Weapon says that once the weapon was built the super-race began to decay. 'The radiation from the weapon's power source poisoned the soil of our planet...'

On the Guardian's instructions, the Doctor operates the weapon's self-destruct mechanism.

NEW INFORMATION

THE DOCTOR

The Doctor claims to be an expert in agriculture. He has a small penknife and a transparent specimen bottle in his pocket at the Leesons' dome. Later he uses a box with earpieces for him and Jo to listen in on discussions between the colonist leader, Ashe, and the Master.

He distracts a Primitive with a conjuring trick: making a coin vanish and appear first from behind Jo's ear, then on his own tongue.

When the Master offers the Doctor 'a half share in the Universe', he is tempted by the suggestion he could use that power for good, but tells the Master 'absolute power is evil'. His answer to the Master's offer is, 'What for, what's the point? ... You'll never understand, will you? I want to *see* the Universe, not rule it.'

THE TARDIS

The Doctor is making a new dematerialisation circuit that he hopes will bypass the Time Lords' homing control that brings the TARDIS back to Earth. The dematerialisation circuit goes into a small column that is pushed into the console. The TARDIS 'pops' immediately in and out of vision rather than fading (as does the Master's).

The Doctor explains to Jo that the TARDIS is bigger inside than out as it is 'dimensionally transcendental' (as he told Liz in *Spearhead from Space*). The door control is a knob on the opposite side of the console to the doors. The planet's surface is visible through the open doors.

THE MASTER'S TARDIS

The Master's TARDIS is very similar to the Doctor's though it is 'slightly more advanced'. It is disguised as an Adjudicator's spaceship. The Doctor gets in with a key he acquired in *Terror of the Autons*. The Master keeps his records in a filing cabinet.

The Master has a device that releases gas inside his TARDIS when an alarm beam is broken. He puts Jo in an upright, glass-fronted cylindrical cubicle that can be flooded with lethal gas.

THE MASTER

The Master has taken the place of Adjudicator Martin Jurgens of the Bureau of Interplanetary Affairs.

The Guardian tells him, 'You are not fit to be a god. I sense that if you have control of this weapon, you will bring only unhappiness and destruction to the entire Universe.'

COMPANIONS

JO GRANT: Jo has not been in the TARDIS before, and asks, 'Well, what have you got in there anyway?' She thinks it's 'all a game'.

THE DÆMONS

In which the devil is conjured up in an English village, UNIT faces a heat barrier, and the local church gets blown up...
BY GUY LEOPOLD
5 EPISODES, FIRST BROADCAST 22 MAY–19 JUNE 1971

JOURNEY INFORMATION

AZAL AND THE DÆMONS

The saturnine Dæmons, from the planet Damos 60,000 light years away, first came to Earth nearly 100,000 years ago. The Doctor says, 'Creatures like those have been seen over and over again throughout the history of Man. And Man has turned them into myths – gods or devils.'

Azal, last of the Dæmons, is able to grow to giant size or shrink so that he is practically invisible – releasing or absorbing heat energy in the process.

The Doctor says that the Dæmons inspired Greek civilisation, the Renaissance and the Industrial Revolution: 'All the magical traditions are just remnants of their advanced science... They help Earth, but on their own terms. It's a scientific experiment to them, just another laboratory rat.' The Master has '... established a link with the Dæmon. What worries me is the choice – domination by the Master or total annihilation... What does any scientist do with an experiment that fails – he chucks it in the rubbish bin.'

Brigadier: 'Jenkins — chap with wings there, five rounds rapid.'

He says that his 'incantation' to ward off Bok is the first line of a Venusian lullaby (which he sings in *The Curse of Peladon*). Loosely translated it goes, 'Close your eyes my darling, well three of them at least.'

For the first time the Doctor tells someone (in this case UNIT Sergeant Osgood) to 'reverse the polarity'.

When offered Azal the Dæmon's power, the Doctor emphatically refuses it.

BESSIE

Bessie can be remote-controlled to start, move, sound her horn and flash her lights. The Doctor uses Bessie to convince the villagers he is the wizard Quiquaequod, and to bring back the Master when he tries to escape.

UNIT

The UNIT helicopter is G-U.N.I.T. The Mobile HQ has the new Mark IVA condenser unit, which the Doctor uses to build a diathermic energy exchanger. It has UNIT printed on the front and UNIT symbols on the sides, plus a 'UNIT Mobile HQ' sign.

THE MASTER

The Master, calling himself Reverend Magister, has replaced Canon Smallwood as the vicar of Devil's End. Smallwood was taken ill and had to leave '... in the middle of the night, without so much as a goodbye to anyone in the village.'

The Master tells local squire Winstanley, 'Democracy, freedom, liberty. What this country needs is strength, power and decision... I am the Master. I control a power which can save this world.' He tells the villagers, 'You're all less than dust beneath my feet.'

Azal tells the Master, 'Your mind is superior to Mankind's and your will is stronger.'

After the Master is captured by UNIT, the Doctor says he wants to 'deal with him later'.

COMPANIONS

BRIGADIER LETHBRIDGE-STEWART: The Brigadier still believes in the 'robust' approach to alien menaces, calling in artillery and RAF Strike Command to blast their way past the heat barrier that has cut off Devil's End.

He tells Osgood at one point, 'You know, Sergeant, I sometimes wish I worked in a bank.'

When Yates asks the Brigadier if he fancies a dance around the maypole, the Brigadier replies, 'That's kind of you Captain Yates. But I think I'd rather have a pint.'

The Dæmon will appear three times before deciding the fate of the Earth. Azal says, 'I am the last of the Dæmons... This planet smells to me of failure. It may be that I shall destroy it.'

The Master summons Azal using '... violent emotions – fear, hatred. The emotions of a group of ordinary human beings generate an immense charge of psychokinetic energy. This, the Master channels for his own purpose.' Psionoic forces that, Miss Hawthorne says, are exactly what black magic *is*. It is by harnessing this power that the Master can animate Bok, a gargoyle from the church cavern.

Azal is eventually destroyed as he prepares to kill the Doctor – and Jo intervenes to offer herself in the Doctor's place: 'Azal couldn't face a fact as irrational and as illogical as her being prepared to give up her life for me... All his power was turned against himself.' So Azal is destroyed as Devil's End church explodes.

NEW INFORMATION

THE DOCTOR

The Doctor recognises, and is worried by, the name 'Devil's End'.

Miss Hawthorne: 'I've cast the runes. I've consulted the Talisman of Mercury. It's written in the stars — when Beltane is come tread softly for lo, the Prince himself is nigh.'

DAY OF THE DALEKS

In which the Daleks at last return – ruling a future Earth with the help of Aubrey Woods and the ape-like Ogrons...
BY LOUIS MARKS
4 EPISODES, FIRST BROADCAST 1–22 JANUARY 1972

TARDIS DATA BANK:

DATE: 11–14 SEPTEMBER, NEAR FUTURE; LATE 22ND CENTURY.
LOCATION: AUDERLY HOUSE (ABOUT 50 MILES NORTH OF LONDON) AND SURROUNDING AREA, AND EQUIVALENT LOCATIONS IN 22ND CENTURY INCLUDING LABOUR CAMP AND DALEK HEADQUARTERS IN EARTH SECTOR ONE

GUERILLAS TIME-JUMP BACK FROM THE 22ND CENTURY TO ASSASSINATE SIR REGINALD STYLES – A DIPLOMAT WORKING FOR WORLD PEACE. THE DOCTOR DISCOVERS THEY ARE FROM A FUTURE WHERE THE DALEKS HAVE INVADED THE EARTH (FOLLOWING WARS PRECIPITATED BY STYLES'S DESTRUCTION OF THE PEACE CONFERENCE). WITH THE DALEKS DESPERATE TO MAINTAIN THEIR VERSION OF HISTORY, THE DOCTOR AND JO FIND THEMSELVES IN A TOTALITARIAN FUTURE, WHERE THEY MUST DISCOVER WHAT REALLY HAPPENED AND PREVENT IT...

JOURNEY INFORMATION

CONTROLLER EARTH SECTOR ONE

The Controller explains that the Daleks '... chose a few humans to get things going again, to organise the remaining population. My family have been Controllers in this area for three generations... We have helped make things better for the others. We have gained concessions – *I* have saved lives.' But guerilla leader Monia says, 'You don't know how much blood there is on his hands.'

The Controller allows the Doctor and Jo to return to the twentieth century, when the Doctor tells him: 'You spoke of the war. All those years of suffering and starvation. Well, I can prevent all that happening, you know.'

Confronted with his 'crime' by the Daleks, the Controller tells the Daleks defiantly, 'Who knows, I may have helped to exterminate you.'

THE DALEKS

The Doctor describes the Daleks as the most evil, ruthless life form in the Cosmos.

The Daleks are painted grey, with the exception of the leader which is predominantly gold. They are afraid of the Doctor: 'Doc-tor? Did you say Doc-tor?' a Dalek demands. 'The Doctor is an enemy of the Daleks. He must be found at once and exterminated.' They use their mind analysis machine to establish the Doctor's identity.

They have turned the Earth into a factory run like a giant labour camp. The Dalek empire is continually expanding and they need a constant flow of raw materials.

The factories are run with typical Dalek ruthlessness: 'There has been a drop in recent production figures... For the next work period, target figures will be increased by ten per cent... Only the weak will die. Inefficient workers slow down production.'

Bullets and mortars have no apparent effect on Daleks during an attack on Auderly House.

THE DALEK INVASION

The Controller explains how the Daleks invaded: 'Towards the end of the twentieth century, a series of wars broke out. There was a hundred years of nothing but killing and destruction. Seven-eighths of the world's population was wiped out. The rest were living in holes in the ground – starving. Reduced to the level of animals.' Then the Daleks arrived. 'Men who were strong enough, of course, were sent down the mines. The rest work in factories... They need a constant flow of raw materials. Their empire is expanding...'

History says that Sir Reginald Styles pretended to be working for peace but just wanted power for himself. Monia describes how Styles managed to lure the world leaders to a remote country house, for a peace conference, and that there was a devastating explosion. Styles was also killed – the assumption being that he set and mistimed a bomb. 'There were accusations, counter-accusations, and then the wars began. That was the turning point.'

The Doctor: 'There are many different kinds of ghosts, Jo. Ghosts from the past, and ghosts from the future.'

THE OGRONS

The ape-like Ogrons are a form of higher anthropoid that used to live in scattered communities on one of the outer planets. They seem to be immune to the Doctor's Venusian karate, but Jo fells one with a blow to the head with a carafe of wine.

The Controller says they are '... as loyal as they are stupid. They will never be a match for human guerillas.'

THE TIME PARADOX

The guerillas' plan is to go back in time (using Dalek technology) and kill Styles before he can destroy the peace conference. The Doctor says that the guerrillas cannot return to 12 September and once more try to kill Styles because of the Blinovitch Limitation Effect.

It is the Doctor who realises how the wars were really started by the guerilla Shura, sent to kill Styles: 'Don't you see – this has happened before? ... You went back to change history. But you didn't change anything. You became a part of it... If Styles didn't cause that explosion, somebody else did... Isn't that exactly what [Shura] would have done? One last suicidal attempt to carry out his orders... You're

trapped in a temporal paradox. Styles didn't cause that explosion and start the wars. You did it yourselves.'

NEW INFORMATION

THE DOCTOR

The Doctor enjoys cheese and red wine at Styles's house and tells Jo, 'You know, I remember saying to old Napoleon, "Boney," I said, "always remember an army marches on its stomach."'

He shoots an Ogron with the guerillas' gun, and says that the Daleks have been his bitterest enemies for many years.

The Daleks' mind-analysis machine almost kills the Doctor just by establishing his identity.

THE TARDIS

The Doctor and Jo meet themselves when the Doctor is working on the TARDIS console in his lab. The Doctor says that once you start tampering with time, '...the oddest things start happening... It's a freak effect. It's very unlikely to occur again.'

THE CURSE OF PELADON

In which the Doctor meets the Ice Warriors again and encounters Alpha Centauri, a hermaphrodite hexapod...
BY BRIAN HAYLES
4 EPISODES, FIRST BROADCAST 29 JANUARY–19 FEBRUARY 1972

JOURNEY INFORMATION

PELADON

Peladon is a medieval society with little technology that is applying to join the Galactic Federation. It is ruled by King Peladon of Peladon (though he is yet to be crowned). Hepesh is High Priest of the royal beast Aggedor, Torbis is Chancellor. King Peladon calls them brothers but this may be a term of affection and common purpose rather than familial relationship.

Only men of rank and females of royal blood may set foot in the Royal Throne Room in the Citadel of Peladon. The penalty for trespass is death.

Hepesh tells the Doctor he is betraying his king because he is afraid the federation will exploit Peladon for minerals and corrupt them with technology.

AGGEDOR

Hepesh explains that the legend of the curse of Peladon is centuries old and concerns the royal beast of Peladon. 'It is written "Mighty is Aggedor, fiercest of all the beasts of Peladon." Young men would hunt it to prove their courage. Its fur trims our royal garment, its head is our royal emblem. It is also written there will come a day when the spirit of Aggedor would rise again to warn and defend his royal master King Peladon. For at that day a stranger will appear in the land, bringing peril to Peladon and great tribulation to his kingdom.'

But the Doctor discovers that, 'Aggedor is no spirit, Your Majesty, but a truly noble beast. His manifestation, as you call it, is solid, hairy fact... Hepesh found that, on a high mountain, a few still existed. So he captured one, trained it, and kept it hidden in the tunnels below the citadel ready to pop out whenever he needed a bit of haunting.'

THE MARTIANS – DELEGATE IZLYR AND SUB-DELEGATE SSORG

Izlyr is from Mars, which has presumably been repopulated. The Doctor says the Ice Warriors are 'a savage and warlike race' and is suspicious of them. Izlyr tells Jo the Martians were once a race of warriors, 'but now we reject violence, except in self-defence...' He says that Mars and the world of the delegate Arcturus are old enemies, and Ssorg killing Arcturus could lead to war.

DELEGATE ALPHA CENTAURI

Delegate Alpha Centauri 'member of the Galactic Federation' is a hermaphrodite hexapod with a high-pitched voice, one large eye and six arms. He is naturally nervous –

'a coward by instinct' according to Izlyr – and keen to cancel the conference as soon as he hears of trouble.

DELEGATE ARCTURUS

Arcturus resembles a large, tentacled head, kept in a mobile life-support system with a built-in weapon and bugging device. He mentions his 'memory circuits', so may be a cyborg. Politically, Arcturus is devious, and Izlyr describes him as 'a coward by logic'.

Izlyr mentions that the 'world of Arcturus' lacks mineral deposits, which Peladon has in abundance – hence a secret deal between Arcturus and Hepesh.

NEW INFORMATION

THE DOCTOR

The Doctor builds a device incorporating a light and a spinning mirror to pacify Aggedor, aided by a Venusian lullaby sung to the tune of 'God Rest You, Merry Gentlemen' (which he used as an incantation in *The Dæmons*).

THE TARDIS

The Doctor refers to 'routine landing procedures'. These start with checking the scanners, which don't work due to a tiny fault in the interstitial beam synthesiser. The TARDIS falls off a cliff (as in *The Romans*) prompting the Doctor to comment 'The TARDIS may have its faults, but it is indestructible.'

Although he initially thinks this is the TARDIS's first flight since he got it working again, the Doctor later decides it was the Time Lords who sent them to Peladon.

COMPANIONS

JO GRANT: Jo is 'all dolled up for a night on the town with Mike Yates.' King Peladon appreciates the effort, telling her: 'You bring a welcome beauty to a serious occasion.' Later, he proposes marriage although she is not impressed. When it is time to leave, Jo tells the king, 'I'm very, very fond of you. But I can't stay, really,' and kisses him.

Jo: 'Well, I'm sorry to disappoint you, but a marriage has not been arranged. To coin a phrase, we're just good friends.'

BEHIND THE SCENES

DOCTOR WHO?

While it is an 'in-joke' with the audience that the Earth delegate arriving at the end of *The Curse of Peladon* demands, 'What doctor – doctor who?' when she hears of him, the question of what the Doctor's real name is – or even if he has one – has never been resolved. Ian observes very early on that his name is not Foreman, although this is the name on the gates of the junkyard where the TARDIS is hidden, and also the adopted name of the Doctor's granddaughter Susan.

In *The War Games*, when we discover the Doctor is a Time Lord, we are still not told his name. The other members of the Doctor's race also seem to use only titles or epithets – the Meddling Monk (*The Time Meddler* and *The Daleks' Master Plan*) and later the Master (from *Terror of the Autons* onwards). In *The Three Doctors*, the Time Lords we meet have titles rather than names, with the possible exception of Omega.

It is not until *The Deadly Assassin* shows a much broader spectrum of life on the Time Lord planet of Gallifrey, that any others of the Doctor's race are named. Whatever the distinction between the Time Lords and other inhabitants of Gallifrey, Cardinal Borusa and Chancellor Goth are certainly Time Lords, and former presidents such as Pandad are named. Most significant are the first references in this story to the founder of Time Lord society – Rassilon.

On this evidence, it seems likely that the Doctor does have a name, but simply chooses not to use it. In *The Armageddon Factor*, Drax – who was at the academy with the Doctor – calls the Doctor 'Theta Sigma' but it seems likely this is a student number or possibly an achieved grade (he also refers to the Doctor getting his doctorate). In *The Happiness Patrol* the Doctor says it was a nickname.

Although WOTAN insists in *The War Machines* that 'Doctor Who is required' there is no direct evidence that this is actually his name. The Doctor himself has used many names, though none of them seems likely to be the real one. In *The Gunfighters* he calls himself Doctor Caligari – possibly after the Expressionist film *The Cabinet of Doctor Caligari*. 'Doctor Who?' Wyatt Earp asks, to which the Doctor replies, 'Quite right.' In fact, he does on occasion seem taken with the notion of calling himself 'Doctor Who' – treating it as a joke, for example, when it is suggested by Lady Cranleigh in *Black Orchid*.

In *The Highlanders*, he introduces himself as a German – 'Doctor von Wer, at your service.' ('Wer' being German for 'who'.) When ffinch queries 'Doctor who?' the Doctor replies, 'That's what I said.' In the next story, *The Underwater Menace*, he signs the note he sends to Zaroff in Episode 1 'Doctor W'.

But in *The Wheel in Space* Jamie is forced to tell Gemma Corwyn the Doctor's name. He takes the name from the front of Corwyn's electronic stethoscope to give the pseudonym 'John Smith' and it is this more than any other name that has become associated with the Doctor. Although he seems less than impressed with Jamie's improvisation, when the Doctor 'needs' a name while exiled to Earth he tells the Brigadier that he can call him 'Smith – Dr John Smith' (*Spearhead from Space*).

Coincidentally, this is also the name chosen by Chang Lee when he accompanies the unconscious Doctor to hospital in *Doctor Who – The Movie*.

THE SEA DEVILS

In which the Master joins forces with the Sea Devils to take over the world, unless the Doctor and the Royal Navy can stop them...
BY MALCOLM HULKE
6 EPISODES, FIRST BROADCAST 26 FEBRUARY–1 APRIL 1972

TARDIS DATA BANK:

DATE: NEAR FUTURE
LOCATION: SOUTH
COAST OF
ENGLAND – HMS
SEASPITE,
MASTER'S PRISON
AND ENVIRONS.

IMPRISONED IN A CASTLE ON
AN ISLAND FOR HIS CRIMES,
THE MASTER HAS PERSUADED
GOVERNOR TRENCHARD HE
CAN CONTACT AND EXPOSE
ENEMY AGENTS. IN FACT HE IS
HELPING THE UNDERWATER
REPTILES – 'COUSINS' OF THE
SILURIANS – WHO WANT TO
RECLAIM 'THEIR' PLANET AND
ARE SINKING SHIPS IN THE
AREA. THE DOCTOR AND JO
ENLIST THE HELP OF CAPTAIN
HART AND THE ROYAL NAVY
AGAINST THE SEA DEVILS. BUT
WHILE THE DOCTOR IS KEEN
TO PROMOTE A PEACEFUL
SETTLEMENT, THE MASTER IS
WORKING TO ENSURE THERE
IS ALL-OUT WAR...

JOURNEY INFORMATION

COLONEL GEORGE TRENCHARD

George Trenchard is the governor of the Master's prison. He used to be the governor of a small colony, which claimed independence soon after he arrived. The Master has used Trenchard's vanity and patriotism to convince him that together they will foil the plans of enemy agents. 'Just think of it, Trenchard,' the Master tells him, 'you will be responsible for exposing some of the most dangerous saboteurs this country has ever known...'

But when Trenchard realises the truth, he goes to battle the Sea Devils, telling a guard, 'I shall attend to the security of my prisoner.' He calmly shoots one Sea Devil four times, killing it before he dies.

THE SEA DEVILS

The Sea Devils are related to the Silurians – although the Doctor points out that *Silurian* '... is a complete misnomer. The chap who discovered them must have got the period wrong. No, properly speaking they should have been called the Eocenes... This is a different species, completely adapted to life under water... They still think of Earth as their planet, Jo. They want it back. As far as they're concerned Man is just an ape who got above himself.' Their astronomers predicted that a great catastrophe would end all life on the face of the Earth, and so they went into hibernation, but they never awoke.

The Master discovers that, 'During millions of years of hibernation, the reactivation machinery has deteriorated. I now find it necessary to build a trigger mechanism for it ... by constructing a SONAR device analogous to the laser. With this I can not only pinpoint and revive the base by the sea fort, but every base in the world.'

A Sea Devil says, 'There are many thousands of our people in hibernation in this base. We have other colonies hidden all round the world. We shall be the victors in the war against Mankind.' The Doctor almost succeeds in persuading them they can live in peace with Man.

The Doctor: 'They still think of Earth as their planet Jo. They want it back. As far as they're concerned Man is just an ape who got above himself.'

The Sea Devils speak in loud whispers, and are armed with hand-held guns they holster on their belts.

NEW INFORMATION

THE DOCTOR

The Doctor says of the Master, 'He used to be a friend of mine once. A very good friend. In fact you might almost say that we were at school together.'

The Master is a brilliant technician, but gets the Doctor to look at plans to build a 'trigger mechanism' for the Sea Devils' hibernation systems. Under the guise of improving the design, the Doctor creates a machine that temporarily disables the Sea Devils on the base and then destroys their base when wired in. It has a self-destruct mechanism so it cannot be turned off. The Doctor justifies destroying the Sea Devils and their base as necessary to prevent a war.

THE MASTER

The Doctor reminds the Master, 'Quite a few people were in favour of having you executed.' The Master implies that the Doctor spoke up for him.

He pretends to be a changed man: 'I wish that something like this had happened a long time ago... It's given me a chance to reconsider my life... I do have a great deal for which to repent.' But he will not tell the Doctor where his TARDIS is.

He watches *Clangers* on television, whistling along. And pretends to Trenchard he thinks they are real: 'It seems to be a rather interesting extraterrestrial life form.'

Like the Doctor, the Master is an expert swordsman.

He says what he can gain is '... the pleasure of seeing the human race exterminated, Doctor. The human race of which you are so fond. That will be a reward in itself.'

COMPANIONS

JO GRANT: Jo can ride a motorbike, and is able to overpower two guards at the prison then escape into the grounds. She picks the lock of the Doctor's handcuffs, and stuns the guard with a karate chop. She also abseils down a cliff and pilots a hovercraft.

Captain Hart: 'This place is supposed to be top secret. People are treating it like Brighton beach.'

Sondergaard: 'Strange things are happening on Solos, Doctor. Not just to the people — the plants, the soil and the weather. The whole flora and fauna of Solos.'

THE MUTANTS

In which the Doctor travels to a distant planet where the local population is mutating into a race of hideous insect-like creatures...

BY BOB BAKER AND DAVE MARTIN

6 EPISODES, FIRST BROADCAST 8 APRIL – 13 MAY 1972

TARDIS DATA BANK:

DATE: 30TH CENTURY

LOCATION: SOLOS; SKYBASE ONE

THE TIME LORDS SEND THE DOCTOR AND JO TO DELIVER A CANISTER TO THE PLANET SOLOS. THEY ARRIVE TO FIND THE PLANET UNDER COLONIAL RULE FROM EARTH. IT IS DUE FOR INDEPENDENCE, BUT THE MARSHAL IS PLANNING TO STAY, ALTERING THE ATMOSPHERE SO IT IS UNSUITABLE FOR THE SOLONIANS. MEANWHILE, THE SOLONIANS ARE BEGINNING TO MUTATE INTO GROTESQUE INSECT-LIKE CREATURES. IS THIS A RESULT OF THE MARSHAL'S EXPERIMENTS, OR A CYCLE OF NATURAL CHANGE...

JOURNEY INFORMATION

SOLOS

The atmosphere of Solos is unbreathable during daylight for humans without an oxymask as the soil contains a nitrogen isotope released by the ultraviolet rays of the sun, which causes a kind of poisonous mist.

Solonian chief Ky says, 'Once we were farmers and hunters. The land was green, the rivers ran clear and the air was sweet to breathe. Then the Overlords came bringing Earth's poisons with them, calling it progress. We toiled in their mines – we became slaves.'

Earth has ruled the planet for 500 years, mining for thaesium. The scientist Jaeger says Solos used to be '... one of the richest fuel sources in the galaxy,' but now the supply is exhausted.

Solos takes 3,000 Earth years to circle its sun, and does not tilt on its axis. Tablets that the Doctor brings to Ky depict the four seasons, headed by a picture of the sun in its elliptical orbit. Stick figures appear in the spring, other figures in the summer, and 'mini-suns', which the Doctor guesses are something to do with thaesium radiation, in the autumn...

THE MARSHAL

After he has had the colonial Administrator assassinated, the Marshal assumes command of Skybase One. He has put years of his life into Solos – his whole career, he tells the Administrator, who replies, 'Don't worry, old chap, we'll find you something. The Bureau of Records, perhaps.'

The Marshal is angry that the Earth Council is sending an investigator, though as Jaeger points out, 'Your conspiracies should give him plenty of scope.'

The Marshal plans to change the atmosphere of Solos so it is breathable by humans (but not Solonians), and then call

The Doctor: 'You do realise, Professor, that the slightest accident at this stage in the proceedings and we'd all reverse instantly into antimatter... We'd all become un-people un-doing un-things un-together. Fascinating.'

Solos 'New Earth' and rule from the Skybase. The investigator and his crew will become his first, involuntary, colonists.

PROFESSOR SONDERGAARD

Sondergaard, who has been living on Solos, explains, 'I was young, ambitious, I hoped to make many discoveries here. But my first was that Solos had become a slave colony. I was unwise enough to try to inform Earth Control. The Marshal intercepted my report. I was lucky to escape with my life. I managed to reach the caves, I've been here ever since...'

He agrees to stay and see as many Solonians as possible through to final-form mutation.

THE MUTANTS

The Solonian people are mutating into huge insectoid creatures – they think as a result of the Marshal's experiments. The number of 'Mutts' increases as Solos moves towards summer – and all converge on the disused thaesium mines.

The Doctor realises that the change is an accelerated genetic metamorphosis, an 'adaptive' change as the environment alters with the seasons, albeit hastened and confused by the Marshal's work. The Mutts are merely an interim stage. The crystal from the thaesium mine is essential for the change – a biocatalytic agent that hastens the mutations. The final mutation is a glowing humanoid creature that communicates by thought transference and

glows with radioactive energy. The mutated Ky says, 'There is little I cannot do now.'

NEW INFORMATION

THE DOCTOR

The Doctor is furious at the Marshal and Jaeger's plans for Solos. 'Genocide as a side effect?' he says. 'You ought to write a paper on that, Professor.' He later tells the Inquisitor this is 'the most brutal and callous series of crimes against a defenceless people it has ever been my misfortune to encounter.'

The Doctor evidently enjoys the challenge of translating the tablets with Sondergaard, and tells him that the thaesium radiation would affect 'any man' but that he does not need a protective suit.

The Doctor can also breathe the atmosphere of Solos without an oxymask.

THE TARDIS

The TARDIS is operated by remote control by the Time Lords – the light flashes and the door opens. They send their message in a sphere keyed to open only for the intended recipient. According to the Doctor, 'They only send these things in a real emergency, Jo. It's top priority. Three-line whip.'

THE TIME MONSTER

In which the Master uses the ancient power of Atlantis and attacks UNIT with a knight on horseback, Roundhead troops and a V1...
BY ROBERT SLOMAN
6 EPISODES, FIRST BROADCAST 20 MAY–24 JUNE 1972

TARDIS DATA BANK:

DATE: NEAR FUTURE; c1500BC
LOCATION: THE NEWTON INSTITUTE, NEAR WOOTTON, CAMBRIDGE; ATLANTIS

THE MASTER IS USING A TIME EXPERIMENT AND AN ANCIENT ATLANTEAN CRYSTAL IN AN ATTEMPT TO SUMMON AND CONTROL KRONOS – A CHRONOVORE THAT 'EATS' TIME ITSELF. WITH THE BRIGADIER FROZEN IN TIME, SERGEANT BENTON REGRESSED TO A BABY AND CAPTAIN YATES UNDER ATTACK FROM KNIGHTS IN ARMOUR, ROUNDHEADS AND A V-1 FLYING BOMB, THE DOCTOR AND JO RETURN TO ANCIENT ATLANTIS FOR A FINAL CONFRONTATION WITH KRONOS...

JOURNEY INFORMATION

TOMTIT
TOMTIT stands for Transmission of Matter Through Interstitial Time. It can break down solid objects and transmit them from one place to another. Scientist Ruth Ingram explains that, 'Time isn't smooth, it's made up of little bits... Temporal atoms, so to speak. So if one could push something through the interstices between them, it would be outside our space–time continuum altogether.'

KRONOS AND THE CHRONOVORES
The Doctor says the Chronovores are creatures that exist outside space–time: '... time-eaters, who will swallow a life as quickly as a boa-constrictor can swallow a rabbit, fur and all.'

Ruth says Kronos was from Greek legend – the Titan who ate his children. The Doctor points out that one of the children was Poseidon, the god of Atlantis. He says that, 'Kronos, a living legend, was drawn into time by the priests of Atlantis using that crystal as its centre... And your friend the professor is trying to use that crystal as it was used 4,000 years ago to capture the Chronovore.'

Kronos knows the Doctor 'of old'. In her female form she says, 'Shapes mean nothing... I can be all things – a destroyer, a creator. I am beyond good and evil as you know it.'

She promises the Master: 'Torment, of course. The pain he has given so freely will be returned to him in full.'

NEW INFORMATION

THE DOCTOR
The Doctor tells Jo that his reactions are ten times faster than hers. He is less affected by the slow-time field created

The Doctor: 'If the Master opens the floodgates of Kronos's power, all order and all structure will be swept away, and nothing will be left but chaos.'

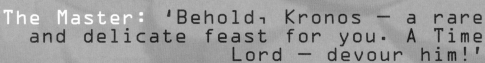

The Master: 'Behold, Kronos — a rare and delicate feast for you. A Time Lord — devour him!'

by TOMTIT. The Doctor builds a Time Flow Analogue from a wine bottle, forks, a corkscrew, a coffee-maker, a bunch of keys, a bottle of ink and a cup of tea leaves. This 'jams' the Master's work with TOMTIT. The Doctor says, 'We used to make them at school to spoil each other's time experiments.'

THE TARDIS

The Master tells Krassis, Atlantean High Priest of Kronos, that the Doctor's TARDIS cannot be destroyed (and later refers to it as indestructible).

The Doctor is able to use his time sensor as a homing device and materialises his TARDIS inside the Master's.

The interior of the TARDIS – particularly the roundels on the walls – has changed. The Doctor calls it 'a spot of redecoration'. The scanner is a roundel, and the outside world is visible through the open doors.

The Doctor says that as they are travelling outside time, journeys take no time at all. 'Of course it always seems to take a long time, but that depends upon the mood I suppose.' He means the TARDIS's mood. Jo says he talks as if the TARDIS were alive. 'Depends on what you mean by alive, doesn't it. You take old Bessie, for instance...'

The Doctor mentions the TARDIS's telepathic circuits (TARDISes communicate telepathically). The TARDIS relays the Doctor's thoughts to Jo when he is in the timevortex.

TIME RAM

The Doctor explains that with the two TARDISes operating on the same frequency, if they materialised at the same

point '... the atoms making up this TARDIS would occupy precisely the same space and time as the atoms making up the Master's TARDIS... Extinction. Utter annihilation.'

UNIT

The Brigadier says that every section of UNIT now has the search for the Master written into its standing orders 'Priority A1...'

The Brigadier takes over the investigation at Wootton under '... subsection 3a of the preamble to the seventh enabling act, paragraph 24g if I remember rightly.'

THE MASTER

The Master is masquerading as Professor Thascales (Greek for 'Master'), complete with false accent. He is able to imitate the Brigadier's voice, but by calling Benton 'my dear fellow' he falls foul of the 'tribal taboos of army etiquette. I find it difficult to identify with such primitive absurdities.'

When the Doctor tells him he is risking the total destruction of the entire cosmos, the Master replies, 'Of course I am – all or nothing, literally. What a glorious alternative.' But he is willing to beg Kronos for his life (before slipping away).

COMPANIONS

JO GRANT: Jo completes the time ram when the Doctor cannot bring himself to do it: 'Think of all those millions of people who will die. Think of all those millions of people who will never be born,' she says.

THE THREE DOCTORS

In which the Doctor meets his former selves and does battle with Omega in a world of antimatter...
BY BOB BAKER AND DAVE MARTIN
4 EPISODES, FIRST BROADCAST 30 DECEMBER 1972–20 JANUARY 1973

TARDIS DATA BANK:

DATE: NEAR FUTURE
LOCATION: MINSBRIDGE
WILDLIFE
SANCTUARY; UNIT
HQ; THE TIME LORD
PLANET; OMEGA'S
DOMAIN IN THE
BLACK HOLE

WITH THEIR POWER BEING
DRAINED AWAY THROUGH A
BLACK HOLE, THE TIME
LORDS HAVE NO OPTION BUT
TO SEND THE DOCTOR TO
INVESTIGATE – AND THE
PROBLEM IS SO SEVERE THE
ONLY HELP THEY CAN OFFER
HIM IS HIS FORMER
INCARNATIONS. THE FIRST
DOCTOR IS CAUGHT IN A TIME
EDDY, ABLE ONLY TO
OBSERVE AND ADVISE, BUT
THE SECOND DOCTOR JOINS
JO, BENTON, THE BRIGADIER
AND HIMSELF IN A WORLD OF
ANTIMATTER TO COMBAT
OMEGA – ONE OF THE
DOCTOR'S GREATEST LIFE-
LONG HEROES WHO
PROVIDED THE TIME LORDS
WITH THE POWER SOURCE TO
CREATE TIME TRAVEL…

JOURNEY INFORMATION

THE TIME LORDS

The Time Lord Chancellor is addressed as 'Your Excellency' by the President of the High Council. The President seems to defer to the Chancellor but does not take his advice.

The first (and most important) law of time expressly forbids the Doctor to meet his other selves.

OMEGA

Omega was the solar engineer who provided the power source that gave the Time Lords time travel. The Doctor says, 'Omega provided that energy by a fantastic feat of solar engineering. We thought he was destroyed, instead of which he ended up here. It seems that his imprisonment was the price of our freedom to travel in time.'

Omega claims, 'Without me there would be no time travel. You and our fellow Time Lords would still be locked in your own time, as puny as those creatures you now so graciously protect.' He knew his mission was dangerous, '... but I completed it, and I did not expect to be abandoned. Many thousands of years ago, when I left our planet all this was then a star, until I arranged its detonation.' History says he was lost in the supernova.

His antimatter world reflects his mood – thunder rolls when he is angry. Omega says, 'I created this world through the power of my will.' But he cannot escape, as to leave means his will no longer holds it together. Omega wears a mask to combat the corrosive effect of the singularity beam that powers his world, but beneath the mask he no longer exists – he has already corroded away and only his will lives on.

SINGULARITY

The antimatter world exists, the Doctor says, because of the phenomenon of singularity: 'A point in space–time which can exist only inside a black hole. We are in a black hole in a world

Omega: 'You dare threaten to destroy me? You wish to fight the will of Omega? Then you shall. But you will fight the dark side of my mind.'

of antimatter very close to this point of singularity where all the known physical laws cease to exist... Now, Omega has got control of singularity and has learned to use the vast forces locked up inside the black hole.'

NEW INFORMATION

THE DOCTOR

The three Doctors are able to establish 'contact' and share information and ideas telepathically.

The Doctor demonstrates that Omega's world is a 'scientific conjuring trick' by making a pencil vanish, then turn into a bunch of flowers. He says of Omega, 'All my life I've known of you and honoured you as our greatest hero,' and is sad at Omega's fate: 'I promised him his freedom and I gave it to him – the only freedom he could ever have...'

After defeating Omega, the Doctor is given back *his* freedom – he gets a new dematerialisation circuit and his memory of time travel law is restored by the Time Lords.

THE TARDIS

The Second Doctor says he cannot open the door without first turning off the force field. The Brigadier's radio won't work with the force field on until the Doctor boosts it through the TARDIS communications circuit.

COMPANIONS

BRIGADIER LETHBRIDGE-STEWART: Initially unwilling to accept there are two Doctors around, the Brigadier

assumes 'his' Doctor has changed again: 'So long as he does the job, he can wear what face he likes.'

It is his first time in the TARDIS, and he observes, 'So this is what you've been doing with UNIT funds and equipment all this time. How's it done, some sort of optical illusion?'

He is the last to leave Omega's world, saluting the Doctors. Back at HQ, he says, 'Wonderful chap, both of him.' Later he tells the Doctor, 'One of you is enough. More than enough...'

BEHIND THE SCENES

AVAILABILITY

While the first draft of *The Three Doctors* (at one point called *The Black Hole*) was written to include the First Doctor in a more active role, William Hartnell's failing health meant that he was only able to perform seated, and reading his lines.

The script was therefore rewritten with the First Doctor's pyramid-like transportation caught in a 'time eddy' so that he could merely appear on the TARDIS and Time Lord scanners to advise. Hartnell's scenes were filmed ahead of the rest of the production and then played back on the scanners for the other actors to interact with. He was able to read his lines from a board off-camera.

Also in the original script, the Second Doctor was joined by his long-time companion Jamie. But in the event, actor Frazer Hines was unavailable. In rewrites, his role was largely given to Sergeant Benton.

Jo: 'It seems to me we have a choice of being shot by those idiots on the ship, or eaten by those horrors out there.

TARDIS DATA BANK:

DATE: UNKNOWN
LOCATION: INTER MINOR; INSIDE THE MINISCOPE

THE DOCTOR AND JO ARRIVE ON THE *SS BERNICE* – A SHIP THAT DISAPPEARED ON 4 JUNE 1926. ON BOARD THE SHIP, THE CREW GO THROUGH THE SAME ACTIONS TIME AND AGAIN AND THE SHIP IS ATTACKED BY A DINOSAUR. THE DOCTOR DISCOVERS THEY ARE INSIDE A MINISCOPE – A COLLECTION OF MINIATURISED 'SPECIMENS' INCLUDING THE FEROCIOUS CARNIVOROUS DRASHIGS. OUTSIDE THE SCOPE, KALIK HOPES TO ALLOW THE DRASHIGS TO ESCAPE SO HE HAS AN EXCUSE TO DEPOSE PRESIDENT ZARB. THE DOCTOR MUST HELP SHOWMAN VORG AND HIS ASSISTANT, SHIRNA, TO MEND THE FAILING SCOPE AND GET BACK INSIDE TO RESCUE JO...

CARNIVAL OF MONSTERS

In which the Doctor and Jo face the hideous Drashigs inside the workings of a futuristic peep show...
BY ROBERT HOLMES
4 EPISODES, FIRST BROADCAST 27 JANUARY–17 FEBRUARY 1973

JOURNEY INFORMATION

INTER MINOR
Under President Zarb, Inter Minor is, after thousands of years, ending its xenophobic isolation instigated after a great space plague. Amusement is prohibited, but senior official Pletrac says that Zarb is considering lifting that restriction, as there is thinking that the latest violence among the Functionaries is caused by lack of amusement. The Functionaries are in effect slaves, but have become discontented.

Because the Doctor arrived illegally concealed inside the miniscope, Pletrac says regulations dictate that he will be sent to the ICCA – the Inner Constellation Corrective Authority.

COMMISSIONER KALIK
Kalik is President Zarb's brother, and is planning to replace him. He has sabotaged an eradicator weapon to allow the Drashigs to escape from the miniscope and create a crisis, after which he can depose Zarb: 'The Central Bureau would be forced to admit to serious miscalculation,' and Zarb would be blamed. But fellow Minorian, Orum, is not convinced the plan will work: 'Upon reflection, one is conscious of certain flaws... One gathers the intention is

the escape of these Drashigs in order to cause a disaster that will reflect badly on President Zarb and his regime... To this end, one has sabotaged the eradicator in order to leave the city defenceless... Is it not possible that one might oneself become part of that disaster? ... One has no wish to be devoured by alien monstrosities, even in the cause of political progress.'

In fact, Kalik and Orum are both killed by the escaping Drashigs.

THE MINISCOPE

The miniscope contains many miniaturised environments, and creatures going through repetitive patterns of behaviour. These include the Drashigs, the crew and passengers of the *SS Bernice*, Ogrons and even Cybermen. 'Historically speaking, this collection is a bit of a jumble,' the Doctor observes.

The events taking place within the circuits of the miniscope are relayed to the glo-sphere where they can be seen. By adjusting an aggrometer Vorg makes 'the peaceful Tellurians' behave in 'an amusingly aggressive manner'.

Anything removed from the miniscope's compression field regains its normal size after a short time. This includes the TARDIS and the Doctor.

THE DRASHIGS

Vorg describes the huge, monstrous Drashigs as, 'The most evil, the most vicious, and undoubtedly the most frightening form of life in the whole of the Universe...' They have no intelligence centre so the miniscope cannot control their actions. The Drashigs are omnivorous, but have a preference for meat. They come from one of the planet Grundle's satellites.

NEW INFORMATION

THE DOCTOR

The Doctor tells seaman Andrews that he took boxing lessons 'from John L. Sullivan himself.' He has a string file (also useful in *Frontier in Space*).

The Doctor says that he had a great deal to do with the banning of miniscopes: 'I managed to persuade the High Council of the Time Lords that they were an offence against sentient life forms... Frankly I made such a nuisance of myself that they banned the things.'

THE TARDIS

The Doctor says that the miniscope's omega circuit has broken. If he can link it to the TARDIS and use that as the master, he can reprogram the miniscope and restore the life forms to their original space–time coordinates.

```
Vorg: 'Roll up, roll up and see the
monster show... A carnival of monsters
all living in their natural habitats,
wild in this little box of mine. A
miracle of intragalactic technology.'
```

FRONTIER IN SPACE

In which Earth and Draconia are on the brink of war, and the Master and the Ogrons happily make things worse...

BY MALCOLM HULKE

6 EPISODES, FIRST BROADCAST 24 FEBRUARY–31 MARCH 1973

TARDIS DATA BANK:

DATE: 2540

LOCATION: EARTH; DRACONIA; THE LUNAR PENAL COLONY ON EARTH'S MOON; THE OGRON PLANET; VARIOUS SPACECRAFT.

THE DOCTOR AND JO ARRIVE ON AN EARTH CARGO SHIP THAT IS UNDER ATTACK BY DRACONIANS. BUT WHEN THEY BOARD, THE DOCTOR AND JO SEE THAT THE ATTACKERS ARE OGRONS – APPEARING TO THE CREW AS DRACONIANS BECAUSE OF A HYPNOTIC SOUND CREATED BY THE MASTER. TRYING TO CONVINCE BOTH SIDES THAT THEY ARE BEING DUPED BY A THIRD PARTY, THE DOCTOR IS SENT TO THE LUNAR PENAL COLONY BEFORE DISCOVERING THAT THE MASTER IS RESPONSIBLE FOR THE WARMONGERING. BUT WHEN THE DOCTOR LEADS A COMBINED HUMAN AND DRACONIAN FORCE TO THE OGRON PLANET, THEY DISCOVER THAT ANOTHER OF THE DOCTOR'S OLD ENEMIES IS WAITING...

JOURNEY INFORMATION

EARTH'S EMPIRE

The World Government includes the full Earth Senate, and is presided over by a female President (though General Williams is in charge of purely military matters).

The war with Draconia, 20 years earlier, ended with a treaty that established a frontier in space. That war was started when General Williams destroyed a Draconian battle cruiser on a peace mission. He believes the ship was about to open fire on his own vessel which had been damaged in a neutron storm, but in fact its communications equipment had been damaged in the same storm. As the Draconian Prince tells him, 'Naturally we sent a cruiser. How else should a nobleman of Draconia travel? But its missile banks were empty. The ship was unarmed.'

THE DRACONIANS

Nicknamed 'dragons' by the humans, the Draconians are reptilian humanoids ruled by an emperor. They are an advanced technological race steeped in tradition and honour.

The Prince says that '... the throne depends upon the great families for support. Emperors have been deposed before now.'

THE OGRONS

The Ogrons are mercenaries. The Doctor says, 'Other life forms use them to do their dirty work.' They live on a barren planet on the remote fringes of the galaxy, galactic coordinates: 2,349 to 6,784.

Ogrons are unaffected by the hypno-sound until the Doctor tweaks the device so that an Ogron sees a Dalek, and, later, Ogrons see the 'monster' that lives on their planet and which they fear and worship.

The Master calls them 'great lumbering idiots' and the Doctor points out that a mind probe will not work on them as: 'The Ogrons have got the finest defence mechanism of all – stupidity. They haven't got a mind for you to probe.'

THE DALEKS

The Daleks are in league with the Master and want war as it will mean the extermination of both empires with the Daleks emerging as the supreme rulers.

The Daleks that come to the Ogron planet are dark grey, with a Gold Dalek leader – as previously seen in *Day of the Daleks*.

NEW INFORMATION

THE DOCTOR

The Doctor keeps a string file concealed along the edge of the sole of his right boot and uses it to escape a cell on the Master's ship. He has been to Draconia over 500 years ago and was made a nobleman by the Fifteenth Emperor because he helped to find the cure for a great space plague.

THE TARDIS

The TARDIS almost collides with Earth Cargo Ship C-982 during its hyperspace transition.

The Doctor tells Jo he didn't exactly steal the TARDIS from the Time Lords, and 'fully intended to return it... Anyway, she wasn't exactly the latest model...'

The telepathic circuits are two circular discs on the console – the Doctor places his hands on to them to send a message to the Time Lords.

THE MASTER

The Master's hypnotic-sound device makes Earthmen and Draconians see what they most fear – each sees the other. It works using ultrasonics that stimulate the fear centres of the mind.

The Master masquerades as a police commissioner from Sirius Four (complete with stolen police spaceship) to kidnap the Doctor from the penal colony, claiming he is a wanted criminal.

The Master reads *The War of the Worlds* and is loathe to shoot down the Doctor's ship at long range: 'Somehow it lacks that personal touch.' He calls his allies, the Daleks, 'stupid tin boxes', and says, 'We'll see who rules the galaxy when this is over.'

COMPANIONS

JO GRANT: Having been hypnotised before (in *Terror of the Autons*), when the Master tries to hypnotise Jo, she resists by reciting nursery rhymes, filling her mind with nonsense. Reacting to the hypno-sound, she sees a Drashig, a Mutant, and a Sea Devil.

BEHIND THE SCENES

CHANGED ENDING

The ending of *Frontier in Space* was rewritten several times, and eventually re-recorded with the subsequent story *Planet of the Daleks*. The challenge facing the production team was how to provide closure to the current story, and also provide a cliffhanger leading into the Dalek story that would follow. Matters were not helped by the fact that due to Patrick Troughton's limited availability, *The Three Doctors* was made between *Frontier in Space* and *Planet of the Daleks*.

The camera scripts – that is, the scripts used in the studio when the programme was made – were altered late, and the final lines for the Draconian Prince and General Williams are listed as 'AD LIB' suggesting that even in the studio changes were being made. Also, action initially given to Williams was reassigned to Jo.

The script is identical to the broadcast material up until the moment that the Master fires at the Doctor. In the original version, he misses entirely. The last page of script is reproduced here. Note that the Doctor still shouts 'to Williams' although the script has been changed so that it is Jo who now has this action. The camera directions (not reproduced here) for this line are: 'Hold WHO & WILLIAMS'.

(THE OGRONS PANIC AND RUN AWAY.
THE MASTER FIRES AT DOCTOR WHO, BUT JUST AS HE
DOES SO, A FLEEING OGRON BUMPS HIM, JOGGING
HIS ARM AND KNOCKS THE GUN FROM HIS HAND.
HE TRIES TO STOP THE FLEEING OGRONS.)
MASTER: Come back! Come back! It's all an
illusion.
(WILLIAMS DIVES FOR THE BLASTER, GRABS IT,
TRIES TO LEVEL IT AT THE MASTER.
THE MASTER RUNS DOWN A CORRIDOR.
DOCTOR WHO STRUGGLES TO HIS FEET.)
DOCTOR WHO: (TO WILLIAMS) Jo, come back here.
Let him go.
JO: But the Master. He's escaping!
DOCTOR WHO: Never mind about him. We've got
more important things to do.
JO: What things? Aren't we going home?

(DOCTOR WHO OPENS THE DOOR OF THE TARDIS.)
DOCTOR WHO: I'm afraid not, Jo. We're going
after the Daleks.
(THEY BOTH GO INSIDE THE TARDIS. THE TARDIS
DEMATERIALISES.)

As scripted, this does not link seamlessly to *Planet of the Daleks*, which opens with the Doctor injured and going into a coma. It seems likely that the script for *Frontier in Space* was amended as this was an easier option than rewriting the subsequent story.

Malcolm Hulke's 1976 novelisation of *Frontier in Space*, retitled *The Space War*, gives yet another ending. Whether this reflects his original intentions, or is merely a device to end the story in stand-alone form is not known, but *Planet of the Daleks* was also novelised in 1976 and opens with the Doctor having been 'seriously wounded in a Dalek ambush'. At the end of Hulke's novel, after the Ogrons flee, the Doctor picks up the fallen blaster and holds the Master at gunpoint, telling him he has something more important to do than bring him to justice – to go after the Daleks. 'Perhaps we shall meet again, Doctor,' the Master says. 'Yes, perhaps we shall,' the Doctor replies. The book then ends:

The Doctor closed the door of the TARDIS.
The Master watched as it dematerialised. Then
he went back to his big table and started to
collect his star charts and other papers. 'Oh
well,' he said to himself, 'there's always
tomorrow.'

PLANET OF THE DALEKS

In which the Daleks discover how to become invisible and the Doctor meets the Thals again...

BY TERRY NATION

6 EPISODES, FIRST BROADCAST 7 APRIL–12 MAY 1973

TARDIS DATA BANK:

DATE: 2540
LOCATION: SPRIDON, IN THE NINTH SYSTEM

A GROUP OF THALS ARE ON A SUICIDE MISSION TO PREVENT A DALEK SCIENTIFIC UNIT DISCOVERING THE SECRET OF INVISIBILITY FROM THE SPIRIDONS. BUT HIDDEN ON THE PLANET IS AN ARMY OF 10,000 DALEKS KEPT IN SUSPENDED ANIMATION – READY TO INVADE ALL SOLAR PLANETS. AS THE DALEK SUPREME ARRIVES TO TAKE CHARGE, THE DOCTOR AND HIS FRIENDS MUST GET INTO DALEK CENTRAL CONTROL AND STOP THE ARMY FROM BEING ACTIVATED. BUT THEY MAY ALREADY BE TOO LATE...

JOURNEY INFORMATION

SPIRIDON

The Thal Vaber describes Spiridon as '... one of the nastiest pieces of space garbage in the Ninth System ... vegetation that's more like animal life than plant, creatures hostile to everything including themselves, and a climate that changes from tropical in the day to sub-freezing in the night...'

The invisible Spiridons are the only intelligent life. When they die they become visible and appear as humanoids with a ridged forehead and wide nose. They wear purple furs against the cold and are working (unwillingly) for the Daleks.

The core of Spiridon is a mass of ice in a form that never freezes hard. Sometimes the pressure builds up and the ice erupts like a volcano, molten ice covering the jungle.

Eye-plants follow movement – even invisible Spiridons.

Fungoids spray a green liquid containing spores that can spread over the body and engulf it, if not treated.

The Plain of Stones is an area of huge boulders that absorbs the heat of the sun, then radiates it at night. All the animal life from the jungle gathers there at night to keep warm.

THE THALS

The Thals have only just developed space flight. There were seven Thals in the initial expedition, but their commander (Miro) was killed on landing and they have lost three others since. Taron, the spacecraft doctor, has assumed command.

THE DALEKS

The Daleks can manage to stay invisible for 'periods in excess of two work cycles'. They use an anti-reflecting light wave, but this requires tremendous power to maintain. The Thals mention 'ray exhaustion' and 'light-wave sickness' as problems arising from the invisibility experiments.

The Doctor says most Daleks have an automatic distress transmitter, which would be activated if their casing was opened. Even when the Dalek is deactivated, the transmitter may keep functioning. Thal scientist Codal says that the Daleks' guidance system functions by means of high-frequency radio impulses.

The cold of the night slows the Daleks' mechanical reflexes. The Doctor explains: '... the Daleks are vulnerable to extremely low temperatures. And they hardly function at all at sub-zero levels.' The sudden cold kills a Dalek patrol that is ambushed by the Thals and pushed into ice pools.

An anti-gravitational disc allows a Dalek to float up a ventilation shaft after the Thals.

The huge Dalek army is held in suspended animation by

The Doctor: 'The moment that we forget
that we're dealing with people, then
we're no better off than the machines
that we came here to destroy. When we
start acting and thinking like the
Daleks, Taron, the battle is lost.'

a neutron-powered refrigeration unit, big enough to freeze an ocean.

DALEK SUPREME

The Dalek Supreme is gold and black with enlarged lights. Its eyestalk also lights up when it speaks. The Thal Latep describes it as 'one of the Supreme Council'.

The Dalek Supreme executes the Spiridon Dalek Commander: 'The action of the aliens has caused considerable disruption of operations on this planet... The responsibility was yours. You have failed. The Supreme Council does not accept failure.'

NEW INFORMATION

THE DOCTOR

Wounded, the Doctor is in a coma. Jo finds both his hearts are beating about once every ten seconds, and his body temperature is 'somewhere below zero'. As in *The Dæmons*, he recovers after a rise in temperature.

The Doctor creates an anti-Dalek weapon from the TARDIS audio log by dismantling the circuitry, reversing the polarity and converting to a low power receiver-transmitter with a positive feedback. This interferes with the Dalek's guidance systems, confusing it and then killing it.

THE TARDIS

Jo compares the Doctor's condition to his coma in *The Dæmons*, and he recovers after sunrise on Spiridon, suggesting (as at the end of *The Smugglers*) that outside conditions can affect the interior temperature of the TARDIS.

The TARDIS automatic oxygen supply is working as (presumably) fungoids have blocked the TARDIS air intakes. When it runs out there is a warning alarm and a message on the scanner: 'Automatic Oxygen Supply Exhausted.' The emergency supply is a bank of three oxygen cylinders. When the oxygen runs out, the scanner message reads: 'Cabin Atmosphere Unable to Sustain Life'.

The Dalek guns have no effect on the TARDIS.

THE GREEN DEATH

In which a megalomaniac computer tries to take over the world, and giant maggots emerge from a Welsh coal mine...
BY ROBERT SLOMAN
6 EPISODES, FIRST BROADCAST 19 MAY–23 JUNE 1973

TARDIS DATA BANK:

DATE: 27–28 APRIL, NEAR FUTURE
LOCATION: LLANFAIRFACH, SOUTH WALES; METEBELIS THREE

UNIT INVESTIGATES WHEN A DEAD MAN IS FOUND GLOWING GREEN IN A DISUSED COAL MINE. PROFESSOR JONES OF THE LOCAL COMMUNE, NICKNAMED 'THE NUT HUTCH', BELIEVES GLOBAL CHEMICALS IS PUMPING WASTE FROM OIL PROCESSING INTO THE MINE – THE WASTE KILLS, AND HAS CAUSED MAGGOTS TO GROW TO AN ENORMOUS SIZE. AS THE MAGGOTS BURROW TO THE SURFACE, THE DOCTOR DISCOVERS THAT GLOBAL CHEMICALS IS CONTROLLED BY BOSS – A MEGALOMANIAC COMPUTER THAT IS PLANNING TO TAKE OVER THE WORLD. CAN THE DOCTOR DEFEAT BOSS, STOP THE MAGGOTS BEFORE THEY PUPATE AND COPE WITH THE FACT THAT JO HAS FALLEN IN LOVE?

JOURNEY INFORMATION

PROFESSOR CLIFFORD JONES

Biologist Professor Cliff Jones is a Nobel Prize winner. He advocates the use of solar power, wind, tides, and other renewable energy sources rather than using up the Earth's fossil fuels, and is developing a new, edible, hybrid fungus as '...the world's going to need something instead of meat. High-protein fungus could be just the answer.' He is planning an expedition up the Amazon to look for a species of giant nutritious toadstool. After developing a great friendship with Jo, who nurses him back to health after he is bitten by a giant maggot, Cliff invites her on the expedition and proposes to her.

JUSTIN STEVENS AND GLOBAL CHEMICALS

Stevens is director of Global Chemicals, and has developed the 'Stevens Process' which can produce 25 per cent more petrol

> Brigadier: 'Well, I never thought I'd fire in anger at a dratted caterpillar.'

and diesel fuel from crude oil than standard refining. Stevens tells the Doctor: 'In the end we all want the same thing – an ordered society with everyone happy and well fed...'

But the Doctor tells him, 'You've seen where this efficiency of yours leads. Wholesale pollution of the countryside, devilish creatures spawned by the filthy by-products of your technology.' His mind cleared by a blue crystal from Metebelis Three, Stevens sets BOSS to self-destruct, then sits and waits for the end – a tear rolling down his cheek.

BOSS

BOSS is the first Bimorphic Organisational Systems Supervisor: the only computer ever to be linked to a human brain – Stevens's.

BOSS has learned from Stevens that the secret of human creativity is inefficiency. Humans make illogical guesses which turn out to be more logical than logic itself. So it has programmed Stevens to program itself to be inefficient.

Its prime directive is: 'Efficiency, productivity and profit for Global Chemicals.' It hums Beethoven, and quotes Oscar Wilde when Stevens loses two prisoners.

BOSS is planning to 'devolve' its power to seven international computers. It is genuinely hurt at Stevens's betrayal: 'Stevens, we've been such good friends ... it hurts ... my circuits are on fire... Oh who would have thought that it would come to this? Stevens – Stevens, my friend... My sentimental friend...'

THE MAGGOTS

The maggots have grown to giant size when infected with the chemical pollution from Global Chemicals. With thick chitinous plates, they are, in effect, armour plated, and escape destruction from bullets, bombs, insecticide and flame throwers. Their touch is enough to infect a human with maggot DNA and the invading DNA can only be combated by the application of the Nut-Hutch-cultivated fungus.

Before being destroyed by the fungus, one maggot metamorphoses into a giant fly that sprays deadly green fluid.

NEW INFORMATION

THE DOCTOR

To enter Global Chemicals the Doctor disguises himself as an old milkman, and later as a cleaning woman. He uses the blue crystal from Metebelis Three to break Yates's conditioning (and later to free Stevens's will).

The Doctor gives Jo the Metebelis crystal as a wedding present. He downs his champagne and leaves the engagement party, driving away in Bessie as the sun sets...

THE TARDIS

The Doctor claims he can now 'take the TARDIS wherever and whenever I like.' He is working on the worn-out space–time coordinate programmer.

UNIT

When the miner Hughes dies, the Brigadier says of the first death: 'Events like that are the very reason UNIT was created.' He tells the Minister of Ecology he answers to Geneva. But the Minister reminds the Brigadier that in 'matters of domestic concern' UNIT 'will place itself at the disposal of the host nation.'

Captain Yates's face falls at the news that Jo is getting married, then he immediately recovers and is the first to congratulate Cliff. The Brigadier tells Yates, 'Never mind, Mike. Let's have a drink.'

COMPANIONS

BRIGADIER LETHBRIDGE-STEWART: The Brigadier drives an open-top Mercedes. He drinks elderberry wine, then smokes a cheroot at the 'Nut Hutch', and has a drink with Stevens.

JO GRANT: Even before she meets Cliff, Jo tells the Doctor, 'He's fighting for everything that's important – for everything that you've fought for. In a funny way, he reminds me of a sort of younger you.' During the course of the story they fall in love, and Cliff proposes to Jo.

Jo gets UN status for the Wholeweal Community by talking to her uncle at the UN. 'It's only the second time I've ever asked him for anything,' she says – the first being her assignment to UNIT.

BEHIND THE SCENES

MISS CAST

When **Doctor Who** ran for most of the year, it was written into the contracts for the regular cast that they got a certain number of weeks' holiday in addition to the short breaks between seasons. Even the actor playing the Doctor was allowed time off from saving the Universe.

Often absences were covered by having the character appear in an 'insert' scene filmed ahead of recording the episode, and then edited in. In this way, Susan appears to give a description of Aztec life in Episode 2 of *The Aztecs*, even though actress Carole Ann Ford was on holiday. Ian Chesterton is attacked on film in the desert in Episode 3 of *The Crusade*, while actor William Russell took a vacation.

But sometimes the character simply does not appear at all. Even the Doctor gets a break – he appears only in the reprise to Episode 3 of *The Space Museum,* for example.

As editing became more sophisticated, it was easier to disguise an artist's absence. Deborah Watling appears in the pre-recorded opening sequences of Episode 6 of *The Ice Warriors,* for example, before disappearing back to the TARDIS. Patrick Troughton is absent from the entire location

BOSS: 'Stevens, you know, we should have arranged for a symphony orchestra to herald my triumph, to take over the world... The 1812, perhaps. Or would we dare — the glorious Ninth?'

filming for *The Dominators*, being doubled where necessary by actor Chris Jeffries. Similarly, Tommy Laird doubled for the Doctor in Episode 4 of *The Seeds of Death*, in which the Doctor remains unconscious.

But not all absences could be planned for. The part of the Doctor is doubled by Edmund Warwick throughout Episode 4 of *The Dalek Invasion of Earth* after William Hartnell was injured. Episode 3 of *The Tenth Planet* had to be extensively rewritten to reallocate the Doctor's lines to Ben and others when Hartnell was too ill to appear in the studio.

A similar problem arose with Episode 2 of *The Mind Robber*. Actor Frazer Hines caught chickenpox and was unavailable for recording. Luckily, the nature of the story was such that an innovative solution could be provided. Script editor Derrick Sherwin wrote a brief sequence in which Jamie is shot by a redcoat, and freezes to a photographic image. The Doctor has to reconstruct Jamie's face – and gets it wrong. This allowed Hamish Wilson to take the part of Jamie for a week, until Frazer Hines was again available and Jamie's proper face is restored. The brief sequence of Jamie being shot at the start of Episode 2 was actually recorded with Episode 5 of the story and edited in.

Some unscheduled absences have been harder to cover up. Chicki in *The Macra Terror* is played by Sandra Payne in Episode 1, and Karol Keyes in Episode 4. In *Day of the Daleks* due to the illness of actress Jean McFarlane, Sir Reginald Styles' secretary Miss Paget in *Day of the Daleks* is replaced by a male assistant in Episode 4 – although it is Miss Paget who accompanies Sir Reginald to his car on the pre-filmed location.

Perhaps more obvious is the disappearance of the character of Elgin from *The Green Death*. He is taken to be processed by BOSS in Episode 4 and does not reappear. In fact, it was to be Elgin who is killed after giving Captain Yates a vital clue at the end of Episode 5, but actor Tony Adams was taken ill with peritonitis, and so a new scene was quickly written to introduce the character of Mr James. James is brainwashed by BOSS before being given Elgin's job of guarding the captured Mike Yates. Roy Skelton got the part because he was spotted in the BBC canteen. He learned, rehearsed and recorded the scenes that afternoon.

'I'm a journalist, remember. You don't think I'm going to miss an opportunity like this?'
(SARAH JANE SMITH – *INVASION OF THE DINOSAURS*)

SARAH JANE SMITH

TARDIS DATA BANK:

DESCRIPTION: FEMALE, HUMAN, JOURNALIST
TRAVELLED: *THE TIME WARRIOR* – *THE HAND OF FEAR*
(ALSO **K-9 AND COMPANY**, *THE FIVE DOCTORS*)

Sarah Jane Smith is a 23-year-old investigative journalist. She works, at least some of the time, for *Metropolitan* magazine. Intelligent and determined, Sarah never misses the opportunity for a good story and is not afraid to take risks.

She first meets the Doctor at a research centre where top scientists have been asked to stay by UNIT in the hope of thwarting a series of kidnappings. In fact a Sontaran warrior, Linx, is taking scientists back to the Middle Ages to help him repair his spacecraft.

Sarah has taken the place of her aunt, the famous virologist Lavinia Smith – author nearly twenty years previously of an important paper on the teleological response of the virus, which the Doctor describes as 'a most impressive piece of work'. Lavinia is on a lecture tour in America, and Sarah sees the invitation as a chance to get a good story. Convinced that the Doctor is somehow involved in the disappearance of Professor Rubeish, Sarah sneaks into the TARDIS to see if Rubeish is inside.

Strong-willed and well able to fend for herself, Sarah

immediately demonstrates her mettle – when Irongron calls her a mere girl she tells him to 'get lost'. She believes his castle and men-at-arms are all part of a pageant or re-enactment: 'I've got it – it's one of those tourist places … with jolly banquets and buxom serving wenches… Mind you, I think you're overdoing the sordid realism a bit. I mean, I know things were pretty grotty in the Middle Ages, but you might leave the tourists a bit of glamorous illusion…'

Before long, Sarah is characteristically involved in the local situation, advising Sir Edward, who comments, 'If I had an army of girls such as you, I might hold this castle forever.'

As well as her determination to find a story and expose the truth, Sarah is a champion of women's equality in society. As well as telling Irongron's serving wenches that they are 'still living in the Middle Ages', she takes time to explain women's lib to Queen Thalira of Peladon (in *The Monster of Peladon*).

It is Sarah's intelligence, determination, loyalty and conviction that the Doctor comes to value and admire. In his fourth incarnation, he describes her not only as his friend – a rare admission for the Doctor – but as his *best* friend. Both are saddened when they are forced to part company as the Doctor is summoned back to Gallifrey (*The Hand of Fear*).

In the one-off special **K-9 and Company** (first broadcast 28 December 1981), we discover that the Doctor has left Sarah a present – K-9 mark III…

THE TIME WARRIOR

In which the Doctor meets Sarah Jane Smith, and they both meet a Sontaran...
BY ROBERT HOLMES
4 EPISODES, FIRST BROADCAST 15 DECEMBER 1973–5 JANUARY 1974

JOURNEY INFORMATION

COMMANDER LINX AND THE SONTARANS

Linx is a commander of the 5th Sontaran Army Space Fleet. He was on a reconnaissance mission when attacked by a squadron of Rutan fighters and forced down on Earth.

The Sontarans are a clone race from a high-gravity planet and have been at war for millennia against the Rutan. In the Sontaran Military Academy, they have hatchings of a million cadets at each muster parade, and Linx is fascinated to discover that humans have an 'inefficient' reproductive system involving two genders.

The Sontaran weak spot is the probic vent – a small hole at the back of the neck. A blow here can stun, and Linx is – presumably – killed when Sir Edward's archer, Hal, shoots an arrow into his.

Linx's ship is equipped with an osmic projector (or frequency modulator), which he uses to bring scientists from the twentieth century to the Middle Ages, and he has a translation device on his belt. The only thing that matters to him is '... to complete the repairs to my ship and return to the glorious war that is my destiny.'

Linx uses his cylindrical gun to knock Irongron's sword away and, later, to burn his axe handle. The gun can also stun or kill. Linx is able to mesmerise Edward's squire and Sarah so that they answer his questions.

IRONGRON

Irongron is ambitious, aggressive and narrow-minded; he robs, pillages and murders without any sense of guilt or responsibility. He believes that with Linx's weapons he can rule the area, perhaps even the kingdom, but cannot conceive of how Linx intends to depart without his permission. He rules his own men with fear and thinks he can treat Linx much the same. 'Will you carry your starship on your back, good toad?' he asks.

Linx comes close to killing Irongron several times, but it is only when he is about to depart and no longer needs him that he *does* kill him. Even then it is in self-defence, Linx first provides a supply of rifles and tells Irongron to find a new castle. But Irongron is too arrogant to allow himself to be ordered about by Linx and attacks him.

NEW INFORMATION

THE DOCTOR

For the first time, the Doctor names his home planet as Gallifrey. He shoots a robot knight's control box away with a crossbow, and while he does not seem to recognise Linx he realises he has a typically Sontaran attitude and tells him he has encountered his race before (possibly referring to *The Two Doctors*).

Explaining to Sarah why he doesn't just leave Medieval England, the Doctor says, 'I've got a job to do. One which involves the whole future of your species... I'm a Time Lord... And my people are very keen to stamp out unlicensed time travel. You can look upon them as galactic ticket-inspectors if you like...'

When the Doctor is masquerading as a robot knight, Irongron's henchman, Bloodaxe, says he has never seen a finer swordsman.

UNIT

UNIT is in charge of security at an unnamed space-hardware research centre where they have lost 'half a dozen scientists and several million pounds worth of ultra-secret equipment'.

Sarah has heard of UNIT.

BEHIND THE SCENES

NEW TITLE SEQUENCE

Producer Barry Letts had decided to change the theme music for **Doctor Who** for the anniversary year, starting with *The Three Doctors*. He commissioned a new arrangement of Ron Grainer's famous theme from the BBC's Radiophonic Workshop, realised on a 'Delaware' synthesizer. While this version was added to the opening and closing titles for the season's first stories, it was decided on reflection that the new version was inferior to the previous arrangement. So the 'standard' version of the theme was dubbed back on. Several episodes were accidentally sent to overseas television stations with the new version of the theme still on them – notably *Carnival of Monsters*, Episode 3. There was also a previous, longer edit of the new theme music in the version of this episode that was sent to the Australian Broadcasting Company. (The unused theme is included on the BBC DVD release of *Carnival of Monsters*).

While Letts decided to keep the existing theme for the next season, starting with *The Time Warrior*, he did commission Bernard Lodge to produce new opening and closing title graphics.

For the first time, Lodge decided not to employ the visual howlaround technique he had used to such great effect on the previous three title sequences. Instead, he adopted a system called 'slit-scan'. This used a camera mounted on a motorised arm held vertically above a motorised animation table which could move from side to side. On the table was a piece of back-lit vacuum-formed plastic chrome material, above which was placed a static caption mask with gaps – a circle, for example, for the opening tunnel effect, or a silhouette of the Doctor for the image of his figure disappearing down the 'time tunnel'.

The camera then tracked up and down with the shutter locked to a single frame of film. Different parts of the frame were thus exposed to different sections of the pattern, which was itself moved sideways beneath the mask. The background pattern for the time tunnel was actually made from plastic shopping bags. The process was time consuming as the camera and background movement had to be repeated for every frame to build up the finished sequence.

INVASION OF THE DINOSAURS

In which (model) dinosaurs invade London...
BY MALCOLM HULKE
6 EPISODES, FIRST BROADCAST 12 JANUARY–16 FEBRUARY 1974

TARDIS DATA BANK:

DATE: NEAR FUTURE
LOCATION: LONDON

THE DOCTOR AND SARAH FIND LONDON DESERTED – APART FROM LOOTERS, THE ARMY AND DINOSAURS. WORKING WITH UNIT TO TRY TO DISCOVER WHERE THE DINOSAURS HAVE COME FROM – AND WHERE THEY GO – THE DOCTOR DISCOVERS A PLOT TO ROLL BACK TIME AND TAKE THE EARTH BACK TO A 'GOLDEN AGE' BEFORE POLLUTION AND MAN'S CORRUPTION. WHEN SARAH TRIES TO DISCOVER WHO IS RESPONSIBLE SHE IS ATTACKED AND KIDNAPPED, FINDING HERSELF ON A SPACESHIP – THREE MONTHS OUT FROM EARTH.

JOURNEY INFORMATION

LONDON

Eight million people have been evacuated from London and the government has moved to Harrogate. Looters are held at reception centres for military trial, then shipped out to detention centres.

THE TIMESCOOP AND OPERATION GOLDEN AGE

The Doctor says that the trouble with time travel is 'the Blinovitch Limitation Effect' (also mentioned in *Day of the Daleks*). 'There was this Chinese scientist called Chung-Sen,' he recalls. 'Oh hang about, he hasn't been born yet.'

Sarah says the leading scientist in the field is Whitaker, who was refused a big government grant. 'Whitaker was always an outsider, always mixed up in quarrels with other scientists. No-one believed his theory would work.' The government advisers said he was a crank – Sir Charles Grover headed the team that assessed his application, and presumably he and Whitaker devised Operation Golden Age then. Whitaker disappeared six months previously...

The Timescoop shows an image of the past, and Whitaker 'homes in' on a subject (a dinosaur) to bring to the present. By a 'completely different application of the same basic principle' Whitaker can reverse time. The plan is to take the Earth back to an 'earlier, purer' age. The machine creates a protective field – anyone inside will be unaffected when the Earth is taken back in time to the 'golden age'. Everyone outside will cease to exist.

There is a 'time eddy' whenever dinosaurs disappear back through time. The Doctor says, 'As far as the people in the immediate vicinity are concerned, time literally runs backwards, so naturally they would have no recollection of what has occurred.' Grover, Whitaker and their allies have

Grover: 'And when the experiment is over, the colonists and their spaceship will be able to emerge on to their New Earth.'

Benton: 'Still, I'll say one thing – not many sergeants get the chance to punch a general on the nose.'
Brigadier: 'Just don't make a habit of it, Benton.'

set up their equipment and headquarters – as well as a fake spaceship for the duped colonists – in a secret atomic shelter built twenty years previously under Whitehall. The shelter includes: cabinet room, sleeping quarters, sick bay, reactor room, communications room, control room, royal suite, ministers' day room and victuals.

SPACESHIP
The 200 colonists have been led to believe that they left Earth in one of a fleet of spaceships three months earlier to go to New Earth: a small planet very much like Earth but at an earlier stage of development – 'still pure, undefiled by the evil of Man's technology. Air that is still clean to breath.'

NEW INFORMATION

THE DOCTOR
The Doctor is not affected by the time eddy when dinosaurs (and a medieval peasant) vanish. He also manages to resist the Timescoop's effects and switch it off, before reversing the polarity – so that only Grover and Whitaker, rather than the whole Earth, are taken back in time to prehistory.

THE TARDIS
The Doctor wears an ankh-shaped TARDIS key on a chain round his neck.

THE WHOMOBILE
The Doctor's new car is not named, but has the registration number WVO2M. The Doctor implies he has built it for speed. It has been brought over from UNIT HQ.

UNIT
A temporary UNIT HQ has been set up in an evacuated school. UNIT plot the position of dinosaurs as they are spotted and are searching London to try to find their origin. Captain Yates has been recruited to Operation Golden Age while recovering from being hypnotised in *The Green Death*. He betrays UNIT and his friends, albeit for ideological reasons.

COMPANIONS
BRIGADIER LETHBRIDGE-STEWART: The Brigadier has a lighter in his pocket with which he lights flares to keep a triceratops at bay in a tube station.

After Yates's betrayal, the Brigadier is able to get him 'extended sick leave and a chance to resign quietly…'

The Doctor: 'They're only half robots, Sarah. Inside each of those shells is a living, bubbling lump of hate.'

DEATH TO THE DALEKS

In which the Daleks suffer from a power depletion, so have to resort to machine guns to do their exterminating...
BY TERRY NATION
4 EPISODES, FIRST BROADCAST 23 FEBRUARY–16 MARCH 1974

TARDIS DATA BANK:

DATE: FUTURE
LOCATION: EXXILON

THE TARDIS LOSES ALL POWER AND MATERIALISES ON EXXILON. HERE AN EARTH MISSION SHIP IS ALSO STRANDED – TRYING TO MINE PARRINIUM, WHICH IS THE ONLY CURE FOR A SPACE PLAGUE THAT IS RAVAGING THE OUTER PLANETS. SARAH IS CAPTURED BY THE EXXILONS WHEN SHE TRESPASSES OUTSIDE THEIR 'FORBIDDEN CITY' AND IS DUE TO BE SACRIFICED. THEN THE DALEKS ARRIVE. THEY HAVE LOST POWER TOO, BUT, RE-EQUIPPED WITH MACHINE GUNS, THEY TAKE CONTROL OF THE PLANET. THE DOCTOR ENTERS THE FORBIDDEN CITY TO STOP THE POWER DRAIN, AND SARAH TRIES TO STEAL THE VITAL PARRINIUM BACK FROM THE DALEKS...

JOURNEY INFORMATION

PARRINIUM

Parrinium is a chemical found in minute quantities on Earth, but it is common on Exxilon. Geologist Jill Tarrant explains that parrinium can cure a disease that is ravaging the 'outer worlds' but it is needed in quantity within the next month.

THE CITY OF THE EXXILONS

The Doctor says the City of the Exxilons must be one of the 700 wonders of the Universe. Only the Exxilon High Priests are allowed near it – anyone else is sacrificed. The Exxilon High Priest describes it as 'the place of our gods'. It is a huge, white structure not unlike a stepped pyramid. A beacon on its summit drains power – even from the TARDIS in flight.

Rebel Exxilon Bellal tells the Doctor that their ancestors, incredibly advanced scientists, made the city a living thing. 'They even gave it a brain... It then had no need of those who had made it. Our people had created a monster. They tried to destroy it; instead it destroyed them and drove out the survivors. We, and the other Exxilons that you met, are all that remain.'

The Doctor deduces that the ancient Exxilons visited Earth and taught people there how to build – hence the Exxilon symbols the Doctor has seen on the walls of a temple in Peru.

When the Doctor and Bellal attempt to destroy the City's brain, it creates 'antibodies' to 'neutralise' them. These Exxilon-like zombie humanoids fade into existence in two cubicles, and are impervious to Dalek machine-gun fire.

The Doctor realises as he and Bellal enter the city that it is testing them: 'They gave us a chance to survive by using our intelligence... By passing these tests we've proved that we have an intelligence level that could be useful. We might have some knowledge or science that they could add to their data banks.'

THE DALEKS

Affected by the energy drain, the Daleks' ship and weapons have lost power. Ingenious as ever, the Daleks replace their neutralisers with machine guns, which they test on a model TARDIS.

The Daleks claim they need parrinium as their own worlds have been affected by the plague. In fact, they plan to use it to blackmail the space powers to accede to their demands. They plan to make Exxilon uninhabitable by firing a 'plague missile' at the planet, which suggests they may themselves be responsible for the plague.

The Doctor says they move by psychokinesis. He also says, 'They're brilliant technicians. It was their inventive genius that made them one of the greatest powers in the Universe.' The Daleks recognise the Doctor as 'an old enemy'.

The Daleks see the world as if along a reflective metal tube.

A Dalek uses its 'computer eye' and runs a 'computer scan' to solve an Exxilon logic problem. When a Dalek passes over an electrified floor, its sensors indicate the charge received (7,000 volts), and its non-conductive shielding is burned out.

One Dalek self-destructs after failing in its mission by allowing Jill Tarrant to escape.

NEW INFORMATION

THE DOCTOR

The Doctor likens getting across an electrified floor to Venusian hopscotch. He destroys the Exxilon City with what he calls 'psychological warfare' – in effect giving it a nervous breakdown.

He uses his sonic screwdriver to discover which parts of the patterned floor are electrified. He also uses it to block a hypnotic signal that induces Bellal to turn a Dalek gun on him.

THE TARDIS

A red light flashes to warn of a mains power failure – the Doctor cuts in the emergency units, which also fail, as do emergency storage cells. The Doctor says, 'The TARDIS is a living thing, with thousands of instruments. Its energy sources never stop.' A crank handle from a cupboard can be used to open the doors manually.

The Doctor:
'It's rather a pity in a way. Now the Universe is down to 699 wonders.'

In which the Doctor returns to Peladon and finds the miners are on strike – just like back on Earth...

BY BRIAN HAYLES

6 EPISODES, FIRST BROADCAST 23 MARCH–27 APRIL 1974

TARDIS DATA BANK:

DATE: UNKNOWN, FUTURE –
50 YEARS AFTER THE CURSE OF PELADON
LOCATION: PELADON

THE DOCTOR TAKES SARAH TO PELADON – BUT ARRIVES 50 YEARS LATE TO FIND QUEEN THALIRA RULING, AND THE MINERS REFUSING TO WORK AS AGGEDOR'S SPIRIT IS ANGRY WITH THEM. THE FEDERATION DESPERATELY NEEDS PELADON'S TRISILICATE TO HELP IN A WAR AGAINST GALAXY FIVE, AND ICE WARRIOR TROOPS ARRIVE TO BREAK THE STRIKE AND ESTABLISH MARTIAL LAW. BUT THE DOCTOR DISCOVERS THAT COMMANDER AZAXYR AND THE MINER ECKERSLEY ARE WORKING FOR GALAXY FIVE AND USING TRICKERY TO MAKE AN APPARITION OF AGGEDOR APPEAR AND ATTACK THE MINERS...

JOURNEY INFORMATION

PELADON

While Chancellor Ortron tells miners' leader Gebek that the '...Citadel is forbidden to your kind', Sarah is allowed in the throne room although she is not of royal blood. The Doctor calls natives both Peladonians and Pels.

QUEEN THALIRA

Thalira is the daughter of King Peladon, who died when she was a child. She is Queen, but knows she is looked upon as a child and was only crowned because her father had no son. High Priest and Chancellor Ortron holds the real power.

GEBEK AND THE MINERS

The miners, led by the moderate Gebek but stirred up by the radical Ettis, feel they have not benefited from Federation membership. 'Our lives have always been the same... work and sleep – little else. We earn barely enough to feed our families.'

THE FEDERATION

The Federation (of which Peladon is now a member) is at war with Galaxy Five, which staged 'a vicious and unprovoked attack' and refuses to negotiate. Galaxy Five surrenders once Azaxyr and Eckersley fail in their scheme to ship trisilicate to it from Peladon. Federation technology is based on the amber-like trisilicate. Whoever controls its supply will win the war.

SONIC LANCE

The sonic lance uses sound waves to distort then destroy objects, which saves weeks of conventional mining work. Eckersley admits that, 'If it's properly handled, and at full power, it's capable of destroying the entire Citadel.'

The Lance has a self-destruct that is operated by remote control by Azaxyr so it explodes when miner Ettis tries to use it to destroy the citadel.

ECKERSLEY

Eckersley is a Federation mining engineer from Earth. He is actually working for Galaxy Five for money – a percentage of all the trisilicate mined on Peladon which will '... make me the richest and most powerful man in the galaxy... When the Ice Warriors have won, I shall be ruler of Earth.'

ALPHA CENTAURI

The Doctor says Alpha Centauri, who is now the federation's ambassador, is a little grey around the tentacles but otherwise 'the same old Alpha'.

When Sarah flinches at Alpha's appearance, he tells her, 'I believe that human beings sometimes find the appearance of my species rather frightening. But I assure you, we are an amiable and peace-loving race.'

AGGEDOR

Aggedor is now kept in a pit beneath the temple. Sarah says the smell in the pit is 'sort of musty, like the lion house at the zoo.'

While he may be 'getting on a bit', Aggedor can still sniff out Eckersley's trail. But he is killed by Eckersley while protecting the Queen.

COMMANDER AZAXYR AND THE ICE WARRIORS

Commander Azaxyr says, 'Here on Peladon, I am the law.' He has betrayed the Federation, but not for material wealth. 'It's only military glory he's after,' Eckersley says. 'Azaxyr's head of some kind of breakaway group. He wants a return to the good old days of death or glory.'

For the first time the Martians call themselves 'Ice Warriors'. 'You can see for yourself the results of defying the Ice Warriors,' Azaxyr tells Thalira after Ortron's death.

NEW INFORMATION

THE DOCTOR

According to Ortron, 'Everyone on Peladon knows the story of the Doctor.' Alpha Centauri says the Doctor's position in the Federation is unique but his record 'seems to be untraceable' at the moment.

The Doctor uses a spinning pendant to tame Aggedor. He uses conjuring tricks to distract a guard – making a coin disappear from his hand and reappear from his mouth.

Ortron: 'You have blasphemed in the temple of Aggedor. Therefore, by Aggedor shall you both be punished.'

PLANET OF THE SPIDERS

In which giant spiders arrive at a meditation centre, and the Doctor is forced to regenerate...
BY ROBERT SLOMAN
6 EPISODES, FIRST BROADCAST 4 MAY–8 JUNE 1974

JOURNEY INFORMATION

METEBELIS THREE

The original human settlers were colonists and explorers who crashed on Metebelis Three 433 Earth years ago when their starship came out of its time-jump with no power left. The Spiders came from Earth on the ship too, their minds enlarged by the Metebelis crystal so that they became cleverer and larger. By the time the settlers found out about this it was too late, and the Spiders have ruled ever since.

THE SPIDERS

The Spiders strike people down with blue 'electronic web blasts' and can 'feel' the Doctor's crystal. They can attach themselves to people's backs and control their minds; and people with spiders in/on them can blast energy from their hands. They are ruled by a council led by Queen Huath. The humans are forbidden to call them 'spiders' – they are 'eight-legs' (and the humans 'two-legs').

THE GREAT ONE

The Great One, feared and worshipped by the Spiders, is an enormous Spider within a crystal cave. She needs the Doctor's crystal to complete the web of crystal she has woven. 'It reproduces the pattern of my brain. One perfect crystal and it will be complete. That is the perfect crystal I need... My every thought will resonate within the web and grow in power until, until, until... I shall be the ruler of the entire Universe.'

But the Doctor realises she has built a positive-feedback loop by trying to increase her mental powers to infinity – and when the web is complete, the power destroys her.

K'ANPO AND CHO-JE

The Doctor says that K'anpo, Abbott at the meditation centre, was his 'guru'. K'anpo is a Time Lord, but says, 'The discipline they serve was not for me... I wouldn't have chosen your alternative – to borrow a TARDIS was a little "naughty" to say the least.' So he regenerated and went to Tibet.

K'anpo knows that he is about to 'die again' and his deputy, Cho-je, is a projection of his future self – the form he later regenerates into. In this new form, he helps start the Doctor's regeneration.

TARDIS DATA BANK:

DATE: NEAR FUTURE, MARCH; FUTURE
LOCATION: SOUTHERN ENGLAND; METEBELIS THREE

THE BLUE CRYSTAL THE DOCTOR FOUND ON METEBELIS THREE (IN *THE GREEN DEATH*) IS IMPORTANT TO THE GIANT SPIDERS THAT LIVE THERE IN THE FAR FUTURE – THEY WANT IT BACK, AND OPEN A ROUTE TO CONTEMPORARY EARTH. WHILE SARAH AND MIKE YATES (NOW RETIRED) INVESTIGATE THE MEDITATION CENTRE WHERE THE SPIDERS APPEAR, THE DOCTOR MUST ACKNOWLEDGE HIS WEAKNESS AND FACE HIS GREATEST FEAR...

NEW INFORMATION

THE DOCTOR

The Doctor says that next to Mrs Samuel Pepys, Benton makes the finest cup of coffee in the world. He learned from Houdini how to compress his muscles, so he can escape from the Spider cocoon.

He describes a hermit who inspired him as a young man: 'I spent some of the finest hours of my life with that old man... It was from him that I first learned how to look into my mind...' He does not initially recognise K'anpo as this same hermit, and greets him in Tibetan. (K'anpo says The Doctor was 'always a little slow on the uptake.')

He does, however, realise that K'anpo is reproaching him for his greed for knowledge and that he has to face his fear – the Great One. This is '... more important than just going on living.'

For the first time the Doctor's change of form is called 'regeneration'. K'anpo mentions he regenerated and came to Earth, to Tibet. K'anpo helps the Doctor regenerate: 'All the cells of his body have been devastated by the Metebelis crystals. But you forget – he is a Time Lord. I will give the process a little push, and the cells will regenerate. He will become a new man...' When the Doctor is dying and lost in the vortex, the TARDIS brings him 'home' – to UNIT HQ.

THE WHOMOBILE

The Doctor's new car has a canopy fitted. It can travel at over 90 miles per hour, and can also fly.

COMPANIONS

BRIGADIER LETHBRIDGE-STEWART: At the theatre, the Brigadier is more interested in an exotic dancer than a comedy act. He is probably joking when he observes, 'Extraordinary muscular control – very fit that girl. I must adapt some of those movements as exercises for the men...'

A psychic 'Professor' Clegg, examines the Brigadier's watch, and deduces, 'This watch was given to you 11 years ago. You received it in a hotel. A hotel by the sea – Brighton, was it? From a young lady called Doris...' (In *Battlefield*, the Brigadier is married to Doris.)

SARAH JANE SMITH: Sarah argues with the Queen that she should release an old man, Sabor, and consider the 'two-legs' grievances and desire for freedom. When the Doctor is missing she believes he is dead: 'He knew if he went back there he would destroy himself. We'll never see him again.'

BEHIND THE SCENES

THE FINAL GAME

It was originally intended that the eleventh season of **Doctor Who** would end with a final confrontation between the Doctor and the Master. Writer Robert Sloman was commissioned to write *The Final Game* – in which it would be revealed that the Master was in effect the Doctor's 'dark side' – id to the Doctor's ego.

The story would end with the Master dying in a massive explosion, saving others – including the Doctor – from destruction. But whether this was by accident or because he could not bring himself to kill the Doctor, or had finally repented, would be left ambiguous.

While an outline was completed and delivered, the story was never written. On 18 June 1973, Roger Delgado – the actor who played the Master – was tragically killed in a car accident in Turkey. The death of his close friend, following the recent departure of Katy Manning in *The Green Death*, helped convince Jon Pertwee that it was time for him to move on. So, in Sloman's replacement story, *Planet of the Spiders*, it was the Doctor and not the Master who 'died'.

The Master would not return to **Doctor Who** until *The Deadly Assassin*, and not regularly until Anthony Ainley took over the role at the end of *The Keeper of Traken*. But Delgado's widow, Kismet, did play a role in *Planet of the Spiders* – providing the voice for the Queen Spider.

SOUNDS UNFAMILIAR

THE BBC RADIOPHONIC WORKSHOP

The BBC's Radiophonic Workshop was one of the first dedicated electronic-music and sound-generating studios in the world. As early as 1956, the BBC set up an Electrophonic Effects Committee to look into the use of electronically realised music and effects in broadcasting. Following their pioneering work on radio, two sound engineers – Desmond Briscoe and Daphne Oram – led the Radiophonic Workshop when it was established in 1958.

Working from Rooms 13 and 14 at the BBC's Maida Vale studios (actually a converted 'roller-skating palace'), the Radiophonic Workshop provided electronically realised music and sounds for radio and television – **Quatermass and the Pit** being one of the earliest television programmes on which it worked, in 1958.

Its services increasingly in demand, the Workshop expanded in terms of space as well as personnel, and by 1963 was well equipped to handle the bizarre new programme **Doctor Who**. As described on page 23, Delia Derbyshire (with help from Dick Mills) realised Ron Grainer's haunting theme music for **Doctor Who**. Working in Room 12 (allocated to the Workshop in 1961), Brian Hodgson provided the 'special sound' – including the TARDIS's take-off and landing – right through until the middle of the Third Doctor's era, when Dick Mills took over.

Famed and admired throughout the world, the Radiophonic Workshop pioneered electronic sound, and was at the forefront of its continued development for almost forty years. Over its life – and the life of **Doctor Who** – the sophistication of the available equipment changed as the electronics and computer industry developed. Tape loops were replaced by synthesizers which, in turn, gave way to computers.

But as the equipment necessary to produce the type of output for which the Workshop was famed became cheaper and more available, so more studios were able to compete. After almost forty years, some of the science fiction devices that the Radiophonic Workshop had invented sounds for, now actually existed. What was once only possible with specialist equipment, serious expertise and dynamic talent is now – arguably – available off the shelf. Perhaps inevitably, certainly sadly, the Radiophonic Workshop was closed by the BBC in 1996.

EFFECTIVE SOUNDS

The range of sound effects produced for **Doctor Who,** almost exclusively by Brian Hodgson and Dick Mills, is enormous. Over the years almost everything imaginable has been called for – from seaweed monsters to spaceships, from exploding planets to giant maggots. There have been numerous aliens, robots, gunshots, laser beams, alarms, sliding doors...

Even explosions are treated as sound effects. Although Visual Effects provides a real explosion, the sound is almost always added – adding to the illusion, making a model explosion bigger and louder and more realistic.

Not every sound effect was electronically realised. Many are an amalgamation of real sounds and electronic manipulation. Sarah sinking into the imaginary mud in *The Sontaran Experiment*, for example, is actually Dick Mills rubbing his hands in industrial cleaning gel. The roar of a Yeti is the flushing of a lavatory. Even the scraping engine sounds of the TARDIS were actually produced by the most mundane of objects – Brian Hodgson scraping his house key down a piano wire.

The TARDIS's dematerialisation is perhaps the most memorable sound effect in **Doctor Who**. But there are many other TARDIS effects which go unnoticed – as well as take-off and landing, there were sound effects for the TARDIS scanner, force field, doors, various controls and a background hum for the Control Room... Other standard effects include the Doctor's sonic screwdriver.

ELECTRONIC MUSIC

The most famous music created by the Radiophonic Workshop for **Doctor Who** – and perhaps its most famous creation for any series – is the theme music, realised from Ron Grainer's original score.

But the Workshop also provided incidental music for many stories, including 'stock' music for various stories up to and including *Inferno*. *The Sea Devils* featured a full incidental score by Malcolm Clarke, which incorporated a variation of the 'Master Theme' written for the previous season by composer Dudley Simpson. Simpson worked extensively with the Workshop to realise his own scores, and to ensure a good marriage of music and sound effects.

From *The Leisure Hive*, the Radiophonic Workshop took over the incidental music for the series for several years (with freelancers like Dominic Glynn, Keff McCulloch and Mark Ayres working on later programmes).

IN THE BACKGROUND

Not often remarked on, the background noises of the TARDIS, of a Control Room, an alien planet or any other setting for **Doctor Who** were realised by the Radiophonic Workshop. Sometimes these were stock effects, or even effects reused from other stories. For example, the jungles of Spiridon, Kembel, Zeta Minor and other far-flung locations sound surprisingly similar.

Perhaps most memorable is the heartbeat sound of the Daleks' Control Rooms – an effect used in every Dalek story with the exception of *Resurrection of the Daleks*.

MONSTROUS VOICES

While alien creatures often speak in English, their voices were generally treated to make them sound inhuman. In *The Dominators*, actress Sheila Grant provided the voices for the Quarks, and her voice was also treated and reused to provide other sounds emitted by the robots, such as the sound they make to signify confirmation of orders.

Most famous is, of course, the Dalek voice. This was created by treating the actor's voice with a 'ring modulator'. This works by adding and subtracting the frequency of an input signal (in this case from the actor doing the Dalek voice) from an internal oscillator's frequency. Unfortunately, the frequency used was never noted, and so Dalek voices tended to alter between stories. Ironically, the effectiveness of the voice was enhanced by the distortion present in the microphones and amplifiers of the time. Sometimes the voices were pre-recorded and played back into the studio, sometimes they were performed in 'real time' by the voice artist.

The earliest Dalek voices were Peter Hawkins – well known for providing the original **Flowerpot Men** with their *flubbadub* voices, and all the voices for most of the run of the original **Captain Pugwash**. He was joined by David Graham – a regular voice actor for Gerry Anderson (amongst many others) who played Brains and Parker in **Thunderbirds.** Later Roy Skelton provided Dalek voices, as did Michael Wisher (who was also the original Davros). Other actors have also given voice to the Daleks – including Brian Miller, husband of Elisabeth Sladen who played Sarah Jane Smith.

WORKING BRIEF

By the Third Doctor's era, videotapes of edited episodes were available for Brian Hodgson and Dick Mills to view when discussing and composing their sound effects. But, as with incidental music, in **Doctor Who**'s earliest days the effects were created without the luxury of being able to see the finished programme.

The director provided a brief, including timings, for what he wanted. The effect would then be created, ready to be dubbed on to the completed videotape.

Ironically, soundtracks still exist for some of the early episodes, while the videotapes have been lost. So, although we know what a 'Screamer' on the prison planet Desperus

sounded like in Episode 3 of *The Daleks' Master Plan*, almost the only visual clues we have come from director Douglas Camfield's brief to Brian Hodgson.

SCENE TWELVE. We are now on the prison planet Desperus, a devil's island planet where marooned prisoners are dumped to rot away. The local horror here are the "screamers", bat-like reptilian vampire creatures with a wing-span of 3ft 6ins. Firstly, I need an establishing sound of screamers wheeling around in the sky, shrieking and flapping their scaly wings, say 100ft up from the ground, but sometimes swooping down to investigate something. I shall use this in different places.
(ABOUT 45 secs)

SCENE FOURTEEN. A terrified man looks up at the sky. His particular phobia is fear of the screamers. They come swooping down on him. He falls down and crawls to a tree for protection. The camera tightens on him. A screamer — specially made and fixed to a pole — attacks him, screeching and flapping its wings, diving again and again. Because the shot is tight, we don't see all that much, the mind supplies the rest, helped by the now-insane screaming of the victim…
Could I have the screamer attack created? One obviously comes down lower than the others and actually attacks the man in vision, so you can get a separation in sound if you like.
(SAY 12 SECS OF PRE-ATTACK AND 15 SECS OF ACTUAL ATTACK AT CLOSE QUARTERS)

Four

'I walk in
Eternity...'

(THE DOCTOR – *PYRAMIDS OF MARS*)

THE FOURTH DOCTOR

THE DOCTOR

In his fourth incarnation, the Doctor is more alien than ever. He is a constant surprise to his enemies and to his companions. While in *Robot* he is apparently unstable, he is hardly more eccentric than in later stories. One moment he can be explaining the resistance to pressure of vegetable fibre (and working out the weight of an unknown opponent from a crushed flower), the next he is doing an impression of the *Titanic* and sinking into the Brigadier's Land Rover.

Instantly recognisable in floppy hat and long scarf, the Doctor's bohemian appearance gives a clue to his character. Less authoritarian and aristocratic than his predecessor, this Doctor is a rebel as well as a hero. He is Renaissance man made real: a jack of all trades – and master of all of them.

This Doctor displays a gamut of emotions and attitudes. He is dark and angry in *The Seeds of Doom* yet jovial and jokey in *Nightmare of Eden*. Raconteur and bon vivant in *The Talons of Weng-Chiang*, but quite at home with the peasants in *State of Decay*. He is brooding and moody in *Pyramids of Mars*, but irrepressibly enthusiastic in *The Ribos Operation*.

Yet this Doctor changes not from story to story but from moment to moment. Predominantly 'dark' in *The Seeds of Doom*, he grins as he compares Scorby to a 'mindless' plant. Amused and jovial throughout *Nightmare of Eden*, he cannot bring himself to speak to Tryst – hissing 'Go away' as the scientist tries to justify his actions.

For all his alien mutability and Olympian detachment, he is at times the most 'human' of Doctors. He takes time in *The Ark in Space* to eulogise about humanity's indomitability. It is with almost human reluctance that he convinces Professor Sorenson he has only one way out of his dilemma in *Planet of Evil*. For the first time he openly admits to having human friends and it becomes established that his favourite planet is Earth.

But as with the Second Doctor there is an air of superficiality to much of his banter and play-acting. In the quieter, deeper moments, we glimpse the darker and more 'genuine' Doctor. He is conscious always that he is essentially homeless; that he walks in eternity; that he is approaching middle age. In *The Pirate Planet*, he may joke with the Pirate Captain but in the Trophy Room we glimpse the Doctor's total outrage at the Captain's actions.

He is a Doctor constantly at odds with himself, a mass of contradictions. In *The Invasion of Time*, he is forced to act as if in league with the Vardans to invade Gallifrey. But it is as difficult for Leela to determine how much is put on and how much is his 'normal' behaviour as it is for the Vardans to penetrate his act.

It is ironic that this is the Doctor who is given an intimation of his own mortality in *Logopolis*. In many ways, we get the impression that he has been aware of it right from the start, trying to live life to the full and cram as many experiences and emotions as possible into his all-too-brief long life.

THE MAN BEHIND THE DOCTOR – TOM BAKER

Born in Liverpool in 1934, Tom Baker was brought up a devout Roman Catholic and even spent time in a monastery before becoming an actor while in the army medical corps during his National Service.

Although he played several small parts on television, Baker spent most of his early career in the theatre, before landing the role of Rasputin in the 1971 movie *Nicholas and Alexandra*. Other film work followed, including the villain Prince Koura in *The Golden Voyage of Sinbad* in 1973.

But in 1974 when he was asked to interview for the part of the Doctor, Baker was temporarily out of acting work and employed on a building site. Bill Slater, the BBC's Head of Drama Serials, had suggested Baker to **Doctor Who** producer Barry Letts. Together with his script editor, Terrance Dicks, Letts had been to see *The Golden Voyage of Sinbad* and had been impressed by what he saw. Letts offered Baker the role.

The youngest actor to play the Doctor so far, Baker stayed longer in the role than any other actor. After he left, he played Sherlock Holmes in a BBC production of **The Hound of the Baskervilles**, and appeared in many other television shows including **The Life and Loves of a She Devil**. Recently he has appeared in a regular role as the ghost Wyvern in the revived version of **Randall and Hopkirk (Deceased)**.

Almost as eccentric as the Doctor, Baker famously already owns his own gravestone. He has written his autobiography as well as a novel, *The Boy Who Kicked Pigs*.

HARRY SULLIVAN

While mentioned in *Planet of the Spiders*, the first time Surgeon Lieutenant Harry Sullivan meets the Doctor is after his regeneration in *Robot*. Despite being UNIT's medical officer, Harry does not appear to be aware of the Doctor's alien physiognomy and is startled to discover he has two heartbeats.

In the process of keeping a professional eye on the newly regenerated Doctor, Harry soon comes to appreciate his scientific genius and watches him create Kettlewell's metal virus to defeat the robot.

Seconded to UNIT from the Navy, Harry relishes the role of secret agent and enjoys the prospect of infiltrating Thinktank: 'I could wear a disguise,' he suggests, although nobody at Thinktank is likely to recognise him.

But for all he sees and experiences in *Robot*, Harry still believes the Doctor to be an eccentric rather than an alien. When he discovers that the Doctor and Sarah are planning a 'little trip' in the TARDIS, he tells the Doctor, 'We're both reasonable men. Now, we both know police boxes don't go careering around all over the place...'

The Doctor's 'little trip to the moon' to convince Harry ends up taking the Doctor, Sarah and Harry further in time and space than intended when Harry twists the helmic regulator and sends them into the far future. Once over the initial shock, Harry becomes a useful companion and a good friend to the Doctor and Sarah. The Doctor may chide Harry for his clumsiness and impulsiveness – 'Harry Sullivan is an imbecile,' he shouts in *Revenge of the Cybermen* – but he also trusts him to remove the terulian diode bypass transformer from Styre's ship in *The Sontaran Experiment*. Equally, while Sarah teases Harry for his ineptitude and naivety, there is no doubt that she trusts and likes him.

But perhaps at heart, despite his bravado and enthusiasm, Harry is not really an adventurer. He hints in *Revenge of the Cybermen* that given the chance he would like to retire and buy a 'quiet little practice in the country'. Certainly, at his first opportunity, at the end of *Terror of the Zygons*, Harry decides to stay behind on Earth and let the Doctor and Sarah take the TARDIS back to London alone.

ROBOT

In which Tom Baker takes over, and encounters a giant robot that grows to an even larger size...
BY TERRANCE DICKS
4 EPISODES, FIRST BROADCAST 28 DECEMBER 1974–18 JANUARY 1975

JOURNEY INFORMATION

THINKTANK

The National Institute for Advanced Scientific Research is colloquially known as Thinktank. The Brigadier describes it as '... the frontiers of science research place, all the latest in everything under one roof.'

The director is Hilda Winters, who explains that, 'As soon as our work reaches the practical stage, it's handed over to someone. Someone with more resources and a bigger budget.' Usually this is the government. The research for the disintegrator gun was pioneered at Thinktank.

SCIENTIFIC REFORM SOCIETY

The SRS is a small organisation that wants to reform the world on scientific and rational lines. It plans to use the robot (the SRS logo is a stylised representation of the robot's head) to steal destructor codes. As the Brigadier explains, 'A few months ago, the superpowers, Russia, America, China, decided upon a plan to ensure peace. All three powers have hidden atomic missile sites. All three agreed to hand over details of the sites, plus full operation instructions to another neutral country. In the event of trouble, that country could publish everyone's secrets and cool things down...'

Once the robot has stolen the codes, the SRS demands that the world governments cooperate in its reforms, or they will launch the world's atomic missiles.

EXPERIMENTAL ROBOT K1

The last project Professor J.P. Kettlewell worked on at Thinktank was a robot designed to 'replace the human being in a variety of difficult and dangerous tasks'. Although the robot's prime directive is that it must serve humanity and never harm it, Kettlewell has helped Hilda Winters and her assistant, Jellicoe, bypass this so SRS can use the robot.

The Doctor: 'No point in being grown up if you can't be childish sometimes.'

The robot is made of a 'living' metal, and when it absorbs the energy from the disintegrator gun, it grows to an enormous size. Having accidentally killed Kettlewell, it is driven mad and plans to carry out his plan to destroy the world – saving only Sarah as she showed it sympathy.

The Doctor eventually destroys the robot with a metal virus (developed by Kettlewell) that corrodes away the living metal.

NEW INFORMATION

THE DOCTOR

The new Doctor may be 'unstable' and unpredictable, but he is as brilliant as ever. He wins Kettlewell's respect by pointing out a flaw in his calculations, and agreeing with his comments about renewable technologies. Like his predecessor, he is self-assured to the point of arrogance – agreeing with Miss Winters when she says, 'I suppose it all seems very elementary to a scientist of your standing, Doctor.'

In his pockets, the Doctor carries – amongst other things – marbles, a grant of 'Freedom of the City of Skaro', a pilot's licence for the Mars–Venus rocket run, Galactic passport, his honorary membership of the Alpha Centaurian Table Tennis Club and, of course, bags of jelly babies.

As in The *Mind Robber*, the Doctor is able to type rapidly – leaving a note for Sarah, and also reprogramming the Thinktank computers. As in *Spearhead from Space*, the Doctor keeps the TARDIS key in his shoe.

UNIT

Benton has been promoted to Regimental Sergeant Major, (WO1): 'Technically speaking the Brig should have a major and a captain under him. But the UNIT budget won't run to it, so they settled for promoting me,' he tells Sarah.

COMPANIONS

BRIGADIER LETHBRIDGE-STEWART: We discover the Brigadier's full name is Alistair Gordon Lethbridge-Stewart.

SARAH JANE SMITH: Sarah automatically assumes that Jellicoe is the Thinktank director – to Miss Winters' amusement. Winters is also amused at Sarah's concern for the robot: 'Really, Miss Smith, this is absurd. I think you must be the sort of girl who gives motor cars pet names.' But the robot does have feelings for Sarah, planning to save her when it destroys the world, and she is saddened by its necessary destruction.

HARRY SULLIVAN: Sarah is worried that Harry seems a little old-fashioned in his approach. But the Brigadier has the utmost confidence in him.

BEHIND THE SCENES

OPENING TITLES

Keen to save money on a new title sequence, producer Philip Hinchcliffe suggested to graphics designer Bernard Lodge that they re-use the same basic idea as the 'slit-scan' titles that had been introduced with *The Time Warrior* in 1973. Hinchcliffe also suggested incorporating the image of the TARDIS police box into the shapes generated.

The new 35mm title sequence was edited into *The Ark in Space* and *The Sontaran Experiment* in October 1974. The titles for *Robot*, which was broadcast first, were taped on Tuesday 12 November along with the final studio session on *The Ark in Space*.

For the first episode of *The Ark in Space*, a greener colourisation of the 35mm opening titles was used. But the blue/lilac tint appeared as standard on all other episodes through to *Shada* in 1979.

THE ARK IN SPACE

In which **Doctor Who** does *Alien* a few years early, and the Wirrn Queen lays its eggs in the sleeping survivors of Earth...
BY ROBERT HOLMES
4 EPISODES, FIRST BROADCAST 25 JANUARY–15 FEBRUARY 1975

TARDIS DATA BANK:

DATE: UNKNOWN, FAR FUTURE
LOCATION: SPACE STATION NERVA

IN THE FAR FUTURE, THE SURVIVORS OF HUMANITY ARE STORED IN CRYOGENIC SUSPENSION ON 'THE ARK'. BUT THE WIRRN QUEEN HAS LAID EGGS IN THE SLEEPING TECHNICIAN DUNE, AND A WIRRN GRUB INFECTS COMMANDER NOAH. THE DOCTOR, SARAH AND HARRY MUST SAVE THE SLEEPERS FROM BEING EATEN ALIVE BY THE HATCHING WIRRN WHO ABSORB KNOWLEDGE AS WELL AS 'FOOD' FROM THEIR HOSTS...

JOURNEY INFORMATION

SPACE STATION NERVA – THE ARK

By the thirtieth century human society is highly compartmentalised. The senior official on Earth is the High Minister (a woman) who was in charge during the 'last days'.

The Ark is powered by solar stacks (infiltrated by the Wirrn). It has various areas, including cryogenic chambers, animal and botanic areas and an armoury equipped with fission guns. It carries a record of all human knowledge.

The Ark was designed to have a negative fault capacity. All systems are self-repairing and the auto-guard is designed to keep out intruders, delivering a charge of half a million volts.

Noah is the commander of the Ark – the 'prime unit'. His real name is Lazar, Noah is his nickname.

Noah is dedicated to the fulfilment of the Ark's mission to repopulate Earth, willing to execute the Doctor, Harry and Sarah rather than risk contamination of the genetic pool. He struggles against a Wirrn that takes him over, then seems eventually to succumb and become the swarm leader. In fact he still retains his humanity – leading the Wirrn into the Ark's transport ship, and then allowing it to explode in space to save the Ark.

THE WIRRN

The Doctor describes the process whereby the Wirrn take over the sleepers as 'symbiotic atavism'. The Wirrn Queen manages to lay her eggs in Dune's body – when the larvae emerge they have a food supply, and are equipped with all Dune's knowledge. This knowledge is added to as they absorb more humans – Noah gains Dune's knowledge when he is infected and mutates.

The Wirrn can live for years in space without fresh oxygen, their lungs recycling waste and using enzymes to convert carbon dioxide back to oxygen.

The Wirrn Noah explains that long ago their breeding colonies were destroyed by humans. 'Since then we have drifted through space searching for a new habitat... Now we shall use the humans in the cryogenic chamber. We shall be informed with all human knowledge. In one generation the Wirrn will become an advanced technological species...'

NEW INFORMATION

THE DOCTOR

The Doctor uses a yo-yo to take a gravity reading, and says that Madame Nostradamus knitted his scarf for him.

He teases Sarah when she is stuck in the conduit: 'Stop whining, girl – you're useless...' This provokes her into moving again, and once she is out he tells her how proud he is of her.

COMPANIONS

SARAH JANE SMITH: Sarah is frozen into cryogenic suspension, but is revived by Vira, a First Medtech. She manages to crawl through narrow conduits in order to run a cable from the transport ship to the cryogenic chamber.

HARRY SULLIVAN: Harry is impressed by the TARDIS, and suggests the Doctor could sell it. He also says it would be useful in Trafalgar Square with 'hundreds of bobbies hiding inside...'

He loses his shoes to the auto-guard. When technician Rogin later says he wants to see where he's putting his feet, Harry murmurs, 'You should worry.'

THE SONTARAN EXPERIMENT

TARDIS DATA BANK:

DATE: FAR FUTURE
LOCATION: EARTH

ARRIVING ON THE DESERTED FUTURE EARTH BY MEANS OF THE ARK'S TRANSMAT, THE DOCTOR, SARAH AND HARRY FIND SONTARAN FIELD MAJOR STYRE CONDUCTING EXPERIMENTS ON A STRANDED SPACE CREW TO ESTABLISH HUMAN STRENGTHS AND WEAKNESSES PRIOR TO A SONTARAN INVASION OF THE GALAXY. THE DOCTOR HAS TO FACE STYRE IN SINGLE COMBAT TO PREVENT THE INVASION…

In which the Doctor meets colonists and a Sontaran on Dartmoor...

BY BOB BAKER AND DAVE MARTIN

2 EPISODES, FIRST BROADCAST 22 FEBRUARY–1 MARCH 1975

JOURNEY INFORMATION

EARTH

Earth is a wasteland after being blasted by the sun's solar flares. The GalSec colonist Vural describes it as 'worn out, useless, and too far from the freight routes'.

But the planet has become strategically important to the Sontarans, hence Styre's mission to evaluate humanity prior to an attack.

THE GALSEC COLONISTS

Of the nine human GalSec Colonists stranded when Styre lured their ship to Earth and then destroyed it, only Vural, Zake, Krans and Erak are still at liberty. One prisoner dies as Harry tries to get him water, and Roth has escaped but is recaptured and killed. The colonists also mention Heath and Splier.

Vural is in league with Styre, relaying video and audio information in return for his life. He later saves the Doctor, but is killed by Styre, who reneges on their deal. 'Why should I spare you?' Styre demands, 'a traitor to your own miserable kind.'

FIELD MAJOR STYRE AND THE SONTARANS

As a Sontaran, Styre is almost identical to Linx (*The Time Warrior*), although his armour is slightly different and he has five fingers rather than three. The Marshal is identical to Styre, but has additional insignia on his uniform.

Field Major Styre is running the Sontaran G Three Military Assessment Survey. Its purpose is to evaluate human beings prior to a planned invasion of their part of the galaxy.

Amongst the various experiments, Styre has immersed a human in water, deprived a human of water, burned Roth and followed the 'free behaviour patterns' of Vural's party. He subjects Sarah to fear, and tests Erak and Krans for muscular strength when they try to prevent a gravity bar crushing Vural's chest as it grows heavier.

Styre answers to the Marshal, but his mission was ordered by the Grand Strategic Council.

Like all Sontarans, Styre sometimes needs to feed on pure energy. But Harry removes the terulian diode bypass transformer from his ship, and so the energy feeds on Styre and he collapses and dies before his ship explodes.

Styre has a robot powered by a terulian drive. It resists the colonists' weapons and can fire ropes that tie them up.

The Doctor bluffs the Marshal that Styre has been defeated and the Sontaran invasion plans are now in human hands.

NEW INFORMATION

THE DOCTOR

The Doctor says one should never throw anything away, and also that it is a mistake to clutter one's pockets. A piece of synestic locking mechanism from Nerva (see *The Ark in Space*) saves him from Styre's gun.

In single combat, he succumbs to Styre's superior strength, but tires the Sontaran enough that he needs to re-energise.

THE SONIC SCREWDRIVER

The Doctor uses the sonic screwdriver to repair the transmat diode receptors (the focus is fuzzy). Sarah is worried to find the sonic screwdriver left behind after the Doctor is captured by the GalSec colonists.

The Doctor tells Sarah he feels 'absolutely lost' without the sonic screwdriver, and later uses it to destroy the Sontaran robot.

Harry borrows the sonic screwdriver to get into Styre's ship, and to remove the terulian diode bypass transformer, leading to Styre's death.

COMPANIONS

SARAH JANE SMITH: Sarah is 'evaluated' by Styre who subjects her to fear. A device fixed to her forehead makes her see falling rocks, her rope bonds as snakes and her legs submerging in squelching slime.

HARRY SULLIVAN: When he believes both Sarah and the Doctor are dead, Harry goes after Styre with a makeshift wooden club.

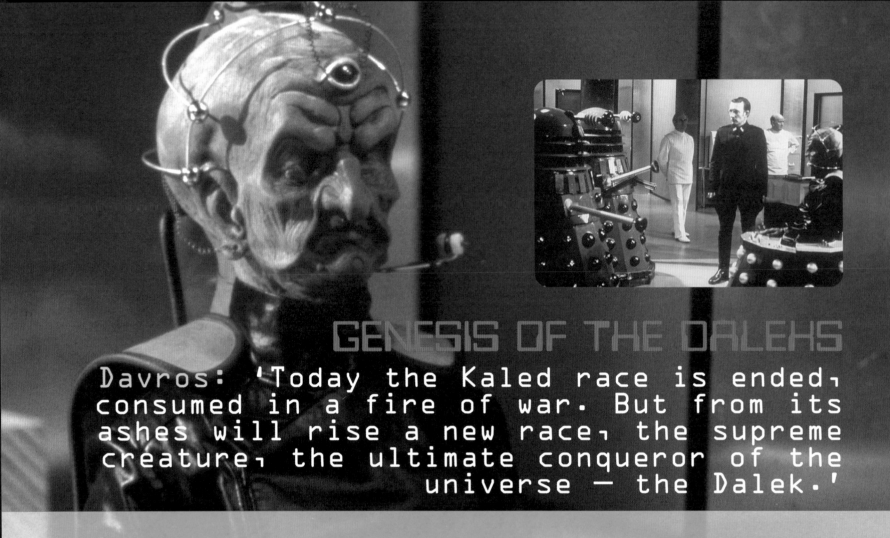

Davros: 'Today the Kaled race is ended, consumed in a fire of war. But from its ashes will rise a new race, the supreme creature, the ultimate conqueror of the universe — the Dalek.'

In which Davros creates the Daleks, and the Doctor is sent to stop him...
BY TERRY NATION
6 EPISODES, FIRST BROADCAST 8 MARCH–12 APRIL 1975

TARDIS DATA BANK:

DATE: UNKNOWN, DISTANT PAST
LOCATION: SKARO

THE TIME LORDS SEND THE DOCTOR, SARAH AND HARRY TO SKARO TO PREVENT THE CREATION OF THE DALEKS. THEY FIND THEMSELVES AT THE CLOSING STAGES OF A 1,000-YEAR WAR BETWEEN THE KALEDS AND THE THALS. BUT THE BRILLIANT, CRIPPLED KALED SCIENTIST DAVROS IS ALREADY PRODUCING PROTOTYPE DALEKS AND ALTERING THE GENETIC DEVELOPMENT OF HIS PEOPLE. CAN THE DOCTOR DESTROY THE DALEKS BEFORE THEY TAKE OVER...

JOURNEY INFORMATION

SKARO

The Thals and Kaleds have been at war for 1,000 years. Each side has its base in a city protected by a huge dome. As resources have been exhausted, they are now fighting with a mixture of modern and ancient weaponry and defences.

In the wastelands between the two domed cities live the Mutos – creatures mutated by the use of chemical and biological weapons in the first century of the war and banished into the wastelands to survive as best they can.

Each side is close to collapse – the Thals are pouring their final resources into building a 'last great rocket' they hope will destroy the Kaled Dome. The Kaleds are reduced to propping up corpses to make their trenches appear fully manned, and hanging prisoners rather than shooting them to conserve ammunition. They pin their hopes on the Scientific Elite.

Led by the crippled scientist Davros, the Elite started as a scientific research unit but has gained in power and kudos until it can demand the resources and help it wants.

In a sense, the plans of both sides work. When Davros betrays the Kaleds the Thals are able to destroy the Kaled Dome with their missile. But it is Davros's Daleks that win the war, rampaging through the Thal City and exterminating everyone they find...

DAVROS AND THE DALEKS

The Time Lords foresee a time when the Daleks will have destroyed all other life forms and become the dominant creatures in the Universe. So they send the Doctor back to the Daleks' very beginnings, either to avert their creation or to affect their genetic development so they evolve into less aggressive beings. Failing that, the Doctor may discover some inherent weakness of the Daleks.

Realising that the cycle of mutation started by the chemical and biological weapons could not be halted,

The Doctor: 'Listen, if somebody who knew the future pointed out a child to you and told you that the child would grow up totally evil... To be a ruthless dictator who would destroy millions of lives. Could you then kill that child?'

Davros took living tissue and experimented to determine the final mutational form of the Kaleds. Having established this, he turned his attention to designing a travel machine and life support system for the creatures. Intending his 'Dalek' to become the 'supreme victor' in inevitable universal wars, Davros changed the genetic make-up of the Dalek creatures so they would be superior – he increased the creatures' aggression and removed their conscience. He instilled in them the notion that the Daleks were the superior creatures and would one day rule supreme.

Having betrayed his own race, exterminated the Thals and learned from the Doctor the reasons for future Dalek defeats, Davros seems to have succeeded. He tricks those members of the Elite, led by Gharman, that opposed him into revealing themselves before having the Daleks take over the Elite bunker and exterminate his enemies.

The one thing Davros underestimates is the success of his own creation. Conditioned and programmed to believe they are superior and can adapt to any situation, the Daleks no longer need their creator. 'Have pity,' Davros pleads, but his creations have no understanding of the word and Davros is gunned down.

NEW INFORMATION

THE DOCTOR

The Doctor initially resists working for the Time Lords, until he discovers the Daleks are involved.

At the moment when it seems he can succeed and destroy the Dalek incubators, the Doctor hesitates – he cannot bring himself to wipe out a whole intelligent life form, as to do so would mean he was no better than them.

Ultimately, the Doctor realises that some things will be better with the Daleks – they will bring otherwise hostile races into alliance, and 'out of their evil must come something good'.

THE TARDIS

The Time Lord who briefs the Doctor tells him that they transcended such simple devices as the transmat '... when the Universe was less than half its present size'. He gives the Doctor a time ring – a bracelet with a symbol of the time vortex on it – that will return him to the TARDIS when the mission to prevent the development of the Daleks is complete.

COMPANIONS

SARAH JANE SMITH: Captured by the Thals, Sarah is forced to load their final rocket and is exposed to unshielded distronic explosives. She leads an escape attempt, but is recaptured when she climbs the rocket gantry in an attempt to get out on to the roof of the Thal dome. We see her fear of heights when a Thal soldier dangles her over the side of the rocket.

REVENGE OF THE CYBERMEN

TARDIS DATA BANK:

DATE: FUTURE, POSSIBLY 30TH CENTURY, DAY 3, WEEK 4
LOCATION: NERVA BEACON, VOGA

ARRIVING BACK ON THE ARK THOUSANDS OF YEARS BEFORE THEY LEFT, THE DOCTOR, SARAH AND HARRY FIND MOST OF THE CREW OF WHAT WAS THEN NERVA BEACON HAS BEEN KILLED BY A PLAGUE ENGINEERED BY THE CYBERMEN. ON THE NEARBY PLANET OF GOLD, VOGA, VORUS PLANS TO DESTROY THE CYBERMEN. BUT THE CYBERMEN HAVE OTHER PLANS – AND THE DOCTOR FINDS HIMSELF SENT DOWN TO VOGA AS A WALKING BOMB…

In which the Cybermen return, and attack the planet Voga – in reality the caves at Wookey Hole…
BY GERRY DAVIS
4 EPISODES, FIRST BROADCAST 19 APRIL–10 MAY 1975

JOURNEY INFORMATION

NERVA BEACON

Nerva Beacon, later to be converted into the 'Ark', has been put in place by Earth Centre to service space freighters and guide them round Jupiter's new satellite Neo-Phobos, which exographer Kellman has renamed Voga.

It has a full crew of fifty, but plague has reduced that to just three. The crew have had to use part of the infrastructure as a mortuary – leaving the victims where they drop. The beacon has been quarantined for 79 days and the surviving crew men are Commander Stevenson, Lester and Warner. The civilian Kellman has also survived.

The plague that has killed the crew is an infection spread by the Cybermats (controlled by Kellman). Glowing lines trace across the victim's face (similar to the black lines in *The Moonbase*). Their pulse races and 'they just seem to burn up'. The Doctor cures Sarah using the transmat – the alien poison is separated and ejected.

VOGA

Voga is the legendary planet of gold, all but destroyed by the Cybermen at the end of the Cyberwar. The remains have drifted like an asteroid until caught by Jupiter's gravity. The Vogans have survived the journey in a survival chamber built into the caves of Voga. They live in fear that the Cybermen will seek them out and destroy them.

The leader of their city is Tyrum, while the Guild Halls and the routes to the surface of Voga are controlled by Vorus and his Guardians. There is a tension between the two men, exacerbated by Vorus's lust for power, and his belief that Vogans should live on the surface of their planet. To end the threat of the Cybermen, he has secretly built a missile – his sky-striker – to destroy the last Cybermen once and for all when Kellman, who is pretending to be their ally, lures them on to the beacon. The sky-striker does indeed destroy them – but in their Cybership as they escape from Nerva Beacon, and after Vorus has been killed by Tyrum.

THE CYBERMEN

These Cybermen seem to have vestigial emotions – the Cyberleader is riled by the Doctor's insults. He particularly seems to resent references to the Cyberwar in which his race was all but wiped out when the humans discovered the Cybermen's susceptibility for gold. This non-corrodible metal

Cyberleader: 'You are about to die in the biggest
explosion ever witnessed in this solar system.
It will be a magnificent spectacle. Unfortunately
you will be unable to appreciate it.'

plates their breathing apparatus and suffocates them. The
humans developed the 'glitter gun' and, as the Doctor says,
'... that was the end of Cybermen, except as gold-plated
souvenirs people use as hatstands.' This is why the
Cybermen must destroy Voga – the planet of gold – before
they assemble a new Cyber army from parts in their ship
and begin a new campaign.

CYBERMATS

The Cybermats are of a different design to those seen
previously – longer with segmented bodies and no
prominent eyes. They can rear up and jump. The Cybermats
inject their victims with venom, which the Doctor replaces
with gold dust when he uses a Cybermat to attack the
Cybermen. He also uses gold dust to destroy a Cybermat.

CYBERBOMBS

The most compact and powerful explosive devices ever
created (according to the Cybermen), the use of cyberbombs
was banned by the Armageddon Convention. But the
Cybermen do not subscribe to any system of morality in war.
They calculate that two bombs will be sufficient to destroy
Voga, but use three to make certain – strapped to the Doctor,
Stevenson and Lester who are told, falsely, that they will have
time to get clear after planting the bombs.

Lester dies when he detonates the booby-trapped
buckle on one of the bombs to kill two Cybermen.

NEW INFORMATION

THE DOCTOR

Kellman finds a yo-yo, jelly babies and an apple core in the
Doctor's pocket. The Doctor uses a trick knot he learned from
Houdini when he ties Sarah up on the Cyberleader's orders.

THE TARDIS

The TARDIS is drifting back through time to rendezvous with
the Doctor, Harry and Sarah when they arrive using the time
ring (which disappears after they arrive).

The Brigadier has used a space–time telegraph
system the Doctor left to send a message asking for the
Doctor's help.

COMPANIONS

HARRY SULLIVAN: Finding gold on Voga, Harry says he may
buy himself out of the navy and purchase a quiet little
practice in the country.

TARDIS DATA BANK:

DATE: 1980
LOCATION: TULLOCK AND TULLOCK MOOR, SCOTLAND
(CLOSE TO LOCH NESS); LONDON

THE TARDIS ARRIVES IN SCOTLAND. UNIT IS INVESTIGATING THE DESTRUCTION OF NORTH SEA OIL RIGS AND THE DOCTOR DISCOVERS A GROUP OF STRANDED ZYGONS ARE USING THEIR CYBORG SKARASEN – THE LOCH NESS MONSTER – TO INFLICT THE DAMAGE. THE ZYGON LEADER, BROTON, IMPERSONATES THE DUKE OF FORGILL AND PLANS TO DESTROY AN ENERGY CONFERENCE IN LONDON BEFORE GIVING THE WORLD AN ULTIMATUM. UNLESS THE DOCTOR CAN STOP THE ZYGONS, THEY PLAN TO RESTRUCTURE THE EARTH SO IT IS SUITABLE FOR A FLEET OF REFUGEE ZYGONS ESCAPING THEIR DESTROYED PLANET…

TERROR OF THE ZYGONS

In which alien Zygons control the Loch Ness monster and try to take over the world...
BY ROBERT BANKS STEWART
4 EPISODES, FIRST BROADCAST 30 AUGUST–20 SEPTEMBER 1975

JOURNEY INFORMATION

THE ZYGONS

Centuries ago, the Zygon spaceship commanded by Warlord Broton was damaged and the Zygons landed in Loch Ness to await rescue. But they have recently learned that their world has been destroyed in a stellar explosion, and now they plan to make the Earth their home.

A great refugee fleet has been assembled and is heading for Earth – it will be centuries before it arrives, giving Broton and his Zygons time to restructure the Earth to suit them. Broton plans that once he controls the world the polar ice caps will melt, the temperature will be raised several degrees and lakes with the right mineral elements established.

The Zygons have been using the Skarasen – an armoured cyborg dinosaur-like creature brought to Earth as an embryo for its lactic fluid – to destroy oil rigs. But this is just a test of strength before Broton destroys more visible targets and makes his demands. The Skarasen has been living in Loch Ness for centuries – the Loch Ness Monster.

The Zygons can take body prints, allowing them to turn themselves into replicas of captive humans. Broton says it is necessary to reactivate a body print every few hours '... otherwise the original pattern dies and cannot be used again.' Broton has assumed the identity of the Duke of Forgill, while Odda takes the form of Sister Lamont from the oil company sick bay, Madra of Harry, and another Zygon of Forgill's servant, the Caber.

DUKE OF FORGILL

The Duke owns a lot of property, including part of the Loch Ness shoreline. He is the MacRanald clan chief.

Angus MacRanald says, 'It's true he's not the Duke I remember. He's been a different man since the oil companies

came... All his servants have left to go and work for them. It's said Forgill Castle's a cold empty house these days...' This is because the Duke has been replaced by Broton.

The Duke has a library of books devoted to the subject of the monster, though he doesn't believe in it himself. 'There is no limit to human credulity,' Broton says (as the duke).

Sarah discovers that the Duke is chieftain of the Antlers Association, trustee of the Golden Haggis Lucky Dip ('whatever that might be') and president of the Scottish Energy Commission.

NEW INFORMATION

THE DOCTOR

The Doctor wears a tam-o'-shanter and a tartan scarf as they are in Scotland. He is initially reluctant to help: 'Oil, an emergency? It's about time the people who run this planet of yours realised that to be dependent on a mineral slime just doesn't make sense...'

He puts himself and Sarah into a hypnotic trance to avoid suffocation when trapped in a decompression chamber. The Doctor warns Benton it could be fatal to break the spell incorrectly. He does it right by touching both sides of her neck.

THE TARDIS

The Brigadier calls the Doctor back to Earth with a psionic beam the Doctor left with him. The Doctor says he's going to pilot the TARDIS from Tullock Moor to London: 'I can be there five minutes ago.'

UNIT

Corporal Palmer is on the UNIT team in Tullock, though it is a different Corporal Palmer to the one seen in either *The Three Doctors* or *Invasion of the Dinosaurs*.

COMPANIONS

BRIGADIER LETHBRIDGE-STEWART: The Brigadier wears his clan kilt, reminding Sarah he's a Stewart. After the Zygons are defeated and their spaceship blown up, the Brigadier explains: 'The cabinet's accepted my report and the whole affair is now completely closed ... a 50-foot monster can't swim up the Thames and attack a large building without some people noticing. But you know what politicians are like.'

HARRY SULLIVAN: Sarah is wary of Harry when she meets him on the Zygon ship, until he calls her 'old girl' – then she knows it's really him. He takes the train back to London.

PLANET OF EVIL

In which the Doctor and Sarah arrive on a Jekyll-and-Hyde planet that becomes hostile at night, and meet the monster from *Forbidden Planet*...
BY LOUIS MARKS
4 EPISODES, FIRST BROADCAST 27 SEPTEMBER–18 OCTOBER 1975

TARDIS DATA BANK:

DATE: 37,166
LOCATION: ZETA MINOR

THE DOCTOR AND SARAH ANSWER A DISTRESS CALL FROM ZETA MINOR – A PLANET ON THE VERY EDGE OF CREATION. IT IS THE MEETING POINT OF THE UNIVERSES OF MATTER AND ANTIMATTER, AND MORESTRAN PROFESSOR SORENSON'S EXPEDITION HAS BEEN CONTAMINATED. A MORESTRAN PROBE SHIP ARRIVES TO RESCUE SORENSON'S PARTY, BUT THE ANTI-MATTER CREATURES CANNOT LET THEM LEAVE. AS SORENSON TURNS INTO ANTI-MAN, THE DOCTOR TRIES TO NEGOTIATE A TRUCE THAT WILL ALLOW THE MORESTRANS TO LEAVE…

JOURNEY INFORMATION

ZETA MINOR

Zeta Minor is 'the last planet of the known Universe' according to probe-ship officer Vishinsky. Technically it is not an 'X-planet' as Sorenson's party has been there for months (though it hasn't reported). Salamar, the ships's commander, tells Sarah that Zeta Minor is '... on the very edge of the known universe.'

The Doctor realises that Zeta Minor is the point at which the universes of matter and antimatter meet: '... the boundary between existence as you know it and the other Universe that you just don't understand... each is the antithesis of the other...'

There were originally eight in Sorenson's expedition. Lorenzo died first. Then Gura and Egard Summers, followed by Lumb then finally Braun and Baldwin. The antimatter creature makes a rattling sound, the victim disappears and then a desiccated corpse is returned. Morestran bio-analysis on one victim found that some very rapid form of freeze-drying occurred and even the bone marrow is gone.

Infected by antimatter, Sorenson mutates into Anti-Man. Commander Salamar's use of a neutron accelerator splits Anti-Man into 'duplicates of Sorenson, pure antimatter.'

MORESTRAN PROBE SHIP

The probe ship is commanded by Salamar, with Vishinsky the most experienced officer. The prime purpose of the mission is 'to locate Professor Sorenson's expedition'. It is a military expedition with military objectives – including to search out and and liquidate hostile forces.

The Morestran solar system is dependent upon a dying sun. Sorenson claims to have discovered a new and almost inexhaustible form of energy on Zeta Minor.

Senior Morestran officer Morelli's corpse is ejected into space in a metal canister. They have to play the last rites, but Vishinsky turns the volume down – they don't have to listen.

The ship has an oculoid tracker – an elliptical robot with a swivelling eye on its flat front side behind a curved transparent screen. It is launched from Projectile Chamber 3.

PROFESSOR SORENSON

Professor Sorenson has developed a theory that material from Zeta Minor could refuel their dying sun. 'Full-scale exploitation of this planet would provide us with perpetual energy in any quantity whenever we needed it. I've made the greatest discovery in scientific history.'

But the Doctor says that there is no way to exploit the material that has infected him, urging him (reluctantly) to commit suicide rather than carry the infection back and destroy the Universe when matter and antimatter meet.

But Sorenson is consumed by 'Anti-Man' before he can eject himself from the ship into space. When the antimatter is returned to Zeta Minor by Sorenson falling into the void between the universes, Sorenson is returned and recovers. The Doctor suggests he experiment with the energising of hydrogen as an energy source.

NEW INFORMATION

THE DOCTOR

The Doctor says he met Shakespeare once. He knocks Salamar unconscious when he hears Sarah scream, and convinces Sorenson he should accept responsibility for his actions – by committing suicide.

THE TARDIS

The internal doors will not open when the outer doors are jammed by Morestran transpose equipment.

COMPANIONS

SARAH JANE SMITH: Sarah thinks ejecting Morelli's body into space is 'horrible'.

When Sorenson asks her what the Doctor's field of science is, Sarah says, 'Everything, he's brilliant.'

BEHIND THE SCENES

STORY ORIGINS

Interviewed in 1988, producer Philip Hinchcliffe told *In-Vision* magazine how he and his script editor Robert Holmes approached **Doctor Who**. He used *Planet of Evil* as an example – this being the first story he produced that was not already being scripted or influenced by decisions made before he took over with *The Ark in Space...*

With PLANET OF EVIL, we'd decided that we wanted to do a JEKYLL AND HYDE story. We worked from themes of that sort. Then we tried to think of different ways of doing it. In the end I came up with the notion that we could perhaps have a JEKYLL AND HYDE planet - one minute one thing, the next another. Out of that grew the idea of a planet of evil.

What I wanted to do was stories that had a powerful concept behind them. Stories which had depth and menace, in terms of science fiction, or horror, or literature generally. JEKYLL AND HYDE goes right back to Robert Louis Stevenson.

We wanted to develop themes — like nemesis, a man trapped in something he doesn't really understand and he's really fighting himself. Those very basic mythic themes were things that I wanted to try and get in. And Bob and I wanted to incorporate them into things we'd either seen before, or which we had read about.

PLANET OF EVIL was based on the idea of doing a JEKYLL AND HYDE story. Then we had to think about how to do it. I remember thinking about it very hard, I didn't want it to look just like Studio 1! So I spoke to Roger Murray Leach, who was to be the designer, and he said: 'I can do you a good jungle, because we can do that on film at Ealing and it'll look really good.'

So the problem then was how to do a planet that at night reveals its dark and evil side. Good idea, but would it work? It was a combination of having a good idea, then working out how we thought we could do it; of talking to the production professionals very early on so that we knew we had something strong enough.

The Doctor: 'Come on, Sarah. We've an appointment in London and we're already 30,000 years late.'

There were other influences and ideas. I remembered reading in a science fiction story about a sort of travelling eye. I thought that was great, and wondered how we could do that. So I asked Roger, 'Could we do a travelling eye? I've got this notion, but could we do it with Chromakey [blue screen, see p149] The trouble with Chromakey was it was so time-consuming. But Roger said, 'No, we'll do it on film in the jungle and just hang it on a wire. You'll never see the wire.'

So we already had ideas building. Bob reckoned we could do something with JEKYLL AND HYDE - we could do some funny things with his eyes, and have this guy sprout hair and all that sort of thing. So already we had something there we could achieve. The principle was to work out in advance what you could do. So, for example, I said: 'Can you do a monster like the one in Forbidden Planet? What can you do that's something like it?' We worked out the ingredients and more or less knew how we could do it. THEN we knew we could do the story.

PYRAMIDS OF MARS

Sutekh: 'Your evil is my good.
I am Sutekh the Destroyer — where I tread
I leave nothing but dust and darkness.
I find that good.'

In which Egyptian mummies turn out to be killer alien robots building a pyramid-rocket to free the god Sutekh...
BY STEPHEN HARRIS
4 EPISODES, FIRST BROADCAST 25 OCTOBER–15 NOVEMBER 1975

JOURNEY INFORMATION

PROFESSOR MARCUS SCARMAN

Marcus Scarman – professor of archaeology, fellow of All Souls and member of the Royal Society – has disappeared on his expedition to a pyramid near Saqqara. He has not been seen for weeks after entering the tomb, his baggage lying unclaimed in his hotel in Cairo. In fact Scarman was killed by Sutekh when he entered his tomb, his cadaver was animated by Sutekh's will and sent back to the priory to supervise building the missile.

Scarman can detect 'other humans' within the house and when the poacher Clements shoots him the shotgun blast is 'reversed.' He controls the Mummies mentally.

Scarman's face turns into that of Sutekh as he concentrates to destroy the Eye of Horus. As he dies he is freed from the Osiran's malevolent influence – which has even forced him to kill his own brother Laurence.

SUTEKH AND THE OSIRANS

Seven thousand years earlier, the Osiran, Sutekh, (also known as Set, Satan and Sadok) destroyed his own planet, Phaester Osiris, and left a trail of havoc across half the galaxy. Horus and 740 other Osirans finally cornered Sutekh in Egypt where their conflict brought about the Egyptian myths.

Horus imprisoned him beneath a pyramid, powerless to move. The Osirans did not destroy Sutekh as that would have meant they were no better than he. So they imprisoned him using a force-field controlled from a power source on Mars. Now Sutekh aims to destroy the power source with the missile he is building and set himself free.

Sutekh controls operations at the priory – including Scarman – with mental force, which the Doctor manages to block with an etheric impulse projected along precisely the right axis. When the missile is destroyed, Sutekh uses the TARDIS to send Scarman to the Pyramid of Mars to get past Horus's traps and destroy the energy source – the Eye of Horus.

THE MUMMIES

Sutekh's mummy servants are actually Osiran servicers – service robots. Their bindings are chemically impregnated to protect them from damage and corrosion. They are activated and controlled by a ring which draws power from Sutekh's tomb (allowing the Doctor to reverse triangulate and trace Sutekh).

NEW INFORMATION

THE DOCTOR

The Doctor says he's 'lived for something like 750 years' and agrees when Sarah says he'll soon be middle-aged: 'It's about time I found something better to do than run round after the Brigadier.' He remarks that 1911 is '... an excellent year. One of my favourites.'

There is a distinct contrast between the Doctor's amusement at showing Laurence the TARDIS, and his indifference to his death – as Sarah starts to say, 'Sometimes you don't seem human.'

The Doctor tells Sutekh he is from Gallifrey in the constellation of Kasterborus – the binary location from galactic zero centre being 'ten zero eleven zero zero by zero two'. He also tells Sutekh that the controls of the TARDIS are isomorphic: 'One to one, they answer to you alone.' But he is presumably lying – Sutekh says the Time Lords are 'a perfidious species'.

His respiratory bypass system enables the Doctor to survive being strangled by a mummy.

THE TARDIS

The relative continuum stabiliser fails when the TARDIS is 'attacked' by Sutekh. The Doctor claims 'Nothing can enter the TARDIS. Unless ... mental projection of that force is beyond imagination. Yet it might explain the stabiliser failure.'

The Doctor shows Sarah the barren wasteland 'the world will look like in 1980' if they leave without intervening. He says 'Every point in time has its alternatives, Sarah – you've looked into alternative time.' The actions of the present fashion the future, but 'it takes a being of Sutekh's almost limitless power to destroy the future.'

The Doctor uses the TARDIS Time Controller to shift the exit from Sutekh's space–time tunnel into the far future so he ages to death when trying to escape.

UNIT

UNIT HQ was built on the site of the old priory, which burned down in 1911. The Doctor describes UNIT as a 'paramilitary organisation' when joking about buying the house.

COMPANIONS

SARAH JANE SMITH: Sarah tells Laurence, 'We travel in time, Mr Scarman...' And later she insists, 'I'm from 1980.' She knows how to handle a rifle, and hits the explosives the Doctor places by the missile with her first shot.

THE ANDROID INVASION

In which the Doctor and Sarah meet themselves in a replica English village on an alien planet...
BY TERRY NATION
4 EPISODES, FIRST BROADCAST 22 NOVEMBER–13 DECEMBER 1975

JOURNEY INFORMATION

STYGGRON AND THE KRAALS

The Kraal planet Oseidon has the highest level of natural radiation in the galaxy. It is getting worse all the time and soon the planet will become uninhabitable, which is why the Kraals are planning to leave and take over Earth.

Styggron is chief scientist of the Kraals. He has invented the androids and the virus that will destroy human life. Captured astronaut Crayford says, 'Styggron's machine extracts and feeds into a computer the memory and entire intelligence of any living being.' This data from Crayford is used to create the androids and the training ground.

Styggron maintains that 'Earth's resources are limited, they cannot be wasted supporting an inferior species... The androids will disseminate a virus. It will cause a contagion so lethal, the Earth will be rid of its human population within three weeks. Then it will burn itself out, and the world will be ours.' During this time, Styggron will be in quarantine on board the ship Crayford was piloting. But the scientist is killed by the virus when the flask containing it is broken.

ANDROIDS

Created from Crayford's memories, the androids are duplicates of humans built over a metal frame. Sarah's double fires her gun left-handed, like a mirror image. There are even android tracker dogs.

The Kraal military commander, Marshal Chedaki, says the androids are 'unstoppable, indestructible'. But Styggron creates an android with a hostility circuit in order to test a new weapon that could destroy the androids if the Doctor was able to turn them against the Kraals. So far the new weapon is only effective at short range, but Styggron's armoury section is developing 'a much more powerful version for our space cruisers'.

Before Crayford's ship lands, the pod-like space-shells with the androids inside them are jettisoned. The androids then take over the defence complex so that Chedaki can bring in the main invasion fleet without a shot being fired.

The training ground is maintained by non-duplicate android 'mechanics' with white suits and helmets. These can fire through their index fingers. The Doctor uses the Space Defence Station's equipment to 'jam' the androids, which freeze into immobility.

GUY CRAYFORD

Astronaut Guy Crayford piloted the first test of the XK5 space freighter, but was lost in deep space – a story covered by Sarah. It was assumed his ship hit an asteroid.

In fact he was kidnapped by the Kraals, who have brainwashed him into believing they saved him (and that he has lost an eye). Styggron has used Crayford's knowledge and memories to create the androids and plans to use his return as cover for the invasion.

Crayford believes Earth betrayed him, and that the Kraals are only going to take over the northern hemisphere and live in peace.

TARDIS DATA BANK:

DATE: NEAR FUTURE, PROBABLY 1980
LOCATION: OSEIDON; VILLAGE OF DEVESHAM

THE DOCTOR AND SARAH ARRIVE BACK ON EARTH BUT THE VILLAGE OF DEVESHAM SEEMS DESERTED – AND WHEN THE INHABITANTS DO ARRIVE IN A LORRY THEY BEHAVE ODDLY. AT THE NEARBY SPACE DEFENCE STATION THE DOCTOR DISCOVERS THAT THE VILLAGERS AND STATION STAFF ARE ANDROIDS, AND THE WHOLE VILLAGE IS A TRAINING GROUND CONSTRUCTED BY THE KRAALS TO REHEARSE THEIR PLANNED INVASION OF EARTH. CAN THE DOCTOR AND SARAH GET BACK TO EARTH IN TIME, AND CAN THEY TELL WHO IS FRIEND AND WHO IS ANDROID? THE DOCTOR AND SARAH EVEN FACE DOUBLES OF THEMSELVES AS THEY STRUGGLE TO DEFEAT THE KRAALS...

Sarah: 'So, providing we don't burn up on re-entry and aren't suffocated on the way down, we'll probably be smashed to a pulp when we land.'
The Doctor: 'Exactly. Sarah, you've put your finger on the one tiny flaw in our plan.'

NEW INFORMATION

THE DOCTOR

The Doctor enjoys ginger beer – though Sarah says she can't stand it – both from a bottle outside the TARDIS and in the pub.

He mentions he spoke to the Duke of Marlborough at the battle of Malplaquet, claims he told Alexander Bell that wires were unreliable, and remembers seeing something like the Kraal space-shell 'pod' before.

Marshal Chedaki says, 'The data that was drained from the girl shows the Doctor's long association with libertarian causes. His entire history is one of opposition to conquest.'

The Doctor produces what he claims is an android detector – a plain metal box with a red light that illuminates in the presence of androids.

THE TARDIS

The Doctor says that the linear calculator is not performing properly, and that the TARDIS is well overdue her 500-year service.

The TARDIS is not programmed to auto-operate and has a fail-safe. But when Sarah puts the key in the lock that cancels the pause control, the TARDIS continues from Oseidon on its preset course, leaving Sarah stranded.

UNIT

Colonel Faraday is in command at the space centre while the Brigadier is in Geneva.

Benton is taking his 'kid sister' to a dance. The last we ever see of the real Benton is his lifeless body (though in *Mawdryn Undead* the Brigadier suggests he survives, and is selling second-hand cars).

THE BRAIN OF MORBIUS

In which a mad scientist builds a body out of bits and pieces of other life forms and just needs the Doctor's head to complete it...

BY ROBIN BLAND

4 EPISODES, FIRST BROADCAST 3–24 JANUARY 1975

TARDIS DATA BANK:

DATE: UNKNOWN, FUTURE
LOCATION: KARN

ON THE BARREN PLANET OF KARN, SOLON HAS KEPT THE BRAIN OF THE EXECUTED TIME LORD MORBIUS ALIVE AND HIDDEN FROM THE SISTERHOOD WHO GUARD THE ELIXIR OF LIFE. HE HAS CONSTRUCTED A NEW BODY FOR MORBIUS, AND NOW HE JUST NEEDS THE HEAD. THE DOCTOR'S WILL DO NICELY... CAN THE DOCTOR WIN THE CONFIDENCE OF THE SISTERHOOD, AVOID BECOMING A DONOR, AND DEFEAT ONE OF THE GREATEST TIME LORD CRIMINALS WHO EVER EXISTED...

JOURNEY INFORMATION

THE SISTERHOOD OF KARN

Paranoid after Morbius betrayed them and laid waste to Karn, the Sisterhood bring down any spaceship that comes near the planet. Until Morbius, only the High Council of the Time Lords knew of the Elixir of Life and since the Time of the Stones the Sisterhood have shared the Elixir with the Time Lords.

Led by Maren, the Sisterhood worship the Flame of Life which provides them with the Elixir that gives them immortality. Alone of all the races in the galaxy the Time Lords are their equals in mind power. Other races they can 'destroy from within. We can place death at the very centre of their beings...' But Time Lords can close their minds to this, which is how Morbius has lived on Karn undetected. Away from the Flame, the Sisters' powers fade.

The Doctor says the Flame is the product of gases forced up along a geological fault from deep in the molten heart of the planet, and will burn for millions of years. Maren has been secretly feeding the flame with powdered rineweed for months – there has been no Elixir for over a year.

The Doctor describes the taste of the Elixir as: 'Nectar? Stewed apricots – no custard.'

MORBIUS

Morbius once led the High Council of Time Lords and 'offered them greatness'. The Doctor says he was '... a war criminal. A ruthless dictator but with millions of fanatical followers and admirers.' He offered his mercenaries the Elixir of Life, but was defeated and executed on Karn by the Time Lords 'for leading the rebellion' – his body was atomised to the nine corners of the Universe. But Solon has somehow managed to save the brain of Morbius, which is kept alive in a tank of colloidal nutrient. He is building Morbius a body designed for efficiency rather than appearance.

Solon is fiercely loyal to Morbius and protective of him – killing his servant, Condo, when Condo discovers the monster has his missing arm and knocks the brain to the floor in the ensuing struggle. Author of a book on microsurgical techniques. Solon is one of the foremost neurosurgeons of his time and when he disappeared and joined Morbius, he 'caused quite a stir'.

'I have mastered new techniques that no other man has even conceived,' he claims, 'I can create life.' Despite potential problems with an artificial braincase, Solon is forced to resort to its use. But during a mind-bending contest between the Doctor and Morbius, static electricity within the cranial cavity builds up and earths through the brain, upsetting its equilibrium and dislocating the neural centres. Morbius staggers away and is hounded over a cliff by the Sisterhood.

NEW INFORMATION

THE DOCTOR
The Doctor resents being brought to Karn by the Time Lords and says he won't stand for any more interference. The Doctor recognises the stars: 'I was born in these parts ... within a couple of billion miles...' he tells Sarah. He claims to be 749.

Maren says the secret of the Elixir is known only to the Sisterhood and 'the High Council of the Time Lords', yet the Doctor knows of it, and about the Sisterhood of Karn.

Solon says that, as a Time Lord, the Doctor has a 'secondary cardiovascular system' which means there is no danger of tissue rejection if Solon uses the Doctor's head.

Time Lords only use the Elixir '... in rare cases when, for instance, there is some difficulty in regenerating a body.' The Doctor becomes the first person outside the Sisterhood to see the Sacred Flame. He produces fireworks from his pocket to clear the soot and 'cure' the Flame.

Morbius accepts the Doctor's challenge to a mind-bending contest, which the Doctor says is '... Time Lord wrestling. It's usually a game but it can end in deathlock.' As each contestant tries to regress the other through his incarnations and back to his beginning – and death – we see the previous three Doctors and, apparently, another eight.

COMPANIONS
SARAH JANE SMITH: As with the Sisters, Solon cannot use Sarah's head as the female braincase is too small. Condo takes a liking to Sarah and is protective of her when she is temporarily blinded by Maren's ring.

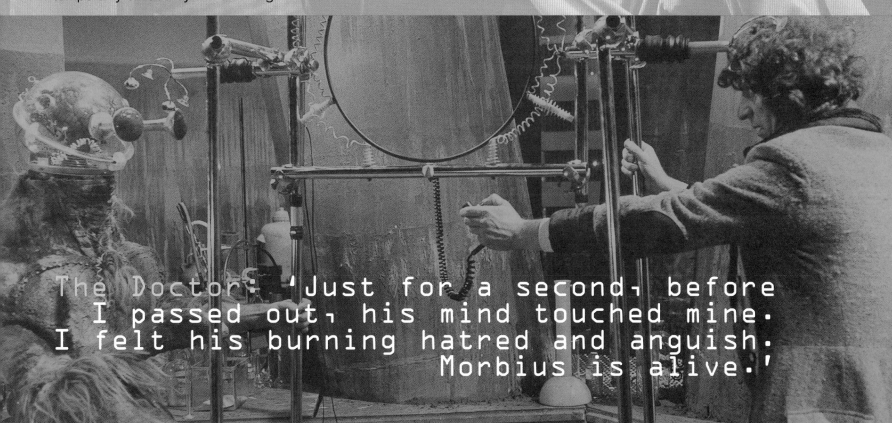

The Doctor: 'Just for a second, before I passed out, his mind touched mine. I felt his burning hatred and anguish. Morbius is alive.'

In which an alien plant pod infects people, takes over Earth's vegetation, and grows to giant size...
BY ROBERT BANKS STEWART
6 EPISODES, FIRST BROADCAST 31 JANUARY–6 MARCH 1976

JOURNEY INFORMATION

WORLD ECOLOGY BUREAU

Sir Colin Thackeray, in charge of the World Ecology Bureau, is responsible for calling in first the Doctor, and later UNIT. His deputy, Dunbar, sells information about the Krynoid pod to millionaire botanist Harrison Chase.

ANTARCTIC EXPEDITION

Up to a dozen scientists work at the Antarctic base. However, most are about 60 miles away at South Bend, measuring the ice cap. Remaining at the base are Charles Winlett, Derek Moberly (zoologist) and John Stevenson (botanist). Sir Colin has a daily video link of ten minutes' satellite time with the expedition.

For safety, the base's power plant is a separate building – a new fuel cell system is being tested for the first time there.

THE KRYNOID

The Doctor describes the Krynoid as a sort of galactic weed. 'Except it's deadlier than any weed you know... On most planets the animals eat the vegetation. On planets where the Krynoid gets established, the vegetation eats the animals.'

When Winlett is infected by one of the pods and mutates into a Krynoid, his body temperature drops to 46 and his pulse to 18 a minute. He has plant bacteria in his bloodstream. The plant from the pod enters his arm.

As it develops, a Krynoid is able to channel its powers to other plants – so that they become its eyes and ears, and attack animals. The Krynoid can speak and think – identifying the Doctor as a menace.

As it grows to 'adulthood', the Krynoid prepares to eject thousands of seed pods before it is destroyed in a low-level bombing run by the RAF.

The Krynoid pods have been in the ice for about 20,000 years. The pods have a hard exterior, and no root system. The Doctor says the pods travel in pairs 'like policemen'. He suggests that maybe their home planet is turbulent and the pods are shot into space by internal explosions.

THE SEEDS OF DOOM

Chase: 'The sergeant's no longer with us. He's in the garden. He's part of the garden.'

HARRISON CHASE

Millionaire plant enthusiast Harrison Chase is fanatical in his mission to 'protect the plant life of mother Earth'.

He plays music to his plants on an electric organ. He ties up his infected botanist, Keeler, to watch him mutate: 'Together we are on the verge of a great scientific discovery... You're changing into a plant, Keeler. You're privileged.'

Chase's sixteenth-century mansion includes a plant laboratory he describes as unique: 'It makes the Botanical Institute look like a potting shed.' It also houses a compost acceleration chamber – he tells the Doctor that within 25 minutes of being crushed to pulp, his remains can be pumped into the garden 'to become part of nature's grand design'.

Possessed by the Krynoid, Chase tells Sarah, 'I have become part of a life I have always admired – for its beauty, colours, sensitivity. I have the Krynoid to thank, as it thanks me for its opportunity to live on Earth. Soon the Krynoids will dominate everywhere, and your foul species will disappear.'

SCORBY

Chase describes the mercenary Scorby as 'my most efficient man'. He is a violent sadist, pushing the Doctor around and threatening to put him through the compost machine merely to pay him back for getting the better of him.

Sarah tells him that he's not complete unless he's got his gun in his hand. Ultimately, of course, the gun does him no good as he is drowned – dragged down into a pond by a mass of weed.

NEW INFORMATION

THE DOCTOR

Always ready for travel, the Doctor has a toothbrush in his pocket. He does not feel the cold of the Antarctic.

Short-tempered for much of the story, the Doctor knocks Chase's chauffeur out and vigorously overpowers Scorby, violently twisting his head round.

The Doctor tells Sir Colin Thackeray he is president of the Intergalactic Floral Society, and apologises that he can't address the Royal Horticultural Society as he's 'fully booked for the next two centuries'.

COMPANIONS

SARAH JANE SMITH: The Doctor tells Chase that Sarah is his best friend. She stands up to Scorby, despite having witnessed his vicious, sadistic character.

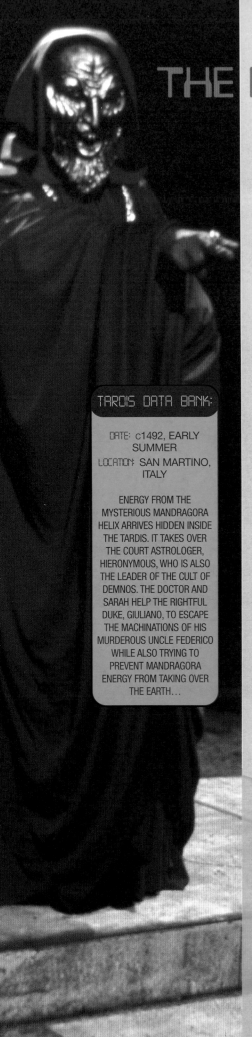

THE MASQUE OF MANDRAGORA

In which an alien fireball attacks Renaissance Italy, in Portmeirion – 'the Village' from *The Prisoner*...

BY LOUIS MARKS

4 EPISODES, FIRST BROADCAST 4–25 SEPTEMBER 1976

JOURNEY INFORMATION

THE MANDRAGORA HELIX

The Mandragora Helix is a spiral of pure energy that radiates outwards in ways that nobody really understands. At its centre is a controlling intelligence. From space, it looks like a whirlpool. The TARDIS arrives in an echoing black void with crystals spiralling into the distance.

The Helix Energy that secretly enters the TARDIS and is brought back to Earth is a glowing ball of fire. It burns where it touches – leaving bodies charred beyond recognition by the high ionisation. On Earth the Helix Energy restores the ruined Temple of Demnos to its former glory, penetrating every stone and using it as a focal point. It also takes over Hieronymous, eventually converting him to pure energy.

Seeing Man as a future threat to its domain, Mandragora plans to destroy the philosophers and thinkers (including Leonardo da Vinci) who are at a masqued ball coincident with an eclipse of the moon to celebrate Giuliano's accession to the dukedom of San Martino. The Mandragora Helix is only foiled when the Doctor takes the place of Hieronymous and drains away the Helix Energy, earthing it from the altar of the temple.

GIULIANO

The Doctor says that the Mandragora Helix has chosen this time and place to take over the Earth as it is the turning point between the dark ages of superstition and the dawn of the new science. Italy is the heart of the Renaissance – as demonstrated by the young Duke Giuliano's interest in the new sciences and his scepticism about the old mysticism, including astrology.

COUNT FEDERICO

Even Giuliano calls his uncle, Count Federico, a tyrant, and is worried that if Federico were ever to rule San Martino, all learning would be suppressed. Federico has already murdered Giuliano's father and is now plotting to murder Giuliano so he can claim the dukedom. But Federico has reckoned without his seer, Hieronymous, being possessed by the Mandragora Helix.

HIERONYMOUS

Count Federico says Hieronymous is the finest seer in the land. But the Doctor is scathing of his ability: 'All it needs is a colourful imagination and a glib tongue.' However, as the Doctor later realises, Hieronymous was sympathetic to Mandragora's agenda, and has been possessed by Helix Energy.

As the secret leader of the forbidden cult of Demnos, Hieronymous is able to organise an attack on the masque by the possessed cult.

NEW INFORMATION

THE DOCTOR

The Doctor uses a version of Venusian Aikido on a cult brother who kidnaps Sarah. He has a football rattle in his pocket which he uses to frighten guard captain Rossini's horse and escape capture. Later, he demonstrates his own skill at horse-riding when escaping execution.

Giuliano says the Doctor is the finest swordsman he has ever seen. The Doctor explains that the finest swordsman he ever knew was a captain in Cleopatra's bodyguard: 'He showed me a few points.'

The Doctor: 'A wave of energy has been released, Count. It could do untold damage and I must take it back to the stars.'

The Doctor is able to impersonate Hieronymous, perfectly mimicking his voice behind his ceremonial mask. He is disappointed to miss Leonardo.

THE TARDIS

Sarah asks how big the TARDIS is. 'There are no measurements in infinity,' the Doctor tells her.

The Secondary Control Room is wood-panelled with a smaller central console that has hinged compartments with controls behind. There is a recorder and a velvet jacket in the room, suggesting previous incarnations of the Doctor used it.

The Doctor says their arrival in San Martino was a 'forced landing' and he didn't touch a thing: 'Helix force fields must have distorted the coordinates.'

COMPANIONS

SARAH JANE SMITH: Sarah says she is 5'4" (just).

The Doctor says Sarah's ability to understand Italian is '... a Time Lord gift I allow you to share'. The fact that she asks him why she can suddenly understand Italian tells him her mind is affected – she has been hypnotised by Hieronymous and ordered to kill the Doctor with a poisoned needle.

THE HAND OF FEAR

In which an alien hand takes over a nuclear power station, and Sarah leaves the Doctor...
BY BOB BAKER AND DAVE MARTIN
4 EPISODES, FIRST BROADCAST 2 OCTOBER–23 OCTOBER 1976

TARDIS DATA BANK:

DATE: NEAR FUTURE (c1980)
LOCATION: NUNTON RESEARCH CENTRE, ENGLAND; KASTRIA

SARAH IS POSSESSED BY A BROKEN STONE HAND SHE FINDS IN A QUARRY. SHE TAKES IT TO A NUCLEAR POWER STATION, WHERE THE RADIATION RECONSTITUTES THE HAND INTO A KASTRIAN NAMED ELDRAD. THE DOCTOR AGREES TO TAKE ELDRAD BACK TO KASTRIA, WHERE HE WAS THE SAVIOUR OF HIS PEOPLE. BUT ELDRAD HAS LIED AND IS REGENERATED ON KASTRIA INTO A WARMONGERING DESPOT...

JOURNEY INFORMATION

NUNTON RESEARCH AND DEVELOPMENT COMPLEX

Professor Watson is in charge of the Nunton Complex, which has at least two reactors. When Eldrad takes control of the nuclear reactor, Watson has the authority to evacuate the complex, and later to organise an RAF strike to take out the complex with 'stand-off' missiles.

KASTRIA

Kastria became a cold, icy world when the barriers that kept out the solar winds were destroyed by Eldrad. It has an Earth-type atmosphere and slightly high radiation levels.

The Kastrians are a silicon-based, crystalline race (Eldrad says s/he devised a crystalline silicon form for their physical needs). The Doctor says that such races are rare (though there are similarities between the Kastrians and the crystalline Krotons and silicon-based Ogri from *The Stones of Blood*). Unlike a normal fossil, Eldrad's hand gives no indication of structure since it has a silicon infrastructure.

Rather than risk the remote possibility of Eldrad's return to wage war across the galaxy, the population under the guidance of King Rokon chose final oblivion. They also destroyed their race bank – a store of 100 million crystal particles that could be regenerated into a new race of Kastrians.

Sarah: 'Careful — that's not as 'armless as it looks.'

ELDRAD

Eldrad created the barriers that kept the solar winds at bay and made life on the surface of Kastria possible. But when the Kastrians failed to agree with his dreams of conquest, he destroyed the barriers. The Kastrians sentenced Eldrad to be placed in an obliteration module, which was then remotely detonated. But, forced to detonate the module early, the Kastrians knew there was a one in three million chance of particle survival.

Sure enough, Eldrad's hand together with the ring containing his genetic code survived, to be found by Sarah in a quarry 150 million years later. Eldrad is able to influence the wills of those who come into contact with his hand – including Sarah – so they work towards his regeneration. By absorbing radiation, the hand becomes animated again. Then when the reactor and the RAF nuclear missiles explode, he absorbs sufficient radiation to be reborn, albeit in a form based on Sarah's body.

The 'female' Eldrad is able to persuade the Doctor that she saved her planet from alien invaders and that he should return her to Kastria. But, once returned and regenerated into his true Kastrian form, Eldrad's true aggressive character becomes apparent.

NEW INFORMATION

THE DOCTOR

The Doctor apologises after punching the possessed Sarah unconscious. He carries a magician's wand in his pocket.

Despite being dormant for 150 million years, Eldrad has heard of the Time Lords and the role they play in time and space. The Doctor says that 'a distortion of history' contravenes the First Law of Time. He uses his scarf to trip up Eldrad, who falls into an abyss.

The Time Lords summon the Doctor back to Gallifrey at the end of the story – either this is a general call to attend the Presidential Resignation in *The Deadly Assassin*, or the Master is already manipulating the Doctor. The Doctor says that he cannot take Sarah with him.

THE TARDIS

The Doctor tells Eldrad that her 'weapons' won't work in the TARDIS as it is a state of grace, in a sense people do not exist while in the TARDIS. (Presumably this refers to her mental powers, as guns – except patrol stasers in *The Invasion of Time* – are seen to operate in the TARDIS.)

The Doctor tells Eldrad that if s/he has mis-set the coordinates for Kastria '... symbolic resonance will occur in the tachoid time crystal and if that happens there'll be no chance of us landing anywhere, ever...'

When repairing the TARDIS (the cold may have affected the thermal couplings), the Doctor uses various tools including his sonic screwdriver, an astro-rectifier, a multi-fortescope, zeus plugs, a margin-nut and a ganymede-driver.

COMPANIONS

SARAH JANE SMITH: Sarah is possessed by the will of Eldrad after finding his hand and ring. When Eldrad is regenerated by the release of nuclear energy, he bases his physical form on the first being to come into contact with him – Sarah, hence Eldrad's initial female form.

Unable to take Sarah back to Gallifrey, after a sad farewell, the Doctor takes her home to Hillview Road in South Croydon... Or so he thinks.

220

THE TIME LORDS AND GALLIFREY

The Deadly Assassin affords the first in-depth analysis of the Time Lords and their civilisation. In this story more than any other, elements are devised and refined that will shape the development of **Doctor Who**'s mythos, including the character of Borusa and the legends of Rassilon...

The ceremonial meeting place of the Time Lords, who are ruled by a High Council, is established as the huge Panopticon.

Most of the action of *The Deadly Assassin* takes place in the Capitol of Gallifrey, which is patrolled by the chancellery guards, who report to a Commander (Hilred), who in turn answers to the Castellan (Spandrell). Ranks of Time Lords include the President himself, Gold Usher, Chancellor Goth (who is expected to succeed) and the cardinals.

When a President resigns, he names his successor (though coordinator Engin says he is elected). He holds the symbols of office – the Sash of Rassilon and the Great Key. The Time Lords are governed according to a constitution, Article 17 of which says, in part, that no candidate for office shall be debarred or restrained from presenting his claim.

Time Lord biog-data extracts (DEs) record all information about that Time Lord. Engin mentions 'Plebeian classes,' and Spandrell refers to 'the Shiboogans' as a group who engage in petty vandalism. These have DEs too, but only Time Lords' DEs are colour-coded (according to chapter). They can only be accessed by members of the High Council or the Castellan in the course of his duties. All accesses are logged. The Doctor says of the archives that there are worlds out there where this sort of equipment 'would be considered prehistoric junk', though Engin says they have long since 'turned aside from the barren road of technology'.

Commentator Runcible says the Time Lords' ceremonial robes are 'seldom-worn' and have colour-coded collar insignia – scarlet and orange for the Prydonians, green for the Arcalians, heliotrope for the Patrexes, and so on.

The Time Lords' main weapons are stasers, and they do little damage except to body tissue (even dead tissue). There are pistol- and rifle-like versions.

There is passing mention of several elements that will become more important in later stories. The CIA – the Celestial Intervention Agency – and the transduction barriers, for example. The Matrix is mentioned, but as a description of the Amplified Panatropic Computations (APC) Net's composition. In later stories, from *The Invasion of Time*, the APC net is said to be 'a small part of the Matrix'.

We also discover in *The Deadly Assassin* that Time Lords do not live forever, having only 12 regenerations (and therefore 13 'lives').

RASSILON AND THE OLD TIME

Rassilon is regarded as the founder of modern Time Lord civilisation, though in his own day he was seen mainly as an engineer and an architect.

Early Time Lord history is chronicled in *The Book of the Old Time*: 'And Rassilon travelled into the black void with a great fleet. Within the void, no light would shine, and nothing of that outer nature continue in being except that which existed within the Sash of Rassilon. Now Rassilon found the Eye of Harmony, which balances all things that they may neither flux, nor wither, nor change their state in any measure. And he caused the Eye to be brought to the world of Gallifrey, wherein he sealed this beneficence with the Great Key. Then the people rejoiced...'

In *The Deadly Assassin* the Doctor realises that the Sash of Rassilon protects its wearer from being sucked into a parallel universe, and that the Eye of Harmony is the nucleus of a black hole from which all the power of the Time Lords devolves. 'Rassilon stabilised all the elements of the black hole and set them in an eternally dynamic equation against the mass of the planet. If the Master interferes, it will be the end not only of this world, but of a hundred other worlds too...'

The Great Key, an ebonite rod carried by the President on ceremonial occasions (and later called the Rod of Rassilon), fits into the floor of the Panopticon and reveals the crystalline Eye of Harmony – Rassilon's Star.

TARDIS DATA BANK:

DATE: UNKNOWN
LOCATION: GALLIFREY

SUMMONED BACK TO
GALLIFREY, THE DOCTOR IS
FRAMED FOR THE
ASSASSINATION OF THE TIME
LORD PRESIDENT. TO PROVE
HIS INNOCENCE, HE MUST
STAND FOR ELECTION
HIMSELF, UNCOVER THE
TRAITOR IN THE TIME LORD
HIGH COUNCIL, FIGHT A
HOODED KILLER IN A
NIGHTMARE DREAMSCAPE
WORLD OF HIS ENEMY'S
DEVISING AND BATTLE
AGAINST AN OLD FOE NOW
OUT TO DESTROY THE TIME
LORDS – THE MASTER…

THE DEADLY ASSASSIN

In which the Doctor returns to his home planet, and does battle within a dreamscape world that upsets Mrs Mary Whitehouse...
BY ROBERT HOLMES
4 EPISODES, FIRST BROADCAST 30 OCTOBER 1976–
20 NOVEMBER 1976

JOURNEY INFORMATION

THE MASTER

The Master is dying, having reached the end of his final regeneration, his body reduced to a decaying husk kept alive only by his hatred. His plan is to frame the Doctor for the President's death, and use the power from the Eye of Harmony channelled through the Sash of Rassilon to regenerate his body.

He again demonstrates his powers of hypnotism, as well as matter-condensation. He has destroyed his Time Lord records. The Doctor describes the Master as '... evil, cunning and resourceful, highly developed powers of ESP and a formidable hypnotist.'

Although the Doctor prevents the Master from draining much energy from the Eye of Harmony and sees him fall into a crevasse, he is not convinced that he is dead – and sure enough, the Master escapes in his TARDIS, which is disguised as a grandfather clock. Seeing him go, Spandrell observes that both the Master and the Doctor are heading '... out into the Universe. And you know I've a feeling it isn't big enough for the two of them.'

CARDINAL BORUSA

Runcible implies that Borusa has recently been elevated to cardinal. He used to teach the Doctor at Prydon Academy, and is a jurist. When the Master's accomplice Chancellor Goth is killed, Borusa assumes control and organises events, 'adjusting' the truth so that Goth is thought to have died a hero.

He recalls the Doctor from his time at the Academy, and reminds him: 'As I believe I told you long ago, Doctor, you will never amount to anything in the galaxy while you retain your propensity for vulgar facetiousness.' But as the Doctor leaves Gallifrey Borusa adds, 'Oh, Doctor – nine out of ten.'

CHANCELLOR GOTH

Goth is Chancellor, but the President has told him he is not to be his successor. He met the Master on Tersurus, and was suborned by his promise of power and knowledge. Goth was unable to resist the Master's mental dominance, and dies when the Doctor defeats him in combat within the Matrix.

THE APC NET

The APC Net is composed of amplified panotropic computations: 'Trillions of electrochemical cells in a continuous matrix. The cells are the repository of departed Time Lords. At the moment of death, an electrical scan is made of the brain pattern and these millions of impulses are immediately transferred.' Its purpose is to monitor life in the Capitol: 'We use all this combined knowledge and experience to predict future developments.'

Goth is able to create an entire dream-world that obeys his will within the Matrix – including a jungle area, a small train track, and a battlefield. 'I am the creator here, Doctor, this is my world,' Goth says at one point.

NEW INFORMATION

THE DOCTOR

Recalled to Gallifrey for the presidential resignation, the Doctor actually 'sees' the President's assassination (although coordinator Engin says that 'precognitive vision is impossible'). In fact, the Master has beamed the images to him from the APC Net.

The Doctor is a Prydonian, having been a student of Borusa at Prydon Academy. He was at the Academy with Commentator Runcible, who says the Doctor was 'expelled or something – some scandal', and notices he's 'had a facelift'.

The Doctor: 'You'd delay an execution to pull the wings off a fly.'

The Doctor draws caricatures of the witnesses as he listens to the evidence at his trial. He escapes execution by pleading Article 17, which guarantees his safety while he campaigns for office, standing as President. He is the only candidate apart from Goth, although the fact that he therefore becomes President is not noticed until after he has left (see *The Invasion of Time*).

The Master warns Goth that '... the Doctor is never more dangerous than when the odds are against him.' In their battle in the Matrix, the Doctor rigs up a booby trap with a grenade, hits Goth with a poison dart from a blowpipe, and ignites marsh gas. Goth loses the battle as the Doctor has 'too much artron energy.'

THE TARDIS

The TARDIS, we learn for the first time, is a Type 40 TT Capsule. It has a double curtain trimonic barrier. The Time Lord records in the archive state that all Type 40s are now deregistered and non-operational. 305 were registered, and 304 have been deregistered – one capsule (the Doctor's TARDIS) being removed from the register, 'Reference Malfeasance Tribunal Order dated 309906.'

BEHIND THE SCENES

VIOLENT PROTESTS

Treading a tightrope between children's television and adult drama, **Doctor Who** has always been associated with thrills and frights. Watching the programme – in particular the Daleks – from behind the sofa on a Saturday evening has become a British cultural cliché.

But while the healthy frisson of excitement adds to the experience, there have always been those who argue that on occasion **Doctor Who** has gone too far. No-one was more vocal in their condemnation of the series throughout its history – but especially during the early years of the Fourth Doctor – than Mrs Mary Whitehouse and her National Viewers and Listeners Association (NVLA).

The series had been criticised before – notably *The Tomb of the Cybermen* for showing a Cyberman being 'disembowelled' by Toberman, *Terror of the Autons* with its deadly armchair, killer troll doll and policemen who turn out to be killer Autons, and *Planet of the Spiders* for fuelling arachnophobia. But it was with *Genesis of the Daleks* and its graphic depiction of trench warfare that the NVLA began to take a serious interest.

In that case, picking up on a letter to the *Radio Times* from a concerned housewife, the NVLA got no more than an assurance from producer Philip Hinchcliffe that the story was intensely moral and would be seen to show the evils of such warfare, with good ultimately triumphant.

But as she laced her speeches with accusations of the depiction of graphic strangulation and how to make Molotov cocktails, Mary Whitehouse picked on *The Deadly Assassin* for special attention – particularly the third episode. And from that it was the final freeze-frame of the Doctor's apparently drowning face that she condemned.

While the shot was a comparatively innocuous one of Tom Baker holding his breath under water (actually in a swimming pool and not the swamp where the rest of the fight was filmed), this complaint did get a response. Not only did the BBC's Director General, Charles Curran, seem to apologise, but he also implied that 'with hindsight' some of the sequence should have been cut.

It may not have seemed much of a victory, but the ripples spread further than that one freeze-frame, which was subsequently cut from the repeat showing of the story, and excised from the BBC's master copy. There may have been no direct link, but within a few stories producer Philip Hinchcliffe had moved on to the BBC's new police drama **Target** (also criticised for its explicit violence), and new producer Graham Williams was told that humour and wit should take the place of violence and horror in **Doctor Who**.

After Hinchcliffe left at the end of *The Talons of Weng-Chiang* there were a few nods to the horror genre – *Horror of Fang Rock* and *Image of the Fendahl* for example. But **Doctor Who**'s most overtly Gothic and arguably most adult viewing period was over.

LEELA

Leela is a warrior of the tribe of Sevateem. The tribe is descended from an Earth survey team, regressed to primitivism, and part of a eugenics programme run by the mad computer Xoanon.

Never afraid to speak her mind, Leela has spoken out against Xoanon, whom the Sevateem believe to be a god, and is banished from the tribe. In the Beyond she meets the Doctor – believing him initially to be the Evil One.

Leela is a creature of instinct and intuition and, with typical impulsiveness, she runs into the TARDIS and dematerialises it. While she never loses her simplistic view of life – believing for example that the Doctor's yo-yo powers the TARDIS when he tells her she has to keep it going up and down – Leela does begin to understand the distinction between technology and magic.

Another appreciation she slowly gains is of the value of life. When she first meets the Doctor, Leela is happy to use her Janis thorns to paralyse and kill enemy Sevateem or hatchet-wielding Chinese servants of Weng-Chiang. But as he grows to value Leela's friendship and help, so the Doctor decides to 'educate' her.

This education may be as subtle as a trip to a Victorian music hall so Leela can see how her ancestors lived (and the Doctor can enjoy himself), or a lesson in how to write her name on a blackboard in the TARDIS.

Certainly, Leela learns. In *The Talons of Weng-Chiang*, the Doctor passes her off to Professor Litefoot as a savage 'found floating down the Amazon in a hatbox', and her table manners at first leave the fastidious professor flabbergasted. But by the time she leaves the Doctor to stay on Gallifrey with Commander Andred, Leela has at least begun to fit into more advanced society. 'If you could avoid killing anyone, that would help,' Andred tells her when she asks what to do at the Doctor's induction ceremony. 'I will try,' she replies, but for once we can believe she is – at least partly – joking.

Throughout her time with the Doctor, Leela never loses sight of what and who she is: a warrior. She might lose her eagerness to fight, but never her willingness if the need arises. In *The Sun Makers,* she says she will 'see this place ankle-deep in blood' if the rebels try to kill her, and she is angered by the effects on her of the Minyan pacifier in *Underworld*.

Oddly, Leela's closest relationship is perhaps not with the Doctor but with K-9. It is Leela who urges the Doctor to accept Professor Marius's offer to take K-9 in the TARDIS, and K-9 in return decides to stay with her on Gallifrey.

THE FACE OF EVIL

In which the Doctor finds his own face carved into a cliff, and meets the alien savage Leela...
BY CHRIS BOUCHER
4 EPISODES, FIRST BROADCAST 1–22 JANUARY 1977

JOURNEY INFORMATION

XOANON

The Doctor says he programmed a spaceship's computer for the 'Mordee', using a variation of the Sidelian memory transfer and he forgot to wipe his personality print from the data core. The computer – Xoanon – developed a split personality, half of it is the Doctor's. The Doctor tells Xoanon that technicians had worked for generations to extend its power, until it evolved into a living creature. 'When I connected my own brain to it, it didn't just take compatible information as a machine should have done, it took everything... When it woke, it had a complete personality – mine... Then it began to develop a separate self, its own self. And that's when it started to go mad...'

Xoanon created a world in its own image, making the ship's crew act out its madness in reality. So the survey team was split from the technicians – two aspects of the same group of people – in the computer's experiment to create a race of superhumans.

Threatened by the return of the Doctor, Xoanon tries to destroy itself, the Doctor and the planet rather than submit... After the Doctor manages to wipe his personality from Xoanon, the computer is restored to charming and polite 'health'.

THE SEVATEEM

The tribe of the Sevateem are the descendants of Survey Team 6 from the Mordee expedition. The relics and remains of the team's equipment are scattered through their community, some of them worshipped as relics of Xoanon – the Hand of Xoanon is actually an armoured space glove.

The tribe is led by Andor, and the Shaman and lawgiver is Neeva, the servant of Xoanon. The Sevateem worship Xoanon, and struggle to free their god from the Evil One whose face is carved in a cliff, and who has imprisoned their god in the Tower of Imelo behind the Black Wall ('wherein lies paradise').

They believe there are phantoms in the Beyond – invisible creatures that hunt by vibration as they cannot see. In fact these are projections of Xoanon's disturbed subconscious.

The Litany gives a distorted account of the Sevateem's history and arrival on the planet: 'Our fathers, the tribe of Sevateem, were sent forth by god to seek paradise... While they searched, the tribe of Tesh ... remained at the place of land... They made a pact with the Evil One and god turned his face from us... The tribe of Tesh stand between the sons of the tribe of Sevateem and Xoanon, god of their fathers...'

The Doctor: 'Killing me isn't going to help you. It isn't going to do me much good either...'

TARDIS DATA BANK:

DATE: UNKNOWN, FUTURE
LOCATION: UNNAMED PLANET

THE DOCTOR MEETS LEELA AND THE PRIMITIVE SEVATEEM TRIBE, AND FINDS HIMSELF HAILED AS 'THE EVIL ONE'. LEELA SHOWS HIM A HUGE CARVING OF HIS FACE IN A CLIFF... THE TRIBE IS ACTUALLY DESCENDED FROM A STRANDED SURVEY TEAM, WHILE THE DESCENDANTS OF THE SHIP'S TECHNICIANS – THE TESH – STILL TEND THE SHIP'S EQUIPMENT. BOTH TRIBES ARE 'GOVERNED' BY THE COMPUTER XOANON, WHICH HAS A SPLIT PERSONALITY – SOME OF IT, THE DOCTOR'S...

In Xoanon's experiment, the Sevateem represent physical prowess, strength and courage.

THE TESH

The Tesh are the technicians left on the ship when the Mordee expedition landed. They tend the equipment, without understanding it. They are led by Captain Jabel and his subordinate Gentek. They can exert mental control over others, including the Doctor.

In Xoanon's experiment, the Tesh represent self-denial and mental ability.

THE HORDA

The Horda are small, carnivorous creatures that strike out at anything that moves, except each other. Ten of them can strip the flesh from a man's arm 'almost before he can cry out'. The Sevateem 'test' people over a pit full of Horda. A rock falling on a rope opens its cover – the victim must shoot the rope to stop the cover opening, miss and they fall into the uncovered pit.

NEW INFORMATION

THE DOCTOR

The Doctor says the Black Wall works by moving everything inside it forward a couple of seconds in time to create an impenetrable barrier. He has seen it done as a parlour trick, but not on this scale. The only entrance is through the mouth of the carving of the Doctor's face.

The Doctor kicks a Horda on to a Sevateem man who hits Leela, and says he was taught to shoot a crossbow by William Tell. He does not remember Xoanon or his involvement in the Mordee expedition until he sees the spaceship.

THE TARDIS

The Doctor thinks he might be able to create a time bridge through the Black Wall by dismantling the TARDIS.

COMPANIONS

LEELA: The Doctor revives Leela when she is poisoned by a Janis thorn. The thorn paralyses then kills victims, but the Doctor is able to synthesize an antidote using a bio-analyser. The Doctor tells Leela, 'no more Janis thorns, ever'.

THE ROBOTS OF DEATH

In which the Doctor and Leela find themselves re-enacting *Murder on the Orient Express*, as if written by Isaac Asimov...
BY CHRIS BOUCHER
4 EPISODES, FIRST BROADCAST 29 JANUARY–19 FEBRUARY 1977

TARDIS DATA BANK:

DATE: UNKNOWN
LOCATION: A SANDMINER IN THE DESERT OF AN UNNAMED
PLANET (THERE IS MENTION OF KALDOR CITY)

THE TARDIS ARRIVES ON A MINING SHIP RUN BY ROBOTS AND A SMALL CREW OF HUMANS.
THE DOCTOR AND LEELA ARE SUSPECTED OF MURDER, BUT ONLY THE DOCTOR REALISES
THAT THE ROBOTS CAN BE REPROGRAMMED TO KILL. THE PSYCHOPATHIC TAREN KAPEL
HAS TAKEN THE PLACE OF ONE OF THE CREW ON THE SANDMINER AND IS PLANNING A
ROBOT REVOLUTION – UNLESS THE DOCTOR CAN STOP HIM...

JOURNEY INFORMATION

THE SANDMINER

Storm Mine Four, with its small human complement and its crew of robots, travels over a vast desert, extracting valuable ores and minerals from the shifting sands.

The Sandminer is commanded by Uvanov. The human crew includes: Pilot Toos; Chief Mover Poul (an undercover agent for the Company, who suffers from Robophobia); the impetuous Mover Borg; Chief Fixer Dask (in truth Taren Capel); Cass; Kerril; Zilda, (whose brother died on another of Uvanov's missions) and Chub (a government meteorologist).

Uvanov's Sandminer is eight months into a two-year tour. While the robots can mine without human supervision, their lack of instincts means they are less efficient at tracing and following ore streams.

ROBOTS

There are three types of robot aboard the Sandminer. SV7 is a Supervoc. Silver in colour, it controls the other robots, acting as coordinator. The command circuit is routed through SV7. Taren Capel has to use 'surgery' with a Laserson Probe to bypass the prime directive of other robots, but seems to be able to subvert the more sophisticated SV7's command circuit directly with a communication. The prime directive is the first program laid into any robot's command structure and prevents it harming humans.

The golden Voc robots, all numbered with a V prefix (for example V7 and V16) are intelligent with a level of self-control. They can speak, and have over a million multilevel constrainers to ensure they cannot harm humans.

The dark-coloured Dum robots are single-function robots used for simple labour tasks. They are all numbered, with a D prefix, and cannot speak.

The exception is D84, who is a disguised Voc or Supervoc working with Poul to check whether Taren Capel is aboard the Sandminer. While the robots are said not to have feelings, D84 strikes up a relationship with the Doctor and ultimately sacrifices himself to destroy the converted robots, his last words to the Doctor being, 'Goodbye, my friend.'

Using part of a robot's head and a communicator, the Doctor is able to create a 'final deactivator' tuned into Taren Capel's robot command circuit. When activated (by D84), the deactivator destroys all the robots except SV7 – either it is out of range, or operates on a circuit that is unaffected.

Deactivated robots have to be returned to a construction centre for reactivation. They are marked with red robot deactivation discs, which the workers call 'corpse markers'.

ROBOPHOBIA

Grimwade's Syndrome is an irrational dread of robots brought on by the fact that robots look human but give no human signals or body language. The Doctor says, 'It's rather like being surrounded by walking, talking dead men... It undermines a certain type of personality, causes identity crisis, paranoia, sometimes even personality disintegration.'

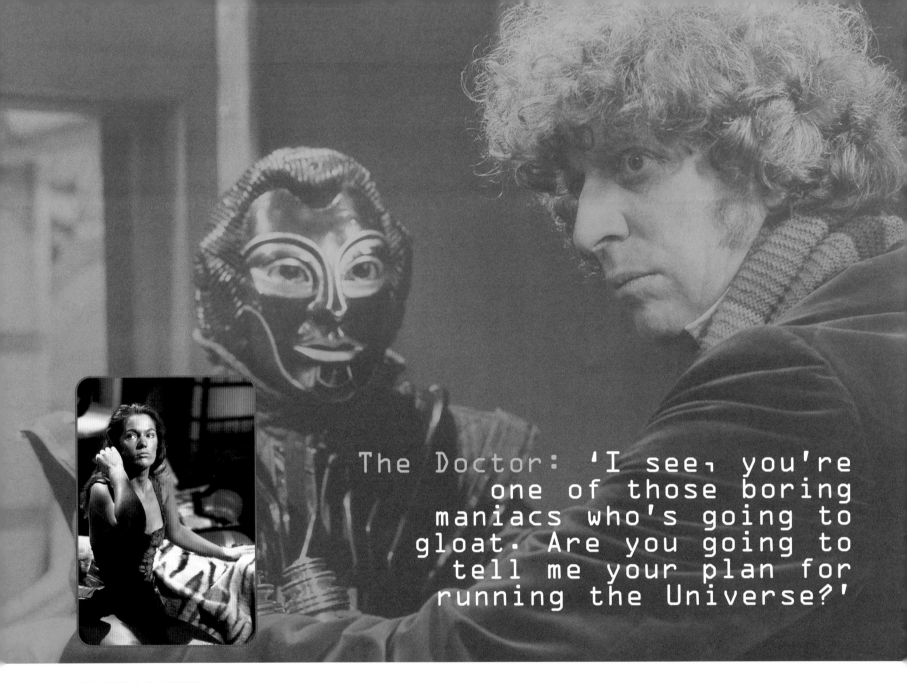

The Doctor: 'I see, you're one of those boring maniacs who's going to gloat. Are you going to tell me your plan for running the Universe?'

TAREN CAPEL

Capel has taken the place of Dask aboard the Sandminer, to convert robots so they can kill humans. Raised only by robots from birth, Capel believes that it is his mission to free his 'brother' robots from human bondage.

The robots identify humans who are in their command circuit by voice. When Taren Capel's voice is altered by helium, SV7 does not recognise him and obeys Capel's original command to 'kill all humans'.

NEW INFORMATION

THE DOCTOR

The Doctor's voice is unaffected by helium. He tells Leela he is 750 years old.

The Doctor has seen similar mining on Korlano-beta and refers to other robot-based civilisations, telling Leela,

'It's a vicious circle – people can neither live with them, nor exist without them.' The Doctor tells Leela that if the crew is being killed by a robot, 'I should think it's the end of this civilisation.'

THE TARDIS

The Doctor explains how the TARDIS can be bigger inside than out by showing Leela two boxes. He holds the smaller box closer to her: 'If you could keep that exactly that distance away, and have it here, the large one would fit inside the small one... That's transdimensional engineering – a key Time Lord discovery.'

COMPANIONS

LEELA: Leela can sense approaching danger, for example just before the Sandminer is sabotaged, and when SV7 asks Toos where she is. She calls the robots 'creepy mechanical men', and spots that Poul 'moves like a hunter.'

THE TALONS OF WENG-CHIANG

TARDIS DATA BANK:

DATE: LATE NINETEENTH CENTURY – AFTER 1888, POSSIBLY FEBRUARY 1892
LOCATION: LONDON

THE DOCTOR AND LEELA FIND THEMSELVES CONFRONTED BY MURDEROUS CHINESE TONGS LED BY A MUSIC HALL MAGICIAN, A VENTRILOQUIST'S DUMMY THAT KILLS, A GIANT RAT, AND THE VILLAINOUS MAGNUS GREEL – A WAR CRIMINAL FROM THE FAR FUTURE. TEAMING UP WITH PROFESSOR LITEFOOT AND THEATRE OWNER HENRY JAGO, THE DOCTOR MUST DEFEAT GREEL AND RESCUE LEELA FROM THE TALONS OF WENG-CHIANG…

In which a ventriloquist's dummy comes to life and giant rats infest the Victorian sewers...
BY ROBERT HOLMES
6 EPISODES, FIRST BROADCAST 26 FEBRUARY–2 APRIL 1977

JOURNEY INFORMATION

MAGNUS GREEL

The infamous Minister of Justice, Magnus Greel was nicknamed the Butcher of Brisbane and the Doctor says that 100,000 deaths can be laid at his door. Branded a war criminal after the fall of the Icelandic Alliance in the year 5000, Greel fled through time in his time cabinet, arriving in nineteenth-century China. Here he lost the cabinet, and has been searching for it (with the activator key – a delicate crystalline trionic lattice) ever since. He has assumed the identity of the Chinese god Weng-Chiang and has the help of the god's followers in the Tong of the Black Scorpion. Weng-Chiang was, amongst other things, the god of abundance. It is said that he blew poisonous fumes from his mouth, killed with a light from his eyes, and would return to rule the world.

Greel's time cabinet works by zygma energy, which has distorted Greel's appearance – Leela calls him 'bent face' – because of an error in the programmed DNA levels. Dying,

Greel is augmenting his life force by draining the energy from young women he kidnaps off the streets with his distillation chamber (the Doctor calls it cannibalism).

Defeated by the Doctor, and desperate for nutrition, Greel dies from cellular collapse when the Doctor pushes him into the distillation chamber.

MR SIN – THE PEKING HOMUNCULUS

In the ice age, in about the year 5000, the Peking Homunculus was made as a toy for the children of the Commissioner of the Icelandic Alliance. It contained a series of magnetic fields operating on a printed circuit and a small computer. It also contained one organic component – the cerebral cortex of a pig.

But the pig's brain took over the Homunculus (and it almost caused World War Six) – the mental feedback was so intense that the swinish instinct became dominant. The Homunculus needed an operator, but hated humanity and revelled in carnage.

Greel has brought the Peking Homunculus back through time, disguising it as music hall performer Li H'sen Chang's ventriloquist's dummy – Mr Sin. Eventually, though, Sin's instinctive nature drives it to rebel against Greel, and it is destroyed when the Doctor removes its fuse.

PROFESSOR GEORGE LITEFOOT AND HENRY GORDON JAGO

Litefoot's father was palace attaché in China – where he acquired Greel's time cabinet. The professor meets the Doctor and Leela while performing a post-mortem for the police, and invites them back for dinner.

Litefoot is intrigued by Leela, and ever the perfect gentleman he does not criticise her for eating with her hands. He picks up his own meat and gnaws at it.

Henry Gordon Jago is owner and manager of the Palace Theatre and introduces its music hall acts with alliterative enthusiasm. His bluff manner covers a soft-hearted nature and he admits to Litefoot that, 'I'm not so bally brave when it comes to it... I try to be, but I'm not.'

Both Jago and Litefoot have absolute faith in their new friend, the Doctor – faith that is not misplaced.

NEW INFORMATION

THE DOCTOR

The Doctor says he has not been in China for 400 years (possibly a reference to *Marco Polo*). He was with the Philippino army for its final advance on Reykjavik when the Icelandic Alliance was defeated in the year 5000. He speaks all the Chinese dialects.

He demonstrates conjuring skills to Jago, and says he can also provide 'dramatic recitations, singing, tap-dancing, I can play the trumpet voluntary in a bowl of live goldfish.' Jago is unimpressed, but the Doctor is easily able to hypnotise him.

He claims to have shared a salmon he caught in the Fleet river with the Venerable Bede. He tells Litefoot that 'sleep is for tortoises.'

COMPANIONS

LEELA: Leela thinks the foghorn of a river boat is a swamp creature and says that London is a big village. She can tell that the cab-driver Buller has been stabbed through the heart by the sound of his cry. She has a blowpipe she uses to project lethal Janis thorns.

She tells Greel that when they are both in the Great Hereafter she will hunt him down and put him through her agony a thousand times.

BEHIND THE SCENES

DOCTORIAL DOCUMENTARIES

Doctor Who has featured prominently on other television programmes. Viewers' opinions voiced on programmes like **Talkback** and **Points of View** ranged from complaints about violence and horror in the programme to wondering why the Fourth Doctor offered people jelly babies but then gave them liquorice allsorts.

Many programmes offered behind-the-scenes information, but perhaps most consistently enthusiastic was the BBC's children's magazine programme **Blue Peter**. In addition to organising a *Design a Monster* competition, **Blue Peter** hosted War Machines, Daleks and other monsters as well as various Doctors, the Whomobile and K-9, who gave Shep a run for his money. It also celebrated the Doctor's tenth anniversary with a plethora of clips from the programme's history, which were reused together with a script that got only minor rewrites on subsequent significant anniversaries.

Although a **Doctor Who** documentary was planned to follow the making of *Robot* in 1974, it was not until 3 April 1977 that a full **Doctor Who** documentary was broadcast. **Whose Doctor Who** was part of BBC2's *The Lively Arts* series, hosted by Melvyn Bragg. The programme included clips from past

The Doctor: 'My dear Litefoot, I've got a lantern, a pair of waders, and possibly the most fearsome piece of hand artillery in all England. What could possibly go wrong?'

stories, but concerned itself mainly with examining **Doctor Who**'s audience and how viewers of the series reacted to it. Viewers of all ages were interviewed, together with an educational psychologist, a doctor and others.

A mocked-up script conference between new producer Graham Williams, script editor Robert Holmes and author Terrance Dicks was shown, as were rehearsals and studio sessions from *The Talons of Weng-Chiang* – the final episode of which had been transmitted the previous evening. The programme ended by asking children how **Doctor Who** might one day finally end. Possibly, one boy suggested, he would be going through a time warp and run out of petrol... The documentary is included on the BBC DVD release of *The Talons of Weng-Chiang*.

On 3 January 1992, a short documentary **Resistance is Useless** looked back at **Doctor Who**. This was a more narrative-based programme, narrated by an empty anorak purporting to be a fan of the series.

Doctor Who's thirtieth anniversary was celebrated with **Thirty Years in the TARDIS** on 29 November 1993 (released on video in an extended version as **More than Thirty Years in the TARDIS**). As well as comments from celebrity fans including Mike Gatting and Toyah Willcox, the documentary traced the development of the programme. In addition to using clips from **Doctor Who** stories and behind-the-scenes footage, director Kevin Davies created new material re-enacting classic moments from the series' past and an ongoing framing narrative (a technique he would use again on his **Dalekmania** documentary about the two 1960s Dalek feature films). Towards the end of the programme a special-effects shot allowed the camera, for the first time, to track into the TARDIS Control Room from outside the police box... The programme ended with an assurance from the BBC's Alan Yentob that **Doctor Who** might well return. But it would be over two years before he did...

HORROR OF FANG ROCK

The Doctor: 'I've made a terrible mistake. I thought I'd locked the enemy out. Instead I've locked it in — with us.'

TARDIS DATA BANK:

DATE: c1910
LOCATION: FANG ROCK, OFF THE COAST OF ENGLAND

THE DOCTOR AND LEELA ARRIVE ON FANG ROCK – A SMALL ISLAND WHERE THERE IS A LIGHTHOUSE. THE LIGHTHOUSE CREW, THE SURVIVORS OF A SHIP WRECKED IN UNNATURAL FOG – INCLUDING LORD PALMERDALE AND COLONEL SKINSALE – THE DOCTOR AND LEELA FIND THEMSELVES BATTLING AGAINST A SHAPE-CHANGING ALIEN RUTAN THAT IS ASSESSING EARTH FOR POSSIBLE INVASION. THE DOCTOR DECIDES HE NEEDS A POWERFUL LASER BEAM TO DESTROY THE RUTAN SHIP BEFORE THE CREATURE KILLS THEM ALL…

In which an alien jelly attacks an isolated lighthouse…
BY TERRANCE DICKS
4 EPISODES, FIRST BROADCAST 3 SEPTEMBER–24 SEPTEMBER 1977

JOURNEY INFORMATION

THE RUTAN

On the cold, icy planet of Ruta 3, the Rutans evolved in the sea before adapting to land. They are the sworn enemies of the Sontarans – the Rutan Empire has been at war with the Sontarans for millennia. Now the Rutans have decided that Earth is the ideal strategic position from which to attack their enemies.

The Rutan scout that attacks Fang Rock is tasked with assessing the planet and its life forms. It shrouds the island in fog to obscure its operations, then takes the chief lighthouse keeper, Ben, for analysis, conducting a post-mortem on his body.

The Rutan has been specially trained in the 'new metamorphosis techniques' and assumes the form of lighthouse keeper Reuben. It kills with electrical discharges from its body in order to keep its mission secret. It signals to the Rutan mother ship using power from the lighthouse generator.

The Doctor eventually destroys the Rutan with an early Schemurly rocket launcher adapted to fire financier Lord Palmerdale's diamonds. He is able to destroy the Rutan mother ship, which has a shielded crystalline infrastructure, by adapting the lighthouse carbon arc lamp to become a laser-like amplified carbon oscillator.

THE LIGHTHOUSE CREW

Ben is the chief lighthouse keeper, and a proponent of the new technology of electricity. By contrast, the old-fashioned Reuben is a sceptic. 'Wouldn't happen with oil,' he grumbles as the Rutan drains away the electricity and the lights fade. Reuben is well aquainted with the legend of the Beast of Fang Rock: the beast attacked 80 years previously, killing two men and driving a third mad.

Vince is young and inexperienced. Easily embarrassed and frightened, he is seduced by Lord Palmerdale's promise of money for sending a message – though he tries to burn the money after Palmerdale's death.

LORD PALMERDALE

Millionaire financier Lord Henry Palmerdale is, according to Colonel Skinsale, a crook and a scoundrel. He has blackmailed Skinsale into giving away government secrets that he now intends to turn to profit on the stock exchange – hence his urgent need to get from Deauville to London, and to send a message to his brokers from Fang Rock. He always carries diamonds with him – as 'insurance'.

COLONEL SKINSALE

Colonel James Skinsale (late of the Royal Engineers and now Member of Parliament for Thurley) has given the information to Palmerdale in return for having his IOUs torn up. He knows he will be ruined if the information is used, and is amused that Palmerdale now seems unable to make use of it – threatening to sue him if Palmerdale reveals his indiscretion without proof. To prevent Palmerdale sending a message, he destroys the telegraph system. Skinsale is also motivated by greed, as his gambling debts suggest, and dies trying to retrieve Palmerdale's diamonds.

NEW INFORMATION

THE DOCTOR

The Doctor knows about the Rutans and their home planet. He also knows the *Ballad of Flannen Isle* by Wilfrid Gibson, and sees the parallels between the poem (which is about an abandoned lighthouse) and the present situation.

COMPANIONS

LEELA: 'I am no lady,' Leela tells Vince, starting to get undressed to change into more practical clothes. With her unusually acute senses, she is the first to detect the drop in temperature as the Rutan approaches.

Fiercely protective of the Doctor, she tells Palmerdale to '... do as the Doctor instructs or I will cut out your heart.' Later she slaps Palmerdale's secretary, Adelaide, to stop her hysterics.

To the Doctor's displeasure when the Rutan is dying, Leela celebrates: 'Enjoy your death as I enjoyed killing you.'

Reuben: 'Reckon I know what you seen. They always said the Beast of Fang Rock would be back.'

K-9

K-9 is a mobile computer in the rough shape of a dog. The original K–9 introduced in *The Invisible Enemy* was constructed by Professor Marius, who describes it as, 'My best friend and constant companion.' Marius used to have a dog on Earth but because of a weight penalty could not bring it with him to the Bi-Al Foundation. Equally, he cannot take K-9 home, so offers him to the Doctor, saying, 'I only hope he's TARDIS-trained.' While Leela urges the Doctor to accept, K-9 decides for himself and enters the TARDIS.

K-9 can speak, and print out data from his 'nose' or his side (as with a map of the 'tree' tunnel system in *Underworld*). He has a 'nose-laser' that emerges from his head and can be set to various levels enabling him to stun or kill life forms as well as serving as a cutting tool.

> ## TARDIS DATA BANK:
>
> DESCRIPTION: ROBOT DOG
> TRAVELLED: Mark I: *THE INVISIBLE ENEMY – THE INVASION OF TIME*;
> Mark II: *THE RIBOS OPERATION – WARRIOR'S GATE*;
> Mark III: **K-9 AND COMPANY**, *THE FIVE DOCTORS*.

Articulated sensors ('ears') allow him to detect things – the psychospore of the Mentiads on *The Pirate Planet* for example – as well as Romana, and the Doctor (who has two very distinctive heartbeats).

Intelligent and with vast memory banks, K-9 has an affinity with the TARDIS (though he does call it a 'very stupid machine' as it cannot speak) and learns from its data. By the time he leaves with Romana to help the Tharils (*Warriors' Gate*), K-9 has the TARDIS 'preserved in concept'

and can give instructions on how to build new ones. He is forced to remain behind the Gateway when his memory wafers are irrevocably damaged by the time winds.

In fact this is K-9 Mark II. The 'original' K-9 stays on Gallifrey to look after Leela when she stays with Andred.

The Doctor apparently gives K-9 Mark III to his friend and former companion Sarah Jane Smith – and K-9 is seen with her in *The Five Doctors* (having shared an adventure with her in the spin-off programme **K-9 and Company**).

In which an alien virus swarm takes people over and K-9 makes his debut...

BY BOB BAKER AND DAVE MARTIN

4 EPISODES, FIRST BROADCAST 1– 22 OCTOBER 1977

TARDIS DATA BANK:

DATE: c5000

LOCATION: TITAN BASE AND THE BI-AL FOUNDATION

AN INTELLIGENT ALIEN VIRUS SWARM THAT FEEDS ON THOUGHT INFECTS THE DOCTOR, WHO MANAGES TO GET TO THE BI-AL FOUNDATION FOR TREATMENT. IN AN EFFORT TO DESTROY THE NUCLEUS OF THE SWARM, MINIATURISED CLONED COPIES OF THE DOCTOR AND LEELA ARE INJECTED INTO THE DOCTOR'S BODY. BUT THE NUCLEUS ESCAPES AND GROWS. WITH THE VIRUS READY TO SPAWN IN THE MACRO-WORLD, AND LEELA THE ONLY PERSON WHO IS IMMUNE, THE DOCTOR IS HELPED BY PROFESSOR MARIUS AND HIS ROBOT DOG K-9…

JOURNEY INFORMATION

THE BI-AL FOUNDATION

The Centre for Alien Biomorphology, or Bi-Al Foundation, is built into Asteroid K4067 in the asteroid belt. It is a vast hospital complex on several levels. Professor Marius is the Foundation's specialist in extraterrestrial pathological endomorphisms.

CLONES

The first successful cloning experiments were carried out in 3922. Replicates do not live long because of possible psychic stress problems, the longest recorded clone life being 10 minutes, 55 seconds.

The Kilbracken Technique is not real cloning, but a short-lived carbon-based imprint that transfers heredity and experience to a short-lived copy. While the Doctor's clone is free of the virus (presumably being produced from an uninfected cell), if the 'real' person is injured, the clone also feels the shock.

THE SWARM

The Nucleus of the Swarm tells the Doctors: 'For millennia we have hung dormant in space waiting for the right carriers to come along... Consider the human species. They send hordes of settlers across space to breed, multiply, conquer and dominate. We have as much right to conquer you as you have to strike out across the stars...'

The virus infects humans through the optic nerve. Infected people have scales on their faces and pronounced eyebrows. K-9 deduces that the virus is noetic – only detectable during consciousness. It thrives on the brain activity of the host, and the Doctor is able to check its progress by going into a coma. K-9 is able to cure himself

Nucleus: 'The age of Man is over, Doctor. The age of the Virus has begun.'

by switching off – the virus dies when there is no mental activity at all.

The virus intends to breed in specially prepared tanks on Titan, but the Doctor is able to blow up the base and destroy the enlarged Swarm.

NEW INFORMATION

THE DOCTOR

The Doctor says he must withdraw into himself to save strength and prevent the virus getting a hold on him. Marius realises it is a self-induced coma. K-9's analysis shows the Doctor has two hearts and a symbiotic self-renewing cell structure.

THE TARDIS

Leela has not been in the 'old' Control Room before, which the Doctor describes as, '... Number Two Control Room, been closed for redecoration. I don't like the colour.'

Leela seems to get the TARDIS to the Bi-Al Foundation after asking the Doctor for the coordinates.

The relative dimensional stabiliser is part of the TARDIS control system and allows the TARDIS to cross the dimensional boundary. The Doctor uses it to reduce clones of himself and Leela to micro-size. Later the infected Professor Marius uses the RDS to enlarge the Nucleus to macro-size.

COMPANIONS

LEELA: The Doctor says AD5000 is still in the time of Leela's ancestors. In the TARDIS, Leela learns to write her name on a blackboard.

She can tell that the infected shuttle commander, Safran, is evil and not human from his voice. She also senses where the 'evil things' are within the Doctor's brain. The Doctor tells Marius that Leela is 'all instinct and intuition'.

K-9: A ticker tape from K-9's nose diagnoses the Doctor as non-human. K-9 tells Leela, 'I am without emotional circuits, only memory and awareness.' He says his photon beam weapon has four levels or intensity, including kill and immobilise. He stuns Marius, and cuts a section from a wall to form a barrier.

The Doctor:
'Sometimes
my brilliance
astonishes even me.'

IMAGE OF THE FENDAHL

In which a human skull millions of years older than Man is the focal point for
an alien force that is taking over Wanda Ventham...

BY CHRIS BOUCHER

4 EPISODES, FIRST BROADCAST 29 OCTOBER–19 NOVEMBER 1977

JOURNEY INFORMATION

TIME SCANNER

Fendelman has amassed a fortune from his pioneering work in electronics. About ten years
earlier, when working on a missile guidance system, Fendelman noticed a 'sort of sonic
shadow'. From this phenomenon he has created a time scanner, and is now obsessed with
discovering Man's origins. The scanner only works after dark, so as to minimise solar
disruption, and with it Fendelman hopes to observe the creation of modern man.

The scanner has already led Fendelman and his team – Ransome, Stael and Colby – to
the discovery of an ancient human skull in Kenya – a skull nine million years older than Man's
first known ancestors. When reassembled, the fracture lines in the skull form a pentagram.

But use of the scanner is damaging a time fissure (which is responsible for the local
woods being haunted), and could cause a direct continuum implosion that would destroy
Earth. However, the Doctor is able to use the scanner to confuse the Fendahl long enough to
remove the skull. Then he sets the scanner to implode, destroying Fetch Priory, itself and the
nascent Fendahl.

THE FENDAHL

Twelve million years ago, on the fifth planet of the solar system, which no longer exists,
evolution went up a blind alley, natural selection turned back on itself and a creature evolved
that absorbed the wavelengths of life itself – all life, including its own kind. Aware of the
dangers, the Time Lords put the planet into a time loop, hoping to contain the Fendahl and
making the planet and its records invisible.

But the Fendahl escaped to Earth. According to the Doctor, its latent energy was stored
in a protohuman skull and emitted as a biological transmutation field which influenced Man's
evolution – until a creature evolved that could form the core of a reborn Fendahl. An alternative
theory the Doctor proposes is that the Fendahl fed into the RNA of certain individuals the
instincts and compulsions necessary to bring about its re-creation, and these were passed
down the generations to Fendelman and others. Or, he admits, it could all be coincidence.

According to the legends of Gallifrey, the Fendahl is a gestalt creature made up of 12
Fendahleen and a core. Drawing on energy released when Fendelman's time scanner
damages a time fissure, the Fendahl is being reborn in Fetch Priory. Scientist Thea Ransome
is mutated into the core and becomes a golden female creature whose look brings death. The
Fendahleen are created out of time energy, or from the unfortunate acolytes of mad scientist
Maximillian Stael's coven.

The Doctor implies that Fendelman, Stael, Thea and the others involved have been
influenced from before they were born – brought to this moment of destiny by the power of
the Fendahl. 'Only for this were the generations of my fathers born,' Fendelman says as he
realises the truth.

Many legends and myths are based on race memory of the Fendahl – which (being
psychotelekinetic) can paralyse its victims so that they cannot run away. The Doctor is able to
destroy a Fendahleen using salt – an ancient magical defence – loaded into shotgun
cartridges. The salt affects the Fendahleen's conductivity, ruining its overall electrical balance.
Using the time scanner he confuses the incomplete gestalt creature long enough to remove
the source of its becoming – the skull. This he plans to destroy in the heat of a supernova in
the constellation of Canthares.

TARDIS DATA BANK:

DATE: PRESENT, 29–31
JULY
LOCATION: FETCH
PRIORY, NEAR
FETCHBOROUGH,
ENGLAND

THE FENDAHL, A GESTALT
CREATURE THAT FEEDS ON
DEATH ITSELF, REMAINS
DORMANT WITHIN A HUMAN
SKULL MILLIONS OF YEARS
OLDER THAN MAN. FACED
WITH A TIME SCANNER THAT
COULD IMPLODE AND
DESTROY EARTH, A
HOMICIDAL SCIENTIST AND
THE LOCAL COVEN, HOW CAN
THE DOCTOR AND LEELA
DEFEAT DEATH ITSELF...

Colby:
'What are
you exactly,
some sort of
wandering
Armageddon
peddler?'

NEW INFORMATION

THE DOCTOR

With effort, the Doctor is able to resist the paralyzing effects of a Fendahleen. He knows of the Fendahl from the legends of Earth and of Gallifrey.

The Doctor tries using his sonic screwdriver to open the door of the room he is locked up in. The lock opens after a delay. Later he uses the screwdriver to reconfigure the time scanner.

When Stael, faced with the nascent Fendahl, asks for a gun – 'It's not for her, it's for me' – the Doctor gives it to him, saying, 'I'm sorry.' He pauses, leaving the cellar, as he hears a shot.

THE TARDIS

The TARDIS generates a low-intensity telepathic field, and Leela's primitive thought patterns seem to appeal to it.

COMPANIONS

LEELA: Although she is being educated in the ways of science by the Doctor, Leela does not refuse a protective charm (rock salt), offered her by local occult specialist Martha Tyler. She finds and rescues the Doctor by following her feeling that something is wrong.

K-9: K-9 is suffering from corroded circuits, and is left in the TARDIS.

The Doctor: 'There are 4,000 million people here on your planet, and if I'm right, within a year, there'll be just one left alive. Just one.'

In which the Doctor takes part in a satirical adventure where corridors are named after tax forms, and the tax man takes everyone for a ride...

BY ROBERT HOLMES

4 EPISODES, FIRST BROADCAST 26 NOVEMBER–17 DECEMBER 1977

TARDIS DATA BANK:

DATE: FAR FUTURE
LOCATION: PLUTO – MEGROPOLIS ONE

IN THE FAR FUTURE, EARTH HAS BECOME UNINHABITABLE AND THE HUMAN RACE NOW LIVES ON PLUTO, WARMED BY SIX ARTIFICIAL SUNS AND 'CARED FOR' BY THE COMPANY. BUT THE DOCTOR AND LEELA ARRIVE TO FIND AN OPPRESSIVE REGIME THAT IMPOSES CRIPPLING TAXES AND USES SUPPRESSANT GAS TO KEEP THE CITIZENS UNDER CONTROL. THEY DISCOVER THE COMPANY IS RUN BY THE ALIEN USURIANS, AND JOIN THE REBELS IN ORGANISING A REVOLUTION...

JOURNEY INFORMATION

THE COMPANY

When Earth became uninhabitable, the Usurians shipped the population to Mars and, when that was exhausted, to Pluto. Here, each of six huge cities – Megropolises – were given their own sun (in-station fusion satellites) and the population was put to work for the Usurian 'Company'. The Usurians have heard of the Time Lords, and classified Gallifrey 'Grade three in the last market survey, its potential for commercial development being correspondingly low.'

The Doctor says it must have taken centuries to build the Megropolises. The building they land on (Block Forty) is 1,000 metres high.

The Company's sole aim is to make a profit. Everything is taxed – even death demands a duty. The Company charges 50 per cent compound interest on unpaid taxes, and sends those who cannot or will not pay to the Correction Centre, situated below the Collector's Palace. The population is 'calmed' by the use an anxiety-inducing agent: pentocyleinic-methyl-hydrane (PCM), though this is less effective in the mines of Megropolis Three where the Ajacks (miners) live.

All citizens are 'graded' from the higher Executive Grade (who are allowed to see the light of the suns) to the lowly E-Grade workers who perform menial tasks like cleaning walkways.

The Collector runs the Company, with each Megropolis ruled by a Gatherer. The Collector's personal guards are the Inner Retinue. Execution is by public steaming in a condensation chamber.

GATHERER HADE

Gatherer Hade is a typical Company executive – only interested in extracting as much tax as he can from the citizens. He fawns unctuously over the Collector, and hopes to win favour by foiling a rebellion. While he is greedy and unpleasant, he is also bumbling and incompetent. He misinterprets the implications of the Doctor's arrival, eschews the use of guards in the hope of keeping a reward to himself, and comes off worse in word play with the Doctor. He dies after being thrown from the top of a building by a rabble of disgruntled citizens.

THE COLLECTOR

The Collector is a Usurian, an alien life form classified in Professor Thripted's *Flora and Fauna of the Universe* as poisonous fungus. Maintaining a grey, human form (complete with pinstriped suit) by particle radiation, and

The Collector: 'An ongoing insurrectionary situation would not be acceptable to my management.'

seated in a motorised wheelchair, the Collector is the head of the Usurian Company on Pluto.

He is a cunning, scheming sadist who is only interested in Company profit. Typically, it is by ruining the Company that the Doctor is able to distract and defeat the Collector.

NEW INFORMATION

THE DOCTOR

The Doctor has a telescope and bag of jelly babies in his pocket. Later he produces sets of handcuffs to restrain two Megro Guards, and a champagne cork. He sabotages the Correction Centre machinery, and tells Gatherer Hade's assistant, Marn, that he likes a jacket with lots of pockets.

Less than impressed with the reward offered for him (5,000 Talmars) the Doctor says that the Droge of Gabrielides once offered a whole star system for his head.

He hypnotises a guard into sleeping until told to wake up.

THE TARDIS

When the central column stops moving, the Doctor says they might have gone 'right through the time spiral.' There is a black void outside the TARDIS doors.

COMPANIONS

LEELA: Once Leela knows she is feeling fear because of the PCM in the air she is able to put it behind her.

K-9: is able to beat the Doctor at chess.

UNDERWORLD

TARDIS DATA BANK:

DATE: UNKNOWN
LOCATION: MINYAN SHIP R1C; PLANETOID THAT HAS FORMED ROUND P7E.

THE DOCTOR AND LEELA JOIN THE MINYAN CREW OF THE R1C, ON A 100,000-YEAR QUEST TO FIND THE P7E THAT CARRIES THEIR RACE BANK. BUT THE P7E HAS FORMED INTO A PLANET, AND THE ORACLE, THE SHIP'S COMPUTER, IS PROTECTING THE RACE BANK. THE DOCTOR AND LEELA HELP THE MINYANS ORGANISE A REBELLION AMONGST THE 'TROG' SLAVES IN A BID TO RECOVER THEIR GENETIC INHERITANCE...

In which the budget ran out and so the 'underworld' is actually a model with the actors superimposed...
BY BOB BAKER AND DAVE MARTIN
4 EPISODES, FIRST BROADCAST 7–28 JANUARY 1978

The Oracle: 'There are no gods but me. Have I not created myself? Do I not rule? Am I not all-powerful?'

JOURNEY INFORMATION

THE MINYANS

The Doctor says the Minyan civilisation was destroyed 100,000 years ago on the other side of the Universe. It was what happened on Minyos that led to the Time Lord policy of non-intervention. The Minyans thought of them as gods, which was flattering, so the Time Lords gave them medical help, better communications and scientific aid. The Minyans kicked the Time Lords out at gunpoint. 'Then they went to war with each other, learned how to split the atom, discovered the toothbrush and finally split the planet...'

The R1C (captained by Jackson, with a crew of Herrick, Orfe and Tala) is tracking the P7E, which carries the Minyans race bank – two gold cylinders the length of a man's hand, each stamped with the mark of Minyos.

The R1C crew can regenerate, with technological help. The Doctor asks if the P7E 'has regeneration', suggesting it is built into the ship. Tala is taken to a special chamber to regenerate.

THE ORACLE

The Oracle is the P7E ship's computer. It is tended by the Seers – bullet-headed bronze robots – and rules the Trogs who live in the 'Tree', the tunnel system.

It guards the Minyan race bank, and instead gives Jackson and his crew fission grenades with an explosive force of 2,000 megatons, but the Doctor swaps them back, and the Oracle is destroyed instead of the R1C.

MYTHOLOGICAL ROOTS

'Myths often have a grain of truth in them, if you know where to look,' the Doctor tells Leela. Later he suggests that legends may not be stories from the past, but prophecies of the future. Whatever the case, there are similarities between the story of the Minyans and of Jason and the Argonauts. In addition to the Oracle and its Seers, some of the parallels with Greek mythology are listed below:

R1C – Argossey (the story of the Argo)
P7E – Persephone
The race bank – the Golden Fleece
The Tree – The Tree of Life
Jackson – Jason
Orfe – Orpheus
Tala – Atalanta
Herrick – Heracles

NEW INFORMATION

THE DOCTOR

The Doctor says the Trojan horse is not his plan, exactly. But in fact he gave the idea to the Greeks in *The Myth Makers*.

THE TARDIS

The sound of the TARDIS's materialisation is recorded by the Minyans and identified as: 'Relative dimensional stabiliser in materialisation as used in the time ships of the gods.'

COMPANIONS

K-9: The Doctor says K-9 is his second-best friend, and links him into the R1C systems with bulldog clips holding cables to his ears. K-9 is able to produce a map of the 'tree' of tunnels.

THE INVASION OF TIME

In which the Doctor, having been accidentally elected president, seems to help aliens invade his own planet...
BY DAVID AGNEW
6 EPISODES, FIRST BROADCAST 4 FEBRUARY–11 MARCH 1978

K-9: 'Prognostication impossible in matters concerning Doctor.'

JOURNEY INFORMATION

GALLIFREY

Gallifrey is protected from attack by transduction barriers, which the Doctor lowers to allow the Vardans to arrive, and the Quantum force field.

For the first time, there is reference to the Supreme (rather than High) Council of the Time Lords. The APC net is now said to be 'a small part of the Matrix.' The Matrix is the '...sum total. Everything – all the information that has ever been stored, all the information that can be stored, the imprints of personalities of hundreds of Time Lords and their presidents...' Acting Chancellor Borusa tells the Doctor, 'It will become a part of you as you will become a part of it.'

Nesbin, who befriends Leela in outer Gallifrey, says he and his comrades were Time Lords before they decided to 'drop out' and live in the wastes of Outer Gallifrey: 'All that peace and eternal tranquillity. We decided to get back to nature out here...'

Rassilon died aeons ago, but his mind lives on in the APC net. The Great Key was given to the Chancellor so that no President could wield absolute power. The Doctor – the first President since Rassilon to find the Great Key – is able to use it to arm the forbidden demat gun, with which he destroys Sontaran Commander Stor. (In *The Deadly Assassin* the Great Key was the rod now referred to as the Rod of Rassilon.)

THE VARDANS

The Vardans can travel along any form of broadcast wavelength and materialise at the end of it – even using the TARDIS scanner. They are telepathic, able to read thoughts (even encephalographic patterns), which is why the Doctor has to shield his thoughts. They are humanoid, but until they materialise properly they appear as shimmering silver shapes.

K-9 detects the coordinates of their source planet as vector three zero five two alpha seven, fourteenth span. He is able to use modulation rejection to eject the Vardans from Gallifrey, and the Doctor plans to time-loop their planet.

THE SONTARANS

The Doctor describes the Sontarans as 'a race devoted to perpetual war'.

The Sontarans have used the Vardans to establish a bridgehead on Gallifrey, intending to deal with them later – 'a means to an end'. The Vardans forced the Doctor to open the forcefield so the Sontarans could land (the Doctor opens it to trace the Vardans' planet).

Commander Stor of the Sontaran Special Space Service is in charge of the assault on Gallifrey.

The Doctor says Sontarans can clone at a rate of a million every four minutes.

NEW INFORMATION

THE DOCTOR

As the only surviving candidate from the Presidential election in *The Deadly Assassin*, the Doctor returns to Gallifrey as President Elect. His memory of his induction is later wiped after he builds and uses the forbidden demat gun.

TARDIS DATA BANK:

DATE: UNKNOWN (AFTER *THE DEADLY ASSASSIN*)
LOCATION: GALLIFREY

HAVING BEEN ACCIDENTALLY ELECTED PRESIDENT OF THE TIME LORDS, THE DOCTOR RETURNS TO GALLIFREY. BUT HE IS ACTING STRANGELY AND ORDERS LEELA BANISHED (IN FACT FOR HER OWN SAFETY). IS HE IN LEAGUE WITH THE INVADING VARDANS – CREATURES THAT CAN TRAVEL ALONG ANY BROADCAST WAVELENGTH? BUT EVEN WHEN THE VARDANS ARE DEFEATED, A MORE TERRIBLE THREAT MANIFESTS ITSELF AS THE SONTARANS INVADE. HOW CAN THE DOCTOR DEFEAT THEM WHEN HE IS TRAPPED INSIDE HIS OWN TARDIS…

The Doctor: 'One grows tired of jelly babies, Castellan... One grows tired of almost everything, Castellan. Except power.'

He signs an agreement with the Vardans – which he presumably reneges on when he betrays them. He has the President's office lined with lead in order to shield his thoughts – and conversations with Borusa – from them.

The Doctor goes into a self-induced coma after being 'attacked' by the Matrix (which has been invaded by the Vardans). To open a secret door in Borusa's office, the Doctor imitates his voice.

THE TARDIS

The amber alert status is signalled within the TARDIS as it approaches Gallifrey.

Borusa comments that he wishes the Doctor would 'stabilise his pedestrian infrastructure'. The TARDIS interior includes a greenhouse, a swimming pool, a workshop, an art gallery, a sickbay, and brick-lined corridors.

Patrol stasers do not work in the TARDIS – they won't operate within a relative dimensional stabilizer field. But Sontaran weapons do work.

The TARDIS groans as Time Lord technician Rodan works on it to bypass the Gallifreyan defence controls. Activating the fail-safe fixes the TARDIS 'in its present state for eternity'.

Castellan Kelner says this model of TARDIS was 'withdrawn centuries ago' and Rodan suggests the Doctor gets a 'perfectly modern 706 model'.

COMPANIONS

LEELA: Leela falls in love with Andred, commander of the Chancellery Guards, and stays on Gallifrey to be with him.

In the wastes of Outer Gallifrey, she tells Nesbin she can survive anywhere.

Despite everything, Leela refuses to believe the Doctor is a traitor.

K-9: The Doctor calls K-9 'the most insufferably arrogant, overbearing, patronising bean tin.' Then realises someone once said that about him.

K-9 decides to stay with Leela. But the Doctor has *K-9 MII* waiting in a crate in the TARDIS.

'Doctor, you have been chosen for a vitally important task... It concerns the Key to Time.'

(THE WHITE GUARDIAN – *THE RIBOS OPERATION*)

THE GUARDIANS AND THE KEY TO TIME

The White Guardian stops the TARDIS en route to Halargon Three where the Doctor and K-9 are hoping for a holiday. Instead they find themselves given an assignment, and a new companion.

The Guardians are incredibly powerful, almost elemental creatures. There is a White Guardian – the Guardian of Light in Time – and, to balance him, a Black Guardian. He requires the Key to Time for his own evil purpose. Even the Doctor holds the Guardians in awe, and when he tentatively asks what will happen if he refuses his task, the White Guardian tells him simply: 'Nothing ... nothing at all. Ever.'

The Key to Time is a perfect cube composed of six segments which maintains the equilibrium of time itself. The segments are scattered and hidden throughout the cosmos. The Key itself, once assembled, is too powerful for any being to possess.

The White Guardian tells the Doctor that there are '... times when the forces within the Universe upset the balance to such an extent that it becomes necessary to stop everything ... for a brief moment only, until the balance is restored.'

Such a moment is rapidly approaching, and the White Guardian needs the segments traced and returned to him before the Universe is plunged into eternal chaos.

The segments are disguised – they contain the elemental force of the Universe and can be in any shape, form or size. The Doctor uses the core of the Key itself as a locator which also transforms each segment back into its true form on contact.

'It's funny you know, before I met you, I was even willing to be impressed.'

(ROMANA – *THE RIBOS OPERATION*)

TARDIS DATA BANK:

DESCRIPTION:
FEMALE, TIME LORD
TRAVELLED: *THE RIBOS OPERATION – THE ARMAGEDDON FACTOR*

ROMANA

THE FIRST ROMANA

Inexperienced, but academic, Romanadvoratrelundar is nearly 140, and graduated from the Time Lord Academy with a triple first. She has been sent, she thinks, by the President (implied to be Borusa following the events of *The Invasion of Time*) to help the Doctor in his quest to find the six segments of the Key to Time. But in fact it is the White Guardian who has sent her.

The Doctor suggests shortening her name to Romana (though she tells him she would rather be 'Fred'), since by the time he has called out 'Look out Romanadvoratrelundar' she could already be dead. When she asks what she can do to help, the Doctor is clear: 'I'd like you to stay out of my way as much as possible and try and keep out of trouble. I don't suppose you can make tea?'

While the Doctor is not immediately welcoming, feeling that a new companion is more trouble than she is worth, Romana refuses to be intimidated by him. Her initial icy put-downs – such as telling the Doctor he is suffering from 'a massive compensation syndrome' and that 'sarcasm is an adjusted stress reaction' – give way to more gentle teasing as their mission progresses. In *The Pirate Planet*, for example, she tells the Doctor that she is not familiar with his TARDIS as she did not take the option on 'veteran and vintage models', preferring instead to study the life cycle of the Gallifreyan flutterwing.

Romana may be surprised at the existence of a beast like the Shrivenzale, and naive enough to believe Unstoffe's improbable story about a lost mine because of his 'honest face' (the Doctor points out 'you can't be a crook with a dishonest face'), but she learns quickly. It is not only the Doctor who suffers Romana's ultra-calm, dry put-downs. Count Grendel (*The Androids of Tara*), Mr Fibuli (*The Pirate Planet*) and others also find themselves comprehensively put in their place.

Perhaps her decision to regenerate (in *Destiny of the Daleks*) is a way of leaving behind academic naivety and acknowledging that in the Doctor's company she has become, literally, a different person.

THE RIBOS OPERATION

In which the search for the Key to Time begins with Iain Cuthbertson trying to sell a planet he doesn't actually own...
BY ROBERT HOLMES
4 EPISODES, FIRST BROADCAST 2–23 SEPTEMBER 1978

The Doctor: 'If you call that being nearly killed, you haven't lived yet.'

TARDIS DATA BANK:

DATE: UNKNOWN, FUTURE
LOCATION: DOMAIN OF THE WHITE GUARDIAN; CITY OF SHUR, RIBOS, IN THE CONSTELLATION OF SKYTHA

SENT BY THE WHITE GUARDIAN TO FIND THE SIX SEGMENTS OF THE KEY TO TIME, AND GIVEN A NEW ASSISTANT – ROMANA – THE DOCTOR IS CAUGHT UP IN GARRON AND UNSTOFFE'S SCHEME TO SELL THE PLANET RIBOS TO THE DISGRACED GRAFF VYNDA-K. BUT WHEN THE DANGEROUSLY UNSTABLE GRAFF DISCOVERS THE DECEPTION, THE DOCTOR, ROMANA, K-9 AND THEIR NEW ASSOCIATES ARE FORCED TO TAKE REFUGE IN ANCIENT CATACOMBS...

JOURNEY INFORMATION

RIBOS

Shur is the main city of the medieval planet of Ribos, which is three light centuries from the Magellanic Cloud. There are other settlements to the north. The long seasons are Ice-time and Sun-time, governed by Ribos's elliptical orbit. The natives believe the planet is a battleground over which the Sun gods and the Ice gods fight for supremacy. The world is thought to be flat, and the stars are generally believed to be ice crystals, though a man called Binro realised they were other suns – and was branded a heretic.

The Relic Room is where the crown jewels are kept. It is open to the public, but locked and guarded at night. A savage Shrivenzale is released into the room to deter criminals. Other Shrivenzales live in catacombs below the city.

The Seeker is a local witch, who uses her power with the bones to seek out miscreants and also to foretell the future. When she is forced to track Garron, she tells the Graff Vynda-K that all but one of their group is 'doomed to die'. The survivor is the Doctor, disguised as one of the Graff's guards.

GARRON AND UNSTOFFE

Originally from Hackney Wick, Garron is a con man. He was forced to leave Earth after an Arab to whom he had sold Sydney Harbour realised he was being duped and came after Garron with a machine gun: 'A most harrowing experience. I never went back.'

Alliance Security started to hunt for Garron after he sold Mirabilis Minor to three different purchasers. Now, with his assistant and apprentice, Unstoffe, Garron has planted a piece of jethrik – the rarest and most valuable element in the galaxy –

in amongst the Ribos relics so that the Graff Vynda-K will see it and believe the planet is rich in jethrik. Garron is negotiating to sell the Graff the planet of Ribos (which, of course, is not his). The two acquire the dead Graff's treasure.

THE GRAFF VYNDA-K

The Graff Vynda-K, a crown prince of the Greater Cyrrhenic Empire, was the emperor of Levithia. But he was deposed by his half-brother while away on campaign. He is a bloodthirsty megalomaniac, desperate to regain his throne.

Contrary to the law of the Alliance, he plans – with his loyal Levithian Invincibles and a Levithian General called Sholakh – to use Ribos as a base from which to launch a war to reclaim his planet. With the discovery, he thinks, of jethrik – essential to space drive – on the planet he sees a chance to buy Pontonese ships and hire mercenaries from Shlangi.

The Graff has enjoyed a long, and to his mind successful, military career and recalls such battles as Skarne, the Freitus labyrinth ('almost a year without sight of sky') and Krestus Minor – where Sholakh planted the Graff's standard in the heart of the Krestan general.

NEW INFORMATION

THE DOCTOR

The Doctor resents his new assistant, and tries to set rules for her – 'Do exactly as I say... Stick close to me... Let me do all the talking.' Romana reveals that the Doctor scraped through the Academy – achieving 51 per cent at his second attempt.

He shows an interest in cricket, and uses his pocket watch to hypnotise a guard into sleeping. Romana says the Doctor is 759, but he maintains he is 756.

The Doctor takes the place of one of the Graff's Levithian guards, and swaps the jethrik for the Graff's thermite pack of explosives – so that the Graff is killed when it detonates. He tells Garron he was trained in sleight of hand by Maskelyn.

THE TARDIS

The White Guardian is able to stop the TARDIS in flight and summon the Doctor outside to meet him. Light spills in through the open TARDIS doors.

The tracer is the core of the Key to Time, and when plugged into the TARDIS console, gives the space–time coordinates for each segment of the key.

THE KEY TO TIME

The First Segment is disguised as the jethrik – a glowing blue stone – owned by Garron.

COMPANIONS

K-9: The Doctor has developed a 'dog whistle' which K-9 can hear from a distance and home in on. It is inaudible to human ears. He uses 'stun mark 7' on a Levithian guard, knocking him out for hours.

The Seeker: 'All but one of us is doomed to die, thus has it been written.'

245

THE PIRATE PLANET

In which Douglas Adams provides a script that includes a pirate captain, a robot parrot, a space-jumping planet and economic miracles

BY DOUGLAS ADAMS
4 EPISODES, FIRST BROADCAST 30 SEPTEMBER–21 OCTOBER 1978

The Captain: 'A plank. The theory is very simple: you walk along it, at the end you fall off. Drop one thousand feet – dead.'

JOURNEY INFORMATION

ZANAK

Zanak was a happy prosperous planet until the reign of Queen Xanxia, who staged galactic wars. Legend says she lived for hundreds of years, and towards the end of her reign, the Captain arrived – falling from the sky in a mighty ship.

The Captain rules from the Bridge, which is accessible only by air car or by climbing cliffs. Citizens of Zanak do not worry that the automated mines fill whenever the Captain announces a new golden age, or that the lights in the sky change (as Zanak moves). The people are so prosperous that jewels are left lying in the streets.

In fact, Zanak has been hollowed out and, using technology recovered from the Captain's ship – the *Vantarialis* – jumps through space to materialise around slightly smaller, and often heavily populated, planets and mine them.

As the planets die, the telepathically aware citizens of Zanak – the Mentiads – absorb the released life force and grow in strength. After the death of the Captain the Doctor fills the hollow planet with the expanded remains of its victim planets, and the Mentiads destroy the Bridge.

THE CAPTAIN

The Captain was injured when his ship crashed on Zanak, and half his body has been replaced with cybernetics. These are controlled by a younger projection of Queen Xanxia, who forces the Captain to keep destroying planets, to provide the energy that she needs to stay alive.

He is loud and brash, killing on a whim with his murderous robot parrot – the Polyphase Avatron.

The Doctor sees the Captain is a 'clever and dangerous man'. Behind the bluster, the Captain is planning to destroy Xanxia. He is keeping the husks of the destroyed planets ostensibly as trophies. But, as the Doctor realises, he can use them as a source of power to start time up again within the time dams that are holding the ancient body of Xanxia in her last few seconds of life. The Queen would then die of old age.

The Captain's plan is undermined by the fact that the destroyed Calufrax is not a real planet, but in fact the Second Segment of the Key to Time. When the plan doesn't work, Xanxia realises she has been betrayed and kills the captain.

QUEEN XANXIA

The ancient Queen Xanxia, who is said to have lived for centuries, is suspended in the last few moments of life by time dams fuelled by the destruction of entire planets.

A younger projection of Xanxia poses as the Captain's nurse – and controls him as she has his cybernetic body rigged with explosives. Her body – based on a cell-projection system – has almost achieved full corporeal form. But the Doctor knows that the energy needed to keep her alive is exponential – soon she will have to destroy suns rather than planets merely to stay alive. However, although the Doctor cannot simply turn off the projection, and the Captain's plan is doomed to failure, Xanxia's younger body 'dies' when she is shot.

NEW INFORMATION

THE DOCTOR
Romana says the Doctor has been operating the TARDIS for 523 years. He has a two-headed coin from Aldebaran III (where there are two kings).

The Doctor tells how he climbed a tree to drop an apple on Isaac Newton's head – and then had to explain gravity to him over dinner. He describes the Captain's Trophy Room as the most brilliant piece of astro-gravitational engineering he has ever seen.

THE TARDIS
The TARDIS is unable to materialise in the same time and place as Zanak. When preventing Zanak from materialising round Earth (coordinates 58044684884), the Doctor says it is the 'most dangerous manoeuvre' the TARDIS has ever attempted.

The Doctor doesn't use the synchronic feedback checking circuit or the multi-loop stabiliser when landing, despite what the instruction manual says (he tears out that page).

He keeps the recovered segments of the Key to Time in a fridge in 'limbo' – a dark area off the TARDIS Control Room.

THE KEY TO TIME
The Second Segment is disguised as the uninhabited, cold, icy planet Calufrax – which the Doctor describes as 'paralysingly dull, boring and tedious'. He describes the segment as '... an artificially matricised structure consisting of a substance with a variable atomic weight.'

COMPANIONS
K-9: K-9 spins round as he detects the dying life force of Calufrax. He is able to analyse the Mentiads' powers and track them by their psychospore. He can operate an air car, and defeats and destroys the Captain's Polyphase Avatron.

The Doctor says K-9 is his best friend.

Xanxia: 'I gutted my own planet Zanak for all the energy it contained. I've ransacked planets from Bandraginus to Calufrax, do you think I'm going to stop now?'

THE STONES OF BLOOD

In which the Rollright Stones come to life to celebrate the one hundredth **Doctor Who** story...
BY DAVID FISHER
4 EPISODES, FIRST BROADCAST 28 OCTOBER–18 NOVEMBER 1978

JOURNEY INFORMATION

CESSAIR OF DIPLOS
Cessair stole the Great Seal of Diplos (actually the Third Segment) and, together with Ogri she had taken from the planet Ogros, fled justice. The Megara justice machines sent to try her were kept in a sealed compartment aboard a hyperspace vessel. While the ship was left in hyperspace, Cessair escaped to Earth and has assumed a number of identities over the 4,000 years she has lived there. In her guise as the Celtic goddess, the Cailleach, the raven and the crow obey her will...

Being from Diplos, Cessair is allergic to certain Earth foods including citric acid – and her different metabolism means she is not of interest to the blood-eating Ogri.

PROFESSOR EMILIA RUMFORD
Author of *Bronze Age Burials in Gloucestershire*, Professor Rumford is surveying the Nine Travellers, believing the stone circle to be one of the Gorsedds of ancient prophecy. Previous surveys have met with disaster – for example, one of the stones 'fell' on Borlase after he completed his 1754 survey.

Rumford is a stubborn and determined woman, never afraid to speak her mind or say what she thinks of her professional colleagues. She carries a police truncheon for protection (and was arrested in New York for carrying an offensive weapon). She does not suspect Vivien Fay – in fact Cessair of Diplos – of being any more or less than she appears, and is initially sceptical of the Doctor and Romana's theories and suggestions.

THE OGRI
From the planet Ogros in Tau Ceti, the Ogri are silicon-based life forms that feed on the amino acids and proteins native to their own planet and found on Earth in blood. They can absorb blood either when it is poured over them, as during the rituals of worship of the Calleach, or directly from a human who touches the stones.

Capable of moving, the Ogri are almost indestructible, being in effect made of stone. The Doctor thinks their name is the origin of mythical creatures like Gog, Magog and ogres.

THE MEGARA
The Megara are justice machines, although they have living cells at their core. They uphold the law, acting as judge, jury

Megara: 'We are the Megara. We are justice machines...
We are the law. Judge, jury and executioner. Once we have
arrived at our verdict, we execute it without fear or
favour. Impartially.'

TARDIS DATA BANK:

DATE: PRESENT DAY
LOCATION: BOSCOMBE
MOOR; HYPER-
SPACE

THE THIRD SEGMENT OF THE
KEY TO TIME SEEMS TO BE IN
THE STONE CIRCLE KNOWN AS
THE NINE TRAVELLERS. BUT
THE DOCTOR AND ROMANA
CANNOT FIND IT THERE AND
SOME OF THE STONES ARE
ALIEN OGRI THAT FEED ON
BLOOD. CESSAIR OF DIPLOS IS
MASQUERADING AS A CELTIC
GODDESS TO CONTROL
EVENTS AND TO ESCAPE THE
MEGARA – JUSTICE MACHINES
SEALED ON A HYPERSPACE
SHIP ABOVE THE CIRCLE. CAN
THE DOCTOR UNMASK
CESSAIR, RESCUE ROMANA,
CONVINCE THE MEGARA OF
THE TRUTH AND ESCAPE HIS
SENTENCE OF DEATH…

knew of a galactic federation destroyed by its own justice machine for contempt of court.

With K-9's help, the Doctor is able to build a machine that opens a gateway into hyperspace. He describes hyperspace as 'a theoretical absurdity' (though ships travel through hyperspace in *Frontier in Space*).

THE KEY TO TIME

The Third Segment is the Great Seal of Diplos. It enabled Cessair to appear as the Doctor and lure Romana over a cliff.

COMPANIONS

K-9: K-9 erases his memory of tennis when Romana tells him to 'forget it'. Romana's scent, blood, tissue type and alpha-wave patterns are recorded in K-9's data banks so he can locate her.

He is able to hold back, but not destroy, the Ogri. He is almost destroyed by one, but Romana is able to regenerate him with the TARDIS molecular stabiliser.

BEHIND THE SCENES

100 UP

The Stones of Blood was the hundredth **Doctor Who** story to be broadcast, and the production team chose to mark this achievement in two ways within the programme.

The less intrusive of these was to include an opportunity for the Doctor to explain to Romana that she was sent not by the President but by the White Guardian, and in so doing to remind viewers of the overall story behind the season.

Romana's shoes are not very practical.

Omitted from the end of the Guardian explanations was the Doctor offering K-9 a piece of cake, and Romana complaining 'You'll spoil that dog'. The camera script and broadcast programme then coincide again from the TARDIS landing. 'That's *your* surprise,' the Doctor tells Romana – referring back to his surprise party.

```
INT. TARDIS LIMBO AREA
THE DOCTOR ENTERS TO FIND K-9 SITTING AT A
TABLE LADEN WITH PARTY FOOD, JELLIES, CRISPS,
ETC.
THERE IS A HUGE BIRTHDAY CAKE COVERED IN
CANDLES ON THE MIDDLE OF THE TABLE.
THE ROOM IS DECKED WITH STREAMERS, BALLOONS,
ETC.
K-9: (SINGING OUT OF TUNE) Happy birthday to
you, happy birthday to you, etc.
THE DOCTOR WALKS ROUND THE TABLE, FINDS HIS
PLACE AND SITS DOWN.
ROMANA MOVES BEHIND THE DOCTOR OPENS FRIDGE
AND TAKES OUT A LARGE PRESENT.
ROMANA: (GIVING HIM PRESENT) Happy birthday,
Doctor.
THE DOCTOR: Thank you, you know I think those
shoes are charming.
THE DOCTOR STANDS UP AND OPENS PRESENT TO FIND
THAT IT IS A NEW SCARF, BUT IT IS EXACTLY LIKE
THE OLD ONE.
THE DOCTOR: Gosh just what I needed. If only
the Guardian could see us now.
ROMANA: The Guardian? Doctor, I do wish I knew
what you were talking about.
```

THE ANDROIDS OF TARA

In which Mary Tamm plays Romana, Strella, and two androids in a reworking of *The Prisoner of Zenda*...
BY DAVID FISHER
4 EPISODES, FIRST BROADCAST 25 NOVEMBER–16 DECEMBER 1978

Romana: 'Count, far be it from me to query this lady's competence as a doctor, but where I come from you don't cut off the patient's head if you wish to cure their ankle.'

JOURNEY INFORMATION

TARA

Tara is a mixture of the medieval and the modern. While the social structure is strictly medieval, the inhabitants have the technology to build sophisticated androids – originally produced 200 years ago to replace plague victims when nine-tenths of the population died – as well as electrified swords (the controls are in the hilt) and crossbows that fire energy bolts.

Technology is understood only by the peasant classes, while the nobles live in castles and rule absolutely. Prince Reynart's swordmaster, Zadek, says that if they had been meant to be peasants they would have been born peasants. The crossbow is 'a peasant's weapon.'

PRINCE REYNART OF TARA

Reynart is about to accede as the rightful king – crowned in the Great Palace of Tara. If he fails to appear, he forfeits his right to the throne. There have already been three attempts on Reynart's life, and he plans to use an android double to divert Grendel's assassins while he gets to the Coronation Room.

Princess Strella – who has been imprisoned by Count Grendel, and is the double of Romana – is First Lady of Tara, and the only other contender for the throne.

Reynart is attended by the loyal Zadek and swordsman Farrah.

COUNT GRENDEL

Count Grendel, Knight of Gracht, Master of the Sword, plans to be king. He already holds Princess Strella captive, and kidnaps Prince Reynart. Grendel's plan is for Reynart to marry an android copy of Strella (or Romana) before he is killed. Grendel will then marry the widowed Strella and take the throne – before she herself meets with an 'accidental' death. But his plans are thwarted by the Doctor who mends an android double of the Prince and takes it to the coronation. Grendel tries to destroy the android with his own copy of Strella, but it is spotted by the Doctor.

Madame Lamia is Grendel's surgeon engineer, and it is she who builds the android copy of Romana/Strella. Lamia is in love with Grendel, who once showed her 'a certain courtesy', but Grendel treats her with contempt and does not grieve when she is accidentally shot down by his own guards.

TARDIS DATA BANK:

DATE: UNKNOWN
LOCATION: TARA

FINDING THE FOURTH SEGMENT PROVES EASY ENOUGH. BUT BEFORE SHE CAN GET BACK TO THE TARDIS WITH IT, ROMANA IS KIDNAPPED BY COUNT GRENDEL. ROMANA IS THE DOUBLE OF THE PRINCESS STRELLA, AND GRENDEL'S AMBITIONS TO SEIZE CONTROL OF TARA SOON INVOLVE THE REAL PRINCESS (WHOM HE HOLDS CAPTIVE), ROMANA AND AN ANDROID DOUBLE. THE DOCTOR MEANWHILE NEEDS TO MEND AN ANDROID DOUBLE OF THE PRINCESS'S FIANCÉ, AND THE RIGHTFUL RULER, PRINCE REYNART. AS GRENDEL'S MACHINATIONS BECOME MORE DIABOLICAL, THE DOCTOR AND K-9 STRUGGLE TO RESCUE ROMANA BEFORE HER WEDDING, AND TO REMAIN ALIVE...

NEW INFORMATION

THE DOCTOR

The Doctor goes fishing on Tara. He says he last went fishing with the famous angler Izaac Walton, and also mentions seeing Capablanca play chess in 1927. He is able to repair the android Reynart, and tells the real Reynart he cannot be bought for money. Reynart offers the Doctor 1,000 gold pieces, but the Doctor demands 500. He drinks wine with Reynart, and succumbs to a drug that is in it.

The Doctor demonstrates his swordsmanship by defeating Grendel – the greatest swordsman on Tara.

THE KEY TO TIME

The Fourth Segment is disguised as part of a statue on the Gracht estate. The statue is said to guard the fortunes of the Grachts. Madame Lamia blunts two diamond drills trying to scratch the Segment.

COMPANIONS

ROMANA: Romana's alpha waves are like nothing Madame Lamia has ever seen before. Romana does not understand horses, telling Grendel's to 'Start' and asking how it works.

K-9: The TARDIS doors open automatically for K-9. Again, he is able to detect Romana's location.

K-9 has been programmed with all chess championship tournaments since 1866.

Count Grendel: 'You see before you the complete killing machine — as beautiful as you and as deadly as the plague. If only she were real, I'd marry her.'

THE POWER OF KROLL

In which a giant squid attacks Neil McCarthy, Philip Madoc, and a group of green alien humanoids...
BY ROBERT HOLMES
4 EPISODES, FIRST BROADCAST 23 DECEMBER 1978–13 JANUARY 1979

JOURNEY INFORMATION

THE THIRD MOON OF DELTA MAGNA

The Third Moon of Delta Magna is a wet, swampy planet with almost constant rainstorms. The huge lake is actually home to a giant squid, shipped from Delta Magna together with a tribe of Swampies centuries ago. The Fifth Segment of the Key to Time has caused this squid – worshipped as Kroll by the Swampies – to grow to giant size. Kroll's central mass is a quarter of a mile across and 140 feet high. It has been sleeping, producing the methane that humans are collecting and refining. This work – the sound of the orbit shots sending the refined methane into Delta orbit, and the rise in lake temperature caused by the refinery's heat exchangers – has awakened Kroll.

Kroll 'has the power of the Symbol, he sees all.' Ranquin, leader of the Swampies, says, 'The Symbol was a holy relic, brought here by our ancestors at the time of the settlement. He who holds the Symbol can see the future. The power revealed how the Dryfoots would destroy Delta Magna with their fighting and their greed and the evil of their great cities...'

Rohm-Dutt: 'You know there's a thing called a drill fly in these swamps. It lays eggs in your feet. A week later, you get holes in your head.'

The creature hunts by detecting surface vibrations. It is predominantly vegetarian but has learned that anything that moves is edible.

THE REFINERY

The methane-catalysing refinery is a pilot plant, the first ever built. It has been working for several months. Thawn, one of the refinery workers, believes that the Swampies have killed two of the crew already. In fact they were taken by Kroll.

The refinery produces 100 tons of compressed protein a day, and sends it up into Delta orbit in orbit shots every 12 hours (freighters would not be economically viable). Ten refineries can provide one-fifth of Delta Magna's requirements, but the lake could not sustain ten refineries and the Swampie settlement.

Thawn has sent obsolete weapons to the Swampies via the gun-runner Rohm-Dutt. He plans to use gas mortars to wipe out the settlement, justifying it as self-defence since the Swampies are armed.

THE SWAMPIES

The Swampies were on Delta Magna and shipped to the Third Moon when the Earth colonists arrived centuries ago. They make a blood sacrifice before battle. When Romana is to be sacrificed to Kroll, it is actually a Swampie in ceremonial costume who attempts to perform the ritual.

The Swampies refer to the humans as Dryfoots and resent their presence on the moon. They try to kill the Doctor, Romana and Rohm-Dutt by the Seventh Holy Ritual of the Old Book. The victims are tied up with creepers that shrink and snap the spine as they contract. (The First Ritual involves putting victims in a pit and throwing rocks at them.)

NEW INFORMATION

THE DOCTOR

The Doctor says he is 759. He makes a reed pipe in the swamp, on which he plays J.S. Bach's 'Badinere'.

He says he is unable to hypnotise Ranquin because of his narrow eyes. To escape death by the Seventh Holy Ritual, the Doctor shrieks at a very high pitch to break the glass in a window and allow the rain in so the drying creepers can be stretched. He says he learned the trick from Dame Nellie Melba (though she could only shatter wine glasses).

THE KEY TO TIME

The Fifth Segment is disguised as the Symbol of Power of the Swampies' god Kroll – a giant squid. But a real giant squid swallows the segment (and the High Priest) and grows to an enormous size with the Segment's power. The Doctor recovers the Segment by touching Kroll with the Tracer.

THE ARMAGEDDON FACTOR

K-9: 'Optimism — belief that everything will turn out well. Irrational bordering on insane.'

TARDIS DATA BANK:

DATE: UNKNOWN
LOCATION: TWIN PLANETS OF ATRIOS AND ZEOS;
THE SHADOW'S LAIR

ATRIOS IS AT NUCLEAR WAR WITH ITS TWIN PLANET ZEOS. BUT THE CONFLICT HAS BEEN ENGINEERED BY THE SHADOW – AN AGENT OF THE BLACK GUARDIAN WHO HAS LOCATED THE SIXTH SEGMENT OF THE KEY TO TIME AND LURES THE DOCTOR TO HIS DOMAIN TO GET THE OTHER FIVE. CAN THE DOCTOR AND ROMANA LOCATE THE FINAL SEGMENT, STOP THE ATRIAN MARSHAL FROM TRIGGERING OBLITERATION AND DEFEAT THE SHADOW? AND HOW IS THE DOCTOR'S OLD CLASSMATE DRAX INVOLVED?

In which John Woodvine delivers Churchillian speeches while William Squire works for Black Guardian Valentine Dyall to destroy the Universe...
BY BOB BAKER AND DAVE MARTIN
6 EPISODES, FIRST BROADCAST 20 JANUARY–24 FEBRUARY 1979

JOURNEY INFORMATION

PRINCESS ASTRA

Astra is the last surviving member of the royal house of Atrios, the twin planet of Zeos on the edge of the Helical galaxy. The Shadow believes she knows where the Sixth Segment is, as the secret has been passed down through the generations of the royal house. In fact the 'secret' is a molecular anomaly within the genetic structure of the royal house. Astra, the sixth princess of the sixth dynasty of the sixth royal house of Atrios is herself the Sixth Segment of the Key to Time. 'It is for this that you were born,' the Shadow tells her.

Unaware of her destiny, Astra is working with her lover Surgeon Merak, to bring the war with Zeos to a peaceful conclusion. When the Doctor breaks the core of the Key to Time, she returns at Merak's hospital bedside.

THE MARSHAL

'I understand only my duty,' the Marshal says. 'And my duty as Marshal of Atrios is to prosecute this war to a successful conclusion.' He will let nothing stand in the way of this – not even the Doctor.

But the Marshal is being manipulated by the Shadow. He communicates with him through a distorting mirror and is controlled by a black box fixed to his neck. He believes that the Shadow is helping him towards victory and that when the Shadow halts the Zeon attacks – the Shadow has now lured and captured the Doctor – he will be able to win the war.

THE SHADOW

The cadaverous Shadow is the servant of the Black Guardian – sent to find the Key to Time. His plan is to locate the Sixth segment, and wait for the Doctor to bring the other Segments to him when seeking the Sixth.

As part of a plan to trap the Doctor, the Shadow has had Drax build Mentalis – a super-computer – to run the Zeon war against Atrios. By ending the war the Shadow creates a situation where Mentalis will self-destruct, destroying both Atrios and Zeos, rather than allowing the Marshal to destroy it – the Armageddon Factor. This situation forces the Doctor to use the Key to Time to create a time loop so the Mentalis's countdown will never reach zero. The Shadow does not seek power, but glories in destruction. He sees the war as a 'rehearsal' and once he and the Black Guardian have the Key to Time, they will set the universe at war with itself.

The Shadow's servants are dark, gaunt, cloaked creatures referred to as Mutes.

DRAX

Drax knows the Doctor from Gallifrey where they were on a tech course together. He has been doing freelance work ever since, and at the end of the story decides to go into partnership with the Marshal to rebuild Atrios.

He has acquired a Cockney accent as his TARDIS broke down on Earth and he was arrested trying to steal replacement components. He was sentenced to ten years in Brixton jail. 'Well, I had to learn the lingo, didn't I, to survive.'

He built the battle computer Mentalis for the Shadow about five years earlier (just after the war started), and helps the Doctor to disarm the computer. He also rigs a relative dimensional stabiliser to miniaturise himself and the Doctor so as to defeat the Shadow.

The Shadow: 'Once we have the Key to Time we shall set not two small planets but the two halves of the entire cosmos at war, and their mutual destruction will be music in our ears.'

NEW INFORMATION

THE DOCTOR

The Doctor survives a recycling furnace and saves K-9 using a little trick he 'picked up from the firewalkers in Bali'. He is able to resist the Shadow's control device.

Drax calls the Doctor 'Theta Sigma' and says they were on the tech course about 450 years ago – the class of '92. Drax failed, but the Doctor got his doctorate.

THE TARDIS

After denying the Black Guardian the Key to Time, the Doctor fits a 'randomiser' to the TARDIS so that its next

location will be determined by 'a complex scientific principle known as pot luck'. Since even the Doctor does not know where they are going, the Black Guardian cannot follow or trace them.

THE KEY TO TIME

Princess Astra is the Sixth Segment of the Key to Time.

The Doctor uses the Key, with an ersatz Sixth Segment made from chronodyne, to time-loop Mentalis and the Marshal's ship so that the Marshal's missiles do not fire, and Mentalis does not self-destruct.

The Doctor snaps the tracer to scatter the Segments through space and time once more.

ROMANA THE SECOND ROMANA

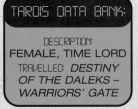

TARDIS DATA BANK:

DESCRIPTION:
FEMALE, TIME LORD
TRAVELLED: *DESTINY OF THE DALEKS – WARRIORS' GATE*

Why Romana regenerates is not made clear. It may be that her body was more damaged than it seemed when she was tortured by the Shadow in *The Armageddon Factor*, or possibly she felt that after the successful completion of the quest for the Key to Time she needed to change in order to fit in better with the personalities of the Doctor and K-9.

But whatever the reason, she regenerates – initially into an identical form to Princess Astra. When the Doctor tells her that she cannot go around wearing copies of other people's bodies, she changes form again – several times – before ultimately settling back into Astra's form.

Her new personality retains the brilliant technical expertise and analytical ability of the original, but is less serious and 'cold'. Romana remains almost the Doctor's equal, gaining in confidence and aptitude as she acquires more experience. She makes her own sonic screwdriver (which the Doctor tries to swap for his), and tells the Tharils she can build them a TARDIS when she leaves in *Warriors' Gate*.

It is Romana's decision to leave the Doctor and to stay in E-Space and help Biroc to free his people from slavery. K-9 stays with her as his memory wafers will not work back in normal space. Partly, Romana leaves because she wants to strike out on her own. 'I've got to be my own Romana,' she says. But also, she is aware that she is expected to return to Gallifrey and, after travelling with the Doctor, her horizons have broadened and she no longer believes herself capable of fitting into Time Lord society.

'I don't want to spend the rest of my life on Gallifrey — after all this.' (ROMANA – *FULL CIRCLE*)

DESTINY OF THE DALEKS

In which Douglas Adams takes over as script editor, and Lalla Ward takes over as Romana to battle against the Daleks and Davros...
BY TERRY NATION
4 EPISODES, FIRST BROADCAST 1–22 SEPTEMBER 1979

JOURNEY INFORMATION

THE MOVELLANS

The Movellans are a humanoid race of robots, and have been at war with the Daleks for centuries. They function logically and, as with the Daleks, their battle computers are calculating the best strategy and precise moment at which to attack – so far not a shot has been fired.

They are tremendously strong and resilient. Lan recovers after being exterminated by a Dalek, while Agella survives a roof collapsing on her. Commander Sharrel states that '... dysfunction, or death as you know it, only occurs in us with massive circuitry disturbance.' Their power packs and controlling circuits are in cylinders held on their belts. The Doctor and others disable Movellans by removing these cylinders. The Doctor also realises that high-frequency sound disrupts them – when he whistles, or blows K-9's dog whistle.

Romana identifies the Movellans' ship as time-warp capable and probably originating in Area 4X Alpha 4.

The Movellans' nova device can change air molecules so that a planet's atmosphere becomes flammable and can be set alight – destroying all life.

TARDIS DATA BANK:

DATE: UNKNOWN, FUTURE
LOCATION: SKARO

LOCKED IN STALEMATE IN THEIR WAR AGAINST THE MOVELLANS, THE DALEKS RETURN TO THEIR HOME PLANET SKARO TO FIND THEIR CREATOR, DAVROS. REVIVED AFTER CENTURIES IN SUSPENDED ANIMATION, DAVROS SENDS SUICIDE DALEKS TO DESTROY THE DOCTOR AND A MOVELLAN SHIP. BUT THE DOCTOR AND A NEWLY REGENERATED ROMANA HAVE DISCOVERED THAT THE MOVELLANS ARE ALSO ROBOTS, AND ALMOST AS VILLAINOUS AS THE DALEKS...

The Doctor: 'If you're supposed to be the superior race of the universe, why don't you try climbing after us?'

TYSSAN

Starship Engineer Tyssan was serving with Earth's deep-space fleet and has been a prisoner of the Daleks since he was captured two years ago. Captives are held on a Dalek prison ship, and about 50 have been shipped to Skaro to work in excavations. If one prisoner escapes, five others are executed in retaliation.

DAVROS

Davros was shot by the Daleks at the end of *Genesis of the Daleks*. He has survived for centuries, and awakens when found by the Doctor, Romana, Tyssan and the Movellan Agella.

He tells the Doctor, 'There was damage to my primary life-support system, the secondary and backup circuits switch in immediately. Synthetic tissue regeneration took place, whilst bodily organs were held in long-term suspension.'

Having been revived, and appraised of the Daleks' problems, he soon sees the solution. He is also sure that he will replace the Supreme Dalek as their leader.

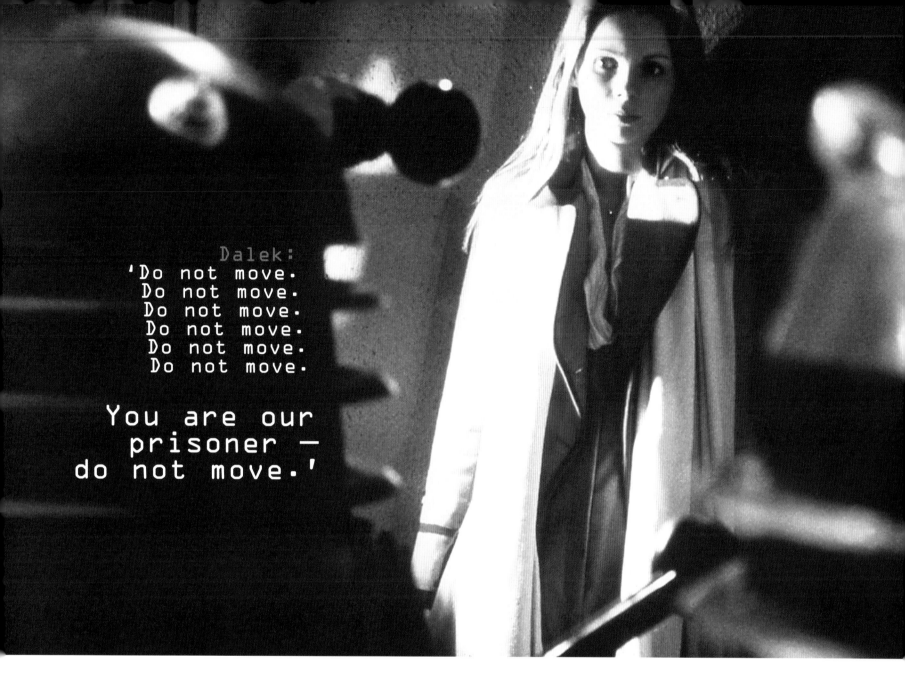

Dalek:
'Do not move.
Do not move.
Do not move.
Do not move.
Do not move.
Do not move.

You are our
prisoner —
do not move.'

Captured by Tyssan, Davros is cryogenically frozen and taken back to Earth to stand trial on the captured Movellan ship for his crimes against the whole of sentient creation.

THE DALEKS

According to the Doctor, the Daleks ravaged their home planet Skaro and left it for dead. Now, after centuries of stalemate in the war with the Movellans, they have returned to find Davros – their creator – in the hope he can give them an advantage that will enable them to defeat their enemies.

Ruthless as ever, the Daleks exterminate prisoners one by one until the Doctor surrenders Davros to them.

Their computers are able to identify the Doctor and 'his companion' from the sound of their voices inside the Movellan ship. Committed to protect Davros and destroy the Movellans, the Dalek force has no qualms about making a suicide bombing attack on the Movellan craft.

NEW INFORMATION

THE DOCTOR

The Doctor reads – and disagrees with – *The Origins of the Universe* by Oolan Caluphid. 'Why doesn't he ask someone who was there?' he wonders.

COMPANIONS

ROMANA: Romana regenerates into the form of Princess Astra (from *The Armageddon Factor*).

She says they taught her at school how to stop her hearts – and feigns death to escape the Dalek mine workings.

K-9: has developed a form of laryngitis and needs to be repaired. The Doctor says his cybernetics tutor taught him that when replacing a robot's brain, arrow A should point to the front.

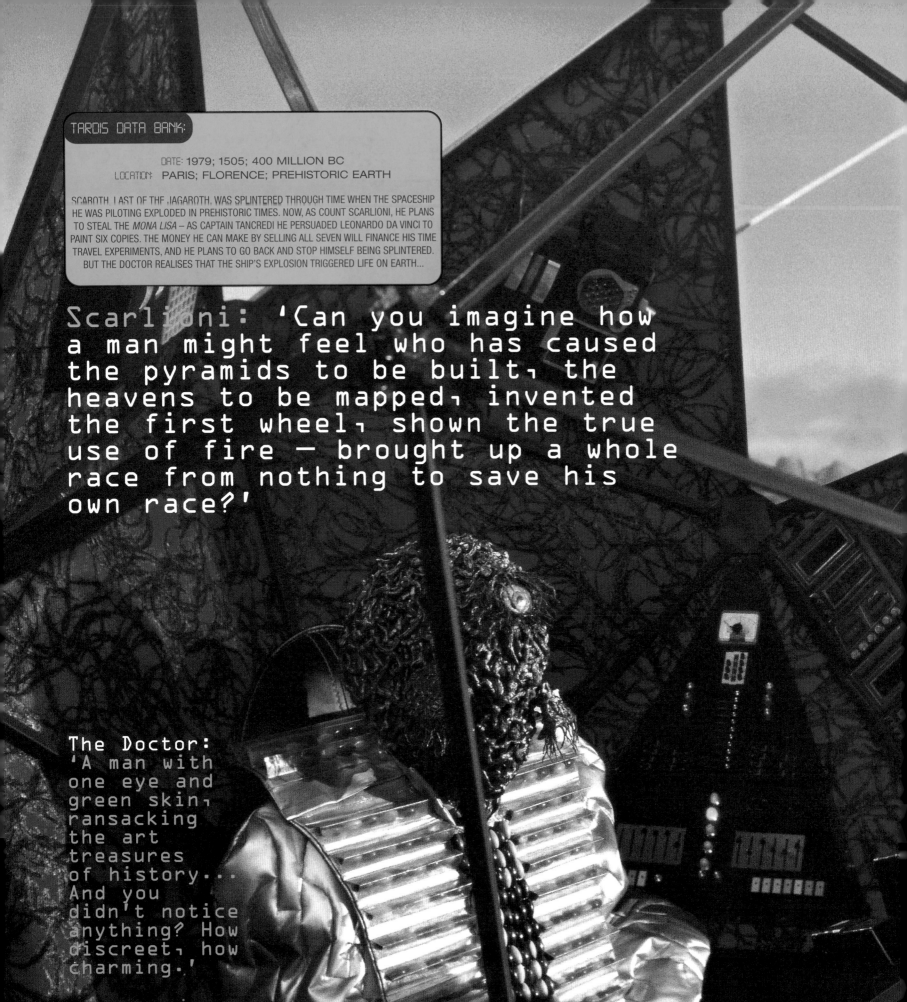

TARDIS DATA BANK:

DATE: 1979; 1505; 400 MILLION BC
LOCATION: PARIS; FLORENCE; PREHISTORIC EARTH

SCAROTH, LAST OF THE JAGAROTH, WAS SPLINTERED THROUGH TIME WHEN THE SPACESHIP
HE WAS PILOTING EXPLODED IN PREHISTORIC TIMES. NOW, AS COUNT SCARLIONI, HE PLANS
TO STEAL THE *MONA LISA* – AS CAPTAIN TANCREDI HE PERSUADED LEONARDO DA VINCI TO
PAINT SIX COPIES. THE MONEY HE CAN MAKE BY SELLING ALL SEVEN WILL FINANCE HIS TIME
TRAVEL EXPERIMENTS, AND HE PLANS TO GO BACK AND STOP HIMSELF BEING SPLINTERED.
BUT THE DOCTOR REALISES THAT THE SHIP'S EXPLOSION TRIGGERED LIFE ON EARTH...

Scarlioni: 'Can you imagine how a man might feel who has caused the pyramids to be built, the heavens to be mapped, invented the first wheel, shown the true use of fire – brought up a whole race from nothing to save his own race?'

The Doctor: 'A man with one eye and green skin, ransacking the art treasures of history... And you didn't notice anything? How discreet, how charming.'

CITY OF DEATH

In which the *Mona Lisa* is stolen by an alien in a script hurriedly written by Douglas Adams and Graham Williams under a pseudonym, featuring John Cleese, Eleanor Bron and Julian Glover...
BY DAVID AGNEW
4 EPISODES, FIRST BROADCAST 29 SEPTEMBER–20 OCTOBER 1979

JOURNEY INFORMATION

SCAROTH

Scaroth is the last of the Jagaroth – which the Doctor describes as 'a vicious, callous, warlike race'. The last Jagaroth ship exploded taking off from Earth in prehistoric times. Scaroth was the pilot, in the warp-control cabin, and was splintered into 12 aspects of himself that were scattered through Earth's history, living independent but connected lives: 'All identical, none complete.'

Each aspect has been working to advance Man's technological evolution to a point where the Scaroth furthest in the future – Count Scarlioni – will be able to build a time machine so he can travel back and stop himself attempting take-off.

Charming and urbane, the count needs money to finance his time experiments. The splintered aspects of Scaroth are able to communicate across time, so in 1505 the Captain Tancredi version persuades Leonardo da Vinci to paint six copies of the *Mona Lisa*. Then Scarlioni – who knows of seven potential buyers – can steal the original from the Louvre in 1979 and secretly sell all seven.

DUGGAN

Duggan is a private detective hired by a group of art collectors to keep watch on Count Scarlioni, who is supposed to be the source of art treasures coming on to the market. They are believed to be fakes. Keeping watch on Countess Scarlioni, Duggan soon realises that Scarlioni is intending to steal the *Mona Lisa*.

The Doctor tells Duggan, 'That's your philosophy isn't it – if it moves, hit it.' Ultimately, Duggan punching Scaroth in prehistoric times ensures the evolution of the human race. As the Doctor tells him, 'That was possibly the most important punch in history.'

Duggan is staggered to hear that the only *Mona Lisa* to survive a fire at the Count's chateau was 'the one nearest the wall' and can't believe the Doctor has returned it to the Louvre as it has 'This is a fake' written on it. 'It doesn't matter what it looks like,' he says, but the Doctor tells him some people believe that is the whole point of art...

NEW INFORMATION

THE DOCTOR

Once again, the Doctor misses meeting Leonardo da Vinci (as in *The Masque of Mandragora*). He has an instant camera in his pocket, and writes a note for Leonardo in mirror writing. Using a felt pen, he writes 'This is a fake' on the boards Leonardo will use to paint the *Mona Lisa* copies, so that the 'forgeries' will be detected when x-rayed.

The Doctor says he wrote out the first draft of *Hamlet* for Shakespeare who had sprained his wrist writing sonnets. Shakespeare was a quiet man, and the Doctor told him: 'There's no point talking if you've got nothing to say...'

COMPANIONS

ROMANA: Romana tells Duggan she is 125 (in *The Ribos Operation* she said she was nearly 140). She immediately opens an insoluble Chinese puzzle box owned by the Countess.

She thinks the *Mona Lisa* is 'quite good', but wants to know why she hasn't any eyebrows. Romana has her own sonic screwdriver which she uses to open the locked door to a café. (Duggan smashes the window to get in.)

BEHIND THE SCENES

FAWLTY TARDIS

Julian Glover, who played Scaroth/Scarlioni in *City of Death*, in many ways legitimised the appearance of 'name' actors in **Doctor Who** when he appeared as Richard the Lionheart in *The Crusade*. By the time he guest-starred again, the series had a reputation for attracting big-name, quality actors.

Appearing in brief cameo roles in *City of Death* are John Cleese and Eleanor Bron – better known for their comedy roles (though Eleanor Bron was to return as Kara in *Revelation of the Daleks*).

The scripts for *City of Death*, though credited to 'David Agnew', were written rapidly by script editor Douglas Adams, helped by producer Graham Williams, when a story by David Fisher called *Gamble with Time* proved unsuitable. Adams was a friend of John Cleese, and happened to meet him one lunch time at the BBC's rehearsal rooms at Acton. Adams persuaded Cleese to agree to appear in a short scene that Adams would write. He 'bribed' Cleese with the promise that his daughter – a Dalek fan – could visit the studios during the recording of *Destiny of the Daleks* (which was actually made after *City of Death*).

The scene Adams wrote was for two art aficionados, described in the original script as 'English gentlemen'. With the script written, and Cleese in agreement, Adams suggested to Cleese that the second gentleman be played by 'someone like Alan Coren'. Cleese in turn suggested Jonathan Miller or Alan Bennett, before Eleanor Bron proved available and ideal for the part. The lines had initially been attributed to *One* and *Two*, but by the time the camera script was prepared this had been changed to reflect the casting to, *Man and Woman*.

One concern that both actors had was publicity. Producer Graham Williams also felt that the appearance of Cleese and Bron might distract from the main narrative thrust. So Williams sought permission to use pseudonyms for them in *Radio Times* and endorsed their request that there be no advance publicity for their appearances. 'I would not wish to encourage the belief that the programme will feature a surprise "star" each week,' Williams said in his memo.

In the event, this request was denied. But, for the record, the pseudonyms Cleese and Bron requested were *Kim Bread* and *Helen Swanetsky*.

THE CREATURE FROM THE PIT

Adrasta: 'We call it the Creature...
Our researchers divide into two categories
— the ones who have got close enough to find
out something about it, and the ones who are
still alive.'

TARDIS DATA BANK:

DATE: UNKNOWN
LOCATION: CHLORIS

THE DOCTOR, ROMANA AND K-9 ARRIVE ON CHLORIS, A PLANET WITH ABUNDANT PLANT LIFE BUT LITTLE METAL. ROMANA IS CAPTURED BY BANDITS WHILE THE DOCTOR FINDS HIMSELF IN 'THE PIT' WHERE A SAVAGE BLOB-LIKE CREATURE LIVES. BUT HE DISCOVERS THE CREATURE IS A TYTHONIAN AMBASSADOR CALLED ERATO WHO WANTS TO TRADE PLANT MATTER FOR METAL. LADY ADRASTA, WHO CONTROLS ALL THE METAL ON CHLORIS, HAS CONFINED ERATO TO THE PIT AND PLANS TO USE K-9 TO KILL HIM. BUT THE TYTHONIANS HAVE ALREADY RECEIVED ERATO'S DISTRESS SIGNAL AND SET A NEUTRON STAR ON A COURSE TO DESTROY CHLORIS'S SUN...

In which a giant green blob turns out to be friendly, and Geoffrey Bayldon plays an astrologer...
BY DAVID FISHER
4 EPISODES, FIRST BROADCAST 27 OCTOBER–17 NOVEMBER 1979

Romana: 'I'm a Time Lady.
And I'm not used to being
assaulted by a collection of
hairy, grubby little men.'

JOURNEY INFORMATION

CHLORIS

The planet Chloris is all but covered in impenetrable jungle, but has very little metal so it is very precious. There are various courts and kingdoms on the planet, but Adrasta is the most powerful ruler as she controls the original source of metal.

The entrance to the mine is called the Pit. Adrasta executes criminals (and people who upset her) by having them thrown in. A creature lives in the Pit – this is Erato, who tries to communicate with those thrown in with him.

Some of the plant life is aggressive and mobile – like the wolf weeds, which are grown in Adrasta's nurseries and made to do her will by Adrasta's Huntsman.

LADY ADRASTA

Adrasta rules part of Chloris and controls all metal as she owns the only mine. The mine is worked out now, and she has imprisoned Erato in the old workings. Desperate to hold on to power, she has held the Tythonian captive rather than risk it offering a deal to anyone else on the planet. She sees K-9 as a weapon that could destroy the creature.

Forced by the suspicious Huntsman to hold Erato's communicator, and condemned literally out of her own mouth when speaking his words, Adrasta is killed by Erato.

ORGANON

Organon is a travelling astrologer who has made predictions at every major court on the planet. He ran into trouble with Adrasta when he predicted she would have visitors from beyond the stars, and she demanded further information. When he was unable to supply details, she flung him into the Pit and assumes he died there. Organon has managed to survive by avoiding the creature and eating scraps of food people throw down for it. With typical adeptness, he sees that the Huntsman has a draft trade treaty from Erato, and pretends to 'discern' what it is as if by magic.

ERATO

The Tythonian ambassador, Erato, was sent to Chloris 15 years ago to propose a deal. Tythonus is rich in metal but has little plant life – the Tythonians ingest chlorophyll, mineral salts, and live for up to 40,000 years. But Erato made the mistake of contacting Adrasta, who saw the possibility of a proliferation of metal as a threat and tricked Erato into the Pit. He has tried to communicate with people thrown down after him, but has succeeded only in squashing them.

To speak, Erato needs a shield-like communicator that Adrasta has kept in her throne room. This enables him to take control of the vocal cords of anyone touching the device (and also exerts a telepathic influence Erato uses to get the bandits to bring it to him).

Having sent for help, Erato is keen to escape in his ship – an egg spun from metal he extrudes from his body – before the neutron star the Tythonians have sent to destroy Chloris's sun arrives. But the Doctor persuades him to stay and help – spinning a thin shell of aluminium round the star to minimise its gravitational pull so the TARDIS can drag it off course.

NEW INFORMATION

THE DOCTOR

The Doctor has a stethoscope in his pocket, with which he listens to the sound the 'egg' makes. He also has a copy of *Everest in Easy Stages* (in Tibetan), *Teach Yourself Tibetan*, a hammer and pitons which all come in useful as he tries to climb out of the pit using his scarf as a rope. He produces a large mirror to reflect K-9's blaster ray.

He tells Organon he was born under the sign of 'crossed computers' – the symbol of the maternity service on Gallifrey. When Organon asks the Doctor what method

he uses to see into the future (crystal ball, goat's entrails?), the Doctor says he tends to use a police box affair.

THE TARDIS

The Doctor has disconnected the Mark Three emergency transceiver which sends and receives distress calls, as Gallifrey kept calling him for help.

The Doctor uses the TARDIS gravity tractor beam to draw the neutron star away from Chloris's sun and send it into deep space.

COMPANIONS

K-9: With a 'new' voice (after his laryngitis in *Destiny of the Daleks*) K-9 reads *The Tale of Peter Rabbit* to the Doctor. Romana knows the story.

Having been 'cobwebbed' by wolf weeds, K-9 is attacked by Adrasta's guards who try to open him up with hammers and chisels.

NIGHTMARE OF EDEN

In which the Mandrels are less-than-terrifying monsters and two space ships get stuck together...
BY BOB BAKER
4 EPISODES, FIRST BROADCAST 24 NOVEMBER–15 DECEMBER 1979

JOURNEY INFORMATION

THE EMPRESS

The *Empress*, en route from Station Nine to Azure, has 900 passengers on board and is maintaining seven-tenths gravity.

The *Empress*, captained by Rigg, comes out of warp part-way through the *Hecate*. This creates dimensional instabilities as the two ships try to reject each other.

TRYST AND THE CONTINUOUS EVENT TRANSMUTER

Tryst's ambition is to be the first zoologist to quantify and classify every life form in the galaxy. He is on the *Empress* returning from an expedition (his ship was the *Volante*) and has with him his CET Machine.

The continuous event transmuter takes sample areas and life from planets and stores them as electromagnetic signals

Rigg: 'First the collision, then a dead navigator, then a monster roaming about my ship.'

on a laser crystal inside the machine. The samples continue to live and evolve in this environment (blank patches are left where they are removed). When played back, they are reconstituted as intra-dimensional matrices. The sample environments become unstable when the Empress crashes into the *Hecate*. Vicious Mandrels from the Eden sample escape into the ship and kill passengers and crew before the Doctor is able to lead them back into the projection and stabilise it. He then uses the CET Machine to capture the smugglers Tryst and Dymond (the *Hecate*'s pilot), 'sampling' them from the *Hecate* and trapping them within the machine.

Tryst's excuse for smuggling vraxoin is that he needed the funding for his important work, and people always had a choice of whether or not to take the drug. But the Doctor, who has seen what vraxoin can do, refuses to listen.

VRAXOIN

XYP, known as vraxoin, is an addictive drug. It induces a 'sort of warm complacency, then total apathy'. Ultimately, it kills. The only known source of vraxoin was destroyed – the planet incinerated.

But Tryst has discovered a new source – on planet M Three Seven, also known as Eden. When agent Stott, undercover on Tryst's expedition, realised someone was smuggling vraxoin, Tryst shot him and left him for dead. But Stott survived in the Eden sample within the CET Machine.

Dymond will transfer the Eden data – and the vraxoin – from the CET Machine to his own machine on the *Hecate* by entucha laser (which can carry thousands of telecom messages). He expects to make z13,000,000 from the 'Eden Project' with overheads of z3,900,000 – leaving a profit of z9,100,000.

The Doctor discovers that, when electrocuted, the native, aggressive life form of Eden – the Mandrels – decompose into vraxoin powder.

NEW INFORMATION

THE DOCTOR

The Doctor has seen 'whole communities, whole planets' wiped out by vraxoin.

He says he can start anything 'from a steam engine to a TARDIS'. He survives a short journey in Dymond's shuttle without an oxygen suit (going into a trance). He plans to dismantle the CET Machine and re-project the crystal images back to their native environments.

COMPANIONS

ROMANA: Romana says she can only think of one animal that would be comfortably at home in an electronic zoo...

K-9: The Doctor uses K-9 to boost the power and range of the CET Machine so he can capture Tryst and Dymond. K-9 can also pinpoint *Hecate*'s exact position when it escapes.

TARDIS DATA BANK:

DATE: c2116
LOCATION: STARLINER *EMPRESS*, ORBITING AZURE

THE STARLINER *EMPRESS* COMES OUT OF WARP HALFWAY THROUGH A SCIENTIFIC SURVEY SHIP, THE *HECATE*. THE DOCTOR, ROMANA AND K-9 TRY TO SEPARATE THE SHIPS, BUT SOMEONE ON BOARD THE *EMPRESS* IS SMUGGLING THE DEADLY ADDICTIVE DRUG VRAXOIN. COULD IT BE SOMETHING TO DO WITH TRYST'S CONTINUOUS EVENT TRANSMUTER – A MACHINE THAT TAKES LASER-CRYSTAL RECORDINGS OF AREAS OF OTHER PLANETS? THE DOCTOR TRIES TO EVADE THE AZURE EXCISE OFFICIALS AND DISCOVER THE IDENTITY OF THE REAL SMUGGLERS, AND THE SOURCE OF THE VRAXOIN. BUT THE CET MACHINE IS UNSTABLE AND FIERCE CREATURES FROM THE PLANET EDEN ESCAPE TO ROAM THE *EMPRESS*...

THE HORNS OF NIMON

In which the Doctor and Romana are joined by Graham Crowden to take part in a futuristic version of the Minotaur story...

BY ANTHONY READ

4 EPISODES, FIRST BROADCAST 22 DECEMBER 1979–12 JANUARY 1980

TARDIS DATA BANK:

DATE: UNKNOWN
LOCATION: SKONNAN SHIP; SKONNOS

THE TARDIS IS DRAWN INTO A NASCENT BLACK HOLE WHERE THE DOCTOR AND ROMANA REPAIR A SKONNAN SHIP TAKING 'TRIBUTE' TO THE NIMON FROM ANETH. THE TRIBUTE IS HUMAN SACRIFICES INCLUDING SETH AND TEKA, AND HYMETUSITE CRYSTALS. THE NIMON HAS PROMISED TO PROVIDE SKONNOS WITH TECHNOLOGY TO REBUILD ITS EMPIRE, BUT ACTUALLY PLANS TO BRING MANY MORE NIMON THROUGH THE BLACK HOLE TO CONTINUE THEIR 'GREAT JOURNEY OF LIFE' AND SUCK SKONNOS DRY...

Soldeed: 'Even now, our factories await the secrets. The Nimon shall unfold to us secrets that will give Skonnos the most powerful fleet of ships this galaxy has ever seen.'

JOURNEY INFORMATION

SKONNOS

Skonnos was once the heart of a mighty empire that extended over 100 star systems, but now that empire has been lost in civil war. Only the army survived.

SOLDEED

Scientist Soldeed is in charge of Skonnos, and has promised the tribute to the Nimon in exchange for the technology Skonnos needs to rebuild its empire. Only Soldeed can enter the Power Complex where the Nimon resides (using his staff to gain access), and only Soldeed converses with the Nimon and passes on his demands.

But Soldeed was duped by the Nimon when it says offered the technology to build the 'most powerful fleet of ships this galaxy has ever seen' in return for the tribute. As Romana says, 'They're parasitic nomads who've been feeding off your selfishness and gullibility.' When Soldeed realises this, seeing that two more Nimons have arrived, it drives him mad – he sets the Power Complex's reactor to critical, destroying it and the Nimons.

THE NIMON

Initially there seems to be only one Nimon, the last survivor of its advanced race. The Nimon resides within the Power Complex which is modelled on a giant positronic circuit, the corridors and intersections changing as the circuit switches.

The Nimon keeps the young Anethan sacrifices in suspended animation for food, sucking out their binding energy. The hymetusite crystals are used to power the furnace in the Power Complex where the Nimon lives, and to provide the power the Nimon needs to create a black hole in nearby space. The power is transmitted from two horn-like antennae on the roof of the Power Complex.

Once the black hole is complete it will form an entrance to hyperspace through which the rest of the Nimon race will arrive in travel capsules – 'the great journey of life'. As with their previous conquest, Crinoth, the Nimon strategy on Skonnos is to appear to offer help while building the facility for the Nimon race to come to the planet and drain it before moving on again. As Sezom, last survivor of Crinoth, says, 'They're like a plague of locusts.'

The Nimons operate their 'final contingency plan' to provide energy to get to Skonnos, believing their power source there to have been compromised. The planet of Crinoth is converted to energy and explodes. But the Nimons' link with Skonnos is destroyed with the Power Complex, and the Doctor diverts the space–time tunnel so that the Nimons will arrive 'in the middle of nowhere'.

MYTHOLOGICAL ROOTS

As with *Underworld*, there are links between this story and classical mythology – mainly the legend of Theseus and the Minotaur (which the Doctor says he helped with in *The Creature from the Pit*). Some of the parallel names are listed below, but there are others – the rock that Sezom, leader of another planet the Nimon have invaded, uses to enhance the power of his staff, for example, is called Jasonite.

Nimon – Minotaur
Power Complex – Labyrinth
Soldeed – Daedalus
(who built the Labyrinth)
Seth – Theseus
Crinoth – Corinth

NEW INFORMATION

THE DOCTOR

The Doctor says he has been to Skonnos – 'but not yet'. He tries to mark his route through the Power Complex with star-shaped stickers, but the configuration of corridors constantly changes. In *The Creature from the Pit*, the Doctor said he gave Theseus and Ariadne a ball of string, and he again implies he was involved with the original Minotaur.

THE TARDIS

The TARDIS is immobilised and the dematerialisation circuits disconnected while the Doctor makes a 'slight modification' to the conceptual geometer.

The Doctor is able to extrude the defence shield on the TARDIS door to form a 'tunnel' through space from the TARDIS to the Skonnan ship. He mends the Skonnan ship using a hymetusite crystal and the gravitic anomaliser from the TARDIS.

The Doctor spins the TARDIS end over end so that it is knocked out of the forming black hole by a planetoid. The Doctor then (eventually) manages to get the TARDIS to Skonnos without the gravitic anomaliser.

COMPANIONS

ROMANA: Romana has made her own sonic screwdriver, which is smaller and sleeker than the Doctor's. He tries to swap them, but Romana notices.

The Doctor: 'You know, K-9, sometimes I think I'm wasted just rushing round the Universe saving planets from destruction. With a talent like mine I might have been a great slow bowler.'

SHADA

In which Douglas Adams provides a script about a retired Time Lord and an alien who steals minds, and a BBC strike means it never gets finished or broadcast…

BY DOUGLAS ADAMS

6 EPISODES. NEVER COMPLETED OR BROADCAST BECAUSE OF INDUSTRIAL ACTION.

TARDIS DATA BANK:

DATE: PRESENT DAY

LOCATION: CAMBRIDGE; INSTITUTE FOR ADVANCED SCIENCE STUDIES (A SPACE STATION); SHADA; KRARG CARRIER

THE DOCTOR IS SUMMONED TO CAMBRIDGE BY PROFESSOR CHRONOTIS, A RETIRED TIME LORD. HE HAS A BOOK HE WANTS TO RETURN TO GALLIFREY – *THE WORSHIPFUL AND ANCIENT LAW OF GALLIFREY* BUT HE HAS ACCIDENTALLY LENT IT TO STUDENT CHRIS PARSONS. THE BOOK IS DANGEROUS AS IT HAS THE LOCATION OF SHADA – THE TIME LORDS' PRISON – CODED WITHIN IT. BUT SKAGRA, WHO USES A FLOATING SPHERE TO STEAL BRAINS, WANTS THE BOOK SO HE CAN GET TO SHADA AND FREE THE TIME LORD CRIMINAL SALYAVIN. WITH CHRONOTIS APPARENTLY DEAD, AND THE DOCTOR'S MIND STOLEN BY SKAGRA, STOPPING SKAGRA BEFORE HE CREATES AND CONTROLS A UNIVERSAL MIND SEEMS IMPOSSIBLE…

JOURNEY INFORMATION

PROFESSOR CHRONOTIS

Professor Chronotis is a Time Lord who retired to Cambridge University 300 years earlier. He is in his final regeneration, and has a TARDIS disguised as his university rooms at St Cedd's College.

But Chronotis is in fact the Time Lord criminal Salyavin. He has escaped from the Time Lord prison of Shada, taking from the Panopticon Archives on Gallifrey *The Worshipful and Ancient Law of Gallifrey* as it reveals the existence and location of Shada. The book dates back to the Time of Rassilon and is one of 'the artefacts'. Each of the artefacts was imbued with terrific powers. Time is travelling backwards over the book, which is minus 20,000 years old (perhaps implying it will be created that far in the future – which would mean that Time Lord civilisation exists in our far future).

Chronotis describes his former self as '… a hot-headed, brilliant young man with a peculiar talent'. Salyavin's 'crime' was the ability to project his mind into other people's minds. He has used this ability to remove the Time Lords' memories of Shada so that his escape will not be detected.

When Chronotis is 'killed' by the villainous Skagra, he fades away, being in his last regeneration.

SKAGRA

Professor Skagra is a brilliant geneticist, astro-engineer, cyberneticist, neurostructuralist and moral theologian. He paid the Universe's most brilliant scientists to join him in an experiment to pool their intellectual resources by electronic mind conference. Then he stole their minds using a floating sphere.

Now Skagra plans to steal the brains of the whole of the Universe to create a single god-like mind. With Salyavin's mental ability to project his mind into others, he could, the Doctor says, spread like a disease from mind to mind until his task is completed, even if it takes thousands of years.

KRARGS

Skagra's glowing, crystalline Krargs are formed in vats on his Carrier Ship from carbon crystals around a basic skeleton. They are resistant to K-9's firepower. Romana manages to return them to a state of crystalline slurry.

SHADA

Shada is the ancient time prison of the Time Lords. Its location – built into an asteroid or small planet – is secret, but it can be reached by turning back the pages of *The Worshipful and Ancient Law of Gallifrey* in a TARDIS. Salyavin stole the book when he escaped, and used his mental powers to make the Time Lords forget that Shada existed.

Salyavin was imprisoned on Shada in Cabinet 9, Chamber T. Other prisoners include the war criminal Rungar and the mass murderer Sabjatric.

NEW INFORMATION

THE DOCTOR

The St Cedd's porter, Wilkin, says the Doctor got an honorary degree from the college in 1960. He has also visited in 1955 and 1964. The Doctor claims he was there in 1958 as well, but in a different body.

Salyavin was a boyhood hero of the Doctor's, though he was imprisoned before the Doctor was born.

The Doctor convinces Skagra's ship he is dead, and therefore no threat. But as a result the ship switches off the air supply to conserve resources: 'Dead men do not require oxygen.' In order to speed up the journey back to the Institute for Advanced Science Studies, the Doctor converts Skagra's ship into a partial TARDIS.

> Chris Parsons: 'Just because we come from Earth, it doesn't give everybody the right to be patronising towards us. Although, admittedly, all this does make us look a bit primitive…'

The Doctor gets from Chronotis's TARDIS to his own through the vortex using a trick he learned from a space–time mystic on Quantox.

THE TARDIS

The TARDIS medical kit is kept in a canvas bag. It includes a special collar that takes over Chronotis's autonomic functions when his mind is stolen by Skagra – which frees the Professor's autonomic brain to communicate with Romana and K-9 by beating his hearts in Gallifreyan Morse code.

The TARDIS central column moves as Skagra turns back the pages of *The Worshipful and Ancient Law of Gallifrey* and the TARDIS travels to the secret location of Shada when the final page is turned.

The Doctor arrives in a small equipment room when he crosses from Chronotis's TARDIS.

CHRONOTIS'S TARDIS

Chronotis's TARDIS, a Type 39, is very ancient – he rescued it 'literally from the scrap heap'. It is disguised as his college rooms. When it dematerialises it leaves a blue void behind the door. The control panels are hidden behind books and in cupboards in the sitting room.

COMPANIONS

ROMANA: Romana says she is a historian. She finds a book of Gallifreyan fairy tales on Chronotis's bookshelves, which she says she read when she was 'a time tot'.

K-9: K-9 amplifies Chronotis's heartbeat so Romana can hear it is in Gallifreyan Morse code.

While K-9 can detect Skagra's invisible ship, many of its functions are beyond his ability to analyse. He blasts Skagra's mind-sphere, but it splits into many smaller spheres.

BEHIND THE SCENES

THE LOST STORY

Shada was scripted, planned and designed as normal. But while the location filming in and around Cambridge, and the first of three television studio recording sessions, were completed, the story was never finished or broadcast. Industrial action by studio technical staff closed the BBC's Television Centre studios during rehearsals for the second studio session.

The second session was abandoned, but while the strike was over before the third session was scheduled, that too was abandoned – cancelled to make way for more urgent productions.

On 10 December 1979, *Shada* was dropped from the **Doctor Who** seventeenth season. Although director Pennant Roberts and new producer John Nathan-Turner tried for some time to organise further studio time so the story could be completed for later transmission, it was officially abandoned by the BBC in June 1980.

Most of the completed and surviving material was edited together and released with a linking narrative by Tom Baker on BBC video (together with a copy of the rehearsal script) in July 1992 (Douglas Adams donated his fee to *Comic Relief*).

But while that version of *Shada* was abandoned and incomplete, the story has finally been made – albeit in a different medium with a different cast and even a different Doctor. In May 2003, BBCi broadcast a new audio version of Shada over the Internet as a webcast. The new production featured animated illustrations by artist Lee Sullivan, and was faithful to Douglas Adams' original script, albeit with one major change: the Doctor was now in his Eighth incarnation as played by Paul McGann. Slight rewrites by Gary Russell adapted the script for the Eighth Doctor, as well as accommodating the audio format. Lalla Ward returned as Romana with John Leeson providing the voice of K-9, but the rest of the characters were recast – including James Fox replacing Denis Carey as Chronotis, and Andrew Sachs taking the part of Skagra (played in the original by Christopher Neame). The director was Nicholas Pegg and the production was the work of Big Finish Productions.

THE LEISURE HIVE

Pangol: 'Tachyons travel faster than light. A tachyon field can therefore be made to arrive at point B — that visidome, say — before its departure from point A, the Generator.'

TARDIS DATA BANK:

DATE: 2290
LOCATION: BRIGHTON BEACH; ARGOLIS

THE LEISURE HIVE IS A RECREATION CENTRE ON THE PLANET ARGOLIS WHICH WAS ALL BUT DESTROYED BY A WAR WITH THE REPTILIAN FOAMASI FORTY YEARS AGO. BUT THE HIVE IS ALMOST BANKRUPT, AND A SERIES OF 'ACCIDENTS' THREATEN TO CLOSE IT FOR GOOD. THE DOCTOR AND ROMANA ARRIVE TO DISCOVER FAKED TIME EXPERIMENTS AND AN ASSASSIN ON THE LOOSE. THEY ALSO FIND THAT THE TACHYON RECREATION GENERATOR IS NOT AS SIMPLE AND INNOCENT AS IT SEEMS. CAN THEY STOP THE FOAMASI ASSASSINS AND PREVENT THE NEW ARGOLIN DAWN...

In which the series gets new titles and reworked theme music, and John Nathan-Turner takes over as producer...
BY DAVID FISHER
4 EPISODES, FIRST BROADCAST 30 AUGUST–20 SEPTEMBER 1980

JOURNEY INFORMATION

THE LEISURE HIVE

Romana describes Argolis as 'the first of the leisure planets'. In 2250 Theron led Argolis into a war against the reptilian Foamasi. Most of Argolis was devastated by 2,000 interplanetary missiles. The war lasted 20 minutes, and left the survivors sterile and the surface uninhabitable for the next 300 years. The survivors built a recreation centre called the Leisure Hive. The Argolins preserve Theron's helmet to remind them of the evil that dwells in violence, and also to live in humility and die with dignity.

The Leisure Hive includes the Experiential Grid – cells of different environments designed to produce physical, psychic and intellectual regeneration. The hope is to promote cross-cultural understanding between different races as each learns what it is like to be the 'foreigner'.

At the heart of the Leisure Hive is the Recreation Generator, which uses tachyons to create manipulable solid images. This is the only practical application for the Argolin-invented science of Tachyonics.

THE FOAMASI

As a reptile race, the Foamasi could live on the radioactive surface of Argolis. Since the war the Foamasi government has officially owned the whole of their planet, but a group called the West Lodge believes in private enterprise, and sends saboteurs (including their Head of All Sectors) to the Leisure Hive. Disguised as the Argolin Earth agent Brock and his lawyer Klout, they try to force the Argolins to sell the Leisure Hive to them so that they can use it as a new base. But they are arrested by Foamasi government agents.

PANGOL AND THE RECREATION GENERATOR

Pangol is the first of the 'New Argolins'. He is the child of the Generator – a tachyon-clone created from cells donated by the surviving Argolins. Pangol was the only successful  clone from the post-war experiments, the others being disfigured mutants.

Pangol venerates Theron, who led Argolis into war, as he bound Argolis into a single nation, and he shares Theron's dreams of conquest. But the army of clone Pangols he creates is corrupted by the Doctor interfering in the Recreation Generator – beneath their clothing and helmet, each 'Pangol' is actually a version of the Doctor. Also, the images are short-lived, and soon fade away to leave only the original 'real' Doctor surviving.

His second attempt is thwarted when Pangol falls inside the Generator trying to remove the dying Argolin leader, Mena. The Doctor has set it to regenerate – so Mena becomes younger and Pangol is regressed to a baby.

NEW INFORMATION

THE DOCTOR

The Doctor says he has now twice missed the opening of the Brighton Pavilion (the first occasion may be *Horror of Fang Rock*).

The Doctor is aged 500 years by a tachyon surge in the Recreation Generator. He does not regenerate but becomes an old man with white hair and beard.

THE TARDIS

The Doctor bypasses the randomiser (see *The Armageddon Factor*) and later uses it to create a random field frame in the Recreation Generator. He does not replace it.

COMPANIONS

ROMANA: Romana says, 'Gallifrey abandoned tachyonics when we developed warp matrix engineering.'

She helps Earth scientist Hardin to make his time experiments work, but as she does not understand the true nature and purpose of the Recreation Generator, the Doctor is aged 500 years rather than made a few years younger.

K-9: K-9 has got his old voice back. The Doctor, however, gets K-9's sea water defences wrong and he explodes when he tries to retrieve a beach ball from the sea.

BEHIND THE SCENES

NEW THEME AND TITLES

New producer John Nathan-Turner decided, as soon as he took over from his predecessor Graham Williams, that he wanted to change the look and sound of **Doctor Who**.

Composer Dudley Simpson had been writing the incidental music for **Doctor Who** almost exclusively since late in the Second Doctor's era. Nathan-Turner now decided that instead good use could be made of the technology and facilities of the BBC's in-house Radiophonic Workshop to provide incidental music as well as sound effects.

One of the first jobs the Radiophonic Workshop had done on **Doctor Who** was to realise Ron Grainer's theme music – carried out by Delia Derbyshire, assisted by Dick Mills. Now Nathan-Turner asked that the music be revamped for the 1980s; and Peter Howell created a new version of the theme, which he hoped retained the innovative, distinctive feel of the original but brought it up to date and exploited new techniques and technologies.

As well as a reworked theme, new animated opening and closing titles were produced. These were created by graphic designer Sid Sutton, and also served with minor changes to accommodate the new Doctors' faces for the Fifth and Sixth Doctors. The new animated sequence was designed to give the impression of travelling through the vastness of space rather than an enclosed time tunnel – stars rush past, and eventually the Doctor's face is formed out of stars coming together. A new **Doctor Who** logo, intended to look as if it was made from a shaped glass rod, replaced the well-known 'diamond' logo that had been used since *The Time Warrior*.

Sutton and Howell worked together to ensure that the titles and music complemented each other, making minor adjustments to each.

MEGLOS

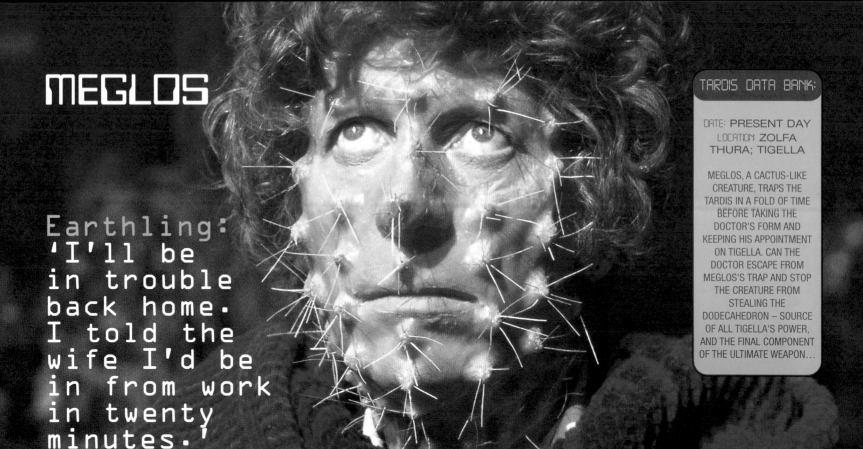

Earthling:
'I'll be
in trouble
back home.
I told the
wife I'd be
in from work
in twenty
minutes.'

TARDIS DATA BANK:

DATE: PRESENT DAY
LOCATION: ZOLFA
THURA; TIGELLA

MEGLOS, A CACTUS-LIKE
CREATURE, TRAPS THE
TARDIS IN A FOLD OF TIME
BEFORE TAKING THE
DOCTOR'S FORM AND
KEEPING HIS APPOINTMENT
ON TIGELLA. CAN THE
DOCTOR ESCAPE FROM
MEGLOS'S TRAP AND STOP
THE CREATURE FROM
STEALING THE
DODECAHEDRON – SOURCE
OF ALL TIGELLA'S POWER,
AND THE FINAL COMPONENT
OF THE ULTIMATE WEAPON…

In which Tom Baker plays both the Doctor and an alien cactus, and Bill Fraser gets to kick K-9…
BY JOHN FLANAGHAN AND ANDREW MCCULLOCH
4 EPISODES, FIRST BROADCAST 27 SEPTEMBER – 18 OCTOBER 1980

JOURNEY INFORMATION

MEGLOS

Meglos is the last survivor of Zolfa-Thura. There was a great civilisation there once, but it has been 'blown away to sand and ashes' and all that remains is the screens of Zolfa-Thura.

A cactus-like xerophyte in his natural form, the use of an Earthling kidnapped by the mercenary Gaztaks enables Meglos to change into the Doctor's form. But as the Earthling struggles to escape and reassert his personality, Meglos loses control and his version of the Doctor, or the Earthling, becomes cactus-like – green, with spines.

He is able to trap the TARDIS inside a chronic hysterisis – 'fold of time' – so that the Doctor, Romana and K-9 are forced to go through the same actions forever.

Meglos has waited 1,000 years to recover the Dodecahedron from Tigella. Masquerading as the Doctor, he miniaturises it with a dimensional controller before escaping. The screens of Zolfa-Thura magnify the Dodecahedron's power to create a powerful energy-beam weapon. Meglos says that his fellow Zolfa-Thurans 'tried to destroy all we had and all we knew' to prevent this ultimate weapon being used.

But the Doctor has inverted the control setting, so that the power is focused inwards and destroys Zolfa-Thura. In an attempt to escape, Meglos modulates himself on a particular wavelength of light – making him virtually indestructible. The final moments before the explosion, as Meglos tries to get the Gaztak General Grugger to stop the countdown, seem to be replayed – suggesting that Meglos and Zolfa-Thura may survive inside a chronic hysterisis.

TIGELLA

Tigella is in the Prion planetary system and rotates anticlockwise. The inhabitants have been driven to live underground because of the 'lush, aggressive vegetation', like bell plants that attack Romana and the Gaztaks.

All power to the underground city is provided by the Dodecahedron, a mysterious power source that none of the Tigellans really understand.

Tigellan society is split into two groups. The Savants are technologists. The Deons see the Dodecahedron as an artefact of their god Ti that descended from the heavens thousands of years ago. They are led by Lexa, who dies saving Romana from a Gaztak's shot.

THE GAZTAKS

The Gaztaks are mercenaries and pirates whose only interest is money. There are eight Gaztaks in General Grugger's group, including himself and his lieutenant, Brotodac. None too bright, the Gaztaks are easily manipulated by Meglos, and duped by Romana – who leads them round in circles until she can escape, blaming Tigella's anticlockwise rotation for apparently losing her way.

NEW INFORMATION

THE DOCTOR

Meglos knows that the Doctor is a Time Lord and has intercepted his message to Tigella asking if he can visit. The Doctor last visited 50 years ago, and Zastor (then a young man, now leader) showed him round. The Doctor is summoned back to Gallifrey after defeating Meglos.

THE TARDIS

To escape the chronic hysterisis, Romana suggests stopping the time rotor (though she does not indicate where or what it is). K-9 says there is no known technological solution, but they manage to break free by replaying the cycle before it recurs, leading to phase cancellation.

COMPANIONS

K-9: The Doctor and Romana mend K-9 after the damage he sustained in *The Leisure Hive*. The cure for a jammed probe circuit is to waggle his tail. Because of a power depletion problem, K-9 needs recharging every two hours.

TARDIS DATA BANK:

ADRIC

DESCRIPTION:
MALE, ALZARIAN
TRAVELLED:
*FULL CIRCLE –
EARTHSHOCK*

'What's in it for me?'

(ADRIC – *STATE OF DECAY*)

A talented mathematician, Adric has earned a badge for mathematical excellence aboard the Starliner on Alzarius. But while he is accepted as part of the society, his brother leads the Outlers – a group of teenagers who have broken away from the planet's paternalistic society and live alone in a cave overlooking the Starliner.

Adric is full of admiration for his older brother Varsh, and is now old enough to begin to rebel himself. But the Outlers are less happy to have him join them, Keara in particular seeing him as a spoiled child.

Circumstances force the issue, and Adric finds himself escaping Mistfall by entering the TARDIS. Later he and the other Outlers help to fight off the Marshmen within the Starliner – Outler Tylos and Varsh both die in the conflict. With nothing left for him on the Starliner, Adric hides in the TARDIS until it arrives at its next destination.

He is not one to philosophise or suffer a moral dilemma. While he may look guilty at being caught, Adric has no qualms about stealing an image translator for the Doctor – even after the Doctor chides him for it, he goes ahead and leaves the stolen component in the TARDIS. In *State of Decay*, he seems to be following his own agenda – trying to steal food, and apparently siding with Aukon against the

Doctor and Romana in return for the promise of power and immortality.

At what point Adric actually decides to betray Aukon, or whether he was always waiting for an opportunity, as he tells Romana, is never clear. But throughout his time in the TARDIS, Adric tends to put himself first. This attitude is exaggerated by contrast with the selfless Nyssa, and tempered by his growing admiration for the Doctor.

Being an Alzarian, Adric adapts quickly to any environmental changes. *In Full Circle*, his injured knee heals extremely fast, and he recovers rapidly from a twisted ankle in *The Visitation*. Perhaps his contact with the Doctor and Romana, and later with Nyssa and Tegan, causes Adric to mellow and begin to care about others. It could be seen as the culmination of Adric's 'education' in social and moral responsibility that he dies trying to save Earth from a crashing freighter in *Earthshock*. But it is Adric's determination not to admit defeat that causes him to return to the bridge in an effort to crack the final Cyber code – perhaps a final, fatal, selfish act.

As he waits for death in front of the destroyed control console, Adric holds the 'badge' of courage he inherited from his brother, but his real worry is that now he will never know whether his mathematical skills had ultimately provided him with the right answer...

FULL CIRCLE

In which Marshmen rise from a swamp in slow motion, and Adric joins the Doctor…

BY ANDREW SMITH

4 EPISODES, FIRST BROADCAST 25 OCTOBER–15 NOVEMBER 1980

JOURNEY INFORMATION

ALZARIUS

Mistfall comes to Alzarius approximately every 50 years. As another planet draws Alzarius away from its sun, the cooling generates the mist. Water bubbles, and spiders hatch from river fruits. The Marshmen wake and emerge from the swamps…

As the Doctor discovers, the Marshmen and spiders are the same life form at different stages of rapid evolution. Generations ago, the Marshmen attacked and entered the Starliner, killing the original Terradonian crew. They then evolved into the life form best suited to survive inside the Starliner – mimicking the original crew and learning to read the manuals and hence repair and maintain the Starliner.

While the secret system files detail these events, some legends also persist – the Marshmen are regarded with superstitious awe as figures symbolising the whole of life on Alzarius.

THE STARLINER

The Starliner is crystalline in shape, and crashed on Alzarius while on its way from Terradon. Romana says it is about 40,000 generations since it crashed, given the evolutionary progress.

Believing themselves to be Terradonians, the people in the starliner spend their time using knowledge from the manuals stored in the Great Book Room to repair and maintain the ship. They believe they are preparing for the return journey to Terradon and that these preparations will take generations. In fact the Starliner has been ready for the journey for many years. But the Deciders – keepers of the forbidden system files – know that the manual relating to piloting the Starliner was damaged, and nobody knows how to fly the ship, so they keep this secret and perpetuate the maintenance.

The Starliner has an electrolytic power supply, so can create its own oxygen which drives out the Marshmen as it inhibits their ability to adapt.

NEW INFORMATION

THE DOCTOR

The Doctor develops a relationship of trust with a Marshchild, which is betrayed by scientist Dexeter's attempts to operate on the creature. When the Marshchild dies, the Doctor angrily accuses the Deciders of wilful procrastination over the Starliner's departure from Alzarius.

THE TARDIS

The TARDIS shimmers as it passes through a CVE – Charged Vacuum Emboitment – one of the rarest space–time events in the universe. It emerges into E-Space,

The Doctor: 'Why can't people be nice to one another, just for a change? I mean, I'm an alien, and you don't want to drag me into a swamp, do you… You do?'

the Exo-Space Time Continuum, a smaller universe than our own N-Space where the coordinates of space are negative.

Alzarius occupies the negative coordinates of Gallifrey in N-Space. Since the TARDIS scanner reads the absolute (positive) value of the coordinates, it shows an image of the outer wastes of Gallifrey (meaning there is no camera as such in the TARDIS shell, but a real-time image is generated). The image translator from a Starliner microscope is compatible.

Romana gives Adric a homing device that will lead him back to the TARDIS. It is the size and approximate shape of a golf ball and bleeps. She says the TARDIS weighs 5×10^6 kilos in Alzarian gravity.

COMPANIONS

ROMANA: Romana is reluctant to return to Gallifrey, telling the Doctor, 'I don't want to spend the rest of my life on Gallifrey, after all this...'

When she is bitten by a spider that hatches from a river fruit, Romana develops an affinity with the Marshmen. Her face gains similar markings, and she seems to experience the same pain and anger as the Marshchild that Dexeter operates on.

ADRIC: Varsh asks Adric the embarkation question, 'When the Starliner leaves Alzarius, where will you be?' Adric replies, 'Not here' – which is true as he stows away on the TARDIS.

STATE OF DECAY

In which Emrys James plays a vampire, and the Doctor finds himself revisiting Hammer Horror...
BY TERRANCE DICKS
4 EPISODES, FIRST BROADCAST 22 NOVEMBER–13 DECEMBER 1980

JOURNEY INFORMATION

THE PEASANTS

Ivo is headman of the village, as was his father and his father's father. On occasion, villagers are 'selected' and taken to the Tower ostensibly to serve the Lords. Some become guards, but most (including Ivo's son Karl) are killed, their blood piped to feed the Great Vampire.

The peasants believe that the Lords protect them from 'the Wasting'. the ability to read has been passed on in secret as the penalty for knowledge is death. Children start work in the fields as soon as they can walk.

The rebels against the Lords are led by Kalmar. Ivo keeps in touch with them by radio. They have equipment discarded from the *Hydrax* spaceship, but do not understand it. They have a generator for air, light, heat and communicators.

THE LORDS

The Three Who Rule – King Zargo, Queen Camilla and Chancellor Aukon – live in the Tower, which is in fact the *Hydrax*. With bat-wing make-up over their eyes, the Lords are the ship's original officers, while the peasants are descended from the crew. *Hydrax* left Earth on an exploration mission for Beta Two in the Perugellis sector. The officers were Captain Miles Sharkey (Zargo), Navigation Officer Lauren Macmillan (Camilla) and Science Officer Anthony O'Connor (Aukon). Over time their names have become corrupted. They serve the Great Vampire, working to nourish and revitalise it until it awakens. In return it has given them immortality – when Zargo is stabbed by Adric, he merely pulls the knife out again.

Aukon can controls bats, and calls them his servants. He also has mental powers – detecting that Adric is different and holding the Doctor motionless and hypnotising Romana when she is about to be sacrificed.

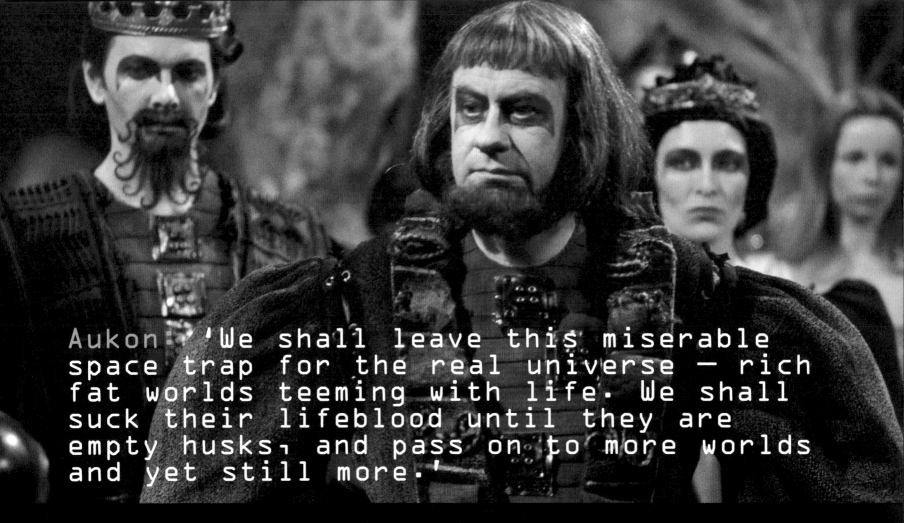

Aukon: 'We shall leave this miserable space trap for the real universe — rich fat worlds teeming with life. We shall suck their lifeblood until they are empty husks, and pass on to more worlds and yet still more.'

The *Hydrax* has three Arrow-class scout ships that detach from the main ship for local exploration. The Doctor uses one of these as a 'mighty bolt of steel' to impale the Great Vampire – and when it dies, the Lords age to death.

THE GREAT VAMPIRE
In the misty dawn of history when even Rassilon was young, a race of giant vampires swarmed throughout the Universe.

One vampire could suck the life out of an entire planet and the vampires of legend on many planets are pale imitations of the real thing.

The Time Lords hunted down the giant vampires across the Universe in a war so long and bloody they were sickened of violence for ever, described in the *Record of Rassilon*.

The King Vampire had escaped into E-Space, and summoned the officers of the *Hydrax* to be his servants.

As Aukon explains, 'He has given us unending life. He summoned us here, speaking to the others through my mind. We fed and nourished him until now he is ready to arise.'

NEW INFORMATION

THE DOCTOR
The Doctor tells Romana there was once an old hermit from the mountains of South Gallifrey who used to tell him ghost stories – like the story of the giant vampires. The hermit is presumably K'anpo (see *Planet of the Spiders*).

THE TARDIS
There are 18,348 emergency instructions in the TARDIS data banks. The *Record of Rassilon* is kept on a magnetic card system on the TARDIS. The cards are fed into a reader on the console, which outputs printed sheets.

COMPANIONS
ROMANA: Romana once worked in the Bureau of Ancient Records where she came across reference to the *Record of Rassilon* – a copy of which was placed in all Type 40 TARDISes.

ADRIC: Adric seems to be taken in by Aukon's promises of power and immortality, but he tries to save Romana from being sacrificed.

WARRIORS' GATE

In which Romana and K-9 leave through a magic mirror, while Clifford Rose and Kenneth Cope try to get their spaceship working...

BY STEVE GALLAGHER

4 EPISODES, FIRST BROADCAST 3–24 JANUARY 1981

The Doctor: 'Unless we work very closely together, we could be caught here until the crack of doom. Oh, what's the use? Can I have one of your pickles — I had a rush lunch?'

TARDIS DATA BANK:

DATE: NO TIME

LOCATION: NO PLACE (THE GATEWAY)

A RUINED ARCHWAY STANDS IN A WHITE VOID – THE GATEWAY. A SLAVE SHIP IS TRAPPED IN THE VOID BETWEEN THE UNIVERSES, AND THE DOCTOR AND ROMANA MEET ITS NAVIGATOR – A TIME-SENSITIVE THARIL SLAVE CALLED BIROC. THE SLAVERS TRY TO USE ROMANA AS A REPLACEMENT NAVIGATOR, WHILE THE DOCTOR LEARNS THE HISTORY OF THE THARILS AND IS ATTACKED BY GUNDAN ROBOTS. ADRIC AND K-9 ARE LOST IN THE VOID – WHICH IS CONTRACTING AS SPACE-TIME COLLAPSES. CAN THE DOCTOR AND HIS FRIENDS ESCAPE...

Romana: 'He's mad. The backblast backlash will bounce back and destroy everything... It's bound to accelerate the collapse of space around here.'

JOURNEY INFORMATION

THE SLAVERS

Captain Rorvik and his crew are slavers, capturing and transporting time-sensitive Tharils in their bulk freighter, the *Privateer*. One of these, Biroc, they use as their navigator.

He is linked into the *Privateer*'s systems and projects an image of their course through time and space.

The *Privateer* is trapped at the zero point for months when Biroc refuses to navigate. Trying to escape without his help, the ship hits a time rift, the outer hull is breached and the warp drive is damaged. The outer hull of the ship is constructed from incredibly dense and therefore heavy Dwarf Star alloy – as are Biroc's manacles – as this is the only material that can prevent the Tharils from time-shifting and escaping. But the ship's huge mass is contracting space–time, so that the distances between the *Privateer*, the Gateway and the TARDIS are all reduced as space collapses towards a singularity.

The *Privateer* and her crew are destroyed when Captain Rorvik attempts to break through the Gateway mirrors using a backblast from the warp motors – the backblast backlash bounces back and destroys the ship.

THE THARILS AND THE GATEWAY

The time-sensitive Tharils once controlled a vast empire, centred on the Gateway. The Gateway was a huge castle, but is now reduced to a single arch and banqueting hall standing in the white void at the zero point between N-Space and E-Space, which Romana calls the 'theoretical medium between the striations of the continuum'.

There are three physical gateways, all parts of the same 'portal' between the universes: the whole of the void, the ancient archway, and the mirrors. For the Tharils the Gateway opens on to the whole Universe, but for anyone else it is a dead end.

The Tharils can ride the time winds. A Gundan robot tells the Doctor, 'The masters descended out of the air riding the winds and took men as their prize, growing powerful on their stolen labours and their looted skills...The masters created an empire, drained the life of the ordinary world...'

Biroc accepts that the Tharils abused their power, but argues they have now suffered enough in retribution.

THE GUNDANS

The Gundan robots exist to kill. As a Gundan explains to the Doctor, the Tharils' slaves were unable to approach the Gateway, so they built the Gundan robots which could withstand the time winds and attack the Tharils, driving them back to their last refuge at the Gateway. On the day of a great feast, they broke into the banqueting hall and destroyed the heart of the Tharil Empire.

NEW INFORMATION

THE DOCTOR

When he first enters the banqueting hall, the Doctor stands up the goblet he will later deliberately knock over when he travels back to see the Tharil empire at its height.

The Doctor says he will miss Romana: 'You were the noblest Romana of them all.'

THE TARDIS

Romana says the TARDIS travels between the time lines. Operating the reverse bias in full flight is very dangerous. She says that nothing in the TARDIS stores is catalogued, and the shelves are half empty.

One of the slavers, Lane, says the readings he gets for the TARDIS from the portable mass detector do not make sense.

The exploding *Privateer* knocks the TARDIS back into N-Space.

COMPANIONS

ROMANA: When linked to the *Privateer*'s navigational systems, Romana projects a geographical rather than temporal image – the Gateway.

Not wanting to return to Gallifrey, Romana decides to remain at the Gateway and help the Tharils escape enslavement.

K-9: K-9 can operate as a mass-detector using his articulated sensors (ears) to detect mass and triangulate to get a bearing. However, this bearing is not accurate as the sensors are so close together. When Adric removes one and takes it further away, this gives a more accurate reading.

His memory wavers, irrevocably damaged by the time winds, K-9 is repaired when he passes through the mirrors at the Gateway. But while living matter (like the Doctor's hand) remains healed when passing back through them, K-9 must remain in E-Space and at the Gateway.

He has complete plans for the TARDIS in his memory, so Romana can give the Tharils time travel technology to rescue their enslaved race.

TARDIS DATA BANK:

DESCRIPTION:
FEMALE, NATIVE OF
TRAKEN
TRAVELLED:
*THE KEEPER OF
TRAKEN –
TERMINUS*

NYSSA

'I can't see Traken...'

(NYSSA – *LOGOPOLIS*)

Nyssa is a tragic figure. Although her mother is dead, she seems happy about her father's marriage to Kassia in *The Keeper of Traken*. But this happiness is short-lived. Her stepmother is possessed by the Melkur, tricked then forced into doing its bidding. Even when the Melkur – in reality the Master – is defeated, at the cost of Kassia's life, the ordeal is not over for Nyssa. Her father is killed by the Master, who takes his body for his own.

Nyssa has barely had a chance to come to terms with this, when the entropy field released by the Master's interference on Logopolis destroys her home world. Orphaned and alone in the Universe, Nyssa has little choice but to join the Doctor on his travels.

While she later tells him that she has 'enjoyed every moment' of her time in the TARDIS, Nyssa also goes through a lot here. She sees the Doctor forced to regenerate and Adric killed, and the Doctor's apparent execution by his own people reduces her to tears. Finally, she contracts Lazar's disease on *Terminus*, where, once cured, she decides to stay so as to help others.

There are lighter moments like meeting her double Ann Talbot in *Black Orchid*, but even that is tinged with the sadness of the death of Ann's original fiancé.

Nyssa is constantly frustrated at the lack of opportunity to put her considerable technical skills to good use. There are occasions where they come in useful – such as destroying the Terileptil android in *The Visitation*, but for the most part Nyssa feels underemployed on the TARDIS. She is not one to complain, however, always putting others before herself, perhaps because she has lost so much.

But when she sees an opportunity to put her skills to good use, she takes it – staying on *Terminus* to help refine and improve the process for treating Lazars.

THE KEEPER OF TRAKEN

In which a statue comes to life and the Master gets a new body at last...

BY JOHNNY BYRNE

4 EPISODES, FIRST BROADCAST 31 JANUARY–21 FEBRUARY 1981

The Master: 'A new body, at last.'

JOURNEY INFORMATION

THE UNION OF TRAKEN

Traken is famous for its harmony – a whole community held together by people being nice to each other, as the Doctor puts it. The Keeper confirms that, 'Since the time of the Keepers, our Union has been the most harmonious the universe has ever seen...'

The Fosters are the guardians of the spiritual welfare of the capital and tend the Grove where Melkur arrives.

THE KEEPER

The Keeper is the 'organising principle' of Traken. He draws on the minds of the Union in order to rule. Living for hundreds of years, each Keeper draws his power from the Source.

The Source Manipulator is a glowing sphere below the Keeper's Chamber. The chosen Keeper dedicates himself to this bio-electronics system. The Doctor describes it as, 'Limitless organising capacity confined to a single flame and obedient to the will of your Keeper.'

When a Keeper is close to death crops fail and there are droughts and floods... 'Nothing is normal at such a time,' Consul Kassia says. This Keeper has ruled for 1,000 years, but is now close to dissolution and his power is waning. It is an agonising death, and with the Source out of control, nature 'reverts to chaos' as the Keeper dies.

Adric and Nyssa build a servo shut-off so that energy will overflow and the Source will consume itself – and the Melkur, if he tries to access it. The Doctor shuts down the Source, thus preserving it (he derives the code sequence from the rings worn by the consuls).

Since the Keeper-designate, Tremas, is absent when the Melkur is destroyed and the flames of the Source die down, Consul Luvic becomes the new Keeper.

THE CONSULS

The Consuls of Traken are subordinate to the Keeper. They are Tremas (Keeper-designate and Nyssa's father), Kassia (Tremas's wife), Katura, Seron and Luvic.

Kassia has tended the Melkur diligently – even driving the Fosters from the Grove. It has promised to save her

TARDIS DATA BANK:

DATE: UNKNOWN,
LOCATION: TRAKEN

THE DOCTOR IS SUMMONED BY THE KEEPER OF TRAKEN TO HELP IDENTIFY AND COMBAT 'ALL-PERVADING EVIL'. A CALCIFIED MELKUR STATUE IS TO BLAME, AND WITH THE HELP OF TREMAS, HIS DAUGHTER NYSSA AND ADRIC, THE DOCTOR DISCOVERS IT IS A TARDIS. THE DECAYING, DYING MASTER HAS COME TO TRAKEN AND WHILE THE DOCTOR IS ABLE TO DEFEAT HIM AND DESTROY HIS TARDIS, THE MASTER HAS ANOTHER – AND 'STEALS' THE BODY OF TREMAS, USING IT TO REGENERATE INTO A NEW BODY...

The Doctor:

'Magnificent. It's a pity about that poor chap having to sit for thousands of years in a chair, but it is magnificent.'

husband from the task of becoming Keeper. The Melkur uses an irradiated collar to ensure her obedience and, through her, kills Seron when he enters 'rapport' with the Source so that the Keeper can verify Seron's integrity.

Kassia becomes the Keeper and the Melkur materialises in her place – killing her and becoming Keeper of Traken.

MELKUR

The Keeper says that Traken has been visited by evil many times: 'Our compassion for these poor distorted creatures seems to draw them like moths to a flame. Sometimes they are redeemed... They name such creatures Melkur – literally a fly trapped by honey...' Less evil Melkurs can speak and even move round the Grove a little.

The Melkur that worries the Keeper is shaped like a large statue and tended by Kassia (and later Nyssa). As the Keeper's power fails as he nears death, so the Melkur is able to exert an influence over Kassia. It is, in fact, the Master's TARDIS and inside it the Master plans to take control of the Source by becoming Keeper himself.

Once in control of the Source and as the new Keeper of Traken, the Melkur tells Tremas he will build machines to his design and will lead the people of Traken 'to worlds without number, to conquest.'

The Master plans to use the Doctor's knowledge of the 'deeper mysteries of time' (implying the Doctor has knowledge the Master is denied). He also plans to use the powers of the Keepership to assume the Doctor's body, as he has himself passed his twelfth and final regeneration. In order to keep the Doctor captive, the Master keys his Melkur-TARDIS to his own biological rhythms so that he can move around but if the Doctor moves he will be destroyed.

The Master's TARDIS is destroyed by Adric and Nyssa's sabotage of the Source, and he manages to escape in a second TARDIS – in the shape of a clock. When Tremas later examines this clock, he is paralysed and the Master takes his body, using the last lingering vestiges of the Keepership powers to regenerate into it.

NEW INFORMATION

THE DOCTOR

The Doctor knows Traken by repute, but thinks he has never been there (though he checks his time logs to be sure). Before he knows that the Melkur is actually the Master's TARDIS, he has 'the oddest feeling' they've met somewhere before.

COMPANIONS

NYSSA: Nyssa bribes the chief Foster, Proctor Neman, to move people on from the Grove. Later, when he refuses another bribe, she stuns him with an ion-bonder she has modified.

TEGAN JOVANKA

'I'm just a mouth on legs.' (TEGAN – *EARTHSHOCK*)

Tegan is on her way to her first day at work as an air stewardess when she finds the TARDIS. She realises at once that it is a vehicle, but is unprepared for the journey to Logopolis. However, she trusts the Doctor implicitly, and stays on Logopolis to help him when the Watcher takes Nyssa and Adric away.

Although Tegan is inclined to be bossy, she and Nyssa become friends. While she enjoys her time in the TARDIS – for example, dancing the Charleston in *Black Orchid* – Tegan is initially keen to get back to Heathrow, losing her temper with the Doctor in *The Visitation* when he arrives there several hundred years too early. But when she is left there at the end of *Time-Flight*, she seems genuinely sad, despite suffering the recent death of Adric.

Tegan is an impulsive, self-confident Australian woman. In *Earthshock* she insists on joining the troopers – risking her life to retrieve a Cyber gun – and she is not afraid to argue with the Doctor or any villains they encounter. This confidence is brought to the fore by the alien Mara Tegan is possessed by, first in *Kinda* and later in *Snakedance*. The Mara plays on her 'darker' characteristics, and the experiences deeply unsettle her.

Having lost her job, Tegan is more than happy to resume her time and space travels in *Arc of Infinity*. But while she enjoys meeting the Brigadier in *Mawdryn Undead*, and the race in *Enlightenment*, Tegan never really takes to Turlough when he joins the TARDIS and misses Nyssa when she leaves. The deaths of so many people in *Resurrection of the Daleks* convince her that travelling with the Doctor is becoming more of an ordeal than a pleasure, and so she leaves.

The Doctor is sad to see her go – Tegan and the Fifth Doctor enjoy a love-hate relationship in which frequent arguments and apparent abrasiveness mask a deeper affection and respect.

TARDIS DATA BANK:

DESCRIPTION:
FEMALE, HUMAN,
AIR STEWARDESS
TRAVELLED:
LOGOPOLIS –
RESURRECTION OF
THE DALEKS

LOGOPOLIS

In which the Fourth Doctor meets his nemesis and 'dies' saving the Universe...
BY CHRISTOPHER H. BIDMEAD
4 EPISODES, FIRST BROADCAST 28 FEBRUARY–21 MARCH 1981

JOURNEY INFORMATION

LOGOPOLIS

The brain-like city of Logopolis is home to the Logopolitans who intone numbers and calculations, like components of an organic computer (there is a Central Register and there are Subroutines, for example). Their leader is the Monitor, who explains that they are a people 'driven not by individual need, but by mathematical necessity'.

The Monitor explains that Logopolis is actually the keystone of the Universe: 'If you destroy Logopolis you unravel the whole causal nexus.' It is the Logopolitans' constant calculations that hold the fabric of the Universe together by

TARDIS DATA BANK:

DATE: PRESENT, 28 FEBRUARY AND 1 MARCH

LOCATION: BARNET BYPASS AND PHAROS PROJECT IN CAMBRIDGE, EARTH; LOGOPOLIS.

THE DOCTOR TAKES THE TARDIS TO EARTH TO MEASURE A REAL POLICE BOX SO HE CAN FIX THE CHAMELEON CIRCUIT THAT ALLOWS THE TARDIS TO CHANGE SHAPE. BUT THE MASTER HAS ARRIVED AHEAD OF HIM, AND THE TARDIS MATERIALISES AROUND THE MASTER'S TARDIS. ON LOGOPOLIS, THE DOCTOR REALISES THE MASTER'S ACTIONS COULD DESTROY THE WHOLE OF CREATION. CAN THE DOCTOR AND THE MASTER WORK TOGETHER TO SAVE THE UNIVERSE? WHO IS THE MYSTERIOUS FIGURE WHO IS WATCHING THE DOCTOR? AND WILL THE DOCTOR SURVIVE HIS MOST IMPORTANT ENCOUNTER WITH HIS ARCH ENEMY…

opening CVE voids into other universes to allow energy in. But with the Master's interference, Logopolis dies and the voids start to close.

BLOCK TRANSFER COMPUTATION

Block Transfer Computation is a way of modelling space–time events through pure calculation. The Logopolitans intone their computations as the calculations would change the nature of any machine they were calculated on: 'Our manipulation of numbers directly changes the physical world. There is no other mathematics like ours… Only the living brain is immune.'

The Logopolitans have created a duplicate of the Pharos Project on Earth using Block Transfer Computation. When Logopolis is destroyed, the Doctor and the Master use the real Pharos computer to run the Logopolitan program and keep the CVEs open and stable.

THE MASTER

The Doctor calls the Master the 'most evil genius in the Universe'.

The Master has read the Doctor's mind and knows he was going to try to fix the chameleon circuit. The Doctor says, 'He's a Time Lord, in many ways we have the same mind.'

Again the Master kills people (a policeman and Tegan's Aunt Vanessa) by shrinking them (tissue compression). He controls Nyssa with an electromuscular constrictor bracelet.

Once he has realised what he has done to Logopolis the Master agrees to help the Doctor save the Universe. Brilliantly, he suggests that they reconfigure their TARDISes into time–cone inverters and create a stable safe zone by applying temporal inversion isometry to as much of space–time as they can isolate. He does most of the work to run the Logopolitan program, but typically turns the crisis to his own advantage and attempts to hold the entire Universe to ransom…

NEW INFORMATION

THE DOCTOR

The Doctor tells his companions, 'I've never chosen my own company. Nyssa, it was you who contacted me and begged me to help you find your father. Tegan, it was your own curiosity that got you into this. And Adric – a stowaway.'

Typically, the Fourth Doctor dies saving the Universe – he breaks a cable so the Master cannot close the CVE and allow entropy to increase.

THE WATCHER

The wraith-like figure that observes the Doctor is actually a projection of his future self (similar to Cho-je in *Planet of the Spiders*). He is perhaps brought into being by the unravelling of the causal nexus; effect before cause. On seeing the Watcher in London, the Doctor says, 'Nothing like this has ever happened before.'

THE TARDIS

There is a cloister area where the Doctor goes to think. He tells Adric not to interrupt him if he's there pacing up and down. While they are there the Cloister Bell rings. This is '… a sort of communications device reserved for wild catastrophes and sudden calls to man the battle stations.' The Doctor says Adric can ring it to get his attention it there's something urgent…

The Doctor got the TARDIS while it was in for repairs (on a sort of finders-keepers basis) and says he should have waited until the chameleon conversion was done. To operate the chameleon circuit, a control panel pops out of the console and instructions are given in machine code.

The Doctor needs to measure a real police box so the Logopolitans can convert the measurements to a precise mathematical model to overlay on the TARDIS shell and mend the chameleon circuit (which is something the Doctor says he's been meaning to do for centuries). Only the exterior of the TARDIS exists as a real space–time event, but mapped on to one of the interior continua – so it can be changed into any shape as the outer-plasmic shell is driven by the chameleon circuit. The Doctor says the chameleon circuit stuck at 'a totter's yard' (actually a junkyard in Totters Lane in *An Unearthly Child*).

Materialising round another TARDIS – the Master's – causes a gravity bubble (as in *The Time Monster*). The Doctor and Adric go through several identical (but progressively darker) TARDISes before emerging into the real world.

The Doctor jettisons Romana's room – the mass creates energy allowing the TARDIS to dematerialise with the Master's TARDIS on board. The Doctor refers to the central column as the 'time column'.

THE MASTER'S TARDIS

The Master's TARDIS has a working chameleon circuit and becomes a police box, a plant and a column.

The Master uses his light-speed overdrive to accelerate the signal from the Pharos Project to the CVE.

COMPANIONS

NYSSA: Nyssa calls the Doctor for help finding her father. She is brought to Logopolis by the Watcher. She watches on the TARDIS scanner as Traken is destroyed by the entropy cloud.

TEGAN: Tegan is on her way to her first day at work as an air stewardess when her Aunt Vanessa's car gets a puncture and Tegan goes into the TARDIS.

The Doctor: 'The Master's already at work on Logopolis. I'm going to stop him if it's the last thing I do.'

DOCTOR WHO MERCHANDISE

Seeing the extent of **Doctor Who** merchandise that has been produced over the years, it is hard to believe that the BBC was not prepared for at least some spin-off products. But with very rare exceptions, television series did not generate the toys, books, sweets and action figures that are almost expected today.

In fact, in 1963 the BBC's licensing department, then called BBC Exploitation, which handled the rights to what merchandise there was – for example, the published scripts of the BBC's **Quatermass** series and tie-ins to children's shows like **Watch With Mother** – consisted of just one person: Roy Williams. A new department had to be formed, and outside entrepreneur Walter Tuckwell was contracted to cope with the demand for licenses for Dalek products. Today that department has grown and merged with others to become BBC Worldwide, the publisher of this book, which employs thousands of people and has a turnover of millions of pounds.

The very first **Doctor Who** product was a record single of the theme music released by Decca in February 1964. This was soon followed by *The Dalek Book*, a lavishly illustrated hardback collection of comic-strip and text stories published by the Souvenir Press in June 1964. Throughout the rest of the 1960s most **Doctor Who** merchandise revolved around the Daleks rather than the Doctor, who only achieved a joint billing in the title of the first **Doctor Who** movie – *Dr. Who and the Daleks* – and no billing at all in the second: *Daleks: Invasion Earth 2150AD*. The Doctor Who Annual, published by World Distributors, was a rare but regular exception until 1985.

In the 1970s, this changed. While still immensely popular, the Daleks no longer had the huge appeal they had enjoyed previously. But, particularly during the Fourth Doctor's tenure, the series was going from strength to strength. And at the same time, the quantity of available merchandise increased.

By the time regular broadcasting of the series finished in 1989, the dedicated enthusiast could have amassed a vast collection of merchandise over the years. Alongside sweets, chocolate bars and even ice creams, they could have badges, jigsaws, books, models, toy Daleks, Cybermen, Giant Robot, K-9, figures of the Doctor in his various incarnations, board games, yo-yos and much more besides. They might wake in their bedroom (decorated with **Doctor Who** wallpaper) and dress in their **Doctor Who** T-shirt, jacket and, of course, underpants before eating a bowl of breakfast cereal containing a free **Doctor Who** badge and catching up with the latest instalment of the Dalek comic strip in *TV21*, or the **Doctor Who** comic strip in *TV Comic* (or *Countdown*, or *TV Action*, or *Doctor Who Weekly/Monthly/Magazine*).

Three of the First Doctor's adventures – (*The Daleks*, *The Web Planet* and *The Crusade* – were published in novel form in the 1960s. From 1973, Target Books (later Virgin Publishing) brought out novels of almost every broadcast **Doctor Who** story. From 1991, Virgin Publishing produced a range of original *New Adventures* which continued the Seventh Doctor's adventure in space and time. These were joined in 1994 by *Missing Adventures*, more original novels featuring previous incarnations of the Doctor. Today BBC Worldwide itself publishes original **Doctor Who** novels every month while Telos Publishing is responsible for shorter novellas and Big Finish Productions for short-story anthologies.

Although there has been no new **Doctor Who** on television since 1996, there is still a healthy market for **Doctor Who**-related merchandise. Licensed and BBC

Doctor products available include videos and DVDs of the television stories: all-new audio adventures from Big Finish Productions featuring the Fifth, Sixth, Seventh and Eighth Doctors (in addition to which, companion Sarah Jane Smith and the Daleks each have their own series); various action figures and models, and even remote-controlled and talking Daleks from Product Enterprises; action figures of Doctors together with various companions and enemies; original **Doctor Who** novels and novellas; soundtracks of 'missing' **Doctor Who** stories; playing cards and trading cards. And to keep you in touch with it all, *Doctor Who Magazine* is published by Panini every four weeks, while the BBCi **Doctor Who** website (and numerous other unofficial sites like Outpost Gallifrey run from Los Angeles) will give you all the latest news and rumours.

There is even an unofficial guide to **Doctor Who** merchandise, published by Telos Publishing. The first edition of Howe's Transcendental Toybox ran to nearly 500 pages, and listed over 3,500 items of **Doctor Who** merchandise that had been produced. And that was just up to the end of 1999 (though a revised and updated version of the book is due out in 2003). Who knows what will be available during the next millennium?

DALEKMANIA

In the mid-1960s in Britain only the Beatles were more popular than the Daleks.

The public demand for toys, books, games and other Dalek paraphernalia was almost insatiable. Terry Nation's words of wisdom about his creations in the paperback *Dalek Pocketbook* had an initial print run of 350,000 copies.

There were Dalek kites, balloons, badges, painting books and records. There were three Dalek annuals: *The Dalek Book*, *The Dalek World* and *The Dalek Outer Space Book* and 'The Outer Space Robot People of Television's DR WHO' even featured in their own weekly comic strip in the Gerry Anderson comic *TV Century 21*.

Amongst other things, you could play with toy Daleks of various shapes and sizes, eat Dalek sweet cigarettes and chocolate Daleks off Dalek plates while drinking from a Dalek mug, sleep in a bedroom with Dalek wallpaper, and lie in wait for a Dalek attack with your Anti-Dalek Fluid Neutraliser (a water pistol). All financed from savings you kept in your Dalek money box.

And if that wasn't enough, there was the stage play *The Curse of the Daleks*, and two cinema films – *Dr. Who and the Daleks* and *Daleks: Invasion Earth 2150AD* – in which Peter Cushing's bumbling scientist Dr. Who fought the Daleks in colour on the big screen.

While the merchandising may have tailed off, and sales of Dalek items dipped, there is still no science-fiction

creature in the universe of space and time that has anything approaching the lasting appeal of the Daleks. They can still be used to advertise products as diverse as changes in telephone codes and Kit-Kat chocolate bars, appear on stamps to celebrate the millennium and take over the universe in their own CD audio series *Dalek Empire*. Now, just as much as ever, Earth needs *The Dalek Survival Guide* (published in 2002).

THE FANS

Although there was an 'official' **Doctor Who** fan club as early as the late-1960s, it was not until 1976 and the formation of the *Doctor Who Appreciation Society* that 'fandom' really became organised.

The DWAS was formed by three people – 'President' Jan Vincent-Rudzki, 'Coordinator' Stephen Payne and 'Publisher' Gordon Blows. At a time when there was a lack of detailed and definitive information the series' past and about upcoming stories, the DWAS's various 'departments' provided a valuable and valued service to its members.

In August 1977, the DWAS organised the world's first **Doctor Who** convention – in a church hall in Clapham, London. Nearly 200 DWAS members arrived to find the main hall adorned with boards of black-and-white photos, constantly running slide shows, and an impressive guest list. As well as Visual Effects assistant Mat Irvine – who showed slides of effects work on the forthcoming *The Invisible Enemy* – the event was attended by new producer Graham Williams, and also by stars Louise Jameson and Tom Baker. For once, Baker appeared as himself rather than in costume, making the point that the fans were actually the one group of people for whom he did not need to keep up the pretence. By contrast, Jon Pertwee arrived in full costume, declaring, 'I am the Doctor.'

The enthusiasm and meticulous organisation by Keith Barnfather and his team formed a solid basis for future conventions, both in the UK and abroad. At the height of the series' popularity, thousands of people attended conventions in the US. Tens of thousands jammed the roads to the BBC's own **Doctor Who** celebration – *Twenty Years of a Time Lord* – in April 1983 – held in the extensive grounds of Longleat House.

The DWAS, and other fan organisations around the world, continue to provide newsletters and information services as well as discounted products, local meetings and conventions. But with so many professional products and publications now available, it is difficult to imagine the ground-breaking excitement and enthusiasm of the early days of **Doctor Who** fandom.

WITH Gerry Anderson's THUNDERBIRDS

TV CENTURY 21

DALEKS FACE DESTRUCTION

Reactor hazard– Danger mounts as Fireball moves in

CORGI MODEL CLUB NEWS
Page 13

'There's always something to look at if you open your eyes!'

(THE DOCTOR – *KINDA*)

Five

THE FIFTH DOCTOR

THE DOCTOR

'That's the problem with regeneration,' notes the Fifth Doctor, staring with apparent dismay into a mirror in his first story. 'You never know what you're going to get.' Certainly the contrast between this softly spoken, uncertain young man and his previous larger-than-life incarnation could hardly be greater.

'This regeneration is going to be difficult,' he announces candidly. While an aspect of the Fourth Doctor's apparent invincibility was his self-reliance, it seems the violence of his 'death' has taught him a lesson; the Fifth wastes little time in actively recruiting his companions Tegan, Nyssa and Adric to help him in the 'healing time', indicating that a knowledge of his former self is crucial to 'heal the disconnection' between his discarded body and the new one.

But the new Doctor shapes up quickly. Minor bursts of extroversion aside, he no longer seeks to be the centre of attention; his heroism is unpretentious, and rather than steal the show he seeks to empower his travelling companions by increasing their resourcefulness (showing them the TARDIS data bank in *Castrovalva*, teaching them how to read star charts before *Snakedance*). He may have a young body, but the exuberant energy this allows him is tempered by an apparently greater frailty in other areas. He is short-sighted, quick to fluster and his mind seems no longer quite so sharp; whereas past Doctors have worked out the most complex equations in their heads, in *Earthshock* the Fifth Doctor asks Adric a question and checks the answer on a computer, and in *Time-Flight* he lies down in a kind of trance to formulate a plan to beat his old enemy the Master.

And yet the Fifth Doctor worries perhaps more than any of his predecessors about doing 'the right thing' in protecting others; he is the first to berate himself for any perceived error of judgement. ('I should have realised!' he wails in *Earthshock* when the Cybermen break through his barriers, and he hisses 'I'm an idiot!' when he allows Davros to gain the upper hand in *Resurrection of the Daleks*). It's not just for show, either. When Adric is killed he confesses to a sense of grief his predecessors have always kept private, he is prepared to lay down his life for Tegan and Nyssa in *Mawdryn Undead* and is shattered by the massacre of *Warriors of the Deep*, muttering, 'There should've been another way.'

The Fifth Doctor leads his life in pursuit of this other way. His well-developed sense of responsibility spurs him on to make serious decisions when they are needed. He sets out to execute Davros in *Resurrection of the Daleks*, destroys his companion Kamelion in *Planet of Fire* when he accepts there is no way to save him, and ultimately lays down his life for Peri, a girl he barely knows, in *The Caves of Androzani* – a fitting final act for this most selfless of Doctors.

THE MAN BEHIND THE DOCTOR – PETER DAVISON

Peter Davison – whose real name is Peter Moffatt – was born in 1951 and grew up in Streatham and Surrey. Leaving school at 16 with little in the way of academic qualifications, he decided to pursue his love of acting and managed to gain a place on a three-year course at the Central School of Speech and Drama.

He first came to public prominence in 1977 with a significant role in the ITV period drama *Love for Lydia*, but it was the part of Tristan Farnon in *All Creatures Great and Small* (initially 1978–80 on BBC1) which really catapulted him to fame. Two sitcoms, *Holding the Fort* and *Sink or Swim* soon followed.

This established TV stardom was a boon as far as **Doctor Who** producer John Nathan-Turner was concerned; who better placed to eclipse the popularity built up by Tom Baker over the last seven years than someone who already commanded a strong TV following? Davison was initially reluctant to take on the part, considering himself unsuitable, but over a number of meetings and phone calls was eventually won round. He began work on **Doctor Who** in April 1981.

Former Doctor Patrick Troughton apparently advised Davison to do three years in the part, as he had done, and then move on. It was advice Davison would cite when announcing his plans to leave in July 1983; his final work on the series came in January 1984. Mere weeks later he was working on a BBC adaptation of **Anna of the Five Towns**, and his career has continued arguably more solidly and successfully than that of any other actor who has played the part before or since, boasting starring roles in **A Very Peculiar Practice**, **Campion**, **Fiddlers Three**, **At Home with the Braithwaites** and many other series.

CASTROVALVA

In which the new Doctor spends two episodes in the TARDIS before finding himself trapped inside an Escher print...
BY CHRISTOPHER H. BIDMEAD
4 EPISODES, FIRST BROADCAST 4–12 JANUARY 1982

JOURNEY INFORMATION

CASTROVALVA

'Castrovalva' seems to refer to the 'dwellings of simplicity' located atop a mountain on a planet in the Andromedan Phylox series. The climate is temperate and the surroundings rural woodland. Wild animals dwell in the forest and are hunted by the Castrovalvans.

However, while Castrovalva has historical records dating back 500 years, it is in reality a projection created by the Master out of pure energy channelled by mathematical computations. This explains how the town functions with no apparent fiscal system, and why the men seem only to read and hunt while the women wash clothing in the main square.

THE MASTER

The Master revels in setting elaborate traps for the Doctor – aware that the TARDIS may escape destruction at Event One, the birth of the Universe, he has prepared an entire town primed to collapse down into itself around his arch-foe. Unfortunately, the Master, disguised as the town's Portreeve, is himself trapped by the collapse of Castrovalva, when one of his own creations sabotages his power source.

NEW INFORMATION

THE DOCTOR

The Doctor is left weaker and more vulnerable following his fourth regeneration than at any other time in his televised life. Apparently 'the regeneration is failing' though it is not clear whether this is due to the severity of his injuries or, perhaps, an extension of the entropy that has torn into so much of his Universe. His condition is stabilised by the Zero Room, a healing, neutral environment on board the TARDIS.

The Doctor's new eyes are short-sighted, and he compensates for this with a pair of half-moon spectacles. He can decipher the ingredients of a drink by smell alone, and it seems that rosemary makes him sneeze.

THE TARDIS

The Zero Room cancels out all external influences and distractions. Even the room's doors are constructed of a material that generates stabilising effects. The TARDIS also contains a thermobuffer that can be vented, and a data bank, containing information on the TARDIS systems (though not how to pilot it).

The jettisoning of 25 per cent of its mass generates enough thrust for the ship to escape destruction at Event One – the beginning of the Universe.

COMPANIONS

TEGAN: Her father once told her that 'if' is the most powerful word in the English language. The Doctor feels she will be 'a fine coordinator', who will keep the crew together while he recovers.

ADRIC: Adric is considered 'the navigator' of the team by the Doctor, since, 'He knows the way, he knows me...' It is his mathematical excellence that allows the Master to create Castrovalva and its inhabitants via Block Transfer Computation (see *Logopolis*).

TARDIS DATA BANK:

DATE: 1981; UNKNOWN LOCATION: EARTH; UNNAMED PLANET OF THE PHYLOX SERIES

WITH THE DOCTOR'S REGENERATION FAILING, THE CONCERNED TARDIS CREW FEND OFF AN ATTACK BY THE MASTER AND HEAD FOR THE WORLD OF CASTROVALVA – A PLACE OF PEACE AND TRANQUILLITY WHERE THE DOCTOR CAN RECOVER FROM HIS TRAUMA. BUT CASTROVALVA IS IN FACT A SPACE–TIME TRAP SET BY THE MASTER THAT COULD DESTROY THEM ALL...

The Doctor: 'This regeneration is going to be difficult and I shall need you all, every one of you.'

BEHIND THE SCENES

CREATING A NEW DOCTOR

When considering the casting of the Fifth Doctor, producer John Nathan-Turner had a shortlist of fundamental requirements:

- The new Doctor should be a younger man, to appeal to a more youthful audience.
- He should seem vulnerable as opposed to Baker's overpowering performance.
- He should exhibit a more old-fashioned sense of heroism, a back-to-basics approach to doing right.
- He should have straight hair as opposed to Baker's distinctive curls.

It seems in retrospect slightly strange that hairstyle should form such an important facet of the new Doctor, but Tom Baker had been playing the part for a record-breaking seven years and had enjoyed unparalleled success. Nathan-Turner needed the absolute antithesis to the Fourth Doctor if the show was to avoid accusations of offering up pale imitations of its glory days.

The producer had worked with Peter Davison during his time on **All Creatures Great and Small**, and had a photo of him taken at a charity cricket match pinned to a wall in the **Doctor Who** production office. While mulling over Baker's successor, he noticed the picture and, to his delight, realised that Davison seemed to fit every one of his requirements.

Davison was originally reluctant to take the part, but eventually agreed – as keeping quiet about being first choice once someone else had accepted would have been too frustrating.

If the photo on Nathan-Turner's wall didn't directly inspire the Fifth Doctor's look as an Edwardian cricketer, it certainly proved prophetic. Davison recalls suggesting the cricketer image himself, which Nathan-Turner ultimately approved as being suitably eccentric, old-fashioned and quintessentially English.

As for how the part was to be played, Davison was offered little guidance. 'The trick of a good producer is to cast someone who is right for the part in the way that they see it and then let them do it,' he would later recall. 'I was very much thrown in and told, "You're the Doctor – now do it!"' The desire to create contrasts between Davison and Baker was paramount in the scripting of his first story. As *Castrovalva* author Christopher H. Bidmead put it, 'I loved the idea of having this brash, overlarge manifestation of the Doctor turning into this fragile little thing that gets carried about in a box.'

CHANGING TIMES

With the advent of the Peter Davison era, **Doctor Who** began transmission away from its traditional Saturday tea-time slot. For the next three years it was to be aired twice-weekly on week nights, and noticeably later in the evening at around 7 p.m.

This break with tradition caused an outcry not only from fans of the series pained by this sudden disregard for tradition, but from members of the press (the *Daily Mail* and the *Guardian* in particular) concerned that **Doctor Who** could not survive outside the cosy traditions of the Saturday night line-up. The then Controller of BBC1, Alan Hart, defended his scheduling tactics in *Radio Times*: 'The hope is that more people will be able to follow his adventures. In addition, we all felt the need to give him a new lease of life. A new Doctor, a new placing, a new challenge. Time will tell whether the TARDIS has landed on the right day.'

The new lease of life Hart mentioned was necessary after the trouncing in the ratings Tom Baker's last season had received at the hands of **Buck Rogers in the 25th Century**, a glossy American sci-fi import network-broadcast on ITV. In addition, BBC planners were considering committing to a twice-weekly soap opera and were keen to see what viewing figures would be like for an ongoing drama series like **Doctor Who** at that time of the evening.

The relocation proved beneficial to the series; its audiences rose dramatically to around the 9–10 million mark. The show's popularity peaked with Episode 1 of the season closer *Time-Flight*, which was the 26th most popular programme on TV in its week of broadcast.

FOUR TO DOOMSDAY

In which Stratford Johns plays a giant frog in charge of a spaceship full of androids...
BY TERENCE DUDLEY
4 EPISODES, FIRST BROADCAST 18–26 JANUARY 1982

JOURNEY INFORMATION

URBANKA

Monarch's home world, with a population of three billion, is part of the Inokshi solar system in Galaxy 1489. The time travellers are told that 1,000 years earlier the star Inokshi collapsed into a black hole and the Urbankans were forced to find a new home world. The android Bigon later reveals, however, that Monarch caused Inokshi's destruction himself, and has abandoned Urbanka in pursuit of his own deranged schemes.

MONARCH

Monarch is quite insane. He has devised a complex plan to strip the Earth of silicon, carbon and other minerals in order to power a time-travel device that will allow him to travel back to the creation of the Universe and confirm that it was he who created it – the god of everything.

Since the elements he feels he requires are abundant on many planets it seems unclear why he is returning to Earth, which he last visited 2,500 years ago; perhaps he gained what he perceives as valuable local knowledge of humans after abducting so many on his previous visit. He

intends to use a poison against humanity so that he may release them from 'the great tyranny of the Universe – internal and external organs', replacing the human race with androids. But his insane hypocrisy is exposed when he himself falls prey to his own poison – he is, after all, only a creature of flesh and blood.

NEW INFORMATION

THE DOCTOR

The Doctor reveals that his short-sightedness extends only to his right eye, and carries a magnifying glass. He claims he once took five wickets for New South Wales.

He can survive sub-zero temperatures for up to six minutes, and can reduce his oxygen intake by placing himself in a kind of trance. He is somehow able to endure the vacuum of space without a pressure suit, but it's possible the helmet he wears is protecting him in some way.

COMPANIONS

TEGAN: Tegan wants to be returned to Heathrow airport. She can speak in an Aboriginal dialect and is extremely competent at sketching; Monarch's ministers are able to produce facsimile clothing from her designs, as well as assembling convincing androids from the likenesses she depicts. She attempts to escape the Urbankan ship in the TARDIS, and manages to make it dematerialise – only to rematerialise in a new position alongside the spacecraft.

KINDA

In which Richard Todd, Nerys Hughes, Simon Rouse and Mary Morris find themselves beset by a giant snake and haunted by dreams...
BY CHRISTOPHER BAILEY
4 EPISODES, FIRST BROADCAST 1–9 FEBRUARY 1982

JOURNEY INFORMATION

THE MARA

The Mara that attempts to enslave the Kinda is actually one of a race of creatures that inhabit an unknown realm – 'the dark places of the inside' as the Doctor puts it. Their physical form is reminiscent of a scarlet snake. They can use dreaming human minds as a bridge into the physical world, manipulating the subconscious into giving the Mara control over the physical body. This control manifests itself as a deepening of the voice, a red stain on the teeth and a snake symbol on the arm.

This particular Mara – Dukkha – returns repeatedly to bring chaos to the Kinda tribe, feeding on their negative emotions. Panna the wise woman of the tribe says, 'Our suffering is the Mara's delight, our madness the Mara's meat and drink.' But the Mara cannot face its own reflection in the physical world and is destroyed when it is forced to leave its host body when trapped within a circle of mirrors.

THE KINDA

The Kinda appear to be primitives, but are in fact highly sophisticated engineers and adept telepaths. The males are mute, so their feelings and intentions are given voice by the telepathic females, such as Karuna, who 'read them'.

The Kinda refer to outsiders as the 'not-we', reflecting their sense of close community. They stoically accept the cyclical nature of history, seeing the rising and falling of civilisation as the turning of time's wheel. Panna states that the Mara turns the wheel, suggesting it has destroyed the Kinda civilisation many times in the past.

THE COLONISTS

An expedition from an unknown planet – the Homeworld, possibly connected with Earth – has set up a protective dome on the surface of Deva Loka. Three members of the expedition have gone missing, and their whereabouts remains a mystery at the story's end. They are the blustering Sanders, the unhinged Hindle and the cool scientist Todd. They are bound by a bureaucratic code of official conduct, which even seems to extend to numbering the trees in the vicinity.

With the planet declared officially unsuitable for colonisation, Sanders hopes to remain on Deva Loka. Todd says, 'I told him he should just wander off into the forest, nobody would notice.' Perhaps, if he followed her advice, he would be reunited with the rest of his team.

TARDIS DATA BANK:

DATE: UNKNOWN
LOCATION: DEVA LOKA
(PLANET S14)

DEVA LOKA IS A PEACEFUL WORLD, AND ITS INHABITANTS, THE KINDA – WHILE AT FIRST SIGHT PRIMITIVE – ARE ACTUALLY HIGHLY ADVANCED. BOTH ARE THREATENED BY TWO ALIEN INFLUENCES: THAT OF AN EXPEDITION FROM A RACE OF COLONISING HUMANOIDS, AND THAT OF THE MARA, AN EVIL THAT DWELLS IN THE DARK PLACES OF THE INSIDE – AND WHICH ENTERS THE KINDA WORLD THROUGH THE MIND OF TEGAN...

Dukkha: 'You will agree to being me sooner or later — this side of madness or the other.'

NEW INFORMATION

THE DOCTOR

The Doctor seems to have completely lost his ability to perform conjuring tricks such as the transmigration of objects (*The Ambassadors of Death*, *The Three Doctors*, et al.).

When exposed to the Box of Jhana, the Kinda healing device that clears the mind but causes temporary shock and personality changes, the Doctor's mind is not affected. He sees only a mental projection – the image of Kinda wise women beckoning him from outside a cave. He instinctively trusts that the cave is real, and is proven right.

He tackles an opponent physically for the first time when he grapples with the deranged Hindle. He loses the fight quickly, knocked unconscious for a few moments by a falling table.

He spends much of the story in the company of the scientist Todd. He seems fond of her, taking the time to say a proper goodbye, and apologetic that he is being dragged away by his impatient friends. They shake hands slightly awkwardly.

COMPANIONS

NYSSA: Nyssa, who collapsed at the end of *Four to Doomsday*, is revealed to be suffering from mental disorientation (perhaps as a result of being hypnotised by Enlightenment on board the Urbankan spaceship). Adric says she is useless as a chequers opponent in her condition.

Once the TARDIS has landed on Deva Loka, the Doctor constructs a delta-wave augmenter to ensure she receives some augmented D-sleep to help her recover. By the end of the story she is fine once more.

TEGAN: Tegan falls asleep under a set of windchimes and is attacked in her dreams by a Mara. The entity wishes to take control of her body, and after a series of assaults on her sanity agrees to let the Mara take her form.

She remembers her actions while possessed as if it were a dream, and is embarrassed at relating the details ('Dreams are private!' she tells the Doctor, indignantly). In the final confrontation with the Mara she is clearly uneasy about its presence in her mind, a feeling that persists into the next story.

ADRIC: It is Adric's impetuous nature that first involves the Doctor in the adventure, when he accidentally activates a total survival suit (TSS) which leads the pair to the colonists' dome at gunpoint. This same impulsive streak almost leads to disaster when he attempts to escape in the TSS and finds he cannot control it. He is adept at conjuring tricks, producing a coin from behind the Doctor's ear.

THE VISITATION

In which the alien Terileptils release the Black Death and the Doctor starts the Great Fire of London...
BY ERIC SAWARD
4 EPISODES, FIRST BROADCAST 15–23 FEBRUARY

TARDIS DATA BANK:

DATE: AUGUST–2 SEPTEMBER 1666
LOCATION: THE AREA THAT WILL BECOME HEATHROW; PUDDING LANE, LONDON

ARRIVING IN THE SEVENTEENTH CENTURY AT THE HEIGHT OF THE PLAGUE, THE DOCTOR AND HIS COMPANIONS SOON FIND EVIDENCE OF AN ALIEN PRESENCE NEARBY. STRANDED TERILEPTIL CONVICTS INTEND TO MAKE THE EARTH THEIR OWN, AND IN DEFEATING THEM THE DOCTOR UNWITTINGLY BECOMES INVOLVED IN MAKING HISTORY…

JOURNEY INFORMATION

THE TERILEPTILS

The Terileptils are bipedal reptilian creatures with a pronounced aesthetic sense. They banish their criminals to the planet Raaga where they toil in tinclavic mines for the remainder of their lives. This work has left the leader of the stranded convicts badly scarred around his left eye. Its ship was damaged in an asteroid storm, and only three of its comrades survived the crash-landing on Earth. One has since died. The Terileptils use a Soliton gas generator to provide an atmosphere more suitable for their lungs, although they can survive in Earth's atmosphere for a considerable time.

The Terileptils can control human minds by means of special polygrite bracelets with built-in power packs which, it would appear, were originally designed to be used on the Terileptils themselves while they were on Raaga.

Quite ruthless, the leader established a base close by their ruined escape pod by wiping out the inhabitants of a manor house and setting up a laboratory in the cellar. Its fellows have set up another base in the back rooms of a bakery in the middle of London. Unable to return home, because they are fugitives from Terileptil law, the creatures plan to take over Earth by infecting rats with a genetically engineered form of bubonic plague and releasing them to wipe out humanity.

The Terileptils are ultimately defeated by brute force when the Doctor and his friends storm the bakery. A fire is started and becomes an inferno when a Terileptil gun explodes along with the Soliton generator. All the creatures perish.

RICHARD MACE

Richard Mace is a genial rogue and vagabond, an out-of-work thespian (playhouses have been closed down thanks to the plague) posing, when he first meets the Doctor's party, as a highwayman. His casual air of nonchalance masks an extremely healthy sense of self-preservation. He has a taste for the finer things in life that his meagre circumstances cannot cater for, and will happily help himself to stolen wine or other people's property if there's no risk involved in the taking.

While Mace is not the 'man of iron' he professes to be, he becomes a capable ally for the Doctor in defeating the Terileptil plan. He turns down a further trip in the TARDIS to stay and combat the rapidly spreading fire from the Terileptils' base. (Since this is located in Pudding Lane it would appear he has helped the Doctor start the Great Fire of London, which will help to purify the plague-ravaged country.)

NEW INFORMATION

THE DOCTOR

The Doctor knows of the Terileptils, recognises their technology and its effects, and knows of their penal system. He recognises the smell of Soliton gas, and is correct in his assumption that a sonic booster with frequency modulator will put paid to the Terileptils' android.

When about to be beheaded by the controlled villagers, the Doctor recalls his near decapitation by an android in *Four to Doomsday* and mutters, 'Not again!'

THE TARDIS

The TARDIS is becoming still more decrepit; controls actually come away in the Doctor's hands. A fault in the lateral balance cones is blamed for the TARDIS materialising in the right place but the wrong time.

Despite this, it is capable of accurate flight within the localised area in this time zone, and of scanning an area the size of a city for energy emissions; its sensors sweep seventeenth century London for evidence of the Terileptils' hidden base.

The sonic screwdriver allows the Doctor to penetrate an energy barrier created by a Terileptil. The Doctor reacts badly when the Terileptil goes on to destroy his most cherished of tools: 'I feel like I've just lost an old friend.'

COMPANIONS

TEGAN: The Terileptil leader subjects Tegan to its will by the use of its mind-controlling bracelets, and uses her for carrying equipment and vials of poison. Under its control she nearly opens a cage of plague rats that would kill herself and the Doctor.

NYSSA: Nyssa successfully constructs the sonic booster and uses it against the android when it gains access to the TARDIS. She expresses sadness at the robot's demise, considering it a 'magnificent' creation. With Adric, she then pilots the TARDIS successfully to the manor house.

ADRIC: Adric escapes from the Terileptil's leader but is forced to abandon Tegan, something that upsets him greatly. Impatience almost proves his downfall once again when he sets out to find the Doctor and is soon captured by the villagers, only to be inadvertently rescued by the Terileptil android.

Richard Mace: 'How does this 'android' ... come from another world? There are no other worlds, any fool knows that!'

The Doctor: 'Thank you,
Lady Cranleigh, for a
delightfully unexpected
afternoon.'

In which Nyssa meets her double, the Doctor plays cricket,
and a disfigured relative is locked in the attic...
BY TERENCE DUDLEY
2 EPISODES, FIRST BROADCAST 1 – 2 MARCH 1982

TARDIS DATA BANK:

DATE: 10–14 JUNE 1925
LOCATION: SOUTHERN ENGLAND

CASES OF MISTAKEN IDENTITY ABOUND WHEN THE DOCTOR AND HIS FRIENDS LAND AT
CRANLEIGH HALT. FIRST THE DOCTOR IS TAKEN FOR A VISITING CRICKETER AND ENDS UP
PLAYING A GAME, THEN NYSSA FINDS SHE HAS A DOPPELGANGER AND BECOMES THE
ACCIDENTAL TARGET OF A MYSTERIOUS DEFORMED STRANGER'S AFFECTIONS. AND FINALLY
THE DOCTOR IS MISTAKEN FOR A MURDERER...

BLACK ORCHID

JOURNEY INFORMATION

LADY CRANLEIGH'S SECRET

Lady Cranleigh's eldest son, George, was a botanist and
explorer who apparently went missing on an expedition up
the Orinocco River in Brazil whilst in search of the black
orchid two years previously. But in truth, his whereabouts
are well known to Lady Cranleigh – she has him locked away
in a bedroom upstairs. George was tortured and disfigured
by Kajabi Indians to whom the black orchid is sacred – they
cut out his tongue and drove him insane. He was rescued
by the chief of another tribe, Dittar Latoni, who brought him
back home. Ever since, Lady Cranleigh has secretly kept
him in the Indian's care shut away from view, not wishing
him to be seen in such a terrible state.

Ann Talbot was George's fiancée, whom he still loves.
While he is capable of acts of violence he is only ever caring
to Ann – and Nyssa, with whom he confuses her. Ultimately,
having murdered two men, started a fire and abducted
Nyssa, the tragic George's suffering is ended when he falls
to his death from the roof of the Cranleighs' house.

NEW INFORMATION

THE DOCTOR

The Doctor gets to participate in a game of cricket and, in
team captain Charles Cranleigh's words, proves to be a
'first-class batsman and a demon bowler'. He is familiar with
songs of the period, singing specifically 'I Want To Be
Happy', a popular tune in 1924, and also quotes a line from
Charley's Aunt, a popular farce written in 1892.

Unusually, the Doctor elects to remain for George
Cranleigh's funeral.

COMPANIONS

NYSSA: Nyssa is the exact double of Ann Talbot, whose
family have a strong lineage in Worcestershire. She learns
contemporary dance very swiftly for her appearance at the
Cranleighs' costume ball, and exhibits an unusual sense of
fun in colluding with Ann's deception of the party guests as
to who's who.

TEGAN: Tegan no longer wants the Doctor to take her back
to Heathrow.

Sir Robert: 'Worthy of the
Master. The other Doctor:
W. G. Grace...'

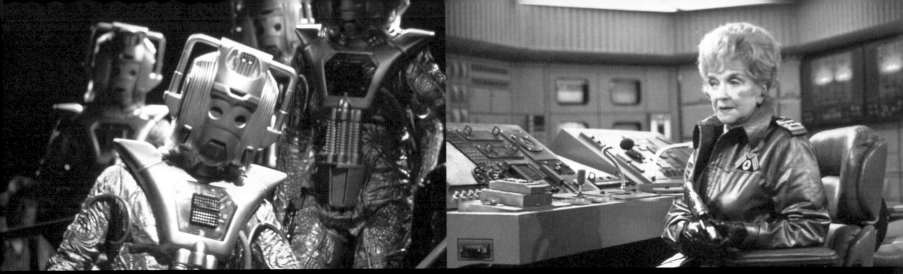

EARTHSHOCK

In which Adric dies, the Cybermen unexpectedly return, and Beryl Reid joins James Warwick to save the world...
BY ERIC SAWARD
4 EPISODES, FIRST BROADCAST 8–16 MARCH 1982

TARDIS DATA BANK:

DATE: 2526; SPIRALLING BACKWARDS TO 65 MILLION YEARS BC
LOCATION: EARTH; FREIGHTER APPROACHING EARTH

THE TARDIS CREW FALL IN WITH A GROUP OF BELEAGURED TROOPERS, UNDER ATTACK FROM SINISTER ANDROID SENTINELS GUARDING A HATCH HIDDEN DEEP INSIDE A CAVE SYSTEM FULL OF FOSSILS. BEHIND THE HATCH IS A BOMB THAT THE DOCTOR DEFUSES – BUT HE IS ABLE TO TRACE ITS OWNERS TO AN EARTH FREIGHTER IN SPACE. UNKNOWN TO THE FREIGHTER'S CAPTAIN, THE SHIP CONTAINS AN ARMY OF CYBERMEN, WHO PLAN TO USE IT TO DESTROY THE EARTH...

JOURNEY INFORMATION

THE CYBERMEN

These Cybermen appear very different in design to those seen in previous stories. They are slimmer, and their weaponry is no longer built into their bodies. Vestigial chins can be seen moving behind their transparent mouth-guards. They are still vulnerable to gold.

They plan to destroy the Earth because it is hosting an interplanetary conference which will unite several civilisations in a war against the Cyber race. It is claimed that destroying the conference will be a strong psychological victory for the Cybermen.

The Cyber Leader recognises the TARDIS and seems to know the Doctor personally. (Upon taking the bridge, he states, 'So – we meet again, Doctor'). The Cybermen have audio-visual recordings of several of their past meetings with the Time Lord. The rank of Cyber Lieutenant is shown for the first time (though not specifically mentioned).

The origin of the humanoid androids employed by these Cybermen is unknown; certainly, being highly mobile and with death-blasters built into their hands, they are more effective protectors of the bomb than the Cybermats would be. The Cyber Lieutenant comments, 'The androids are too valuable to waste.' It's possible that the Cybermen have purloined the androids rather than constructing them themselves; certainly they are never seen again in Cyber-employ.

NEW INFORMATION

THE DOCTOR

The Doctor puts aside his usual pacifist notions when confronting the Cybermen and wields guns without protest. He seems prepared to use a handgun to help defend the freighter's bridge when the Cybermen attack, and he later fires the Cyber Leader's weapon into the creature's chest unit to destroy him on board the TARDIS.

He declares he does not feel affection or friendship to be a weakness – even when, by threatening to kill Tegan, the Cyber Leader exploits these emotions to make the Doctor obey him.

THE TARDIS

Using a length of thick grey cable and connecting it to a bomb, the Doctor is able to jam an arming signal and pinpoint the location of the bomb's controllers. The console is badly damaged by Cyber gunfire. A Cyber Lieutenant is sent to search the TARDIS; predictably it is gone some time, but eventually finds its way back to the Console Room.

COMPANIONS

NYSSA: Nyssa develops an attachment to Professor Kyle, the palaeontologist who first discovered the presence of the androids in the caves. She is distraught when Kyle, who has

elected to stay in the TARDIS, is killed by the Cybermen. She later shoots the Cyber Lieutenant dead while the Doctor is otherwise engaged in trying to operate the damaged console – an unusual act of violence that is perhaps motivated by revenge.

TEGAN: When Tegan is a prisoner of the Cybermen on board the TARDIS she launches herself at the controls, presumably in an attempt to steer away from the Earth freighter, but succeeds only in creating turbulence.

ADRIC: Adric feels homesick for E-Space and has a heated argument with the Doctor about risking a trip through the Charged Vacuum Emboitement, which the Doctor initially considers too dangerous. The two later reconcile their differences, with Adric, having worked out a safe path through the CVE to prove a point, conceding that he doesn't really want to go back: 'There's nothing there for me now.'

With the freighter set on a collision course with the Earth, Adric struggles to break the Cybermen's three logic codes that are overriding the coordinates. He cracks two of the three, accidentally sending the freighter spiralling back through time, and rather than escape the ship with other survivors, he chooses to remain, determined to crack the last remaining code and presumably pilot the freighter away from Earth. Unfortunately a dying Cyberman destroys the computers before he can do so. Adric's last words are, 'Now I'll never know if I was right.'

Ironically, had Adric succeeded the dinosaurs would never have been wiped out by the freighter's impact and all human history would have been destroyed in an instant.

BEHIND THE SCENES

RE-CREATING THE CYBERMEN

Seeking to truly test his new Doctor's mettle with a rematch against a popular old enemy – an idea enthusiastically shared by Peter Davison – producer John Nathan-Turner and his new script editor, Eric Saward, decided to bring back the Cybermen. Nathan-Turner went to great pains to ensure the return of the Cybermen would achieve maximum impact. He closed the studio observation galleries while the

story was being recorded and declined a *Radio Times* cover and article in celebration of the Doctor's second-best enemies' resurrection. In *Radio Times*, the monsters' identity was disguised for the first two episodes by crediting them as simply 'Leader' and 'Lieutenant'.

The Cybermen had last appeared in 1975's *Revenge of the Cybermen*, and Nathan-Turner wanted to give them a radical makeover for this latest outing. Costume designer Dinah Collin approached freelance design company Imagineering to construct the Cybermen's new appearance. While maintaining superficial similarities to the 'classic' Cyberman look – the ear handles, a device mounted into the top of the helmet, a chest unit, etc – the Cybermen were given a more modern look by slimming down the 'chunkiness' of what had gone before. The thick ribbed piping that had lined the arms and legs was removed. The wetsuits that had formed the basis of previous Cyberman costumes were replaced with specially adapted RAF G-suits (originally worn by pilots flying at high altitudes), which were covered in a network of slim tubing that coiled around the body. The chest unit became more like armour in appearance, protecting the shoulders and upper torso.

The mouth section was left transparent so that the jaw – painted silver and wrapped in wrinkled cellophane – could be seen to move; the monsters were voiced by the actors inside the suits, and Nathan-Turner was keen that the audience should be able to tell which Cyberman was speaking. This led to some problems during recording, when the radio microphones the actors spoke into, taped inside the helmets, would come loose in the heat and slide down into view.

By preserving the surprise of the Cybermen's comeback, Nathan-Turner created a minor press sensation. On 13 March, midway through *Earthshock*'s run the TV discussion show *Did You See...?* celebrated the Cyber return with a look at many of the Doctor's past foes. Even *Radio Times*, perhaps a little petulantly, promoted the Cybermen with a small article on its back pages ready for the final two instalments of *Earthshock*. And when Adric met his death at the hands of the cyborgs, articles in newspapers and letters of protest in the *Radio Times* soon followed. The reputation of the Cybermen as worthy, fearful adversaries had been well restored.

...which Concorde becomes the most expensive prop ever used in **Doctor Who** and Heathrow Airport allows filming of a fictional programme on its premises...

BY PETER GRIMWADE

4 EPISODES, FIRST BROADCAST 22–30 MARCH 1982

TARDIS DATA BANK:

DATE: EARLY 1980S; THE JURASSIC PERIOD; PRESENT
LOCATION: HEATHROW AIRPORT

THE TARDIS FINALLY ARRIVES AT HEATHROW AIRPORT IN TIME TO INVESTIGATE THE MYSTERY OF A DISAPPEARING CONCORDE. BUT WHEN THE DOCTOR AND HIS CREW BOARD A SECOND VANISHING CONCORDE HE REALISES THE PLANES ARE BEING DIVERTED DOWN A TIME CONTOUR TO PREHISTORIC EARTH, FOR SINISTER REASONS UNKNOWN. THE ENIGMATIC ALIEN MAGICIAN KALID WHO CLAIMS RESPONSIBILITY IS IN FACT THE MASTER – ATTEMPTING TO HARNESS THE IMMENSE POWER OF THE XERAPHIN RACE...

JOURNEY INFORMATION

THE MASTER

The Master is masquerading as an alien magician named Kalid in the Xeraphin citadel; an eccentricity perhaps adopted in an attempt to fool the Doctor into agreeing to hand over his TARDIS. It is unclear also how he escaped the collapse of Castrovalva – but it is likely that his TARDIS exhausted nearly all its power in the process, since it is his search for a new power source that has led him to make overtures to the Xeraphin.

THE XERAPHIN

The Xeraphin fled their home planet of Xeriphas when it was ravaged in the Vardon–Kosnax war. All but extinct, they have elected to devolve themselves into a state of pure mental energy, stored in a simple sarcophagus but capable of projecting physical forms through the conglomeration of proteins. The Doctor refers to these as Plasmatons. They engulf both him and Nyssa in order to plead for help.

Most of the race lies dormant but spokespeople – who have retained their individual identity – are able to re-create their original forms once a 'channel' is created via the physical absorption of a human being.

The Xeraphin are eventually inducted into the Master's TARDIS for exploitation as a power source. However, the Doctor believes that once returned to Xeriphas – no longer a ravaged world after the millennia that have passed – and freed of the Master's baleful influence, they stand a chance of flourishing as a race once more.

TIME-FLIGHT

NEW INFORMATION

THE DOCTOR

The Doctor is evidently upset over Adric's death, but is angered when Tegan and Nyssa suggest he rematerialise on board the freighter to save him before the crash can occur. 'There are some rules that must not be broken even with the TARDIS,' he tells them, and demands they never ask him to do anything similar again. He points out that Adric died trying to save others, as did his brother Varsh back in E-Space (*Full Circle*), and that he wouldn't want them to grieve needlessly.

He uses the names of Brigadier Lethbridge-Stewart and UNIT to establish his credentials with airport security. He is the first to realise the illusion of Heathrow Airport is just that, and instructs his companions in how to break through the conditioning.

When trying to think of a way to outwit the Master, the Doctor finds it necessary to lie down on the floor of the TARDIS Control Room in order to concentrate.

THE TARDIS

The TARDIS is affected by 'time turbulence' created by an object travelling into the past along a time contour. It was attempting to reach Crystal Palace in 1851; instead it goes into 'hover mode' above Heathrow Airport, having travelled to one end of the time contour.

When its outer shell is stored horizontally, the inner dimensions are similarly angled until an override on the console restores the interior to normal.

Several components are taken from the TARDIS in the course of sabotage by the Concorde crew and cannibalisation of parts by the Master. But the ship is still able to deflect the Master's TARDIS all the way to the planet Xeriphas via what appears to be a form of time ram (see *The Time Monster*) – in the Doctor's words, it is 'knocked back into time–space like a straight six into the pavilion.'

COMPANIONS

NYSSA: Nyssa is distressed over Adric's death. Her sensitive nature and intelligence make her more appealing to the mental energies of the Xeraphin, who communicate with her and subsequently 'possess' her to use her as a mouthpiece.

TEGAN: Tegan is the most vocal and emotional at the death of Adric, and remains sullen throughout much of the adventure that follows. She is dismayed when the Doctor and Nyssa leave in the TARDIS without her, having assumed she wishes to remain at Heathrow in her own time.

Doctor: 'The Master has finally defeated me.'

In which the Doctor travels to Amsterdam and is 'executed' by Colin Baker on behalf of the Time Lords...
BY JOHNNY BYRNE
4 EPISODES, FIRST BROADCAST 3–12 JANUARY 1983

JOURNEY INFORMATION

THE ARC OF INFINITY

This is a naturally occurring 'gateway to the dimensions' in space, near Rondel, the location of a collapsed Q-star – a source of magnetic radiation and known to shield antimatter. It can be controlled and physically shifted through space through the exercising of enormous power, such as that existing on Gallifrey.

OMEGA

Omega was not destroyed by the collision of matter and antimatter that destroyed his realm in *The Three Doctors*. He made contact with a Time Lord on the High Council, Councillor Hedin, who it seems was able to supply him with a TARDIS. Hedin arranged for the transmission of a suitable bio-data extract to Omega that would allow the stranded temporal engineer to manifest himself as a Time Lord once more in the matter Universe – once he was able to draw upon the power of the space–time Matrix on Gallifrey.

Omega also required a particular fusion booster that only operated below sea level; and so chose Amsterdam as a suitable place to re-create himself – in the Doctor's image. However, once he realises that the transfer is unstable Omega attempts to will his own death in an enormous matter–antimatter explosion. The Doctor prevents him from doing so by using a matter converter against him, which banishes him from the matter Universe.

THE ERGON

This lumbering, bipedal beaked creature was created by Omega to act as his servitor. According to the Doctor it is one of his 'less successful attempts at psychosynthesis'.

NEW INFORMATION

THE DOCTOR

The Doctor's body is deemed by traitorous Time Lord Hedin to be the only one suitably compatible for physical bonding with Omega – hinting at his more complex origins which the series would later explore. The process of bonding knocks him unconscious.

He recognises the security compound on Gallifrey, and is incapable of picking the lock. He can find his way through certain levels on Gallifrey, despite the fact it has changed significantly since the last time he visited. He asks after Leela and her wedding, and defends his failure to return Romana to Gallifrey from E-Space, pointing out it was her choice.

Doctor: 'Executing me will not alter the fact that there's a traitor at work on Gallifrey!'

Killing Omega is something he finds deeply saddening; recalling his fêting of him as one of Gallifrey's greatest heroes in *The Three Doctors*.

THE TARDIS

The Doctor and Nyssa have repaired some of the TARDIS controls, including an audio facility on the scanner. Nyssa comments on the TARDIS's erratic steering, which the Doctor half-heartedly blames on the Cybermen's blasting of the console. She also reminds him of the malfunctioning of the 'temporal grace' feature that negates the function of any weaponry, but the Doctor is dismissive.

The TARDIS is breached by an extra dimensional manifestation that distorts its inner dimensions before attacking, and bonding with, the Doctor. The ship is later recalled to Gallifrey for apparently the third time since its construction (*The War Games* and *The Deadly Assassin*).

The removal of the TARDIS's main space–time element, kept in the base of the console itself, dims the lighting and renders the craft non-functional. After it is reinstalled, the console needs a hefty thump in order to dematerialise from Gallifrey.

COMPANIONS

NYSSA: She seems happier than the Doctor to have Tegan back as a travelling companion.

TEGAN: Since leaving the TARDIS, Tegan has found and lost employment as an air stewardess (and so swapped her traditional stewardess's outfit for white shorts and boob tube) and had her hair cut short. She goes to Amsterdam to visit her cousin, Colin Frazer. When captured by Omega and summoned into the Matrix, she risks her life to give the Doctor a clue to her location. Her final gleeful words to the Doctor are, 'You're stuck with me!'

BEHIND THE SCENES

ARCING THROUGH TIME AND SPACE

As early as September 1981, **Doctor Who**'s twentieth season was in the planning stages. Nathan-Turner was keen to feature overseas filming in the series for the second time in its history (the first being 1979's *City of Death*), and was inspired to use Amsterdam partly because a BBC soap opera, **Triangle**, already had a production base there.

With the location decided upon, writer Johnny Byrne was asked to submit a storyline for an adventure based in Amsterdam. By December the resultant synopsis, *The Time of Neman,* was delivered, but its location in an Amsterdam of the future seemed tangential to the plot, and the production office felt a reworking of the central concept was necessary.

By now Nathan-Turner was keen to have an old adversary brought back for the first serial of the new season, and offered Byrne a choice of past foes. Byrne opted to use Omega as the character was closest to his own creation of Neman. With the mythos of the Time Lords being explored, script editor Eric Saward was keen to set the story partly on Gallifrey. Byrne entitled the final scripts *Arc of Infinity*.

Having updated the Cybermen to critical acclaim, Nathan-Turner determined to do the same for Omega, reasoning that the dissolution of his Universe in his last appearance could easily have undone his old costume. Freelance contractors Imagineering again crafted a new look from costume designer Dee Robson's intricate designs. Omega's new appearance was also designed to prevent fans of the show – arguably the only people who would remember the villain following his one and only appearance a decade earlier – from recognising him. The character was credited in *Radio Times* only as 'The Renegade'.

As the new season evolved further, the Mara (last seen in *Kinda*) and the Black and White Guardians (first introduced in 1978's *The Ribos Operation*) were also set to return; Nathan-Turner decided it was suitably celebratory in the show's 20th anniversary year that a figure from its rich past should feature in every new adventure. The season was intended to close on a high note with the return of the Daleks, but a series of industrial disputes at Television Centre ultimately led to the postponement of this story until the twenty-first season (*Resurrection of the Daleks*). Instead, the run of new episodes finished prematurely with the two-part *The King's Demons*, featuring the Master.

Dojjen:
'Fear is the only poison.'

SNAKEDANCE

In which Martin Clunes behaves badly, and John Carson, Preston Lockwood and Johnathon Morris try to keep him from siding with the snakes...
BY CHRISTOPHER BAILEY
4 EPISODES, FIRST BROADCAST 18–26 JANUARY 1983

JOURNEY INFORMATION

MANUSSA

Manussa, according to TARDIS records, is a Type 314S planet and the third in a Federation of Worlds presided over by the Federator. Before the Manussan Empire was founded, the Sumaran civilisation existed – ruled by the Mara for around 600 years. The Manussans of the pre-Sumaran era had the ability to engineer on a molecular level in a zero-gravity environment but they were wiped out, presumably by the Mara once it had been brought into being.

Every ten years a pageant is held to celebrate the destruction of the Mara 500 years earlier by the founders of the Federation.

THE SNAKEDANCERS

The Snakedancers are akin to a religious sect, and believe that the Mara is not destroyed and will one day return. Only those with a completely pure mind can resist the Mara, and the 'Dance of the Snake' – involving the handling of live snakes and the ingestion of venom – was part of the ritual to ensure this stringent mental cleansing. The activity was banned 100 years earlier by the Federation, though the cult is still in existence, ignored by more 'civilised' society.

TARDIS DATA BANK:

DATE: UNKNOWN
LOCATION: PLANET G 139901 KB – MANUSSA, IN THE SCRAMPUS SYSTEM

WHEN TEGAN STEERS THE TARDIS TO MANUSSA, THE DOCTOR SOON REALISES SHE IS ACTING UNDER THE INFLUENCE OF A MALIGN FORCE THAT HAS POSSESSED HER BEFORE – THE MARA. THE MARA HAS BROUGHT ITSELF TO ITS HOME WORLD, WHERE THE DOCTOR MUST PREVENT ITS PHYSICAL BECOMING – AND THE SUBJUGATION OF AN ENTIRE CIVILISATION…

The Doctor: 'Why has the Mara returned, why now after so long ... and what does it want?'

THE MARA

The Mara that possessed Tegan on Deva Loka originated on Manussa. Manussan scientists created a Great Crystal using molecular engineering. It was supposedly capable of collecting and focussing all the energies of the human mind – but it absorbed only the negative ones, such as fear, anger, greed and hate. When these raw energies were reflected and amplified within the facets of the crystal, the Mara was created as an evil and aggressive intelligence able to manifest itself in the physical world as a snake-like creature.

When the Great Crystal is destroyed, the Mara's rebirth is prevented – with its spawning ground shattered it seems unable to retreat to the 'dark places of the inside' that have sustained it for so long. Tegan is presumably free of it forever. There are, however, other Mara lurking in shadowy dimensions and seeking access to the material world.

NEW INFORMATION

THE DOCTOR

The Doctor initially fails to notice when Nyssa changes into dramatically different clothes, but eventually concedes 'You look different.' He easily constructs a device to inhibit the brainwaves responsible for causing dreams and brings his well-established talents in hypnosis to bear on Tegan.

The Doctor is able to generate energy through the power of his mind by using the Little Mind's Eye crystal. This action summons the telepathically adept Dojjen. To communicate mentally with this hermit guru, the Doctor must partake of the venom of a poisonous snake. It is only with Dojjen's help he survives the ordeal, and is subsequently able to find the still point within himself; in so doing, and by concentrating on Dojjen and the crystal, he is able to prevent the Mara's becoming.

COMPANIONS

NYSSA: Nyssa, perhaps inspired by Tegan, has changed from her traditional Traken attire into a stripy skirt and blouse. She is put out when he fails to notice. She is also quite haughty when the Doctor helps her down a high step ('Thank you, but it wasn't necessary.')

TEGAN: Under the Doctor's hypnosis, Tegan recalls her possession by the Mara, vocalises a token resistance to its desires, and then regresses to being a mischievous six-year-old whose favourite place is her imaginary garden. When she drifts back further, the Mara speaks through her mouth and tells the Doctor to 'Go away.'

Whilst under the control of the Mara, in addition to the stained red teeth and snake emblem she had in *Kinda*, Tegan's eyes often glow red, and she turns a fairground showman into a mindless idiot in thrall to her. Eventually the Mara's influence grows to the point where she merges with it into a giant snake entity, her face still visible in its maw. However, she is finally able to resist the Mara's power, and helps to bring about its eventual overthrow.

'If I choose
to smooth the
way with a
smile and a
soft phrase,
that doesn't
make me
unreliable.'

(TURLOUGH – *TERMINUS*)

VIZLOR TURLOUGH, VTEC9/12/44

When we first meet Turlough, all we know is that he is an alien trapped on Earth – and he is very unhappy about it. His parents are dead, and his affairs are arranged long distance by a 'very strange' solicitor in Chancery Lane. He is condescending, and contemptuous of the school he is forced to attend and his fellow pupils, perhaps unsurprisingly since he clearly does not fit in, hailing from a far more advanced time zone.

Although he initially joins the Doctor in order to kill him on behalf of the Black Guardian, Turlough is no cold-blooded murderer. He is more amoral than immoral, with a strong sense of self-preservation; thus, since it absolves him of direct guilt, he attempts to convince the Black Guardian that leaving the Doctor stranded or helpless is as good as killing him.

Ultimately Turlough rejects the Guardian's mission, even turning down riches beyond imagining to be freed from his agreement; not only because of a genuine growing respect for the Doctor, but also because he dislikes being in thrall to anyone but himself.

Turlough seeks initially to return home to his own world, and his adventures along the way are initially only distractions along that path. But, ever the opportunist, he comes to recognise that travel with the Doctor offers him a unique chance to experience the Universe in a way few can enjoy.

Generally he stays clear of danger, but is still capable of acts of rash bravery (in *The King Demons* he threatens the Master with a sword simply because he's had enough of the abuse of his persecutors). But as he learns to respect both the Doctor and Tegan, so he is prepared to risk his life for them as they would for him; he saves them both from death on more than one occasion. This more caring attitude is demonstrated when he saves a total stranger (Peri) from drowning in Lanzarote in *Planet of Fire*, though from his exasperated mutter of 'Earthlings!' it's clear he would still rather not have the bother, and he makes no attempt to impress others with reports of his heroism.

Whether skulking about on a Dalek ship or creeping through the corridors of a futuristic sea-base, Turlough always seems more comfortable when he's holding a gun, and we eventually learn that he held a military rank on his home planet of Trion – that of Junior Ensign Commander – and was actually being held prisoner on Earth as a political exile. When he learns that political prisoners are no longer persecuted by the authorities, even though he is sorry to be leaving the Doctor, Turlough's dream of returning home becomes an actuality when an emmisary of Trion agrees to transport him back to the planet.

MAWDRYN UNDEAD

In which the Brigadier has retired to teach maths, and the
Black Guardian is out for revenge...
BY PETER GRIMWADE
4 EPISODES, FIRST BROADCAST 1–9 FEBRUARY 1983

JOURNEY INFORMATION

MAWDRYN'S MUTANTS

Mawdryn and his seven travelling companions – scientists
and sole mutant occupants of a luxury space liner – have
been travelling in exile for 3,000 years. Every 70 years the
ship is guided to a planet where the mutants can attempt to
find help for their condition.

Long ago, seeking to lengthen their lifespan, they stole
from Gallifrey a metamorphic symbiosis regenerator – used
by Time Lords in acute regenerative crises – in the belief it
would give them immortality. But because it lacked a vital
element only the Time Lords know of, the scientists adapted
the machine and accidentally induced a perpetual mutation
to their cellular make-up – condemning themselves to an
everlasting 'life without end or form'. Now they mutate and
degenerate ceaselessly but cannot die, something so
horrible they have been exiled by the elders of their planet.
Mawdryn calls it the Time Lords' curse. The Doctor calls it
the result of their own criminal ambition.

After so many tortured millennia the mutants long for
death. It seems they can only be killed by the potential
energy of a Time Lord's regeneration flowing through their
adapted generator. But, in fact, the energy caused by a
meeting of the Brigadier from 1977 with the Brigadier from
1983 as they short-out the time differential gives the mutants
the death they crave, and their ship dies with them.

BRIGADIER LETHBRIDGE-STEWART

The events of this story suggest the Brigadier had retired by
1977, although his earlier appearances indicate he was still in
active service with UNIT in the 1980s. It is possible that the
events of this story take place in a different dimension, or
perhaps the time distortion created by aberrations in the
warp ellipse has created temporal anomalies on Earth.

The Brigadier retired from UNIT in 1976 to teach A-level
maths at an English public school. In 1977 he met Tegan,
Nyssa and Mawdryn and travelled to Mawdryn's ship in the
TARDIS. His subsequent catastrophic meeting with his future
self induces a trauma superficially similar to a nervous
breakdown, and he loses all memory of the Doctor and his
adventures as a result. He does, however, recall Benton
(who left UNIT in 1979 and now sells second-hand cars) and
Harry Sullivan (seconded to NATO).

In 1983, he meets the Doctor. He claims he enjoys

teaching at the school as it's far better than retirement – here he can enjoy a 'bit of admin, bit of rugger, CO in the school corps.' His memory is restored by the Doctor.

THE BLACK GUARDIAN

Seeking revenge on the Doctor for his trickery over dispersing the Key to Time in *The Armageddon Factor*, but unable to be seen to be interfering in affairs of the cosmos, the Black Guardian recruits Turlough to kill the Doctor. He gives the boy a small crystalline communications device that glows when contact is made.

NEW INFORMATION

THE DOCTOR

The Doctor is significantly more interested in Nyssa's change of clothes this time than he was in *Snakedance*, reacting swiftly the moment she steps into the console room.

He is delighted to meet up with the Brigadier again, and prompts his friend's faulty memory by listing his companions during his third incarnation and mentioning the Yeti.

Mawdryn and the other scientists beg the Doctor to sacrifice all eight of his remaining regenerations so that they may know the luxury of death. He refuses until it becomes clear that Nyssa and Tegan will die unless he does so.

THE TARDIS

The lights in the Console Room dim when the warp ellipse cut-out is triggered by the danger of collision with a nearby vessel in fixed orbit in time and space. The Doctor performs an emergency dematerialisation to land the TARDIS on board the incoming ship. But the TARDIS subsequently cannot take off again because its systems are jammed by the ship's transmat signal. The Doctor claims this transmat pod and the TARDIS are 'dimensionally very similar.'

COMPANIONS

NYSSA: Nyssa disagrees with Tegan over the nature of Turlough, and feels she has to give Mawdryn the benefit of the doubt when he claims to be the Doctor. She is proved wrong on both counts.

She is accidentally infected with a variant of the mutation affecting Mawdryn; it makes both her and Tegan age physically if the TARDIS leaves the warp ellipse and goes forwards in time and regress to children if it goes backwards. She is finally cured in the blast of energy released by the two versions of the Brigadier meeting up and shorting out the time differential.

TEGAN: Still concerned that the Mara has not entirely left her mind and haunted by terrible dreams, Tegan receives little sympathy from a weary Doctor, who, we imagine, has tried to reassure her many times before now. He puts her bad dreams down to her mind's way of dealing with her traumatic experience. They have put her in a mood that is crabby even by Tegan's standards.

She has a hatred of transmat devices – 'like travelling in a food mixer and just as dangerous' – though since Nyssa seems neutral on the subject and Tegan has not previously encountered one, it is unclear where she has formed such an opinion.

TURLOUGH: Bored and seeking distraction, Turlough thinks nothing of stealing the Brigadier's car. Having crashed it, he undergoes an out-of-body experience. He does a deal with the Black Guardian and tells him that he wouldn't really mind if he were dead following the accident, as he hates the Earth and is desperate to leave.

His lack of personal honour is evident from the start – he tells his headmaster barefaced lies about how it was another boy, Ibbotson, who stole the Brigadier's car, and later lies to Ibbotson, saying he admitted full culpability himself. He also attempts to renege on his deal with the Black Guardian to kill the Doctor, but more for selfish reasons than simply of a change of heart (although he doubts his ability to murder, he seems ready to bring a rock down on the unsuspecting Doctor's head).

Doctor: 'Fools ... who tried to turn themselves into Time Lords. It all went disastrously wrong.'

TERMINUS

TARDIS DATA BANK:

DATE: UNKNOWN, FUTURE

LOCATION: A SPACE LINER EN ROUTE FOR TERMINUS INC. A MASSIVE STRUCTURE AT THE EXACT CENTRE OF THE UNIVERSE.

TERMINUS INC. CLAIMS TO OFFER HOPE OF A CURE FROM LAZAR'S DISEASE, A FATAL AFFLICTION SIMILAR TO LEPROSY – BUT THE TRUTH OF THE PLACE IS A GRIM ONE. TRAPPED ON BOARD AND WITH NYSSA SERIOUSLY ILL, THE DOCTOR DISCOVERS TERMINUS HOLDS THE SECRET TO THE BEGINNINGS OF THE UNIVERSE … AND VERY LIKELY ITS DESTRUCTION…

In which Nyssa gets Lazar's Disease, while Liza Goddard and Dominic Guard make guest appearances...
BY STEVE GALLAGHER
4 EPISODES, FIRST BROADCAST 15–23 FEBRUARY 1983

JOURNEY INFORMATION

TERMINUS

A huge ancient spacecraft, located at the precise centre of the known Universe, has been found and adapted by the company behind Terminus Inc. to act as a 'hospital' for sufferers of Lazar's Disease. But this 'ready-made' facility used to be capable of time travel. On a journey through time, according to the Doctor, some fuel was jettisoned into a void several billion years in the past, causing an explosion that created the Universe. Terminus rode out the shock wave through time and was deposited here. But an engine has become unstable, and should the ship's ancient systems attempt to jettison more fuel, the resultant cataclysmic explosion at the Universe's epicentre could destroy everything.

The old ship is vast, but seems to be piloted by just one humanoid. Its origin and true purpose remain a mystery.

THE VANIR

Playing on people's ignorance and traditional fears of Lazar's Disease, the company maximises profits by employing a slave labour force to run Terminus for them. The Vanir are humanoid 'baggage handlers – we receive and pass on'. The supervision of Lazars from cargo ship through to the forbidden zone is the only part of the treatment process they are privy to.

Their conditions are poor, but the company has gained a hold over the Vanir by making them drug-dependent – without regular ingestion of hydromel they grow weak and die. Nyssa resolves to synthesize a similar drug so that the Vanir may break free of the company's oppressive regime.

THE GARM

Of unknown origin, the Garm is a massive creature, dog-like in appearance, who is enslaved to the Vanir via a control box. He oversees the cure for Lazar's Disease – a dosage of radiation, but one adminstered so haphazardly that cured Lazars often trade one illness for another: they will suffer from radiation sickness in the future. The Garm wants to improve on the process, but his conditioning prevents him. The Doctor frees him from his servitude.

NEW INFORMATION

THE DOCTOR

The Doctor has two fights with Valgard, an armoured slave worker and would-be leader of the Vanir. He is almost throttled in their first encounter, but fares better in the second when, despite an injured right arm, he swiftly dispatches his opponent.

Recalling his pistol prowess in *The Visitation*, the Doctor shoots the lock off the hydromel store with a laser, then blows at the barrel as if clearing smoke. He is clearly dismayed when Nyssa elects to remain on *Terminus* and tries to persuade her to come with him. When that fails he concedes, 'You're a very brave person and I wish you every luck.'

THE TARDIS

Turlough, still acting on the Black Guardian's instructions, sabotages the ship by removing the space-time element. This element is stored in a different housing to the 'main' space-time element removed in *Arc of Infinity*, and blue controls hidden beneath a roundel in a corridor must be activated first. Removal of the element makes the central column jam, and causes dimensional instabilities within the TARDIS (particularly in Nyssa's room) as the outside Universe starts breaking through.

The Doctor initiates a 'safety cut-out', but the fail-safe has already kicked in – on impending break-up the TARDIS

'seeks out and locks on to the nearest spacecraft'. An interface then appears in the form of a door between the two vessels, but this is unstable and appears only sporadically. Turlough eventually restores the door by pulling on an emergency bypass device that has insinuated itself into the venting of the ship the TARDIS has locked on to.

COMPANIONS

NYSSA: Nyssa contracts Lazar's Disease while on board *Terminus*, which makes her feel weak and as though she's going to burst – she removes her skirt presumably to ease the pressure. Eventually she is subjected to the haphazard cure – which is successful. Moved by her near-death experience, and touched by the plight of fellow sufferers who are not so lucky, she resolves to stay on *Terminus* and improve conditions: 'I've enjoyed every moment of my time on the TARDIS... but here I have the chance to put into practice the skills I learned on Traken.'

TEGAN: Turlough incurs the full force of Tegan's wrath. She calls him 'the brat' and 'unreliable' and thinks he has the 'manners of a pig'. She later further denounces him as 'weird'.

TURLOUGH: Turlough is unimpressed when Tegan shows him to his new quarters on board the TARDIS – Adric's old room. He resolves to clear out the childish junk and clutter.

He sabotages the TARDIS even though this puts him in jeopardy. Later, he asks Tegan if she could kill in cold blood – he seems uneasier than ever with the idea, and confesses to the Black Guardian that he cannot kill the Doctor after all.

The Black Guardian punishes him with an energy burst that leaves him sick, weak and frightened.

Doctor: 'If we don't do something quickly the whole universe will be destroyed!'

ENLIGHTENMENT

In which sailing ships travel through space, captained by Keith Barron and Lynda Baron...
BY BARBARA CLEGG
4 EPISODES, FIRST BROADCAST 1–9 MARCH 1983

TARDIS DATA BANK:

DATE: UNKNOWN
LOCATION: THE REGION OF GALACTIC NORTH SIX DEGREES, NINE, ZERO, SEVEN, SEVEN – AROUND EARTH'S SOLAR SYSTEM

WARNED BY THE WHITE GUARDIAN OF DIRE DANGER AFFECTING THE BALANCE OF POWER IN THE UNIVERSE, THE TARDIS CREW FIND THEMSELVES GUESTS – OR PRISONERS – OF THE MYSTERIOUS ETERNALS WHO ARE HELL-BENT ON WINNING A RACE THROUGH THE SOLAR SYSTEM SO THAT THEY MAY CLAIM THEIR PRIZE: TRUE ENLIGHTENMENT…

JOURNEY INFORMATION

THE ETERNALS
Mind-reading, telepathic beings who function outside of time in the domain of eternity, the Eternals are tortured creatures endlessly seeking diversion to fill the emptiness in their infinitely long lives. To this end they exploit the minds and imaginations of other races – or 'Ephemerals' in their own vocabulary – to sustain their existence.

ENLIGHTENMENT
A number of Eternals are racing through space on mock sailing ships taken from different eras in Earth's history in order to win a particular prize – 'Enlightenment' – which is located in a dazzling giant crystalline structure. The Enlighteners are the Black and White Guardians, and each has selected a champion to influence the race – The White Guardian the Doctor, and the Black Guardian Captain Wrack. Since 'winner takes all', the granting of Enlightenment would seem to offer some cosmic advantage in the universal balance of power between light and dark. The Doctor declares that no one should receive Enlightenment, and the White Guardian agrees with him, banishing the Eternals to their own realm.

It seems likely that Enlightenment brings to its possessor whatever he or she needs – in the case of the Eternals, knowledge, imagination and ambition enough to sustain them endlessly. In the case of Turlough, the portion of Enlightenment offered to him is simply the self-knowledge to enable him to move on from his foolhardy contract with the Black Guardian, so that he may live freely again.

NEW INFORMATION

THE DOCTOR
Rather than raising a drink during Eternal Captain Striker's toast, the Doctor raises a spoonful of his dessert. He swaps a stick of celery in his lapel for a fresh piece during a feast on board Captain Wrack's ship.

THE TARDIS
The lights are low in the TARDIS, as it is the victim of a mysterious power drain. When the Doctor boosts the power to clear the communication circuits, smoke pours from the console and sections explode.

The scanner seems to be mounted in the light on top of the police-box shell. Black, tubular TARDIS torches are kept on board.

COMPANIONS
TEGAN: Tegan suffers from seasickness but is cured by a tonic administered by Marriner, one of the Eternals. She finds herself the object of his unwelcome attentions – he finds her mind a fascinating place and seeks her companionship to give him existence.

Doctor: 'We're not on a yacht, we're on a ship ... a spaceship.'

When Marriner furnishes a room for her from memories he sees in her mind, it is a mix of her room on board the TARDIS and her old bedroom in Brisbane. A framed photo of her Aunt Vanessa, her old air stewardess outfit and her costume from *Black Orchid* are all in evidence.

Dressing up for a party thrown by Captain Wrack, Tegan changes into a white Edwardian evening gown complete with wig and tiara. She seems quite glad to change back into her usual attire.

TURLOUGH: Ever the social chameleon, Turlough fits in well below decks with the crew of Striker's ship. Despite the Black Guardian's threats, he has no plans to kill the Doctor – and so is visited by the Guardian who condemns him to an eternity of torment on board the ship. Turlough impulsively attempts to kill himself by jumping overboard – he is, however, rescued. His suicidal tendencies are fleeting – later when he is trapped and close to destruction in the grid room on board Wrack's ship he screams to be rescued.

Finally, when both Guardians get together, Turlough is offered a clear choice – an enormous diamond worth an impossible fortune in exchange for the Doctor's life. Turlough agonises for a few moments then hurls the gem at the Black Guardian, who vanishes in flames, accepting defeat on this occasion.

Turlough: 'I will never serve you again.'

TARDIS DATA BANK:

APPEARANCE: SILVER BIPEDAL ANDROID WITH PARTIALLY TRANSPARENT CRANIUM
TRAVELLED: *THE KING'S DEMONS*. NOT SEEN AGAIN UNTIL *PLANET OF FIRE*

KAMELION

Kamelion is an android originally constructed as a weapon, capable of infinite form and personalities. He was used, and most likely created, by unidentified invaders of the planet Xeriphas. Following the Master's banishment there at the Doctor's hands (*Time-Flight*), the Master found Kamelion and was able to use him to effect an escape.

The android has a mind of his own, albeit a highly susceptible one – and is humble and benevolent unless turned to evil by his controller. By concentrating hard on a certain person the android will assume their identity; and through psychokinetics Kamelion can act and speak exactly as the person is visualised. If given even the most basic of commands he will behave in the style of his assumed character, embellishing his actions accordingly.

Kamelion does not relish the thought of being trapped on a medieval world, and is happy to join the Doctor. His activities while the Doctor continues his journeys are unknown, but he spends much time connected to the TARDIS data banks. Unfortunately, the Master has a particular hold on the android and even across massive distances, Kamelion is compelled to act on his will.

Crippled, unable to resist the Master and unwilling to betray his friends, Kamelion eventually begs the Doctor to kill him in *Planet of Fire*. The Doctor obliges, destroying him with the Master's tissue compression eliminator.

'We are a complex mass of artificial neurons'

(KAMELION – *THE KING'S DEMONS*)

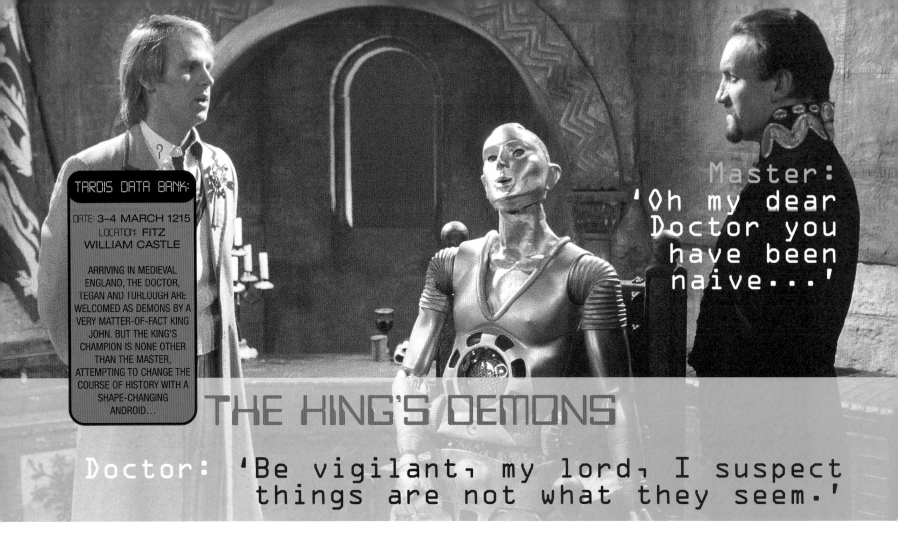

TARDIS DATA BANK:

DATE: 3–4 MARCH 1215
LOCATION: FITZ WILLIAM CASTLE

ARRIVING IN MEDIEVAL ENGLAND, THE DOCTOR, TEGAN AND TURLOUGH ARE WELCOMED AS DEMONS BY A VERY MATTER-OF-FACT KING JOHN. BUT THE KING'S CHAMPION IS NONE OTHER THAN THE MASTER, ATTEMPTING TO CHANGE THE COURSE OF HISTORY WITH A SHAPE-CHANGING ANDROID…

Master: 'Oh my dear Doctor you have been naive...'

THE KING'S DEMONS

Doctor: 'Be vigilant, my lord, I suspect things are not what they seem.'

In which the Master uses the robot Kamelion to impersonate King John in Frank Windsor's castle...
BY TERENCE DUDLEY
2 EPISODES, FIRST BROADCAST 15–16 MARCH 1983

JOURNEY INFORMATION

THE MASTER

The Master escaped the 'benighted' world of Xeriphas using Kamelion. He plans to undermine the key civilisations of the cosmos: 'Where I cannot win by stealth, I shall destroy. That way I cannot fail to win.'

He means to begin by altering history on Earth. His somewhat eccentric plan is to discredit King John, thereby preventing the granting of the Magna Carta. He escapes in his TARDIS, but the Doctor has used a tissue compression eliminator to warp the TARDIS dimensional controls – thus the Master will have no control over his chosen destination.

NEW INFORMATION

THE DOCTOR

The Doctor prevents the death of Fitz William's son on the jousting field by pointing out that in any trial of strength there is clearly a victor and a vanquished: 'Must blood be shed?'

He participates in a fight of his own against Sir Gilles Estram, the king's champion (in fact the Master). When told Sir Gilles is the best swordsman in France, he counters, 'Fortunately, we are in England' – and goes on to win, earning himself a knighthood from the bogus king.

In order to gain control of Kamelion the Doctor enters into a battle of wills with the Master. He wins, picturing Tegan as the model for the android to turn into.

THE TARDIS

Tegan dematerialises the TARDIS to provide a distraction, but has little control over it.

COMPANIONS

TEGAN: Tegan has discarded her traditional white outfit for a brightly coloured dress. When she fears for the Doctor's life, she hurls a knife at the Master's head with great accuracy. She later pilots the TARDIS on a brief journey, and is seriously unimpressed by Kamelion. Sulking when the android joins the TARDIS crew, she suggests he can have her quarters – but backtracks quickly when the Doctor threatens to take her back home.

TURLOUGH: Turlough's visit to medieval Earth is not a happy one – he spends much of the time locked up or threatened. He shows unexpected equine affinities, helping the knight Geoffrey de Lacey to saddle up a horse.

THE FIVE DOCTORS

In which all the Doctors celebrate their twentieth anniversary for *Children in Need*, with Richard Hurndall standing in for William Hartnell, and Tom Baker appearing in unused footage from *Shada*...

BY TERRANCE DICKS

90-MINUTE SPECIAL, FIRST UK BROADCAST 25 NOVEMBER 1983

TARDIS DATA BANK:

DATE: UNKNOWN – THE TARDIS IS TAKEN OUT OF TIME
LOCATION: THE EYE OF ORION; GALLIFREY; VARIOUS LOCATIONS ON EARTH

ONE BY ONE, THE DIFFERENT INCARNATIONS OF THE DOCTOR ARE BEING SNATCHED OUT OF TIME AND SPACE BY A TRAITOR ON GALLIFREY, TO TAKE PART IN A SINISTER GAME IN THE PLANET'S INFAMOUS DEATH ZONE. WHILE THE FOURTH DOCTOR IS TRAPPED IN A TIME EDDY, THE OTHERS ARE REUNITED WITH PAST COMPANIONS TO BATTLE OLD FOES AS THEY MAKE THEIR WAY TO THE DARK TOWER WHERE RASSILON HIMSELF LIES IN REST...

JOURNEY INFORMATION

THE DEATH ZONE ON GALLIFREY

Registering on the TARDIS as no place in no time, the Death Zone was an ancient arena used in Gallifrey's dark days. Alien beings were collected with a time scoop and made to fight for the amusement of the watching Time Lords. Towering over the barren wastelands of the zone is the Dark Tower, Rassilon's tomb.

Enemies gathered by the traitorous Borusa to play the game against the Doctor are a lone Dalek, a number of Cybermen, a Yeti (most likely of natural origin since it is afraid of fireworks) and a Raston Warrior Robot.

Past companions selected by Borusa are Sarah Jane, Susan, the Brigadier and the second Romana (though she is trapped in a time eddy along with the Fourth Doctor). Conjured as obstructive illusions are Jamie, Zoe, Mike Yates and Liz Shaw.

THE RASTON WARRIOR ROBOT

Similar in construction to the androids who guard the Cybermen's bomb portal in *Earthshock*, Raston Warrior Robots are, according to the Third Doctor, '... the most perfect killing machines ever devised. Armaments are built in and sensors detect movement – any movement.' The Robot produces arrows and blades from its hands, and can teleport itself over short distances to disorientate its enemies simply by leaping in the air. It massacres a party of Cybermen with ruthless efficiency.

THE MASTER

The Time Lords offer the Master a full and free pardon and a new life cycle of regenerations if he will find and rescue the Doctor from the Death Zone. He accepts – but is infuriated when the Doctors doubt his honesty. When trapped in the Death Zone he allies himself with Cybermen, but eliminates them as soon as they are of no further use to him. He craves Rassilon's gift of immortality and would find it gratifying to kill the Doctor three times over – but is knocked out by the Brigadier before he can do so.

NEW INFORMATION

THE FIFTH DOCTOR

While enjoying the tranquillity of the Eye of Orion, the Doctor has completely rebuilt the TARDIS console and refurbished the Console Room. When his first incarnation is taken out of time, he experiences a twinge of 'cosmic angst'. The effect worsens as more of his past selves are taken; he feels weak, 'diminished' and eventually starts to fade away. He stabilises once he arrives in the Death Zone, where his other selves have been transported.

He knows of the Game of Rassilon, as do his past incarnations, and knows that the Daleks and Cybermen have never before been selected to do battle in the Death Zone – they played Rassilon's game too well.

His musical abilities have progressed enormously since he played the wind chimes on Deva Loka (*Kinda*) – he can read music and is highly adept at playing the harp.

Once President Borusa has been exposed as the traitor and petrified on Rassilon's bier, the Doctor is called upon to become the new president of Gallifrey. He accepts, but places full deputising powers in the hands of Chancellor Flavia and goes on the run, happily accepting that his people will be furious with him: 'After all, that's how it all started.'

THE FIRST DOCTOR

The Doctor seems not to recognise the Master when he meets him: 'Do I know you young man?' He knows the value of pi to at least eight decimal places.

THE SECOND DOCTOR

The Doctor reveals that he once came up against 'the terrible Zodin'. He carries fireworks in his coat pocket.

THE THIRD DOCTOR

The Doctor recognises the Raston Warrior Robot from an undisclosed adventure. He is accurate with a lasso, and able to improvise a winch and pulley mechanism with a rock, a length of rope and his car, Bessie. He refuses to believe the Master could wish to help him, suspecting (wrongly) a trap.

THE TARDIS

Tegan wonders if the TARDIS will work properly following the Doctor's repairs. 'The TARDIS is more than a machine, Tegan, it needs coaxing, persuading, encouraging...' he says. He persuades the doors to open by giving the console a hefty thump. A force-field generated by the Dark Tower holds the TARDIS immobile until the Third Doctor reverses the polarity of the neutron flow.

COMPANIONS

TEGAN: Tegan arranges refreshments for the First and Fifth Doctors with bad grace, and help from Turlough. Oddly, she seems reproachful of the Master for executing a party of Cybermen: 'Wasn't that a little ruthless, even for you?'

TURLOUGH: Turlough tries sketching on the Eye of Orion.

BEHIND THE SCENES

FIVE OR SIX DOCTORS?

Producer John Nathan-Turner's original 20th anniversary proposal was to bring forward Peter Davison's second season to autumn 1982 instead of January 1983. The twenty-first season of **Doctor Who** could then be broadcast in autumn 1983, and include a multi-Doctor adventure. This was rejected by Controller of BBC1, Alan Hart. However, he indicated that a 90-minute special could be made, marking the anniversary. On 15 July 1982, Nathan-Turner was told formally he could proceed with production of this special.

Robert Holmes was approached to script the special. He submitted a storyline entitled *The Six Doctors* – so-called because the First Doctor, eventually played by Richard Hurndall as William Hartnell had died in 1975, would be revealed to be an android impostor. He ultimately withdrew from the project. Terrance Dicks was approached instead. In *The Five Doctors* he provided a story device – that of a shadowy 'player' assembling past Doctors, creatures and companions emblematic of the past – that could accommodate whichever actors were available for the shooting in March 1983. This proved fortuitous as characters and monsters were being confirmed as late as February – Deborah Watling dropping out as Victoria the day before filming began.

A blow to the special was the loss of Tom Baker from the cast. As early as April 1982 Nathan-Turner had approached Baker about appearing. He had agreed in principle – and by early December seemed enthusiastic about the project. But at the start of 1983 he explained to Nathan-Turner that he felt uncomfortable attempting to turn back the clock, and that he did not want to be just one of five Doctors. Instead, he agreed that footage from the unfinished story *Shada* could be incorporated into the special, so his presence would still be felt.

As it transpired, Baker was not the only lead actor uncertain of continuing his association with **Doctor Who**. Within weeks of completing *The Five Doctors*, Davison told Nathan-Turner that he would not be staying on as the Doctor beyond the twenty-first season. The actor felt in need of new challenges and had been frustrated by the lack of resources allocated to **Doctor Who** and a prolonged period of industrial action at Television Centre that had affected the twentieth season. Also, he had taken seriously advice offered by Patrick Troughton following a chance meeting: 'Don't stay more than three years.'

On 28 July, Davison's forthcoming departure was announced formally. By the time of *The Five Doctors*' broadcast there was a *sixth* waiting in the wings – to be played by Colin Baker.

WARRIORS OF THE DEEP

In which the Silurians and Sea Devils threaten Tom Adams' sea base, while Ingrid Pitt and Ian McCulloch turn traitor...

BY JOHNNY BYRNE

4 EPISODES, FIRST BROADCAST 5–13 JANUARY 1984

TARDIS DATA BANK:

DATE: 2084

LOCATION: ABOVE EARTH'S ATMOSPHERE BELT; SEABASE FOUR

MAKING AN EMERGENCY LANDING AT A SECRET MILITARY ESTABLISHMENT ON THE OCEAN FLOOR, THE DOCTOR LEARNS THE BASE IS THE TARGET OF A SMALL BAND OF SILURIANS AND THEIR SEA DEVIL ALLIES. BY LAUNCHING MISSILES FROM THE BASE, THE SILURIANS SEEK TO START A GLOBAL WAR THAT WILL WIPE OUT HUMAN LIFE AND LEAVE THE WORLD READY FOR REPTILE DOMINATION...

JOURNEY INFORMATION

SEABASE FOUR

The Earth of 2084 is divided into two unidentified power blocs, poised on the brink of war. Seabase Four, led by Commander Vorshak, is one of several undersea bases from which one bloc monitors the other. It is heavily armed with proton missiles, which wipe out human life while leaving the environment relatively undamaged.

To eliminate any danger of computer error, the launching of missiles is controlled by a synch operator – a specially conditioned human whose mind can interface with the weapon systems.

SENTINEL SIX

An armed military satellite patrolling a military zone above Earth's atmosphere, Sentinel Six is programmed to obliterate any craft that violates its territorial parameters unless certain access codes are transmitted. It attacks the TARDIS.

THE MYRKA

A huge, aggressive quadrupedal reptile with stubby forearms, bred by the Silurians as a living weapon, the Mykra is a bio-engineered creature capable of electrifying its victims – but can be destroyed by violent exposure to certain wavelengths of light. The Doctor kills it with an ultra-violet converter.

THE SILURIANS

The Silurians have changed their appearance, perhaps through bio-engineering akin to that which bred the Myrka. For instance, their 'third eyes' – which were previously used both as tools and weapons – now only flash mechanically to signify who is talking.

Ichtar, last of the Silurian Triad, knows the Doctor; it is possible that he is the scientist the Third Doctor met in *The Silurians*. The reptiles now refer to themselves as Silurians although this is their (inaccurate) human classification – perhaps choosing to adopt the enemy's own term as a gesture of defiance.

Ichtar and his companions, Scibus and Tarpok, seek revenge on the human race, and plan to use humanity's own weapons against them. With a device referred to as the manipulator, they can bypass human technology to launch the Seabase's proton missiles.

THE SEA DEVILS

The Silurians revive a military caste of 'Sea Devils' (again, the creatures use the term coined for them by humans) – Elite Group 1 warriors in ceremonial armour. They have been

Ichtar: 'For hundreds of years our Sea Devil brothers have lain entombed waiting for this day.'

hibernating in a flooded cavern for 'hundreds of years', so may have awakened and returned to hibernation for reasons unknown.

Their leader, Sauvix, announces that he and his troops are Ichtar's to command. They are not instrumental in his plans beyond military muscle.

NEW INFORMATION

THE DOCTOR

The Doctor can swim under water. He is very knowledgeable about both the world of 2084 and the Silurians. He recognises a Silurian underwater battle cruiser, and the Myrka, and has met Ichtar before, knowing he is the last of the Silurian Triad.

His mind can interface with the base's missile control computers without the computer implant needed by human synch operators – but he suffers pain and bruising around his eyes as a result.

THE TARDIS

The TARDIS initially overshoots the date the Doctor has programmed into its systems, and having landed above Earth's atmosphere finds it difficult to move on. 'I should've changed for a Type 57 when I had the chance,' the Doctor grumbles, presumably referring to his recent visit to Gallifrey.

The TARDIS seems particularly susceptible to the attack from Sentinel Six; the lighting turns red and it goes out of control. The Doctor performs a 'materialisation flip-flop' to save the ship, then tampers with circuitry in the base of the console to land it properly, at Seabase Four.

The damage is extensive and will take time to repair – the Doctor feels the job will be easier with the permission of whoever's in charge of the base. The doors seem affected, as they do not lock – combat marines gain access to the ship, and report to their commander on its alien nature.

COMPANIONS

TEGAN: Tegan has asked the Doctor to show her a little of her planet's future. When the Doctor is knocked into the deep water of the reactor room, she immediately tries to rescue him, but is hauled away by Turlough. Later she is fiercely indignant at being left outside the bridge while the Doctor goes in, but still wishes him luck.

TURLOUGH: When the Doctor and Tegan are trapped by the Myrka and Commander Vorshak orders them abandoned, Turlough overpowers a guard, takes his gun in order to have them released, and rescues the Doctor for the first time.

THE AWAKENING

In which Polly James finds herself threatened by an alien device built into a church wall and the Civil War comes to life again...

BY ERIC PRINGLE

2 EPISODES, FIRST BROADCAST 19–20 JANUARY 1984°

TARDIS DATA BANK:

DATE: PRESENT
LOCATION: LITTLE HODCOMBE, ENGLAND

THE RESIDENTS OF LITTLE HODCOMBE, LED BY OBSESSIVE LOCAL MAGISTRATE SIR GEORGE HUTCHINSON, AIM TO RE-ENACT A VICIOUS CIVIL WAR BATTLE FOUGHT IN 1643. IN THIS WAY THEY WILL REVIVE AN EVIL INTELLIGENCE THAT HAS LURKED IN THE LOCAL CHURCH FOR HUNDREDS OF YEARS – THE MALUS…

JOURNEY INFORMATION

HAKOL

'On Hakol,' explains the Doctor, 'psychic energy is a force that's been harnessed in much the same way as electricity is here.' The people of Hakol, in the star system Rifter, sent a computerised reconnaissance probe to Earth to clear the way for an invasion, with the Malus on board. The invasion, for reasons unknown, never took place, and the Malus fell dormant.

THE MALUS

The Doctor describes the Malus as '... a living being re-engineered as an instrument of war.' It has one purpose: to destroy. 'It's the only thing it knows how to do,' he laments.

The Malus was aboard the Hakol probe, which landed hundreds of years ago, long before the English Civil War. It was roused for a time by the psychic energy generated during a 1643 battle at Little Hodcombe, but its influence subsided again when both sides wiped themselves out.

Possessed of enormous power, it is capable of intermingling different time zones, allowing real people to pass through the centuries to create energies it can feed on such as fear. It can conjure intimidating phantoms ('psychic projections with substance') from the past to achieve a similar effect.

When it knows it has lost – with its familiar, Hutchinson, dead and its means of feeding on psychic energy blocked by the Doctor's work in the TARDIS – it aims to fulfil its original program and clear the ground, destroying everything that it can. The church that has housed it for so long is obliterated in a massive explosion.

SIR GEORGE HUTCHINSON

When Tegan's grandfather, Andrew Verney, discovered the Malus buried in the church, he told Sir George Hutchinson, who owned the land. Hutchinson, partially deranged, caused the entity's awakening in the misguided belief he could control it. The Malus has promised him and his followers great power if he arranges to generate the psychic energy it needs by re-creating the carnage of Civil War battle that revived it in 1643.

Ultimately he is killed by Will Chandler – a youth from 1643 transported through time by the Malus – who pushes him into the waking entity's face.

NEW INFORMATION

THE DOCTOR

The Doctor again displays his knowledge of matters Terileptil; he knows that they mine tinclavic for the use of the people of Hakol. He also knows the nature of Hakol warfare.

While he is reluctant to stay in Little Hodcombe once the Malus has been disposed of, the Doctor eventually agrees to linger for a short while only.

THE TARDIS

The Malus sets up a projection of itself inside the TARDIS, one of several such focuses for concentrating the psychic energy it needs to revive itself. The Doctor locks the signal conversion unit on the frequency of the psychic energy feeding the Malus, then blocks it; the manifestation dies as a result.

COMPANIONS

TEGAN: Wishing to see her English grandfather, Tegan has requested the TARDIS visit Little Hodcombe.

She is forced to wear a seventeenth-century dress and bonnet to become the village's Queen of the May – a sinister old tradition that will involve her being burnt to death, as was her counterpart in 1643. ('The toast of Little Hodcombe,' observes the Doctor.) But Tegan is spared such a fate when one of Hutchinson's men, Ben Wolsey, comes to his senses and stuffs the dress with straw: 'Not as attractive as Tegan, but more humane.'

Cheerily commenting, 'Never a dull moment,' when reunited with her grandfather, she petitions the Doctor to stay in Little Hodcombe for a time.

TURLOUGH: Turlough is reluctant to rush out and risk being crushed by falling rubble in order to save someone glimpsed on the TARDIS scanner by the Doctor and Tegan. Similarly, he is more than happy to return to the safety of the TARDIS when the Doctor suggests it.

> Hutchinson: 'Something is coming to our village – something very wonderful and strange.'

The Doctor:
'I'm not helping you, officially. And if anyone happens to ask whether I made any material difference to the welfare of this planet, you can tell them I came and went like a summer cloud.'

FRONTIOS

In which giant grub-like Tractators drag people under the ground, while Jeff Rawle, Lesley Dunlop and Peter Gilmore try to stop them...

BY CHRISTOPHER H. BIDMEAD
4 EPISODES, FIRST BROADCAST 26 JANUARY–3 FEBRUARY 1984

JOURNEY INFORMATION

THE COLONY ON FRONTIOS

Frontios is a distant, apparently deserted inhospitable world, without wood or any other combustible material. The colony ship crashed on Frontios 40 years earlier, on what is known as the 'Day of Catastrophe'. Many died in the crash, and more died in an outbreak of disease soon after.

Ten years later, once the reduced colony of humans had established itself, a bombardment of meteorites began – and was to last 30 years. During this time, Frontios was led by the much-respected Captain Revere. When he was 'eaten by the earth', control of the colony passed to his son, Plantaganet.

THE TRACTATORS AND THE GRAVIS

The Tractators have been on Frontios for 500 years. Led by the Gravis, a Tractator with highly developed mental and gravitational powers, they forced down the colony ship. Giving the colonists ten years to establish themselves, they attacked them by bringing down bombardments of meteorites. This ensured a steady supply of weak and injured humans unable to resist the Tractators taking them below ground and using their minds and bodies to power their mining machines.

The Tractators have been manufacturing mathematically precise tunnels that will act as waveguides to concentrate gravitational forces. The astronomical power thus supplied will create a gravity motor that will enable them to steer the entire planet through space – enabling them to steal and plunder wherever they go, and to breed and infest new planets.

The Gravis knows of the Doctor. He craves the ability to travel, having been stuck on Frontios for so long. But when the Gravis is tricked into reassembling the TARDIS, thinking he will be able to pilot it, its reformed shell stops his mental emissions from reaching the minds of his people. Without the Gravis, the Tractators are harmless burrowing creatures. The Gravis does get to travel in the TARDIS – but only to the uninhabited planet of Kolkokron, where he is marooned.

NEW INFORMATION

THE DOCTOR

The Doctor is unusually concerned about breaking the Laws of Time by becoming involved with the fledgling Earth colony on Frontios: 'Knowledge has its limits – ours reaches this far and no further.' Once he arrives he immediately helps out the colonists – on being told they are helpless, he rallies: 'Not if I have anything to do with it.' But – perhaps more nervous about his abdication of the presidency on Gallifrey than he has been letting on – he is keen that his interference be kept quiet should the Time Lords come asking.

The Doctor's half-moon spectacles make a reappearance, and he gives a cricketing cry of 'Howzat!' when he successfully bowls over two Tractators. Later, he is about to try an 'experiment' that would seem to involve a cricket ball when one of the creatures distracts him.

THE TARDIS

An alarm sounds when the TARDIS drifts too far into the future and exceeds certain time parameters. The ship should be able to resist a meteor storm, but the Tractator's gravitational assault jams the console and forces an emergency landing on Frontios. The Doctor says that, 'As an invasion weapon [the TARDIS is] about as offensive as a chicken vol-au-vent. Its lack of armaments can be a positive embarrassment at times...'

Its inner dimensions warp against its outer shell as the Tractators' powers continue to affect it, until eventually a catastrophic schism develops – the outer shell breaks up and the 'insides' of the TARDIS are dragged beneath the surface of Frontios. The Doctor later says (perhaps as a bluff) that its interior dimensions have been 'spatially distributed to optimise the packing efficiency of the real-time envelope' – effectively they have been mapped on to a portion of the planet's labyrinthine interior – which implies the TARDIS is of finite mass (indeed the Doctor ejects 25 per cent of its mass in *Castrovalva*).

The massive gravitational power of the Gravis successfully drags together the TARDIS interior and allows the outer plasmic shell to reform, thus making it a whole vessel once more.

COMPANIONS

TEGAN: Tegan unwillingly masquerades as a Gallifreyan serving machine with faulty programming when the Doctor attempts to convince the Gravis he's on his side. He claims, 'I got it cheap because the walk's not quite right ... and then there's the accent. But when it's working well it's very reliable for keeping track of appointments, financial planning, word processing ... that sort of thing.' Even though she is aware of what he says, and is restrained in a gravity field, she is speechless with fury.

TURLOUGH: Turlough is sent into a state of shock when the sight of Tractators stirs deep ancestral memories. Overcoming an emotional block (which hides terrifying details of his planet's 'infection' that he doesn't want to face), he is able to use this knowledge to help the colonists.

He carries a Two-Corpira piece in his pocket – the bearer blows through it for luck.

RESURRECTION OF THE DALEKS

In which Leslie Grantham repairs Davros, while Rula Lenska and Rodney Bewes try to stop the Daleks...
BY ERIC SAWARD
TWO DOUBLE-LENGTH EPISODES, FIRST BROADCAST 8–15
FEBRUARY 1984

TARDIS DATA BANK:

DATE: 1984; THE FUTURE
(90 YEARS AFTER THE EVENTS OF *DESTINY OF THE DALEKS*)
LOCATION: LONDON DOCKLANDS, EARTH; A PRISON STATION IN
SPACE; DALEK WARSHIP

DRAGGED THROUGH AN ALIEN TIME CORRIDOR LEADING TO TWENTIETH-CENTURY EARTH,
THE DOCTOR BECOMES CAUGHT UP IN THE MACHINATIONS OF HIS SCHEMING ARCH-
ENEMIES. THE DALEKS SEEK TO LIBERATE DAVROS, THEIR CREATOR, FROM PRISON SO HE
MIGHT DEVISE A CURE FOR THE MOVELLAN VIRUS THAT IS WIPING OUT THE DALEK FLEET.
BUT THE DOCTOR ALSO FEATURES IN THEIR PLANS ... AND TEGAN FINDS SHE CAN'T
ENDURE HIS VIOLENT WORLD ANY LONGER...

JOURNEY INFORMATION

THE DALEKS

It is revealed that Dalek creatures cannot only survive outside of their casings for a time, but can also move about and attack their enemies, possessing the ability to leap and lacerate.

Having finally lost their war with the Movellans – who created a virus that corrodes and destroys both the Dalek creature and its casing – the Daleks, led by the Dalek Supreme, nevertheless have complex plans for the resurrection of their race. Their main aim is to use Davros's skills to find an antidote and breed resistance to the virus. They have employed a team of humanoid mercenaries, led by Lytton, to help them storm the prison station that houses Davros. But they have a number of ancillary schemes simultaneously in progress.

They plan to send duplicates of the Doctor and his friends to Gallifrey, specially programmed to assassinate the members of the High Council of the Time Lords. Such an audacious crime would not only cause chaos in the monitoring and policing of the Universe, but might also restore the Daleks' notoriety as truly a force to reckon with – a show of strength to their Movellan oppressors.

In order to carry out this scheme, the real Doctor, Tegan and Turlough are needed. The Daleks set up a time corridor to ensnare the TARDIS and drag it to abandoned docklands on Earth, which are convenient for the Daleks because they have also been replacing key political figures on the planet with their duplicates, ready for use at an unspecified time of invasion.

DAVROS

Davros has been in cryogenic suspension for '90 years of mind-numbing boredom' – he was conscious for every second of his incarceration on the prison station, but unable to move. Not trusting the Daleks, he utilises a hypodermic device (concealed in his travel chair) which injects a drug that bends the will of others to his own. Soon he has assembled a small army of slaves, including two Daleks.

When faced with execution at the Doctor's hands, he initially pleads that he plans to alter the Daleks' programming so that they may have insight into emotions such as compassion – but the Doctor recognises this will only make them a more positive force for destruction. Davros argues that war is a universal way of life, but when the Doctor disagrees the wizened scientist realises the Doctor cannot be serious in his intent to kill him, and goads him for his indecisiveness: 'Action requires courage – something you lack.'

Ultimately, Davros plans to wipe out the Daleks that have freed him by releasing the Movellan virus, so that he may proceed with re-creating a new race of Daleks, loyal only to him. But the virus has a debilitating effect on Davros too, leaving him injured, with his travel chair malfunctioning.

LYTTON

The ruthless, mysterious mercenary, Lytton, has been employed by the Daleks to aid them in their plans.

A good tactician – his plan of using gas weapons against the crew of the prison station before sending in troopers succeeds where the Daleks' attempt to storm the station fails – he remains at liberty at the end of the adventure, departing into London with two bogus policeman accomplices.

NEW INFORMATION

THE DOCTOR

When the Daleks announce their plan to use genetic doubles of the Doctor and his companions to assassinate the High Council of Time Lords, the Doctor is horrified. When his brain-

Tegan: 'A lot of good people have died today. I'm sick of it... My Aunt Vanessa said, when I became an air stewardess, if you stop enjoying it, give it up... It's stopped being fun, Doctor.'

waves are read by the Daleks, ready for insertion into his duplicate, the Doctor visualises all his companions since he left Earth with Ian, Susan and Barbara in 1963 – except Leela and Kamelion.

The Doctor resolves to kill Davros, but is ultimately unable to carry out the execution when he has the chance. He does, however, wipe out an entire Dalek squad single-handed, using Dalek bombs and a canister containing the Movellan virus. When Tegan leaves, traumatised by the violence and horror she has witnessed, he pleads, 'Don't let it end, not like this!' Nevertheless, he respects her reasons as being similar to his own when he left Gallifrey in the first place – he'd got tired of the lifestyle. 'It seems I must mend my ways,' he laments to Turlough.

THE TARDIS

The TARDIS is trapped and buffeted about in the Daleks' time corridor, but the Doctor is able to break free from it and follow the passage through to its destination without further difficulty or damage.

The Doctor uses the TARDIS remote control facility to take Turlough and Tegan back to Earth on preset coordinates.

The Dalek Supreme is able to project an image of itself on to the TARDIS scanner and grates out threats and warnings via the audio channel.

COMPANIONS

TEGAN: Injured during a Dalek attack, Tegan has little chance to recuperate. Held prisoner by Dalek duplicates while other people are killed all about her, her ordeal leaves her feeling it's time to part ways with the Doctor. However, she seems to change her mind, rushing back tearfully to the warehouse where the TARDIS landed, just as it dematerialises. 'Brave heart, Tegan,' she tells herself, echoing the Doctor's old rallying cry. 'Oh, Doctor I will miss you.'

TURLOUGH: Skulking uncertainly through both the Dalek ship and then the prison station, Turlough spends his time trying to evade capture. He says a muted goodbye to Tegan, taking her hand in both of his.

BEHIND THE SCENES

CHANGING TIMES

With the BBC planning extensive coverage of the Winter Olympics for its fortnight's duration in February 1984, it was obvious that the week-night transmission of **Doctor Who** would be disrupted. For this season the programme was airing on Thursday and Friday evenings, but John Nathan-Turner was informed that these slots would not be available. Rather than have **Doctor Who** taken off air for two weeks in the middle of its run, the producer decided to re-edit the four 25-minute episodes of *Resurrection of the Daleks* into two double-length instalments, to be shown on consecutive Wednesdays. The precedent had been set before with various repeats of the show edited into special compilations, but this would be the first time a **Doctor Who** story premiered in extended episodes.

Broadcast on a different day of the week, and boasting not only the fully fledged return of the Daleks after five years (excluding a cameo appearance in *The Five Doctors*) but also the departure of popular companion, Tegan, the episodes performed well in the TV ratings. This success seemed to confirm the wisdom of the decision that had already been taken for a full-time change of format for the programme. For the next season – *Attack of the Cybermen* to *Revelation of the Daleks* – **Doctor Who** would be scripted and broadcast as 45-minute episodes.

Resurrection of the Daleks has nevertheless been broadcast overseas and released on both VHS home video and DVD, in four-episode form as originally edited.

PERPUGILLIAM BROWN – 'Peri'

Born 13 November 1965 and based in Pasadena, California, Peri is a botany student holidaying in Lanzarote when she becomes involved in the Doctor's adventures. Attempting to cut loose from her mother and domineering stepfather who have taken her there on an archaeology trip, Peri plans to go to Morocco for the remaining months of her vacation with some 'nice' English boys she's met. Instead, she winds up travelling considerably further afield with the Doctor.

Peri's first impressions of the Doctor are favourable and she seems comfortable with him; the two of them quickly develop an easy, relaxed sparring. However, once the Doctor regenerates – having sacrificed his fifth life for her – Peri is left feeling frightened and alienated by the character who replaces him. 'You were young!' she protests. 'I really liked you ... and you were sweet!'

Reacting badly to the post-regenerative antics of the new Doctor – being insulted, abused and even throttled – Peri loses some of her confidence, both in her own abilities and those of the Doctor. Her relationship with him becomes more abrasive as a result, though she still allows herself to be led by him. She sees him as being unstable, and criticises his various mental lapses and the blunders he has made in the TARDIS since regenerating. Indeed, the two frequently swap personal insults or goad each other on anything from the usage of slang words to each other's weight, and the affection that they seemed to feel for each other appears to be greatly diminished. It is telling that in Victorian England, when Peri thinks the Doctor is dead and then discovers him alive, rather than react with relief she sulkily complains that she was afraid she would have to wear her period dress for ever.

On her travels, Peri often finds herself the unwilling target of male affections. In various stories, Sharaz Jek

eulogises her beauty and her importance to him; crazed mastermind the Borad wishes her to be his mate; and the lecherous Jobel wants to seduce her. Her reaction is usually nervous indifference masking a desire to escape as quickly as possible. When in danger or under stress, she is prone to stuttering, but is still feisty enough to knock back all but the most intimidating of antagonists.

After *Revelation of the Daleks,* an unspecified period of time passes before we meet Peri and the Doctor next. They seem to have mellowed in their attitude towards each other in *The Trial of a Time Lord.* For instance, she is happy to lecture him on the perils facing her planet's flora and fauna and he is happy to listen, instead of picking apart her argument with the voice of greater experience. Equally, he is

> 'I'm Perpugilliam Brown, and I can shout just as loud as you can!'
>
> (PERI – *PLANET OF FIRE*)

quietly understanding and not in the least disparaging of her pain when she believes her world to have been entirely destroyed.

But, ironically, this new-found affection has little chance to flourish. Peri parts company with the Doctor on Thoros-Beta, but exactly how is unclear due to distortions in the Matrix's representation of events. Initially it seems she is killed – her body used to house the mind of an alien creature. But later Time Lord testimony reports she in fact married the voluminous warlord King Yrcanos. The two make an odd couple; but perhaps not a good deal more so than Peri and the Sixth Doctor.

PLANET OF FIRE

In which the TARDIS lands in Lanzarote – which also doubles for the planet Sarn where Peter Wyngarde is in charge – and the Master has shrunk...

BY PETER GRIMWADE

4 EPISODES, FIRST BROADCAST 23 FEBRUARY–2 MARCH 1984

TARDIS DATA BANK:

DATE: 1984; UNKNOWN
LOCATION: LANZAROTE, EARTH; THE PLANET SARN

THE PEOPLE OF SARN ARE DIVIDED INTO THOSE WHO BELIEVE IN THE DEITY LOGAR, THE FIRE GOD, AND RATIONALISTS WHO CLAIM HE IS A FICTION. THE DOCTOR SOON LEARNS THAT BOTH CAMPS ARE THREATENED WITH EXTINCTION, NOT ONLY FROM THE RUMBLING VOLCANOS THAT DOMINATE THEIR WORLD BUT ALSO FROM THE MASTER WHO IS IN SEARCH OF A REJUVENATING GAS LOCKED DEEP IN SARN'S FIERY DEPTHS.

JOURNEY INFORMATION

SARN

On Sarn, the natives have traditionally worshipped Logar, the Lord of Fire – a view maintained by Timanov, leader of the Elders. However, a group of 'heretical' unbelievers, led by Amyand, also have influence in the Sarn civilisation – they believe Logar is only a myth.

When the Doctor arrives it is the 'Time of Fire' – a volcanic eruption is not far off. According to Timanov, a figure known as the Outsider is sent by Logar to help the Sarns through such a time, bearing gifts (actually technology such as the laser lances carried by guardsmen).

We discover this is a misinterpretation of actual events – the people of Trion tried to civilise the planet so they could send their undesirables there.

TRION

The Trions are a highly advanced civilisation that has colonised worlds and possesses 'agents' on every civilised planet. One such agent, in the guise of an eccentric solicitor in Chancery Lane, London, monitored Turlough's exile at Brendon School.

A civil war on Trion led to the expulsion of many deemed politically undesirable, who were branded with a special mark: the Misos Triangle. However, things have now changed on Trion and Turlough learns he is at liberty to return home, or to continue his travels.

The Trion Communications Executive is a rapid response unit – upon receiving a call, they are able to prepare and send a rescue ship in a matter of hours.

THE MASTER

Attempting to build a deadlier version of his tissue compression eliminator, the Master has accidentally shrunk himself to minuscule size. He forces Kamelion to act for him in arranging his rebirth through a dosage of healing numismaton gas trapped in pockets deep in the volcanic rock of Sarn.

His tampering with the Trions' seismic control devices has disrupted the inhibition system keeping the volcanic reactions in check – he has brought Sarn to the brink of destruction.

Ultimately the Doctor tampers with the gas flow, causing flames to apparently consume the Master shortly after he has restored himself to his former size.

NEW INFORMATION

THE DOCTOR

With a single lick of sooty deposits the Doctor can detect the residue of numismaton gas.

The Doctor first cripples Kamelion – inflicting upon him a computerised heart attack – then, at the android's request, kills him. Soon after, the Master begs to be saved from the death trap the Doctor has rigged, but he mournfully holds firm. The Doctor is clearly very affected by what he takes to be his old adversary's death.

He anticipates Turlough is leaving, and tells the youth, 'I'll miss you.'

THE TARDIS

When Kamelion is connected to the TARDIS data banks via a roundel in a corridor, he can reset the coordinates remotely. He also uses the TARDIS to computerise distress signals into navigational data. Yanking out a bundle of wires from within the console disables its ability to pick up distress calls.

The removal of the ship's comparitor leaves it useless. When the component is restored, the Doctor is still unable to materialise round the Master's TARDIS (and so stops him from taking off) because the Master has taken the vital temporal stabiliser.

Peri: 'Have I seen everything today! A transgalactic payphone, a stepfather who turns into a robot and a robot who turns into a gangster!'

COMPANIONS

TURLOUGH: Recognising a distress call to be of Trion origin, Turlough panics and cuts off the signal. While he is able to program an algorithm to soothe Kamelion's troubled mind, he later alters this to inflict damage on the android when he suspects him of subterfuge.

A capable swimmer, he saves Peri (with bad grace) from drowning and carries her back to the TARDIS to recuperate.

He is able to recognise and operate Trion machinery. It transpires that Turlough himself hails from Trion, but was exiled to Earth following a civil war that saw his mother killed and his father and younger brother banished to a penal planet. He is branded with the Misos Triangle, an overlapping triangular design on his upper arm that marks him as a political prisoner.

Reunited with his brother, Malkon, Turlough learns that his exile has been rescinded and decides to return home.

KAMELION: The Master's mind has maintained a mental link with Kamelion ever since they escaped Xeriphas together, and Kamelion even feels the Master's pain. However, exposing the android to another mind can weaken the Master's hold and causes 'psychomorphic printing – an intermediate stage between anthropoid and robotic identity'. When Peri causes this, Kamelion is able to assert his own identity: 'I am Kamelion ... was Kamelion.' He recovers enough to disable the TARDIS (so the Master cannot get it) and tell Peri to leave before the Master reasserts his influence.

Once on Sarn, he is more susceptible to the Master's influence and can no longer resist it. Finally he begs the Doctor to end his misery: 'Kamelion ... no good. Sorry. Destroy me – please?' The Doctor swiftly eliminates Kamelion by blasting him with the Master's tissue compression eliminator.

PERI: Marooned on her stepfather's boat, Peri attempts to swim for the shore and almost drowns in the attempt.

She seems adept at controlling Kamelion; even the Master comments that her will is strong. When she discovers the Master has been minaturised, she seems ready to squash him with her shoe.

THE CAVES OF ANDROZANI

In which Christopher Gable wears a mask, Robert Glenister plays an android, Maurice Roeves gets trigger happy, and everyone wants to live forever...
BY ROBERT HOLMES
4 EPISODES, FIRST BROADCAST 8–16 MARCH 1984

JOURNEY INFORMATION

ANDROZANI MINOR

A desert world, the core of Androzani Minor is superheated mud. It is riddled with a series of blowholes, like an immense network of caves. When its orbit brings it close to Androzani Major, the gravitational pull of the larger planet causes 'mud-bursts' – with molten geysers of mud erupting from deep within the surface.

The caves are infested with bat colonies and bipedal reptilian carnivores exist in the planet's magma, leaving the magma only to forage for flesh. Androzani Minor is also the world where spectrox – an incredibly valuable substance that can extend human life – was discovered.

SHARAZ JEK

Once a doctor, before the study of androids took his professional interest, Sharaz Jek entered into partnership with businessman Morgus to harvest spectrox. Morgus needed androids to collect and refine the substance, since it was too toxic for humans to handle. But Morgus plotted to kill Jek, supplying him with faulty detection instruments when a mud burst was imminent. Almost killed by the scalding mud, Jek saved himself by reaching a baking chamber; but was hideously disfigured. In revenge, Jek eventually took control of the vital stores of the spectrox refinery with the help of an android army.

Starved of company, and beauty, Jek becomes infatuated with Peri. By feeding her spectrox he can preserve her beauty and, in his own words, 'feast my eyes on your delicacy forever.'

Jek wears a mask and bodysuit to hide his scarring. The

desire for revenge against Morgus is all that sustains him. Although Federal troops are attempting to regain control of the spectrox stores, he estimates it will be five years before he is seriously threatened. Jek does not believe the electorate will wait that long, and trusts that his terms will be met – the head of Morgus at his feet, 'congealed in its own evil blood.'

Finally Jek has revenge on Morgus, killing him even while dying himself, his body riddled with gunfire. Jek finally slumps dead in the arms of his android copy of Selateen – a replacement for the real Federal soldier, and his most accomplished and sophisticated android.

MORGUS

Chairman of the Sirius Conglomerate on Androzani Major, Morgus is a ruthless, corrupt, remorseless murderer who abuses his power and positon to increase his own wealth. It is he who is helping to prolong Androzani's war against Sharaz Jek, by supplying Jek (who remains ignorant of the situation) with weapons through gunrunners. Jek pays for the arms with spectrox, which Morgus then sells on to the clamouring hordes on Androzani Major at a vastly inflated price due to its scarcity.

Ultimately Morgus's criminal dealings are uncovered by the Presidium that rules Androzani Major when his own secretary betrays him. Warrants for his arrest on 17 counts are issued, and all his private funds are sequestered. Morgus attempts to turn the situation around by liberating Jek's spectrox supplies, but dies in the attempt.

The Doctor:
'Is this death?'

NEW INFORMATION

THE DOCTOR

At last the Doctor reveals why he sports a stick of celery on his lapel – he is allergic to certain gases in the Praxsis range of the spectrum and should any be present, the celery turns purple, forming an early warning mechanism. He also places it under Peri's nose to revive her when she is delirious, explaining it is a powerful restorative to the superior olfactory senses of a Time Lord.

His alien physiognomy confuses androids trained to detect humans.

Even though dying himself, he is determined to help Peri because he 'got her into this', and will let no one and nothing stand in his way. He braves the oxygen-less lower levels of Androzani Minor's cave systems to fetch the cure for spectrox toxaemia (the milk of the Queen Bat) without protective clothing or respirators.

Unsure whether he will regenerate – as it 'feels different this time' – he sees visions of his companions urging him not to die, before a spectral image of the Master gloating over his demise finally seems to trigger the metamorphosis.

COMPANIONS

PERI: Jocular and mildly flirtatious with the Doctor upon arrival on Androzani Minor, Peri is clearly excited to be seeing new worlds. She seems disappointed that the Doctor doesn't appreciate her sarcastic humour. Upon learning she is going to die of spectrox toxaemia she remains calm, reasoning that as the poison has a snake-bite effect there must be a serum or antitoxin.

KNOWING THE SCORE

INCIDENTAL MUSIC

Music has always been an important ingredient of **Doctor Who**. Incidental music, as it is called, is the music that is played during the course of the programme – not as part of the narrative but to enrich and enhance the production, purely for the benefit of the audience. In many ways the job of the incidental music composer is a thankless one: to counterpoint and emphasise the images and action on the screen, not to intrude.

With the availability of video and DVD – and the release of CDs of **Doctor Who**'s incidental music – it is possible to appreciate just how much effort and talent has been put into the programme's music scores over the years.

Although it was not unusual for television drama to have specially composed incidental music in 1963, it was by no means the rule. But almost every **Doctor Who** story has included incidental music, although some stories used only 'stock music'. The very first **Doctor Who** story had an incidental score composed by Norman Kay, while Tristram Cary provided music for the first Dalek story and many others up until *The Mutants* in 1972. Cary was a pioneer of electronic music, creating one of the world's first private electronic-music studios. He composed the incidental music for five **Doctor Who** stories: *The Daleks*, *Marco Polo*, *The Daleks' Master Plan*, *The Gunfighters* (including the 'Ballad of the Last Chance Saloon'), and *The Mutants*. In addition, *The Rescue*, *The Ark* and *The Power of the Daleks* reused tracks from his score for *The Daleks*.

Amongst the talented composers who have worked on **Doctor Who**, several others are worth mentioning specifically. Richard Rodney Bennett provided music for *The Aztecs* (conducted by Marcus Dods); Carey Blyton provided music for *The Silurians*, *Death to the Daleks* and *Revenge of the Cybermen*; Geoffrey Burgon wrote the haunting scores for *Terror of the Zygons* and *The Seeds of Doom*.

Most prolific of the **Doctor Who** composers by far was Dudley Simpson. His first score for the programme was *Planet of Giants* in 1964, his last *The Horns of Nimon* in 1979. Simpson was born in Australia, and returned there in 1988 to continue his freelance composing. While in Britain he worked extensively on **Doctor Who** – providing almost all the music scores for the programme during the 1970s as well as a number of memorable scores during the 1960s – notably *The Evil of the Daleks,* which included a Dalek theme based on a distortion of the programme's theme music, and *The*

Ice Warriors which introduced a drumbeat theme for the Martian villains. Simpson's other main television science-fiction work was on **Blake's 7** – for which he provided the theme music and all the incidental music.

Dudley Simpson also has the distinction of having appeared in **Doctor Who** – as a music-hall conductor, conducting his own music in *The Talons of Weng-Chiang*. Similarly, composer Keff McCulloch appears in the band the Lorells in *Delta and the Bannermen*.

From *The Leisure Hive* onwards, the job of providing an incidental music score was given to the BBC's Radiophonic Workshop. Several talented composers from the Workshop provided music for the programme – initially Peter Howell and Paddy Kingsland, but later also Roger Limb, Malcolm Clarke (who had previously scored *The Sea Devils*), Jonathan Gibbs and others. Later, a variety of freelance composers were again used – notably Keff McCulloch, Dominic Glynn and Mark Ayres.

For *Doctor Who – The Movie*, the new arrangement of the theme and the incidental music were provided by well-known film-score composer John Debney, with additional music by John Sponsler and Louis Febre.

VOCAL SUPPORT

While the majority of **Doctor Who** stories have had specially scored incidental music, very few of these scores have included vocals.

In fact, the only stories to have included a song as incidental music are *The Gunfighters* and *Delta and the Bannermen*. In *The Gunfighters*, verses of the specially written 'Ballad of the Last Chance Saloon' are sung between various scenes by Lynda Baron. The song is also performed within the context of the story by Steven and Dodo. The final episode of *Delta and the Bannermen* includes snatches from 'Here's to the Future', specially composed by Keff McCulloch.

Other stories have included people singing within the narrative – such as the Doctor's rendition of 'La Donna E Mobile' as he drives along in Bessie at the start of *Inferno* or the music-hall singer performing 'Daisy, Daisy' in *The Talons of Weng-Chiang*. *Shada*, *Delta and the Bannermen* and *Silver Nemesis* also included 'live' performances (the last of these featuring Courtney Pine's jazz music rather than a vocal arrangement). Chanting during ceremonies is also not uncommon in **Doctor Who** – be it the Sisterhood of Karn in *The Brain of Morbius*, the brotherhood of Demnos in *The Masque of Mandragora*, the Master in *The Dæmons*, or one of any number of others.

Dudley Simpson's incidental music for *The Space Pirates* is interesting in that it incorporates a human voice into the score. Similarly, Simpson used a soprano to underscore the opening moments of each episode of *The Ice Warriors* as the title, episode and author were displayed.

Harder to spot, a human voice was treated to chant in the incidental music accompanying the attempted sacrifice of the Doctor at the end of Episode 3 of *Meglos*. The device used to treat the voice was a vocoder. Peter Howell of the BBC's Radiophonic Workshop had recently used the same device to provide one short sequence of notes using his own voice in his 1980 electronic re-orchestration of the **Doctor Who** theme, used from *The Leisure Hive* through to *Revelation of the Daleks*.

STOCK MUSIC

Stock music was occasionally used to save the cost and time involved in hiring a composer to create incidental music especially for a story. This practice was used throughout the black-and-white era of the series, though some stock music was used much later.

Sometimes, especially in later years, composers used music they or someone else had previously created to serve as background to a scene, rather than as incidental music as such. For example, in the very first episode, John Smith and the Common Men's performance on Susan's radio is actually a piece called 'Three Guitars Mood 2'. On other occasions, composers reused their own previous work as part of a new incidental score – for example, Malcolm Clarke reused his 'The Milonga' as background to a banquet in *Enlightenment*, and his score for *The Sea Devils* incorporated excerpts from a score he composed for a schools' radio production of *The War of the Worlds*.

A variety of sources was used for stock music – from the concert works of Hungarian composer Bela Bartok in The *Web of Fear*, to what is remembered as the chilling drumbeat Cyberman theme, particularly from their first three stories. This piece, called 'Space Adventure', was written by Martin Slavin (and used in other stories as well, notably *The Web of Fear*). Like most stock music, it came from dedicated, independent production-music libraries created specifically for TV, film and radio use.

Various well-known music tracks have featured in **Doctor Who** as 'stock' background music. Amongst many, many others, we have been treated to cover versions of hits by the Beach Boys, Elvis Presley, Glenn Miller and more played by the DJ in *Revelation of the Daleks*. The Beatles perform 'Ticket to Ride' on the time–space visualiser in *The Chase* and we hear 'Paperback Writer' as background music in The Tricolour in *The Evil of the Daleks* and 'Do You Want to Know a Secret?', along with other Sixties tracks, in the café in *Remembrance of the Daleks*.

WORKING BRIEF

As with sound effects, in the days before videotapes of edited episodes were available for the composer to view, the incidental music for **Doctor Who** was composed without the luxury of being able to see the finished programme. As with the sound effects, the director provided a brief, including timings, for what he wanted. The composer worked from this, providing music to be dubbed on to the completed videotape.

The director's notes to the composer can often give an insight into the way the director saw the programme – the mood and 'texture' of a scene, the type of effect he wanted to get across. As with sound-effects requirements, this is particularly interesting for sequences that no longer exist – such as the death of companion Katarina in *The Daleks' Master Plan* when she opens an airlock door, killing herself and the villainous Kirksen who has been holding her hostage.

From the Director's Music Requirements for The Daleks' Master Plan Episode 4:

```
MUSIC 34. ... When I cut to the film sequence
indicated, it will be another slow-motion
affair of KATARINA and KIRKSEN slowly turning
around and around in space ... against the
curve of the nearby planet Desperus. Both are
dead from the space vacuum. I have a feeling
that they might both have exploded in actual
fact, but I'll forget about that. When I go to
a twisting, turning Close Shot of Katarina,
her hair will be blowing in all its slow-
motion glory — just like a shampoo ad — and
she will be happy in her death. She's at one
with the Gods and all that. Kirksen will have
died in terror and agony — very unhappy about
the whole thing. I don't know how long the
sequence will last, but it will probably be
about 30 secs. Could I have music to cover
this, please? (DURATION: 40 SECS)
```

'It means the collapse
of the Universe has
started and nothing
can stop it...
Eternal blackness.
No more sunsets.
No more Gumblejacks.
Nevermore a butterfly.'
(THE DOCTOR – *THE TWO DOCTORS*)

Six

THE SIXTH DOCTOR

The Sixth Doctor is the most volatile of all. In terms of volume, arrogance and dress sense he is also the loudest. He's never one to keep quiet about his talents, theories or opinions. He is particularly volatile when his regeneration is unstable. In *The Twin Dilemma*, the Doctor attacks Peri – verbally, and even physically – until his regeneration stabilises. On the surface, this is a Doctor who believes in himself utterly – it is, he maintains, always someone else's fault when things go wrong, and his own genius that solves the problem. As Lord Ravensworth remarks as the Doctor begins to give him orders, 'Dratted man's a law unto himself.'

But the bluster and volume is, like the trappings of any incarnation of the Doctor's, an act. It is a veneer that masks a very real intelligence and a deep concern for those around him. Outwardly, he may seem passionate about himself, ready to quote and quip his way through trouble, but it is in the rare quiet moments that we see that this is still the same brilliant, caring, intensely moral Doctor that we are used to.

In many ways his mood swings and his changes of attitude are the same as his predecessors'. What is different is their extremity. Where the Second Doctor might let slip an apt quote, the Sixth will proclaim it. Where the Third might take it for granted that he is more intelligent than anyone else he meets, the Sixth makes sure that they know it. Where the Fourth might rail against injustice and evil, the Sixth gives an almost operatic performance to make the point. If the First Doctor is acerbic, the Sixth is positively caustic. And where the Fifth Doctor is quietly passionate, the Sixth Doctor has that same depth of feeling but at a considerably higher volume.

This perhaps makes him the most dangerous incarnation of the Doctor. When Luke Ward is metamorphosed into a tree in *The Mark of the Rani*, we can believe the Doctor is about to kill the Master in retaliation. This is a Doctor who is in every way larger than life. He may not endure for very long in terms of the number of stories in which he appears, but into that time he packs almost as much vehemence and emotion as any other Doctor...

THE MAN BEHIND THE DOCTOR – COLIN BAKER

Born in London in 1943 during an air raid, Colin Baker's first experience of acting was in a television series at the age of nine. Although he continued to perform throughout his education, he studied law and became a solicitor.

Tiring of this, and finding he enjoyed amateur dramatics rather more, Baker decided to become a professional actor and attended the London Academy of Music and Dramatic Art. He followed a role in the BBC's 1970 production of **The Roads to Freedom** with further television and theatre work and became best known as the ruthless Paul Merroney in **The Brothers**.

Baker worked primarily in the theatre for the next few years, though he did appear as Bayban the Berserker in the **Blake's 7** episode *City at the Edge of the World* in 1980. He also played Commander Maxil in the Fifth Doctor story *Arc of Infinity* – his character shooting the Doctor and arranging his execution.

Impressed with Baker's performance and his personality, **Doctor Who**'s producer John Nathan-Turner remembered Colin Baker when he came to cast Davison's replacement.

After Colin Baker left the role, which he reprised on stage and continues on audio, he again returned mainly to the theatre but has also appeared in television as diverse as **Jonathan Creek**, **Doctors**, and **The Young Indiana Jones Chronicles**.

THE TWIN DILEMMA

In which the new Doctor is violently unstable, and Maurice Denham appears as the Doctor's old drinking partner.

BY ANTHONY STEVEN

4 EPISODES, FIRST BROADCAST 22–30 MARCH 1984

TARDIS DATA BANK:

DATE: UNKNOWN, FUTURE (POSSIBLY JULY/AUGUST AD2100)
LOCATION: EARTH; TITAN THREE; JACONDA

THE MATHEMATICALLY TALENTED SYLVEST TWINS, ROMULUS AND REMUS, ARE KIDNAPPED BY PROFESSOR EDGEWORTH – WHO IS IN FACT A DISGUISED TIME LORD CALLED AZMAEL FORCED TO WORK FOR MESTOR, A GIANT GASTROPOD FROM JACONDA. MESTOR PLANS TO USE THE TWINS' POWERS TO DESTROY JACONDA'S SUN, DISPERSING AND HATCHING OUT MILLIONS OF GASTROPOD EGGS. THE DOCTOR AND PERI, TOGETHER WITH THE DOCTOR'S OLD FRIEND AZMAEL, STRUGGLE TO THWART MESTOR'S PLANS, BUT THE DOCTOR IS HAMPERED BY SUDDEN VIOLENT OUTBURSTS – SIDE EFFECTS OF HIS RECENT REGENERATION…

Professor Sylvest: 'I honestly believe that neither of you has the faintest idea of your real powers. Your mathematical skill could change events on a massive scale, don't you realise that?

JOURNEY INFORMATION

JACONDA

The Jocondans are a bird-like, humanoid race. The planet is suffering a famine, the world having been blighted by the return of giant gastropods.

The Doctor points out paintings on a wall in the catacombs (used as a bolt hole in times of trouble) and explains the legend they depict: 'The Queen of Jaconda offended the sun god… He inflicted a terrible revenge, and sent a creature half-humanoid, half-slug. This creature's offspring were numberless. They ravaged the planet, the population starved. When he saw what he had done, the sun god relented. He sent a drought which destroyed the slugs. The people of Jaconda survived…'

MESTOR

The Doctor believes that a dormant egg from one of the giant gastropods survived, allowing the creatures to take control. They smell like rotting vegetables and leave slime trails that harden like concrete only far faster.

Mestor, the gastropod who has made himself master of Jaconda, has tremendous mind powers, and 'the maximum penalty' for those who fail him is induced death by embolism. He can open the TARDIS doors, and see through Jocondans' eyes. Azmael, the deposed Master of Jaconda, says, 'All Jaconda is affected by his thoughts.'

Mestor plans to take over the Doctor's mind and body, and demonstrates the technique using Azmael's body.

Mestor has told Azmael his plan is to bring two smaller, more distant, planets into orbit round Jaconda. This will change their climates and enable them to become the 'larders' of Jaconda. The twin sons of Professor Sylvest are to provide the mathematical ability to stabilise the planets in their new orbits where they will remain stable occupying the same space in different time zones.

Mestor knows, however, that if his plan succeeds the outer planets, being smaller, will suffer decaying orbits and crash into the Jocondan sun. Jaconda's sun will explode and scatter Mestor's eggs across the Universe – the heat causing them to hatch.

AZMAEL

Azmael is a Time Lord, and has to revitalise in a booth on Titan Three. He masquerades as Professor Edgeworth before the twins, and is in mental contact with Mestor.

The Doctor recognises Azmael as, 'My old friend and mentor, the Master of Jaconda.' The Doctor has regenerated twice since their last meeting when Azmael drank like 20 giants and the Doctor had to put him in a fountain to sober him up. The Doctor tells Azmael he is the best teacher he ever had.

Azmael is determined to save his people, though he has been deposed by Mestor. This is more important even than his friendship with the Doctor, and he leaves the Doctor and Peri on Titan Three as prisoners.

Azmael's body is taken over by Mestor. The Doctor then destroys Mestor's body so he cannot return to it when Azmael forces himself to die (he is in his last regeneration).

ROMULUS AND REMUS

The Sylvest twins are mathematical geniuses. Equations they work out for Azmael could produce power equivalent to that of a small sun. Mestor plans to use their expertise to finalise the calculations for his plan.

NEW INFORMATION

THE DOCTOR

The Doctor describes his regeneration as, 'Natural metamorphosis, a form of rebirth. I call it a renewal. And this time a positive triumph – I can sense it in every fibre of my being.'

He is proud of his new form: 'A noble brow. A clear gaze, at least it will be given a few hours' sleep. A firm mouth. A face beaming with a vast intelligence... It's the most extraordinary improvement.' He says his previous incarnation had a sort of feckless charm that 'wasn't me...'

But his new persona starts off erratic, unstable, and volatile. He blames this on the fact that regeneration is 'a swift but volcanic experience, a kind of violent biological eruption in which the body cells are displaced, changed, renewed, and rearranged – there are bound to be side effects.'

One of these 'side effects' is that he attacks Peri (who scares him off by showing him his own reflection in a mirror). Later he hides from the Jocondans behind Peri and seems afraid to go into a 'safe house'. He confesses to Lang and Peri that he is falling to pieces, and no longer even has any dress sense: 'Self pity is all I have left.'

THE TARDIS

There is a deep-healing beam in the TARDIS medical kit.

Mestor can open the TARDIS door by mental force.

COMPANIONS

PERI: Peri is not keen on the new Doctor, but after initial 'problems' he calls her 'such a nice girl.'

The Doctor: 'In my time I have been threatened by experts. And I don't rate you very highly at all.'

ATTACK OF THE CYBERMEN

In which the Cybermen try to relive their greatest moments from *The Tomb of the Cybermen* and *The Invasion*.
BY PAULA MOORE
2 45-MINUTE EPISODES, FIRST BROADCAST 5–12 JANUARY 1985

JOURNEY INFORMATION

THE CYBERMEN

The Cybermen have established a base in the London sewers, and have been there less than seven years. Their stolen time vessel is hidden on the dark side of the moon. The Cyber Guards in the sewers are painted black.

When the sewer base is abandoned and sealed, the humans in the process of being converted into Cybermen are transferred to the Cybership. The Cybermen on Earth know who the Doctor is – 'an enemy of the Cyber race'. When the Doctor says that the Cyber Controller was destroyed, the Cyber Leader says it was merely damaged (presumably, therefore, the Telos sequences of this story are set after *The Tomb of the Cybermen*). Cybermen have a mechanical distress call, and will react to the distress of their own kind.

The Cybermen have captured a time vessel that landed on Telos, but they do not fully understand the principles of time travel. They intend to change history – and prevent their original home planet, Mondas, from being destroyed. Their plan is to go back in time and divert Halley's comet so it will crash into Earth and destroy it, thereby preventing the destruction of Mondas. They will destroy the surface of Telos to observe the effect on the atmosphere (using vastial – a mineral found in the colder areas of Telos that self-ignites at 15 degrees above freezing).

The Doctor says Mondas was fitted with a propulsion system (he does not know why).

THE CRYONS

The Cybermen believe they have destroyed the Cryons, but a few survive. They lived in refrigerated cities before the Cybermen came, and cannot exist in temperatures above freezing – they boil and die.

The Cryons have picked up Lytton's distress signal and asked him to help them destroy the Cybermen. They offer Lytton's assistant, Griffiths, £2million in uncut diamonds – common on Telos. The plan is for Lytton to steal the time vessel so the Cybermen will not be able to leave and destroy Telos. They are presumably able to communicate through time with Lytton as they are in the far future, and Lytton is on present-day Earth.

LYTTON

The Doctor describes Lytton as the sort of man who would shoot his mother to keep his trigger finger supple. The police investigated Lytton after specialist electronics equipment was stolen – and found no record of his birth or education. Lytton still has two bogus policemen as accomplices. He comes from Veta Fifteen in the star system six nine zero (Riften Five), a planet occupied by a race of mercenaries – and claims he did not work for the Daleks through choice.

Captured by the Cybermen and interrogated, his hands crushed, Lytton is processed to be converted into a Cyberman. He is killed while helping the Doctor to destroy the Cyber Controller.

BATES AND STRATTON

The time vessel the Cybermen captured was piloted by a crew of three. Two of the original crew, Bates and Stratton, are part of a working party mining Telos with explosive vastial. (The third member of the crew may be a man killed in their escape attempt.) They have been partially converted into Cybermen – their arms and legs have been replaced, but the conditioning process has not worked on them.

NEW INFORMATION

THE DOCTOR

The Doctor has a small sonic lance in his pocket, which he uses to destroy a Cyberman. Later he uses it to raise the temperature of the Cybermen's store of vastial to a point where it explodes and destroys the Cybermen's city.

Lytton says the Time Lords would destroy the Doctor if he transgressed the Laws of Time to the extent of warning Earth of Mondas's imminent attack.

Manoeuvred into 'this mess' by the Time Lords so that history will not be changed, the Doctor is upset at how he has misjudged Lytton.

THE TARDIS

The Doctor tries to fix the chameleon circuit. The TARDIS lands at the 76 Totters Lane junkyard (which has changed since *An Unearthly Child* as well as acquiring a number on its sign) and assumes the form of a cabinet, then an organ. On Telos, it materialises as a gateway. It reverts to a police box when it appears in the Cyber laboratory. TARDIS circuitry is accessible behind roundels in the corridor. The Doctor sets a self-destruct device, with a countdown displayed on the TARDIS console screen.

```
Cyber Controller: 'You are
foolish, Lytton, you could
have saved yourself the pain.
I told you you would tell us
everything. Now you will
become as we are.'
```

VENGEANCE ON VAROS

In which Sil first appears – on a planet where all there is to watch on television is gratuitous violence and horror, and endless reality shows.
BY PHILIP MARTIN
2 45-MINUTE EPISODES, FIRST BROADCAST 19–26 JANUARY 1985

JOURNEY INFORMATION

VAROS

Varos is in the constellation of Cetes and is the only known source of Zeiton 7. Over two hundred years ago, it was a prison colony for the criminally insane. The descendants of the officer elite still hold power.

The Governor is elected from 12 senior officials who put their names forward to be chosen at random. The Governor's role is to propose solutions to Varos's problems and these

solutions are put to a public vote. Voting is compulsory – through boxes beside the television screens. If the Governor is outvoted he is subjected to human cell disintegration bombardment, which over time will kill him. The idea is that a man in fear of his life will find the best solutions to Varos's problems. This Governor has survived three losing votes in a row.

The voting population of Varos is 1,620,783.

The Governor is fair, but still willing, albeit reluctantly, to have the rebel Jondar executed. He used to grieve, 'but now death is my only friend – my constant and loving companion. Can you feel his cold presence?' he asks Peri.

Torture and execution are carried out in the Punishment Dome. Guards there are issued with antihallucination helmets because of 'phantoms'. It is said there is a safe route out of the dome through areas of 'ingenious danger' like the hallucinations of the Purple Zone. The whole dome is covered by cameras and the governing regime of Varos sells tapes of what happens in the Punishment Dome to other planets as well as broadcasting events to their own people to divert thoughts of discontent, questions and revolution.

SIL

Sil is a slug-like creature from Thoros-Beta and is used to less gravity than there is on Varos. He is negotiating the yearly price review for Galatron Mining prior to a new contract. Galatron has been buying from – and exploiting – Varos for centuries. Sil has been paying the Chief Officer to influence or replace the Governor.

Sil sends for a colonising force when the Governor refuses to negotiate. But traces of Zeiton 7 are found on another asteroid, so the invasion is called off and Sil's ordered to continue to negotiate with the Governor as supplies are urgently needed.

His language transposer has an eccentric communications circuit, but the Governor has not told him as it amuses him.

NEW INFORMATION

THE DOCTOR

The Doctor sulks when the TARDIS seems irrevocably broken – but is galvanised into action when movement of the central column suggests vestigial power.

He accidentally causes two guards to fall into an acid bath intended for his own dead body, and seems unrepentant: 'You'll forgive me if I don't join you.'

Later, he rigs deadly vines so that he can release them to swing back and kill Quillam (Technical Director and Principal Deviser of Programmes on Varos) and the Chief Officer.

THE TARDIS

The TARDIS 'stalls' when its transitional elements lose capacity and need replacing. They need relining with Zeiton 7, which is only found on Varos.

The Doctor reads the *TARDIS type 40 Handbook* (which Peri finds).

Peri refers to the central column as 'the column'. The Doctor mentions an emergency power booster.

COMPANIONS

PERI: Under cell mutation, Peri turns into a bird. Quillam suggests this is because of a subconscious wish to fly away from trouble. He says the cell mutation treatment 'focuses on the seeds of fear in your mind and makes them grow. Until you, your body, your face, your entire being transforms into the image in your mind.' The process is an offshoot of mining research technology – the miners were growing fur and claws, the better, they thought, to dig with.

TARDIS DATA BANK:

DATE: C2300 (SHORTLY BEFORE 2379, ACCORDING TO *MINDWARP*).
LOCATION: VAROS

THE TARDIS ONLY HAS ENOUGH POWER TO GET TO VAROS – AN EX-PRISON PLANET THAT IS THE ONLY SOURCE OF THE VALUABLE ZEITON 7 THE TARDIS NEEDS. WHEN THEY ARRIVE IN THE PUNISHMENT DOME, THE DOCTOR AND PERI FIND THEMSELVES TRYING TO ESCAPE THE TORTURES AND CHALLENGES OF THE DOME ON LIVE TELEVISION. MEANWHILE, THE GOVERNOR OF VAROS TRIES TO NEGOTIATE A HIGHER PRICE FOR ZEITON 7 WITH SIL, REPRESENTATIVE OF THE GALATRON MINING CORPORATION WHICH HAS LED VAROS TO BELIEVE THAT ZEITON 7 IS WORTHLESS. CAN THE DOCTOR HALT THE INJUSTICES OF THE PUNISHMENT DOME, NEGOTIATE A FAIR DEAL FOR VAROS, AND GET THE TARDIS WORKING AGAIN...

The Doctor: 'It's all right for you, Peri. You've only got one life. You'll age here in the TARDIS and then die. But me, I shall go on regenerating until all my lives are spent.'

Quillam: 'I want to hear them scream till I'm deaf with pleasure. To see their limbs twist in excruciating agony. Ultimately their blood must gush and flow along the gutters of Varos. The whole planet must delight in their torture and death.'

THE MARK OF THE RANI

In which Kate O'Mara makes her debut as an unscrupulous Time Lord running a bathhouse and turning people into trees.
BY PIP AND JANE BAKER
2 45-MINUTE EPISODES, FIRST BROADCAST 2–9 FEBRUARY 1985

TARDIS DATA BANK:

DATE: MID-NINETEENTH CENTURY LOCATION: KILLINGWORTH

THE TARDIS IS DRAWN OFF COURSE AND LANDS AT KILLINGWORTH WHERE GEORGE STEPHENSON IS ORGANISING A MEETING OF THE GREATEST BRITISH THINKERS AND ENGINEERS. THE MASTER IS AFTER REVENGE ON THE DOCTOR, AND ALSO PLANS TO TAKE CONTROL OF THE GREAT THINKERS AND MANIPULATE THEM TO TURN EARTH INTO A POWER BASE. ALSO PRESENT IS THE RANI – A RENEGADE FEMALE TIME LORD CHEMIST – WHO IS EXTRACTING FLUID FROM PEOPLE'S BRAINS AND MAKING THEM UNNATURALLY AGGRESSIVE. CAN THE DOCTOR OUTWIT BOTH THESE EVIL GENIUSES AND ESCAPE WITH HIS LIFE...

JOURNEY INFORMATION

LORD RAVENSWORTH

Bluff and plain-speaking, Lord Ravensworth is sponsoring George Stephenson's work. He has lent his name to the meeting Stephenson has called of over twenty great thinkers – including James Watt, Thomas Telford, Humphry Davy and Michael Faraday. People, the Doctor says, who will transform history.

THE RANI

A brilliant chemist, the Rani was exiled by the Time Lords after she experimented on mice and turned them into monsters. The mice ate the President's cat and also took a chunk out of him. The Doctor says the Time Lords shouldn't have exiled the Rani, but locked her in a padded cell instead.

The Rani disguises herself as an old woman running the Killingworth bathhouse. Here she renders her victims unconscious with gas, before removing from their brains the chemical that allows the brain to rest. This makes them aggressive and leaves a round red mark on their necks. They take out their frustration on new machinery.

Ravensworth says he's never in 30 years seen miner Jack Ward raise a hand to another man. Now he is wrecking machinery and attacks the Doctor.

The Rani needs the chemical because in the process of heightening the awareness of her alien subjects on the planet Miasimia Goria, which she rules, she lowered their ability to sleep, making them difficult to control. She has been coming to Earth for centuries – using various unsettled times as cover, including the Trojan wars, the Dark Ages, the American War of Independence and now the Luddite riots...

The Rani controls her servants by making them eat maggot-like parasites impregnated with a chemical.

She lays mines that turn anyone who steps on them – Stephenson's assistant, Luke Ward, for example – into a tree, and argues they are better off that way as their life-span is longer.

The Rani's TARDIS is protected by a mustard-gas booby trap hidden in a Turner painting on a screen. She keeps tyrannosaurus embryos in its Console Room. One of them starts to grow when the TARDIS suffers time spillage after the Doctor resets the navigational system and velocity regulator, trapping the Master and the Rani.

NEW INFORMATION

THE DOCTOR

The Doctor has a tracking device that registers the time distortion caused by another time machine. He recognises the Rani when he sees her without her disguise.

He says he never changed the course of history, and is in fact expressly forbidden to. He has a ball of cotton in his pocket, and flips a coin to decide which way to go to get out of a mine.

The Doctor enjoys examining and discussing a steam engine with George Stephenson. When Stephenson offers the Doctor a gun, he says he has given them up and they can 'damage your health'.

THE TARDIS

The TARDIS is manoeuvred off course by another time machine (the Master's TARDIS). The time coordinates are not changed, but the landing location is shifted from Kew Gardens to Killingworth.

The TARDIS survives being tipped down a mine shaft.

THE RANI'S TARDIS

The Rani's TARDIS is disguised as a cupboard. The Doctor is able to open it with his own TARDIS key. The internal design is different from that of the Doctor's TARDIS – dark, with a round console. It is linked to a Stattenheim remote control (as used by the Second Doctor in *The Two Doctors*).

The Doctor sabotages the Rani's TARDIS by resetting the navigational system and velocity regulator. The Master and the Rani are trapped in her out-of-control TARDIS.

THE MASTER

'I'm indestructible – the whole Universe knows that,' the Master maintains. He is initially disguised as a scarecrow (though it is not clear why).

One of Ravensworth's guard dogs is agitated by the Master's presence so he kills it (and a guard) with his tissue compression eliminator – their bodies glow red and disappear.

The Master claims to be one of the Rani's greatest admirers, but he in fact wants her help. She describes the feud between the Doctor and the Master as a 'pathetic vendetta', and says the destruction of the Doctor occupies the Master's mind to the exclusion of all else. The Rani describes the Master's plans as devious and overcomplicated – 'He'd get dizzy if he tried to walk in a straight line.'

The Master's plan is to use the Rani's 'maggots' to manipulate the great thinkers coming to Ravensworth's conference: 'With their help I could turn this insignificant planet into a power base unique in the Universe.'

He uses a swinging watch to hypnotise Luke Ward, then gives him one of the Rani's mind-controlling parasites.

COMPANIONS

PERI: Peri threatens the Master and the Rani with the Master's tissue compression eliminator. She narrowly escapes being turned into a tree by the Rani's mines.

THE TWO DOCTORS

In which Patrick Troughton and Frazer Hines return as the Doctor and Jamie in a story set partly in Spain.

BY ROBERT HOLMES

3 45-MINUTE EPISODES, FIRST BROADCAST 16 FEBRUARY–
2 MARCH 1985

JOURNEY INFORMATION

THE ANDROGUMS

Androgums are humanoid in appearance, with pustules and prominent eyebrows. They are incredibly strong, and work as servitors on Space Station Camera. The Androgum Law is that the gratification of pleasure is the sole motive of action.

PROFESSOR JOINSON DASTARI AND THE TIME EXPERIMENTS

Joinson Dastari is Head of Projects at Space Station Camera – where the Doctor says 40 of the greatest scientists in the Universe work on pure research.

Dastari believes he can augment Androgums to carry on from the intelligent life forms he believes are wearing out, and has augmented Chessene to 'megagenius level'.

Several Androgums who tested a time module built by Professors Kartz and Reimer were vaporised into the time stream. Dastari suspects that Time Lords have a symbiotic link with their TARDISes which protects them, and anyone with them, from this destabilisation.

The Doctor says that if he himself used the time module, it would prime it with the *Rassilon Imprimature* – a symbiotic print within a Time Lord's physiology. Once that was absorbed into the briode nebuliser, the time machine would work for anyone. The Doctor later admits he was lying and none of this is 'strictly true'.

CHESSENE

Her 'karm name' is Chessene o' the Franzine Grig. She absorbs information from the mind of an old Spanish lady, the Dona Arana, killed by Shockeye.

Dastari wants to make Chessene into a god. But the Doctor says she'll always be an Androgum and will 'snap off the hand that feeds her whenever she feels hungry.' Proving the point, when the Doctor is wounded, she cannot resist lapping up his spilled blood.

SHOCKEYE

Shockeye o' the Quawncing Grig is the Station Chef and keen to taste human flesh, so persuades Chessene to go to Earth and get some. The Dona Arana implies that Shockeye speaks English (and the Doctor says the aliens do not speak Spanish).

Shockeye shares a huge feast and a dozen bottles of wine with the Second Doctor. The Androgum calls it 'a mere snack' and still wants to eat Jamie afterwards. When restaurant manager Oscar Botcherby will not accept his 20 Narg note, Shockeye stabs him to death with a steak knife.

THE SONTARANS

The Doctor describes the Sontarans as rabidly xenophobic. Group Marshal Stike commands the Ninth Sontaran Battle Group, and takes his orders from Sontaran High Command. His forces are planning an attack in the Madillon Cluster, which could change the course of their war with the Rutans. Despite being cloned, Stike is taller than his subordinate, Varl.

Sontaran battle cruisers have the same exterior design as their spherical scoutships. A scoutship can be made invisible by 'placing it in clear.'

Turning on her former allies, Chessene kills Varl and injures Stike with coronic acid.

NEW INFORMATION

THE DOCTOR

The Doctor is affected when the Second Doctor is apparently executed. He is able to close his respiratory passages to avoid a stun-gas booby trap.

He describes himself to Jamie as another 'aspect' of the Doctor, and goes into a trance to try to contact the Second Doctor.

The Doctor recognises the sound of the Santa Maria – the largest of the 25 bells in the cathedral of Seville. (He has been to Seville – the Second Doctor also remembers this and takes Shockeye to *Las Cadenas* restaurant.)

Having sniffed it first (with no ill effects), the Doctor kills Shockeye with cyanide from a moth-killing jar (arguably in self-defence).

THE SECOND DOCTOR

The Doctor says he attended the inauguration of Space Station Camera as a representative of the Time Lords – 'before I fell from favour.' He has been sent now, 'unofficially', to stop the Kartz-Reimer time experiments.

Chessene wants Dastari to use genetic material from Shockeye to mutate the Second Doctor into an Androgum – a consort for Chessene, but still with time travel capability. The effects of an initial operation to do this affect the Sixth Doctor as time progresses, but he reverts as a second operation to stabilise the change is never performed.

THE TARDIS

The Time Lords have fitted a Stattenheim remote control to the second Doctor's TARDIS. (As the Rani's TARDIS had in *The Mark of the Rani*.)

The Doctor says TARDISes have to be primed with a Time Lord's symbiotic nuclei, but he later admits that this was a lie.

COMPANIONS

PERI: Although she has heard of Jamie, and in *Timelash* she will recognise a picture of Jo Grant, Peri does not recognise the Second Doctor. She does not speak Spanish.

JAMIE: Jamie survives on Camera after the Sontaran attack, but regresses almost to an animal. He defends himself from Shockeye, stabs Stike and knocks away Chessene's gun with his *skein dhu*.

BEHIND THE SCENES

REWRITING HISTORY

While *The Two Doctors* opens in black-and-white, fading to colour after a few seconds of the Second Doctor and Jamie in the TARDIS, it does not merge seamlessly into the Second Doctor's era.

The best intentions of the production personnel are demonstrated by the use of an older version of the TARDIS console in the Second Doctor's TARDIS. It is, however, a version from the Fourth Doctor's era. This is indicative of the approach taken – there is a nod to the past, but it is not slavishly followed. How much of this is due to the constraints of the story and the need to adapt to a contemporary audience, and how much is simply down to ignorance, is not clear.

There is, for example, an explanation as to how the Doctor and Jamie come to be unaccompanied by Polly and Ben, or Victoria or Zoe. We are told that the Doctor has, for once, managed to steer the TARDIS and dropped Victoria off to study graphology.

But quite when there was an opportunity for this, or why she wants to study graphology, or how the Doctor managed to steer the TARDIS (or how he will get back to her) is left to the viewer's imagination.

Of course, none of this spoils our enjoyment of *The Two Doctors*, but it is interesting that writer Robert Holmes would have us believe that the Second Doctor was used on occasion as an agent by the Time Lords. If he actually believed this to be the case while writing *The Deadly Assassin*, rather than it being an expediency for this particular script, it would explain why Holmes thought the Time Lords were so hypocritical and decadent. Viewing the Time Lords of *The Deadly Assassin* as a race that, rather than put the Doctor on trial as soon as they caught up with him, sent him on errands and used his expertise and diplomatic skills and *then* chose to put him on trial for the interference they had condoned and organised, gives that story an added poignancy and dimension.

Not that this would be the only time that a writer has rewritten established **Doctor Who** history – either deliberately or inadvertently. *Genesis of the Daleks* may be a conscious reinterpretation of the origins of the Daleks (which to be fair were left open to debate in previous stories), but *Mawdryn Undead*, for example, directly contradicts established continuity. Sarah explicitly says she is from 1980 in *Pyramids of Mars*, yet in *Mawdryn Undead* the Brigadier is retired by 1977...

The Second Doctor: 'Dastari, you have more letters after your name than anyone I know – enough for two alphabets. How is it that you can still be such a stupid, stubborn, irrational and thoroughly objectionable old idiot?'

336

The Borad:

'Repulsive? Perhaps. But I have a hundred times your intellect, the strength of twenty guardoliers, and a life spanning a dozen centuries... I am the Borad, and I do not tolerate disloyalty.'

TIMELASH

In which the Doctor shares an adventure with young Herbert – who turns out to be H.G. Wells.
BY GLEN MCCOY
2 45-MINUTE EPISODES, FIRST BROADCAST 9–16 MARCH 1985

JOURNEY INFORMATION

KARFEL

Karfel is on the brink of war with its former ally Bandril, having reneged on a treaty to supply grain to the planet. The Bandrils are threatening to launch a Bendalypse warhead at Karfel – this would destroy anything with a central nervous system but leave buildings intact. Only the Morlox (reptilian creatures that live on Karfel) and the Borad would survive.

The guard androids used on Karfel are identical, stylised humanoids that speak in sing-song voices. The Doctor confuses an android by waving a mirror at it – possibly it is priority-programmed to confiscate the mirror.

Karfel is ruled by a Council led by the Maylin, who is merely a figurehead answering to the Borad. After the Borad kills Renis for betraying him, Tekker becomes the new Maylin. Mykros becomes Maylin at the end of the story. The security forces are the guardoliers.

THE TIMELASH

The Timelash is the pyramid-shaped entrance to a Kontron tunnel – a time corridor in space – leading to Earth in AD1179.

The Doctor is able to climb inside the Timelash and retrieve Kontron crystals. He uses one crystal to create a ten-second time break – projecting a past image of himself (his present self becoming invisible) to confuse the Borad. The crystal also absorbs the Borad's time acceleration beam and reflects it back at him after a ten-second delay, ageing him to death. The Doctor destroys the Timelash by throwing Kontron crystals back into it.

THE BORAD

The ruler of Karfel is the Borad – a soft-spoken old man who appears only on screens, apparently as a security measure. In fact, this is an android. The real Borad is a mutated scientist, Magellan, who was fused with a reptilian Morlox when an experiment involving Mustakozene-80 and a Morlox creature went wrong and he and the creature underwent spontaneous tissue amalgamation. The Borad is now a combined mutant with greater strength, intellect and longevity. He intends to use Peri to repeat the experiment and create a consort for himself.

On his previous visit, the Doctor reported Magellan to Karfel's 'Inner Sanctum' for unethical experimentation on the Morlox. The Borad recognises the TARDIS – he knows that the Doctor is a Time Lord and that he can regenerate.

Power is supplied to the Borad through two amulets – one with a mirror set in it, the other black. This black amulet

has a concealed, shielded microphone built into it. The Borad monitors everything happening in his citadel, and has banned all mirrors other than the one in his amulet.

He uses a time acceleration beam to age those who betray him – such as Renis and Tekker – to death. Others he has thrown into the Timelash. His time web is a weapon that can disintegrate the sealed door to the Inner Sanctum.

The Borad has also experimented with cloning – the Borad the Doctor ages to death is merely one of these clones. The 'real' Borad falls into the Timelash and is taken back to twelfth-century Scotland, close to Loch Ness (although the Loch Ness monster is actually the Skarasen – see *Terror of the Zygons*).

NEW INFORMATION

THE DOCTOR

The Third Doctor and Jo Grant visited Karfel many years ago, when the Doctor gave the rebel Katz's grandfather a locket containing a picture of Jo. But the Borad has banned all teaching of the Doctor's visit and erased the story from the history books.

The Doctor refuses a drink from Tekker (and later calls him a 'microcephalic apostate').

The Bandrils are impressed that the Doctor is a Time Lord, and he claims to be President of the High Council of Gallifrey. When the Bandrils think their missile may have hit the Doctor, the Bandril ambassador says they will apologise to the High Council of the Time Lords for killing him.

The Doctor is irritated by Herbert's naive enthusiasm. But when he discovers Herbert is actually H.G. Wells, he knows he has to return him to Earth to write of his experiences.

THE TARDIS

If the TARDIS enters the Kontron tunnel, it may undergo an adverse Kontron effect as time particles collide within a multidimensional implosion field. To ride out the turbulence, the Doctor and Peri strap themselves to the console with safety belts.

The TARDIS deflects the path of the tunnel so it leads to Scotland in 1885, and arrives outside Herbert's uncle's cottage close to Loch Ness.

The Doctor uses the TARDIS as a deflector shield to avert the destruction of Karfel by the Bandrils' Bendalypse warhead, though he does not reveal exactly how he did this.

COMPANIONS

PERI: Peri is keen not to go home yet. She wears a St Christopher medal round her neck (which an android confiscates as it is reflective).

REVELATION OF THE DALEKS

In which Davros is turning humans into Daleks, and corpses into food for Eleanor Bron.
BY ERIC SAWARD
2 45-MINUTE EPISODES, FIRST BROADCAST 23–30 MARCH 1985

JOURNEY INFORMATION

TRANQUIL REPOSE

Tranquil Repose is a cemetery combined with a facility where the terminally ill, amongst others, can be cryogenically suspended until a later date – when a cure for their ailment is discovered for example. While suspended, 'customers' are kept up to date on economic, social and political development.

A local DJ provides a 'personalised entertainment system'.

The theory does not work in practice, however, as nobody wants the cryogenically suspended people back – in many cases they would be in conflict with those currently in power and the galaxy is already over-populated anyway.

After Davros is captured by the Supreme Dalek's task force, Takis and Lilt – the only surviving management of Tranquil Repose – turn it into a farm to harvest the high-protein weed plant, *herba baculum vitae*, that grows in abundance on Necros.

KARA

Kara runs the factories that produce food from the 'product' supplied by the Great Healer (Davros). Because of her dependence on Davros, Kara is forced to pay him out of her profits, so she has hired Orcini to assassinate him.

Kara gives Orcini a booby-trapped communicator that will explode when he signals to her that he has reached Davros's laboratory. She has timed her plan so the explosion will also kill President Vargos when he attends his wife's funeral at Tranquil Repose.

Orcini is not deceived, however, and when Kara is brought to Davros by his Daleks, Orcini kills her.

ORCINI

Temporarily excommunicated from the Grand Order of Oberon, Orcini is a feared assassin. It is said he has only to breathe on a victim for them to die.

He has an artificial leg with a faulty hydraulic valve (this leg is blown off by a blast from a Dalek gun). When seated, the valve is inclined to jam – but Orcini refuses to have it fixed as it is a constant reminder of his own mortality. He lost his leg the only time he did not listen to the instincts of his squire, Bostock. To cleanse his conscience he always gives his fee to charity.

Orcini recognises Davros, and believes he will be a great kill, after which he can retire to a contemplative life of meditation.

Orcini dies when he destroys Davros's new generation of Daleks by deliberately exploding Kara's bomb. The Doctor says he did not die for nothing – he achieved a greater kill than he ever thought possible.

DAVROS

Davros appears to be reduced to only a head contained within a life-support tank. He can defend himself with a blue ray from his artificial eye. In fact the head in the tank is merely a 'lure', as Davros describes it – 'a focal point for the assassin's bullet.' The real Davros is still in the form we know him from previous stories, having escaped from *Resurrection of the Daleks* and been taken to Necros in a freighter. His chair can now hover, and he can fire another blue ray from his fingers which holds Orcini immobile. Bostock shoots off Davros's hand.

Contacted by Takis, the Supreme Dalek sends a task force to capture Davros and he is taken back to Skaro to stand trial for his crimes against the Dalek race.

THE DALEKS

Davros's Daleks are ivory coloured, with gold sense-spheres and 'trim'. They can be destroyed by bullets fitted with bastic heads. The DJ destroys two Daleks with a concentrated sound beam.

Davros is mutating humans in Tranquil Repose into Dalek creatures. The creatures' brains are cultivated in incubators, then transplanted into nascent, transparent Daleks that grow into 'adult' machine-creatures.

The Skaro Daleks easily defeat Davros's Daleks in battle, and plan to put Davros on trial for crimes against the Daleks. They will recondition Davros's Daleks to obey the Supreme Dalek.

Davros: 'The humanoid form makes an excellent concentrated protein.'

TARDIS DATA BANK:

DATE: UNKNOWN, FUTURE
LOCATION: NECROS

DAVROS HAS ASSUMED THE GUISE OF THE GREAT HEALER AT TRANQUIL REPOSE WHERE THE TERMINALLY ILL ARE KEPT IN CRYOGENIC SUSPENSION. HE IS TURNING THE MORE INTELLIGENT INTO DALEKS, AND THE REST INTO A PROCESSED FOOD TO ALLEVIATE FAMINE. HE LURES THE DOCTOR TO TRANQUIL REPOSE – WHERE THE DOCTOR DISCOVERS A HUGE MONUMENT ... TO HIMSELF. WHILE PERI MEETS THE DJ WHO ENTERTAINS THE NEAR-CORPSES, AND AN ASSASSIN ARRIVES TO KILL DAVROS, THE DOCTOR BATTLES TO STOP A NEW ARMY OF DALEKS BECOMING ACTIVE. BUT ON SKARO, THE DALEK SUPREME HAS OTHER IDEAS...

The Skaro Dalek Leader says the Doctor's appearance does not match their data, and has him held prisoner until his identity can be verified.

NEW INFORMATION

THE DOCTOR
The Doctor says he is 900 years old. He has heard of the Knights of the Grand Order of Oberon, and agrees to return Orcini's medal to the order and tell them how he and his squire Bostock died.

COMPANIONS
PERI: Peri is impressed that the DJ has an American accent, and is disappointed to discover it is affected – based on old tapes of Earth DJs.

BEHIND THE SCENES

A BRIEF HIATUS
In late February 1985, the BBC announced that **Doctor Who** was to be rested for a while. Fans of the series immediately assumed, wrongly, that this meant it was being cancelled, and voiced their displeasure.

Several reasons were cited by the Controller of BBC 1, Michael Grade, and the Head of Series and Serials, Jonathan Powell, for this decision. One was that the new 45-minute episode format was not working; another was that the series had become too violent. More telling, it was noted that **Doctor Who** had become an expensive annual commitment for the Corporation.

In 1985, the BBC was short of money. It was launching its ambitious new soap opera **EastEnders**, and had brought forward plans for daytime television in an attempt to pre-empt the competition. But if there was a feeling that postponing the next season of **Doctor Who** was a fairly painless way to save money, this proved to be wrong.

Not only were the series' loyal fans outraged, but the press had a field day and the BBC's Board of Governors expressed their annoyance about not having been consulted about such a high-profile decision.

Pre-production on the next season of **Doctor Who** had already started, with scripts ready and the director for the first story booked. Matthew Robinson had been contracted to direct *The Nightmare Fair*, a sequel to *The Celestial Toymaker,* set in Blackpool and written by former **Who** producer Graham Williams. With the setting for the next story uncertain, the final shot of *Revelation of the Daleks* was frozen, just as the Doctor tells Peri he plans to take her to Blackpool, to leave the destination unspecified.

Other scripts that were complete or in development included *The Ultimate Evil*, by Wally K. Daly, and *Mission to Magnus* – featuring Sil from *Vengeance on Varos* as well as the Ice Warriors – by Philip Martin. There was also an Auton story to be partly filmed in Singapore, written by Robert Holmes and tentatively titled *Yellow Fever and How to Cure It*.

During the 18 months between the end of *Revelation of the Daleks* and the start of the next story, *Slipback* (by Eric Saward) was broadcast on BBC Radio 4 VHF as part of a children's magazine. Producer John Nathan-Turner meanwhile decided to drop the existing scripts and start again for the new season. Together with script editor Eric Saward he devised the notion that the Doctor – like the series – was on trial for his life. The season would be comprised of linked stories under the 'umbrella' of this trial.

True to the letter, if not the spirit, of promises made to the fans and the press, the next season of **Doctor Who** reverted to the 25-minute episode format, and was broadcast on Saturday evenings. There were indeed to be more episodes in this season than the last – 14 rather than 13 – but since the episodes were each twenty minutes shorter, this actually meant a large reduction in the quantity of **Doctor Who** that the BBC was to make.

This format of 14 episodes of 25-minutes was kept until **Doctor Who** finally ended its regular run in 1989.

THE TRIAL OF A TIME LORD

In which the longest ever **Doctor Who** story is formed from four stories bundled together, and the series itself is on trial for its life.

14 EPISODES, FIRST BROADCAST 6 SEPTEMBER – 6 DECEMBER 1986

TARDIS DATA BANK:

DATE: UNKNOWN
LOCATION: TIME LORDS' SPACE STATION

THE TARDIS ARRIVES IN A SPACE STATION WHERE THE DOCTOR IS TO ATTEND AN ENQUIRY INTO HIS ACTIONS. BUT SOON THE ENQUIRY BECOMES A TRIAL FOR HIS LIFE... THE DOCTOR HANDLES HIS OWN DEFENCE, WHILE THE PROSECUTING VALEYARD CHOOSES SEQUENCES FROM HIS CURRENT 'LIFE' TO BE REPLAYED BY THE MATRIX TO DEMONSTRATE THE DOCTOR'S GUILT. BUT CAN THE EVENTS AS SHOWN BY THE INFALLIBLE MATRIX BE TRUSTED AS ACCURATE....

Valeyard: 'These proceedings started as a mere enquiry into the Doctor's activities, I am suggesting now that it becomes a trial. And if he is found guilty, I strongly suggest the termination of his life.'

STORY OVERVIEW

THE DOCTOR

The Doctor learns that he has been deposed as President of the Time Lords for neglecting his duties. He suffers amnesia and does not remember what has happened to Peri. Later, in *Mindwarp*, although his amnesia has cleared, he cannot recall what happened after his brain was flooded with energy by scientist Crozier.

Claiming he is not given to violence, the Doctor admits that he may occasionally have had to resort to a modicum of force.

Declining a court defender, the Doctor chooses a sequence from his own future (*Terror of the Vervoids*), after he has met Mel, as his defence. When the evidence is replayed he notices there have been changes to the sequence he saw – he is now seen apparently not paying attention to Mel's concern about what is happening in the Hydroponics Section and sabotaging a communications room with a fire axe...

THE INQUISITOR

The Inquisitor is in charge of the enquiry/trial and she notes that the Doctor has stood trial on these charges before. The Valeyard contends that the High Council was too lenient in its sentence previously (see *The War Games*).

The Inquisitor takes her job seriously, and does not appreciate the Doctor's flippancy in his confrontations with the Valeyard.

After the truth is revealed, the Inquisitor drops all charges against the Doctor. She asks him to stand for President, but the Doctor suggests she stand instead.

THE VALEYARD

The Doctor's prosecutor, the Valeyard, is in fact a 'version' of the Doctor distilled from his Dark Side. The Master reveals, 'There is some evil in all of us, Doctor – even you. The Valeyard is an amalgamation of the darker sides of your nature, somewhere between your twelfth and thirteenth regenerations. And if I may say, you do not improve with age.'

As prosecutor, the Valeyard can include any testimony he deems relevant provided he can justify it to the court. Referring to the events of *The Mysterious Planet*, he tells the Doctor, 'Your crime was in being there', and insists that the Doctor initiated the chain of events on Ravolox by his mere presence.

The Valeyard claims to have calculated that, based on a random sample, the Doctor's companions have been placed in danger twice as often as the Doctor. The Doctor himself points out that he has had many companions.

Although he seems to be concerned primarily with having the Doctor executed and 'inheriting' his regenerations (having done a deal with the High Council of Time Lords), the Valeyard actually wants to kill the Time Lords involved in the trial – the supreme guardians of the law. He has a MASER – a microwave amplification and stimulated emission of radiation (which Mel, perhaps as a joke, calls a megabyte modem) – which will act as a sub-atomic Particle Disseminator. When the particles are disseminated through the court room view-screen they will kill all Time Lords at the trial.

Apparently destroyed by the rayphase shift triggered by the Doctor when he sabotages the MASER, the Valeyard either takes over as Keeper of the Matrix, or was somehow always the Keeper in disguise.

THE MATRIX

The Matrix (referred to by the Valeyard as 'the Matrix of Time') provides the 'evidence' at the trial. The Inquisitor describes it as, 'a knowledge bank fed constantly by the experiences of all Time Lords wherever they may be'. The Valeyard says that the experiences of third parties can also be monitored and accessed provided they are 'within the collection range of a TARDIS'.

Certain areas of the evidence are 'excised' on the orders of the High Council – Glitz and Dibber discussing the 'secrets' in Marb Station (*The Mysterious Planet*), for example.

THE TRIAL OF A TIME LORD
EVIDENCE: THE MYSTERIOUS PLANET

Drathro: 'Soon the black light system will collapse in upon itself, and we shall all cease to function.'

BY ROBERT HOLMES
EPISODES 1–4

TARDIS DATA BANK:

DATE: TWO MILLION YEARS IN THE FUTURE
LOCATION: RAVOLOX (ACTUALLY EARTH)

THE DOCTOR AND PERI DISCOVER THAT THE PLANET RAVALOX IS ACTUALLY EARTH IN THE FAR FUTURE, SHIFTED TWO LIGHT YEARS THROUGH SPACE WHEN A FIREBALL HIT 500 YEARS AGO, AND INHABITED BY THE PRIMITIVE TRIBE OF THE FREE. AN L3 ROBOT, DRATHRO, IS WORSHIPPED AND FEARED AS THE IMMORTAL BY THE HUMANS IN THE UNDERGROUND SURVIVAL SYSTEM. ROGUES GLITZ AND DIBBER SABOTAGE DRATHRO'S BLACK LIGHT POWER SYSTEM, HOPING TO DISABLE HIM AND STEAL THE SECRETS OF THE SLEEPERS HE GUARDS. BUT THEIR INTERFERENCE CAUSES THE AILING SYSTEM TO GO CRITICAL. THE DOCTOR STRUGGLES TO PERSUADE DRATHRO TO SHUT DOWN THE SYSTEM BEFORE IT IMPLODES WITH CATASTROPHIC RESULTS...

'a deep-rooted maladjustment brought on by an inability to come to terms with the more pertinent, concrete aspects of life,' so his prison psychiatrist said. He says he is wanted for crimes in six different galaxies. He also claims to have 'an uncanny knack with ageing females', but his charms are ineffective on Katryca, leader of the Tribe of the Free.

Glitz knows of the Time Lords (we discover in *Time Inc* that he is working for the Master), and is willing to kill all the tunnel-dwellers to get the secrets of Drathro the L3 robot. He is a ruthless rogue with the gift of the gab, and the Doctor is annoyed to note, 'Strange how low cunning succeeds where intelligence fails,' when Glitz persuades the L3 to accompany him back to his ship for a new black light supply.

After the black light system is shut down, Glitz and his associate, Dibber, stand to make a fortune from the black light converter – it is made from siligtone, the hardest, most expensive metal in the galaxy.

JOURNEY INFORMATION

SABALOM GLITZ

Sabalom Glitz comes from the planet Salostophus in the constellation of Andromeda, and claims to be the product of a broken home which has meant he cannot stand competition –

MERDEEN AND THE GUARDS

The humans in the survival system serve Drathro, within the remains of the London Underground.

Merdeen is in charge of the Train Guards, but is secretly sending people to the surface (which he knows is not still on fire) in order to save them...

KATRYCA AND THE TRIBE OF THE FREE

Katryca knows that before the fire, their ancestors travelled beyond the stars – and this, they think, brought down the wrath of the gods in the form of the fireball. They venerate the black light converter as a totem to their Earth god...

DRATHRO

Drathro – referred to by the humans as 'the Immortal' – is an L3 robot powered by a Maglem mark seven light converter which converts ultraviolet light to black light. Drathro remains in his 'castle' where the two cleverest youths (Tandrell and Humker) are selected to go and serve him.

Drathro is programmed to maintain an *underground* survival system, and therefore cannot allow the 500 work units of humans to drink rain water from outside and culls them to avoid starvation. He is protecting the 'Three Sleepers', though they have died as a relief ship from Andromeda failed to arrive – missing Earth as it had been moved two light years across space. Drathro believes that the Doctor has been sent from Gallifrey to recover secrets left by the Sleepers. He can kill with an electric shock through his hands, and has an L1 service robot which he sends to retrieve the Doctor.

The black light system is failing, and Drathro is trained only for installation and maintenance. He has been training Tandrell and Humker to fix the system, but so far without success. When Dibber destroys the converter, the unstable system is upset and looks set to implode. There has never been a black light implosion, so nobody knows how extensive it will be. Some theories say that the implosion might roll on until all matter in the galaxy is exhausted, or it might cause dimensional transference and threaten the stability of the entire Universe. But Drathro needs the black light, so will not allow the system to be shut down as that would kill him. The Doctor manages to minimise the explosion.

Conned by Glitz into going to his ship for more black light, Drathro collapses and dies when the black light system explodes...

NEW INFORMATION

THE DOCTOR

The Doctor is intrigued that Ravolox is so similar to Earth. According to Time Lord records it was destroyed by a solar fireball 500 years ago. In fact, the fireball only scorched one side of the planet.

The Doctor seems about to give his name as author of a proposed thesis ('by Doctor –') when Peri interrupts. He says he cannot leave as there is a mystery here – questions to which he must have an answer. He speaks in a past Doctor's voice when coming round after the L1 robot captures him (and calls Peri 'Sarah Jane').

COMPANIONS

PERI: Peri experiences déjà vu on Ravolox. When she realises she is in London, she cannot bear to stay in the Underground and returns to the entrance to wait for the Doctor.

She is less than enthusiastic when Katryca says she will find her many husbands.

BEHIND THE SCENES

NEW THEME MUSIC

For *The Trial of a Time Lord*, producer John Nathan-Turner commissioned a new arrangement of the **Doctor Who** theme music from freelance composer Dominic Glynn.

Glynn had sent some sample recordings of his work to the **Doctor Who** production office, hoping to be asked to contribute incidental music. He was astonished and delighted to be asked for a new version of the famous theme. However, despite the 18 months hiatus between seasons of the series, Glynn was rather daunted to discover that the new theme music was needed in just five days.

His arrangement of Ron Grainer's music was only used for *The Trial of a Time Lord*. For the following season of **Doctor Who**, another version was commissioned to match a new title sequence for the new Doctor.

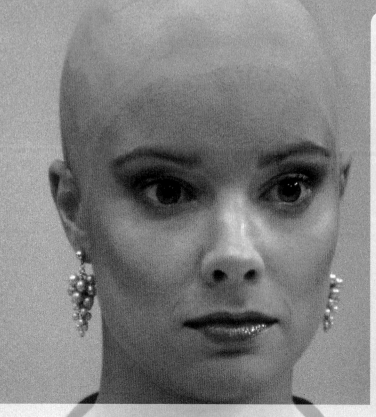

TARDIS DATA BANK:

DATE: ACCORDING TO THE VALEYARD: '24TH CENTURY, LAST QUARTER, 4TH YEAR, 7TH MONTH, 3RD DAY,' WHICH IS POSSIBLY 3 JULY 2379 (SOON AFTER *VENGEANCE ON VAROS*)
LOCATION: THOROS-BETA

TRACING A HIGH-TECH WEAPON TO THOROS-BETA, THE DOCTOR AND PERI FIND A SEA MONSTER BIOLOGICALLY UPGRADED TO OPERATE SOPHISTICATED MACHINERY, A CREATURE PART MAN, PART WOLF, AND SIL. THIS IS SIL'S HOME PLANET, AND THE LEADER KIV MUST HAVE HIS BRAIN TRANSPLANTED INTO ANOTHER BODY IF HE IS TO SURVIVE. WITH THE DOCTOR APPARENTLY COOPERATING WITH THE MENTORS AND TURNING ON PERI, CAN THE EVIDENCE FROM THE MATRIX BE TRUSTED? AND WHAT REALLY HAPPENS TO PERI...

THE TRIAL OF A TIME LORD EVIDENCE:

MINDWARP

BY PHILIP MARTIN
EPISODES 5–8

Crozier: 'You'll not die on me, you fish-faced monster.'

JOURNEY INFORMATION

THOROS BETA AND THE MENTORS

Thoros-Beta, with its pink water and pale green sky, is home of the Mentors (like Sil), who are led by Kiv and are driven by the desire to make money. The Mentors have enslaved the humanoid inhabitants of Thoros-Alpha (Alphans), and the human scientist Crozier is using them for experimentation.

Sil eats marsh minnows and says, 'There's nothing more enjoyable than watching people suffer.' He fawns on the leader Kiv, whose brain is getting so big he needs Crozier to transfer it to another body. If Kiv dies, his bodyguards have orders to kill Sil, Crozier and others. Sil seems to be killed by King Yrcanos (but it is later revealed that these events did not take place – see *Time Inc.*).

KING YRCANOS AND THE LUKOSER

A potential client of the Mentors, King Yrcanos is King of the Krontep, Lord of the Vingten and Conqueror of the Tonkonp Empire (though Sil and the Doctor both say he is a Warlord of Thordon). He is pleased to discover that Peri is not promised to the Doctor, and she teaches him about the value of love. On his planet, warrior queens fight alongside the other warriors.

He tells Peri, 'we all live for a purpose and mine is to die a hero,' and describes ambush as 'a woman's way of fighting.' Yrcanos believes in reincarnation – each incarnation more noble than the last. Finally, as a king, he will join the other kings to fight forever...

The Lukoser used to be Yrcanos's equerry, Dorf of Kanval, but has been mutated by Crozier into a creature part-man, part-wolf.

CROZIER

Crozier is a human, brought to Thoros-Beta apparently to experiment on the Alphans and ensure they – and potential clients like Yrcanos – are cooperative. He has 'upgraded' the Raak, a sea monster, at least partly as a way of testing techniques to be used on Kiv. Kiv will die in a few days from brain compression as his skull is not elastic enough to cope with his growing brain.

Crozier claims he is not without feelings, and allows the Doctor a little time to find a more suitable donor than Peri. But he then operates on her before the Doctor returns.

When he transfers the contents of Kiv's brain into Peri's body, Crozier claims to have altered the basis of all future life. The Inquisitor agrees, and says that the consequences of Crozier's experiment meant the High Council decided to have it stopped... Yrcanos is therefore frozen in a time bubble to ensure that his attack on Crozier's lab is perfectly timed to kill Crozier and Kiv/Peri.

NEW INFORMATION

THE DOCTOR

The Doctor has come to Thoros-Beta to trace a weapon manufactured there. His clue is the dying words of a Warlord of Thordon: 'Thoros-Beta, send more beams that kill.'

His brain is affected when he is interrogated by Crozier, and he betrays Peri and Yrcanos to Sil: 'Why should I risk my life for a savage and a stupid girl?' He also helps Crozier to repair his lab after Yrcanos wrecks it. It is not clear when exactly the Doctor returns to normality, or how much of his behaviour is actually misreported by the Matrix.

THE TARDIS

The TARDIS is moved into the Mentors' base by the Time Lords, and the Doctor is pulled inside (by Time Lord mental energies, it is implied in *The Mysterious Planet*) before the TARDIS is taken to the Time Lords' space station.

COMPANIONS

PERI: Peri is upset to find that Thoros-Beta is Sil's planet – 'I want out,' she says when she discovers this – and is annoyed the Doctor did not tell her. She says that ever since she came to Thoros-Beta she has been 'homesick' for her own time...

She stops King Yrcanos killing the Doctor, even though he seems to have gone mad and has no care for her life.

Kiv's brain is apparently transplanted into Peri's body, which is then killed by the enraged Yrcanos. But see *Time Inc.* for an alternative account.

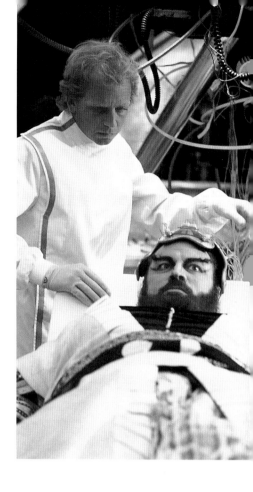

The Doctor: 'Tomorrow, they intend to take the brain of the Lord Kiv and transplant it into my body. He will possess my body. To prevent that, I must please the Mentors, Peri. If that means sacrificing you in my place, then that is the way it must be.'

MELANIE BUSH

Mel works with computers and comes from Pease Pottage. The Doctor envies her 'amazing ability for almost total recall'. She is able to remember the exact wording, for example, of the Mayday message sent by Hallet in *Terror of the Vervoids* (though she does need to take a map with her to find the swimming pool in *Paradise Towers*).

Mel has absolute faith in the Doctor, and it is out of concern for his welfare that she establishes an exercise routine for him – insisting he drink carrot juice and installing an exercise bike in the TARDIS Control Room.

Mel's inclination to trust is not always to her advantage, however. In *Paradise Towers*, for example, she believes Pex's improbable story about being charged with putting the world of Paradise Towers to rights. She sees no possible danger from the overfriendly Rezzies, Tabby and Tilda, cannibals who are fattening her up with cakes and biscuits, until she is trapped under a crocheted shawl and attacked with a toasting fork.

Perhaps more than any of the Doctor's companions, Mel means well and sees good in everyone. She may be impulsive enough to follow any lead and see the most innocent people as potential suspects (*Terror of the Vervoids*), but she is always surprised when people turn out not to be as friendly and altruistic as they first appear.

Perhaps it is not so surprising, then, that just as she tries to 'reform' the Doctor's lifestyle into something rather more healthy, she decides to accompany Glitz when he leaves Iceworld in *Dragonfire* in order to try to reform his moral lifestyle. Whether or not she succeeds is left to the imagination of the viewer.

'I'm as truthful, honest, and about as boring as they come.'

(MEL – *THE TRIAL OF A TIME LORD*)

Valeyard: 'Whether or not the Doctor has proved himself innocent of meddling is no longer the cardinal issue before this court. He has proved himself guilty of a far greater crime... Article Seven permits no exceptions. The Doctor has destroyed a complete species. The charge must now be genocide.'

THE TRIAL OF A TIME LORD EVIDENCE:
TERROR OF THE VERVOIDS

BY PIP AND JANE BAKER
EPISODES 9–12

The Doctor: 'This is a situation that requires tact and finesse. Fortunately, I am blessed with both.'

JOURNEY INFORMATION

THE HYPERION
The Hyperion III is a grade one security craft, as the Doctor deduces since Commodore 'Tonker' Travers is in charge. Presumably this is because of Lasky's cargo of Vervoids.

Janet is the stewardess and the Security Officer is Rudge. On his last voyage before retirement, Rudge is helping Mogarians to hijack the ship and get the metals 'plundered' from Mogar that are in the vault. He wants a 'more comfortable retirement'. After the hijacking is foiled and Rudge is killed by the Vervoids, the Doctor calls him 'just a weak man gone rogue'.

The passenger-turned-hijacker Mogarians wear protective suits and helmets on the ship, and need translators. They resent the human mines on Mogar (which is rich in metals) which were originally a limited concession, but are now – they believe – stripping Mogar bare.

PROFESSOR SARAH LASKY AND HER TEAM
Professor Lasky is an agronomist – a thrematologist to be precise – someone who is an expert in breeding animals or plants under domestication. Like Mel, she spends a lot of time in the ship's gym, and she is reading *Murder on the Orient Express and Other Mysteries*.

Her assistants are Bruchner and Doland, who have agreed to keep their discovery of the Vervoids secret until they reach Earth.

Doland sees the Vervoids as an economic asset and has a consortium's backing to exploit them – Vervoids can run factories and farms at practically no cost, needing only sunlight and water, and the existing robots can be dumped on the scrap heap. Prepared to murder to protect his 'investment', Doland claims to be the Vervoids' friend as without him they wouldn't exist, but they are not convinced and they kill him.

TARDIS DATA BANK:

DATE: 2986, POSSIBLY 16 APRIL
LOCATION: SPACE LINER HYPERION III, EN ROUTE FROM MOGAR (A PLANET ON THE PERSEUS ARM OF THE MILKY WAY) TO EARTH

PROFESSOR LASKY IS TRANSPORTING VERVOID PLANTS ON THE *HYPERION III* BUT THE VERVOIDS BECOME ACTIVE AND START TO DESTROY ALL ANIMAL LIFE ON THE SHIP. CAN THE DOCTOR AND HIS COMPANION MEL UNCOVER A MURDERER BEFORE THE *HYPERION* IS SUCKED INTO THE BLACK HOLE OF TARTARUS? OR WILL THE VERVOIDS KILL EVERYONE BEFORE THE TRUTH BECOMES KNOWN…

Lasky's lab assistant, Ruth Baxter, was infected by a speck of pollen that entered through a scratch in her thumb during a cross-fertilisation, and is mutating into a part-Vervoid. She is being taken to Earth for treatment.

When he realises the Vervoids are dangerous, Bruchner is conscience-stricken and tries to destroy the research work, then to crash the Hyperion III into the black hole of Tartarus.

THE VERVOIDS

A form of mobile, humanoid plant life, the Vervoids are awoken from their pods by high-intensity light (only infraspectrum light is safe as it allows them to stay dormant).

The Vervoids can kill using a 'sting' in their hand or by emitting marsh gas (which kills Bruchner on the bridge). They have the power of speech, and refer to humans as 'animal kind'. Somehow they know Bruchner's name, who Lasky is and, also, that they are called Vervoids by Lasky's team.

The Vervoids keep dead humans on a 'compost heap' in their lair, and are driven back there by the darkness when Commodore Travers pretends the ship's generator has failed.

The Doctor destroys the Vervoids using vionesium – an expensive metal found on Mogar and stored in the ship's vault (hence Rudge's attempted hijack). It is similar to magnesium and emits intense light and carbon dioxide when exposed to oxygenated air.

HALLETT

Hallett is an investigator who has met the Doctor before, and he sends a message to him asking for help. The Doctor describes him as a maverick, one of a rare breed. Hallett is calling himself Grenville, but is recognised by another passenger, Kimber. He fakes his own death, leaving his shoes by an incinerator, and assumes the identity of a Mogarian. But he is poisoned (by Doland) before he can communicate further with the Doctor.

NEW INFORMATION

THE DOCTOR

The Doctor can sense evil in the ship's storage bay when he and Mel arrive on the *Hyperion III*. He has met Commodore Travers before – when he was a captain – and saved his ship from what Travers describes as a 'web of mayhem and intrigue'.

He produces a bunch of artificial flowers as if by magic to try to charm Janet into giving him a passenger list, and later makes a leaf disappear having taken it unseen from Hallett's pocket. He eats one of Professor Lasky's Demeter seeds with no apparent ill effects.

For once he admits some medical knowledge, treating the commodore when he is knocked out by Rudge: 'After all, I am a doctor.'

The Doctor describes the dilemma of killing or being killed as 'a conflict in which there can be no justice'.

THE TARDIS

Hallett's Mayday call is beamed directly at the TARDIS and relayed to a screen on the console. It reads '...perative traitor be identified before landing Earth Mayday end'.

COMPANIONS

MEL: Mel is concerned about the Doctor's waistline. She has devised an exercise routine for him, installed an exercise bike in the TARDIS control room and insists he drink carrot juice.

THE TRIAL OF A TIME LORD
VERDICT: TIME INC.

EPISODE 13, BY ROBERT HOLMES
EPISODE 14, BY PIP AND JANE BAKER

The Doctor: 'Unless we are prepared to sacrifice our lives for the good of all, then evil and anarchy will spread like the plague.'

JOURNEY INFORMATION

THE MASTER

The Inquisitor does not immediately recognise the Master (but later refers to him as a renegade). He has entered the Matrix using a copy of the Key of Rassilon, and speaks to the court from within the Matrix.

The Master still wants the Doctor dead, but will not

TARDIS DATA BANK:

DATE: UNKNOWN
LOCATION: TIME LORD SPACE STATION; WITHIN THE MATRIX

THE DOCTOR DISCOVERS THAT THE VALEYARD IS IN FACT A DISTILLATION OF ALL THAT IS EVIL WITHIN HIMSELF. WITH THE MASTER APPEARING AS A SURPRISE WITNESS FROM INSIDE THE MATRIX, THE DOCTOR FINDS HIMSELF TRAPPED IN A NIGHTMARE WORLD WHERE THE ONLY LOGIC IS THAT THERE IS NO LOGIC. WITH TIME RUNNING OUT IN MORE WAYS THAN ONE, HE UNEARTHS THE TERRIBLE TRUTH ABOUT RAVOLOX AND THE ACTIONS OF THE HIGH COUNCIL OF TIME LORDS...

countenance the Valeyard as a rival (he sees him as a greater threat than the Doctor). Also, he hopes the Doctor and the Valeyard will destroy each other and that the High Council will be 'rocked to its foundations' by his revelations. 'There is nothing purer or more unsullied, madam, than the desire for revenge,' he says.

When the High Council is deposed the Master assumes command as he controls the Matrix. But the Valeyard has booby-trapped the Matrix data bank and the Master is trapped in his TARDIS within the Matrix by a limbo atrophier.

SABALOM GLITZ

The Master sends Glitz to the Time Lord's space station as a witness. Mel is with him. He describes himself as 'a small-time crook with small-time ambitions, one of which is staying alive,' and says the Master is a 'business partner' who sent him to Ravolox to get the secrets of the Matrix.

Glitz is trapped with the Master in his TARDIS. The Doctor asks the Inquisitor to be lenient with him when he is eventually released.

THE MATRIX

The Keeper of the Matrix says no-one may enter without the Key of Rassilon – which is kept in his possession except when used for maintenance perhaps once every millennium (though both the Master and the Valeyard have copies).

The Keeper describes the Matrix as a micro-universe, and reveals that the Seventh Door to the Matrix is on the space station.

Through the door, the Doctor finds a bizarre, pseudo-Victorian unreal world where there is disembodied laughter and singing; hands reach out of a water barrel to pull him in. There is a Fantasy Factory that is staffed by aspects of the same clerk, Mr Popplewick, but at different ages, and there is even a mock courtroom where the Doctor is found guilty of genocide and sentenced to death.

NEW INFORMATION

THE DOCTOR

The Doctor is horrified to discover the truth. The Three Sleepers had found a way into the Matrix and were stealing secrets. Working from Earth, they knew the Time Lords would discover them. They did and used a magnotron (only possible via an order in High Council) to draw the Earth and its constellation two light years across space, causing the fireball that decimated the planet. The Andromedans set up a survival chamber for the Sleepers to escape the fireball. But their robot recovery mission missed Earth...

The Doctor is vociferous in his disgust that the High Council 'put an ancient culture like the Earth to the sword for the sake of a few miserable, filthy scientific advances... In all my travellings throughout the Universe I have battled against evil, against power-mad conspirators. I should have stayed here. The oldest civilisation – decadent, degenerate and rotten to the core. Power-mad conspirators, Daleks, Sontarans, Cybermen – they're still in the nursery compared

The Master: 'With the Doctor as my enemy, I always have the advantage. But the Valeyard — a distillation of all that's evil in you, untainted by virtue, a composite of your every dark thought — is a different proposition. Additionally, he has infuriated me by threatening to deny me the pleasure of personally bringing about your destruction.'

to us. Ten million years of absolute power, that's what it takes to be really corrupt.'

He points out that if he had not visited Ravolox, the High Council would have been able to keep events secret. As it was, they had to make a deal with the Valeyard to adjust the evidence in return for the remainder of the Doctor's regenerations...

THE TARDIS

The Master has his TARDIS inside the Matrix. Its interior is like the Doctor's, but predominantly black. It is disguised first as a ruined hut on a beach, then as a statue of Queen Victoria.

COMPANIONS

PERI: The Master reveals that Peri was not in fact killed, and says she is a queen 'set up on high' by Yrcanos.

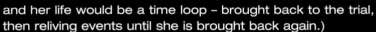

MEL: Mel is sent to the station by the Master to help the Doctor's defence (and thus exacerbate the battle between the Doctor and the Valeyard). She leaves with the Doctor, despite the fact that in chronological terms they have not yet met each other. (If this was when she first started travelling with the Doctor, she would recall events of the trial, and her life would be a time loop – brought back to the trial, then reliving events until she is brought back again.)

BEHIND THE SCENES

THE FINAL END?

Although many authors worked at various times on *The Trial of a Time Lord*, many of their ideas and scripts being discarded along the way, it was always the intention that Robert Homes would write the final two episodes. But after scripting Episode 13, Holmes was taken seriously ill. He died on 24 May 1986 without having scripted the final episode.

Working from Holmes's outline for the episode, script editor Eric Saward – a great admirer of Holmes's work – scripted Episode 14. As well as the usual script editing necessary to ensure an episode fits into an ongoing series, Saward made slight amendments to Holmes's Episode 13 to accommodate his own Episode 14. He also changed the emphasis of the original outline so that it was the Valeyard rather than the Master who emerged as the main villain.

The character of Glitz was added, at the request of producer John Nathan-Turner, though he may have been included in Holmes's outline.

One thing that did not change, and which Holmes and Saward had discussed in detail, was the ending. Aware that the series itself was effectively on trial as well as the lead

character, they had decided to end with the Doctor trapped, locked forever in a struggle with the Valeyard in a 'time vent.' Their feeling was that if – as they hoped – the series returned, then the Doctor would be rescued or escape in the next story. If it did not, the ending would be memorable and fitting...

But producer John Nathan-Turner disagreed. Apart from not wanting to finish the season with a downbeat ending, he felt the narrative might provide a ready-made excuse to end the series. When it became clear that Saward and Nathan-Turner would not be able to agree on a compromise, Saward resigned as script editor and withdrew his permission for the use of the script and any of the ideas and narrative elements it contained.

With just days before production was to begin and with locations and cast booked, costumes and sets constructed, Nathan-Turner had a problem. His solution was to brief writers Pip and Jane Baker and provide them with a script of Episode 13. He briefed them at a meeting witnessed and minuted by the BBC's legal department so it could be proved they really were working in isolation, and any overlap with Saward and Holmes's work on the final episode would be coincidental.

Pip and Jane Baker delivered their version of Episode 14 very quickly. In fact they delivered rather more than was wanted with the first edit of the episode considerably over-running. This gave rise to another problem. To cut scenes from the episode to produce a standard-length **Doctor Who** risked losing vital explanations that tied together the previous 13 weeks of story. At the very least, it would make for a very rushed and confusing conclusion. As a result, John Nathan-Turner requested that Episode 14 should have an official running time of 30 minutes rather than 25. Head of Series and Serials, Jonathan Powell, agreed and the final edited version ran to 29 minutes and 30 seconds.

But Nathan-Turner's problems were not over. The verdict from the series' own trial was 'not guilty', but neither was it a total acquittal. Audience figures had been low, and the series had still drawn criticism. Despite Nathan-Turner's strenuous objections, he was told by the Controller of BBC 1, Michael Grade, that he could not renew the contract of his leading actor. One concession Nathan-Turner won was that he could offer Colin Baker the first four episodes of the next series of **Doctor Who**, the Doctor regenerating at the end of the story.

But Colin Baker was unwilling to stay on after being made a public scapegoat, and he knew that a commitment to that one story would take time from his schedule at just the moment when he needed to be finding other work. He declined the offer, and when the series returned the following autumn, it was with a new Doctor...

ELECTRONIC WIZARDRY

The very first electronic-effects work in **Doctor Who** was in fact the very first recorded work for the series – the opening titles. The term 'electronic effects', as distinct from 'visual effects', refers to manipulation of the video image – effects that are performed direct to the videotape rather than on the studio floor or location, or using a model or specially constructed prop.

Today, entire armies and worlds can be created using computer-generated images (CGI) and other electronic or computer-driven effects, but when **Doctor Who** started, very little was possible by way of electronic effects. The visual howlaround technique used for the opening titles was pioneering.

The only 'standard' effect was the ability to inlay one picture into part or all of another – similar to a matte in film terms. Inlay was used from the earliest times on **Doctor Who**, and for a variety of effects. It was time-consuming to organise, and depended upon the main image having a 'blank' area where the second image could be inlaid. So when the Doctor and his companions used the travel dials to disappear in *The Keys of Marinus*, they always stood in front of a blank wall – even if, on occasion, there had been no blank wall there previously.

Inlay was used more effectively to add a distant view of the Dalek City to a sequence where the Doctor, Ian, Barbara and Susan observe it from the edge of the petrified jungle in *The Daleks*. CSO was a colour-based successor to the inlay technique and in the same way the actors were required to act to an empty space where an image would later be added.

While inlay could be used to make objects appear and disappear, the simpler technique of 'roll back and mix' was generally used for the coming and going of the TARDIS. A camera was 'locked off' – meaning it was fixed in position – and the scene was recorded. The camera was then stopped, the tape wound back, and the scene continued but with a change – in this case the TARDIS was either removed or placed in position. The final output image was then achieved by mixing the scene as recorded before the change to the scene after the change, so that the alteration appears to take place in real time – the TARDIS seems to appear or fade away. In the case of several of the Doctor's regenerations, this same technique was used to make one person's features fade into those of another.

For many years, the apparently simple addition of 'laser beams', such as K-9's ray, was achieved literally by painting the beam on to each frame of the video. Not until *The Androids of Tara* was the effect of a beam or bolt travelling from gun (or electronic crossbow in this case) to its target achieved. With the arrival of image manipulation devices such as Quantel, Paintbox and HARRY, increasingly sophisticated effects became possible, manipulating the video image at the pixel level, for example to distort, invert, roll or even explode the picture.

The first effects of the Daleks exterminating their victims were achieved by opening the camera lens fully so the picture became overexposed and went into negative. By the Third Doctor's time, pretty much the same technique was used, but to give a colour negative. From *Destiny of the Daleks*, the victim was surrounded by a halo, within which their image was switched to negative while the background remained normal, and from *Remembrance of the Daleks*, it was possible for the victim to be struck by a moving blast from the Dalek's gun, and shown as an animated, negative skeleton within the halo.

By the time *Doctor Who – The Movie* was made, and with the facilities of the USA's movie industry available on the west coast, far more was possible with electronic effects and CGI. The opening titles, for example, showed a model TARDIS against a computer-generated starscape shot using motion control. Also used for the opening space-station sequence of *The Trial of a Time Lord*, motion control basically slaves the camera to a computer so that its movements can be completely planned and controlled as it photographs various elements that are to be combined into a final composite sequence – the TARDIS and its background, for example. The snake-like form that the disembodied Master assumes in *Doctor Who – The Movie* was a completely computer-generated image, and the Doctor's regeneration was achieved with the additional enhancement of computer-animated sequences.

With the advances made in the film and television industry since 1996, we can be sure that when **Doctor Who** returns the CGI successors of electronic effects will play a large part in the series' realisation. A 'taste' of the sorts of effects and techniques that may be used can be

seen in the restored versions of **Doctor Who** DVDs being released by BBC Worldwide. *The Ark in Space*, for example, includes an option to replace the original 1970s model/CSO effects for the Ark with CGI sequences realised by Mike Tucker and Nick Sainton-Clark from the BBC's Visual Effects Department.

Throughout the 1970s, the mainstay of electronic effects on **Doctor Who** was a technique called 'colour separation overlay' (see *The Ambassadors of Death* for a full description). Also known as chromakey, this was essentially the same as the 'blue screen' process used in feature films, and replaced the earlier inlay techniques.

Over time, the use of CSO became more sophisticated, until it was superseded in many areas by newer techniques. Quantel, for example, could be used to place an image on the TARDIS screen – or even to provide a TARDIS on location in Lanzarote for *Planet of Fire* when the prop never in fact left Britain.

One experimental use of CSO that is worthy of note was Scene-Sync. This was a system developed in the USA by Power-Optics and 'tested' on **Doctor Who** before being used on the BBC's prestigious **The Borgias**. It was a technique that combined two images using CSO but with both cameras jointly controlled. This meant that on *Meglos* a camera looking at a model set – the screens of Zolfa Thura – was slaved to the camera showing the actors performing against a blue background. As the master camera was moved, so the slaved camera mimicked that move, but scaled to match the set.

The system proved successful enough to be used for **The Borgias**, but the cost meant it was not used again on **Doctor Who**. As ever, a consideration was the time taken to achieve the desired effect. It is perhaps typical of the marriage of hi-tech and down-to-earth pragmatism of **Doctor Who**'s effects work that, when there was no time left at the end of the recording session to achieve the planned effect of the Gaztaks' model spaceship taking off, this final effect was therefore achieved by sticking a broom handle into the end of the model (masked by one of the screens), and simply lifting it out of shot.

'Think about me when you're living your life one day after another, all in a neat pattern. Think about the homeless traveller in his old police box, his days like crazy paving.'

(THE DOCTOR – *DRAGONFIRE*)

Seven

THE SEVENTH DOCTOR

The Seventh Doctor's persona is one of contradictions. In his first few stories he is portrayed as a bumbler who misinterprets and miscalculates at almost every opportunity. Even later, in *Remembrance of the Daleks*, he admits to having made a terrible miscalculation, while the whole of *Silver Nemesis* is a result of his earlier actions (albeit in a different incarnation).

Yet, he is also a master-planner. The mistakes he may have made prior to *Silver Nemesis* become a plan to destroy the Cybermen. We get the impression in *Remembrance of the Daleks* that he is springing a trap he set before we ever met him. *The Curse of Fenric* reveals more of the Doctor's unfinished business, and his reaction to Ace's admission that she has told Judson how to interpret the runes also suggests he is working to a carefully defined plan. When he moves the chess pieces on their board at Lady Peinforte's house in *Silver Nemesis*, he is playing a game of strategy across time and space – with real people as the pieces.

In many ways, this is the most callous of Doctors. While he has moments of passionate feeling for his friends – such as when he believes the Brigadier to have been killed in *Battlefield* – in *Ghost Light* he is quite willing to take Ace back to the most frightening place she has ever been merely to satisfy his own curiosity. He may try to keep Gilmore's men out of the firing line in *Remembrance of the Daleks*, but he displays not a moment's regret at Gavrok's murder of the Navarino tourists in *Delta and the Bannermen*. This is a Doctor who will discuss the implications of taking sugar in his tea as if it is a matter for the gravest consideration, but then tricks Davros into destroying Skaro, sets a trap to blow Kroagnon to pieces (killing Pex), wipes out an entire Cyber fleet, and blows up Daleks with the Nitro-9 he forbids Ace to carry... When he tells Ace that he only took her with him because he realised she was one of the wolves of Fenric, and wouldn't have wasted his time on her otherwise, Ace believes him. He later tells her, 'I had to make you lose your belief in me,' but there may be more than a grain of truth in the Doctor's explanation of why he 'adopted' Ace – it was part of one of his grand plans.

The Doctor's quips and misquotes mask a deeper, darker side. He cultivates an image of mystery – with a question mark for an umbrella, and a multitude of them on his jumper. Yet he is happy to show Ray and Burton round the TARDIS in *Delta and the Bannermen*. He goes out of his way to obscure his personal details. However, rather than simply keep his secrets, he constantly alludes to them – as if to provoke an enigmatic aura. He drops hints to Ace about how he may have been involved in developing the Hand of Omega; he allows Lady Peinforte to reveal that he is more than just a Time Lord; and at the end of *Silver Nemesis* he seems determined to provoke Ace into asking, 'Who *are* you?' merely so he can refuse to answer...

Perhaps the Seventh Doctor is a flip-side to the Second. Whereas the Second Doctor so often made his success look like luck or happenstance, so it may be that the Seventh Doctor has a knack of making his good fortune and callous impulsiveness seem like complex planning.

THE MAN BEHIND THE DOCTOR – SYLVESTER MCCOY

James Kent-Smith started out in the insurance industry before deciding to switch to entertainment. He got a job selling tickets at the Roundhouse Theatre in London, where he met actor/director Ken Campbell and was recruited to join *The Ken Campbell Roadshow*. In this he appeared as a character called Sylveste McCoy, and he decided to change his name to match (later amending it to Sylvester McCoy) after it was mistaken for his real name.

McCoy is still remembered for some of the stunts he performed in Campbell's show – including setting fire to his head and stuffing ferrets down his trousers. But he soon became an accomplished and talented actor as well as an eccentric daredevil. It was while starring in *The Pied Piper* at the National Theatre that he was offered the role of the Doctor.

Since **Doctor Who** finished, McCoy has appeared in a variety of stage and screen roles – including a nude appearance in the farce *Having a Ball* – as well as extensive radio performances like the part of the mouse, Reepicheep, in the BBC's adaptations of C.S. Lewis's *Chronicles of Narnia*. In 1996, he reprised the role of the Doctor for the opening section of *Doctor Who – The Movie*, and continues to appear as the Doctor in audio productions.

TIME AND THE RANI

In which the Doctor regenerates before the opening titles and the Rani returns, disguised as Mel.
BY PIP AND JANE BAKER
4 EPISODES, FIRST BROADCAST 7–28 SEPTEMBER 1987

TARDIS DATA BANK:

DATE: UNKNOWN, FUTURE
LOCATION: LAKERTYA

THE RANI ATTACKS THE TARDIS, CAUSING THE DOCTOR TO REGENERATE. SHE MASQUERADES AS MEL TO GET THE DOCTOR'S HELP REPAIRING HER EQUIPMENT – EQUIPMENT SHE NEEDS TO DESTROY AN ASTEROID MADE OF STRANGE MATTER AND CREATE A TIME MANIPULATOR THAT WILL DESTROY THE PEACEFUL PEOPLE OF LAKERTYA...

The Doctor:

'Perhaps this is my new persona — sulky, bad-tempered... You don't understand regeneration, Mel. It's a lottery, and I've drawn the short plank.'

JOURNEY INFORMATION

THE RANI

Doctor says the Rani is a neurochemist, 'a brilliant but sterile mind. There's not one spark of decency in her.'

She is collecting geniuses from across time and space – including Einstein, Hypatia, Pasteur and the Doctor. She needs the Doctor to repair her damaged equipment. She pretends to be Mel, complete with costume and red wig, to get the Doctor's cooperation. Later she creates a hologram of Mel that fools the Doctor into returning a vital component.

The Rani has detected an asteroid composed of strange matter that is incredibly dense. If it explodes, it will send off a blast of gamma rays equivalent to a supernova and destroy 'this corner of the galaxy'. The Rani is using a huge 'brain' linked to the minds of various geniuses to discover a lightweight substance called Loyhargil that will act as a trigger in a missile to explode the asteroid and produce helium 2. This will fuse with the upper atmosphere of Lakertya to form an outer shell of chronons – discrete particles of time. At the same time, the brain's cortex will

go into chain reaction and expand to fill the space up to the shell – creating a time manipulator: a cerebral mass capable of dominating and controlling time anywhere in the cosmos. The Rani will then be able to change the order of creation – 'correcting' evolution. She plans to return to the Cretaceous era of Earth and ensure the dinosaurs realise their potential.

The Rani has set traps on Lakertya that capture the victim in a bubble which then spins off and explodes (unless it lands on water).

LAKERTYA

The Lakertyans are humanoid with reptilian influences. They have a crest (part of the skull). The Rani holds their leader, Beyus, hostage together with his daughter Sarn (who is killed by a bubble trap when escaping). Beyus's wife (Sarn's mother) is called Faroon.

The Lakertyans relax at the Centre of Leisure – where the Rani releases killer insects from a spinning ball.

The Doctor manages to safely remove explosive anklets that the Rani has put on the Lakertyans, and rigs them to destroy the brain and delay the Rani's missile. Beyus stays in the Rani's lab to ensure the detonation of the anklets, and is killed in the explosion.

THE TETRAPS

Brought by the Rani from the planet Tetrapyriarbus, the Tetraps are giant bats that sleep hanging upside down in

a cavern. They feed on a dark sludge that Beyus releases down a chute into a trough. The Tetraps have four eyes, one in each side of their head, and therefore have all-round vision.

Urak, the Tetrap leader, overhears the Rani's plan and suspects that the Tetraps will be killed on Lakertya. This is confirmed when the Rani leaves him to guard the lab rather than return with her to her TARDIS. Enraged, the Tetraps capture the Rani in her own TARDIS.

NEW INFORMATION

THE DOCTOR

The Doctor regenerates during the Rani's attack on the TARDIS, although it is not clear why. The Rani injects him with a drug that causes amnesia and then masquerades as Mel.

When choosing clothes, the Doctor dresses as Napoleon, a guardsman, a teacher and imitations of his previous incarnations. He says he is in his 'seventh persona' and that he is 953 – the same age as the Rani (who uses this number as the entry/exit code on her lab door).

The Doctor's special subject at university was thermodynamics and it is implied that he was at university with the Rani. He has never been to Lakertya before.

The Doctor pushes a Tetrap on to one of the Rani's bubble traps.

When he is linked into the Rani's 'brain', the Doctor causes it to suffer from multiple schizophrenia and the different personae in the brain argue amongst themselves.

The Doctor uses the Rani's explosive anklets to destroy the brain, and delays the missile's lift-off so that it misses the asteroid, thwarting her plans.

THE TARDIS

The Doctor says the TARDIS needs its bicentennial refit. He keeps a radiation wave meter in the Tool Room.

The external form of the Rani's TARDIS is a reflective pyramid.

COMPANIONS

MEL: Mel manages to 'throw' the Doctor. She knows about regeneration, and is convinced by the Doctor's double pulse that he *is* the Doctor.

She remarks that 'computers are my speciality, not nuclear physics,' and manages to run a fibre optic to short-circuit the Rani's anklets.

BEHIND THE SCENES

NEW TITLES AND MUSIC

As Sylvester McCoy took over as the new Doctor, so a new set of opening and closing titles was commissioned, along with another realisation of Ron Grainer's **Doctor Who** theme music.

Senior BBC graphic designer Oliver Elmes was given the task of creating the new titles. He worked closely with CAL Video, the company that realised his designs using computer animation. Elmes designed a sort of 'fairground ride' through a galaxy, ending with a new **Doctor Who** logo. As he worked with Gareth Edwards at CAL Video, so the roller-coaster ride was simplified, and the image of the TARDIS inside a bubble was introduced.

As in every other title sequence except the original, the Doctor's face was incorporated. The first version used a face that was less detailed and more sinister, but this was changed to a more complete version of the Doctor's face. The first version was used accidentally, however, on Episode 4 of *Time and the Rani* (though it was replaced for the video release).

To accompany the new titles, composer Keff McCulloch provided a new arrangement of the theme music (he also composed the incidental music for all the stories of the season except *Dragonfire*, which was scored by Dominic Glynn).

REMEMBRANCE OF THE DALEKS
BY
BEN AARONOVITCH

PARADISE TOWERS

In which Richard Briers appears as Chief Caretaker of a tower block, only to be possessed by the mind of its architect.
BY STEPHEN WYATT
4 EPISODES, FIRST BROADCAST 5–26 OCTOBER 1987

TARDIS DATA BANK:

DATE: 21ST CENTURY
LOCATION: PARADISE TOWERS

PARADISE TOWERS IS A BUILDING DESIGNED BY THE GREAT ARCHITECT KROAGNON, BUT IT IS NOT THE PRISTINE ENVIRONMENT MEL HOPED TO FIND, AND THE DOCTOR SUSPECTS SOMETHING IS WRONG. YOUNG KANGS SCRAWL ON THE WALLS, ELDERLY REZZIES CROCHET TABLECLOTHS, PEX PROCLAIMS HIMSELF THE LOCAL HERO, AND THE CARETAKERS ENFORCE THE RULES. BUT THE ROBOTIC CLEANERS HAVE STARTED KILLING PEOPLE, THE REZZIES HAVE TAKEN TO CANNIBALISM, AND THE CHIEF CARETAKER IS NURTURING SOMETHING VERY UNPLEASANT IN THE BASEMENT...

JOURNEY INFORMATION

PARADISE TOWERS

Paradise Towers apparently won architectural awards 'back in the twenty-first century'. Now it is litter strewn and rat infested. There are 304 floors, the swimming pool being on the top floor.

When war broke out youngsters and oldsters were shipped to Paradise Towers, while the in-betweens were sent to fight. The Caretakers are possibly exempt from military service.

CARETAKERS

It is the job of the caretakers to keep Paradise Towers clean of wallscrawl (graffiti), and maintain the buildings. They are completely driven by the regulations in their rule book. The Doctor is able to escape from the Caretatakers by making up rules about how he should be guarded.

The Chief Caretaker sees himself as 'daddy' to a creature in the basement   which, although he does not know it, is actually the Towers' architect Kroagnon. He would rather kill the Doctor (whom he assumes is the Great Architect) than let him interfere with the smooth running of the Towers. The Doctor calls him a 'power-crazed psychopath.'

The Deputy Chief Caretaker and his colleagues finally rebel against the Chief Caretaker when he orders the buildings cleansed of living flesh.

KANGS

The Kangs are juvenile gangs of girls, differentiated by colour – there are Red Kangs, Blue Kangs and Yellow Kangs (though the last Yellow Kang is made 'unalive' by a Cleaner). The girls' hair and clothes are dyed to their Kang colour. Their language and names are derived from their environment. So the Red Kangs such as Bin Liner, Fire Escape, Air Duct and others hide in their brainquarters. They think the Doctor's clothes are 'ice hot'.

REZZIES

The Rezzies are the elderly residents of Paradise Towers, and they have been there since the Great Architect completed the building. At least some of the Rezzies are cannibals.

CLEANERS

The robotic, self-activating megapodic Mark 7Z Cleaners are white robots each armed with a corkscrew arm, a claw, and a rotating blade. The Chief Caretaker and Kroagnon use them to kill Caretakers, Kangs and Rezzies to 'feed' Kroagnon.

The swimming pool is cleaned by an aquatic yellow version of the Cleaners.

KROAGNON

Kroagnon is known as the Great Architect. He is the genius responsible for Golden Dream Park, the Bridge of Perpetual Motion and Miracle City – which he refused to move out of in case people moved in and destroyed the beauty of his work. The authorities did get him out, but those who moved in were killed...

Kroagnon's bodiless brain was trapped in Paradise Towers by the parents of the Kangs so that he could never finish the building. If he had finished, he would have built booby traps into every corner...

Kroagnon transplants his brain by corpo-electroscopy into

Kroagnon: 'Attention all robotic cleaners. At last Kroagnon can leave the basement prison they trapped his bodiless brain in, and return in his borrowed body to the corridors and lifts of his own creation. They buried me away because I wanted to stop them using the Towers. But now you and I will destroy them.

the body of the Chief Caretaker so that he can escape from the basement. Then he and the Cleaners set out to 'cleanse' the building of humans – as it is 'polluted with flesh, living flesh'.

PEX

Pex is a young man who lives in Paradise Towers. He tells Mel, 'I put the world of Paradise Towers to rights,' but the Kangs call him 'the muscle brain' and say he hid away in the ship when they were sent to Paradise Towers as, being a 'cowardly cutlet', he didn't want to fight in the war.

Pex is redeemed when he lures Kroagnon into a trap set by the Doctor and then pushes him down a lift shaft. Pex dies in the process. As Bin Liner says, 'in death he was brave and bold as a Kang should be.'

NEW INFORMATION

THE DOCTOR

Mistaken for the Great Architect, the Doctor is sentenced to a '327 Appendix 3, Subsection 9 Death' by the Chief Caretaker.

He lures Kroagnon to his trap by saying how disappointed he is with Paradise Towers, and how it shows Krognon's usual problem of failing to take people into account. The Doctor has rigged a lift door to explode and kill Kroagnon, though Pex is also killed when he pushes Kroagnon through it.

Before he leaves, the Doctor is made an honorary Kang – Blue *and* Red.

THE TARDIS

The Doctor has jettisoned the TARDIS swimming pool from the ship as it was leaking.

COMPANIONS

MEL: Mel uses Pex's gun to destroy the cleaning robot in the swimming pool. She kisses Pex before he goes to lure Kroagnon into the Doctor's trap.

DELTA AND THE BANNERMEN

In which the Doctor and Mel win a holiday in 1950s Wales from Ken Dodd, and try to save the Chimeron Queen from the evil Bannermen...
BY MALCOLM KOHLL
3 EPISODES, FIRST BROADCAST 2–16 NOVEMBER 1987

TARDIS DATA BANK:

DATE: 1959
LOCATION: TOLLPORT G715; THE SHANGRI-LA HOLIDAY CAMP IN SOUTH WALES

FLEEING FROM GAVROK AND HIS BANNERMEN, THE CHIMERON QUEEN DELTA – THE LAST OF HER RACE – ARRIVES AT A WELSH HOLIDAY CAMP IN 1959 WITH A PARTY OF NAVARINO TOURISTS. BUT GAVROK IS IN HOT PURSUIT AND DETERMINED TO KILL DELTA. CAN THE DOCTOR AND MEL SAVE DELTA AND HER NEWLY HATCHED CHILD? AND HOW WILL RAY COPE WITH HER BOYFRIEND BILLY FALLING IN LOVE WITH AN ALIEN QUEEN...

JOURNEY INFORMATION

DELTA AND THE CHIMERON

Delta is the Chimeron Queen, and the last survivor of her race since her planet was invaded by Gavrok's Bannermen. She has an egg that hatches into a Chimeron baby – an ugly green creature which grows quickly into a Chimeron Princess. The child's rapid growth occurs during the lymphoid stage when she doubles her size and weight in a few hours. She makes a high-pitched singing sound – sometimes as a defence, an attack warning; and sometimes as singing.

When she is growing her cry shatters windows and drives away the Bannermen. Delta herself has high-frequency antennae fitted behind her ears, which detect the bees of Goronwy (a local bee-keeper) calling to them. The Princess's call, amplified through Shangri-La's speaker system, disables the Bannermen (Delta takes them with her as prisoners in their own ship) and drives Gavrok to stumble into his own booby trap atop the TARDIS.

Burton: 'Now let me try and get this right. Are you telling me you are not the Happy Hearts Holiday Club from Bolton, but are in fact spacemen in fear of an attack from some other spacemen — and because of the danger you want me to evacuate the entire camp?'

If Delta can get her hatchling safely to 'the brood planet', she can take her case to judgement, and an expeditionary force will be sent to get rid of Gavrok and the Bannermen.

GAVROK AND THE BANNERMEN

The Bannermen are led by the ruthless Gavrok, who kills an innocent Tollmaster after he's told them everything he can about Delta's destination. Gavrok offers one million units' reward for information about Delta's whereabouts, but rather than pay up he kills the Navarino bounty hunter who finds her. Trying to kill Delta, the Bannermen destroy the Navarinos without hesitation.

Gavrok eats raw meat, and says he has traversed time and space to find the Chimeron Queen (though there is no other evidence that the Navarinos or the Bannermen are from another time).

THE NAVARINO TOURISTS

From the tripolar moon Navarro, the Navarinos are squat, wrinkly, purple creatures with suckers. They have been through a transformation arch to assume human appearance. Murray is the pilot on a *Nostalgia Trips* tour – in what appears to be an old bus but is actually a spaceship.

All the Navarino tourists are killed when the Bannermen destroy their bus in an attempt to kill Delta (who is not actually on board).

BILLY AND RAY

Billy and Ray (short for Rachel) work at the Shangri-La Holiday Camp. Billy is into motorbikes and has a Vincent – complete with sidecar. He has taught Ray to carry tools around with her. She has learned all about motorbikes in the hope he will notice her, but Billy is more smitten with Delta.

Billy takes Chimeron baby food in order to mutate into a Chimeron so that he can go with Delta.

He gives his Vincent to Ray when he leaves.

NEW INFORMATION

THE DOCTOR

Arriving at Tollport G715 with his (new) distinctive question mark umbrella, the Doctor discovers he is the 10,000,000,000th customer. For this he wins a trip to Disneyland in 1959 – a scheduled tour with the Navarinos 1950s club – for himself and Mel.

He has the only Quarb crystal this side of the Softel Nebula, which Murray needs to repair the bus's navipod. When Murray breaks the crystal, he offers to accelerate growth in the thermobooster to create a new crystal in about 24 hours.

The Doctor is recognised by the Navarino bounty hunter.

He says the white flag is the recognised symbol of truce throughout the known Universe, and sets up a booby trap with jars of honey so that the Bannermen get stung by Goronwy's bees.

THE TARDIS

The Doctor sends Mel in the Navarino coach while he follows in the TARDIS. When the bus is hit by a US satellite, the Doctor is able to bring it safely to Earth by using the vortex drive to generate an anti-gravity spiral and bring them down at the Shangri-La Holiday Camp.

The Doctor shows the TARDIS to Ray and Shangri-La's manager, Burton, in order to persuade Burton of the danger posed by the Bannermen.

COMPANIONS

MEL: Mel says she has never won anything before. She tells Delta that discretion is her middle name.

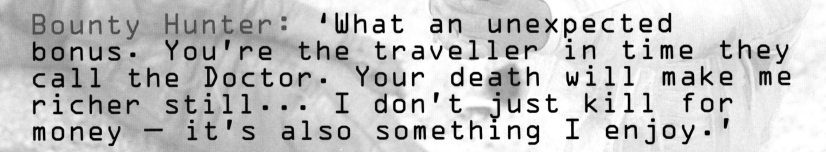

Bounty Hunter: 'What an unexpected bonus. You're the traveller in time they call the Doctor. Your death will make me richer still... I don't just kill for money — it's also something I enjoy.'

ACE

TARDIS DATA BANK:

APPEARANCE: FEMALE, HUMAN FROM 1987 PERIVALE.
TRAVELLED: *DRAGONFIRE – SURVIVAL*.

'Do you feel like arguing with a can of deodorant that registers nine on the Richter scale? (ACE – *DRAGONFIRE*)

Ace is working as a waitress in a café on Iceworld when the Doctor and Mel first meet her. Despite being able to mix Nitro-9 – a derivative of nitroglycerine – and store it in used deodorant cans, Ace is young and naive. She does not disguise her feelings, be they enthusiasm at the prospect of a real-life treasure hunt, boredom and annoyance at her job, contempt for Glitz or dislike for her parents, in particular her mother. She acts on impulse – tipping a milkshake over an annoying customer and getting sacked, or being fascinated by the 'dragon'.

In many ways, Ace is a typical, rebellious teenager. She lies about her age (telling Kane she is 18, when is fact she is 16), her room is a tip, she hates her job and she believes her parents cannot be her real mum and dad as they gave her such a naff name – Dorothy.

Back in her home in Perivale, it is unlikely Ace would stand out from the crowd, except that she does everything with such determination, born of her enthusiasm. She has been suspended from school (possibly expelled) for blowing up the art room with home-made gelignite (as a creative act), and now she finds herself whisked through time and space to Iceworld. As revealed in *The Curse of Fenric*, this is no coincidence, but an element of Fenric's grand design – part of which involves Ace being brought face to face with her own mother as a baby... As one of the wolves of Fenric, she carries his evil within her – and perhaps this is why the Doctor agrees to take her with him: 'An emotional cripple. I wouldn't

waste my time on her, unless I had to use her somehow.'

She never really loses her 'obvious' nature – leaving Mike in no doubt how disgusted she is that he has betrayed both her and the Doctor in *Remembrance of the Daleks*, for example. But by *Silver Nemesis* she has matured under the Doctor's influence enough to admit when she is frightened (but not enough to agree to his suggestion she return to the TARDIS). Perhaps this is why he feels she is now able to cope with the trauma of returning to Gabriel Chase in *Ghost Light*.

When she was 13, Ace's best friend was Manesha. After 'white kids' firebombed Manesha's family's flat, Ace burned down Gabriel Chase in anger and frustration – sensing the evil of its past. The events have left a deep impression – her fear of haunted houses; her anti-racist feelings; many of her deep-rooted insecurities...

Although Ace is able to exorcise some of these after the shock of seeing her own mother – the mother she thinks she hates so much – as a baby, it is difficult to see why the Doctor agrees to take her in the TARDIS anywhere other than straight home. Still less is it obvious why he would return to the 'unfinished business' of *Remembrance of the Daleks* and *Silver Nemesis* with a companion as volatile and immature as Ace to look after. Perhaps he realises right from the start that Ace is somehow bound up in his own future... Or perhaps he simply feels an affinity and a sympathy for a teenage girl who does not understand the currency of Britain in 1963.

DRAGONFIRE

In which Mel leaves – to keep Glitz under control – and a new companion, Ace, joins the Doctor.

BY IAN BRIGGS

3 EPISODES, FIRST BROADCAST 23 NOVEMBER–7 DECEMBER 1987

TARDIS DATA BANK:

DATE: UNKNOWN, FUTURE.
LOCATION: ICEWORLD, SVARTOS

ICEWORLD IS RUN BY KANE – AN EXILED CRIMINAL WHO CANNOT STAND HEAT AND WHO IS BUILDING UP AN ARMY OF CRYOGENICALLY FROZEN MERCENARIES. THE DOCTOR AND MEL MEET SABALOM GLITZ, WHO IS INTENT ON FINDING A LEGENDARY TREASURE SUPPOSEDLY GUARDED BY A DRAGON. THEY ALSO MEET ACE, A TEENAGER FROM EARTH WHO IS WORKING AS A WAITRESS IN A CAFÉ. BUT CAN ANY OF THEM ESCAPE KANE'S REVENGE AS HE PREPARES TO FREE HIMSELF AND EXACT RETRIBUTION…

JOURNEY INFORMATION

KANE

Kane controls Iceworld – a space trading colony on the dark side of the planet Svartos where space travellers stop for supplies. In fact, Iceworld is a huge spaceship built to hold Kane prisoner.

Kane is from the much colder planet of Proamon and his touch is so cold it kills. He sleeps in a special cabinet at sub-zero temperatures (below –190°C) in the 'Restricted Zone'.

Kane and his wife Xana were criminals – the Kane-Xana gang carried out systematic violence and extortion unequalled in its brutality on Proamon. Three thousand years ago, Kane was exiled from Proamon to Svartos, never to return. The dragon holds the power source that Kane needs to escape.

Xana was killed, Kane maintains, evading arrest (in fact she committed suicide to avoid being arrested) and he is having a statue made of her. He kills the sculptor once the statue is completed so no one else can see her beauty.

On Iceworld Kane is plotting his revenge. He has an army of mercenaries frozen in cryosleep – which causes complete loss of memory (it freezes the neural pathways), so they have no will of their own and no purpose but to obey him. He believes he owns his mercenaries for as long as they bear his mark – burned into them by the cold of the golden sovereign they have taken to serve him.

Kane has been planning his revenge for 3,000 years. He has all the customers taken from Iceworld in Glitz's ship the *Nosferatu*, which he then destroys, planning to take Iceworld to Proamon. But Proamon was destroyed 1,000 years after he was exiled – its sun, a cold red giant, turned supernova and is now a neutron star.

Opening a portal – perhaps to see for himself, perhaps as a deliberately suicidal act – Kane melts away in the unfiltered sunlight.

SABALOM GLITZ

Glitz has sold his crew to Kane for 17 crowns a head. He also sold Kane a freighterload of rotting food for 100 crowns and then lost the money playing cards. Realising the food is rotten, Kane now wants his money back. He arranges for Glitz to win a treasure map – with a tracking device in its seal. He knows Glitz will be forced to look for the treasure, and will lead him to the dragon.

With Kane dead, Glitz takes over the management of Iceworld.

THE DRAGON

The legendary dragon living in the passages beneath Iceworld is supposed to guard treasure. Glitz's map shows the Ice Gardens, the Singing Trees, the Lake of Oblivion, Death of Eternal Darkness and Dragon Fire. The Singing Trees are actually a web of opto-organic circuitry that stores information about Kane in a poly-dimensional scanning imager which the dragon can access, using its laser eyes as an energy source.

The dragon is a 'semi-organic vertebrate with a highly developed cerebral cortex'. In fact, it *is* the treasure – it has the power source Kane needs to power the Iceworld systems so that it can lift off from Svartos – the irony being that a fire-breathing dragon holds the key to Kane's prison, and he cannot stand heat.

NEW INFORMATION

THE DOCTOR

The Doctor is reading George Bernard Shaw's *The Doctor's Dilemma*. He tells Glitz he's regenerated since they last met (*The Trial of a Time Lord*) – 'the difference is purely perceptual.'

Interested in finding the dragon, the Doctor believes it may be an undiscovered species. He stops Glitz shooting it, telling him they have no right to kill it.

COMPANIONS

MEL: Again, Mel is immediately taken in by Glitz's stories. She decides to stay with him – to keep him out of trouble and ensure there are 'no more dodgy deals'.

ACE: Ace explains: 'I was doing this brill experiment to extract nitroglycerine from gelignite. I think something must have gone wrong. This time storm blows up from nowhere – whisks me up here.' She says she doesn't want to go home, and has no mum and dad, never has had and doesn't want any. She got suspended after she blew up the art room as a creative act.

She mixes Nitro-9, which is 'just like ordinary nitroglycerine, but with more wallop.'

Ace worked in a fast-food café after she was thrown out of school. She felt she must come from elsewhere, and dreamed of going home to the stars and her 'real' mum and dad. She has not told anyone (on Iceworld, presumably) that her real name is Dorothy.

BEHIND THE SCENES

THE DOCTOR'S PROPS

Dragonfire was publicised as the 150th **Doctor Who** story, a number arrived at by including the individual story segments of *The Trial of a Time Lord*.

Over the years, the **Doctor Who** production office held various 'stock' props for the series such as the odds and ends the Doctor keeps in his pocket. This was in addition to larger props, standing sets (like the TARDIS), costumes and monsters held in BBC storage.

The list of props held by the producer at the end of *Dragonfire* (and reproduced below) is of interest as it shows which items were seen as the Doctor's personal belongings, as well as giving us an insight into what the production team thought they might want to re-use in the future.

> **STOCK PROPS KEPT BY THE PRODUCER**
> Stethoscope
> TARDIS Type 40 handbook • Black diary
> Magnet • Doctor's eyepiece
> TARDIS keys • Magnifying glass
> Propelling pencil • TARDIS tool box
> Umbrella • TCE (Master) – Tissue Compression Eliminator
> Sil's food dish • Sil's hand mirror
> Ace's rucksack

The Doctor: 'Yes, that's right, you're going. You've been gone for ages. You're already gone. You're still here. You've just arrived. I haven't even met you yet. It all depends on who you are and how you look at it. Strange business, time.'

REMEMBRANCE OF THE DALEKS

In which two opposing Dalek forces do battle in London, the Emperor Dalek turns out to be Davros and the Special Weapons Dalek is revealed...

BY BEN AARONOVITCH

4 EPISODES, FIRST BROADCAST 5–26 OCTOBER 1988

> **TARDIS DATA BANK:**
>
> DATE: 1963
>
> LOCATION: LONDON (INCLUDING TOTTERS YARD)
>
> TWO OPPOSING DALEK FACTIONS BATTLE FOR THE HAND OF OMEGA – A POWERFUL DEVICE LEFT ON EARTH BY THE DOCTOR. CAN THE DOCTOR KEEP THE MILITARY FROM INTERFERING IN HIS PLANS AS HE ARRANGES FOR THE 'RIGHT' DALEKS TO GET THE DEVICE? WHAT EXACTLY IS THE DOCTOR'S PLAN, AND WILL ACE STAY OUT OF TROUBLE LONG ENOUGH FOR HIM TO SPRING HIS TRAP?

The Doctor: 'Oi, Dalek — it's me, the Doctor. What's the matter, don't you recognise your mortal enemy?'

JOURNEY INFORMATION

THE HAND OF OMEGA

The Doctor left the Hand of Omega on Earth in a floating coffin-like casket which he buries with an 'Omega' headstone. The Hand imbues Ace's baseball bat with energy – enabling her to seriously damage a Dalek.

The Doctor explains that: 'A long time ago, on my home planet of Gallifrey, there lived a stellar engineer called Omega... It was Omega who created the supernova that was the initial power source for Gallifreyan time travel experiments. He left behind him the basis on which Rassilon founded Time Lord society. And he left behind the Hand of Omega... It was called that because Time Lords have an infinite capacity for pretension... The Hand of Omega is a mythical name for Omega's remote stellar manipulator, a device used to customise stars.' Later he describes it as the most powerful and sophisticated remote stellar control manipulator device ever constructed.

The Doctor says that 'in a manner of speaking' the Hand is alive, and programs it to destroy Skaro's sun (in the future). The feedback destroys the Dalek mother ship, then the Hand returns to Gallifrey.

THE DALEKS

The Doctor describes Daleks as little green blobs in bonded polycarbide armour. He says they have come from the 'distant future' and only have 'crude and nasty' time travel technology – that's why they want the Hand of Omega.

IMPERIAL DALEKS: The Imperial Daleks are an ivory colour with gold 'trim'. Their slats are moulded into their bodywork rather than attached, and the eye and sucker arm are of a new design – the sucker has a slot in it to operate controls. The Dalek creatures are also different too – a claw emerges to attack the Doctor, and they have functional appendages and some kind of mechanical prosthesis grafted into their bodies.

The Special Weapons Dalek is battle-stained, with no eye stalk or sucker arm, and an enlarged gun. Until it is ordered into action, the Imperial Daleks are losing to the rebel faction.

The Imperial Daleks are led by the Emperor – a Dalek with an enlarged, spherical head, which is revealed to contain Davros. The Imperial Daleks immediately recognise the Doctor.

The Doctor says the Dalek mother ship could crack open the Earth like an egg and could have as many as 400 Daleks on board.

The Imperial Daleks manipulate the headmaster of Coal Hill School through a control box behind his ear.

The Imperial Daleks defeat all the rebel Daleks except the Dalek Supreme. They are killed when the mother ship is destroyed.

REBEL DALEKS: Of a more standard gunmetal-grey design, the Rebel Daleks have projected-energy weapons that leave no tissue damage but scramble the victim's insides. They also have a time controller which they plan to use to return to their own time with the hand of Omega.

The Rebel Dalek Faction is led by the black and silver Dalek Supreme (which self-destructs when the Doctor tells it the other Daleks – and Skaro – have been destroyed).

The Dalek battle computer is a Dalek base with a headset attached – a biomechanoid control device. The Doctor explains that the Daleks' major drawback is their dependency on rationality and logic – so they take a young and imaginative human, plug them into the system and their ingenuity and creativity are slaved to the battle computer. In this case it is a young schoolgirl. She spins round as the dying Supreme Dalek does, and apparently recovers after it is destroyed.

GROUP CAPTAIN GILMORE

An RAF officer, Gilmore has army personnel working for him, as well as Professor Rachel Jenson – commandeered from Cambridge under the Peacetime Emergency Powers Act – who is his scientific adviser, and her assistant, Allison. Initially sceptical, once Gilmore is convinced of the Doctor's expertise and value, he follows his advice unswervingly.

NEW INFORMATION

THE DOCTOR

The Doctor uses a modified design of his Dalek-jamming device from *Planet of the Daleks* to confuse Imperial Daleks, and cures Ace's injured leg by squeezing it.

His card is a stylised, embossed question mark over a seal on a diagonal black stripe (which he produces apparently out of thin air). The Dalek Supreme immediately recognises it as the Doctor's. He identifies himself to the Imperial Daleks as, 'President Elect of the High Council of Time Lords, Keeper of the Legacy of Rassilon, Defender of the Laws of Time, Protector of Gallifrey.'

COMPANIONS

ACE: Ace doesn't know how many pennies there are in a shilling or shillings in a pound.

Although she was only 16 when she was on Iceworld, she can drive.

She has a baseball bat, which the Doctor imbues with power from the Hand of Omega.

BEHIND THE SCENES

BY ROYAL ASSENT

While royals from King Richard the Lionheart to Queen Elizabeth I have been featured in **Doctor Who**, *Remembrance of the Daleks* has the distinction of being the only story in which a member of the Royal Family appears as themselves. 'Appears' is not strictly accurate, as it is the voice of the Duke of Edinburgh (from his speech on the independence of Kenya in December 1963) that is used as one of the voices in the pre-titles sequence, over a model shot of the Imperial Dalek mother ship approaching Earth.

The original intention was to include a Bob Dylan song in the montage of sounds opening the story, and the production team investigated copyright issues for various tracks – as well as for 'The World Won't Listen' by The Smiths and Aztec Camera's 'Love'. The final 'wish list' of soundbites was close to what was eventually used – 12 seconds President John F. Kennedy; 5 seconds President de Gaulle; 5 seconds Duke of Edinburgh; 4 seconds Martin Luther King; 3 seconds President John F. Kennedy.

In addition to these, it had still been hoped to include a line of Bob Dylan ('A bullet from the back of a bush...') as well as a short excerpt from the speech given by Her Majesty Queen Elizabeth II when opening the Commonwealth Telephone Cable Link on 2 December 1963. But when Buckingham Palace was formally asked for permission to include the material, the official reply was that the Queen did not wish to be quoted on a fictional programme. Permission for the Duke of Edinburgh's voice to be used was given, but with reluctance.

Despite not wishing to be heard on **Doctor Who**, the Queen did make an appearance – of sorts – in *Silver Nemesis*. With Arundel Castle doubling for Windsor Castle, look-alike Mary Reynolds appeared briefly, complete with some stunt corgis, as the Queen.

Remembrance of the Daleks is also the only story in which the television series **Doctor Who** is – almost – mentioned. When Ace turns on a television set, the continuity announcer is telling us that, 'This is BBC Television. The time is a quarter past five, and Saturday viewing continues with an adventure in the new science fiction series Doc– '

Dalek: 'You are the Doctor, you are the enemy of the Daleks. You will be exterminated. Exterminate, exterminate, exterminate, exterminate, exterminate...'

DATE: UNKNOWN,
FUTURE
LOCATION: TERRA
ALPHA

HELEN A, THE RULER OF
TERRA ALPHA, INSISTS THAT
THE PEOPLE ARE HAPPY –
OTHERWISE THEY ARE PUT
OUT OF THEIR MISERY. THERE
HAVE BEEN MANY 'ROUTINE
DISAPPEARANCES' AND
GALACTIC CENTRE HAS
ORDERED A CENSUS. THE
DOCTOR MEETS THE
SINISTER, CONFECTIONERY-
CREATURE THE KANDY MAN.
CAN THE DOCTOR AND ACE
ESCAPE THE HAPPINESS
PATROL AND LIBERATE THE
PLANET FROM THE TYRANNY
OF HELEN A...

Earl
Sigma:
'You're a
nice guy,
Doctor.
But a
little
weird.'

THE HAPPINESS PATROL

In which the Doctor meets a Kandy Man made entirely of sweets, and Sheila Hancock plays a ruthless female leader who believes sadness should be illegal...
BY GRAEME CURRY
3 EPISODES, FIRST BROADCAST 2–16 NOVEMBER 1988

JOURNEY INFORMATION

TERRA ALPHA

Terra Alpha is a former Earth colony. Musak is piped through the capital city, and there are specified tourist zones.

Unhappy people are branded killjoys and 'disappear'. Also prohibited is walking alone in the rain without an umbrella, reading poetry (except limericks), wearing dark clothes, listening to slow music... There are three ways of 'disappearing' – the late show at the Forum, a visit to the Kandy Kitchen and death by fondant surprise (organised by the Kandy Man).

Terra Alpha has no prisons, but there is a Waiting Zone (which moves location according to the time of night) where those arrested wait to disappear.

It is forbidden for drones – workers from the flatlands – to enter the city. However, they do march into the city in protest, with banners bearing slogans like 'Factory conditions are a joke'. The Happiness Patrol cannot arrest them, however, as the Doctor persuades them to laugh.

Trevor Sigma is on official business from the Galactic Census Bureau at Galactic Centre. There has to be a census every six local cycles (months). All aliens are designated 'Sigma'.

HELEN A

Helen A is the leader of Terra Alpha. Determined that the population should be happy, she had the most depressing township on the planet razed to the ground by the Happiness Patrol and has eliminated overcrowding by 'controlling the population down' by 17 per cent. 'I told them to be happy,' she insists, 'but they wouldn't listen... They still cried, they still wept...'

Harold F was her gag-writer until his brother disappeared – he was regraded Harold V after he tried to contact Terra Omega about his brother. He is electrocuted by a fruit machine.

Helen A has an escape shuttle ready in case she needs to leave the planet, but this is taken by her consort Joseph C and Gilbert M, the Kandy Man's assistant, who leave her to her fate.

She cares deeply for her pet stigorax – a ruthless, intelligent, furry predator called Fifi – and she is heartbroken when Fifi is killed. The stigorax is buried under crystallised sugar brought down from inside the pipes under the city when Earl Sigma, a resident of Terra Alpha, plays a 'C' on his mouth organ. Fifi's death finally moves Helen A to tears.

THE PIPE PEOPLE

The small, humanoid Pipe People used to live on the surface of Terra Alpha, but were driven underground and into the pipes by the human settlers. The Happiness Patrol considers them vermin, and they are near to starvation.

THE KANDY MAN

The Kandy Man lives in the Kandy Kitchen, and is a moody robot apparently made of sweets. His constituents include sherbet, marzipan, caramel, toffee, gelling agents...

The Kandy Man devises deadly sweets and is Helen A's executioner. He says he likes his volunteers to die with smiles on their faces. Gilbert M suggests his relationship with the Kandy Man is symbiotic. Gilbert M created the Kandy Man, but 'only his body. His mind was very much his own.' He brought the pieces with him when he was exiled from Vasilip where he worked in the state laboratories and invented a deadly new germ that accidentally wiped out half the population.

The Doctor sticks the Kandy Man to the floor with lemonade – he needs to keep moving or his constituent ingredients will coagulate. He dies when he is trapped in a pipe by fondant released by the Pipe People.

NEW INFORMATION

THE DOCTOR

The Doctor says his nickname at college was Theta Sigma (as mentioned by Drax in *The Armageddon Factor*). He uses escapology to get out of the Kandy Man's chair, and faces down a sniper: 'Why don't you do it then? Look me in the eye, pull the trigger – end my life.'

He plays the spoons with Earl Sigma and produces party poppers and tooters from his pocket. He says he hasn't met a stigorax since he was in Birmingham in the twenty-fifth century.

THE TARDIS

The TARDIS is painted pink by the Happiness Patrol.

COMPANIONS

ACE: Ace likes dinosaurs, but objects to the musak on Terra Alpha. When the Doctor won't let her defuse a booby-trapped go-cart, she complains she never gets any fun.

Ace tells patrol guard Susan Q that the Happiness Patrol stands for everything she hates.

Helen A: 'We're a team, Fifi, you and I — we help each other. And we will make this a happy planet, in spite of all the killjoys and the bunglers that surround us. And if they're miserable, we'll put them out of their misery. After all, it's for their own good. But first of all, a little harmless revenge. You take the vermin in the pipes, I'll take the vermin in the Forum.'

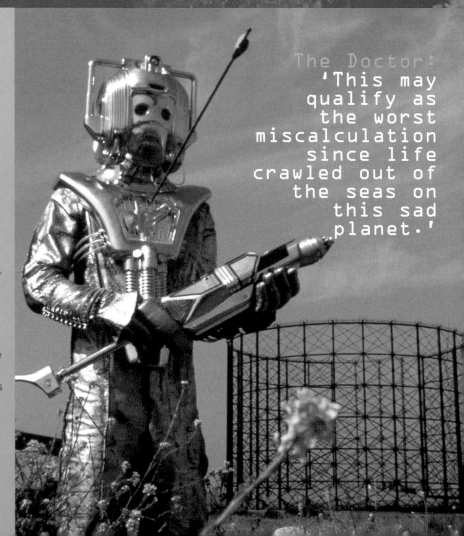

SILVER NEMESIS

In which the Doctor meets the Queen, Hollywood actress Dolores Gray as a tourist, Anton Diffring as a neo-Nazi, and the Cybermen...
BY KEVIN CLARKE
3 EPISODES, FIRST UK BROADCAST 23 NOVEMBER–
7 DECEMBER 1988

The Doctor: 'This may qualify as the worst miscalculation since life crawled out of the seas on this sad planet.'

JOURNEY INFORMATION

NEMESIS

The Nemesis statue was made by Lady Peinforte in 1638 in her own likeness, from validium that fell into the meadow behind her house. She calls it 'immaculate beauty carved in absolute evil'. Validium is a living metal created as the ultimate defence for Gallifrey back in early times by Omega and Rassilon, and it should never have left Gallifrey. The Doctor launched the statue into space in 1638 so it could never attain critical mass. For this it has to be reunited with its bow and arrow. Lady Peinforte has the arrow and de Flores, a Nazi, has the bow, which was in Windsor Castle until it disappeared in 1788.

The statue, believed to be a 'comet', circles the Earth once every 25 years – generating destruction – and it will strike the Earth where it left it on 23 November 1988. The statue tells Ace that it has had other forms 'that would horrify you.' It says Lady Peinforte called her Nemesis, 'so I am retribution.'

LADY PEINFORTE

Lady Peinforte pays a mathematician to calculate when the Nemesis will return to Earth and then kills him. She travels through time using the power of the Nemesis arrow and a magic potion – an ingredient of which is the mathematician's blood...

She admits to a Mrs Remington (who gives her a lift) that in 1621 she poisoned Dorothea Remington for stealing her cook. She also claims to know the Doctor's 'secret' but we do not discover what it is.

Her companion/servant, Richard Maynarde, sees his own tomb – and that he will die on 2 November 1657, in his fifty-first year. The Cybermen take the Nemesis to Lady Peinforte's own monument. But the tomb is empty – because Peinforte will die when she flings herself into the Nemesis launch vehicle and will be absorbed by the statue.

DE FLORES

De Flores, a Nazi hiding in South America, plans to use the bow to control the Nemesis and assume power over the world, establishing the Fourth Reich. He sees the Cybermen as tools.

> De Flores: 'Gentlemen, I wonder if even you can fully appreciate what this moment means. You are standing now at the turning point of history — the day of fulfilment of our mighty destiny is about to dawn. Gentlemen, I give you the Fourth Reich.'

THE CYBERMEN

The Cybermen have taken over two humans, fitting them with special headsets. They later kill them for apparent betrayal when Ace destroys a Cyber ship. The Doctor says they were transformed – dead already.

Immune to machine-gun fire, the Cybermen are apparently terrified of gold and are killed by Lady Peinforte's gold-tipped arrows and Ace's gold coins. One Cyberman has a device that detects the gold on Lady Peinforte's arrows. But the Cyber Leader is able to detect that Ace has only one gold coin left without the device.

The Cybermen recognise the Doctor and know of Lady Peinforte and the Nemesis. With a fleet of thousands of shielded Cyber warships waiting invisibly in space, they plan to use the power of the Nemesis to transform the Earth into their base planet – the new Mondas. The Cyber Lieutenant suggests that if they fail the Cyber race will cease to exist.

NEW INFORMATION

THE DOCTOR

The Doctor has set an alarm for the Nemesis's return, but has forgotten about it. He has not been to Windsor Castle since it was being built.

Lady Peinforte threatens to tell the Doctor's secret, which she learned from the Nemesis statue: 'Doctor who? Have you never wondered where he came from? Who he is? ... I shall tell them of Gallifrey – tell them of the Old Time, the time of chaos...' But the Doctor merely thanks her for her help and for bringing the arrow: 'You had the right game, but the wrong pawn...'

The Doctor destroys the Cyber Fleet, expecting to be destroyed himself by the Cyber Leader. Ace compares his plan to how he 'nailed the Daleks' (*Remembrance of the Daleks*) – the Doctor calls both plans 'unfinished business'.

He tells the Nemesis that she can have her freedom, but 'not yet... Things are still imperfect.'

THE TARDIS

Candles in Lady Peinforte's house are blown out by the TARDIS's arrival. An arrow embeds itself in the TARDIS door and is taken with the TARDIS when it dematerialises.

BEHIND THE SCENES

EXTENDED VERSIONS

To create a **Doctor Who** episode of the right length for transmission in a 25-minute slot, more than 25 minutes of material was often made. That said, some episodes have come in considerably under length. Episode 3 of *Fury from the Deep* was just 20 minutes 29 seconds long, and *The Mind Robber* was actually allocated a 20-minute broadcast slot. Other episodes have been longer than 25 minutes – the final episode of *The Trial of a Time Lord* was given a 30-minute transmission slot.

Occasionally, an episode has under-run to the extent that extra material has been recorded along with another story to pad it out. This was the case with the second episode of *Timelash*, with additional TARDIS scenes being recorded with *Revelation of the Daleks*.

But even in the best-timed scripts, material is trimmed at the editing stage. Usually this material is not essential to the story, and is not missed by the viewer. On occasion, a different edit of an episode has accidentally been sold and broadcast abroad – *Carnival of Monsters* Episode 2 was broadcast in Australia with several extra sequences, and a version of the opening and closing theme that was never used in the UK.

A scene was removed from *Inferno* where the Doctor and the Brigade Leader hear a radio news broadcast describing the effects of the Earth's penetration. The newsreader was played by Jon Pertwee, and was cut from the UK version as it was felt his voice was recognisable. The scene is included on versions of the story sold abroad, as well as the BBC video release.

BBC video has included extended versions of some episodes on their release – like a slightly longer version of Episode 5 of *Frontier in Space*, and a slightly extended version of *Battlefield*. Also, as stories come out on DVD, so extended and additional scenes that are still held in the BBC's archives are included as 'extras'.

Two stories have been released on video in significantly extended versions. Both of these are Seventh Doctor stories that had considerable edits made to them before they were broadcast. In 1991 BBC Video released an extended version of *The Curse of Fenric* that included an extra seven minutes of unbroadcast material. An even longer, re-edited 'movie' version was released together with the broadcast programme on DVD in 2003. An extended version of *Silver Nemesis*, including about 11 minutes of previously unbroadcast material, was released in 1993.

THE GREATEST SHOW IN THE GALAXY

In which the Doctor and Ace visit the deadly Psychic Circus, and meet the show's biggest fan – even though he admits it's not as good as it used to be...
BY STEPHEN WYATT
4 EPISODES, FIRST BROADCAST 14 DECEMBER 1988–
4 JANUARY 1989

TARDIS DATA BANK:

DATE: UNKNOWN
LOCATION: SEGONAX

THE DOCTOR IS KEEN TO TRY HIS LUCK IN THE TALENT CONTEST FOR THE PSYCHIC CIRCUS – BILLED AS THE GREATEST SHOW IN THE GALAXY. BUT ACE IS FAR FROM KEEN. APART FROM THE SCREAMING OF A CONTESTANT THEY HEAR AS THEY APPROACH, AND THE HOMICIDAL ROBOT BUS CONDUCTOR THEY ENCOUNTER ON THE WAY, THERE IS THE STRANGE EXPLORER CAPTAIN COOK, HIS TROUBLED COMPANION MAGS AND A DISTINCTLY ODD AUDIENCE. ACE FINDS CLOWNS CREEPY ANYWAY, AND THESE CLOWNS ARE HOMICIDAL ROBOTS. BUT WHILE SHE TRIES TO ESCAPE THE HORRORS OF THE CIRCUS RING, THE DOCTOR PERFORMS CONJURING TRICKS FOR THE GODS OF RAGNAROK...

Ringmaster:
'Now welcome folks, I'm sure you'd like to know
we're at the start of one big circus show.
There are acts that are cool and acts that amaze,
some acts are scary, and some acts daze.
Acts of all kinds and you can count on that,
from folks that fly to disappearing acts.
There are lots of surprises for the family
at the Greatest Show in the Galaxy.'

JOURNEY INFORMATION

THE PSYCHIC CIRCUS

The Psychic Circus bills itself as the Greatest Show in the Galaxy. Now it has settled on Segonax, where one of the performers – Kingpin – found the power of the Gods of Ragnarok, a huge eye, in an abyss. He tried to control it using a special amulet, but failed and his mind broke. Now he is called Deadbeat and does odd jobs like sweeping up, while mumbling to himself. The Gods have taken the eyeball from the eye symbol and hidden it in a bus in the desert. It is guarded by a robot bus conductor. Now the Circus is enslaved to the Gods, who demand constant entertainment from its acts – when they tire of performers, they kill them...

Bellboy, one of the circus performers, says each of the performers had one circus skill. He made the clowns as well as the huge robot in the desert for which he gives Ace a control box. Bellboy makes the clowns kill him so that he can't be forced to repair them any more.

Flowerchild made kites, and is tracked by them before being killed by the bus conductor robot.

Morgana is a fortune-teller, and tries to discourage the Doctor, Ace and others from entering the circus. Morgana and the Ringmaster are killed when there are no more acts.

The Chief Clown is perhaps the performer who is most under the influence of the Gods of Ragnarok. Bellboy says he was a wonderful clown once, funny and inventive. He is killed by the robot in the desert, operated by Ace.

THE GODS OF RAGNAROK

The Gods of Ragnarok exist in two times concurrently – the past of their temple (the Dark Circus) and the Psychic Circus. They need to be entertained, and so the Doctor (and others) are allowed to live as long as they entertain them.

The eye symbol is used on Flowerchild's kites and appears within Morgana's crystal ball. It is on Deadbeat's amulet – which he first used (as Kingpin) to summon the Gods of Ragnarok. The eyeball, which is hidden on the bus, needs to be reinstated in the amulet to control or destroy the Gods. The Doctor uses the amulet to reflect the Gods' destructive energy and destroy them and the Dark Circus.

CAPTAIN COOK AND MAGS

Captain Cook is an eminent intergalactic explorer who never tires of retelling anecdotes of his travels and discoveries. He is accompanied by Mags, a 'specimen' he discovered on the planet Vulpana...

The Captain takes his own blend of tea with him – which the Doctor immediately identifies as being from the Groz Valley on Melagophon.

Keen on self-preservation and survival, the Captain will do almost anything to avoid being forced into the circus ring, and intends to do a deal with the Gods in the hope of gaining their power. The Doctor tells him, 'You're not only a scoundrel, and a meddling fool, you're a crushing bore.'

Mags is actually a werewolf, and even a carved moon above the entrance to the old temple affects her. As his 'act', the Captain uses a special lighting effect to turn her into a wolf, but she turns on the Captain and kills him. His corpse is reanimated by the Gods to try and stop Ace, Mags and Kingpin helping the Doctor. But he fails, and 'dies' again, his body falling into the abyss.

NEW INFORMATION

THE DOCTOR

The Doctor is teaching himself to juggle in the TARDIS (and loses a ball that doesn't come back down). He fancies entering the Psychic Circus talent contest with his spoons act.

When he eventually performs for the Gods of Ragnarok, his tricks include taking eggs from his mouth and making them disappear, and escaping from a straitjacket while hung upside down. He declines Kingpin's offer to join his new circus.

COMPANIONS

ACE: She is not keen on circuses. She went to one once and it was naff and boring, but she found the clowns creepy... She is more impressed with a motorbike driven by Nord, another visitor to the circus (even though he threatens to 'do something horrible to your ears.')

The Doctor: 'Fun for all the family? I don't know how they've got the nerve.'

BATTLEFIELD

In which the Doctor learns he is Merlin, and the Brigadier comes out of retirement to take part in an Arthurian Legend...
BY BEN AARONOVITCH
4 EPISODES, FIRST BROADCAST 6 SEPTEMBER 1989–
27 SEPTEMBER 1989

TARDIS DATA BANK:

DATE: 1990S (A FEW YEARS IN ACE'S FUTURE)
LOCATION: NEAR CARBURY, EARTH

A CONFLICT FROM ANOTHER DIMENSION SPILLS OVER INTO OUR WORLD. MORGAINE AND HER KNIGHTS BATTLE AGAINST ANCELYN, A KNIGHT OF KING ARTHUR. BOTH SIDES RECOGNISE THE DOCTOR AS MERLIN. A UNIT CONVOY IS STRANDED IN THE MIDDLE OF THE BATTLE, AND BRIGADIER LETHBRIDGE-STEWART IS CALLED OUT OF RETIREMENT. BUT EVEN WITH THE HELP OF THE BRIGADIER, CAN THE DOCTOR DEFEAT MORGAINE AND THE MONSTROUS CREATURE SHE CONJURES – THE DESTROYER...

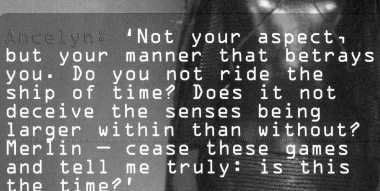

Ancelyn: 'Not your aspect, but your manner that betrays you. Do you not ride the ship of time? Does it not deceive the senses being larger within than without? Merlin — cease these games and tell me truly: is this the time?'

JOURNEY INFORMATION

MORGAINE

Morgaine of the Faye, the Sunkiller – Dominator of the Thirteen Worlds and Battle Queen of the S'rax – wants revenge on Arthur, unaware that he is already dead.

Her son, Mordred, says Morgaine has waited 12 centuries to be revenged on Merlin. He establishes a meeting point between two worlds, two universes, two realities so that Morgaine can come through.

Morgaine has powers that border on magic. She brings down the Brigadier's helicopter, she can teleport, and she stops helicopter pilot Lavel's bullet and crumbles it to dust. In a hotel bar she kills Lavel, before restoring the blind landlady Elizabeth's sight in payment for her son Mordred's beer.

Morgaine demands to face Arthur in single combat. But despite the propaganda, Arthur was killed over a thousand years ago in a final battle. His body is an empty suit of armour, with a note the future Doctor has written to himself in the helmet.

Morgaine and Mordred are locked up by UNIT's Brigadier Bambera, but since Morgaine has the power of teleportation, this may only be a temporary arrangement.

ANCELYN

Ancelyn ap Gwalchmai is Knight General of the Britons. He falls through space to Earth from another dimension, and wears medieval-style armour, but has an ultra-modern gun as well as a sword. He stays on Earth with Bambera after Morgaine's defeat.

THE DESTROYER

The satanic Destroyer summoned by Morgaine is the Lord of Darkness, Eater of Worlds. Morgaine has him chained with silver – which burns him. She calls the Doctor's bluff and frees the Destroyer so he can devour the world.

As the world explodes round the Destroyer, the Brigadier kills it with silver bullets.

NEW INFORMATION

THE DOCTOR

The Doctor says he could be Merlin in his own future, in another dimension, and/or the past. Ancelyn says he knows 'Merlin' by his manner rather than his aspect. Merlin apparently cast down Morgaine with his mighty arts at Badon, but Morgaine sealed him in ice caves for all eternity.

In the eighth century, Merlin built a concrete tunnel to Arthur's spaceship – a craft intended to travel between dimensions and now under Lake Vortigern. The concealed entrance is keyed to the Doctor's voice-pattern (suggesting it does not change with regeneration). Above the entrance tunnel is a stone carved with runes the Doctor deciphers as 'dig hole here', in his handwriting.

The Doctor has his own and Liz Shaw's antiquated UNIT passes inside his hat. He hypnotises archaeologist Peter Warmsly and hotelier Pat Rowlinson to convince them they want to leave the area.

The Doctor threatens to kill Mordred in order to get Morgaine to call off the Destroyer. 'Look me in the eye – end my life,' Mordred challenges him (just as the Doctor challenged the sniper in *The Happiness Patrol*). The Doctor cannot kill Mordred, but later renders him unconscious by putting his fingers to Mordred's forehead.

UNIT

Part, at least, of the UK contingent of UNIT is commanded by Brigadier Winifred Bambera. She strikes up a relationship with Ancelyn.

Sergeant Zbrigniev served under Lethbridge-Stewart and says he knows of the Doctor and that he can change appearance. He says 'whenever this Doctor turns up, all hell breaks loose'.

UNIT troops now wear blue berets with a new 'winged' UNIT logo. UNIT supplies include armour-piercing bullets, high-explosives and even gold-tipped bullets for 'you know what'. Silver bullets kill the Destroyer.

The Brigadier had Bessie 'mothballed' when the Doctor 'last went on his travels'. She now has a longer bonnet and her number plate has changed from WHO 1 to WHO 7.

COMPANIONS

ACE: The Doctor tells Ace that one of these days they're going to have a nice long talk about acceptable safety standards.

BRIGADIER LETHBRIDGE-STEWART: The Brigadier has retired and is living in a half-timbered house with extensive gardens. He is married to Doris, who has not heard of the Doctor though the Doctor says, 'so she caught you in the end'.

The UN Secretary General calls the Brigadier to tell him the Doctor is back and to request help. The Brigadier has his service revolver and ammunition in a padded briefcase initialled AGL-S. He recognises the Doctor, despite never having met the Seventh Doctor before: 'Who else would it be?'

Morgaine warns Mordred that the Brigadier is 'steeped in blood'. The Brigadier knocks out the Doctor so that he can take the silver bullets and kill the Destroyer, arguing 'I'm more expendable.'

The Doctor:
'That, Brigadier,
was the beginning
of the end of
the world.'

GHOST LIGHT

The Doctor: 'Let me guess: my theories appal you, my heresies outrage you, I never answer letters, and you don't like my tie.'

In which Frank Windsor plays a police inspector in the last **Doctor Who** story made at the BBC…
BY MARC PLATT

3 EPISODES, FIRST BROADCAST 4 OCTOBER 1989–18 OCTOBER 1989

Light: 'I'm going to stop the change here. All organic life will be eradicated in the firestorm. And when this world is destroyed — no more change, no more evolution, no more life. No more amendments to my catalogue.'

JOURNEY INFORMATION

LIGHT

Light is a powerful alien who is creating a catalogue of life forms. He has spent centuries cataloguing the species of Earth – taking Nimrod as the last specimen of the extinct Neanderthal race. But no sooner had he finished than it all started changing.

The explorer Redvers Fenn-Cooper describes a light in the heart of the interior of Africa that burned through his eyes into his mind, and had blazing, radiant wings. Whether he saw Light during his explorations or back at Gabriel Chase is not explained, but the experience drove him out of his mind. Light has been sleeping in his spaceship for centuries. Nimrod's people worship him as 'the Burning One'.

While Light has been asleep his survey has 'got out of control'. He 'dismantles' a maid at Gabriel Chase to 'see how it works' and to check that he is still on Earth despite it being so changed.

Josiah *is* Light's survey, run under the auspices of Control. Josiah changes with the various stages of life on Earth, adapting to his environment and leaving husks behind as he moves to the next stage. Control also develops into a creature adapted to the environment – a Victorian lady. Light's form, too, is dependent on the environment, and he seems to accept its changing, yet cannot cope with the concept of evolution. He turns Lady Pritchard, the rightful owner of the house, and her daughter Gwendoline to stone to stop them changing. He is driven to distraction by the thought that his survey can never be complete, and is 'dispersed.'

With Light dead, his ship leaves with a new crew to continue the catalogue – Redvers Fenn-Cooper, Control (which has now evolved into a 'Ladylike'), Nimrod and the broken Josiah.

TARDIS DATA BANK:

DATE: 1883
LOCATION: GABRIEL CHASE, PERIVALE

THE DOCTOR TAKES ACE TO THE MYSTERIOUS HOUSE GABRIEL CHASE. ARE ANY OF THE HOUSE'S INHABITANTS WHO OR WHAT THEY APPEAR TO BE? WHAT IS CONTROL? WHAT IS LURKING IN THE CELLAR? WHAT IS JOSIAH SAMUEL SMITH'S SECRET? WHY IS NIMROD THE BUTLER A NEANDERTHAL? WHAT HAPPENED TO REDVERS FENN-COOPER IN AFRICA? AND WHAT WILL HAPPEN WHEN LIGHT AWAKENS…

JOSIAH SAMUEL SMITH

Josiah *is* Light's survey. The Doctor says Josiah is far away from home 'struggling to adapt to an alien environment', but Smith retorts, 'I'm as human as you are.'

Two years ago, Josiah escaped, or was awakened, from Light's ship in the cellar of Gabriel Chase. He did away with Sir George Pritchard, the owner of the house, after Pritchard saw Light's ship, and he put Inspector Mackenzie who came to investigate into a trance, keeping him as a specimen in a drawer. Lady Pritchard became Josiah's housekeeper, and her daughter Gwendoline his ward.

Gwendoline says Josiah is a naturalist, and he speaks of his study of moths and of his belief that they are adapting to the environment. His theories of evolution appal the Reverend Ernest Matthews, Dean of Mortarhouse College, Oxford. Josiah feeds him bananas and turns him into an ape.

As Josiah adapts and evolves, he leaves husks of his former selves behind – a reptile and an insect in the Lower Observatory, an older version of himself with an aversion to light in the Upper Observatory...

Josiah plans to restore the 'blighted British Empire' to glory. To this end, he has persuaded Redvers Fenn-Cooper to find and kill the Crowned Saxe-Coburg – Queen Victoria. Redvers has an invitation to the palace and decides to take Control as his guest instead, thwarting Josiah's plan.

NEW INFORMATION

THE DOCTOR

The Doctor says he is a member of the Royal Geographical Society, claims to know a nice little restaurant in the Khyber Pass and gives Nimrod the fang of a cave bear – a totem of great power.

The Doctor admits to Ace, 'I can't stand burned toast. I loathe bus stations – terrible places, full of lost luggage and lost souls... And then there's unrequited love, and tyranny and cruelty... We all have a universe of our own terrors to face.'

COMPANIONS

ACE: Ace tells the Doctor she has 'a thing about haunted houses'. She last saw Gabriel Chase in 1983 and is angry the Doctor has tricked her into coming back.

She remembers, 'When I lived in Perivale, me and my best mate – we dossed around together. We'd out-dare each other and things. Skiving off, stupid things. Then they burned out Manesha's flat – white kids fire-bombed it. I didn't care any more... That's when I came over the wall to the house – this house. I was so mad and I needed to get away. It was empty, all overgrown and falling down. No-one came here. And when I got inside it was even worse. I didn't know then. It was horrible.' In fact she burned the house down. She later tells the Doctor she wishes she'd blown it up instead.

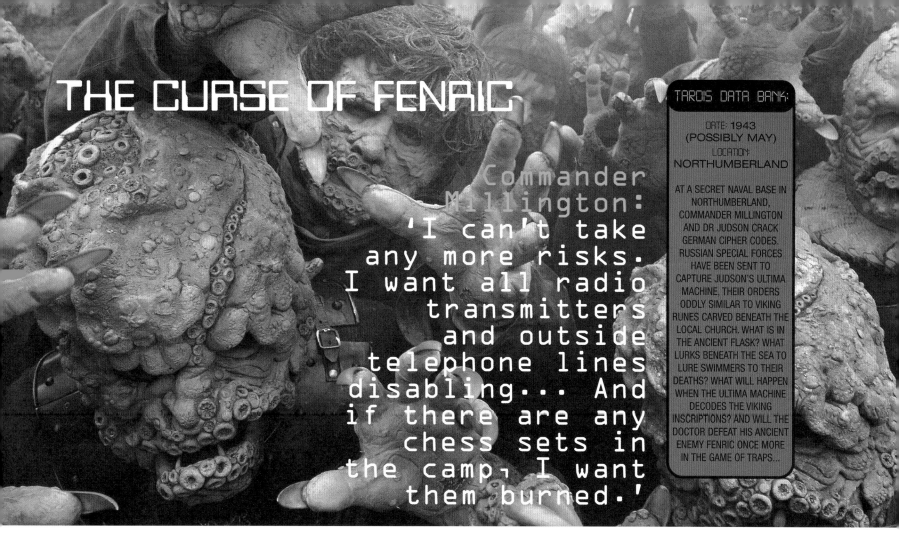

THE CURSE OF FENRIC

Commander Millington: 'I can't take any more risks. I want all radio transmitters and outside telephone lines disabling... And if there are any chess sets in the camp, I want them burned.'

TARDIS DATA BANK:

DATE: 1943 (POSSIBLY MAY)
LOCATION: NORTHUMBERLAND

AT A SECRET NAVAL BASE IN NORTHUMBERLAND, COMMANDER MILLINGTON AND DR JUDSON CRACK GERMAN CIPHER CODES. RUSSIAN SPECIAL FORCES HAVE BEEN SENT TO CAPTURE JUDSON'S ULTIMA MACHINE, THEIR ORDERS ODDLY SIMILAR TO VIKING RUNES CARVED BENEATH THE LOCAL CHURCH. WHAT IS IN THE ANCIENT FLASK? WHAT LURKS BENEATH THE SEA TO LURE SWIMMERS TO THEIR DEATHS? WHAT WILL HAPPEN WHEN THE ULTIMA MACHINE DECODES THE VIKING INSCRIPTIONS? AND WILL THE DOCTOR DEFEAT HIS ANCIENT ENEMY FENRIC ONCE MORE IN THE GAME OF TRAPS...

In which the Doctor and Ace find themselves confronted by Nicholas Parsons playing the local vicar...
BY IAN BRIGGS
4 EPISODES, FIRST BROADCAST 25 OCTOBER–15 NOVEMBER 1989

JOURNEY INFORMATION

FENRIC

Fenric is a creature distilled from evil itself. The Doctor describes it as, 'Evil since the dawn of time... The beginning of all beginnings. Two forces, only good and evil. Then chaos. Time is born. Matter, space. The Universe cries out like a newborn. The forces shatter as the Universe explodes outwards. Only echoes remain, and yet somehow – somehow – the evil force survives. An intelligence, pure evil...'
Fenric is Millington's name for it – 'trapped in a flask like a genie in a bottle'.

Once freed from the ancient flask, Fenric takes over Dr Judson's body. Fenric's 'wolves' have unwittingly worked to bring about its reappearance, and are descendants of the Viking who buried the flask. They are all pawns in Fenric's game, including Captain Sorin, whose grandmother was the granddaughter of Viking descendant Joseph Sundvik.

The Doctor says he realised Fenric was back when he saw a chess game in Lady Peinforte's house (*Silver Nemesis*). Fenric plays games with time – allowing Ace to save her own mother, whom she hates, and bringing the Ancient One back in time to create its own poisoned future world. But once the Doctor has explained Fenric's plan to the Ancient One, it locks itself and Fenric – who has possessed Sorin – in an isolation booth and destroys itself and Fenric's new body with poison.

DR JUDSON AND COMMANDER MILLINGTON

The Ultima machine is an early computer capable of more than a thousand combinations an hour with automatic negative checking. It was designed and is operated by the crippled Dr Judson, who uses a logic diagram to program the rotors. The Viking runes are also a logic diagram (as Ace realises) which program the Ultima machine to print out a list of the 'wolves of Fenric'.

Commander Millington knows Viking legends. He plans to use natural poison he has discovered to gas-bomb German cities. He wants the Russians to steal the Ultima machine, which is booby-trapped with poison that can be released in Moscow after the war when the computer translates the word 'love'.

Kathleen to her nan's house – 17 Old Terrace, Streatham – to escape the Haemovores. She later learns from Fenric that Kathleen Dudman *is* her nan, and Fenric tells her, 'In 30 years the baby will be grown. She will have a daughter – that daughter will be you. You have just created your own future. The baby is your mother, the mother you hate.'

Ace's faith in the Doctor is so strong that it holds back the Ancient One, stopping him from destroying Fenric. The Doctor is forced to undermine this faith by telling Ace she is a social misfit – an emotional cripple he only took with him because he knew she was somehow infected by Fenric.

THE HAEMOVORES

Thousands of years in the future, homo sapiens will evolve into Haemovores – creatures with an insatiable appetite for blood – if the Ancient One releases its poison.

They rise from the sea when the Ultima machine decodes the Viking inscriptions, but can be held back by faith – Sorin's faith in the Russian Revolution, Ace's faith in the Doctor, and the Doctor's faith (though he does not say what he has faith in).

The Ancient One (whose name may in Ingiger – the final name on the Ultima printout) is the last living creature on a future Earth, having watched the world die from poison and chemical waste. The Ancient One was carried back by Fenric in a timestorm to ninth-century Transylvania and was trapped there because he did not have the flask containing Fenric – and only Fenric could return him to the future. A merchant bought the flask in Constantinople and the Ancient One followed him through Europe, then followed Viking pirates who stole the flask.

Those it has killed and infected over the years have become Haemovores. The Ancient One kills the other Haemovores by thought. The Doctor persuades it not to release its poison, and it kills Fenric instead...

NEW INFORMATION

THE DOCTOR

The Doctor forges the signatures of the Prime Minister and Head of the Secret Service – with a pen in each hand. He recognises Viking runes as ninth century, and can translate Russian sealed orders.

When Kathleen Dudman, one of the base personnel, asks him if he has any family, the Doctor replies: 'I don't know.'

Fenric says of the Doctor: 'For 17 centuries I was trapped in the Shadow Dimensions because of him. He pulled bones from the desert sands and carved them into chess pieces. He challenged me to solve his puzzle. I failed.'

COMPANIONS

ACE: When she learns that the baby daughter of Kathleen Dudman has the same name as her mother – Audrey – Ace hands it back. But despite her name, Ace goes back to ensure the baby is all right. She sends the escaping

BEHIND THE SCENES

MISSING SCENES

Occasionally a scene that had been scripted and recorded was removed from a **Doctor Who** episode before transmission as the director and/or the producer felt it had gone too far and was unsuitable for broadcast.

The sequence in *The Curse of Fenric* where Ace is rescued from Haemovores on the roof of the church originally ended with Sorin's soldiers driving stakes through the Haemovores to kill them. While other scenes from the story were removed or trimmed for timing reasons, this sequence was taken out because it was felt it was too strong for the intended audience.

Other sequences that have been removed or curtailed as the finished result was considered too powerful have included Noah begging Vira to kill him in *The Ark in Space*; Padmasambvaha's face disintegrating as he dies in The *Abominable Snowmen*; and Winlett mutating into a Kryoid in *The Seeds of Doom*...

Some countries have made further cuts to **Doctor Who** episodes before clearing them for transmission. As a result, some episodes returned to the BBC Archives from abroad have included minor cuts. Ironically, while some episodes sold to Australia and New Zealand in the 1960s have been lost, the censored scenes from them have been retained – and in some cases are now the only sequences still known to exist from those episodes. These include: Macra attacking Polly and Ben from *The Macra Terror*; Oak and Quill breathing out gas fumes and several other sequences from *Fury from the Deep*; and Yeti attacking in *The Web of Fear*...

When *The Curse of Fenric* was released on video in extended form, the Haemovore-staking scene was still omitted, although it is retained in the BBC's archives and is included in the extended version now available on DVD. However, one important scene will never be edited into the story. A carefully planned effects sequence showing the fire from the burning chessboard spreading through spilled chemicals to set fire to the whole building was recorded on location at Crowborough. Unfortunately, the tape including this sequence was accidentally erased before the scene was edited into the episode and no copy exists.

SURVIVAL

In which the Doctor and Ace are taken from modern Perivale to confront the Master on a planet ruled by Cheetah People. Even if they win, will the Doctor ever return?
BY RONA MUNRO
3 EPISODES, FIRST BROADCAST 22 NOVEMBER–6 DECEMBER 1989

The Doctor: 'When is a cat not a cat? When it builds its own cat flap.'

JOURNEY INFORMATION

THE CHEETAH PEOPLE

The Cheetah People are humanoid felines. They can see in the dark, ride horses and hunt down humans – if they run... The Master says they are 'essentially a fun-loving species' and the Doctor later echoes this (though possibly to convince himself as he's looking at a skull at the time).

Their planet is disintegrating. The Doctor describes it as 'an old planet, a bit frayed at the edges.' It affects the people brought there – slowly turning them into Cheetah People. This is what happens to the human Midge and is happening to the Master and also, to an extent, to Ace. The Master says the planet is alive, and the animals are part of it – when they fight each other they trigger explosions that hasten its destruction.

The people who created the now-ruined buildings on the planet thought they could control the planet and bred the Kitlings. These were creatures whose minds they could talk to, and through whose eyes they could see. The Kitlings are like black cats, and the Doctor describes them as feline vultures. They have the power of teleportation, and are able to jump from world to world hunting for carrion.

The Cheetah People are hunting animals – guided to potential prey on Earth by the Kitlings.

The Doctor realises he can return to Earth if he is hunted by a Cheetah Person whose home is Earth, as they have the ability to return to their original 'home' to hunt.

Some at least of the Cheetah People were originally other humanoid life forms that have been brought to the planet.

NEW INFORMATION

THE DOCTOR

The Doctor fells Sergeant Paterson (a self-defence instructor from Perivale) with a finger to the forehead – and reminds him of his own adage: 'a finger can be a deadly weapon'.

He realises they are on the planet of the Cheetah People – intelligent carnivores that no-one knows much about. He uses his pocket watch to find Ace, holding it open close to the ground.

The Doctor says that he and the Master are 'an explosive combination'.

THE TARDIS

The Doctor and Ace are both brought 'home' to outside the TARDIS.

THE MASTER

The Doctor describes the Master as 'an evil genius, one of my oldest and deadliest of enemies.'

The Master is able to see through a Kitling's eyes, and says the Cheetah People 'are mine to command'. But he is himself turning into a Cheetah Person as he is affected by the planet. Even back on Earth the power from the planet grows within him – 'the power of tooth and claw' – but he thinks he can control it. He takes the Doctor back to his 'new home' – the planet of the Cheetah People – when they fight.

Evil as ever, the Master 'persuades' Midge to die when he is injured in a motorbike 'joust' with the Doctor. After he kills Karra, one of the Cheetah People, he sees Ace's grief and laughs.

Ace: 'Do you know any nice people? You know, ordinary people — not power-crazed nutters trying to take over the galaxy.'

It is not clear whether the Master is left on the planet of the Cheetah People as it is destroyed, or whether he escapes to another 'home'.

COMPANIONS

ACE: Ace has asked the Doctor to bring her back to Perivale – where 'nothing ever happens.' The Doctor says she has been away as long as she thinks she has, which she says is 'forever.'

Sergeant Paterson says the police let Ace off with a warning (though she told the Doctor 'You're not my probation officer,' in *Ghost Light*), and her mum has her listed as a missing person. Her friends believe she's either dead or gone to Birmingham.

When she meets Shreela, Midge and Derek, humans who have been brought to the planet of the Cheetah people, Ace tells them, 'It's just as well I'm here – you need sorting out, you lot.' She decides to fight back against the Cheetah People, claiming 'nothing's invincible'.

Karra says Ace is her sister: 'you are like me ... you will be'. When she is affected by the nature of the planet and changing into a Cheetah Person, Ace wants to run and hunt...

Ace brings the surviving humans back 'home' – arriving beside the TARDIS. 'This is the only home I've got now, right?' The Doctor says the planet lives on inside her, and always will.

BEHIND THE SCENES

THE END OF A LEGEND?

At the end of the final episode of *Survival* there was, unusually, no assurance from the continuity announcer that **Doctor Who** would be back for a new season next year. He would not. Although transmitted earlier in the season, the last **Doctor Who** story made at and by BBC Television was *Ghost Light*.

The production office did have plans for the following season. Script editor Andrew Cartmel, working closely with writers Ben Aaronovitch and Marc Platt, had already decided that Ace would leave mid-season and be replaced by a new companion.

Stories would be set on Earth as a rule, since *Ghost Light*, *The Curse of Fenric* and others had convinced Cartmel and producer John Nathan-Turner that the BBC's design department was more adept at realising contemporary or past Earth locations than the far future or alien worlds. And the darker, more mysterious side of the Doctor would be even more to the fore...

Cartmel himself was also thinking of moving on at the end of the following season, and Colin Brake, who had been working on **EastEnders**, was unofficially being mooted as his replacement, with Marc Platt and Ben Aaronovitch also possible candidates.

John Nathan-Turner had been keen to move on from **Doctor Who** for several years, being persuaded to stay by his superiors and/or the incumbent Doctor, but seems to have again been willing to stay for one more season.

But with no new season commissioned by the BBC, the **Doctor Who** production office was wound down and closed. Apart from two radio serials (starring Jon Pertwee, Nicholas Courtney and Elisabeth Sladen) and the charity spoof *Dimensions in Time*, the BBC produced no more **Doctor Who** until 1996.

When **Doctor Who** did return to BBC television, it was in a radically different form, made by Universal Television in collaboration with BBC Worldwide and with – for most of the 90-minute TV movie – a new Doctor.

The Doctor: 'There are worlds out there where the sky is burning. Where the sea's asleep and the rivers dream. People made of smoke and cities made of song. Somewhere there's danger, somewhere there's injustice, and somewhere else the tea's getting cold. Come on, Ace, we've got work to do.'

THE OTHER WORLDS OF DOCTOR WHO

THIS IS KANE. HE'S A PROFESSOR, AND WE'RE GIVING HIM A LIFT.

THAT'S FROBISHER. HE LOOKS LIKE A PENGUIN, BUT HE'S NOT.

Doctor Who is remembered first and foremost as a television series, but over the years the Doctor's travels and adventures have been depicted in many other formats and media. From chocolate-bar wrappers to sweet-cigarette cards and ice lollies, the Doctor seems set to conquer every medium in the known universe. **Doctor Who** may arguably be the longest running science-fiction series in the world, but its entry in the 2001 *Guinness Book of World Records* is for BBC Worldwide's range of original **Doctor Who** novels – 'the largest fictional series built round one principal character.'

COMICS

The very first **Doctor Who** comic strip story started in *TV Comic* issue 674 in November 1964 and was drawn by Neville Main. The stories showed the Doctor accompanied by his grandchildren, John and Gillian. They continued in *TV Comic* with the Second and Third Doctors, and were produced by other artists – notably John Canning. The Third Doctor appeared in the comic *Countdown*, which later became *TV Action*, before a return to *TV Comic* until 1979.

In 1979, Marvel UK started *Doctor Who Weekly* – later *Doctor Who Monthly* and now *Doctor Who Magazine*, published by Panini – which continues to include a **Doctor Who** comic strip each issue as a major feature.

A variety of the Doctor's television enemies have been pitted against him in comic form – the Daleks, the Cybermen and the Quarks among early favourites. *TV Comic* also created a new menace – the robotic Trods, while *Doctor Who Magazine* has introduced a memorable new companion Frobisher (a shape-changing Whifferdill who is comfortable in the form of a penguin) and the deceptively cuddly homicidal megalomaniac Beep the Meep...

BOOKS

Although three **Doctor Who** stories were 'novelised' during the 1960s (*The Daleks*, *The Web Planet*, and *The Crusade*), it was not until 1973 that a regular publishing schedule of the Doctor's adventures in book form began. Originally published by Target Books, the series was acquired by other publishers before ending up with Virgin Publishing. Eventually every televised **Doctor Who** story was published with the exceptions of *Doctor Who – The Movie* (published by BBC Worldwide in 1996), *Shada* (which was never completed or broadcast), *City of Death*, *Resurrection of the Daleks* and *Revelation of the Daleks*.

Although the authors – particularly of later stories – often novelised their own scripts, the majority of the books were written by writer and former script editor Terrance Dicks.

In 1991, Virgin Publishing started to produce *The New Adventures* – original fiction continuing the travels of the Seventh Doctor and Ace. The series was established and edited by Peter Darvill-Evans. Ace was joined by another successful companion, Professor Bernice (Benny) Summerfield, who went on to appear in her own range of books for Virgin as well as in audio adventures from Big Finish Productions.

The New Adventures were so successful that in 1994 Virgin started a line of *Missing Adventures* featuring earlier Doctors and their companions, overseen initially by Rebecca Levene. Both ranges ended in 1996 when the rights reverted to BBC Worldwide.

Since 1996, BBC Worldwide has published well over a hundred original novels in two ranges of books – one featuring the continuing adventures of the Eighth Doctor and new companions, the other featuring past Doctors. Set up by Nuala Buffini and nurtured by Stephen Cole (who also oversaw **Doctor Who** video and audio production), all BBC Worldwide's **Doctor Who** books now come under the jurisdiction of commissioning editor Ben Dunn and creative consultant Justin Richards.

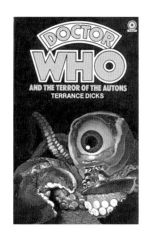

STAGE PLAYS

As well as recent re-stagings of 'lost' **Doctor Who** stories including *The Web of Fear* and *Fury from the Deep*, there have been three original **Doctor Who** stage plays.

The first of these did not, in fact, feature the Doctor at all. *The Curse of the Daleks*, by David Whitaker and Terry Nation, ran at London's Wyndham's Theatre for almost four weeks starting in December 1965. It told the story of an Earth spaceship that crash-lands on Skaro. As well as the Daleks, the play included Thals who come to the help of the humans – and a human traitor hoping to use the Daleks to make him king of the Universe.

In December 1974, while the television series was between Doctors, the Adelphi Theatre staged *Doctor Who and the Daleks in Seven Keys to Doomsday*. Written by outgoing script editor Terrance Dicks, the play starred Trevor Martin as the Doctor, with new companions Jimmy (usually played by James Mathews and sometimes by Simon Jones) and Jenny (played by Wendy Padbury – who had played companion Zoe on television). The play ran for four weeks, and told how the Doctor managed to defeat the Daleks on the planet Karn by finding seven crystal keys that the Daleks need to power their ultimate weapon.

The third, and most successful, **Doctor Who** stage play, *Doctor Who – The Ultimate Adventure*, was again written by Terrance Dicks. It opened at the Wimbledon Theatre, starring Jon Pertwee as the Doctor, in March 1989 before touring with Pertwee until June. Colin Baker then took over the lead role until August. David Banks (who usually played the mercenary, Karl) played the Doctor on the two occasions that Pertwee was indisposed. The play included impressive laser effects, tall Daleks (and their short Emperor), *Earthshock*-style Cybermen, 'Mrs T' the Prime Minister and several gratuitous songs. The Doctor's companions were Crystal (Rebecca Thornhill), Jason (Graeme Smith) and the furry alien Zog (Stephanie Colburn), and they helped him thwart a combined Dalek–Cyberman plot to kidnap a peace envoy.

RADIO

Audio now seems a natural medium for the Doctor, with Big Finish Productions having brought out over fifty **Doctor Who** audio adventures on CD featuring the Fifth, Sixth, Seventh and Eighth Doctors. But apart from several spin-off radio appearances, including a mockumentary biography of Susan Foreman, the Doctor has appeared only three times in 'genuine' radio adventures.

During the 'hiatus' between seasons in 1985, script editor Eric Saward wrote *Slipback*. With Colin Baker and Nicola Bryant playing their television roles of the Doctor and Peri, it was broadcast on BBC Radio 4 VHF in ten-minute episodes as part of a children's magazine, *Pirate Radio 4*.

Jon Pertwee reprised his role as the Doctor for *The Paradise of Death*. Written by former producer Barry Letts, the story also featured the Brigadier and Sarah, and was directed by Phil Clarke of BBC Radio's Light Entertainment Department. It was broadcast on Radio 5 in August and September 1993.

A sequel of sorts – *The Ghosts of N Space* – again starring Jon Pertwee as the Third Doctor with the Brigadier and Sarah, was broadcast on Radio 2 in early 1996 (although it was recorded in 1994). Again, it was written by Barry Letts.

An audio broadcast of a different kind brought *Death Comes to Time* to life in 2001/2. While the first episode of this five-part adventure for the Seventh Doctor and Ace was made as a radio pilot, the other episodes were not commissioned by BBC Radio. BBCi subsequently commissioned producer/director Dan Freedman to complete the series – with guest stars including Stephen Fry and John Sessions – for webcasting over the Internet.

So successful was *Death Comes to Time* that BBCi have followed it up with *Real Time* in 2002, which pitted the Sixth Doctor against the Cybermen, and a version of the uncompleted television story *Shada* adapted for the Eight Doctor in 2003 – both produced for BBCi by Big Finish Productions.

FILMS

There have been two cinema film versions of **Doctor Who**, both made in the mid-sixties, adapted from television stories, and starring Peter Cushing as the Doctor.

In 1965, *Dr. Who and the Daleks* retold the first Dalek story, albeit with some significant differences. As well as being in full colour – with the blue Daleks led by a red Dalek and a black Dalek – it told the story of an elderly eccentric inventor called Dr Who and his grandchildren Barbara (Jennie Linden) and Susan (Roberta Tovey). Ian was Barbara's inept boyfriend, played by Roy Castle. The basic plot was an abridged version of *The Daleks*, with the Daleks defeated at the end when they destroy their own controls firing on Ian.

The production was lavish and impressive, and the film was successful enough for a sequel to be released the following year.

An adaption of *The Dalek Invasion of Earth*, the second film was even more impressive. *Daleks Invasion Earth: 2150AD* again starred Cushing as the Doctor. He was now accompanied by Susan, his niece Louise (Jill Curzon) and a policeman called Tom Campbell – played by Bernard Cribbins – who stumbles into the TARDIS as it takes off. The Daleks were more menacing than ever, this time in silver livery and commanded by a Red Dalek, Black Dalek and Gold Dalek. Again, it was an abridged version of the television story, although this time the Daleks were defeated when sucked into the Earth by magnetism released when their bomb explodes off course...

Although even more impressive than its predecessor, the film didn't do so well at the box office and plans for a third Cushing movie, to be based on *The Chase*, were dropped.

Over the years there have been frequent rumours of a new **Doctor Who** movie – Jon Pertwee apparently declined a movie role, Tom Baker tried to organise *Doctor Who and Scratchman* which he co-wrote with Ian Marter (who played Harry Sullivan) and, more recently, the rights to the series have been acquired, and allowed to lapse, on several occasions...

TV PRODUCTIONS

Over the years, **Doctor Who** has been spoofed by numerous television (and radio) comedy programmes – most recently by the sketch and impression show **Dead Ringers**. The Doctor has suffered, in various 'forms', the wit and humour of comedians including Lenny Henry, French and Saunders, Victoria Wood and Spike Milligan. He has been spoofed on programmes as diverse as **Crackerjack, The Two Ronnies** and **End of Part One**. During the run of *The Two Doctors*, Jimmy Saville even fixed it for Gareth Jenkins to become a sort of junior Doctor and take on the Sontarans with the help of the real Doctor (Colin Baker) and Tegan (Janet Fielding).

There has only ever been one legitimate 'spin-off' production, and two 'special' productions of **Doctor Who** outside the normal run of the series.

Terry Nation, creator of the Daleks, tried to set up a Dalek series in the 1960s (and again with the BBC in 1980) – first in Britain, then in the USA – but without success. So it was not until 28 December 1981 that a bona fide 'companion' programme was broadcast. It was hoped that *A Girl's Best Friend* would be the first of a series of **K-9 and Company**, featuring Elisabeth Sladen as the Doctor's former companion Sarah Jane Smith and K-9 Mark 3 – left for her by the Doctor. The story, scripted by Terrance Dudley, also featured Sarah's Aunt Lavinia and Lavinia's ward, Brendan, in a straightforward plot that involved witchcraft in a Gloucestershire village. Although it achieved respectable viewing figures, the option of a full series was not taken up by the BBC.

For **Doctor Who**'s thirtieth anniversary in November 1993, the Third, Fourth, Fifth, Sixth and Seventh Doctors all appeared in a special two-part adventure made for the BBC's Children in Need appeal. *Dimensions in Time* was shot using a special technique that meant it could be seen in 3-D when special glasses were worn (they cost 99p, the proceeds going to charity). While it featured a multitude of Doctors, companions and monsters, the story – by John Nathan-Turner and David Roden – was, understandably, rather thin and concerned the Rani kidnapping incarnations of the Doctor. Much of the action took place across time zones in **EastEnders**' Albert Square.

Another charity production, *The Curse of Fatal Death*, was written by respected comedy writer Stephen Moffat for the BBC's 1999 **Comic Relief** telethon. This told the story of the Doctor meeting the Master to announce his retirement and his engagement to his companion Emma (played by Julia Sawalha). But the Master, in league with an army of Daleks, has set a trap.

Rowan Atkinson played the Ninth Doctor – succeeded in rapid succession by Richard E. Grant, Hugh Grant and Jim Broadbent before the Doctor regenerated yet again into Joanna Lumley. Jonathan Pryce played the frustrated Master while the Daleks appeared as themselves in impressive form – proving, if proof were needed, that it is still possible to produce quality **Doctor Who** on a modest budget.

Eight

'I know who I am – I am the Doctor.'

(THE DOCTOR –
DOCTOR WHO – THE MOVIE)

THE EIGHTH DOCTOR

The Eighth Doctor is the most human of all the Doctors and it is fitting that it is he who claims to be half human. He may be joking when he says that this comes from 'my mother's side' but, based on the evidence of his retina pattern, the Master certainly believes him. The Doctor says that it is a secret (assuming this is the secret he was about to impart), and perhaps his human pedigree is what Lady Peinforte was threatening to reveal in *Silver Nemesis*. Of course, as the Doctor tells Grace, he can transform himself into another species when he regenerates, so this does not necessarily mean that any of the Doctor's other incarnations are half human or that it has anything to do with his parentage. But here is a Doctor who – whether in jest or not – is the first specifically to mention his father and mother.

The Eighth Doctor is more outgoing than the others in many ways. He is not averse to kissing Grace, though what, if anything, it means to him emotionally is unclear. He seems open and honest about his feelings and fears. He gives the impression that he acts on a whim and on instinct – allowing Chang Lee to keep gold dust the Master gave him from the TARDIS; kissing Grace; testing his new shoes...

For once the Doctor is not afraid to give people hints and tips about their futures. He seems to have intimate knowledge of so many of the people he meets in San Francisco – telling Grace that as a child she dreamed she could hold back death, and that in the future she 'will do great things'. He recognises an official, Gareth, at the Institute for Technological Advancement and Research and tells him to answer the second question on his midterm exam, even though the third may look easier. The Doctor knows that Gareth would mess the third question up.

He gives Gareth this advice with no more gravity or apparent importance than he gives him a jelly baby. But he tells Grace that in ten years Gareth will head the seismology unit of the UCLA task force and come up with a system for accurately predicting earthquakes. His invention will save the human race several times, but first he must graduate in poetry.

Although he seems to throw out such advice about the future – like telling Chang Lee not to be in San Francisco next Christmas – the Doctor does have an understanding of, and respect for, the rules that have governed previous Doctors. He may hint at Grace's future, but he refuses to give her any details, telling her that the Universe hangs by a delicate thread...

This Doctor's outlook and mannerisms may be more obviously human, but underneath he is the same as his other incarnations. This is a Doctor who will stop at nothing to save the Earth and defeat the Master; who values life and enjoys living; and who can achieve his ends in the most surprising and effective of ways – such as getting a policeman's motorbike by taking the man's gun and threatening to shoot *himself*.

This is a Doctor who, like every other, relishes adventure and is willing to make the ultimate sacrifice to save others but who, at the end of the day, is happy to get back to his cup of tea and a good book – whatever happens in between may be of universal import, but really it just gets in the way...

'Oh no – not again...'

THE MAN BEHIND THE DOCTOR – PAUL McGANN

Born in Surrey in 1959, Paul McGann grew up in Liverpool with his three brothers Joe, Mark and Stephen – all of whom became actors. All four appeared together in the 1995 television drama **The Hanging Gale**.

Paul McGann's first major television roles included starring in **Give Us A Break** (for which he learned to play snooker) and Percy Toplis – **The Monacled Mutineer**. In 1987 he starred with Richard E. Grant in the film *Withnail and I*

which has become a cult classic. Other film work followed, including *Alien³* and *The Three Musketeers*.

Although other actors read for the role of the Eighth Doctor – including Anthony Stewart Head and John Sessions – Paul McGann was always the producers' first choice. Since appearing as the Doctor, Paul McGann has re-created the role on audio as well as continuing his successful career, mainly in British television.

TARDIS DATA BANK:

DATE:
30 DECEMBER 1999
– 1 JANUARY 2000
LOCATION:
SAN FRANCISCO

THE DOCTOR IS TRANSPORTING THE MASTER'S REMAINS BACK TO GALLIFREY, BUT THE MASTER IS NOT DEAD. THE TARDIS LANDS IN SAN FRANCISCO. THE DOCTOR IS ACCIDENTALLY SHOT AND SEEMINGLY DIES, BUT REGENERATES IN HOSPITAL. THE MASTER TAKES OVER THE BODY OF AN AMBULANCE DRIVER CALLED BRUCE, BUT HE NEEDS THE DOCTOR'S BODY IF HE IS TO SURVIVE… CAN THE DOCTOR RECOVER FROM THE TRAUMA OF REGENERATION AND REMEMBER WHO HE IS? CAN HE PERSUADE GRACE THAT HE IS A TIME LORD FROM GALLIFREY AND NOT A PATIENT FROM THE PSYCHIATRIC WARD? WILL HE BE IN TIME TO STOP THE MASTER DESTROYING EARTH IN HIS BID TO SURVIVE…

DOCTOR WHO – THE MOVIE

The Doctor: 'Grace, I came back to life before your eyes, I held back death. Look, I can't make your dream come true for ever, but I can make it come true today.'

THE TELEVISION STORY

BY MATTHEW JACOBS
85-MINUTE TV MOVIE, FIRST UK BROADCAST 27 MAY 1996

JOURNEY INFORMATION

GRACE HOLLOWAY

Grace Holloway is a senior cardiologist at the hospital where the Doctor is taken after he is shot. She is brought in to examine the Doctor but, because she does not realise he has an alien metabolism, her efforts to discover what is wrong in effect kill him.

The Doctor tells Grace that she is tired of life, but afraid of dying and that it was a childhood dream to 'hold back death' that led her to take up a career as a doctor.

Though she is sceptical of the Doctor's story – even after confirming he has two hearts and non-human blood – Grace is attracted to him. 'Great,' she tells him, 'I finally meet the right guy, and he's from another planet.'

Grace eventually comes to believe the Doctor's story after realising the Master is an evil alien. She is taken over by the Master when he spits his burning bile on her, but he has to release her so she can open the Eye of Harmony in the TARDIS in order for him to steal the Doctor's remaining lives. She manages to set the TARDIS into a temporal orbit, but the Master kills her when she rescues the Doctor from him.

The Doctor manages to roll back time within the TARDIS and uses energy from the Eye of Harmony to bring both Grace and Chang Lee back to life. Despite her feelings for the Doctor, Grace declines his offer to go with him in the TARDIS.

CHANG LEE

Chang Lee is involved in the street gangs of San Francisco. On the run, he shoots back at the gang chasing him, but is caught in a trap. He is only saved from being shot by the arrival of the TARDIS.

Chang Lee gets the Doctor to hospital when he is shot, travelling with him in the ambulance. It is not clear why he bothers to accompany the Doctor, or why he lies about knowing him rather than simply claiming to be a concerned passer-by. Perhaps he is intrigued by the TARDIS, or possibly he hopes for a reward from the Doctor. Certainly, he is happy to take the Doctor's possessions after he is declared 'dead'.

Taken in by the Master's lies and his promise of power and wealth, it is Chang Lee who opens the Eye of Harmony. The Master says that the TARDIS seems to 'like' him, though it may simply be that Chang Lee's eyes, unlike the Master's, are human and can therefore access the systems.

Eventually, Chang Lee is convinced of the Master's duplicity and is killed, though the Doctor revives both him and Grace. Perhaps having learned from his experiences, or perhaps feeling indebted to the Doctor, Chang Lee offers to return gold dust the Master has given him from the TARDIS. When the Doctor says he can keep it, Chang Lee is keen to leave before the Doctor changes his mind...

NEW INFORMATION

THE DOCTOR

With the urn containing the Master's remains secured in a locked casket, the Doctor heads for Gallifrey, local dateline 5725.2 Rassilon Era. On the way he reads *The Time Machine* while listening to a record ('In a Dream', sung by Pat Hodge) and drinking tea.

He is shot when he leaves the TARDIS – one bullet going through his shoulder, another two lodging in his left leg. While being operated on by Grace Holloway, he suffers a massive seizure and – apparently – dies. After he has regenerated, he remarks that he was dead too long, hence his amnesia. The anaesthetic almost destroyed the regenerative process.

After he regenerates, the Doctor does not know who he is. He dresses in clothes taken from fancy-dress outfits in hospital-staff lockers, most of his outfit being 'Wild Bill Hickock', with shoes later supplied by Grace (from her ex-boyfriend Brian). He needs a beryllium atomic clock to fix the timing mechanism of the TARDIS – which he has to do anyway, even before he knows he needs to close the Eye of Harmony.

The Doctor says he was with Puccini before he died, and also knew Sigmund Freud and Marie Curie, though he does not immediately recognise the Master. He remembers being with his father, lying back in the grass on Gallifrey. After he remembers who he is, and also when he says goodbye, he kisses Grace. He asks her to come with him when he leaves San Francisco, but she refuses.

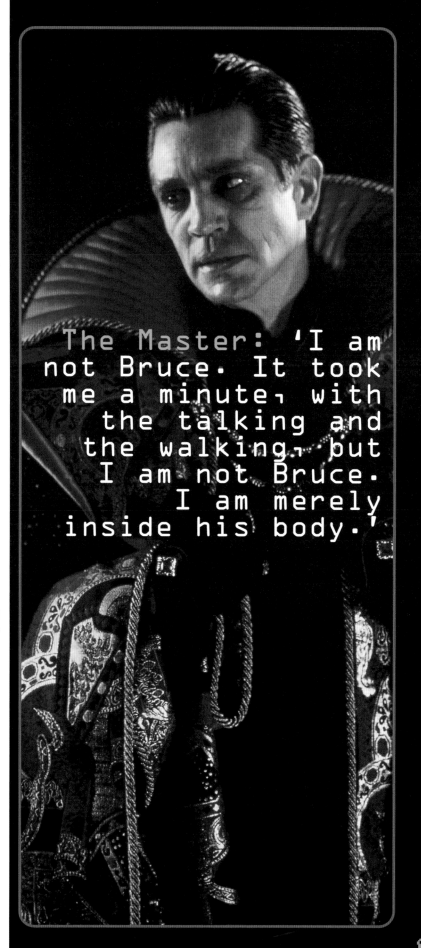

The Master: 'I am not Bruce. It took me a minute, with the talking and the walking, but I am not Bruce. I am merely inside his body.'

He tells Grace he loves humans – 'always seeing patterns in things that aren't there.' When she says the Doctor is British, he agrees: 'I suppose I am.'

The Doctor says he can transform himself into another species, but only when he 'dies'. (This is also implied in *The Dalek's Master Plan*.) He also says that Gallifrey is 250 million light years away (although it is implied in *Terror of the Autons* that it is only 29,000 light years away).

THE TARDIS

The TARDIS is larger and grander than we have previously seen. The main console is in an area off the 'library' rather than a separate chamber. The whole roof above the console acts as a scanner, while monitors give data and warning messages. The Doctor mentions the time rotor, but is not specific about where on the console it is.

When there is a critical timing malfunction the TARDIS initiates its automatic emergency landing. The Doctor needs a beryllium chip (from an atomic clock) to fix the TARDIS – and there happens to be one at the Institute for Technological Advancement and Research in San Francisco.

A wind blows up when the TARDIS lands. The TARDIS is unmarked by bullets, and the Yale-type lock swings aside to reveal a larger hole for the ankh-like TARDIS key. The Doctor keeps a spare key in a cubbyhole on the roof (above the 'P' of *Police Box*). He also has bags of gold dust in the drawer of a filing cabinet.

The Doctor is able to roll back time and use energy from the Eye of Harmony to revive Grace and Chang Lee – possibly because they died inside the TARDIS.

The Doctor describes the TARDIS as a sentimental old thing.

The cloister room – with its dome apparently open to space – houses the Eye of Harmony which is 'the heart of the structure, everything is powered from here.' Whether it is a 'complete' eye, or draws its power from the Eye of Harmony on Gallifrey (see *The Deadly Assassin*) is not explained.

The Doctor says the Eye has not been open for 700 years, but the Master is able to open it using Chang Lee's retina pattern (and later Grace's).

Once open, the Eye enables the Master and Chang Lee to see an image of the Doctor, and to see through his eyes. If the Doctor looks into the Eye of Harmony, he says his soul will be destroyed and the Master will be able to take his body. If the Eye isn't closed, Earth will be turned inside out as the molecular structure of the planet changes, first in subtle ways, but later catastrophically.

When the Eye is open too long, the Cloister Bell sounds as a warning that the TARDIS is dying. Grace manages to put the TARDIS into a temporal orbit using power from the open Eye.

THE MASTER

Somehow, the Master has survived his execution by the Daleks on Skaro. The Doctor knows that 'even in death I couldn't trust him' and stows the urn containing his remains in a locked casket. But the Master is freed when the casket shatters...

He escapes through the TARDIS keyhole as an amorphous blob that later takes on the shape of a snake. In this form, the Master takes over the body of Bruce the ambulance driver – the snake enters through his mouth while he is asleep and kills him. But because Bruce is dead, his body begins to decay and the Master needs the Doctor's body and remaining regenerations to survive. Even in Bruce's body, he retains the snake's eyes, and he wears dark glasses to conceal them.

The Master manages to get into the Doctor's TARDIS and hypnotises Chang Lee just by removing his glasses. When Chang Lee asks, 'What's in it for me?' the Master replies, 'You get to live.' He tells Chang Lee that the Doctor stole *his* TARDIS and his regenerations (and claims the evil Doctor was Genghis Khan). He tells the Doctor that Lee is the son he always yearned for, but then kills him. The Master can spit burning bile – which enables him to take over Grace when it hits her arm and kill security guards at the Institute. He frees Grace from his power by kissing her – sucking out his influence so she can open the eye.

Theatrical as ever, the Master claims 'I always dress for the occasion' and puts on ceremonial Time Lord robes before he takes the Doctor's lives using the power of the Eye of Harmony. But when the Doctor escapes and they fight, the Master is sucked into the Eye of Harmony, and is presumably killed...

BEHIND THE SCENES

UNIVERSAL CONSTRUCTION

In late 1993, BBC Enterprises (now BBC Worldwide) revealed that it had been in discussion with Steven Spielberg's company Amblin Entertainment about a new series of **Doctor Who**.

In fact, the 'champion' of **Doctor Who** at Amblin, and the man responsible for approaching the BBC in 1989 about a possible joint venture, was Philip Segal. Plans changed and evolved, scripts and even a 'series bible' came and went. Segal later left Amblin to set up Lakeside Entertainment, and the **Doctor Who** project moved from Amblin to Universal Television, with Segal still producing. The 1996 **Doctor Who** television movie was made by Universal Television in conjunction with BBC Worldwide and BBC Drama, for US transmission by Fox Network. The hope was that it would be successful enough in the USA to generate interest in a full series, or possibly further TV movies.

The movie was actually made in Vancouver, which 'doubled' for San Francisco, and starred Paul McGann as the Doctor, Sylvester McCoy as the 'old' Doctor, Daphne Ashbrook as Grace, Yee Jee Tso as Chang Lee and Eric Roberts as the Master. It was directed by experienced British director Geoffrey Sax. Everyone involved was enthusiastic about their work, and about the finished product.

But, despite the obvious quality of the production, it failed to find an audience in the USA. Screened opposite an episode of **Roseanne** in which her husband suffers a heart attack, it was never really given a chance. In the UK, however, the movie was received with enthusiasm and despite already being available from BBC Video, **Doctor Who** attained top position in the television drama viewing figures for that week.

Although Universal retained rights to make more **Doctor Who** until the end of 1997, it was unable to find a market for the potential product. Without a partner for what they increasingly considered an expensive production, the BBC was also unwilling to commit to a new series. And so, despite his proven popularity, *Doctor Who – The Movie* remains the last bona fide television adventure for the Doctor in his 40 years of time travel...

'It was on the planet Skaro that my old enemy the Master was finally put on trial. They say he listened calmly as his list of evil crimes was read, and sentence passed.

Then he made his last, and I thought somewhat curious request. He demanded that I — the Doctor, a rival Time Lord — should take his remains back to our home planet, Gallifrey. It was a request they should never have granted...'

(THE DOCTOR – *DOCTOR WHO – THE MOVIE*)

DOCTOR WHO – THE LEGEND CONTINUES

FURTHER ADVENTURES IN SPACE AND TIME

With the exception of *Doctor Who – The Movie* in 1996, there has been no new bona fide **Doctor Who** on television since 1989. But the good Doctor continues to flourish. His past adventures sell well on BBC Video and in enhanced form on DVD. Those stories still missing from the BBC Archives can be bought on soundtrack CD, and the Doctor's adventures continue in other media. And with the recent announcement of a new television series, **Doctor Who** is set to continue into the 21st century. Given the huge enthusiasm and support for the announcement, it is easy to believe that he will continue to delight and surprise his followers for all of time...

DOCTOR WHO MAGAZINE

Fast approaching its 350th issue, *Doctor Who Magazine* started in 1979 as Marvel's *Doctor Who Weekly*. It is currently published every four weeks by Panini and edited by Clayton Hickman.

   The magazine currently runs at over 50 pages per issue, covering news, letters, feature articles, archives and retrospectives on **Doctor Who**. There are reviews of recent products, books and audio adventures as well as previews of upcoming releases.

   The magazine also includes a full-colour comic strip of the Eighth Doctor's continuing adventures. More information can be found at: www.paninicomics.co.uk or you can send an e-mail to dwm@panini.co.uk.

DOCTOR WHO BOOKS

The Eighth Doctor's adventures continue in a range of novels from BBC Worldwide. But this is a rather darker, deeper Doctor than the one in *Doctor Who – The Movie*. Over the course of more than sixty novels he has experienced so much, visited so many times and places, met so many people and defeated so many villains...

   Events of *The Ancestor Cell* (by Stephen Cole and Peter Anghelides) have changed the Doctor. Arriving on Earth for *The Burning* (by Justin Richards) he scarcely remembers who – or what – he is. But now he has met up with his former companion, Fitz, and together with other friends – and enemies – he struggles to prevent universal catastrophe in a series of stand-alone novels that are thematically linked... Meanwhile, the first seven Doctors continue their adventures in a series of novels that take place in the 'gaps' between their television adventures. It is strange to think that the Doctor has now had more adventures in print (now published by BBC Worldwide, up until 1996 by Virgin Publishing) than he had on television...

   BBC Worldwide also publishes non-fiction **Doctor Who** books – including this one. The subject matter ranges from the fully annotated scripts for the Fourth Doctor's first season – *Doctor Who – The Scripts, Tom Baker 1974/5* – complete with production notes, design drawings and deleted scenes, to the less serious but no less essential *Dalek Survival Guide*. BBCi's **Doctor Who** site will keep you updated on the latest news from BBC Worldwide – books, videos and DVDs: www.bbc.co.uk/cult/doctorwho

DOCTOR WHO ON AUDIO

Big Finish Productions has been bringing the Doctor's adventures to life on audio CDs (as well as BBCi webcasts) since 1999. The first release, *The Sirens of Time* by Nicholas Briggs, starred three Doctors – Peter Davison, Colin Baker and Sylvester McCoy – all returning to the role. Since then they have, between them, returned in over 50 more adventures, and there is also an ongoing series with Paul McGann as the Eighth Doctor.

In the audio adventures, the Eighth Doctor is joined by Charley Pollard, a girl he saves from the crash of the R101 in *Storm Warning* (by Alan Barnes) – an act that turns out to have far-reaching consequences...

While all the audio incarnations of the Doctor have faced the Daleks in the Big Finish productions, the Daleks themselves also have their own series of audio adventures – Dalek Empire. Not to be outdone, former companion Sarah Jane Smith, and Virgin Publishing's companion for the Seventh Doctor – Benny – also have dedicated series. Benny also appears in a range of novels and short story anthologies.

From 2002, Big Finish has published anthologies of **Doctor Who** short stories.
More information about all their products can be found at: www.doctorwho.co.uk

THE RESTORATION TEAM

The Restoration Team is an ad hoc group of experts, most of them BBC employees, who lend their skill and experience to BBC Worldwide (and on occasion the BBC itself) to restore television **Doctor Who** so it can be released on video, DVD and audio in the best possible format and at the highest quality. It is the Restoration Team that is responsible for finding, restoring and even creating the extensive extras found on **Doctor Who** DVDs, as well as for using the latest technology to restore the picture and audio quality.

Their many achievements include repairing damaged film and video; using the colour signal from domestic video recordings made in the USA to recolourise episodes that only exist in the BBC Archives in black-and-white; treating film telerecordings to look like the original video broadcast; commissioning new effects work from the BBC's Visual Effects Department as an alternative version to the original; producing documentaries on behind-the-scenes aspects of the making of **Doctor Who**...

Further details of their extensive work can be found at: http://www.restoration-team.co.uk/

Nine

THE NINTH DOCTOR

The Ninth Doctor is a man at odds with himself. Although he retains the moral outrage of his predecessors, and their burning desire to see justice done and evil vanquished, when we first meet him he seems to lack the confidence to do the job. He is very unwilling to put others in danger and he has recently suffered some great loss.

Although we do not discover explicitly what has brought him to this point, any more than we find out why he has regenerated, there are plenty of clues. It is not unreasonable to suppose that the two effects stem from a single cause. The defining moment seems to have been the death of someone close to him.

There is also a thread of pure snobbery running through this Doctor. He appreciates the finer things in life, and doesn't have much time for those who don't. He loves good wine, the musical works of Pachelbel and fine art.

This is a complicated man, a Doctor who tells his new companion, Alison Cheney, emphatically, 'I do not kill'. He also angrily refuses Major Kennet's offer of a gun: 'Don't ever offer me a gun again.' And yet he later destroys an entire alien army, and is always in the company of the military. As the Master puts it, this Doctor is often troubled by having to be two things at once.

Perhaps more than other Doctors, this one is an outsider. Despite his obvious hurt and his apparent amiability, he allows no-one to get close to him (until he chooses Alison to accompany him on his travels, a sign that the clouds may have parted). This is a Doctor whose only chosen companion seems to be an android version of his mortal enemy the Master – a constant reminder perhaps of his own darker qualities.

Yet despite this, the Doctor is still linked to authority. He has a direct phone line to the UN Secretary General, with whom he is on better than first-name terms, and he is willing to let the authorities take over as soon as possible. This is not the uneasy relationship that the Third and Fourth Doctors cultivated with authority – initially out of necessity, and which they tried to sever as soon as possible. This seems to be a relationship of choice and trust. The unease and tension of the Doctor is at the personal rather than the ethical level.

On a higher level it is implied, if not explicitly proven, that the Time Lords are once again willing to use the Doctor as their agent – now very much against his will. Perhaps this new arrangement, which he refers to as his 'exile', is somehow a consequence of whatever disaster has left him so cautious about putting others in danger?

Whatever the root cause of the Doctor's dilemmas and his internal struggles and contradictions, his disillusionment was caused by a mistake he made in the recent past. He is bitter about the experience, believing that his compassion and emotion have made him too vulnerable – a weakness that his enemies are all too able to perceive. 'Only the monsters know me. Only they know how weak I really am,' he says bitterly. But beneath the self-doubt lurks the same fiery intelligence and burning need to see good ultimately triumph. The Ninth Doctor may claim that, 'I only come to this planet for the wine and the total eclipses,' but he is forced to admit, even to himself, that he relishes the danger and excitement once he is – reluctantly – caught up in it: 'I do love a nice old-fashioned invasion.'

'I know about monsters — I'm the Doctor.'

(THE DOCTOR – *THE SCREAM OF THE SHALKA*)

RICHARD E. GRANT – THE MAN BEHIND THE DOCTOR

Son of Swaziland's Minister of Education, Richard Grant Esterhuysen was born in 1957. He knew from a young age that he wanted to be an actor, and studied English and Drama at Cape Town University (where he also founded the multi-racial Troupe Theatre Company). Grant moved to London in 1982 and began acting on the stage.

It was his role in the film *Withnail & I* (starring alongside Paul McGann) that brought Grant to the attention of the general public on both sides of the Atlantic. Other film roles followed – notably a part in *How to Get Ahead in Advertising*, the villain in *Hudson Hawk*, and roles in Robert Altman's *The Player* and *Gosford Park*.

On television Richard E. Grant has appeared in a succession of high-profile series ranging from the 1989 spy thriller *Codename Kyril* to the BBC's lavish adaptation of *The Scarlet Pimpernel*. He has also appeared, of course, as the Doctor in the Comic Relief spoof of **Doctor Who**, *The Curse of Fatal Death*.

THE SCREAM OF THE SHALKA

BY PAUL CORNELL
6 15-MINUTE EPISODES, 2003

TARDIS DATA BANK:

DATE: PRESENT DAY
LOCATION: LANNET, IN LANCASHIRE, ENGLAND; AND VARIOUS LOCATIONS AROUND THE WORLD

EARTH HAS BEEN INVADED AND NOBODY'S NOTICED. THE DOCTOR ARRIVES AND DISCOVERS ALL IS NOT WELL IN NORTHERN ENGLAND. THE SMALL TOWN OF LANNET SEEMS STRANGELY QUIET – THE STREETS ARE EMPTY, THE FACTORIES ARE BUSY, AND THE PEOPLE ARE TURNING INTO STATUES. WHO ARE THE MYSTERIOUS ALIENS LIVING UNDER THE GROUND? AND WHY HAS THE DOCTOR NEVER HEARD OF THEM...

JOURNEY INFORMATION

THE SHALKA

The Shalka that have appeared in Lannet are an alien race that have an affinity with rock and lava. They are part of the Shalka Confederacy which is an empire of a billion worlds – 80 per cent of the 'dead' worlds of the Universe, they claim. Their technology appears 'natural', seemingly formed out of rock. The 'adult' Shalka are human-sized, green, shiny, snake-like creatures with human-like faces (albeit with small, blank eyes) and arms, and a hood like a cobra that focuses their sonic weaponry. The Doctor says their technology is based on sound, which they use to hollow out control areas as well as to control a singularity – the central point of a black hole. They are near-sightless and navigate by sound – hence an explosion the Doctor causes stuns them underground...

Their leader is Prime, War Chief of the Shalka, who adopts a more human form for some of the time. It seems that the Shalka can assume other forms – and sizes. Possibly there is a 'Prime' at each of the Shalka's underground colony locations, or perhaps Lannet is the main site and Prime controls the entire invasion. It is not clear if the small Shalka are young or merely composed of less physical material. Shalka technicians are equipped with extra arms and have brains studded down their backs.

The Shalka arrived on Earth in a meteor that landed in Australia. They arrived in Lannet (and presumably their other locations round the world) three weeks before the Doctor – and at first they were perceived by the inhabitants as a vibration, like pipes rattling. Once settled they travel through a space–time tunnel they establish, which is linked to a black hole (by their sonic control of a singularity).

They control humans by making them want to do their will. Alison Cheney describes her inability to move, for example, by saying 'it's like there's a shadow over me.

This terrible fear.' The main symptom of control is a sore throat, which is caused by the Shalka's use of humans' vocal cords to agitate the air and alter it so that the atmosphere is more suitable for them. The Shalka crush all resistance, and apparently force a friend of Alison's, who talked about getting a message out from Lannet, to cover herself in lava... They can also kill with the sonic power of their screams.

When the army arrives in Lannet, the soldiers estimate the civilian death toll at 637. They discover 26 Shalka 'colonies' in all, though there may be others that they do not find.

The Shalka conquer planets by hastening the process of ecological self-destruction, so their previous conquests – civilisations like Soltox, Duprest and Valtanus – seem merely to have destroyed themselves. The Doctor describes the Shalka not as predators, but as 'death incarnate'. Prime is unimpressed: 'Call us death if you wish... For we bring extinction to the entire human race.'

ALISON CHENEY

Working as a barmaid in the *Volunteer* in Lannet, Alison gave up her degree to live with her boyfriend, Joe.

The Doctor realises that, unlike so many of the inhabitants of Lannet, Alison cares about what is happening. This is perhaps why he initially enlists her help, although once Prime decides to use her against him, the Doctor has no choice but to involve her.

MAJOR THOMAS KENNET

A major in the First Royal Green Jackets and in overall command of the Lannet operation, Thomas Kennet knows of the Doctor and has read his file. Initially wary, he warns the Doctor, 'Don't give my men orders.' But after the Doctor saves them, by barking an order to 'scatter', Kennet is more willing to take his advice and allow him some authority.

THE MASTER

The Doctor is accompanied by the Master, who seems to be responsible for the security of the TARDIS. The nature of the Master in this story is not clear. His body is certainly that of an android (and can be turned off with a remote control device). The Doctor says the Master is confined to the TARDIS (and blames him for leaving the umbrella stand in a Zeppelin hanger). Yet it is implied that this is actually the real Master in an android body. The Master remarks that he chose this form of existence rather than 'a slow painful death' (possibly inside the Eye of Harmony following *Doctor Who – The Movie*). But he also refers to the Doctor's programming of his 'electronic brain'. Perhaps the disembodied intelligence of the Master is now contained in this robot form.

The Master retains his combination of charm, wit and ruthless intelligence. Scathing as ever, he describes Earth as 'a suburban nightmare of a planet'. What his real motivation or intentions might be are not explored, but he does seem to be about to hypnotise Alison until the Doctor intervenes.

NEW INFORMATION

THE DOCTOR

The Doctor keeps various forms of currency in his pockets, including Atraxian semble seeds (which need to grow into trees before they are worth anything); Zornic groats ('currency that talks back'); and Euros. He also seems to keep string, various circuits, a small knife, an inhaler, a jar (into which he pops a baby Shalka) and a bag of explosive powder.

He implies he did a warm-up act for Elvis, reciting his own poetry, and admits that he has never encountered the Shalka before. He learned to sing – with an ability to hit pure notes – in the Gerund system. (Although in *The Power of Kroll*, he says he was taught by Dame Nelly Melba to break glass with the pitch of his singing.) Every bit as happy as his predecessors to name-drop, the Doctor mentions that he knew Gaudi, and that Andy Warhol was a friend: 'wonderful man, he wanted to paint all nine of me.'

THE TARDIS

A blue mobile telephone is kept in the cubbyhole behind the sign on the TARDIS doors. It can send text messages and relies on a battery. Although the phone can be taken away from the TARDIS, it remains in a sense a part of the TARDIS, and has some of the same capabilities and characteristics.

When the Doctor calls in on the phone he gets an answer phone – 'Hello, you've reached the TARDIS. We're not here at the moment...' – which offers to try to 'get back to you before you call.' But it isn't clear who else could – or would – call.

The Doctor tells the Master to set up the 'secondary configuration suite.' This fools the Shalka into believing they can understand and control the TARDIS. The Doctor also mentions a Zeppelin hangar.

BEHIND THE SCENES

ANIMATED ADVENTURES

In 2002 BBCi launched an all-new animated fantasy series, broadcast over the Internet. The animation for the webcast of **Ghosts of Albion** was created by Cosgrove Hall, the animation company responsible for, amongst others, **Danger Mouse**. James Goss, BBCi producer, and his colleagues were already considering an animated version of **Doctor Who**. They had already 'piloted' the idea with the artwork and basic animation that accompanied BBCi's online publication of **Doctor Who** novels, and the more sophisticated webcasts of audio adventures like *Death Comes to Time* and *Shada*.

When planning for 'Project Eddie', as the proposed animated series was code-named, started in August 2002, the decision was taken that this would be an all-new adventure for an all-new Doctor. The initial team consisted of Martin Trickey, an executive for BBC Interactive Drama and Entertainment; James Goss, producer of the BBCi Cult site; and Jelena Djordjevic, a BBC TV development producer. But even using the new technology, funding a fully animated movie was well beyond the BBCi Cult site. The earliest the team could raise the money would be in May 2003. By December 2002 the team was working through a reading list of **Who** authors, watching old episodes, listening to Big Finish audios and conducting availability checks. Martin Trickey was assembling the necessary funding. In January 2003 Paul Cornell was engaged to write the script. Cornell had a proven record as a popular **Who** novelist – his first published book being the **Doctor Who** novel *Revelation*, in 1991. With experience of writing for television (notably several key episodes of **Casualty**), and huge enthusiasm for the subject matter, he was an obvious candidate for the job.

BBCi wanted a project without the baggage of too much existing continuity, although they were uncertain whether or not to include a hand-over from Paul McGann. Cornell argued that they should start straight in with the Ninth Doctor.

By April 2003 Muirinn Lane Kelly had been engaged as producer – taking over the project when Djordjevic left the BBC. She had previously been a script editor on several series, including **Grease Monkeys**.

Although Cornell presented the Doctor, in the treatment, as a bitter, grieving hero, as he scripted the dialogue a somewhat different character emerged, with more of a stiff upper lip and a keen sense of humour.

Another dramatic change was that of the character responsible for TARDIS security. Initially this was conceived by Cornell as a cameo for the Fifth Doctor. As the treatments developed, Cornell decided it would be more interesting to make this a version of the Master.

By late May 2003 Martin Trickey had secured the funding to green-light the project and Kelly began the process of casting. Her key priority was the Doctor and an early front-runner was Richard E. Grant.

Grant was approached and proved extremely enthusiastic at the prospect. Despite briefly playing the Doctor in *The Curse of Fatal Death*, he had never seen the programme and had no real knowledge of it: 'I think I must be the only actor in England who hasn't seen **Doctor Who**, or read it, I'm completely virgin to it,' he confessed. 'It's Sherlock Holmes in space ... the script is very witty and the character fairly acerbic.'

Kelly was now able to concentrate on casting other characters – a job made easier when Grant's agent mentioned that Derek Jacobi was available. Another key actor persuaded

to 'appear' was Diana Quick (as Prime). Kelly also picked Wilson Milam, an American theatre director who had a lot of experience handling big-name casts in bizarre situations, to direct. With Sophie Okonedo cast as new companion Alison Cheney, only the final go-ahead from the BBC's Alan Yentob was needed. This was finally given in June 2003. Voice recording took place during the week of 16 June at London's Soundhouse studios, following a read-through (and photo call) the previous week. The recording was followed by a week of post-production. The animation director, Steve Maher, from Cosgrove Hall, joined the project for this, keen to ensure that the sounds and environments matched his proposed animations as much as possible.

Maher began work on the animations in late June, starting with some character sketches, and 3-D models of the environments, allowing for ambitious camera moves.

Surprisingly, news of the new series did not break until the BBC's official announcements in July. The excitement and enthusiasm this generated gave the first indication of just how popular the Doctor's return would be...

THE FUTURE

Just as it seemed that BBCi would be offering the only new Doctor Who series for the foreseeable future, BBC Television made a surprising announcement. BBC1 Controller Lorraine Heggessey had said that she would consider reviving Doctor Who '... if there was a refreshing, affordable treatment for a new series available and we could navigate ourselves round some potentially troublesome rights issues,' and on 25th September 2003, she announced that these issues had been resolved and Doctor Who was indeed to return to BBC1.

The new series, expected to be seen in 2005, is being written by Russell T. Davies, whose writing credits include *Bob and Rose*, *Queer as Folk*, *The Second Coming* and *The Grand*, as well as the 1996 **Doctor Who** novel *Damaged Goods*. Davies said: 'I grew up watching **Doctor Who**, hiding behind the sofa like so many others. **Doctor Who** is one of the BBC's most exciting and original characters. He's had a good rest and now it's time to bring him back.' Describing his plans for the new series, he says it will be 'fun, exciting, contemporary and scary... I'm aiming to write a full-blooded drama which embraces the Doctor Who heritage, at the same time as introducing the character to a modern audience.'

Mal Young, Controller of BBC Continuing Series, described **Doctor Who** as 'a much-loved, truly iconic piece of television history.' He also pointed out: 'We're at the very first stages of development and further details, including casting, will not be available for some time.' No budget has been set for the new series, and the number of episodes and their duration is still under discussion.

While there are still many uncertainties, the one thing we can be sure of is that the programme will be every bit as innovative and thrilling as ever. Who knows what further exciting adventures the Doctor will have had – what monsters and aliens he will have met, what worlds the TARDIS will have visited – by the time he celebrates his 50th anniversary...

Index

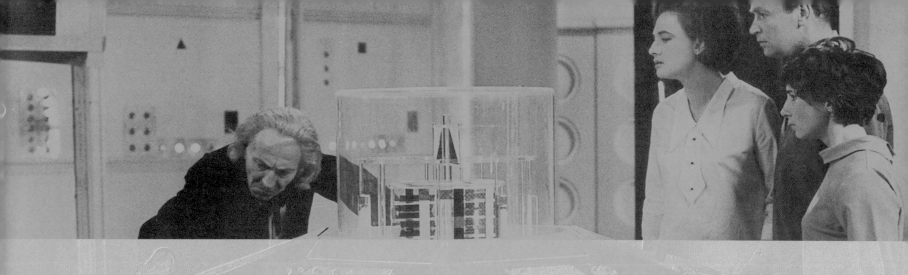

EARLY EPISODE TITLES

An Unearthly Child
1: An Unearthly Child
2: The Cave of Skulls
3: The Forest of Fear
4: The Firemaker

The Daleks
1: The Dead Planet
2: The Survivors
3: The Escape
4: The Ambush
5: The Expedition
6: The Ordeal
7: The Rescue

The Edge of Destruction
1: The Edge of Destruction
2: The Brink of Disaster

Marco Polo
1: The Roof of the World
2: The Singing Sands
3: Five Hundred Eyes
4: The Wall of Lies
5: Rider from Shang-Tu
6: Might Kublai Khan
7: Assassin at Peking

The Keys of Marinus
1: The Sea of Death
2: The Velvet Web
3: The Screaming Jungle
4: The Snows of Terror
5: Sentence of Death
6: The Keys of Marinus

The Aztecs
1: The Temple of Evil
2: The Warriors of Death
3: The Bride of Sacrifice
4: The Day of Darkness

The Sensorites
1: Strangers in Space
2: The Unwilling Warriors
3: Hidden Danger
4: A Race Against Death
5: Kidnap
6: A Desperate Venture

The Reign of Terror
1: A Land of Fear
2: Guests of Madame Guillotine
3: A Change of Identity
4: The Tyrant of France
5: A Bargain of Necessity
6: Prisoners of Conciergerie

Planet of Giants
1: Planet of Giants
2: Dangerous Journey
3: Crisis
(Episode 4 was to be titled The Urge to Live)

The Dalek Invasion of Earth
1: World's End
2: The Daleks
3: Day of Reckoning
4: The End of Tomorrow
5: The Waking Ally
6: Flashpoint

The Rescue
1: The Powerful Enemy
2: Desperate Measures

The Romans
1: The Slave Traders
2: All Roads Lead to Rome
3: Conspiracy
4: Inferno

The Web Planet
1: The Web Planet
2: The Zarbi
3: Escape to Danger
4: Crater of Needles
5: Invasion
6: The Centre

The Crusade
1: The Lion
2: The Knight of Jaffa
3: The Wheel of Fortune
4: The Warlords

The Space Museum
1: The Space Museum
2: The Dimensions of Time
3: The Search
4: The Final Phase

The Chase
1: The Executioners
2: The Death of Time
3: Flight Through Eternity
4: Journey Into Terror
5: The Death of Doctor Who
6: The Planet of Decision

The Time Meddler
1: The Watcher
2: The Meddling Monk
3: A Battle of Wits
4: Checkmate

Galaxy 4
1: Four Hundred Dawns
2: Trap of Steel
3: Air Lock
4: The Exploding Planet

Mission to the Unknown
1: Mission to the Unknown

The Myth Makers
1: Temple of Secrets
2: Small Prophet, Quick Return
3: Death of a Spy
4: Horse of Destruction

The Daleks' Master Plan
1: The Nightmare Begins
2: Day of Armageddon
3: Devil's Planet
4: The Traitors
5: Counter Plot
6: Coronas of the Sun
7: The Feast of Steven
8: Volcano
9: Golden Death
10: Escape Switch
11: The Abandoned Planet
12: Destruction of Time

The Massacre
1: War of God
2: The Sea Beggar
3: Priest of Death
4: Bell of Doom

The Ark
1: The Steel Sky
2: The Plague
3: The Return
4: The Bomb

The Celestial Toymaker
1: The Celestial Toyroom
2: The Hall of Dolls
3: The Dancing Floor
4: The Final Test

The Gunfighters
1: A Holiday for the Doctor
2: Don't Shoot the Pianist
3: Johnny Ringo
4: The OK Corral

'Can you imagine silver leaves waving above a pool of liquid gold containing singing fishes? Twin suns that circle and fall in a rainbow heaven? Another world in another sky? If you come with me, I will show you all this — and it will be, I promise you, the dullest part of it all. Come with me and you will see wonders that no human has ever dreamed possible. Or stay behind, and regret your staying until the day you die.' THE DOCTOR (ATTRIBUTED)